15.⁰⁰

LIEBLING ABROAD

LIEBLING ABROAD

A. J. LIEBLING

INTRODUCTION BY RAYMOND SOKOLOV

WIDEVIEW
BOOKS

Most of the material in this book originally appeared in *The New Yorker*.
The Road Back to Paris copyright © 1939, 1940, 1941, 1942, 1943, 1944 by A. J. Liebling
Mollie & Other War Pieces copyright © 1943, 1944, 1945, 1946, 1964 by A. J. Liebling
Normandy Revisited copyright © 1955, 1956, 1957, 1958 by A. J. Liebling
Between Meals copyright © 1959, 1962 by A. J. Liebling

Manufactured in the United States of America

Library of Congress Cataloging in Publication Data

Liebling, Abbott Joseph, 1904–1963.
    Liebling abroad.
        CONTENTS: Sokolov, R. Introduction.—The road back to Paris.—Mollie & other war pieces.—[etc.]
        1. Liebling, Abbott Joseph, 1904–1963.
2. World War, 1939–1945—Personal narratives, American. 3. Normandy—Description and travel. 4. Gastronomy. 5. Cookery, French. I. Title.
D811.5.L518   1981b   940.54′81′730924   80–28902
ISBN 0–87223–643–9 (pbk.)

Design by Tere LoPrete

Contents

INTRODUCTION

Raymond Sokolov

A. J. Liebling embarked on his first foreign assignment for *The New Yorker* in 1939, arriving in Paris just in time for the *drôle de guerre,* the phony war, that quiet, tense winter and spring before Hitler's forces overran Paris. The assignment was the biggest break of his career; it transformed him from a writer of New York City features into that most glamorous of journalistic creatures, a foreign correspondent, just in time to cover the choicest of all foreign stories, a major war.

Looking back on this wonderful stroke of good fortune, Liebling tried to make it sound as if he had conned the magazine into sending him. "I attracted the assignment," he wrote, "by telling McKelway* how well I could talk French. McKelway could not judge. Besides, I was a reasonable age for the job: thirty-five."

He was also an ideal choice. He could definitely speak French, with a fluency picked up during many youthful vacations in Europe when his prosperous parents had taken him along with them on grand tours of the Continent, a fluency perfected during a year spent as a student in Paris in the midtwenties.

France had become a second home for him. He had hiked across Normandy on a semiserious scholarly research project, hunting for traces of a mythical medieval poet who had supposedly lived at Vire. There, and in the small but soigné and hearty bistros of prewar Paris, he had educated his palate and primed his appetite for substantial, serious food. And in a Left Bank café he met Angèle, the first important woman of his complex amatory career.

France had also seduced Liebling's intellect years before she got to his body. A fancy set of Maupassant on the family's shelves in the wealthy new Long Island suburb of Lawrence was this precocious boy's introduction to "adult" literature. Later, at the Columbia Journalism School, an

* St. Clair McKelway, an older writer at *The New Yorker.*

unwilling apprentice to his future craft, Liebling cross-registered for a literature course that covered Villon and the early French classics. As a young reporter he read and reread Stendhal, who prepared him for battle.

War, indeed, had preoccupied Liebling from earliest boyhood. He memorized all the names of the marshals of France, and when, in 1916, at the age of eleven, an attack of typhoid nearly killed him, he fell into delirium and dreamt that he was a military horse decorated for valor with the Médaille Militaire by General Nivelle, the French commander at Verdun.

Probably neither St. Clair McKelway nor *The New Yorker*'s editor Harold Ross knew about any of these special credentials. Nevertheless, they did not blunder into their choice for the Paris posting. In Joe Liebling they knew they had one of the great reporters of the day. He had been seasoned by several hundred human-interest, "low-life" assignments at the New York *World-Telegram* before he switched over to America's smartest, smoothest magazine. And at *The New Yorker* Liebling had polished his technique, first as a Talk of the Town reporter, then as an increasingly skillful hand at longer features and profiles of figures in the New York entertainment world and its sleazier, Barnumesque peripheries. Liebling could report; he could write; and he knew how to function among ordinary people. Liebling did not resemble Richard Harding Davis. He was myopic and overweight and had weak feet. But Harold Ross was not looking for a swashbuckler. He wanted good, solid reporting about the everyday life of Europe in wartime, from the street and from the trenches. Liebling was his man, better than he could have hoped for.

Liebling covered the war as Ross wanted him to, from the front lines, and got the enlisted man's point of view. He found plenty of color and sharp detail of daily life, fleeing Paris in 1940, crossing the Atlantic in a submarine, dodging airborne strafers on North African airfields, surviving the London blitz, and landing on the Normandy beaches on D day. But he did much more than bring *The New Yorker* manner to the European theater. He brought himself, a fiercely committed Francophile with a novelist's skill for crystallizing his day-to-day experiences into a profound chronicle of a "world knocked down."

In particular, it was the "world" of France that Liebling wanted fiercely to restore. Although he was a patriotic American, he viewed World War II almost exclusively as a campaign to free France. And once he had entered Paris just behind General Leclerc on liberation day, the war was essentially over for him. He stayed for a few months and then went home, well before V-E Day.

He had the French view of things, no doubt about it. And if it was a seriously limiting view, it gave unique clarity to his war reporting, which was later collected in two classics of the genre.

The Road Back to Paris and *Mollie and Other War Pieces* will not instruct the young and curious who want to learn the grand outlines of the war in Europe. Liebling made no attempt to write conventional history; he did not even try to set the events he saw into their larger historical perspective, any more than he had tried to set Tallulah Bankhead in the larger perspective of Anglo-American theater and post-Reconstruction southern aristocratic eccentricity when he did a piece about her for the *World-Telegram*. He took the context for granted and then brought the reader inside it, made him feel the ominously languorous pace of battle, those still days of dreary tenting suddenly blasted into frenzy.

By the 1960s the New Journalists were claiming Liebling as their godfather. He was certainly a personal journalist, taking pages to tell New Yorkers how he bought eggs in the "foamy fields" of Tunisia and then hit the dirt when the enemy dived down and shot up his makeshift desert kitchen. But the personal flavor never overwhelms the observation, the careful witnessing. Never pontificating about the progress of the battle, which he could not see himself, he focused on the things he could see. Liebling keeps himself so strictly in the background that when he does permit himself a general reaction—usually a modest one—it acquires a peculiar force. Watching the aerial bombardment of Normandy from a farmhouse window, he wrote:

> The only residents of the farm who seemed uncomfortable were a great, long-barreled sow and her litter of six shoats, who walked about uneasily, shaking their ears as if the concussions hurt them. At brief intervals, they would lie down in a circle, all their snouts pointing toward the center. Then they would get up again, perhaps because the earth quivering against their bellies frightened them. Puffs of black smoke dotted the sky under the first two waves of bombers; one plane came swirling down, on fire and trailing smoke, and crashed behind the second ridge of poplars. White parachutes flashed in the sun as the plane fell. A great cloud of slate-gray smoke rose from behind the trees where it had gone down. Soon after that the flak puffs disappeared; the German gunners either had been killed or, as one artillerist suggested, had simply run out of ammunition. The succeeding waves of planes did their bombing unopposed. It was rather horrifying at that.

As he followed the advance of the Allies through Normandy, Liebling eventually came into Vire. Friendly fire had almost totally leveled the center of the town which he remembered so vividly from student days. In order for Liebling's France to be preserved, the part of it he cherished most had to be destroyed.

The irony stuck with him for the next decade, which he spent in New York as a press critic and boxing writer. These were eventful years for Liebling, who is perhaps best known today as the author of *The New*

Yorker's Wayward Press column. His incisive comments on newspaper stories and the role of the press in American life have made him a hero for all journalists. And his ringside reports of the great fights of the postwar period went beyond blow-by-blow accounts to take in the whole special world of the "sweet science," its training camps, its sociology and lingo. He became the best boxing writer in a century. But he had not forgotten his old passion; he yearned to see France again. Further prompted by the claims of the Internal Revenue Service (which offered a $20,000 deduction for expatriates) and by his second wife, who wanted a separation, Liebling went abroad again in the middle fifties.

Foreign correspondent redux, he covered British elections and racing and the Suez crisis, but his main preoccupation during this period was himself and his France. He wrote two very different books about this obsession. *Normandy Revisited*, the crowning work of his career, is a Proustian exploration of the past, of his student time in Normandy and his wartime incursions, compared to his middle-aged return, as a successful writer going over the same ground in a hired limo. Those three points in time coexist in *Normandy Revisited* in a beautifully controlled pattern of nostalgia and regret.

The second book was Liebling's last. *Between Meals* came out in 1962, the year before its author died. By then he already knew that decades of self-indulgence at the table had virtually destroyed his physique. With typical perversity, he continued to gorge, and, between meals so to speak, he produced a defiant memoir of his gastronomic career. It begins with a portrait of another glutton, a Frenchman whose health fell apart only after he followed medical advice and cut back on his prodigious menus. The rest of *Between Meals* is a memoir of a great eater's best times in Paris before the war. No one has ever written with more zest and intelligence about the act of eating. *Between Meals* is more than a gourmand's diary, however; it is a heroic refusal to cut down or cut back on a lifetime commitment to the epicurean life even in the jaws of death.

Liebling left several million words behind. Most of them were written about his native city, New York. But his best work, the books in which he found himself and his style most completely, was done 3,000 miles east of *The New Yorker*'s offices. Liebling abroad was Liebling at the peak of his form. All four books are here under one cover, in print again at last.

Feast.

THE
ROAD BACK
TO PARIS

To

H. S., Horse Watkins

and

Pinky Johnson

Contents

BOOK III
THE WORLD GETS UP

BOOK I

The World Knocked Down

1 / The Shape of War

Two NEGRO SOLDIERS sat with their legs dangling into two deep parallel slit trenches in the dead-looking land between Gafsa and Sened Station one morning last winter. Each was eating a cold mixture of meat and beans out of a small shiny tin can capable of reflecting the sun's rays to a distance of several miles in that flat country, and each turned his face upward periodically, with mouth full, to stare into the hot aluminum-colored sky. When I walked up to the end of one trench its proprietor, a tan man, looked at me while the other soldier continued to regard the sky. Then the tan man looked up at the sky, and his companion looked at me. "We was dive-bummed yesterday," this second soldier, a very dark man, said to me. "Driving the infantry up to the line in two-and-a-half-ton trucks. Dive-bumming makes me sick to my stomach." I tried to sound hearty and casual as I asked, "What outfit you men out of?" "Rolling Umpty-seventh," the tan man said while the dark man took his turn looking at the sky. The Umpties are a motor-truck regiment whom I had first met under happier circumstances, in England. "How you doing?" I asked, for want of a better question. "Really, sir, I don't belong on this battlefield at all," the tan soldier answered. "I'm strictly a non-combat man." I thought to myself we were two of a kind.

It was the second day of an offensive that we had started in the direction of Maknassy, the first all-American venture of the Tunisian campaign. Sened Station was the first objective. The bulk of Rommel's army was still only a little west of Tripoli, and there was a long, tempting, thinly held corridor between him and Von Arnim. The men making the attack believed that they would go on from Sened to Maknassy and from Maknassy to the coast of the Gulf of Tunis, cutting Rommel's line of supply and retreat. The major general in command had told the war correspondents he was going on to Maknassy at least and "draw the pucker string tight." We had understood from his manner that he meant to go farther than that if he got the chance.

I asked the colored soldiers how far the front of the battle was from where we then were. I put into my voice an implication that I wanted to rush right into the middle of things. The men did not know exactly where the battle was. Soldiers seldom and war correspondents almost never do. I learned afterward that the Umpties' vehicles, returning after unloading the infantry, had frightened a couple of my most dashing colleagues completely out of the battle area. They had mistaken the approaching trucks for a German tank column.

I walked back from the twin slit trenches to the jeep that had carried me out from Gafsa. Another correspondent was at the wheel. "They don't know where the battle is," I said to this other fellow. "Maybe we had better go ahead further." He said all right, so we started out across the sand again. We kept off the one road between Gafsa and Sened because there were trucks on it and they sometimes attracted strafers. The line of telephone poles along the side of the road gave us our general direction. When we had gone a short way I saw a couple of jeeps coming toward us, and we stopped. There were a couple of officers and eight men in the jeeps, all belonging to a tank-destroyer battalion that had lost its equipment earlier in the campaign. They were serving as battlefield military police, guiding traffic and waiting for prisoners to take charge of. The officers didn't know exactly where the front was either, but they invited us to have a can of coffee by a mud house a couple of miles away where the M.P.'s had set up their headquarters. There were a few scraggly olive trees around this house and a low mud wall around the trees, presumably to prevent the sand from blowing away from their roots.

One of the soldiers put a mixture of sand and gasoline in a couple of the shiny ration cans and lighted them. He filled two more ration cans with water from his canteen and placed them on the burners, and then when the water came to a boil he divided a packet of soluble coffee between the two improvised coffeepots. "The Statler people would give a million dollars to get hold of this process," he said. When the coffee had been drunk he started another batch. While I was waiting for my coffee I stood on the mud wall with one of the M.P. officers and looked over the country around. The railroad paralleled the highway, and we could see a station building with some trees around it about five miles away. It was an intermediate stop between Gafsa and Sened, needed God knows why. "Our guns were out behind there early this morning, and Jerry dropped a few shells in among those trees," the officer said, "but then our guns moved forward, 'way up toward Sened. I think you can go ahead eight or ten miles at least before you have to start to look around. You missed a good show this morning, though. About twenty Stukas came over, and a dozen P-40's bounced them and shot down about eight. Boy, they were falling all over the place. They'll be back, though!" he added cheerily. When we had had our coffee we climbed back into the jeep and started forward again. The mud-house grove seemed in retrospect a pretty nice place to spend the day. Sened Station lies in a gap between two bare east-west ridges. As we moved toward it we spotted a number of dispersed scout cars and wireless-equipped jeeps, the vehicles characteristic of a reconnaissance troop. "A recon outfit!" my companion said knowingly, then, "Aren't they usually pretty well out in front of everybody?"

We drove over within fifty yards of one of the scout cars and climbed out. There were a couple of soldiers sitting with their backs against the wheels of the car, reading paper books. They had their slit trenches ready dug beside them. I walked up to them and said, "What outfit is this, soldier?" One of the men, a corporal, looked up and said, "Sorry, sir, but you got any identification?" He reminded me of a stage doorman. We showed our identification cards, and the corporal explained that the recon outfit had been all the way around the enemy's position on the previous day and night and had come back to report and await another assignment. "We could have took the place, I guess," he said, "but that would not have seemed important enough." He was wrong, but reconnaissance troops, like small terriers, must have their illusions or they would lose their dash.

My companion, Boots Norgaard, who worked for the Associated Press, started taking down the names and home towns of recon soldiers. This is always a fruitful procedure for a press-association man, because he can load up his dispatches with the names and the member papers in the home towns are glad to use them. Every soldier, when he named his home town, said, "And I wish I was there now," or, "Boy, how I wish I was there this minute!" The corporal I had first spoken to asked me if it was true that Bing Crosby was dead. I said I did not know, and he asked me if Groucho Marx was dead. He said he had heard that they were and that Jack Benny was dead too. The army in Tunisia was always full of rumors about well-known people who were supposed to have died at home. Battlefields, for that matter, are always ranged by false rumors about people supposed to have died in the immediate vicinity. When my companion had written down the names of enough towns like Owensboro, Kentucky, and Central Falls, Rhode Island, we moved on again.

We had a clear view of the ridge north of Sened Station, and after we had driven a mile or so forward we saw a number of tanks coming around the end nearer us, just below the crest, and snaking down the southern slope of the ridge toward the station. There were occasional puffs of gray smoke on the slope above them, where the enemy was lobbing shells over. We could hear our own guns up ahead quite loudly now. Then we wandered in among the ammunition half-tracks of an artillery outfit. The soldiers told us that the reconnaissance troop we had just left in good health had been annihilated on the previous day. They also said that a tank-destroyer outfit had lost all its vehicles. This was a reference to the tank-destroyer battalion the military policemen belonged to. The vehicles had been lost in a quagmire in northern Tunisia a month ago, but an artillerist, garbling some conversation with an M.P., had come up with the more fascinating report that the tank busters had been ambushed during this present action. I never like the vicinity of ammo during a battle. The soldiers said two batteries out of their battalion were a mile or two ahead of us. The guns were armored 105's, six to a battery.

We came eventually to a place on the plain where a tall captain with a Red Cross brassard was standing between two jeeps both carrying Red Cross flags. We stopped to talk to him, too. The guns were in sight now, about four hundred yards farther on. The captain, whose name I remember was Bradbury, said he was battalion surgeon. Each of the jeeps had two litters slung to its sides, and when dive bombers or German counter-battery caused a casualty among the gunners Bradbury would run up in one of the jeeps and get the wounded man. He stood there looking at the guns like a spaniel watching for a ball to retrieve. "Yesterday I had seventeen," he said, "including several from the infantry that happened to be hit near us. Only three so far today. None in this position so far—we've moved half a dozen times since daybreak." All the shots we heard were going out, "boom-scream," and none coming in, "scream-boom," so we were unworried. I got out a can of Spam, and we ate it cold before continuing our advance.

"Maybe they have pulled their stuff out of Sened already," Norgaard said optimistically. I had watched the sky all day while he drove, some-times looking straight up for Stukas and at others into the sun for strafers, but nothing had happened, and I began to hope that the P-40's had polished the local Luftwaffe off for the day.

When we had finished the Spam and said so long to Bradbury, we went on up to the guns and stopped the jeep behind them. They were in the open, because there was no cover anywhere around. They had quit shoot-ing for the moment, probably changing a range or target, and we walked up to one gun crew who were smoking cigarettes beside their piece. As soon as we reached them an officer shouted over to them from an armored half-track to their right rear to get our identifications. "I'm sorry, sir," one soldier said, "but after all, how do we know who you are? We got no time for Ayrabs or casual strollers." We showed our identification cards, and the soldier, looking at mine, which describes me as correspondent of the *New Yorker*, said, "Huh, a *paesano*, practically. I'm from New York, too. Fourteent' Street and Avenue A. I wish I was dere now. At a movie, wit' my shoes off." Then they had to start shooting again, and we walked back toward the half-track, which we recognized from its high radio antenna as a command vehicle.

The officer who had shouted to the gunners was a square-faced fair-haired major who told us his name was Burba, executive officer of the battalion. He was in command of the two batteries, since his C.O., a lieutenant colonel, had been wounded. Major Burba said he was from McAlester, Oklahoma. He was a cool, methodical officer who looked as if he would have definite information about everything, so I asked him what his battery was shooting at. "Enemy guns in the grove of trees back of

Sened," he said. "We think their infantry has pulled out of the town already." I asked him what range he was firing at, and he said five thousand yards. "I have one battery here," he said, "and another over about a mile to the right and slightly forward—you can see them over there," and he pointed. "Every fifth shell we fire is a smoke shell so we can see where we are hitting, and the fire of the two batteries is converging on that grove of trees. When we get all our fire together and just right, we will come down on them, and that will be the end of the battle." "Where is our infantry?" I asked in a careless tone, because I could not see any troops out in front of us. "There are two battalions in echelon in those two olive groves to the right and forward of the other battery," Burba said, pointing again. "When we have knocked out all resistance they will go forward and occupy the town. Or maybe the tanks will get there first."

The tanks, as a matter of fact, were already trying to get to the town before the infantry. They were crawling down off the southern side of the ridge where my colleague and I had observed them earlier, moving out in front of the 105's, reminding me of a file of mechanical toys that a street peddler winds up and sets down on a sidewalk. When they had deployed in front of us they turned left and rolled on toward the town. They must have been a couple of thousand yards ahead of us when something began kicking up dust and smoke, sometimes in front of and sometimes behind them. "It's those Jerry eighty-eights," Burba said. "They've got the tanks under a crossfire. We'll fix that in a few minutes." The tanks were now rolling back toward us, except for one which remained motionless out on the plain. "That's the way the infantry was yesterday," one of Burba's junior officers said. "They went up toward the firing line in trucks, and three or four of the trucks got dive-bombed before the fellows could get away from them. It was a mess. After that they couldn't get anybody back into the trucks for a while. After we knock out the opposition they will all be heroes."

"That eighty-eight's a great gun," Burba said admiringly, looking at the motionless American tank through his binoculars. "Ripped that thing just like a G.I. knife does a tin can. Flat trajectory. High muzzle velocity." "Pretty long range, hasn't it?" I asked. "Thirteen thousand five hundred yards," Burba said heartily, as if he were a salesman pushing the German gun on a reluctant prospect. Our six guns loosed off as one and the other battery followed.

Just then there was a prolonged shrieking noise and something monstrous landed a hundred yards behind us and ricocheted off toward Gafsa. It kicked up a lot of dust. It must have been an armor-piercing solid shot, because there was no explosion. Burba said, "Let's get behind the half-track," in the same tone he might have said, "Let's get out of this wind," so we moved over behind the vehicle. Something else shrieked past, through the interval between the two guns on the right flank of the battery, I thought, and I had a bitter intuition that while Burba had been explaining to us what we intended to do to the Germans, some equally competent, equally stolid German artillery officer had been outlining his plans of what he intended to do to us. "He should have snapped into it and not wasted his time talking to war correspondents," I reflected severely. But my colleague and I had an embarrassing feeling that we were not helping the battery by our presence and that if we got hit we would cause them a lot of extra trouble. We were also embarrassed by the thought that if we left too abruptly, Burba and the others might think us fair-weather friends. My colleague reminded me that he really had to get back to headquarters at Gafsa by five so he could get a fill-in on the general picture for the dispatch which he must file to catch the six-o'clock courier car to Tebessa. From there a plane would take it to the cablehead at Algiers. I didn't work for a press association and so had no bulletin to file, but we had only one jeep, and I decided that I couldn't expect the other fellow to wait. So I said, "I guess we may as well go, Major. See you some other time." Norgaard said something to the same effect, and we walked away feeling as sheepish as we ever have in our lives. We got in our jeep and drove back past the patient, expectant Captain Bradbury. We paused for a moment to say good-by to him, and I looked back and saw a column of black smoke rising from one of the gun positions, where the enemy had evidently got a hit.

Each knot of soldiers that we had passed on the way going out had seemed a friendly island that invited a prolonged stay. We were not tempted to stop to talk to any of them on the way back. "Tomorrow we will get an early start and bring out blanket rolls," I said to my companion. "That way we will be able to see more of the battle and not have to go back to Gafsa at night." He agreed. As we entered the center of Gafsa and were about to park our jeep opposite the town's one European-style hotel, which was serving as American headquarters, we saw in the street the major general who commanded the whole operation and who forty-eight hours earlier may have been thinking his name would live with Stonewall Jackson's. We stopped to ask him if the infantry had as yet entered Sened—we had been two hours on the way home—and he said they had, and Sened Station was now in our hands. "The only damned trouble," he said, "is that First Army has called off the whole offensive because there has been some kind of threat in the north. I guess we're going to play it safe and wait for Montgomery." At that time American troops were still under direct control of the British First Army. The greater part of an armored division which had been held in reserve just outside Gafsa to exploit our initial gains was sent north that night without having fought, and the great offensive went into the record as a raid.

The feeling I had had when I left the guns was the sort of thing that demands a rationalization, and I arrived at one while I was sitting on a ridge overlooking Gafsa on St. Patrick's Day, watching our people recapture the place. We had evacuated it a fortnight after the aborted offensive. The region is full of prehistoric artifacts and pieces of them, and I was trying to put together some kind of a form out of bits of flint I found on the hill. I never finished the job, but I think the result would have been ugly if I had. I thought then that I had viewed this war so long that it would be a shame to be knocked in the head before I had patched all my glimpses of it together and tried to reconstruct the shape of the beast.

2 / Reflections in a Cul-de-sac

THERE IS AN OLD PROVERB that a girl may sleep with one man without being a trollop, but let a man cover one little war and he is a war correspondent. I belong to the one-war category. I have made no appearances for Mr. Colston Leigh, the lecture agent, either in a gas mask or out of one, and I have no fascinating reminiscences about Addis Ababa or the Cliveden set. Prior to October 1938 my only friends were prize fighters' seconds, Romance philologists, curators of tropical fish, kept women, promoters of spit-and-toilet-paper night clubs, bail bondsmen, press agents for wrestlers, horse clockers, newspaper reporters, and female psychiatrists. I was writting excellent pieces about sea-lion trainers and cigar-store proprietors for the *New Yorker*, and I was happy.

Hitler had seemed to me revolting but unimportant, like old Gómez, the dictator of Venezuela. I habitually compared him in conversation to a boor who tortured his own family because he could not cope with the outside world, a classic German type. It never occurred to me that he might destroy France, because it would have been as hard for me to prefigure a world without France as survival with one lobe of my brain gone. France represented for me the historical continuity of intelligence and reasonable living. When this continuity is broken, nothing anywhere can have meaning until it is re-established. After the Munich settlement I began to be anxious.

On Sunday, September 3, 1939, everybody with the price of a newspaper knew that Great Britain and France were about to declare war on Germany, which had already invaded Poland. I was living down on East Thirty-third Street then, but I drifted up toward the *New Yorker* office because I thought that even though it was a Sunday I might find someone there to talk to. It was a hot afternoon, I remember. Wolcott Gibbs had a radio going in his office. I went down the fire escape from the main editorial office on the nineteenth floor to the cell on the seventeenth where I did my writing and sat there for a while, at moments glad because France still had pride, at others feeling guilty because I would not share the fight or the risk. I was sorry that I had left daily newspaper work four years before then, because if I had stayed on a paper I might have a chance to go to the war. The *New Yorker* appeared a cul-de-sac.

As I sat there I thought of M. Lebourgeois, a traveling salesman I had met in the billiard room of the Hôtel du Cheval Blanc at Vire in 1926, and also of M. Perrin, the *patron* of the hotel in the Rue de l'Ecole de Médecine at Paris, where I had lived for two years while pretending to study medieval literature, and my good friend Henri, who was the French representative of an American silk firm. All three had shared the quality of having escaped from a great danger with honor intact. None of them had come through the war unwounded, and none had achieved any great position since the armistice of 1918. But each took immense pleasure in not having been killed and in not having to be ashamed of himself.

When M. Lebourgeois had patted his stomach, while telling me of the table d'hôte at a favorite hotel in his territory, he had clearly been glad that the stomach had survived—the bullet had broken his left leg, which bothered him hardly at all except in wet weather. The merchants of the United States, M. Lebourgeois had told me, had absolutely the right idea—*le big business*. Undoubtedly, in that country of large orders, he had said, it was a pleasure to be a salesman. The retailers had vision; they were not like these retrograded types of the Department of Calvados, who bought a few articles at a time and those only with the most apparent misgivings. He had had one period of relative affluence, he had said— almost *le big business*, it had been—directly after the war, when he had gone about selling to small communities those life-size cast-iron figures of poilus which served as war memorials in most of rural Normandy. On the base of each statue was the inscription *"Morts à l'Ennemi,"* and under it the twenty or thirty names of the late heroes. The figure of the poilu was always poised on the ball of the right foot, the bayonet stuck out before him, the iron face constricted in defiance. "These opportunities don't recur often in a man's lifetime," M. Lebourgeois used to say when he told about it. "Figure to yourself—it is necessary to have a war before you can sell something in this bugger of a department." If M. Lebourgeois was sufficiently fortunate to survive this new war, he might make more sales, I figured to myself.

M. Perrin, my landlord, had taken a Chinese pleasure in disingenuous self-abasement. It was a privilege he had earned in the war. If he had deprecated himself before that, nobody would have contradicted him, because, as he used to say, he was a small, insignificant man without capacity or cultivation. Then, in order to survive, it would have been necessary for him to assert himself. He would have disliked that. But he had won the Legion of Honor for bravery under fire, and although he always shrugged away references to his decoration, he never left the ribbon off his coat. Also, he had been a captain. Intelligence is not requisite for a captain of infantry, he used to assure me. An officer of artillery or engineers, *that* required culture, but a captain of infantry, and especially one who began the war as a private, might be very stupid. It was a matter of luck, of survival, one might say. We would sit at a table in front of the Soufflet—which was later to be replaced by a gigantic modernistic chain-store café called Dupont—watching the Danish and Rumanian students and their girls, and the little waiter with the reddish eyes and the carroty mustache would not be so brusque with M. Perrin as with the other clients. M. Perrin's suits had been shiny, but the ribbon had given him an air. Almost, one would say, an instructor at the Ecole des Chartes near by. The instructors' suits were shiny too. The possibility of such a mistake had flattered M. Perrin, and he had tried by his manner to convey to strangers the idea that his ribbon was an academic honor.

M. Perrin was a native of Lille. He had lived with his wife, a large, hot-tempered Orleanaise, his mother, who was very old, and his daughter, who was adolescent, on the street floor of the hotel. Without the red ribbon to enhance his dignity, without the head wound he had received at Douaumont to explain his flightiness, M. Perrin, it was easy to see, would have been familially submerged. "My wife is very bitter after gain," he had sometimes said over the *apero*. But he had never refused to accept payment of a bill which she had harried some student into meeting. His mother had been in Lille during the occupation of 1914–18. Her confidence had never wavered, she had once told me, since the day when she had seen some German officers eating lettuce. "They put sugar on it," she said, an indication to her of cretinism on a national scale. The reason I thought so long of M. Perrin was that he had lived in what he and I and everybody else had thought was a comfortable aftermath. Another decoration would bring him no satisfaction commensurate with the first. Neither would another head wound.

Henri had been most pleased to survive the war of any of them, because to him it had seemed especially horrible. He was a sensitive man, extremely tall, with a long, doleful countenance, watery blue eyes, and a great, drooping Gallic mustache. In 1914 he had been in the United States—it was there I had first known him—and he had returned to fight. Sometimes I used to have dinner with Henri's family in their apartment on the Avenue de la Motte-Picquet, a neighborhood roughly equivalent to Central Park West, and after we had eaten, Henri would tuck a violin under his chin and his daughter Suzette would go to the piano, and then he would play and sing "J'Avais Perdu la Tête et Ma Perruque," from *Les Cloches de Corneville*. His son Jean, who had spent most of his young life in America, would sit silent, uninterested, and slightly embarrassed. Jean liked to talk about automobile engines, using a good deal of American slang. "He should be a handy man around a tank now," I thought, "he's just the right age." Henri had preferred to talk about "before the war," a period, he would say, when Paris really had been fit to live in. Eglée, his wife, had sometimes pretended to be bored by his reminiscences. I reflected that Henri, with luck, would be able to talk someday about "before the war before last." As a matter of fact he was not to survive this second war. He was to die of cold and malnutrition and chagrin, "but principally of chagrin," his daughter would later write to me, in Paris in February of 1941.

I began to think of Vire, where I had met M. Lebourgeois. It is a little city built of gray granite, and its principal street passes under a great gray clock tower that was once a gate in a wall, but all the rest of the wall is gone. The clock strikes every quarter-hour all through the night. There are two little rivers that join within the city limits, one the Vire and one the name of which I could not recall, and there is the Street of the Dyers along the bank of one of them, with old granite houses that jut over the water and low granite porches on the water level. I had once told the mayor, an anticlerical old doctor, that this street was fine, and he had said it was "an infection, a nest of microbes," and that the sooner somebody blew it up with dynamite the better it would be. The vales, *vaux*, of the two little rivers, *les vaux de Vire*, lent their names to form the word vaudeville, according to a plausible but I am now convinced inaccurate theory I had once heard told in a course in Old French at Columbia. I had arrived in Vire for the first time in 1926 because of that odd bit of information. I had always loved vaudeville at the Palace in New York. Besides, Henri had told me that during the last war he and another sergeant had brought some German prisoners from the front to a camp on the west coast, and that on the return trip they had stopped off at Vire, which was the other sergeant's home town, and that they had descended at the Cheval Blanc and eaten and drunk wonderfully well. Since I was an amateur medievalist and a vaudeville fan *and* a glutton, I had gone to Vire. On the first Sunday after my arrival I had attended some mounted trotting races that local farmers were holding at a village four miles from the city. The great heavy men on their great heavy horses—bred for sale to the field artillery—went thundering in a rough semicircle about a great cow pasture. It was easy to lose count of the number of rounds. The crowd stood inside the semicircle, most of the men amiably drunk, the women scarlet-cheeked and out of their heads with excitement, cheering their favorites. One fellow in a plaid cap led for several rounds, then his horse, a brown with a long barrel and short legs, broke into a canter. The man sawed at the horse's mouth to get it back into a trot, he kicked violently, and the horse broke into a sidling gallop and then began trying to throw him. Meanwhile another farmer, on a bay, took the lead easily without pushing his horse. The farmer had thick legs and a great heavy belly that rode in front of him like a sack of grain. He had a red face and a long mustache that drooped like a ship's ensign in a dead calm. He and his bay stallion were unexcited. They trotted in by fifty lengths. A tall old peasant standing next to me hit me on the back of the neck with the heel of his hand, a cordial gesture in Vire. "Pichart wins again!" he shouted. "It never pays to abuse a horse or a woman!"

I remembered M. Hédouin, the municipal librarian of Vire. The combined library and museum was a sort of annex of the City Hall. It was officially closed during the summertime. So I had had to pay M. Hédouin twenty francs an hour to open it for me and find books. He was a small, bent, wispy man, old, but not at all doting. There had been an early-fifteenth-century poet named Olivier Basselin in Vire, according to the *vaux-de-vire* theory which dated from about 1825. His drinking songs had become known as *vaux-de-vire*, by a transference easy to understand. Then the *r* had become an *l*, and then vaudeville had come to be a term for any gay song. The main evidence for this theory was a whole volume of Olivier Basselin's drinking songs, printed in the seventeenth century. There was no surviving manuscript. In order to have survived for two centuries outside of manuscript, the argument ran, the songs must have been very popular indeed. M. Hédouin told me that a nineteenth-century critic named Armand Gasté, a native of Vire and a professor at the University of Caen—there was a street in Vire named after him—had already disposed of the question in two or three volumes. M. Hédouin fished them out of the stacks for me.

M. Gasté demonstrated by a study of the texts that the poems had been written in the seventeenth, not the fifteenth, century and by a lawyer named Jean Le Houx of Vire. Le Houx had been an outwardly serious chap who had not wanted to be known as a composer of drinking songs. He had therefore invented Basselin, as Chatterton invented Rowley and MacPherson invented Ossian, and had published his "discovery." Since the term *vaux-de-vire* had never been applied to songs before Le Houx's time, the etymology for vaudeville from *vaux-de-vire* was almost impossible, Gasté noted. The word vaudeville already occurred in the seventeenth century and was probably derived from *voix de ville*, the voice of the city. I remembered only one of his textual arguments: "Basselin" in one song compared his own nose to the red wattles of a turkey. Turkeys had not been introduced into France until well after the discovery of America, Gasté pointed out. "It was all a humbug," M. Hédouin had told me with a New England kind of malicious pleasure in destroying a pretty story. What I remembered most keenly was the play of intelligences across time, like a wireless chess game. The seventeenth-century attorney and the nineteenth-century professor had played, the old librarian in the twentieth century had marked the score.

I did not think about Germany. When I was a small child I had had a succession of German governesses all indistinguishably known to me as *Fräulein*. They had been servile to my parents and domineering to me, stupid, whining, loud, and forever trying to frighten me with stories of children who had been burned to a crisp or eaten by an ogre because they had disobeyed other Fräuleins. The fairy tales of anthropophagic stepmothers and princes turned into white mice gave me nightmares. Once when I was very small I was escorted by the current Fräulein through the torture tower in Nuremberg and made to look down a deep well into which, she told me, it was customary to throw bad little boys. It was really the place where the jolly Meistersingers had been accustomed to drop the mangled corpses of people who disagreed with them, like a slot for used razor blades. She had bought me a little miniature of the Iron Maiden as a souvenir of our promenade, complete in detail, she liked to point out. Only Germans could be so thorough, she said with pride—there were miniature spikes inside the hollow maiden's hollow eyes, just like the spikes in the big one, that pierced the victim's brain. I suppose German-lovers would have called it *gemütlich*. Banse and Goebbels and their war by fear are in the main line of German culture, not twentieth-century deviations. Only people with hollow hearts can so count on the fears of others. The Fräuleins had shared a national habit of digging their finger-nails into the flesh of my arm. When I was five years old I would rather have died with my milk teeth in a governess' ankle than tie the kind of bow in my shoelaces that she had wanted to make me tie. Anybody who had had a German governess could understand Poland.

3/Toward Paris: 1939

THE NEW YORKER turned out to be the best possible place for a reporter who had to see the war. The magazine had always considered London and Paris, although not Newark or Chicago, within its sphere of inaction. It had run a weekly or fortnightly letter from each of these capitals for years, with an occasional Letter from Salzburg, or Megève or Berlin (during the 1936 Olympics) or Bayreuth as a seasonal variant. The editors, although annoyed by the war because it posed new problems in the selection of comic drawings, thought that the Paris-London aspect of it ought to be covered as thoroughly as a Schiaparelli opening. Harold Ross did not think we would need much on the front, because he had been on the staff of *Stars and Stripes* in Paris in 1918 and felt he knew all about the fighting end, so that it was unnecessary to send out a military expert to represent us. This was lucky for me. The trouble with the *New Yorker* from my point of view as of September 1, 1939, was that all our European coverage was already being done by Janet Flanner, who signed her dispatches "Gênet," and that I could not conceive of a reporter com-ing away from a story just as it broke. Unfortunately for everybody but me, Miss Flanner's mother in California got sick and Miss Flanner noti-fied the office that she wanted to come home. I got the Paris assignment because I had spent several man-hours of barroom time impressing St.

Clair McKelway, then managing editor, with my profound knowledge of France. At about the same time the *New Yorker*, through a London literary agent, acquired the services of Mollie Panter-Downes to do the London Letter. No one in the office at the time of the hiring had ever seen Mollie—the whole transaction was a great boost for the pin-through-the-program system of picking winners at horse races.

I knew very little about Lady Mendl, Elsa Maxwell, Mainbocher and Worth the dressmakers, Mr. and Mrs. Charles Bedeaux, or a number of other leading characters in Gênet's Paris dispatches, but since it seemed probable that they would lam anyway, Ross was willing to overlook this deficiency and even agreed in a halfhearted way with McKelway's idea that I write about the reactions to war of ordinary French people. "But for God's sake keep away from low-life," Ross said. Meyer Berger had once written a *New Yorker* profile of a man who fished for lost coins through subway gratings, and Ross had been trying for months to disinfect the magazine by running pieces about Supreme Court justices and the Persian Room of the Plaza. I promised to keep my end of the war reasonably clean and high-class, and the office booked me a passage on a Pan American Clipper to Lisbon. It was not hard to get an eastbound ticket that season; there were only eight passengers on my plane, including me.

After I had got what I wanted and was sure to go, I had a couple of misgivings. German planes had not yet bombarded French cities, but people here thought that they eventually would, and I shared the general Sunday-supplement idea of what bombing could accomplish. I remember a sequence in a newsreel that September that showed the panic of a London crowd when some crank started throwing rubber balls about. The people had got the idea that there was a raid on; I remember one woman throwing her children on the ground and covering them with her body. I was never to see people so frightened during a real bombing. Walking down Lexington Avenue with Joe Mitchell of the *New Yorker* one warm night shortly before I was scheduled to take off, I said, "I bet I'll wish I was back on Lex a lot of times before this thing is over." The more a man sees of war the more immediate danger has to be before he starts worrying about it. I was talking last spring to a major in Leclerc's Fighting French column who was taking a sun bath in a cup in the hills during the battle of Enfidaville. We were all temporarily trapped by mortar fire, but none of the shells had yet landed in the hollow. They were bursting on the other side of the hill, fifty yards away. I still trepidate at fifty yards, so I said to this major, "That makes me a droll of an effect." He said, "It is all a question of habit," and continued to take his sun bath. In 1939 a lot of us scared at four thousand miles.

A couple of weeks after I talked to the sun-bathing major I met a 59-year-old second lieutenant in the Corps Franc d'Afrique who was on his way to lead an infantry attack, and he said courage was a question of digestion. On the morning of October 9, 1939, when I took off for the war my digestion was excellent, but I was nervous as hell.

At that period—it sounds like talking about stagecoach days—the Clippers still left from a yacht-club setting at Port Washington, Long Island. A friend of mine named Fred Schwed, a romantic soul who had been reared on Richard Harding Davis, although in early manhood he had switched to Scott Fitzgerald, had asked to drive me out to my plane in the early morning. Passengers were supposed to be at the plane with their luggage at eight o'clock. Schwed picked me up at an hour I never had experienced while sober, at the door of the house where I was living, and headed in what I took to be the direction of Long Island because the sun was rising over it. He drove me over one bridge, which was all right, and then around a wild farming country, in which I distinctly saw a hen and on another occasion what I took to be a cow—in one jump more I figured he would have me among the coyotes and Republicans—and then over another bridge, which was all wrong because it landed us in Westchester County. By then I had only an hour or so to catch the plane, so I began to curse, which I do well. The secret of good cursing lies in cadence, emphasis, and antiphony. The basic themes are always the same. Conscious striving after variety is not to be encouraged, because it takes your mind off your cursing. By the time Schwed got me to the landing he felt what a proper swine he was for having gotten up early in the morning to take me to the plane, and if the experience had broken him of volunteering to do favors for people it would have been worth while. I rushed into the dinky frame ticket and customs office they had there, still drooling obscenity, and saw my mother, who had gotten up early in another part of Long Island and come out to see me off. Sucking back four bloody oaths that I could already feel pressing against the back of my teeth, I switched to a properly filial expression, embraced the dear woman, and got aboard the Clipper feeling like Donald Duck.

There was one woman among the passengers, a myopic young American married to a fifty-year-old Englishman who told me he raised vast quantities of broad-*a* tomatoes in the Canary Islands. The tomatist boasted of having financed Franco's airplane trip from the Canaries to Spain at the beginning of the Spanish counter-revolution. He evidently thought it had been a brilliant idea. They had a stateroom, a fact I note for its antiquarian interest: I have seldom traveled since in a plane that wasn't crowded beyond seating capacity. We all floated in luxury on that trip, with two stewards to take care of the eight of us, soundproofing that has since been eliminated even from Clippers to keep down non-essential weight, and Pullman-style berths to sleep in. The most notable passenger was a French stage and screen star going back to report for military service because, he explained to me, a French movie star who remained in Hollywood during the war would lose his popularity at home.

Since he was fifty years old there was not much chance he would be taken into the army, but he had a faithful public in France which thought he was a good deal younger than that. It startled me to see him making up his face in the morning when he climbed out of his berth, but he was a nice civilized Joe. It was the first time he had ever been in an airplane, and he was pleased and excited. "Poor, sick old Europe," he kept saying to the rest of us between slugs of scotch, "poor, sick old Europe." He had just been married in America and thought it was the only country in the world that had a future. We also had on board a professional correspondent named Bob Nixon, of International News Service, a rich Peruvian kid who was going back to Paris to finish a course at the Sorbonne, a German Jew who was a naturalized Cuban citizen and on his way to France to sell the Government a kind of blue paint to put over headlights so they would give full light but would not gleam in the blackout—there was a fortune in it, he told us all, if he could make the right connections—and a brocade manufacturer from Zurich who was going home to take up his reserve commission in the Swiss Army. The Peruvian was quiet and apparently airsick all the way across. The Swiss was a solid sort who told me that the German-speaking cantons were more anti-Nazi than the French cantons. He said he thought Switzerland could maintain her neutrality indefinitely because her army could make invasion expensive for anybody. I found this hard to believe.

When I got tired of talking to the other passengers I thought about women. I frequently do this for hours without becoming bored; they are much pleasanter than sheep to think of when you are trying to fall asleep. Thinking about women also makes you insensible to mild fright or minor discomforts. Once I was sleeping with another fellow under a pup tent in a rainstorm in Tunisia, and at about two o'clock in the morning he woke me up. I said, "What's up?" and he said, "The tent's just blown away." The rain had turned into a cloudburst, and my blankets were soaked through. I got into the front seat of a jeep and wrapped the wet blankets around me. The top and windshield afforded some help, but the water lashed in from both sides. I thought about women for four and a half hours and never even caught cold.

The Frenchman and Nixon and I took the train north from Lisbon the day after we landed. The German-Cuban had no French visa, the Peruvian had disappeared, the Swiss was to take an Italian plane to Rome and go on from there; the tomato twosome were staying on in Lisbon. There was no more feel of war—or rather, since I did not know what war felt like, of difference from peace—in Lisbon than there had been in Port Washington. As soon as the train crossed the Portuguese-Spanish frontier at Fuentes de Oñoro we recognized by the atmosphere that we were in a belligerent country. The train passed camps surrounded by barbed wire and populated either by Republican prisoners of war or Franco soldiers. The victors were so miserably dressed that it was impossible for a stranger to tell them from the vanquished. The station platforms were crowded with soldiers in cotton uniforms and canvas shoes and with officers in boots and Sam Browne belts. The officers, who paid no fare, made a practice of boarding the train and riding for a couple of stations in the wagon-restaurant, where they regaled themselves on black bread, green apples, and imitation coffee, evidently a cut above what they ordinarily got at mess. An obvious flatfoot in plain clothes stood at the end of the corridor of our first-class carriage and watched the door of our compartment, and the bare rocky country through which the railroad passed stank of poverty and ruin. At Irun all the passengers bound for France were marched through the streets to the villa of the fascist governor and kept waiting in the garden for a couple of hours until an assistant had gone through our passports. From the manner of these strutting sparrows of men you might have got the idea that they had defeated France, the United States, and Great Britain, which they had in a way, of course, but by default, and that we were captives. After the tomato fancier's protégés had finished with us, the French actor, Nixon, and I walked across the international bridge to La Hendaye. Since the Pan American people had limited us to fifty-five pounds of luggage we had no trouble carrying our stuff with us. Coming into France, where there was no strain in the faces of the lazy-looking customs guards and where there were few soldiers in evidence and plenty to eat, was like arriving in a neutral from a belligerent country.

After we had gone over to the French *gare* and gotten aboard the Sud-Express for Paris we stood looking out the carriage window at France before the train started. The actor called my attention to an erect, worthy-looking old man in a derby hat and pepper-and-salt topcoat who stood on the platform, waiting to get aboard the train. He had a clipped white mustache and a fine, honest face. The actor was much moved. "It's Pétain!" he said. "He's ambassador to Spain now. Madame lives at La Hendaye." The movie actor had been an ordinary soldier in the other war. "What a fine old boy!" he said with emotion. I had not recognized the marshal, because I had always thought of him with the long, down-sweeping mustaches of his World War I photographs. I felt constrained to agree with my companion. "A great old gent!" I said. He was the first marshal of France I had seen, and his presence seemed a link with Napoleon and a happy augury. "He is young for his age!" the actor said with admiration. I had to admit that he didn't look a day over seventy-five.

The Sud-Express, except for the blacked-out windows and the dim blue lights in the corridor after nightfall, was as fine and punctual a train as it had ever been. The only person aboard who appeared affected by the war was an attendant whom I asked for a couple of bottles of Vichy Célestin. He said, "We have only Vichy Saint-Louis on the train now. You can't get everything you want now, there's a war on!" He wore the same expression of desolation as a waiter at Lüchow's in New York last summer telling me that there was no more Gaspé salmon, only Nova Scotia salmon, on account of the war.

The train arriving at Paris stopped at the Gare d'Austerlitz, far from the center of the city, and it took me a couple of minutes to get a taxicab, but the city, a considerable portion of which we had to traverse to reach my hotel, looked much as it had in 1927 except for the strips of paper pasted across shop windows to keep the glass from flying in case of a bombardment. I don't know yet whether this dodge is of any use. I can't remember seeing any on London shops and don't know whether they gave it up before I got there or just never tried it. The taxis I had seen outside the station were all ridiculously old *tacots*, which is French for jalopies, because the newer cars had been requisitioned by the Government. They had the old-fashioned hand horns that figure in the orchestration of *The Last Time I Saw Paris*.

I had decided on the Hôtel Louvois, facing the Bibliothèque Nationale, across the little Square Louvois. The façade and the square had always attracted me when I was a student. The Louvois would have been no good for me then, being on the Right Bank, and besides the allowance that my father sent me in those days would never have permitted such an expenditure—the Louvois was marked at least *tout confort* and possibly even *deuxième catégorie* in the Hachette Guide Bleu. I figured that as a war correspondent, however, I would be able to afford it. Room and bath cost me eleven dollars a week. I took a room that fronted on the square, overlooking the fountain with heroic allegorical figures representing the rivers of France. There were four statues, all expansively female and symbolizing, I think, the Seine, Rhone, Loire, and Garonne. From my balcony on the second floor of the hotel I had a fine view of the Garonne's navel, which was nearly big enough to hold a baseball. There were twenty-one trees, an even greater number of flowers, in season, and a *pissoir* and a *chalet de necessité* in the little park. There were also benches where lovers and nursemaids came to sit. The Rue Richelieu runs along the Bibliothèque side of the square; the Rue Chabanais with its meretricious associations begins on the hotel side. On the other two sides there were six-story buildings, one of them a hotel, with people living in them whom I saw principally when some event of general interest like a wife-beating was going on in the square, when they would all appear on the little balconies in front of their windows.

In a general way I felt that my quarter included everything between the boulevards and the river, from the Place de la Concorde around to the Place de la Bastille, but my home province in this empire was roughly bounded by Rue Saint-Augustin, Rue Sainte-Anne, Rue Richelieu (with Rue Montpensier and the Palais Royale on the other side of it), and the Place in front of the Comédie Française, with the Café de la Régence on the other side. A province of two hundred acres that included the national library, the national theater, and the national lupanar, all a bit overlaid

with dust and tradition, but still sound. It was part of the Second Arrondissement, represented in the Chamber of Deputies by Paul Reynaud.
He had been elected by seventeen votes. I often reflected, after he became President of the Council in March, that any nine electors from among
the pharmacists' assistants, bistro proprietors, and sporting girls I got
to know in the quarter might have changed the history of France and of
the world by their votes.

After I had left my bag and typewriter at the hotel I went around to
the Paris branch of the Guaranty Trust to get some money on a letter of
credit, and met Theodore Rousseau, the director, who had once been a
New York newspaperman and then secretary to Mayor John Purroy
Mitchel and had since married the Princesse de Broglie. Rousseau invited
me to a wartime lunch at Larue's—it turned out to be just Marennes,
Pouilly Fuissé, *caille vendangeuse*, and Grands Echezeaux—and then
said, "You may have got here too late, old fellow. There's a strong tip on
the Bourse this morning that the war's going to be called off."

4/ My Generals, My Generalissimo

WHEN I FIRST ARRIVED IN FRANCE I was told that there were two institutions
beyond suspicion, the Church and the professional army. The Church did
not interest me, but the generals did. The interest did not date back only
to the beginning of the war. Even at college I had occasionally risked the
contempt of my fellow liberals by reading a book about a soldier. Perhaps
it was because in childhood I had owned a picture book illustrated with
plates representing Napoleon's battles (the Pyramids, with the Little Corporal surrounded by Mamelukes, was my favorite, and the Retreat from
Moscow broke my heart) and had later read Dunn-Pattison's *Napoleon's
Marshals*. I could once name all twenty-six of them—Augereau, Berna-
dotte, Berthier, Bessières, Brune, and then I lose the alphabetic thread.
The first French general I had ever seen was Joffre, in New York during
the other war; I had felt very knowing every time I referred to him as
"Popper." The first I had ever spoken to was old Gouraud, who was on
some sort of a cultural lecturing tour in 1928 when I met him on his way
to Woonsocket, Rhode Island, which has a large French population. I was
then in exile as a reporter on the Providence *Journal* and *Bulletin*; I had
been fired from the sports department of the New York *Times* for frivolity, but in Providence I got all assignments bearing on European affairs
because they knew I had been in Paris.

The general's train had pulled in from New York during the night, and
he was sleeping in a Pullman car on a siding. I wanted to get him in time

for a first-edition story for the *Bulletin*, so I went into the car and woke him up. He was in a lower berth, and his whiskers were hanging over the edge of it. I shook him by the shoulder and said firmly, *"La presse!"* He got the idea and started to get up right away. I guess he had had a lot of arguments with out-of-town reporters already. *"Nous débutons, messieurs!"* he sang out. He had a half-dozen officers concealed in uppers and lowers all around the car, and they all got up. He gave me an exclusive interview, saying he liked Americans and France wanted to be friends with the United States. I took it that it would be all right with him to say he liked Woonsocket, although he had not yet been there, so I put that in the story too, although I worried about the journalistic ethics of the procedure. In those days I was as ethical as Westbrook Pegler, although poorer.

All this will explain why I was predisposed in favor of French generals when I got to Paris in 1939, and why I have been ever since. A fellow who wanted to keep abreast with French history during the following years could not have picked a better specialty. The first project I had brought from New York with me was to write a *New Yorker* profile of General Gamelin, and that necessitated an orientation in his milieu. I looked forward to it with pleasure, like doing a piece about prize fighters or sporting women. Some fellows like to write about the stage or screen, but I never understood why. Others can contemplate without repugnance doing a profile of a politician, a newspaper publisher, or even an advertising man or somebody in the radio business, but my tastes do not run that way. Like Edward Gibbon, a military buff although he never licked anybody himself, I like to hear talk about fighting. The most sensible talk I ever heard on the subject was from Sam Langford, the old Boston Tar Baby; but a French general has something genteel and old-worldly about him that Sam lacks. A good specimen combines the charm of Raymond Weeks, my old professor of philology, and Tex Grenet, the courtly old man who used to make the morning line for the bookmakers before the pari-mutuel came to the New York tracks. Maybe it's a father fixation.

Thucydides and Plutarch saved anecdotes about generals; why should I be proud? A general once told me one about General Mittelhauser, who will be remembered only because he succeeded Weygand in Syria and then declined to continue the war by General De Gaulle's side. Mittelhauser and an aide were returning to Paris by air when the plane developed engine trouble. It began to lose altitude. Mittelhauser looked at his aide, the aide was calm. Mittelhauser thought, "There can't be anything serious. I will not show this young man I am alarmed." The aide looked at Mittelhauser. Mittelhauser appeared calm. The aide thought, "I will not show the boss I am alarmed." The pilot made a crash landing in an orchard; the plane ran between two trees and lost both wings. "Then," said the general who told me the story, "Mittelhauser and the aide knew there had been something serious." The aide pulled Mittelhauser out of the wrecked plane. Mittelhauser said, "When does the next train leave for Paris?" The aide said, "My general, I don't even know where we are." Mittelhauser shouted in a rage, "Imbecile! You never know anything!"

Another general told me another anecdote about Weygand in the First World War. The general who was telling me the story had then been a lieutenant colonel of artillery; Weygand had been Foch's chief of staff. The artillerist had participated in an unsuccessful attack on a little hill; Weygand asked him why his guns had not been able to knock out the enemy's machine-gun positions. "Because they could not be brought to bear at that angle, my general," the artillerist had said. "You are of those who believe that infantry unsupported by artillery cannot take such positions?" "I am of those, my general." "Then bugger off," Weygand had said indignantly and stalked away.

Another old general, a fine old specimen who had been of Gamelin's *promotion* at St. Cyr, was telling me about 1894, when the Dreyfus case had split the French Army wide open. This general, by exception, had been a *Dreyfusard* as a young officer. His best friend at St. Cyr had been an anti-Dreyfusard. They had quarreled, and from that day they had stopped speaking to each other. After the war, in which both had distinguished themselves, my general was riding in a railroad train when at a station the compartment door opened and in walked his former friend, who now had 110 per cent disability for war wounds. My general had 120 per cent. The other officer sat down on the bench opposite my general without saying a word, and they glared at each other for about fifty miles. At last the former anti-Dreyfusard extended his hand and said, "Will you at least shake hands with me?" My Dreyfusard general said, "If you have arrived at better sentiments, yes."

If these stories amuse you, you may understand my obsessional interest in French generals; if not you may consider it a hobby without apparent charm, like peridromophily, which is the collection and classification of street-railway tickets.

I knew that it would be hard to get an interview with the generalissimo of all the Allied Forces while he was running such a large war, so I bespoke the good offices of William C. Bullitt, the United States ambassador, in obtaining it. Gamelin, in all the fall of 1939, granted only one interview, and that a mass affair for all the American correspondents. Bullitt had himself been the subject of a flashy profile by Gênet. He did not know whether it had been flattering or not, and neither did I after having read it only once, but it was expedient for both of us to act as if it had been, he in order to maintain his standing as man of the world and I because I wanted him to do me a favor. He was at any rate a *New Yorker* reader; so, I afterward learned, was Paul Reynaud, and I have sometimes wondered whether Reynaud got his copies regularly in his prisons after the Armistice. I reminded Bullitt that the *New Yorker*, despite its relatively small circulation for a national magazine, went to some pretty literate people all over the country, and that our stuff was filtered down through word of mouth and reprint until it had an effect on public opinion disproportionate to the number of first readers. He said he thought the interview could be arranged, if I wasn't in too much of a hurry. He sent me to Colonel Horace A. Fuller, the military attaché, now a major general commanding a division somewhere in the Pacific, and Fuller promised to talk to Colonel Jean Petibon, Gamelin's *chef de cabinet*, for me. Before interviewing Gamelin I knew that I would have to document myself on his views, his past, and enough of his technical background and jargon to make him feel that I knew what he was talking about. The preparation is the same whether you are going to interview a diplomat, a jockey, or an ichthyologist. From the man's past you learn what questions are likely to stimulate a response; after he gets going you say just enough to let him know you appreciate what he is saying and to make him want to talk more. Everybody with any sense talks a kind of shorthand; if you make a man stop to explain everything he will soon quit on you, like a horse that you alternately spur and curb. It is all in one of Sam Langford's principles of prize fighting: "Make him lead." Only instead of countering to your subject's chin you keep him leading. Once I asked Sam what he did when the other man wouldn't lead, and he said, "I run him out of the ring." This is a recourse not open to the interviewer.

In the summer of 1940 I went up to the Hotel Carlton in Washington to talk to General John J. Pershing about the subject of a profile I was then working on. I did everything I could to get the old man to loosen up, including pretty obvious flattery. "When they started to cut down the Army after the Armistice in 1918, General," I said, "you were against it, weren't you, because you foresaw this new European crisis?" The old boy looked at me in an angry, disgusted manner and said, "Who the hell could have foreseen this?"

The worst thing an interviewer can do is talk a lot himself. Just listening to reporters in a barroom, you can tell the ones who go out and impress their powerful personalities on their subject and then come back and make up what they think he would have said if he had had a chance to say anything. One of the best preps I ever did was for a profile of Eddie Arcaro, the jockey. When I interviewed him the first question I asked was, "How many holes longer do you keep your left stirrup than your right?" Most jockeys on American tracks ride longer on their left side. That started him talking easily, and after an hour, during which I had put in about twelve words, he said, "I can see you've been around riders a lot." I had, but only during the week before I was to meet him.

A profile of course is more than a well-prepared interview. You try to get anecdotes and objective views of the subject from people who have known him at various stages of his life, and then you fit the whole business together. I figured correctly that I would have plenty of time to dig up background before I would be allowed to see the generalissimo. I began by asking M. André de Laboulaye, a former French ambassador to the United States who was now the titular head of the American section at the Hôtel Continental, to recommend a general as a guide to higher strategy and tactics. Old M. l'Ambassadeur, who had some of the charm but none of the decisiveness of a general himself, sent me to General Pujo, who had retired from the command of the Army of the Air only a year before the war began.

General Pujo was a fine average specimen of a general, with ice-blue eyes, a firm chin, a good handshake, and a vast, high-ceilinged apartment in the Rue de l'Arcade with rooms full of Sèvres vases and Empire furniture. All generals, naturally, have a tendency to furnish in Empire because that was a period when generals were appreciated. His conversation was full of nice homely phrases like "we will have them" and "we will not let go the morsel." He said that General Gamelin, an old acquaintance of his, was a man of "tranquil luminosity of mind." Finally he recommended that I buy the *Instruction for the Handling of Large Units*, a publication of the French General Staff which set forth for commanding officers the official tactical doctrine. It had been prepared while Weygand was still commander in chief of the French Army and published in 1936, but the doctrine, Pujo said, had not changed under Gamelin, Weygand's successor. He gave me a note of introduction to Berger-Levrault, the great military booksellers on the Boulevard Saint-Germain.

Berger-Levrault was a fascinating shop, surprisingly like Champion, the publisher of medieval texts on the Quai Voltaire, where I had spent good hours in my earlier Paris time. The clerks, male and female, in their gray linen dusters reminded me of Champion's. They had the same complete knowledge of stock and mental catalogue of regular customers. They regarded newcomers with the same suspicious indifference, but an introduction "*de la part du Général Pujo*" had the same effect as a *de la part* of Joseph Bedier's would have had at Champion's in 1926. The French made the art of war so intellectually fascinating that the study must have stolen any reasonable general from the practice. I went in for documentation on a massive scale, putting my purchases on my expense account. General Gamelin had commanded a campaign against the Druses in the twenties; I bought and read a magnificent history of the Druses, an interesting if repulsive people, by the way, and then a detailed military history of the campaign. When I at length met the generalissimo I asked him one question based on this mass of stimulating reading, and used about one line of what he said about it.

Gamelin himself had done a bit of writing, like most French generals, and I searched Berger-Levrault's stock for Gamelin items. One phrase of his, from a textbook, particularly impressed me: "Experience should be a springboard under our feet, and not a ball and chain at our ankles." There was also a paragraph that seemed slightly stuffy in an intelligent way: "It is natural that the immediate collaborators of higher officers be allowed to

THE ROAD BACK TO PARIS /31

express their opinions freely, it being understood that each must bow in just intellectual discipline once the decision has been made. Initiative, within the frame of intellectual discipline, is the strength of armies."

There was some difference of opinion about the generalissimo among officers of the French Army even in the early days of the war, although all admitted he was bright. The discontent came chiefly from two sources— partisans of General Weygand, who had been retired for age in 1935, and those of General George, chief of the armies in the war zone and heir apparent to Gamelin's job. The generalissimo had in turn recently attained the retirement age of sixty-seven, both parties pointed out, but they based different arguments on this fact. The Weygandists said that if the Government was going to overlook technicalities about age their man should have been kept on, especially since he was so chipper that he had been recalled at the beginning of the war and placed in command of the Army of the Levant. The Georgists said that Gamelin should have retired gracefully and handed over to George.

The only man to whom I spoke who even then predicted disaster was Charles Sweeny, an American who had been at various times a colonel in the Foreign Legion, a correspondent for the New York *World*, and a promoter of ice hockey at the Palais de Glace. He had white hair which he wore cut in a Roman bang, and he aspersed his conversation with allusions to the campaigns of Lucullus and Sulla, which perhaps led me to minimize the importance of what he said. He said that the Army was rotten because the officers were afraid to work the men hard; energetic officers were curbed by their superiors, who lived in fear of politicians. Colonel Sweeny thought also that the ten francs a day which in this war was the pay of men under fire was excessive and would lead to drunkenness and mutiny. Having all this money to spend did not seem to affect the fighting quality of French troops in Tunisia later, however, while the English have been able to fight pretty decently under the triple handicap of three bob, or sixty cents a day. The Americans have not been stopped by still higher pay, and the Australians have done all right with the highest scale of all. I think that Sweeny's political was better than his economic reasoning. At any rate he said the Army was nothing like as sound as the Army of the last war and that it would collapse at the first push. It did. Colonel Sweeny affected me like the dilapidated stranger who appears at least once in most racegoers' lives and tries to tout them onto a twenty-to-one shot, which then wins. I paid no attention to him.

My interview came to pass about two months after I had opened negotiations for it. Colonel Petibon, a hard-looking, hard-driving officer whose arrival at a colonelcy at the age of forty-five was considered precocious in the French Army, had first interviewed me in an office like a monastic cell off a long corridor of the Hôtel des Invalides, early in November. The colonel told me that he was a *New Yorker* reader too. He evidently decided I was all right and said I must not leave town; he

would call me when the generalissimo could see me. It was just about
four weeks later that he telephoned to me at my hotel.

Gamelin's headquarters was at Vincennes, which was a semi-public
secret, but he seldom received there. When he was in Paris he used as
his office a paneled Louis XV room at the Ecole Militaire which for years
had served as Joffre's study. Joffre, of course, had been Gamelin's *grand
patron*. Gamelin had risen under his aegis in the other war, serving him in
the same capacity that Petibon now served Gamelin. The square on which
the Ecole stands was renamed the Place Maréchal-Joffre after the First
World War, and an equestrian statue of the marshal, who rode regularly
and grimly to keep his weight down, stands in the center of it, or at least
did then. The ivory-tinted walls of the generalissimo's suite, still decorated with crowns and fleurs-de-lis in gold, displayed large paintings of
the battles of Fontenoy and Lawfeldt, eighteenth-century victories of the
French Army. It was a raw day, and the room was heated by a small gas
fire. In the anterooms were steel engravings of difficult Alpine defiles
captured by the French in 1800. The entire place was reminiscent of an
ancient, successful business house.

Gamelin fitted perfectly into the vaguely Dickensian setting. He is five
feet four inches tall, which is not conspicuously short for a Frenchman.
He has a good round Flemish head, his hair was blond and parted in the
middle, his cheeks were rosy pink, and he wore a sandy mustache which
had recently taken an optimistic, upward curl. The generalissimo seemed
to me to have the face of a skeptical but indulgent Dutch uncle in a Frans
Hals painting, although in newspaper photographs he often had appeared
grim and strained. I consider him one of the most intelligent and sensitive
men I ever met.

Gamelin did not favor the defensive *per se*, any more than an experienced automobile driver favors always going in one sense of the compass.
He believed that an attack upon Germany would have no chance of
success until the Allies had accumulated a superiority of material, including airplanes, and that only the defensive was feasible in the interim. The
strategic concept was not bad. It was that upon which Great Britain was
to fight the war after the fall of France. But Gamelin's correct conclusion
was based on a false premise; Great Britain and France together, with the
factories they had working for them in the United States, were not out-
producing Germany then. Great Britain was not training troops as fast as
Germany. The discrepancy of men and materials in the Germans' favor
was increasing. It is hard to believe that the generalissimo did not know
this; harder to believe that, knowing it, he could have seemed so optimistic, like a somnambulist jauntily strolling off a roof. Old schoolmates of
the generalissimo had told me that Gamelin from the moment of his first
arrival at St. Cyr had made the same impression as an ambitious young
seminarist who his colleagues at once feel is destined for a high place in
the hierarchy. They had said, "He would rather be generalissimo than

anything else in the world." But he could not have wanted to be remembered as the commander of a disaster.

"You can't get out of the concrete," he said to me regretfully. "There isn't enough heavy artillery in the world to get out of the concrete." This respect for fortification hardly jibed with his omission of it on the north of his line. His failure was not of concept but of execution. "Twenty-five per cent for the theoretical solution of the problem," Foch, his old professor at the War College, had told him often enough, "seventy-five per cent for the application in battle." Then, in the spring, the Allies were to abandon even the strategic defensive and move into the Low Countries.

It is not enough to say that the French paid too little attention to the use of tanks and bombers by the Germans in Poland. They believed in anti-tank defenses, in anti-tank guns, in a strong tactical air force which would control the sky over the battlefield at least, in such elementary conservative chores as keeping the men supplied with food and small-arms ammunition. Their deficiencies in all these matters had nothing to do with strategic doctrine. But in retrospect it is hard for me to associate the calm little man in the big old-fashioned room with omissions in the most elementary parts of war. It is as if I had had a long conversation with a novelist—perhaps M. Jules Romains—and a couple of years later somebody came to me and said, "You remember M. Romains? He was an illiterate."

5 / Bajus Disappointed

THE WAR OF COURSE was not called off, but there were few indications that it was on. Paris was a city in which people were tentatively picking up the threads of ordinary existence—tentatively and a little sheepishly, as if ashamed of their initial agitation. Several million Frenchmen had been mobilized, thirty-eight Communist Deputies had been put in jail, and the newspapers carried a daily communiqué which sometimes chronicled "operations" as small as the shooting of an enemy messenger dog. People distrusted the calm, but there was nothing they could do about it except talk. During each fortnight the city lived through two or three periods of intense preoccupation with the war and as many of groping toward an approximation of peacetime life.

Only the women clung to the hope of a continuing miracle—a war without hard fighting. "Hitler will surely blow out his brains," they said, or "Just think how much money the English must be spending for the revolution in Germany." They circulated with grave optimism the story that a gipsy woman had got into an autobus and sat down next to a Parisienne who had moved her handbag out of the gipsy's reach. The gipsy had then said, "Why do you do that when you have only eighteen francs in your bag?" The woman had exactly that sum. Then the gipsy told each of the other passengers how much he or she had, down to the last *sou*. "Since you know so much," one passenger had asked, "tell us when Hitler will die." "On December second," the gipsy had said, and had got out at the next stop. A story like that gained currency not because Frenchwomen were silly but because they refused to believe that their sons and husbands would be killed—those sons and husbands who until then had been so miraculously preserved, it seemed. Miracles are perhaps to be distrusted; the men were being preserved for the bitterest destiny an army ever had, but nobody then divined it. The book of Michel Nostradamus, the old astrologer, had become a best seller. According to the exegetes of the full-length thirty-franc version I acquired, he had predicted the destruction of Paris by "birds from the East," and its reconquest a year later by a French king after a great victory in the Valley of the Loire, but there was some confusion about the dates for which he had predicted these events. Maybe Hitler will die on a December second—the odds are only 364 to 1 against it; perhaps there will be a battle of the Loire on the way back to Paris. Then the gipsy woman and Nostradamus will get credit for having seen clear, like experts on European affairs.

I was told that in September there had been emotion manifest in Paris; air raids had been expected hourly, reservists went to the front expecting to be hurled into counterattacks against an invader; the Poles had been the darlings of the public. But now that was all over. When people thought of the war it was with cold exasperation; there was a self-conscious distrust of phrases like "heroic poilu," "sacred soil," and "accursed Boche," but it had become clear that as long as Germany was free to mess up Europe every twenty years life would be barely supportable. Not quite everybody realized that life would not be supportable at all. It was the psychology of a defensive war; none other is possible to a decent people until it has suffered much, when a retributive counteroffensive spirit can be aroused. If all the newspaper files and foreign correspondents' books and White and Gray and Mauve Papers of a dozen governments were to be destroyed forever, the fact that the French fought would remain as proof they must have been right. They hated it so, and in the beginning they had had so clear an idea of the odds against them.

André Chamson, in his journal of the war at the front, wrote, "Hitler thought he would have us as he had had the Social Democrats—without fighting. He awaits the disintegration of the last man. But here around me the world is full of men." The Poles and the French had ended the sequence of conquests by bluff, and in doing so made Hitler's end inevitable. His capacity for bluff had been infinite; his capacity for conquest by arms, although great, was insufficient.

In Paris it was the great age of the strategists of the Café du Commerce, the French term for the armchair kind. And the hot blood that had rushed toward the national head during the month of September receded in October toward the feet already chilled by the overtures of a winter of rationed fuel. Behind the blacked-out windows of the cafés in the evenings there was some of the promiscuous sociability of speakeasy days in prohibition-time New York and, I am told, of air-raid shelters during the London blitz. Anybody at all was willing to tell you how the war could be won, but a majority favored gradual methods like the starvation of German war industry.

General Robert-Georges Nivelle, little remembered outside France then or now, had left a deep trace upon the feeling and thinking of his country. It was Nivelle who had talked his countrymen into the great offensive in the Champagne in April of 1917, remembered as the "great bloodletting." When a café strategist complained of seeming inaction in 1939, a confrere had only to wave a finger and say, "Nivelle," to shut him up. In six days in Nivelle's battle in 1917 the French had lost 35,000 killed and 80,000 wounded. As a measure of comparison, we had less than 15,000 casualties, not counting prisoners of war, in the whole African campaign. There were no hospitals reasonably near the battlefield for so many wounded, so they had to be distributed all over France; the trains of mangled men spread despair through the country. Mutinies had followed; every Frenchman of an age to be in civilian clothes in 1939 remembered that awful time. Eventually the Germans would have to attack, the café strategists said, but then we would have them.

Sometimes there was visible a bit of the surface ebullience that my friends told me there had been in Paris in the other war. One Sunday I was walking in Montmartre with my old Henri, whose American silk firm had folded its Paris office during the depression and who had lost all his money, and on the Place Blanche we saw a great crowd of soldiers and strollers around a song plugger who was selling a new ballad. The plugger, a youth about fifteen, wore four hats one on top of another and howled into a megaphone with indelicate gaiety:

"*Hitler n'en a pas,*
Du tout, du tout!
Hitler n'en a pas,
Pas même un tout p'tit bout!"

The lyrics were about things like ammunition and beefsteaks and gaiety. The plugger's gestures weren't included in the lyrics.

There was an evening when I heard two pimps arguing about the war in the bar of a brothel. Each was in fact the protector of one of the two *sous-maîtresses* of the house, and each was waiting until his particular protégée accumulated enough capital and good will to start in business for herself. So they were men with an assured future. It must have been in early October, when the French still held a minuscular strip of German territory in the Saar. "Them, they're not here!" one pimp shouted. "Us, we're there! So we must be winning." A moment later, to emphasize some point or other, he started showing off his World War I wounds and yelled, "I bet I am the only pimp in France with three citations." The proprietor of the house in which they were arguing was a naturalized Italian who, his wife always said, was a perfect gentleman because he never drank anything but champagne. "Not even in the morning!" Madame Lucie would say, looking adoringly at the fat procurer—"not water, not coffee, not beer, not even *mousseux* have I ever seen him drink!" I sometimes used to watch a drop of sweat gleaming on his fat ear and wonder if it tasted of Irroy '28, his favorite. Madame Lucie never told me.

Nearly four years later I was to meet a colleague of the boys under a field ambulance tent on the way to Mateur and Bizerte. He was in the Corps Franc d'Afrique, a volunteer shock-troop outfit. When the nurses had cut his uniform jacket away they had found a tricolor wrapped around his chest. It sounds like the verse of a maudlin song, but it's true. A hunk of shrapnel had gone through the white part of the flag, which was now rust-red. The lower half of a tattooed female extended down toward his scrotum from the place where the flag stopped. When I asked him where he came from he didn't bother saying "Paris"—just "Nineteenth Arondissement." That's Belleville—the stockyards. He had been wounded in the fighting around La Maison Forestière, in the high brush east of Cap Serrat. He had a mouthful of gold teeth and a tough chin. I asked him, foolishly, what he had done in civil life. He said, "I lived on my income."

I do not want to give the impression that I covered Paris for the *New Yorker* entirely from cafés and brothels. I took the responsibilities of my new career so seriously that I joined the Anglo-American Press Association of Paris and went at least once a week to the Hôtel Continental, where the French had set up their equivalent of the British Ministry of Information, although they did not give it the status of a full ministry until the following spring. My sponsors in the Press Association were H. R. Knickerbocker, then with International News Service, and Percy Philip of the New York *Times*. Knick was by way of being a popular hero in Paris because he had broken a big exclusive story about how Nazi leaders had opened bank accounts in a number of neutral countries, including several they were subsequently to take over. He was enthusiastic about the war, meeting me, his apartment on the Ile St-Louis, the sound of the French language, which he could not speak, and the womanhood of Texas. On subsequent occasions I was to meet him being enthusiastic about Winston Churchill, the heroism of the English people, the inspirational gifts of Major General Terry Allen, and the sweetness and fortitude of American army nurses. He and a rear admiral named Clark Howell Woodward are the only two men I ever met in my life who admitted they liked making speeches.

I went up to Knick's apartment one evening with Robert de Saint-Jean of the American section of the Hôtel Continental. Nobody can say Knick wasn't catholic in his choice of guests; it included Edgar Ansel Mowrer on one end of the political scale and on the other a pathological little Frenchman named Jean Fontenoy who wore a turtle-neck sweater with a lounge suit and moaned, whenever he could collect an audience, because the Government refused to call him up for service in the Army. He had been a notorious sucker-around-Abetz and pro-Nazi before the war, a fellow who wrote books boasting of the misery of his peasant parents and preaching that misery was good for working people. It kept them honest, according to him. He, of course, considered he had had a quasi-divine call to the masters' table. He kept on moaning in drugged tones now because he could not get a commission, but he was destined to make collaborationist speeches in theaters after the Armistice and to be found in the Seine with his throat cut. He was the first overt European-type fascist I had ever seen in the flesh, and he had a horrid fascination for me, like the first man a kid sees wearing lipstick and long black stockings. The tomato man on the Clipper had been respectable by comparison. There were not many like Fontenoy to be seen about Paris, and those who did appear in public pretended, like him, that everything had changed for them with the beginning of the war and they were now great patriots. The uncostumed collaborationist types got along swimmingly. Only the turtle-neck sweater boys got into a little trouble, and they not nearly enough. The others had had sense enough to stop talking when the war began, and newspapers friendly to them urged the Government as a national duty to accept them in positions of trust.

The Communists had been inept; they had publicly announced their position against the war, and they were being hunted down as traitors, in many cases by Rightist policemen who were more dangerous types than their quarry. The Maurrases and Lavals, the blackmailers and libelists of L'Action Française and Gringoire, used the Communists skillfully to divert suspicion from themselves. It was Henri de Kerillis, a Rightist himself, who in a speech in the Chamber of Deputies called attention to "the former apologists for the Nazis who are now trying to turn the whole war into a crusade against Stalin." The press almost unanimously reproved him for endangering national unity.

You cannot keep your mind indefinitely on a war that does not begin. Toward the end of the year many of the people who three months before had been ready to pop into their cellars like prairie dogs at the first purring of an airplane motor, expecting Paris to be expunged between dark and dawn, were complaining because restaurants did not serve beefsteak on Mondays, Tuesdays, and Fridays, and because the season had produced no new plays worth seeing. There was even a certain disappointment among the less reflective elements of the population; the appetite for disaster in some human beings is so strong that they feel let down when nothing terrible happens. Cartoonists had developed a number of wartime civilian characters in the genre of Caspar Milquetoast. One of them, a petit bourgeois called Bajus, was shown in a December comic strip listening to a radio address by Hitler. At each howl from the radio set ("I will destroy England before breakfast," "I will show the French what total war means") little Bajus' hair stood on end, and at the close of the speech he turned to his radio, saying, "Oh, please, Adolf, don't stop; frighten me again." Thousands of Bajuses felt deprived of the terror which had become the most interesting component of their daily lives.

There was, even during the fall and winter of 1939, one occasional feature of Paris life that provided a brief reminder of the war in progress. This was the firing of the anti-aircraft guns at German planes that came over on reconnaissance or to drop dirty pictures. The pictures showed British Tommies making love to naked French girls while a poilu died tangled in barbed wire. They fetched a good price from souvenir collectors. The planes never dropped any bombs, but the sound of guns fired in anger and the sight of searchlights combing the night sky is the beginning of a non-combatant's habituation to war. We were being broken in very gently.

The year slid to an end through a nearly normal Paris Christmas season, with carillons and lifesize mechanical figures in the windows of the Galeries Lafayette, postcard hucksters' stalls along the boulevards, and a special Christmas circus at the Medrano, with the three Fratellinis appearing as guest stars. The Medrano was the most delightful little circus in the world, with one ring that had a cushion around it like a billiard table. The liberty horses waved their hoofs in the faces of the spectators in front-row seats. The clowns, clown proper, *auguste* and *grotesque*, shared the hegemony of the ring with the equestrians, according to tradition. The great Fratellinis were not as limber as they had been in my student time, and they took fewer falls, but they had some good mechanical gags and their marvelous faces. The oldest brother got one of the big laughs of the evening when he made his entrance carrying a gas mask. In September every member of his audience had been carrying a similar affair.

The French like old favorites. They go to see them over and over again to observe how time is treating them, and if a performer appears to be in good health they are delighted. They have a weakness for old generals, too, old frock coats, old airplanes. They forget that even the best material wears out. Once Lieutenant Colonel Vincent Sheean and I were riding in an old French airplane in Algeria and the door blew off. There was no particular reason except that it was an old plane and an old door—the wind blew it away. The co-pilot laughed and grabbed my typewriter just as it was about to slide out of the hole the door had left. The conservative spirit is susceptible of exaggeration.

The Medrano was one of my favorite diversions that year. Another was walking along the quais, where the fishermen and book merchants of the Seine pursued the placid, even tenor of their lives. A third was passing one afternoon a week in the hushed interior of the Hamman, the old Turkish bath behind the opera. The Hamman had a dome of colored glass like a mosque and a plunge three strokes long. The icy water plashed into the plunge through the mouths of metal frogs. When you lay on your couch afterward, dozing, you could hear the soothing, nostalgic water-sound like a broken toilet in a New York rooming house. Old François, my favorite rubber, was a tall, stooped Parisian with a face like a rummy Vercingetorix. He was an urban fellow, like me. One day I told him that I was going to the country. He appeared worried, but finally said, "The country, yes. I have heard that it is simply swarming with oxygen."

6 / Vire Revisited

VIRE, like hundreds of other little French cities, showed little outward evidence of the war. About eight hundred of the 6,900 inhabitants Larousse credited the town with had been mobilized, but since Vire had become the home of 1,400 refugees from the war frontiers it had the largest population in its history. Its history goes back to Robert the Devil, who was William the Conqueror's father. Some of the refugees had money, and they had rented every available house in town; others, called "official refugees," got ten francs (less than twenty-five cents) a day from the Government. The mayor, a tall, desiccated doctor who looked like an old-fashioned New England practitioner, said, "It isn't much, of course, but they get along." He told me he didn't think much of the refugees. Soldiers' wives who were residents of Vire received only eight francs a day for themselves and four for each child. The wives, however, having roots in the district, usually had unmobilized relatives who gave them milk and butter and vegetables, for Vire lies in the best dairy country in France. It rains two days out of three from October until July, and no-body used to complain, because the rain made the pastures lush. Now that the Germans have taken away the cattle the rain may be resented.

The Paris newspapers had been paying a good deal of attention to events in the United States. The repeal of the Neutrality Act had got them started, and they had sent a number of reporters to the United States who promptly filed staggering stories of the vast American aircraft industry which was rolling fighter planes off assembly lines as fast as Fords. One plant a fellow described, I remember, was within a couple of miles of Hollywood, and all the most beautiful stars of the cinema used to come out in their automobiles of great luxury to watch the new planes taking to the air like flocks of birds. I was astonished myself when I got back to New York after the debacle to find that we had been producing less than three hundred planes a month, of all categories, at the period of the *grands reportages*. This sort of thing was to cause a disastrous reaction in the spring, when the ground troops discovered that the flocks of airplanes were a myth.

The press of Vire remained strictly cisatlantic. One of the two weeklies, *Le Bocage*, headed its column of criminal proceedings with the news that butter, jam, cake, and sugar had been stolen from one Madame Grandérie by an eleven-year-old boy from a village called Beauquay who had entered her house by climbing a pear tree and breaking three windowpanes. The next item told of the arrest of Joseph Jegu for mendicancy. "Let us add," said *Le Bocage*, "that the individual had a pocketful of money."

When I got to Vire I went to my old hotel, the Cheval Blanc, but found it had changed proprietors. The new man was not nearly as good a cook as the old, who had gone to Angers and taken over a larger hotel also called the Cheval Blanc, but food was as plentiful as before. Outside the grocery stores hung rows of silvery herrings, each with a nail through its tail; the grocers' windows were full of the black smoked sausages called *andouilles de Vire*; the cabbages and onions grew with tropical eagerness in the kitchen gardens even in November. All the local sauces were based on cream and butter and apple brandy—it was a fat country. I wonder how the Virois eat now.

I asked a postman, whom I saw in the café of the hotel, whether old M. Hédouin, the librarian, was still alive, and he said he wasn't.

The economic pulse was steady, I soon found. The farmers were selling beef cattle and horses to the Army at a fixed price which was not a bad one, and there was a new, mysterious war factory among the *vaux*, a mile or two above the town. The countryside reminded me again of southern New England, with rolling hills, birch and holly, elm and oak, except that in the *Bocage* the people had used granite for building houses and barns instead of walls between fields; they marked their boundaries with bands of standing birch and poplar trees. The wet climate has made the Virois quieter than Frenchmen who live in the sun—and harder drinkers. Apple brandy is their regional tipple, and all apple brandy in France is called Calvados in honor of the department in which Vire lies. All over France men had called on the name of this department at marble-topped tables and zinc-topped bars, twenty-four hours a day almost, counting the Paris marketmen who work all night and are great drinkers. Affectionately they had contracted the name to *Calva*, a beautiful name for a drunkard's girl child if any reader wants a tip.

War was no new or strange word in Vire; the Normans had fought the French there, the French the English, and the Huguenots the Catholics;

one wall of a transept of the twelfth-century church was covered with the names of Virois killed in War '14. The mayor, to annoy the curé, always told visitors to Vire that the church dated only from the thirteenth century. He was a Conservative Republican, the mayor, which put him in about the same category as a Republican in Vermont. There were few Marxians in Vire, where they still talked of the French Revolution as a fairly recent event. But they accepted the fact of the Republic as unquestioningly as Vermont farmers do.

Le Bocage had an opposition weekly, *Croix du Bocage*, dedicated to the Catholic point of view. Both papers printed letters from Virois with the Army who said that they were playing with their regimental soccer teams, or wanted sweaters. Both papers published the citation of a lieutenant, the son of a dentist in a neighboring town, who, in one of the skirmishes of outposts in which the armies sometimes indulged, had led a detachment in the capture of a German blockhouse and had operated a machine gun after the death of the gunner. That sort of thing then seemed to an American Homeric.

Headquarters for civilian strategists in Vire was the Café de Paris, where the proprietor, whom I found playing innumerable games of dominoes with all comers, was Maurice Brocco, a man who once enjoyed immense seasonal fame in New York as the little six-day bike rider the crowds at Madison Square Garden liked above all others. Something about him amused the bleary-eyed nocturnal public, and for a long time after he retired Garden fans continued to yell "Come on, Brocco!" when there was a jam.

Brocco is French; he was born near Reims, in the Champagne, which is a flat country favorable to the development of bicyclists. He found, however, that Italian riders were drawing the gate in New York, and since his name sounded Italian he usually rode on the Italian team. It always tickled him when the Italians in the infield yelled, "*Avanti, Brocco!*" In Vire, as might have been expected, Brocco in his cap and sweater was the pattern of dashing cosmopolitanism. I thought that even the mayor, who referred to Brocco as "that good rooster," was a bit jealous of him. With me to bear him out Brocco told the other customers terrible lies about prohibition in America. The lies reconciled them to the wartime prices of *apéritifs*.

On a hill near the town there still stood part of a castle built by Henry Beauclerc, the youngest son of William the Conqueror; and at the foot of the hill the gipsies still camped as they had done seasonally since the tribe came to Europe, snaring rabbits for their food. I came back from the trip feeling pretty good about France.

The through train from Granville to Paris stopped at Vire. When I got aboard I found in the first-class compartment I entered a short, thick-necked, thick-bodied little captain of an Algerian regiment, a fellow with badger-gray hair and clipped mustache who was reading a worn cloth-bound American edition of *The Man That Corrupted Hadleyburg*. "I reread it often," he said in French, noticing me looking at his book. "It is a taste I took in the Cameroons, where I was in garrison for three years. This volume I acquired on a ship where I was of passage to there. Like so many, I read English but I am afraid to speak it. The book has a theme truly French, and an exquisite 'humor.'"

The little captain's regiment was in the northeast, he said, up beyond the end of the old Maginot Line. He was returning from a visit to two married sisters in Granville. He himself had spent most of his life between wars in the colonies—his regiment belonged to the standing army. "It is a splendid regiment," he said. "No *chichi*—just Normans and Kabyles. Most of the native non-coms fought in the other war. They are hard, like the old Roman legionaries." In the North the French were building formidable field defenses, he said. The captain, like scores of Frenchmen I used to talk to, said that he had been ashamed of the abandonment of the Little Entente. Daladier, on his way back from Munich to Paris, had correctly anticipated this feeling. The anecdote of how he drove from Le Bourget to the Quai d'Orsay expecting catcalls and was astonished by being cheered instead is by now familiar, like his comment, *"Les cons!"* But the "spontaneous" demonstrators in the streets were the same hirelings who led the February 1934 riots, working for precisely the same employers—the eternal Nazi-lovers of the industrial cartels. Men of the caliber of my little captain never went into the streets to yell their thoughts at passing limousines. Daladier, a good Frenchman though perhaps a weak man, was puzzled; within a short while he knew that his first intuition had been right. He could not have abandoned Poland without provoking the disintegration of France.

"From Czechoslovakia the Czechs and Russians, and we from the headwaters of the Rhine—the movement of the shovel, what could have been more simple!" the little captain said. "But it would have meant giving up the concept of a defensive war behind the Maginot Line," he added. "You do not know what the concept means to us. It means the high wall topped with broken bottles that the provincial bourgeois puts around his garden. Behind it he is secure with his cabbages. He can wear his slippers, live the good life without bothering to button all the buttons of his trousers. Because I have lived so long outside metropolitan France I can see this."

7 / Merry Christmas, Horrid New Year

IF YOU WERE A CORRESPONDENT in France in 1939 and wanted to go up to the French front you addressed a letter to Mr. Maynard Barnes at the United States Embassy, telling your place of birth, your journalistic history, some reference, and your reason for wishing to go. Barnes forwarded your request to the Intelligence Section at General Headquarters, and in a week or so you were usually granted a pink paper called "A Special Mission Accorded by the General Staff for the Purpose of Journalism," which was good for a week or ten days. You picked up the paper at the Intelligence Section bureau in the Hôtel Continental, where Madame Gros-Perrin, a stout imperious woman with a good laugh, gave you instructions for getting to the front. She told you to go to Nancy and to wait at the Hôtel Thiers there for a press officer from the Intelligence Section who would have further instructions for you. She told you to carry a gas mask and a field helmet. I already owned a gas mask the first time I went up, but I borrowed an American helmet from Captain Bob Schow, one of the assistant military attachés at our embassy. The American helmet then looked a bit like the British job; our new helmets resemble the German.

I left Paris on my first "mission" on December 23. I took the noon train to Nancy, which rolled at its peacetime express clip until nightfall, when, because of the dimmed signal lights, it dropped into a cautious crawl. Arriving at Nancy that night, I found the town blacked out completely. Luckily the hotel was directly across the street from the station, so I was able to reach it without any trouble. A woman at the hotel desk told me that the press officer had not arrived yet, but if I cared to step into the *brasserie* of the hotel I would find a number of other American and English correspondents awaiting him. I could immediately distinguish the correspondents in the *brasserie* because their uniforms were much more magnificent than those of the French military at the other tables. A particularly tailored-looking uniform on Pashkoff, a photographer for *Life*, had the French officers gnawing their mustaches with envy. The most lavishly accoutered man I have seen in France turned out to be an employee of the Columbia Broadcasting System. Since I was trying to get by in riding pants and a vaguely brownish topcoat, I felt like the only ship passenger in a lounge suit at the captain's dinner. I was cheered by the costume of a Mr. Browne of the *Christian Science Monitor*, who had come to the war in tweeds. After one look at each other, Browne and I decided to stick together so that we wouldn't feel inferior.

Most of the correspondents, it developed, were planning to go to a great Christmas Eve midnight Mass in a fortress of the Maginot Line. Columbia and N.B.C. were to broadcast the Mass, and a number of the newsreel companies were to film it. Before the press officer appeared, I was afraid that I would be packed off to the broadcast with all the others, since the Intelligence Section, I figured, probably thought that all Americans were hysterically fond of *radiodiffusion*. But the officer gave Browne and me permission to take a train to Alsace the next afternoon and visit the front there. An officer would call for us when we arrived at a station the captain named, and in due time we would be allowed to see the front.

When, early the next afternoon, we got to our station, we could see we had arrived at the war, because there were no women in sight. Here, against a background of brown, frozen earth and sleety roads, of trees covered with rime, and of the ugly, amorphous buildings of a railway-junction town, there were only soldiers. Most of the men on our train were *permissionnaires* returning from furlough. They lingered around the railroad station unhappily, like students returning from a holiday, then moved off in the direction of their cantonments. Browne and I didn't bother to look for our officer; we were so incongruous in that crowd that he couldn't possibly miss us. After we had waited awhile, an officer stopped in front of us. He had a square jaw and high Celtic cheekbones, and was about as big as a Brooklyn baseball pitcher. "Lieutenant Sauvageon," he announced as he saluted, "aviation officer of the Divisional Staff." Sauvageon stepped aside, and we could see another officer behind him, a slight, smiling man who carried a bamboo cane and maintained a monocle in his right eye. Introducing him to us, Sauvageon said, "Captain de Cholet is one of the few cavalry men in our sector. He is on the staff also." "I have a horse," the captain said, "but he is in Paris."

A soldier came up, took the one valise in which Browne and I had concentrated our possessions, and carried it to a 1936 Citroën that had a red-and-white-striped pennon on the forward end of the left mudguard. "*Fanion du général,*" the soldier volunteered pleasantly, pointing to the pennon. The soldier's name, we learned, was Siegfried. It was a standing joke with the captain and the lieutenant that Siegfried, who was an Alsatian, had constructed the Siegfried Line. Browne and I rode in the rear with the captain between us, and the lieutenant sat in front with Siegfried, who drove. It was about three o'clock in the afternoon. The road was glassy and the mist was very heavy. "Evidently it is not a good day for observation," said the captain. "Moreover, we are sufficiently distant from anything to observe. Therefore, Lieutenant, where can we buy a drink?" "Siegfried," said the lieutenant, "can you discover the mess of the balloonists?" Siegfried did not answer, but after ten minutes of blind navigation he landed us in front of a shuttered tavern.

We all walked into the taproom, which was decorated with a green tile stove, a Christmas tree, and enough antlers to fit out a small museum. At a heavy, bare table a half-dozen soldiers of the Balloon Corps sat with anilin-dyed apéritifs, wrangling over a card game. A young lieutenant got up from among them to greet us. The officers' mess was upstairs, he explained, but he was the only officer in the house, so he had come down to the bar for company. We invited the lieutenant to join us, and Siegfried took his hand at the card table. We all ordered hot grog, and the drink stimulated Browne to ask the balloonist if he had seen anything of a war which, according to the people in the United States, was at that moment in progress between France and Germany. The lieutenant, it seemed, had actually been under fire. The company had an observation balloon at a near-by field, and twice, when it was up, Messerschmitts had come after it. Both times the ground crew had pulled the bag down safely. Lieutenant Sauvageon said that several German machines had come down in the sector. "Curiously," he added, "three of them were undamaged. The pilots said they were airsick. We reported them as shot down because we did not want their families to have any trouble in Germany."

After talking awhile, we said good-by to the balloonist, wished him a merry Christmas, and went out to the Citroën. By now we might as well have been in somebody's pocket for all we could see, but Siegfried, who knew the terrain, was able to feel his way. "It is now evidently quite impracticable even to try to observe," the captain said, "so we will take you to the fort where you are to lodge tonight. It is an old German fort, one they built after they took Alsace from us. It is not a very good fort, but is comfortable, and when we get there the colonel will buy us a drink." Sauvageon, still seated in front, turned around and said, "We picked this colonel specially for you because he is having a big Christmas party and he will have the best oysters and *foie gras* in the sector, better even than the general's. He is a Parisian and he likes to talk to visitors because he has been in the fort now for four months."

It took a long time to reach the fort, and when we arrived we had to cross a drawbridge spanning a moat to get to it. The forts the Germans built after '71 have the pseudomedieval quality of the National Guard armories in New York City. We entered by a wide, high portal and found ourselves in a thoroughly non-functional place of echoing corridors and vaulted ceilings. It seemed to have been built by people who enjoyed playing soldier. I couldn't help asking the first man to introduce himself to us, an artillery lieutenant, whether the fort had any defensive value against modern ordnance, since Siegfried had informed me we were only about five kilometers from the Rhine. "It would stand up to machine guns and field artillery," he said, "but a heavy shell hitting squarely would go right through the roof to the powder vaults, where there isn't any powder now anyhow. But we wouldn't use the fort to fight from. The regiment is scattered all over this part of the sector by batteries. All we have here is a headquarters company, a medical unit, a telephone central, and a guard-house."

We all went into the mess hall to wait for the colonel, which, we were told, was the warmest place in the fort. There were two clusters of German lances on the wall, left behind by the Imperial Army when the French occupied Alsace. Captain de Cholet looked at them tenderly and said, "I left for the last war carrying a lance. I even managed once to stick a German with one, but later war ceased to be fresh and joyful." Sauvageon nodded sympathetically. Before long the colonel walked in.

He was tall, straight, and consciously picturesque. He wore a brown beret which was barely balanced on the side of his head, like Rodolfo's in *La Bohème*. His cheeks were old rose and his eyes cobalt blue, and his long white mustaches did not droop, but descended in a powerful, rhythmic sweep, like the horns of a musk ox. He was an excellent colonel, we had been informed; he had commanded a large part of the heavy artillery in the campaign around Salonika twenty years ago. Between wars he was a banker in Paris.

"Gentlemen," the colonel said, after we were introduced, "I welcome you to the humble barrack of a sick old man. It is not the Meurice. It is not the Plaza Athénée. The fare is not that of Au Cabaret or the Berkeley." We assured him that his fort would do us very well. A soldier then wheeled over a tea wagon holding about twenty bottles—scotch, port, sherry, and various apéritifs. The colonel took an obvious pride in his gamut of alcohols; it proved he could "defend himself." The verb "*se défendre*" had acquired a very broad meaning in the French Army; it signified "getting along." An officer pulled a pair of old socks over his shoes so that he would not slip on the ice; a private met a stray hen and wrung her neck because otherwise she might fly into Germany; soldiers going on patrol in wooded parts of no man's land set rabbit snares so that on their way back they might pick up a tasty breakfast—all these expedients were part of the French concept of self-defense. It followed logically that a colonel defended himself on a grander scale than a subordinate.

De Cholet and Sauvageon took their leave. The staff, they said, had to accompany the general to midnight Mass. It would not be precisely gay; the general was a great friend of the bishop's. They promised to call for Browne and me early in the morning. As we talked to the colonel, most of the officers of his mess joined us around the tea wagon.

Shortly afterward the officers took their places around a large mess table for dinner. Browne and I were invited to sit flanking the colonel. I had on my right a fair-haired, blue-eyed captain, a Jew from Strasbourg. He said that two uncles and an elder brother of his had deserted from the German Army at the beginning of the war in 1914 and had fought with the French. Being only thirteen years old at the time, he had remained at home. In 1918 he had been conscripted into the German Army and had been stationed in that very fort. In civil life he was an industrial engineer. Most of the officers, he said, were, like himself, reservists, but a number of men from "the active" had been inducted into the regiment at the beginning of the war to set the pace for them. The soldiers were young reservists in the later twenties, and three quarters of them were Alsatians or Lorrainers. "This is a regiment that must be mobilized on the spot at the beginning of a war, because Germany is just across the river," he explained.

Before the dinner could begin, the *popotier*, or mess officer, had to make what I was told was a traditional address. In this particular mess, the popotier was a round, embarrassed little man with bulging eyes. He was an *adjudant* and the only member of the mess who wasn't a fully commissioned officer. "My colonel and gentlemen," he began, standing before his plate at the foot of the table, "I have the pleasure to announce—" He was interrupted by shouts of indignation and, correcting himself, said, "The *honor* and the pleasure to announce to you that the menu tonight, the twenty-fourth of December, will consist of soup of leeks and potatoes [a few scattered shouts of "That's what we had the day before yesterday!"], cauliflower au gratin ["O miserable popotier, without imagination!"], salad, cheese, fruits, and, as wine, Châteauneuf-du-Pape." "Thank you, popotier," the colonel said solemnly, "provided only that the Châteauneuf is tolerable."

The dinner was polished off with businesslike haste because there was a full evening ahead of us. After coffee and armagnac, a Christmas mood began to seem more attainable. We all walked along a corridor and down a flight of stairs to an unused powder vault which the soldiers had turned into a *salle de théâtre*. The walls of the vault had been painted to give a three-dimensional illusion of draperies, and at one end of the room there was a real curtain of the same color as the painted ones.

To one side of the curtain stood a great Christmas tree decorated with lighted candles. An orchestra, made up of a violin, saxophone, and piano, played what most Europeans think is the American anthem, "The Stars and Stripes Forever." There were about two hundred soldiers in the vault, wearing ugly, solid shoes and long khaki overcoats that looked like horse blankets. The men were in a state of juvenile excitement. An evening of amateur entertainment was a great event. The leader of the orchestra was a tall, flat-chested fellow with shiny hair and a receding chin. The surgeon major told me that the man was a Berliner who had acquired French citizenship by serving in the Foreign Legion.

After a long overture, a master of ceremonies appeared before the curtain wearing a Prince Albert coat. "Our first number," he announced, "will be a song by our Alsatian chorus—*Rose des Landes*." The chorus was made up of eleven artillerymen, each standing with feet wide apart and thumbs in his belt. "*Röslein, Röslein, Röslein rot, Röslein auf der Heide*," they sang. The non-Alsatian officers and men applauded mightily. As an encore, the chorus sang a marching song which began, "*O Strassburg, O Strassburg, du wunderschöne Stadt*." Then the choirmaster sang a long folk song about the character of the Alsatian people. I remember only one line: "A donkey is no hummingbird." The blond Jewish captain from Strasbourg said to me, "That is the Alsatian situation in one line. We refuse to be what we are not." Soldiers from Brittany and the Midi sang next, and a Parisian corporal delighted all the provincials by losing his nerve completely and breaking down in the middle of a line, belying the metropolitan reputation for nonchalance.

After the last turn there was a rough-and-tumble drawing of Christmas presents. Then the colonel made a speech. The merriest soldier was the best soldier, he said, but the poor, forlorn fellow on outpost duty on the bluffs rising from the Rhine must not be forgotten. He said he was sure every man there would gladly be killed rather than let the Boches pass. "It is very necessary for us to win this war," he added. I think everybody there agreed with him. "There will be a midnight Mass in our new chapel," he announced, "for those who care to attend. This is a free country." I noticed that almost everyone did go to chapel, including those who didn't cross themselves.

After Mass the officers went back to the mess hall for supper. They were in high spirits because they felt that their men had enjoyed the evening's entertainment. In that phase of the war one of the officers' hardest tasks was to keep their men from getting bored. Now the officers had a chance to enjoy themselves, and they were in such good humor that the popotier got through his ritual speech unheckled. There was a slight commotion among the diners, however, when the mess attendants served the consommé in soup plates. "There is a curse upon the mess!" grumbled the surgeon major. "There are no cups for the consommé!" After oysters and some *foie gras de Strasbourg au Porto*, we all began to drink champagne.

We had been sitting at the table for some time when suddenly the colonel shouted, "The battery departs! At a walk!" Immediately the officers began rapping their knuckles on the table, to produce the effect of horses walking. "At a trot!" the colonel ordered. The tempo of the rapping increased. "At a gallop!" The rapping grew faster. "Halt!" There was a second of silence, and the colonel shouted, "First gun—fire!" All the men brought their right fists crashing down on the table. "Second gun—fire!" "Third gun—fire!" "Fourth gun—fire!" After each "Fire!" the table took a sterner thump. After the fourth gun, the officers began to grin shyly, like small boys anticipating the point of a familiar joke. "Fifth gun!" ordered the colonel. That was the cue for the senior captain to speak up, with considerable gravity. "There isn't any, my colonel." (There are only four guns in a French battery.) The colonel appeared dumfounded. Then he recovered. "That doesn't matter!" he shouted. "Fire!" The officers hit the table with both fists. A glass broke, a bottle rolled onto the floor, one dignified-looking captain, overcome with laughter, fell on the neck of the surgeon major.

The party broke up at five o'clock in the morning. The only officer who seemed mildly unhappy was a gangling, thin-lipped captain, a transfer from the regular army, who said to the colonel doubtfully, "This is all very well, my colonel, but it isn't really war." The colonel, whose chest was covered with campaign ribbons and decorations from 1914–18, stopped chuckling and looked at the captain steadily. "Sometime you may look back on this evening," he said, "and you will say, 'The days at the fort were the good ones.' What the devil! A fellow has to defend himself."

I suppose they have looked back upon that evening infinitely often since the Armistice, when practically all of them became prisoners of war. As far as I could ever learn, the regiment was pulled back from the Rhine in early June of 1940, when the Germans had gotten behind the eastern defenses at both the northern and southern ends. Some of them got back into the Vosges, because Sauvageon the aviator, who was himself transferred from that area before the debacle and so did not become a prisoner, wrote to me that one officer I knew had been killed at Hohwald, a summer resort in the mountains fifty miles from Strasbourg. Long before the war I had stayed at Hohwald and walked over the hills to the monastery of St. Odile to drink the white wine called Lacrimae Sanctae Odiliae.

8 / Colonel Albatross

BROWNE AND I SLEPT BRIEFLY, in a kind of dungeon where the stone walls sweated icicles, after the Christmas Eve celebration. Then Sauvageon and De Cholet arrived to take us to see the Germans.

The bridge across the Rhine between Kehl and Strasbourg remained intact, although for reasons easy to understand traffic over it had been light since the first of September. The mist on the river Christmas morning was so heavy that the French soldiers in the little redoubt on the Strasbourg side were hampered in their game of trying to see Germans through their machine-gun sights. They were not often allowed to shoot, mist or no mist, but at any rate they could look, and the Germans played the same game and sometimes talked to the French in French with a public-address system. The bridge was perhaps eight hundred feet long, and between the French and German redoubts at either end were elaborate festoons of barbed wire, which, when coated with white frost, produced a fine decorative effect.

It was cold on Christmas, and fog had covered the hard earth with a thin glaze of ice. The French soldiers holding the bridgehead were well pleased with themselves, for a young corporal from Lunéville had made his way across the bridge during the night and had stolen a Christmas tree which the Germans had set up in their barbed wire. He had also collected a few German newspapers he found lying about in front of the enemy redoubt, and the tree, decorated with strips of the newspapers, now surmounted the French post. All the company officers, from the captain to the tall, red-bearded second lieutenant who *dans la civile* had been a Protestant pastor, had formally scolded the corporal and then shaken his hand. The corporal, a nineteen-year-old volunteer, said, "What tickles me is that now they'll court-martial the sentinel over there. Those

sentinels think they're wise guys, bawling us out with their loud-speaker."
The troops did not shoot except when they lost their tempers badly, for
they realized that shooting would only increase their common discomfort,
but the lull had if anything increased the antipathy between the two
forces. When I heard how seldom anybody fired I said I wanted to look
over the parapet at the Germans, but the captain at the bridgehead made
me take off my American helmet first. "If they think you are an Englishman they may fire," he said. "They have never seen any Englishmen down
here, so we cannot say what the result would be." I looked over bare-
headed and cannot truthfully say that I observed anybody.

A couple of months later when Sauvageon was in Paris on a ten-day
leave he told me of a curious incident in this sector. There were two
casemates that faced each other like these, but across an even narrower
unbridged stretch of the Rhine. A German colonel, a nasty-looking fellow,
used to come out of the German redoubt every evening to smoke a cigar
by the water's edge and cock a snook at the French. One evening he
started to *pipi* in the river, the better to mark his contempt. A French
lieutenant on the left bank stepped to the loud-speaker and said, "You
exaggerate. Get away from there or I shoot." The colonel cocked another
snook and the lieutenant cut loose on him with a machine gun. The
colonel fell on his back, Sauvageon said, his cigar flew out of his mouth,
he was dead. Then the German loud-speaker was heard. The Germans
said they were coming out to get the colonel's body; they had no hard
feelings against anybody but the lieutenant, they said, but if the French
fired on the men coming out for the body they would make it a general
feud. The French in the casemate were angry at the lieutenant; they
considered him in the light of the man who had shot the albatross that
shielded them from harm. They did not fire on the Germans again, and
they made life so miserable for the lieutenant during the succeeding
weeks that he had to ask to be transferred to another casemate.
Sauvageon said that he considered this an unhealthy *état d'esprit*. So did I.

The holiday season afforded a precious chance to break the monotony
of the long pause, and the army in Alsace was taking full advantage of it.
Hunting, for some ridiculous reason, was against the law in wartime even
for soldiers, but that did not affect the supply of venison at the front. As
one commandant blandly put it, "If deer insist on strangling themselves
on the barbed wire, what can one do?" His explanation of the pheasant
served at his mess was equally ingenuous. "The battalion medical officer
runs over a dozen whenever he goes cycling," he said. "As he is not a
veterinary he is unable to save their lives. So we eat them."

General Pichon, the *divisionnaire* at whose mess we stopped for Christmas supper, told us how he had visited a dugout in a forest and found a
soldier skinning three rabbits he had illegally snared. "Sir," said the startled soldier, "I had just withdrawn my rifle from the loophole when in
jumped these poor rabbits, one after another, and died of fear." "The poor

unfortunates," the general had replied, turning to go out and continue his rounds. "Nature is cruel."

In some regiments in the sector eighty per cent of the men were Alsatians. Some had all their possessions locked away in apartments in Strasbourg, whence their families had been removed to Périgord. Strasbourg, through which our guides had Siegfried drive us, was incredibly sad. Ruins are something anyone can understand; but Strasbourg had simply been emptied of life; the stage and all the properties remained. Hats remained in modistes' windows, and beer glasses still stood on café tables where the drinkers had left them the day the war started. In the Place Kleber, where in other years one of the world's finest municipal Christmas trees had always stood, there was a tiny balsam surrounded by bread crumbs; it was a Christmas tree put up by the military police for the abandoned pigeons of the cathedral. With the Corps Franc in Tunisia long afterward I met a towheaded, blue-eyed sixteen-year-old volunteer. "What are you?" I asked him, because the Corps Franc has many German and Austrian and Dutch refugees in it. "French," the boy said. "What city in France?" "Strasbourg," he said, "the most beautiful." It was more than two years since Goebbels had announced the "incorporation" of Alsace-Lorraine in the Reich—like a louse on a man announcing he had now "incorporated" his host.

After Strasbourg, Nancy seemed feverishly gay. The cafés closed at eight-thirty, the blackouts were much blacker than the Paris kind, but there were still women to see and there was even an English correspondents' mess in the Hôtel Thiers, where, by special dispensation of the police, a visitor might stay up and drink as late as twelve o'clock if the lone, crusty old waiter didn't take it into his head to go home before that.

I spent the next couple of days on a conducted tour of a couple of Maginot Line fortifications near St. Avold in Lorraine. They seemed to me excellently contrived, like all the Maginot forts shown to correspondents. They contained mortars and anti-tank cannon but no heavy artillery. The heavy artillery, my conducting officer explained, was several miles back of the Maginot forts proper. This was so that the big guns might be shifted about on the "interior lines" beloved of military writers. Unfortunately interior lines by definition have to be inside something, and the exterior line of fortifications did not exist from Montmédy to the sea. The Germans were to push through unfortified space until they had got behind the left shoulder of the permanent Maginot Line and take it in reverse. As they approached each fort from the left rear, the heavy artillery would have to be pulled out from behind it. That would have left the men in the fort exposed to continual heavy artillery fire without hope of counter-battery. The fort on the extreme left end of the line was taken in this way. It held out through one hundred hours of continuous shelling. No troops came out alive. I heard about it on June 6 from Meyer Handler of the United Press, who had just returned from that sector. Most of the rest of the line was abandoned without fighting.

I returned to Paris on an express train that still had fine, crowded *wagons-restaurants*. These express trains were reserved for officers and civilians. Across the table from me I had a tall, earnest young lieutenant of an infantry regiment that had distinguished itself in the early fall fighting around Forbach. "There are only two armies in the world," he told me with assurance. "Us and them."

9 / Sample Supermen

A FEW WEEKS after I came back from the Maginot Line I went into Lorraine again to see some Germans in a prison camp.

The staff officer who accompanied me seemed embarrassed because there were no large groups of prisoners to see, as there would have been in the last war. "Unfortunately," he said as we set out from Paris, "we have taken few prisoners—perhaps a couple of hundred since the beginning of the war. It's the same with the Germans, of course. We have only the fellows that we bag on patrols between the lines, and the aviators who are shot down in our territory. You can't get many aviators at a time, though."

My guide had served as an artilleryman at the front from 1914 to 1918; now he had an office in the Ministry of War and spent much of his time journeying about to inspect his customers, as he called the prisoners, and to prepare for the reception of more. The camp we were going to was situated in a small city some fifty miles on the French side of the Maginot Line. In our railroad compartment, as we journeyed, the staff officer told me a good deal about prisoners of war. They are supposed to be treated, he said, in accordance with an international agreement signed at Geneva ten years ago, and since prisoners are, in a way, hostages, the three belligerents on the western front respected its terms. Germany did not show the same consideration for Polish prisoners, of whom there were thousands, he said, her official reason being that she did not recognize the Polish Government-in-exile. The real reason, naturally, was that no Germans were being held prisoner by the Poles. German prisoners who felt they were being abused might appeal to the Reich's "protecting power," which, in the case of France, was Sweden. France's protecting power in Germany was, at the time of my trip, the United States. Moreover, the International Red Cross inspected the camps of both sides, so all in all a reasonably close check was kept on the prison officials of the belligerents, he thought.

According to the Geneva agreement, prisoners of war are entitled to living conditions as good as those enjoyed by the garrison troops of the army that has captured them. The troops guarding the prison camps provide a practical measuring stick in this matter: prisoners have a right to the same rations and the same amount of space per man in their dormitories as their guards, and their beds must be as comfortable. They even receive from their captors the same pay as soldiers of equivalent rank in the army that has made prisoners of them. At the end of the war each side will be expected to reimburse the other for this pay. The scheme had worked out well enough so far between France and Germany, although there had been occasional grumbling among the prisoners themselves. The French at home are normally better fed than the Germans, and the Germans are better housed than the French. The men were sensitive to these differences, and to others which similarly upset their habits. The German prisoners, for example, got a ration of wine they couldn't appreciate, French prisoners got beer they didn't like, and neither French nor German can tolerate the other's smoking tobacco.

What I thought of most, going up on the train, was that I was at last to see some Nazis. I had not been in Germany since 1927, and it had been hard for me to understand how the uncertain-looking people I remembered from that trip had become so formidable. I wondered if I would see anybody resembling the thick-legged, bull-necked Storm Troopers in the cartoons left-wing magazines used to publish before the Reich-Soviet pact, or if there would be any of those German idealists you heard about who would say that Nazism was hollow and false. I asked the staff officer if he had heard of such a case of regeneration in any of the camps, and he looked at me as if he thought me remarkably silly. "No," he said. "Even if a prisoner were against Hitler he wouldn't say so, because he is still under the orders of whatever German noncommissioned officers are also at the camp." Commissioned officers were not quartered with the noncommissioned officers and the rank-and-file prisoners. "Anyway," my guide went on, "most prisoners have families in Germany. None of them argue about politics among themselves, except for some Austrians we have in another camp. They seem to think they would not be in this trouble if it were not for the other Germans, and a while back there was a bit of a row about that. Those Austrians are quite a problem. On the other hand, you will find this lot of prisoners we are going to see a very well-disciplined troop. There is an unusually high ratio of noncommissioned officers to men in this camp—about two to five. That is because many of them are aviation prisoners, and only officers and noncommissioned officers fly." I asked what would happen to a German soldier if, regarding the war as over so far as he was concerned, he told one of his German superiors in prison where to get off. The staff officer looked shocked. "We'd put the soldier in the guardhouse," he said. "It would be insubordination."

An army automobile was waiting when we arrived. It was only a five-minute drive out to the prison, a group of buildings which, I was told, had once been a factory. They were arranged in a rectangle, with a yard in the center and a gate at one end. Most of them had slanting glass roofs and were at least thirty feet high, with concrete floors and no upper stories. Halfway up on their walls were rows of enormous windows. The administration offices were near the gate, in what had been the offices of the firm which occupied the factory. We found the commanding officer waiting for us; he had not yet had enough visitors to be bored by them, and he seemed glad of a break in routine. He was a paternal, red-faced captain who appeared capable of taking a sympathetic view of the plight of a prisoner. Beside him was a tall, kind-looking old major, with a pink, bald head and gold-rimmed spectacles, who was introduced to me as an interpreter. The major said he had lived in Germany a long time and thought he understood the German mentality, although he did not approve of it.

The prisoners, it turned out, were in the section of the factory farthest from the gate, and on our way to see them we—the captain, the staff officer, the major, and I—had a chance to look over much of the plant. As we went from one unit to another we passed guards—men of forty or older, selected from a regiment of reserves. The Quartermaster Corps had fitted them out with antique uniforms of horizon blue, and for hats they had old Tank Corps helmets. Almost all looked like peasants, with long arms and hard muscles, and since all had fought in the last war, they handled their rifles with assurance. The guards saluted dutifully as we passed, and that reminded the captain of something. "Wait till you see the Germans," he said, a trifle apologetically. "They *like* to salute." He showed me the guards' bunkhouse so that I could compare their quarters with those of the prisoners later on. The guards had two tiers of fairly wide bunks with metal frames and straw-filled mattresses; the only other furniture was a row of lockers. We walked on through a series of rooms which had been prepared for the reception of prisoners not yet captured. Barbed-wire fences had been rigged up inside all along the walls to keep prisoners away from the windows.

As we approached the occupied unit I heard a man shouting, and by the time we got inside, the prisoners there had quickly formed a double rank in the center of the room. A young German at the head of the platoon was bawling happily the Teutonic equivalents of "Eyes left! Eyes right! Right dress! Attention!" Spines snapped back convulsively, chins jerked up as if each of the Germans in line had received an invisible uppercut. They seemed to enjoy this rigmarole. Their leader turned to the captain with a magnificent salute, as if he had just performed a difficult trick and expected the captain to throw him a bouquet. The captain said hurriedly, "At ease," and looked flustered by so much attention. The German noncom turned on his men. "At ease," he said in a disappointed voice. The men relaxed, appearing depressed at not being asked to do more tricks. The captain said to me, in the tone of a curator explaining an unusual exhibit, "You see? It is their particular mentality."

I walked around the room, an immense one with a concrete floor and brick walls. There was no barbed wire in this unit; the windows were smaller and placed higher than in most parts of the plant. The Germans evidently spent most of their time in the part of the room nearest the door, to be close to the coal stoves which heated the place. The men's cots were arranged head to head in two long rows; they were not double-deckers, like the bunks of the guards, but had the same sort of frames and mattresses. Beyond the cots were a row of rough tables and several long benches. There were books on some of the beds, on which the Germans had evidently been reclining before we came in, and there were chess sets and playing cards on the tables. These little luxuries, I was told, had been sent to the men by their families, who are allowed to send letters and packages, but not newspapers, to the prison. A narrow shelf, with things on it like tooth powder and combs, ran along part of one wall. Each prisoner had a section of the shelf for his possessions and had written his name under it—Hoffmann, Betz, Keil, Muller E., Muller J. were some I noticed. I also noticed a portrait of Goering, torn out of a German magazine; above the portrait was a chunk of wood with a swastika burned into it. There was another picture, also from a magazine, showing tugboats and ice floes in the harbor of Bremen. Near it was a pencil drawing labeled *"Morgenstund,"* which showed a snub-nosed prisoner, stripped to the waist, brushing his teeth in front of a troughlike sink, with a mustachioed sentry, helmeted and carrying a rifle with fixed bayonet, standing vigilantly in the background.

The Germans, eighty or ninety of them, remained standing at ease. With few exceptions they appeared to be between twenty and thirty years old. Most of them still wore the uniforms in which they had been captured, with the addition, in some cases, of a sweater. A couple of men whose clothes, I suppose, had been in particularly bad condition when they arrived were togged out in French tunics and trousers formerly of horizon blue and now dyed a sickly green. Many of the Germans wore smart-looking knee boots, and their forage caps resembled those of the British Royal Air Force. Their uniforms, those that had survived, were decently tailored and made of good cloth; apparently the ersatz fabrics of which one heard so much in France were for civilians.

I noted a variety of coloration and facial types among the men—more dark hair than blond, about as many round heads as long ones, sometimes slant Mongoloid eyes above a red Celtic beard. Regarded as crusaders for race purity, they seemed a mongrel lot. They were not big. The staff officer noticed this, too. "It's a curious thing," he said. "In the last war the prisoners we took at the beginning were almost all huskies." I suspected that the underfeeding of German children during the last war and in the postwar years might have had something to do with it.

The major was chatting with the noncommissioned officer who had been giving orders, and I joined them. This German, a sergeant pilot, was of medium size but athletic-looking and well fed. He was a classic Saxon type—wavy blond hair, blue eyes, and a complexion like boiled ham. He had been piloting a single-seater Messerschmitt pursuit plane when it was shot down with eight other machines in an air battle in November, and upon arriving at camp he had taken command because he was the senior noncommissioned officer. The pilot said he was twenty-eight years old, came from Leipzig, where he had been graduated from the gymnasium, and had served in Spain and Poland. The Air Force obviously was his career, so there was no reason to ask how he felt about Hitler, who created the Air Force. It was a bore being a prisoner, he said; he found the lack of exercise hardest to bear and complained that there was no sports field for the prisoners. Unlike most of his comrades, he enjoyed wine, having acquired a taste for it in Spain; the food, he said, was all right, but there wasn't enough of it. He certainly did not look thin after five months of prison rations. The major said he thought the pilot only imagined he was hungry because the food was strange; Germans, he explained, are used to dark bread, boiled potatoes, cabbage, and fat, overcooked meats, but in French prisons they get white bread, fried potatoes, leeks, and lean red beef. The pilot did not seem convinced by the explanation.

We started back to the office, where, the captain said, I would find it easier to talk at some length to a couple of the prisoners.

A few minutes after we got there the first prisoner chosen for an interview was brought in. "The pilot was a good example of a reliable Nazi," the major said. "Now take a look at this fellow." The prisoner, who came from Berlin, was one of the bloodless industrial-worker type which the postwar years produced in Central Europe. He was an ugly man with a rueful, conciliatory grin, and he looked middle-aged, although he said he was only thirty. He had worked in a hat factory until he was mobilized on the twenty-eighth of August 1939. He had previously served eight weeks in the army back in 1935, when compulsory service was revived in Germany, and that was all the military training he had had before the war. He had been undramatically captured in the Saarland early in September, when he and some other soldiers were sent out on bicycles to lay small mines. He had had more to carry than the others and, on the return trip, had fallen behind. Taking a wrong turn, he had run smack into a French patrol. That was all. Looking at him, I felt sure he had had just such luck all his life.

The major asked the man what he thought the war was about, and he immediately became voluble. As long as there was capitalism, he said, there would be wars. Capitalistic states had to make ammunition to cure unemployment, and then they had to use the ammunition. It was inevitable. I asked him what he thought of Hitler's Germany, and he said emphatically that he considered it a capitalistic state the same as all the others. Russia, he said, was only another dictatorship; she had made the alliance with Germany so that Germany would feel she could safely fight England; Russia hoped that both England and Germany would become exhausted, and then she would rule the world.

The major asked the prisoner what he thought of the showing the Finnish Army had made against the Russian troops. The man said he didn't believe the Finns had won any battles at all. "In Berlin we used to hear also about the big Red victories in Spain," he said, "but it wasn't true. It wasn't true about Finland, either." We asked him whether he knew that British planes had flown over Berlin, and he grinned incredulously, telling us that the German Air Force was the strongest in the world. "One thing I must say," he went on, as if he believed it. "The English have too many colonies. If they would give some to Germany, maybe even with Hitler I could make a living for my family." After he had left, the major said, "He is a Communist." I wondered what he really was.

The next prisoner to enter was another Berliner, who, like so many of his townsmen, had a Polish name. He was a well-set-up youth, thin but with good shoulders, and he still looked smart in his cap and uniform. He had high cheekbones, an aquiline nose, a thin mouth, which he kept drawn tight in an effort at self-control, and baffled green eyes. He was twenty-seven. Once, he said, he had been a tanner's apprentice, more recently he had become a white-collar worker, and just before the mobilization he had been working as an adding-machine operator. He had been captured while doing patrol duty between the lines. I was astonished to hear that he, too, had had only eight weeks of military training—in 1935. "It's nothing unusual," the major said. "At the beginning of this war the Germans had four eight-week classes in their army—all the men from twenty-seven to thirty—and they had no trained reserves at all between the ages of thirty and forty. It is apparently a very spotty army, with all its strength concentrated in certain *corps d'élite* like the motorized divisions and the aviation. They have worked hard in the last seven months, of course, but so have we."

While we talked in French, the prisoner, tense and frightened, stood watching. He was not a Nazi party member, he told us when we asked him; he had never bothered with politics. He had once belonged to Workman's Sport, an affiliate of the old Socialist party, but that was just for the swimming and water-polo privileges of the organization; he had never been a Marxist. The pact between Germany and Russia didn't bother him. He said it was just for business, and anyway the Russians were all right. He had been in Moscow for four weeks in 1938 with a workmen's swimming team. The major asked him why Germany had gone to war. "Because of poverty," the former adding-machine operator almost shouted. "Germany has been poor all my life because we lost the last war." The major looked at him over his gold-rimmed glasses, like a blasé probation officer questioning an incorrigible. "You think war will cure poverty?" he asked. "What else?" said the puzzled soldier. "If we lose this war, it is the end of Germany. We will be Bolsheviks unless the English give us colonies. Colonies we must have or we will be Bolsheviks." The major interrupted him. "Don't you think," he asked, "that wars always bring poverty, even when you win?" Either this was beyond the prisoner's understanding or he was afraid to consider the question; at any rate, he just shrugged. Perhaps he didn't want to have his last hope destroyed until the slogan-makers had time to offer him another.

I would have liked to listen to more political thought from these men, but the staff officer, who had organized our trip as carefully as an offensive, told me that we had forty-two minutes before the next train back to Paris and that consequently we had thirty-seven minutes left in which to visit the German commissioned officers. I wasn't as interested in them, because aviation lieutenants and infantry subalterns at the beginning of a war are almost certain to be enthusiastic, no matter what army they belong to. If the officer comes from a rich family, he considers the war a lark; if from a poor one, he thinks being an officer is a fine job. The German officers I saw lived up to this rule. They were lodged in what, before the war, had been the city jail. The cell doors were solid, not made of bars like those in an American jail, and the cells were about as large as bedrooms in an average modern apartment house. I don't know what kind of prisoners they had been designed for, but they even had wallpaper.

The pleasantest of the officers I met was a Rhinelander, a tall, blond subaltern who reminded me of the young Germans who used to play deck sports on liners, laughing too loudly and trying with a grim will to win. This man was an artillerist who had had the unfortunate inspiration of going on patrol with the infantry. He was reading a book about golf when we came in. He received a salary of seven hundred francs a month from the French Government, which was the pay of a French second lieutenant "absent from duty." This was not as much as the same French officer would get in active service. The officers were charged three hundred francs a month for their food, so, even if they managed to buy a few incidentals from their guards, they probably saved more than half their pay. The notion of getting rich in prison amused the Rhinelander. "I can't get out to spend it, you know," he said in English.

I next met four aviators who shared a common living room during the day. All had shaved their skulls and grown long, brown beards. When I asked one where he came from he said, "Germany. There are no more Prussians or Bavarians or Saxons. We are all Germans." He said he was a German who happened to live in Berlin, and that was all I could get out of him. Of the others, one said he had been shot down by six Spitfires, another by seven Hurricanes, and a third by a dozen Curtisses. I had never heard such a concerted tribute to Allied superiority in the air; listening to them, I marveled that a Messerschmitt could find its way through the traffic. They were lying, of course.

"You remarked the fellow who said there were no Prussians, no Bavarians, et cetera, the most Nazi of them all, to hear him speak?" the captain said after we had left them; "He came down in an open field behind our lines because of engine trouble, he said, but none of our mechanics could find anything the matter with the plane. Naturally he has to put up a big bluff here or he would be under suspicion. If he sounded lukewarm the other prisoners might suspect the truth and send him to Coventry, or conceivably smuggle into their letters somehow a hint of his treachery and then his family in Germany would lose its pay allotment. But there are also fellows like the sergeant pilot who are really Nazi *cent pour cent;* two classes of cocky prisoners, *les vrais durs* and *les faux durs,* the true hard ones and the fake hard ones."

The proportion of *vrais durs* to *faux durs* among German prisoners in successive phases of the war, I have thought since, is the only significant index to the morale of the German Army. The circumstances of a man's capture are more significant than his tone of voice in replying to the interrogating officer. It is to a prisoner's interest to be cocky, after capture, for he is under the surveillance of his fellows and the governance of superiors whose Naziness is likely to be in proportion with their rank. The Geneva Convention was never drawn up to cover an ideological war; there is no inducement for the German prisoner who is democratic or just anti-war to let anybody know what is on his mind. Vanity also counts in the prisoner's attitude. He likes to think of himself as a Teutonic hero even when he knows he has quit cold.

A friend of mine, a lieutenant colonel with the Eighth Army, once interrogated three German prisoners after the Battle of Akarit in the African campaign, and when he had finished, one of the Germans, drawing himself up to their cataleptic version of attention, asked, "But do you not think we are fine soldiers?" The lieutenant colonel said, "Not especially." He said the Germans looked as if he had hit them with an elephant-hide whip. By this time they have probably complained against him for violation of the Geneva Convention against torture.

10 / The Knockdown: Paris Postscript

THE NEW PHASE of the Second World War began for Paris at daybreak on Friday, May 10, 1940. People had gone to bed Thursday night in their habitual state of uncertainty; the governmental crisis in London which was bringing Winston Churchill to power was still the chief subject of preoccupation. With dawn came the air-raid sirens, startling a city that had heard no *alerte* during the daytime since the first weeks of the war. At once the little Square Louvois in front of my window took on the aspect of an Elizabethan theater, with tiers of spectators framed in the opened windows of every building. Instead of looking down at a stage, however, they all looked up. All wore nightshirts, which, since the prosperity of tenants in a walk-up is in inverse ratio to their altitude, appeared considerably dingier on the sixth and seventh floors than on the second and third.

The anti-aircraft guns were intoning such an impressive overture that startled birds flew out of the trees in at least one of the squares and circled nervously in squadrons over the roofs. As they did so, a large, formless woman in a gray nightshirt, making her *entrée* at a top-floor window, waved her right arm toward them and shouted *"Confiance!"*— putting all her neighbors in hilarious good humor.

The guns kept up their racket, and a number of tracer shells lit up the early morning sky. The noise of the airplane motors was distinctly audible, but in those pre-blitz days we could not distinguish between the sound made by bombers and that of French pursuit planes looking for Germans. At last one airplane appeared, flying so high that it looked like a charm-bracelet toy, and as it passed overhead there seemed to be a deliberate lull in the firing. People stared uneasily at the plane, as they would at a stinging insect near a ceiling, but it went away harmlessly enough, and then the guns opened up again.

The morning air was chilly, so most of the spectators soon closed their windows and went back to bed. In the Square Louvois the neighborhood milkman, with his wagon drawn by two enormous old gray stallions, came along a few minutes after the plane, and the crash of his cans on the cobbles brought a few nervous folk back to their windows under the impression that bombing had begun.

The episode differed so from previous alarms, in which no planes were seen, that nobody seemed astonished to learn from newspapers consisting mostly of headlines that the real war—the war on the western front—had begun. *"Finie la drôle de guerre,"* people said to each other with a kind of relief. Even the *guerre* in Norway had seemed *drôle*, because it was so remote. The rush to news kiosks was such that policemen had to shepherd would-be purchasers into queues, which in some cases were half a block long.

I had a letter from Jean, Henri's son, a corporal in one of the two French armored divisions which were created after the Polish campaign. They were good divisions, and Jean had no way of knowing that the Germans had six times as many. "The real roughhouse is about to begin," he wrote. "So much the better! It will be like bursting an abscess." Jean, whose parents were my oldest friends in France, was a strong, quiet boy

who in civil life had been a draftsman in an automobile factory. He liked
to play ice hockey and collect marine algae. He had not wanted a soft job
in a factory during the war because he did not want to be considered a
coward.

On the same morning I had a telephone conversation with another
friend of mine, Captain de Cholet, who had just arrived from Alsace on
furlough. Upon reaching the Gare de l'Est, he had learned that all furloughs were canceled, so he was going back by the next train. He called
me up to say that he wouldn't be able to go to the races at Auteuil with
me, as he had planned. "It's good that it's starting at last," he said. "We
can beat the Boches and have it over with by autumn."

In the afternoon I went to Auteuil alone. I watched a horse belonging
to Senator Hennessy, the cognac man, win the Prix Wild Monarch for
three-year-old hurdlers. The track was crowded with people whose main
preoccupations seemed to be the new three-year-olds and the new fashions being worn by the women. That day the Germans were taking
Arnhem and Maastricht in Holland and attacking Rotterdam with parachutists. Nobody worried much. Everyone was eager principally to know
whether French troops had yet made contact with the enemy. "The
Boches have business with somebody their own size now!" they said
pugnaciously. "They will see we are not Poles or Norwegians!" It was
conceivable, of course, that the Germans would win a few victories, but it
would be a long war, like the last one. All France, hypnotized by 1918,
still thought in terms of concentrated artillery preparations, followed by
short advances and then, probably, by counterattacks. Even if the Allied
troops should fail to save Holland, they would join the Belgians in holding the supposedly magnificent fortified line of the Albert Canal. At
worst, the armies could fall back to the Franco-Belgian frontier, where,
the newspapers had been proclaiming since September, there was a defensive system practically as strong as the Maginot Line. Confidence was
a duty. The advertising department of the *Magasins du Louvre* had discovered another duty for France. The store's slogan was "Madame, it is
your duty to be elegant!" "They shall not pass" was considered *vieux jeu*
and hysterical. The optimistic do-nothingism of the Chamberlain and
Daladier regimes was, for millions of people, the new patriotism. Ten
days before the war began in May, Alfred Duff Cooper told the Paris
American Club, "We have found a new way to make war—without sacri-
ficing human lives."

The news of the break-through at Sedan, which reached Paris on the
fifth day of the offensive, was, for a few Parisians who were both pessimistic and analytical, the beginning of fear. But it happened so quickly,
so casually, as presented in the communiqués, that the unreflective didn't
take it seriously. The Belgian refugees began to arrive in Paris a few days
after the fighting started. The great, sleek cars of the de-luxe refugees
came first. The bicycle refugees arrived soon after. Slick-haired, sullen

young men wearing pullover sweaters shot out of the darkness with terrifying, silent speed. They had the air of conquerors rather than of fugitives. Many of them must have been German spies. Ordinary destitute
refugees arrived later by train and as extra riders on trucks. Nothing else
happened at first to change the daily life of the town.

Tuesday evening, May 14, I climbed the hill of Montmartre to the Rue
Gabrielle to visit Jean's parents. Henri, Jean's father, had long limbs and
sad eyes; he combined the frame of a high jumper and the mustaches of a
Napoleonic grenadier. He was a good Catholic, and by birth and training
he belonged to the wealthier bourgeoisie. By temperament, which he had
never been allowed to indulge, he was a bohemian. A long struggle to
succeed in business, which he secretly detested, had ended in a defeat just
short of total. When war was declared, he was working for a firm of
textile stylists whose customers were chiefly foreign mills. Since September, business had fallen off drastically and Henri had had nothing to do
except drop in once in a while to keep up the firm's desultory correspondence. Henri spoke English, German, and Dutch in addition to French,
and sometimes sang in a deep voice which sounded like a good but
slightly flawed 'cello. He often said that he was happy to be living, at last,
high on Montmartre, just under Sacré-Coeur. His wife, Eglée, would
never have permitted him to live there for any reason less compelling
than poverty. Eglée, before her marriage to Henri, had been a buyer in a
department store. Recently she had devised a muslin money belt for
soldiers to wear under their shirts. She worked an average of sixteen hours
a day, making the belts with a frantic dexterity, but about once a fortnight she got so exhausted that she had to stay in bed for two or three
days. She had placed the belts in several of the department stores, but her
profit was small. Eglée and Henri were both about sixty years old. For
thirty-five years Henri had pretended to like trade in order to hold his
wife's respect, and Eglée had pretended to loathe trade in order to hold
Henri's affection. Neither had succeeded in deceiving the other. He
brooded, she scolded, he drank a little, they quarreled incessantly, and
they loved each other more than any two people I have ever known.

As I came into their apartment Tuesday night, Eglée was saying she
felt sure Jean was dead. Henri said that was nonsense. She said he was an
unfeeling parent. Henri became angry and silent. Then he said that often,
when he was at Verdun, Eglée had not heard from him for a week at a
time. She said that Henri was always talking about Verdun and belittling
"Jean's war." "To think that after these years of preparing to avoid the old
mistakes," Henri said, "the Germans are now eighty miles from us. If they
get to Paris, it's all over." Eglée said he was a defeatist to mention such an
eventuality. He said, "I am not a defeatist. I am an old soldier and also an
old traveling man, and I know how near they are to Paris." I tried to
console him by saying that the Dutch, at any rate, were fighting better

than anyone had expected. Henri had cousins in Holland. Eglée said the Dutch were Boches and would before long prove it.

The next morning there was a radio announcement that the Dutch had surrendered in Europe but were going to continue the war in the East Indies. In the afternoon some of the American correspondents, including myself, went to the Netherlands Legation to meet Mynheer Van Kleffens, the Netherlands Minister for Foreign Affairs, who had arrived from London to explain the Dutch decision. Van Kleffens, accompanied by the Netherlands minister to France and the Netherlands Minister for National Defense, received us and the journalists of other neutral countries in the Legation garden. While we were talking, sadly and quietly, among the trees, the French were losing the war. On that Wednesday, May 15, the Germans made the deep incision which a few days later was to split the Allied armies.

The Foreign Minister, a blond, long-faced man, had a pet phrase which he repeated many times, as a man does when he is too tired to think of new forms for his thought. "The Germans tried this," he would say, recounting some particular method of the German attack, and then he would add, "It failed." "It failed," he would say, and again, "It failed"— until you thought he was talking of a long, victorious Dutch resistance— and then finally, "But to fight longer was hopeless." "We will fight on" was another recurrent phrase. When we asked him whether the Dutch had any planes left to fight with, he said, "No. We had fifty bombers. The last one flew off and dropped its last bomb and never returned."

Holland, with one tenth the population of Germany but with several times the wealth per capita, had presented fifty bombers against five thousand. It had been comfortable to believe in neutrality, and cheap. Norway, with the fourth largest merchant marine in the world, had not built the few good light cruisers and destroyers which might have barred the weak German Navy from its ports. France herself had economized on the Maginot Line, had decided it was too expensive to extend the fortifications from Luxembourg to the sea. The democracies had all been comfortable and fond of money. Thinking of the United States, I was uneasy. I suspected that in proportion to our wealth we were the nakedest of them all.

The first panic of the war hit Paris Thursday, May 16. It affected, however, only the most highly sensitized layers of the population: the correspondents, the American and British war-charity workers, and the French politicians. In Paris, because of censorship, news of disaster always arrived unofficially and twenty-four hours late. On the evening of the catastrophic May 15, even the neurotic clientele of the Ritz and Crillon bars had been calm. But on Thursday people began telling you about Germans at Meaux and south of Soissons, points the Germans didn't actually reach until more than three weeks later. There was a run on the Paris branch of the Guaranty Trust Company by American depositors. I lunched in a little restaurant I frequently went to on the Rue Sainte-Anne, and after the meal, M. Bisque, the proprietor, suggested that we go to the Gare du Nord to see the refugees. M. Bisque cried easily. Like most fine cooks, he was emotional and a heavy drinker. He had a long nose like a woodcock and a mustache which had been steamed over cookpots until it hung lifeless from his lip. Since my arrival in France in October he had taken me periodically on his buying trips to the markets so that I could see the Germans weren't starving Paris. On these trips we would carry a number of baskets and, as we filled one after another with oysters, artichokes, or pheasants, we would leave them at a series of bars where we stopped for a drink of apple brandy. The theory was that when we had completed our round of the markets we would circle back on our course, picking up the baskets, and thus avoid a lot of useless carrying. It worked all right when we could remember the bars where we had left the various things, but sometimes we couldn't, and on such occasions M. Bisque would cry that *restauration* was a cursed *métier*, and that if the Government would permit he would take up his old rifle and leave for the front. But they would have to let him wear horizon blue; he could not stand the sight of khaki because it reminded him of the English. "They say the English are very brave at sea," he would say, winking slowly, "but who knows? We don't see them, eh?"

The trip to the Gare du Nord was solemn. M. Bisque dragged me to see various mothers sitting on rolls of bedding and surrounded by miauling children; his eyes would water, and he would offer a child a two-franc piece and then haul me to the buffet, where he would fortify himself with a glass of Beaujolais. At the buffet I remember meeting a red-bearded gnome of a colonial soldier who kept referring to himself as "a real porpoise." "Porpoise" was the traditional army term for a colonial infantryman. "A real porpoise," the soldier repeated dreamily, "an old porpoise, and believe me, monsieur, the Germans need somebody to bust their snouts for them." He had two complete sets of decorations, one from the old war and one from the new. He was going north to rejoin his regiment, and he was full of fight and red wine.

Saturday morning I had another note from Jean. He enclosed a bit of steel from a Dornier shot down near him. "How I am still alive I have not time to write to you," he said, "but chance sometimes manages things well." The letter produced the same effect on me as news of a great victory. I called up Henri. He and Eglée had had a letter too.

On Saturday, May 18, I went to a press conference held by the Ministry of Information, which had just organized an Anglo-American press section, with quarters in a vast, rococo ballroom at the Hôtel Continental called the Salle des Fêtes. Pierre Comert, chief of the section, held conferences for the correspondents at six every evening, when he would discuss the day's developments from the Government's point of view. This evening he announced that Paul Reynaud had taken over the Ministry of National Defense. He also announced that Reynaud had recalled Marshal Pétain from Spain to advise him. General Weygand had already arrived from Syria, and it was understood that he would take over the high command in a few days. The two great names, in conjunction, were expected to raise national morale. The two old men, however, were military opposites. Pétain, cautious at sixty, when he had defended Verdun, was at eighty-four incapable of conceiving any operation bolder than an orderly retreat. Weygand believed in unremitting attack. One staff officer later told me, "Weygand's ideas are so old-fashioned that they have become modern again. He is just what we need." Strategically, the two men canceled each other, but politically they were a perfect team. Both were clericals, royalists, and anti-parliamentarians. There is something about very old soldiers like Hindenburg and Pétain that makes democrats trust them. But Pétain was to serve Laval's purpose as Hindenburg had served Hitler's. However, we were cheerful on the evening we heard about the appointments. The German advance was apparently slowing down, and all of us thought that Weygand might arrange a counterattack soon. A week earlier we had been expecting victories. Now we were cheered by a slightly slower tempo of disaster.

There was a hot, heavy pause the next few days. I took long walks on the boulevards and up and down dull, deserted business streets. The wartime population of Paris had slowly increased from late November until April, as evacuated families returned from the provinces, but since the beginning of the offensive the population had again decreased. All the people who had remained in town seemed to concentrate on the boulevards. It gave them comfort to look at one another. They were not yet consciously afraid, however. There were long queues in front of the movie houses, especially those that showed double features. You could get a table at a sidewalk café only with difficulty, and the ones that had girl orchestras did particularly well. One girl orchestra, at the Grande Maxeville, was called the Joyous Wings, and its bandstand and instruments had been decorated with blue airplanes. There were no young soldiers in the streets, because no furloughs were being issued.

It is simple now to say, "The war on the Continent was lost on May 15." But as the days in May passed, people in Paris only gradually came to suspect how disastrous that day had been. There was a time lag between every blow and the effect on public morale. I can't remember exactly when I first became frightened, or when I first began to notice that the shapes of people's faces were changing. There was plenty of food in Paris. People got thin worrying. I think I noticed first the thinning faces of the sporting girls in the cafés. Since the same girls came to the same cafés every night, it was easy to keep track. Then I became aware that the cheekbones, the noses, and the jaws of all Paris were becoming more prominent.

There was no immediate danger in Paris unless the Germans bombed it, and when the news was in any degree encouraging I did not think of bombing at all. When the news was bad I thought of bombing with apprehension. It helped me understand why troops in a winning army are frequently brave and on the losing side aren't. We heard anti-aircraft fire every night now, but there were no air-raid alarms, because the planes the guns were firing at were reconnaissance planes. The heaviest shooting would begin in the gray period just before dawn. You wouldn't really settle down to sleep until the morning shooting was over, and you wouldn't wake up until noon.

On the night of May 21, after Paul Reynaud announced to the Senate that the Germans were at Arras and that France was in danger, I had a *frousse*—a scare—of such extreme character that it amounted to *le trac*, which means a complete funk. It was an oppressively hot night, with thunder as well as anti-aircraft fire, interspersed with noises which sounded like the detonations of bombs in the suburbs. When I lay on my bed face down, I couldn't help thinking of a slave turning his back to the lash, and when I lay on my back I was afraid of seeing the ceiling fall on me. Afterward I talked to dozens of other people about that night, and they all said they'd suffered from the same funk. The next morning's papers carried Weygand's opinion that the situation was not hopeless. This cheered everybody. It has since been revealed that May 21, the day of the great *frousse*, was the day set for the counterattack which might have cracked the Germans. It never came, and by May 22, when we were all beginning to feel encouraged, the opportunity had been missed.

Later that day word got around among the correspondents that negotiations were already on for a separate peace and that if the French didn't sign it the Germans might arrive in Paris in a few days. This counteracted the effect of the Weygand message. Still later I felt encouraged again as I watched a city gardener weed a bed of petunias in the Square Louvois, the tiny park under my hotel window. Surely, I thought, if the old man believed the Germans were coming in he would not be bothering with the petunias.

The greatest encouragement I got during those sad weeks came from Jean. Shortly after the Reynaud speech I went up the hill to Montmartre to take some flowers to Jean's mother. For once, Henri and Eglée were smiling at the same time. "You should have been here early this morning for a good surprise!" Henri shouted. "At five there was a knock at our door." "And who do you suppose it was?" his wife cried, taking over the narrative. "Suzette?" I demanded, naming their married daughter, who lived in Grenoble. I was sure that it had been Jean, but I wanted to prolong Eglée's pleasure. "No," Eglée announced happily. "It was Jean. He was magnificent. He looked like a cowboy." "He came with his *adjudant*," Henri broke in, "to get engine parts they needed for tanks. The boy has no rest, you know," he said proudly. "When the division goes into action he fights. When they are in reserve and the other fellows rest, he is head of a repair section. He is a magician with engines. And his morale is good! He says that the first days were hard, but that now they know they can beat the Boche." "On the first day of the battle, Jean's general was arrested," Eglée said, with a sort of pride. "What *canaille!* Jean said it was fantastic what a traitor the general turned out to be. And there were German spies in French officers' uniforms!" "They met a regiment of artillery without officers," Henri said, "but completely! 'So much the better,' the artillerists said. 'They were traitors anyway. But where in the name of God are we supposed to go?' Fifteen German bombers appeared over Jean's unit. 'We're in for it,' he said to himself. But the boy was lucky. The Germans had dropped their bombs elsewhere. Then Jean's unit met German tanks. He says our fellows rode right over them. 'There may be a great many of them,' he said, 'but we are better than they are. Our guns penetrate them, but they do not penetrate us. As for the spy problem, we have solved that. We simply shoot all officers we do not know.' Jean and the *adjudant* stayed for breakfast. Then they had to go away."

Although I knew that an individual soldier had no chance to understand a military situation as a whole, Jean's optimism raised my spirits considerably. I believed fully the details of the encounter with the German tanks. Jean was of that peculiar race of engine-lovers who cannot lie about the performance of a mechanical thing.

When I returned to my hotel I passed along Jean's confident report to Toutou, the hotel's cashier, with whom I often discussed the war. She was a patriot but a congenital pessimist. All the employees slept on the top floor of the hotel, and as soon as Toutou had read of the German parachutists in Holland she had bought a revolver and cartridges. "If one lands on the roof, I'll pop him!" she had said. "Or perhaps as he descends past my window!"

In each week of disaster there was an Indian summer of optimism. On the third Sunday after the offensive started, I had dinner with Henri and Eglée. We teased one another about our forebodings a fortnight earlier. "Do you remember how sure you were that the Germans would be here momentarily?" Eglée said to me. "And how you were certain that Jean was no longer alive?" Henri asked Eglée. "It seems a year ago," I said sincerely. "I must admit that the French had their heart well hooked on. Any other people would have caved in after such a blow. I wonder where Weygand will make the counterattack." "In Luxembourg, in my opinion," Henri said. "If he made the counterattack too far to the west he would not catch enough Boches. A good wide turning movement, and you will see—the whole band of them will have to scramble off. They will be on the other side of the Albert Canal again in a week."

We talked and listened to the radio, and, as usual, I stayed for tea, then for supper, and then for the final news-bulletin broadcast at eleven-thirty.

The bulletins earlier in the day had been dull. But something in the speaker's voice this time warned us, as soon as he commenced, that the news was bad. We began to get sad before he had said anything important. Then he said, "Whatever the result of the battle in Flanders, the high command has made provision that the enemy will not profit strategically by its result." "What can he mean?" Eglée asked. "He means that they are preparing to embark that army for England," Henri said. "Unless the enemy captures the army, his victory is tactical but not strategical." "But why must they embark?" Eglée asked. "I do not know," Henri said almost savagely. That was the day—though none of us knew it—that King Leopold told his ministers he was going to give up. Eglée began to cry. "Now they are coming to Paris," she said, "now they are coming to Paris."

As late as Monday, May 27, people in Paris still believed that the Allies stood a chance of closing the gap between their southern and northern armies. That evening, Pierre Comert, chief of the Anglo-American section of the Ministry of Information, announced at a press conference I went to that operations in the north were "proceeding normally" and that the high command expected the Battle of Flanders to last at least another two weeks. I slept well that night, awakened only a few times by moderate anti-aircraft fire. In the morning Toutou, the cashier at my hotel, stopped me as I was going out and said, "Did you hear Reynaud on the radio? The King of the Belgians has surrendered his army." She had been crying.

I walked about the streets stupidly the rest of the morning. I had the map well in mind. The Belgians, by their surrender, had laid bare the left flank of the Franco-British armies in Flanders, and I thought the armies would soon be surrounded. Perhaps the French and British in the north would become demoralized and surrender. If they had been seeking an excuse to quit, they had a good one now. People on the streets were saying to each other, "And that isn't the worst of it. All the refugees probably are spies." They did not seem depressed. A fellow wheeling a pushcart loaded with wood stopped and shouted to a colleague on the other side of the street, "Say, old fellow, did you hear the news? Ain't we just taking it on the potato!" In his voice was a note of pride.

I walked around the Place Vendôme a couple of times; the luxury-shop windows had for me a reassuring association of tourists and normal times. Charvet was showing summer ties. I bought a couple from an elegant and hollow-chested salesman. I didn't want to talk to him about the war, because he looked sad enough already, but he began to talk about it himself. "We are an indolent people, monsieur," he said pleasantly. "We need occurrences like this to wake us up." Paris reminded me of that conversational commonplace you hear when someone has died: "Why, I saw him a couple of days ago and he looked perfectly well." Paris looked perfectly well, but I wondered if it might not be better for a city in such danger to show some agitation. Perhaps Paris was dying.

That night, when the shock of the Belgian surrender had begun to wear off, I had a late dinner with two American friends in a little Marseillais restaurant on the Rue Montmartre. We were the only customers. We had Mediterranean rouget burned in brandy over twigs of fennel. Although all three of us knew that the war was lost, we could not believe it. The rouget tasted too much as good rouget always had; the black-browed proprietor was too normally solicitous; even in the full bosom and strong legs of the waitress there was the assurance that this life in Paris would never end. Faith in France was now purely a *mystique;* a good dinner was our profane form of communion.

Incredibly, beginning the day after the Belgian surrender, there was a great wave of exhilaration, based on the heroic action of the British and French armies fighting their way out of Flanders. People with relatives in the northern armies had, when they heard of the capitulation, resigned themselves to the capture or death of the trapped men. The German Government, in radio broadcasts, had threatened that even if the Allies were able to make a stand at Dunkirk the Germans would sink every boat that tried to embark troops. It was one German threat that didn't come off. People in Paris began to receive telegrams from relatives who had safely arrived in England. Several of my acquaintances received such messages, so we assumed that the number of troops saved was very large.

My old friends Henri and Eglée had not worried about their son Jean, because, having seen him on leave since the Germans drove the wedge between the Allied armies, they knew he was south of the Somme. But Henri's brother Paul, who at fifty had been called back into service as a lieutenant of artillery, was with the army in Flanders. One evening shortly after the Belgian surrender I climbed up to the Rue Gabrielle, just under the crest of Montmartre, to visit Henri and Eglée, and found them in a happy mood, because Paul had reached England. I tried to talk to Eglée about what she and her husband would do if the Germans turned toward Paris after they finished the Dunkirk job. Her answer was simply that she had an order from the Galeries Lafayette for five dozen of the soldiers' muslin money belts she manufactured at home and that after she completed the order she would have to wait eight days for payment, so how could she think of leaving Paris? As for Henri, he said he now constituted the whole office force of the textile-design company he worked for and couldn't leave without giving a month's notice. Peacetime thought patterns were mercifully persistent.

Everyone now was doing his best to forget that the Allied forces had had too few tanks and guns to begin with, and that now the evacuated armies had lost what little they had. We consoled ourselves with stories of individual heroism and with the thought that the Allies, after all, controlled the sea. Only when the evacuation was completed did the enthusiastic French suddenly take cognizance of the fact that there were no more

British troops on their side of the Channel. As if spontaneously, the German gibe, "England will fight to the last Frenchman," swam into the popular consciousness and began to seem a portent.

Two kinds of person are consoling in a dangerous time: those who are completely courageous, and those who are more frightened than you are. Fernand, the night porter at my hotel, was completely courageous. "Well, what do you know?" he would ask me when I came home at night. Before I answered, he would say, "We will have them yet, the camels. It takes a few defeats to get our blood up. They poison our lives by provoking the anti-aircraft into making a noise at night. A surprise is preparing itself for those cocos!" It was a pleasure to see him during the frequent early-morning *alertes*. Hearing the sirens, he would go out into the small park in front of the hotel and, shielding his eyes with his hands, search the sky for airplanes. Seeing none, he would shake his head disgustedly and shout up to the female guests at the windows of the hotel, "Do not derange yourselves, mesdames, it is for nothing again!"

The most frightened man I saw in France was a certain well-known French journalist who wrote under various names in a dozen Parisian newspapers of varying political color. He had a broad, paraffin-textured face which, when he was alarmed, appeared to be on the point of melting. Long before the offensive began in May, he had tried to explain to me why Laval, the appeaser, and Paul Faure, the left-of-Blum Socialist, together with Georges Bonnet, representative of the great banking house of Lazard Frères, were all planning a move to get rid of Paul Reynaud in order to liquidate the war as quickly as possible. They wanted to put Daladier back in Reynaud's place because they knew that as long as Daladier headed the Government there would be no effectual war—that eventually the war would die of dry rot, which was what ninety per cent of the French politicians and all the French Communists, along with the Germans, wanted. I had asked naïvely why Laval didn't try to become premier himself. "Because, of course," my journalist friend had said impatiently, "then everybody would *know* he was going to make peace. Then there would be mutiny in the Army." Personally, he used to say, he was a decided partisan of both Reynaud, who wanted to fight, and of Laval, who wanted to make peace. You were always running up against things like that in French politics.

When I met my journalist at lunch one day the first week of June, he was in as spectacular a funk as I have ever observed. "What a terrible mistake to have provoked those people, my dear!" he shrieked. "What madness to concern ourselves with Poland! Laval was so right to have wished to conciliate Mussolini. I am going to give my dog a lethal injection. He could never stand the nervous shock of those bombs that whistle. Working people are so insouciant. They know they have us in their power. I cannot get a man to dig a trench in my garden for me until tomorrow afternoon, and the bombers may be here any minute!" As he stuffed asparagus into his mouth, large tears welled out of his eyes. "Peace, quickly, quickly!" he shouted, after swallowing the asparagus.

Sunday, June 2, I visited the country home of a French newspaper publisher who lived with his large, intelligent family near the town of Melun, thirty miles south of Paris. The countryside, hot and rich and somnolent, and the family, sitting on the lawn after a chicken dinner, made me think of Sundays on Long Island. It was as if no war had ever been. We sat around in lawn chairs, fighting against drowsiness, talking unintently, resisting the efforts of one woman to get up a game like charades. We spoke with no originality whatever of all the mistakes all the appeasers in the world had made, beginning with Ethiopia. We repeated to one another how Italy could have been squelched in 1935, how a friendly Spanish government could have been maintained in power in 1936, how the Germans could have been prevented from fortifying the Rhineland in the same year. We talked of the Skoda tanks, built according to French designs in Czechoslovakia, that were now ripping the French Army apart. The Germans had never known how to build good tanks until Chamberlain and Daladier presented them with the Skoda plant. These matters had become for every European capable of thought a sort of litany, to be recited almost automatically over and over again.

Women in the train which took me back to town that evening were talking about the leaflets German planes had dropped, promising to bombard Paris the next day. The word "bombardment" had a terrible sound, evoking pictures of Warsaw and Rotterdam. In the dimly lighted, carefully curtained compartments of the local train, the women looked tired and anxious rather than refreshed. Boarding the train at a tiny station, they would exchange the usual flippancies with the people they had been staying with. "Thanks for the peonies. I'll put them right in water when I get home," one of them might say, but her voice would be strained. Some of them must have been going back to jobs at the great Citroën plant on the Quai de Javel, where hundreds of women punched out parts of machines and sprayed paint. The train arrived at the Gare de Lyon after eleven. There were no taxis. In the last month they had become increasingly scarce even in the daytime; the drivers simply refused to risk their necks in the pitch-black streets at night. I could not distinguish one street from another. There was a cluster of dim, moving lights at a distance, like a luminous jellyfish seen by another fish at the bottom of the sea. I started toward the lights and tripped over a plank, skinning my knee. When I reached them I found that they came from the electric lanterns of a group of policemen who were stopping pedestrians and examining their papers. They were polite and quiet. One of them told me how to get to my hotel, which took me almost an hour.

Monday was hot, lovely, and until one o'clock, tranquil. People going out to lunch were just beginning to smile knowingly and to say to each other, "See, it was just another bluff," when the air-raid sirens sounded.

At that hour I was of course in a bar, that of the Hôtel Lotti near the Continental, for the *apéritif*. It was a "day without hard liquor," so the apéritif was champagne. The waiters lowered the metal shutters. The bombardment was preceded by a tremendous noise of motors in airplanes too high to be seen, and by the angry hammering of anti-aircraft guns. It was as always hard to distinguish the sound of the bombs from these enfolding noises. After forty-five minutes, the roar of the planes stopped, but the shooting continued awhile, and then the sirens gave the all-clear signal. Everybody I met in the street afterward seemed to know exactly where the bombs had fallen. A taxi driver took me straight to the neighborhood bombed. Some six-story apartment houses in Passy had been shaved down to the first floor, as if by the diagonal sweep of a giant razor. The streets there were covered with broken glass, since every window for nearly a mile around was out, and housewives, not hurt but angry, were already out on the sidewalks sweeping up the glass with brooms. Of two large cafés at an intersection, one had been pretty well outed by a bomb, but the terrace of the other, twenty minutes after the all-clear, was doing a record business with clients who wanted to *"discuter le coup."*

Technically, I was later given to understand, it had been, from the German standpoint, a very good bombardment. Two hundred and fifty planes participated, the largest number that had been assembled for a single operation in the war until then. The bombing, considering the height at which the planes flew—twenty thousand feet—was commendably accurate. However, the results looked nothing like the photographs of Warsaw and Rotterdam, because Paris was reasonably well defended. "The anti-aircraft fire was well nourished," the French said, "so the bombers stayed high." The pursuit squadrons, although they failed to intercept the bombers on their way to Paris, were on their tails so closely that the Germans dropped their bombs quickly and left. If there had been no defending batteries or planes, as at Rotterdam, the bombers would have loafed along a few hundred feet above the main thoroughfares and dropped their high explosives like roach powder. The bombs hit the huge Citroën factory on the Quai de Javel and knocked down a few scattered apartment houses, but the total effect on public morale was tonic. Forty-eight hours after the bombardment, M. Dautry, the Minister of War Industry, took a group of correspondents through the Citroën plant, which had been the chief German objective. There we found a smell of burnt paint, and a great deal of broken glass on the floor, but no serious damage to the great automobile-assembly lines or the part of the plant where shells were made. The women making shells worked on as calmly as girls in an American candy factory.

The day we visited the factory, June 5, was also the day the Germans began their second attack, the push southward across the Somme that was to carry them to the Spanish frontier. "It is the beginning of the second round," Pierre Comert announced at the press conference that evening.

None of us could admit to ourselves that the war in France might be a two-round knockout. The French would surely be dislodged from the Somme-Aisne line, we conceded, but it would take weeks to do it. Then they would defend Paris and the line of the Seine, then the line of the Loire. By that time, perhaps, the British would be able to do something. Even the United States might begin to understand what was at stake and give a pledge which would put new heart in the defenders. But this fight was not to have even a decent second round. The rest after the first round had not been long enough; the French were still out on their feet. Unarmed and outnumbered, they were led by two old men who were at loggerheads. As for Reynaud, he had called into his government Ybarnegaray and Marin, two reactionaries whose only surface virtue was a blustering show of war spirit. Raised to power by Socialist votes, Reynaud had turned toward men whom he trusted because they were of his own Rightist background—Pétain, Mandel, Ybarnegaray, Marin. All his Rightist friends except Mandel joined in smothering him. They felt that by making war against Hitler he was betraying his own class.

After the bombardment the Government began an intensive, almost convulsive effort to get the United States Government to send over some fighter planes and, Reynaud may even have hoped, some pilots under the same sort of arrangement by which German pilots had gone to Franco or the American Volunteer group to China. Perhaps the French Government itself may have been deceived about the number of fighter planes finished or in construction in the United States. A red-haired Jewish captain in the Armée de l'Air, an ace in the other war but now a staff man, took me out to see a pursuit group in the field and show me how badly planes were needed.

11 / Who Do Not Fight, But Run Away

"THE SITUATION IS VERY BAD," said the captain, as we drove into the country, "but it is not hopeless, because it could still be corrected so easily. We don't need anything like magic."

The captain did not appear to be much interested in the fumbling remarks I made about the machinery of Congress and the mysteries of public opinion in the United States. Every Frenchman with an American acquaintance had heard all that before. Over and over again, Americans tried to explain such things, but their voices lacked conviction, and they wondered as they talked whether their words had any real meaning and whether the Danish politicians talked any differently before they rolled over and died.

My companion said he thought we'd be able to get a good lunch in a town along the way. The day was hot and beautiful, and the land seemed very peaceful as our Renault limousine raced smoothly along over some of the world's best roads. "It is a very comfortable automobile," the captain said wryly. "It used to be employed to take deputies on tours of observation at the front. They invariably found everything perfect."

Driving across the plains of Brie and Champagne, we saw peasants working with their chunky horses in the rich, unfenced fields; from time to time we passed canals in which boys were taking bellywhoppers, and occasionally we came upon a young woman pedaling along on a bicycle and smiling good-naturedly at the shouts of the soldiers in the camions. We had a magnificent lunch consisting of cheese tartlets, brook trout *amandine,* gigot, asparagus, cheese, cherries, and coffee, with a good bottle of still champagne, the local wine—all for slightly less than a dollar apiece. Our chauffeur ate with us. Most of the other lunchers were medical officers from a near-by hospital, who succeeded no better than such officers usually do in looking really martial, despite their fiercely scarlet kepis. After our meal we drove on a few miles and came to a town on which the Germans had dropped incendiary bombs early in their offensive. The bombs had ruined the stores and little houses and churches in about four blocks some distance from the town's main thoroughfare; driving straight through the center of the community, you would never know anything had happened.

We drove well on beyond the town and finally turned off the highway onto a dirt road where another Air Force car, a small, camouflaged Citroën, was waiting for us. It led the way for our shiny black limousine. We went down the side road for a mile or so until we came to a small house on the edge of a meadow. This, it turned out, was our destination— the post of command of a group of pursuit fliers. There were no runways or hangars or wind socks anywhere in sight, pursuit groups went about their business incognito. In back of the house was an automobile trailer equipped as a radio station, and stretched out on poles in the meadow were a number of brown canvas awnings, each of them concealing a pursuit plane, and, I was told, practically impossible to spot from the sky. "They bombed this field once," the captain said, "but they didn't hit anything. Sometimes they fly down with machine guns, hoping to shoot our planes on the ground, but our machine gunners drive them off before they are able to find what they are looking for."

An officer came back from the Citroën, presented himself, and then took us into the post of command. The commandant's office and his bedroom occupied the ground floor. On the wall of the office I noticed a bulletin board divided into five columns marked "Ready for Instant Departure," "Quick Departure," "Reserve," "On Mission," and "Out of Service," and hanging on nails under each heading were some tin markers shaped like airplanes. It was the sort of thing you might expect to find in the office of an up-to-date taxi company. To me, the number of markers, even including those under "Out of Service," seemed terrifyingly small. The commandant, a man in his late thirties, I should say, was a dark, good-looking fellow—a bit underweight and obviously tired, but there was something about him that suggested the taut ruggedness of an airplane strut. He was polite enough, but appeared skeptical about American journalists, of whom he had seen several since May 10, when, as he put it, the war began. His name was Murtin; I've since met him in Algiers under circumstances considerably happier.

The two escadrilles in the group and practically every pilot belonging to it, I was told, had been cited and decorated since the beginning of the offensive; for the haggard fellows who had lived around that meadow during the past four weeks, the war had been an alternation of death and felicitations. "In four weeks the group has shot down eighty-eight enemy planes," the commandant said, "but to be honest, we have lost thirty-five. Our losses include machines grounded in our own territory—technically not defeats, you know, but what's the difference, once they're out of commission? Well, you may say, eighty-eight planes shot down is very good. Unfortunately, it's not good enough. The way the Germans keep sending out new ones is unbelievable. To cut down their margin of superiority in numbers appreciably, we would have to shoot down six for one. To hold our own, we must down five for one."

He said that the pursuit force, to hold its own until production picked up, should have just double its present number of planes, a matter of several hundred. "But why talk of Utopia?" he said. "At the beginning of the offensive, we were lucky. A big shipment must have arrived from America just in time; at any rate, I got eight new Curtisses in a batch. Imagine! Eight Curtisses! I have never before or since seen so many new machines all at once. It was the riches of Peru!"

I shook hands with the commandant and went out to the field with the captain and a tall, pleasant second lieutenant who couldn't have been more than twenty and had shot down eight planes. "You mustn't mind the boss," the lieutenant said apologetically. "He just lost a good man for a couple of months. An explosive bullet drove isinglass splinters from the windbreak into the man's face, and he can't see. The boss takes things like that to heart." We walked out across that meadow dotted with canopies, and the boy said, "It is peaceful here in the country. The local people like us very much because they are sure that, with the pursuit group here, they are safe from bombing planes. They say, 'Now we can sleep on both ears.' They don't know that we may attract more bombers, and what's the good of telling them? Might as well let them be happy."

It was about a five-minute walk over to a frame pavilion where the pilots on duty await orders to take the planes up. The building was on a ridge, surrounded by tall beech trees, and its unpainted boards smelled good in the heat. There were several fliers on hand, among them a Czech who was playing the "New World Symphony" on a phonograph. He looked sheepish when he was introduced to me. He felt ashamed, his friends explained, because on his first patrol with their group he had got into a fight with a Messerschmitt and had had to bail out in a parachute. The other aviators had tried to tell him that that didn't matter, that it happened to everybody at one time or another, but the Czech still felt bad. There were a number of Czechs in the group, the lieutenant said, and a couple of them were among the best combat pilots he'd seen.

The senior officer on duty was a first lieutenant, who introduced himself as "Marin." He was Marin de la Meslée, destined to finish that phase of the war as the leading French fighter pilot, with twenty victories, and later resume in North Africa. He wore his flying suit, and his plane was on the field; in an emergency he could be in the air in less than two minutes. He was long-limbed, with an aquiline Yankee face, and he had a stoop which he had probably acquired from squeezing into cockpits. Several of us walked together over to a great, shallow gravel pit where most of the Curtisses were cached, concealed only by the awnings which, in addition to camouflaging them, served as a protection against stones that might be kicked up by a bomb falling in the middle of the pit. "This gravel is ideal as a cushion for bombs," Marin said, "and there is water not far below the surface, which doesn't help the incendiary ones any. They just drop in here, churn up a little gravel, and expire."

We looked at the Curtisses—small, unimpressive things. The total equipment of an escadrille, including thirty planes, probably cost less than two million dollars. One of the fliers pointed out the difference between the Curtisses available when the war started, which had four machine guns, and the improved ones, which had six—two in each wing and two over the propeller. "The new ones are a little faster, too," he said, "but essentially they're the same. We need a model with eight or ten machine guns, because it takes an average of three thousand bullets to bring down a bomber. Most of all, though, we need more speed. These are good old girls, but they drag their feet—three hundred and twenty-five miles an hour doesn't amount to much any more. You see, you used to be able to come at a Heinkel from the tail end and shoot it down. That was all there was to it. Easy. But now they have put machine guns in the tails of the Heinkels, and these make it very disagreeable. The best way to catch a Heinkel now is to go around it and attack it head on, and for that you need a fast plane. Ah, if I only had one of those English planes with fifty miles more an hour and plenty of machine guns!" He spoke as though he were wishing for a fourteen-room suite on top of the Ritz or a date with his favorite cinema actress.

"Some of the German pilots are good, but most not so good," the flier continued. "Nearly all the planes are good, though, and since the man in the plane you're after may by chance be one of the good pilots, you cannot afford to take anything for granted. The German pilots are very wrought up, too, and when we shoot them down, if they land alive, they continue to yell 'Heil Hitler!' One parachuted into the top of a tree, and when our fellows climbed up to help him descend, he shot at them with a revolver." Marin came over then and said, "The situation until the end of July will be very difficult because the Germans are so reckless and have so many airplanes. It is like a parachute jump. If we come out of it, all right."

When I got back to my hotel that night, tired and discouraged, Fernand the porter, looking radiant, said to me, "What they must be digesting now, the Boches!" He showed me a copy of Le Temps, which said the German losses were stupefying. All the attacks had been "contained," but the French Army had executed a slight retreat in good order.

By now there were perceptible changes in the daily life of Paris. There was no telephone service in the hotels, so you had to make a special trip afoot every time you wanted to tell somebody something. Taxis were harder than ever to find. My hotel, which was typical, had six floors. At the beginning of the war in September the proprietor had closed the fourth, fifth, and sixth floors. Now I was the only guest on the second floor, and there were perhaps a half-dozen on the first. The staff, naturally, dwindled like the clientele. Every day somebody said good-by to me. One by one the waiters left, and then it was the headwaiter, who had been kept on after all of his subordinates had been dismissed. The next day it was Toutou, who left the bookkeeping to the housekeeper. A couple of days later, the housekeeper herself left. Finally there were only a porter and one chambermaid in the daytime, and Fernand at night. "Perhaps, if the line holds, there will be an upturn in business," the proprietor said.

It was at about this time that my restaurateur friend, M. Bisque, with whom I used to make the rounds of the markets, decided to close his restaurant. It was not that the Germans worried him, he explained to me, but there were no more customers, and also his wine dealer was pressing him to pay his bill. M. Bisque and his wife, who kept the books, and his daughter Yvette, who possessed the tour de main for making a soufflé stand up on a flat plate, and his son, who had been an apprentice in the kitchen of the Café de Paris, and Marie-Louise, the waitress, were all leaving the city to run the canteen in a munitions factory south of Fontainebleau. I wished them Godspeed.

For a few days I had lacked the heart to visit Henri and Eglée. Then Henri had come to my hotel to tell me joyfully they had had another letter from Jean, who said he had been working twenty-one hours a day repairing tanks for his division. On Sunday, June 9, which was a warm and drowsy day, I returned Henri's call. On the way I stopped at a florist's shop and bought some fine pink roses. The woman in the shop said that shipments from the provinces were irregular, but that fortunately the crisis came at a season when the Paris suburbs were producing plenty of flowers. "We have more goods than purchasers," she said, laughing. When I arrived at the apartment I found Eglée busy making her muslin money belts. Henri was amusing himself by reading a 1906 edition of the Encyclopaedia Britannica, one of his favorite possessions, and drinking a *vin ordinaire* in which he professed to find a slight resemblance to Ermitage. "This time I think the line will hold," Henri said. "I served under Pétain at Verdun. He will know how to stop them. Only I don't like the talk of infiltration near Forges-les-Eaux."

"Infiltration" was a grim word in this war. The communiqué never admitted that the Germans had pierced the French line, but invariably announced, "Motorized elements have made an infiltration. They have been surrounded and will be destroyed." Two days later the "infiltration" became a salient, from which new infiltrations radiated. When I left the apartment Henri walked down as far as the Place des Abbesses with me. He wanted to buy a newspaper. As we stood saying good-by we heard a series of reports, too loud and too widely spaced for anti-aircraft. "Those sound like naval guns mounted on railroad cars," Henri said. "The Boches can't be so far away, then." That was the last time I saw Henri. I had a letter from Suzette a year later, telling me he had died in February 1941.

At six o'clock that evening I went to another Anglo-American press conference at the Hôtel Continental. We were told that the Ministry of Information was planning to provide us with safe-conduct passes to use in case we left Paris. That made us suspect that the Government would move very soon. Then M. Comert told us that Jean Provoust, who had just been appointed Minister of Information, wanted to talk to all the American correspondents. M. Provoust, the dynamic publisher of *Paris-Soir*, received us in his office with the factitious cordiality of a newspaper owner about to ask his staff to take a pay cut. He said that he didn't want the United States to think the situation was hopeless. "From a military standpoint," he said, "it is improving steadily. Disregard reports of the Government quitting Paris. We will have many more chats in this room." John Lloyd, of the Associated Press, who was president of the Anglo-American Press Association, waited to see Provoust after the talk and invited him to be guest of honor at a luncheon the correspondents were having the next Wednesday. The Minister said he would be charmed, and then hurried away.

On my way home I saw a number of garbage trucks parked in the middle of the streets to balk airplane landings. Evidently Paris would be defended. I didn't think, after Provoust's talk, that I would have to leave Paris immediately, but the situation looked so bad that I decided to begin getting my passport in order.

Early the next morning, Monday, June 10, I set out in a taxi—which the porter had taken two hours to find for me—to go to the Spanish Consulate General to obtain a transit visa. This was easy to get if you already had the Portuguese visa, and luckily I had one which was good for a year. My taxi driver came from Lorraine, where, he said, people knew what patriotism meant. He had fought the other war, four years of it. The country needed men like Poincaré, a Lorrainer, now. "The politicians have sold us out," he said. "And that Leopold," he shouted, "there is a fellow they should have got onto long ago!" Now, he expected, the Germans would come to Paris. But it would be defended, like Madrid. "They will come here, the dirty birds," he said, "but they will leave plenty of feathers! Imagine a tank trying to upset the building of the Crédit Lyonnais! Big buildings are the best defense against those machines." He did not know that the real-estate men would never encourage such an unprofitable use of their property. "Even ten centimes on the franc is something," the rich men were already telling one another, "when one has a great many francs."

From the Spanish Consulate I went to the Préfecture of Police, where I asked for a visa which would permit me to leave France. A woman police official, a sort of chief clerk, said, "Leave your passport and come back for it in not less than four days." "But by that time, madame," I said, "the Germans may be here and the Préfecture may not exist." Naturally, I didn't leave the passport, but I was foolish to question the permanency of the Préfecture. The French civil servants are the one class unaffected by revolution or conquest. The Germans were to come, as it turned out, but the Préfecture was to stay open, its personnel and routine unchanged. Its great accumulation of information about individual Frenchmen, so useful for the apprehension of patriots and the blackmailing of politicians, was to be at the disposal of the Germans as it had been at Philippe-Egalité's and Napoleon the Little's and Stavisky's. The well-fed young *agents* were to continue on the same beats, unaffected by the end of the war they had never had to fight in. Yesterday the Préfecture had obeyed the orders of M. Mandel, who hated Germans. Now it would obey Herr Abetz, who hated Jews. Change of administration. *Tant pis.*

Afterward I stopped at the Crillon bar, where I met a Canadian general I knew. "The French still have a fine chance," he said. "I am leaving for Tours as soon as I finish this sandwich." I walked over to the Continental to see if M. Comert had any fresh news. As I arrived at the foot of the staircase leading to Comert's office, I met another correspondent on his way out. "If you're going up to the Ministry," he said, "don't bother. The Government left Paris this morning." Then he began to chuckle. "You remember when John Lloyd stopped Provoust last night and invited him to the Wednesday luncheon?" he asked. Yes, I remembered. "Well," he said, "Provoust was in a hurry because he was leaving for Tours in a few minutes." I said maybe we had better leave too, and we did.

12 / A Man Falling Downstairs

A PROVINCIAL CITY which becomes overnight the capital of a great nation is not like a boom town, because it has no ebullience. People arrive dead tired after a night spent in an automobile or by the side of a road and pass their first hours in town looking for a bed. Finding one is a brief triumph. After a few hours of heavy sleep the new arrival goes out, depressed, to look for other equally sad people whom he has known in the abandoned capital city. With Waverley Root, the correspondent whom I had encountered on the Ministry of Information steps, I entered and left two temporary capitals of France within five days after quitting Paris. Tours was the first.

Root had an old Citroën with a motor that made a noise like anti-aircraft fire and was responsible for a few minor panics during our journey, but it stood up through the constant starting and stopping on the one vehicle-choked road the military authorities permitted civilians to travel south on. John Elliott of the *Herald Tribune* rode with us. He had one of his ankles in a plaster cast; it had been broken when an automobile in which he was returning to Paris from the front had hit a truck in a blackout.

The last impression of Paris we carried with us was of deserted streets everywhere except around the railroad stations, where the crowds were so big that they overflowed all the surrounding sidewalks and partly blocked automobile traffic. About everybody who had any means of transportation, except certain special groups like munitions workers and hospital staffs, whose last-minute evacuation had been guaranteed by the Government, left the city on Monday evening, the tenth of June, or Tuesday, the eleventh. It was exactly a month after the beginning of the attack on the Low Countries. Those who left on Tuesday and re-encountered us at Tours reported a great cloud of black smoke over the city, caused, they thought, by burning villages and farms that had been used one after another as points of support in the retreating battle against the Germans. It seems more probable now that the smoke was a smudge the Germans used to conceal their crossing of the Seine below the city and that was carried on into town by the wind.

The roads leading south from Paris were gorged with what was possibly the strangest assortment of vehicles in history. No smaller city could have produced such a gamut of conveyances, from fiacres of the Second Empire to a farm tractor hitched to a vast trailer displaying the American flag and a sign saying "This trailer is the property of an American citizen." A few men rode horses along the grassy edge of the road, making better progress than the automobiles. During the first few kilometers cars stood still for from five minutes to an hour at a time, moving forward only a few yards to stop again with grinding brakes, a procedure which eventually proved fatal to hundreds of old and overburdened vehicles. The Paris autobuses, requisitioned for the occasion, carried the personnel of government offices and major industrial establishments, and on each bus was a sign saying "*Complet*." Some of the girl stenographers and clerks appeared to be enjoying the excursion.

Although the road originally had been set aside for civilian traffic, we soon met soldiers moving north to Paris as everybody else moved south. They seemed content with what they were doing. There were infantrymen in camions and motorcyclists on their machines, and their faces were strong and untroubled.

Once you have started to leave a place, you become apprehensive. When we were held up in suburban traffic jams we noticed everybody around us looking up at the sky, probably remembering the machine-gunning of civilians on Belgian and Polish roads. But the only planes overhead were French. Not even a German reconnaissance plane appeared.

About twenty-five miles out of Paris the crowd thinned, and the surviving automobiles made pretty good time the rest of the way. Inhabitants of the towns through which the unending caravan passed lined the sidewalks of the long main streets, curious and quiet, probably wondering if they too would have to be on their way soon. In the cities south of Paris where the migrants began to stop at dark, restaurants and hotels were overwhelmed by a rush of business that brought no joy to proprietors who, while they sold much of what they had on hand, thought that in a few days they might have to abandon their establishments. On the first evening we had a late dinner at the Jeanne d'Arc restaurant in Orléans, where an R.A.F. mess was established. The British ate placidly and without apparent pleasure, preparing to quit France with about as much emotion as if it had been Burma. We three Americans were leaving without even having fought. France still hoped for an effectual gesture from our country, so we benefited by a last shred of popularity. Knowing how little the United States was likely to do, however, I wondered whether we should ever to be able to go back to Paris with our heads up.

There wasn't even a vacant sleeping space on the benches of a *brasserie* at Orléans. Remembering old traveling-salesman stories, we thought of going to local bordellos for the night. But all the bordellos were full of earlier arrivals from Paris. "They are so tired," the *sous-maîtresse* of one place, who came to the door, said to me compassionately, "that some of them are actually sleeping." So we had to pass the night in the Citroën.

The selection of Tours appeared to have been a mistake. It was too small and too near Paris. The Government had just begun to arrive there when it became evident that it would have to move again in a couple of days. A direct move to Bordeaux or even better to Biarritz, where there were great hotels that could have been requisitioned for the Government, would have been better psychologically and every other way. The hunted, pillar-to-post feeling that legislators get when they are evacuated twice in one week is an invitation to panic. From an administrative point of view Tours had such limited facilities that the offices of government had to be scattered over twenty square miles of villages, occupying town halls and schoolhouses. Publishing the addresses of government bureaus in the local newspapers was not permitted, on the theory that German agents might get hold of the papers and tip off the Luftwaffe. So much of the time in the new capital was spent in a sort of furious hide-and-seek, trying to find the functionaries with whom one had business. The ministers themselves, arriving from Paris with their flustered and indignant mistresses who put the blame for the whole inconvenience upon them, were unable to find their ministries in some cases. The mistresses occasioned a great deal of trouble; there were not enough suites at the Hôtel de l'Univers to go around. Some of the women had to choose between putting up with a room and bath or going to a second-rate hotel. Naturally they made things unpleasant for the protectors who had subjected them to such a humiliation.

Most of the minor officials of the Government and the inhabitants of Tours as well as all the civilian refugees expected Paris to be defended. When it became plain that it would not be, a great wave of defeatism swept the stop-off capital. The people of the city, unused to air raids and anti-aircraft fire, were hospitable but uneasy. They were also overworked, doing their best to take care of their unprecedentedly numerous friends and customers. Garage proprietors, for example, had to listen to scores of appeals every day from refugees whose automobiles had broken down anywhere within a radius of fifteen miles of Tours, and who begged the garagemen to haul in the cars and repair them. I heard a *garagiste* try to turn down a man from Boulogne-sur-Seine who said he had a wife, an old mother, and a couple of children in his car, with all their possessions. The garagiste, whose best employees had been called up for the army months before this great rush of work, finally agreed to take on one more job. He was already working day and night, like a surgeon in a field hospital during a battle. I talked to an old bookseller, a myopic man who wore a straw boater in his shop. I wanted a book about the period in '70–'71 when the Government had been temporarily at Tours. The old man said he might be able to find such a book for me in a month. "The Germans will not succeed," he said, "because they exaggerate. They lack a sense of measure. All the peoples that lacked a sense of measure perished, monsieur. Look at the Babylonians, the Romans of the late Empire." I left him carefully dusting the backs of an early collected edition of Diderot. The Government remained in Tours for four days, and we followed them out.

"Nous suivons le Gouvernement," we always said to the military police who stopped us along the roads. They seldom made us show our papers. It became a refrain. "We follow the Government."

Anthony J. Drexel Biddle, Jr., who had been appointed envoy extraordinary to the Government of France, was following the Government too. Bullitt had remained in Paris, and Biddle, who as ambassador to Poland had followed the Polish Government to France, seemed to be making a career of pursuit diplomacy. Biddle was keeping Washington informed of the progress of the collapse. His dispatches must have read like a play-by-play account of a man falling downstairs. Paul Reynaud himself, who saw clearly what was happening, was beginning to succumb to self-pity. Hélène de Portes, his since-famous mistress, wept continually and urged him to ask terms from the Germans, with whom she had dubious relations. Reynaud, the small man with a big head, had interested me ever since the day I had first seen him at the American Club of Paris. Speaking in English, he had reminded me of an eager terrier struggling against a strange and heavy leash. Shortly after he had become President of the Council, in March, he had sent for General Giraud, commander of one of the armies in the north, and after their conference a rumor spread through Paris that Giraud was to replace Gamelin as army chief. It would have meant Daladier's resignation as Minister of Defense, and that in turn would have brought a vote in the Chamber which Reynaud was afraid to dare. Giraud had gone back to his post and was now a German prisoner.

One man only showed any hope in Tours—the long-nosed, stork-legged Brigadier General Charles de Gaulle, Under-Secretary for War, who was there chiefly because the field commanders had refused to have him with them. He had offended both Weygand and Pétain in 1934 by advocating a mechanized army with a core of armored divisions. He had until then been considered in the Army as one of Pétain's personal *protégés*. Conventional army officers considered his stubbornness in this dispute proof of lightness and ingratitude. He had not remained within what poor Gamelin called "the just bounds of intellectual discipline." Weygand during the 1940 campaign had once ordered De Gaulle put under arrest unless he left the front.

The armored-division idea had not, as a matter of probability, offered much hope for France. If two nations go in for mobile armor and one nation has only half the industrial capacity of the other, the larger industrial nation will inevitably produce twice as great an armored force as its rival. Tanks cannot defend against tanks, and on the "tankable" terrain over which any Franco-German war must be fought the larger tank force, the German, would win by a quick knockout every time.

Biddle, who saw De Gaulle often in those days, remembers him as a gaunt watchdog in Reynaud's anteroom, sitting with his long legs stretched out before him and his nose and the visor of his kepi, nearly parallel, pointed at a spot on the floor just in advance of his right big toe. Whenever the advocates of surrender left Reynaud for a minute, De Gaulle would squeeze in and insist that now was the moment to begin a massed assault with the remaining French tanks. Reynaud cried at one point, "De Gaulle has the character of a stubborn pig, but he *has* charac- ter." It was more than he could say for the others around him. De Gaulle, in London a year later, told me that he still thought of Reynaud with respect. "He was like a man who knows he must swim a river," De Gaulle said, "and who sees the other bank clear. But he was not strong enough to reach it."

The day came when the Government abandoned Tours, leaving a thin line of impassive Moroccans squatting by their machine guns along the Loire and pretending to ignore their rulers' desertion. The Moroccans stayed and were killed. But we followed the Government.

Bordeaux was the next capital. Reynaud had sent for Biddle when the move from Tours was decided upon, and asked him as a last favor to take Madame de Portes into the ambassadorial automobile and see that she got safely to the second provisional capital. He feared that if she rode in a French car she might be recognized and attacked. "Without her he couldn't have carried on at all, old boy," Biddle, a friendly and decorative diplomat, says now, "so we took her." All the way to Bordeaux she railed against De Gaulle.

Root and Elliott and I had been living in an idyllic little roadhouse on the left bank of the Loire between Amboise and Tours. It had rose bowers and a garden by the riverside, and the bedrooms were what the French call *coquette*. It must have been a pleasant place of assignation in time of peace, but when the Moroccans set up a machine gun in the rose bower we decided it was time to move. The ride down to Bordeaux was not as bad as the one from Paris to Tours. So many cars had fallen by the way; it was like a grim Grand National. Italy was in the war now, not that it made much difference. There was a persistent rumor that some- body had heard a radio speaker announce that Russia and Turkey had declared war on Germany and Italy, but nobody could confirm it, because it wasn't so.

We drove as far as a town called Barbezieux the first day, where we got a good supper but couldn't find any lodging until I began a conversation with the owner of a garage and automobile-parts store who was standing in front of his shop watching the refugees go by. Elliott had his ankle in a pretty spectacular cast. "It wouldn't matter for one of my colleagues and myself," I told the garageman, "but my other colleague there gravely wounded his leg at the front, and if he is compelled to remain in the automobile overnight in a cramped position the limb may be permanently deformed." The *garagiste* said that his wife would put a mattress on the dining-room floor for John. "And in effect, as long as we deprive you of your dining room, my other colleague and I may as well sleep on the floor alongside him," I said. "Do not derange yourself to find us mattresses." "But why not?" the garagiste said. "There are plenty of mattresses." So we all got into the house on John's bad leg. The people wouldn't take any money.

We had our *café au lait* with a professor of the local lycée in the garden of a restaurant the next morning. None of the little people one met, like the garagiste and the professor, considered that France might drop out of the war altogether or that Germany might win it. They took it for granted the Government would retain the fleet, go on to North Africa and fight from there. We weren't so sure. The little people hadn't seen the ministers and their mistresses. Poor Comert, whom I had seen only briefly in Tours, had said, resentfully, "The leaders are not worthy of their people."

Bordeaux was the worst of all. Day after day the exhausted piano player from Harry's New York bar in Paris slept at a table on the terrace of a café, his head cradled in his arms. He typified all uprooted Paris packed into this city of indecision. While there was still a chance that Reynaud would be able to take the Government to Africa to continue the war, Biddle tried his best to support the Premier's prestige by extraofficial means. France had been our dike as well as England's, and poor Biddle was cast in the role of the State Department's thumb, thrust in to stop a breach that was too big for a fist.

The American managed to be seen often in Reynaud's company, or on the way to the Premier's quarters, or returning from them, as if he were conveying some tangible offer from Washington. He was, however, under the handicap common to all American diplomats then of not being able to offer anything more satisfying than good wishes. When admitted to the Premier's presence, Biddle says, he could say only, "*Bon jour, mon pauvre vieux.*" Reynaud would say, "*Bon jour.*" Then they would sit in the office together for ten minutes so that people in the anteroom would think they were discussing something, and after that Biddle would return to the United States Consulate, which he was using as temporary embassy.

There was a climate of death in Bordeaux, heavy and unhealthy like the smell of tuberoses. The famous restaurants like the Chapon Fin had never known such business. Men of wealth, heavy-jowled, waxy-faced, wearing an odd expression of relief from fear, waited for a couple of hours for tables and then spent all afternoon over their meals, ordering sequences of famous claret vintages as if they were on a *tour gastronomique* instead of being parties to a catastrophe. I remember particularly the gay hissing dinner party of the Japanese Embassy at the Chapon Fin. They were having a jolly time. I said to Root and Elliott, "The people here look as if they had been let in on a fixed race. France is out of the war now."

It was on the night of June 16 that Reynaud was finally argued into relinquishing his place and putting the country in the hands of its be-trayers, the representatives of the great industrialists. He did not give up, however, without one more long wrangle in which he found few support-ers of continued resistance among the men he had invited to be his colleagues in the Government. Reynaud sent for Biddle early on the evening of the sixteenth and said to him, "I know you can't do anything tangible for us, but for my sake say you will return at midnight. That will gain six hours for me, during which I may still be able to persuade them to go to Africa." He then appealed to his colleagues to delay their final decision until Biddle had received a message the ambassador expected from Washington. Biddle returned at midnight. The report had got all about the city that he was awaiting word from his Government. Nights, the streets of Bordeaux were full of people; only the wealthiest or luckiest of the refugees could find a bed to sleep in. The rest walked about or sat on the curbstones and talked. As the ambassador's car made its way through the Place de la Comédie on its way to the rendezvous, the crowd packed so closely about it that the chauffeur had to stop for a moment. The people began to cheer. Somebody had started a rumor that the United States had entered the war on the side of the Allies and that was why Monsieur Biddle was on his way to see Reynaud in the middle of the night. "Old boy, I sat there in that car and I had a lump in my throat," Biddle says now. "Because I knew that we weren't going to do a damn thing."

The men served by Laval, Chautemps, and their team of interchange-able shills and blinds at Bordeaux were the chiefs of heavy industry who since late in 1934 had been working for France's subjection to Germany. They preferred that she be brought into the German orbit as a satellite rather than annexed. They wanted to distribute the patronage, subject to confirmation by Germany, rather than have administrators imposed on them direct. They thought that Hitler would leave them their share of Europe and Africa to run, just as their colleagues the German members of the steel and coal cartels, which long antedated Hitler, had left them their share of the business. Theirs was the really dangerous International.

Those German colleagues had been the best missionaries for the Nazi state, which guaranteed profits—consider the Goering works, *mon cher!*—eliminated labor unions, and prevented the people from getting any fool-ish ideas in their heads by simply forbidding them to think. The French are peculiarly susceptible to ideas of justice. The steel masters thought the great stupid mass of Germany was just the anchor the French intelligence needed to keep it below the surface forever. This was the doctrine of the men who paid Laval's bills—heavy ones, but then it pays to patronize the best assassin, like the best dentist, when one has *le fric*.

The army chiefs had provided the defeat; Laval capitalized it for his clients. Laval had been lurking on the fringe of the battle like one of those naked peasants armed with a knife who waited on medieval battle-fields until an armored knight was unhorsed and helpless, when they cut his throat. When France was down, Laval's knife flashed.

On Sunday, June 16, while Reynaud was entering his last fight at Bordeaux, Root and I were at St.-Jean-de-Luz, within a few miles of the Spanish frontier, relaxing. His wife and their baby daughter had been living at St. Jean all spring. There wasn't much war feeling there; the hotels were full of Parisians who had come to get as far from the fighting as they could without a passport. It is the kind of place that people who like Provincetown would like, to me vaguely annoying. Early the next morning the radio in my hotel announced that Reynaud had resigned and that a new government had been formed with Laval and Paul Faure, the Socialist collaborationist, in leading places. Shortly afterward, news got around that the Laval-Faure thing had not come off, that there was a Pétain-Weygand government, and that Pétain had appealed to the Germans for honorable terms. It meant that effective resistance was over. If the German authorities had publicly requested terms on November 4, 1918, the German Army would have dissolved before November 11 of that year. Whatever potentialities of resistance remained to the beaten French Army on June 16, there were none on June 23, when the Armistice was actually signed.

The primary reason for the French military defeat as of June 16 is not obscure; it was the disparity of population and industrial capacity between Germany and France. A great part of the reason for the speed and completeness of the defeat lay in the superior use the Germans made of their already superior potentialities.

But there are other reasons not completely apparent even now. It must have been a little like one of those football games in which one team seems certain in advance to beat the other by two or three touchdowns, but in which the inferior team plays far below its form. The worse the poor devils muck things up the more confidently the destined victors play, and the result is an unwarranted score. The French have an excellent word for this kind of losers' dementia. They call it *la pagaille*. After such a game the spectators always think the winning team much stronger than it really is and the losers weaker than they possibly could have been.

The French strategy had been amorphous, the tactics bad, and the material woefully and unexpectedly deficient, for the men had been assured repeatedly that there was enough of everything. This was worse than telling them from the beginning that they would have to fight barehanded. After a football calamity the professional coach, to save his reputation, sometimes implies his players lacked courage. It would not suit Laval's book to have too much of a scandal about war material, because his clients had supplied it. Nor could Pétain, Huntziger, and Weygand afford to disparage generalship, because they had supplied that. And so Pétain started out to spread the libel of decadence against his own countrymen.

The betrayed people were responsible for everything, he implied. Their morals were bad (this attracted to the new regime the support of the

Catholic hierarchy). They had been in love with soft living (translate decent wages, hours, and housing). "Look at the Germans," the old marshal cackled—"weren't they wonderful?" (Material and generalship had had nothing to do with it.) "And see how many Germans there were! Be like them, breed!" he adjured his compatriots. People must have some pleasure to keep them from thinking, and that is undoubtedly the cheapest.

I wrote a letter of farewell to Sauvageon, who I knew was now with a fighter group at Marseille, and another to Suzette, Henri's daughter, at Grenoble, since I thought it more likely that she had stayed there than that the old people had remained in Paris. Both letters were full of more optimism than I felt. America would avenge France, I said. Damned if I haven't already seen part of it come true.

Then I took a taxi down to the international bridge, at La Hendaye that I had crossed so briskly nine months before, went over to Irun, and bought a ticket and a sleeping compartment to Lisbon on an express train.

13/Once Down Is No Battle

I HAD A FEW HOURS TO SPARE at Irun because the train left in the early evening, so I took a walk about the town, in which the damage done by the Franco people's shells in July 1936 was still unrepaired, and out to Fuenterrabia, an old Gothic town on a hill. A learner was playing a piano inside one of the steep Fuenterrabian houses. The weather, so beautiful all that ghastly spring, was like a false unchanging smile. I walked for the first time in nine months without thinking of France. I became conscious of this and felt guilty, as you do when you walk out of a hospital where your wife is and in a couple of blocks catch yourself whistling.

I had had a fairly adequate lunch, soup and veal, at the hotel in the railroad terminus; the fact that it was possible to get such a meal even at a price far beyond people who lived on Spanish wages appeared to me to mark some kind of advance. In the previous fall it had been impossible to get a satisfying meal at all. When I came back from Fuenterrabia I went into a wine bar on an Irun street for a glass of sherry and got to talking, in English, to a dark and a fair man. The dark man was a Spaniard who had lived in New York; he was rather pleased at what had happened to the French. He made bitter fun of the Italians, though. "The Germans will give them nothing at all," he predicted. The blond fellow was a German who said he had been a merchant seaman for a long time but now had some kind of business in Irun. He said he had been a prisoner in

England in the last war. He asked me what I thought would happen next, and I said I didn't know, but that the United States had better get going before the Germans got around to us.

He said, "My dear sir, Hitler has absolutely no designs on Canada or the United States. He is a fair man who wants only his rights." It recalled what the Germans had said before each of their gobbles. I looked at this undistinguished specimen of a people so mean and stupid that they repeated their lies in unison like a marching song, and I thought of the weak bands of wolfish dolts who had drifted across the boundaries of the Roman Empire with protestations of friendship. Once in, they had looked about them like German servants in a Jewish household picking out objects to steal when the Storm Troopers came. The Germans had never been warriors, properly speaking; they had been the scavengers who plucked the eyes out of sick nations. This was their cultural heritage.

Returned to the railroad station, I found two oldish men who were also bound for Lisbon. One, who was indignant because all the first-class sleeping compartments had already been sold, kept waving a card under the nose of the woman Wagons-Lits agent and shouting in French, "I am the Baron Rothschild." The other, who had his accommodations already, was a Sir Charles Something-or-Other from the British Embassy in France, but no stock-company actor would have dared play the role so obviously. I think that his company on the journey down colored all my thinking about Great Britain with pessimism that was to prove unwarranted.

Lisbon was, for the moment, one of the few remaining comfortable cities left in Europe, but it was not easy in its mind. The events in France had placed a certain restraint on the preparations for the dual celebration of the eighth centennial of Portuguese independence and the third centennial of the "liberation from the Spanish yoke" which terminated a temporary union with Portugal's neighbor. The Portuguese, placid as they are, could not avoid the reflection that now there was nothing much to stop the reimposition of a Spanish yoke whenever Franco felt like it, and they hoped he would not take the festivities in ill part.

The regime of Senhor Salazar, the university professor of political economy turned plain-clothes dictator, had kept Portugal solvent, with one of the lowest living standards and highest venereal-disease rates in Europe, but virtually without armament. Fascist Spain, whose financial position was impossible, as any political economist could explain to you in ten minutes, was bristling with expensive ordnance. Senhor Salazar must have hoped that Franco was grateful for favors received during the Spanish Civil War. He was aware that, for the first time since the Peninsular War, the traditional Portuguese alliance with England had become more of a liability than an asset. But it was not the sort of association that even a dictator could end on short notice, for English was the second language of Lisbon, English banks controlled the country's finances, the English for centuries had been the best customers for port, and Portugal knew that if Great Britain was defeated in the war, the victors would confiscate the Portuguese colonies. Italians were not popular in Lisbon, and neither were Germans, of whom there were a good many. Some weeks before my arrival the police had raided the German club and school and uncovered a lot of arms—almost enough for a Portuguese army.

Few residents of Lisbon could forget this political background for long at a time, but outwardly the life of the town and of the crescent-shaped Portuguese Riviera, which begins just north of the capital and follows the shore for thirty miles, went on exactly as it always had. Windows were not darkened at night, some moving-picture shows started at one in the morning, and the Casino in Estoril, the beach resort, began to be gay at about three. British social life in Lisbon had always had the atmosphere of a colonial governor's garden party, and it continued in the same tenor of dropping cards on fellow residents, amateur theatricals (Sir James Barrie and Ian Hay continued to be the favorite playwrights), and mild gambling at the Casino. The Duke of Kent was expected to help open the centennial show, and a special committee of the Royal British Club was proceeding gravely with preparations for his reception, wondering the while whether Germans or Spaniards would arrive before him. The visit was subsequently canceled.

The Pan American Clippers to New York and the boats to South America were then about the only reliable means of leaving the country, and since the demand for passage to South America was not precisely lively, the hotels were full of Americans from France waiting for a place on a Clipper. The total number, perhaps a thousand, was not impressive, but in proportion to the number of passengers a Clipper could carry—twenty-five was about the maximum for the westbound trip—and to the number of good hotel rooms in Lisbon and near-by Estoril, it seemed large. The *New Yorker* had booked my passage already, and I found a good room in the Grand Hotel at Mont-Estoril, so I had no trouble of any kind. I had five or six days to wait for the Clipper, and I employed them in swimming from the beach at Estoril and playing roulette for small sums at the Casino in the evenings. I also visited a British oil company official I knew, an atypical chap because he had had a Spanish mother, spoke Portuguese well, and spent a great deal of time with the Portuguese, a practice disapproved by his peers. They thought it smacked of going native. He was the "number two" in his firm in Lisbon. His chief was a more conventional Briton; he hardly seemed to think that there was anything to worry about. This irritated but in a way reassured me. All of the Lisbon British were packed to move out on twenty-four hours' notice and go aboard British warships, but at the same time the women of the colony were busy taking care of British refugees from France. And, as I have already said, they went on with their amateur theatricals.

The British went about gravely wagging their heads and saying that it was sporting of Churchill to forego recriminations and that, really, what was left of the French Army should have been evacuated to defend the British Isles. The disappearance of that army had altered the position of every nation on the Continent so drastically that people as yet couldn't get used to the idea; it reminded me of the death of the uninsured breadwinner of a large and helpless family.

On the day after I checked into my hotel I went down to the beach to swim. After swimming I sat on the terrace of the bathing pavilion, drinking vermouth and eating remarkably good olives. The vermouth was called the Vermouth of the Good Jesus. (There is a bank in Lisbon called the Bank of the Holy Ghost and of Commerce.) The pavilion people gave you a whole tumblerful of olives with each drink. There were a few German refugee families about, sitting at little tables under beach umbrellas and tremulous with masochistic fear as usual, happily certain that everything was going to turn out for the worst. An Englishman whom I had met at the bar of my hotel sat down next to me, already tight as a tick although it was just midmorning, and began telling me how he personally had piloted the plane that brought Franco from the Canaries to Spain. This broomstick journey must have been a mass enterprise. "Within three years all Democrats will be shot or in prison!" this lovable character told me. There was a public-address system at the bathing pavilion, and the management played phonograph records over it, usually Carmen Miranda. But just as I was sipping the Vermouth of the Good Jesus and wondering whether I ought to knock out the Englishman's brain with an olive pit, adapting the size of the missile to the importance of the target, the phonograph soloist put on a record of Charles Trenet singing "Boum!" The salt water and the sun and the vermouth had put me in a good frame of mind; the happy Parisian tune and the crazy lyric had an exaggerated effect upon me. I looked at the sadist and the masochists and said to myself, "They will both be disappointed." And I remembered something said to me by an old man who had been the last bare-knuckle lightweight champion of the world and had retired undefeated. This old boy was named Jack McAuliffe, and he had told me, "In Cork, where I was born, there was an old saying:

" 'Once down is no battle.' "

BOOK II

The World on One Knee

14 / No Place Like It

WHEN I WAS GETTING ABOARD the Clipper at the mouth of the Tagus to come home I told the radio operator, who was checking off the names on the passenger list, that I had been in France. "Yeah," he said offhandedly, "it looks like we'll have to beat the hell out of those Germans." I began to understand that Hitler would not have us as he had had the Social Democrats, without fighting. It made me feel better. At that time I may have had an exaggerated idea of the boldness of German strategy. I was sure that we had no ground or air forces that could meet a series of quick landings at widely separated parts of our or the Mexican coast. That was a good guess, because when I talked to General Marshall in Washington several weeks later he told me that we had "the possible equivalent of three divisions" of troops ready to fight, and that included the garrisons of the Canal Zone and Hawaii. I was not at all sure that Germany would not offer, and Great Britain accept, terms for a peace that would leave the British Empire temporarily intact and the Reich free to move against the richest, softest, and most inviting target: us. My estimate of Great Britain had been conditioned by ten months in France; like the French, I thought that the British showing had been halfhearted and ineffectual. The British newspapers flown over to Paris even in the last days we were there had been full of racing and cricket. If they were the expression of a nation, England wasn't even interested. It is unnecessary to state that I was wrong about what Great Britain would do, but I had logical reasons for being so, like poor Gamelin. The real wonder of the world, though, is that Japan didn't hop in then. If she had, the nearly disarmed British would have been simply outclassed, no matter how great their determination. Certainly no reasons of conscience deterred the Japanese. The dictatorships were too timid. They had the world on the point of a knockout, but they "lost" it, the way a novice boxer fails to finish another novice after having him groggy.

Getting off the plane and meeting people who had stayed in America was a strange experience, because they hardly seemed to know that anything was wrong. When you started to tell them they said soothingly that probably you had had a lot of painful experiences, and if you just took a few grains of nembutol so you would get one good night's sleep, and then go out to the horse races twice, you would be your old sweet self again. It was like the dream in which you yell at people and they don't hear you. I went down to Washington to do a profile of General Marshall. The War Department took the situation seriously enough, God knows, but when you had got out of the Munitions Building you were in an unconcerned world again. It reminded me of leaving a feverish last rehearsal in a theater and coming out on a sidewalk where few of the passers-by even know there's a show about to open.

After you had been here awhile you began to get stupid too, and more recent arrivals from Europe began to bore you slightly. Dick Boyer came back from Berlin, where he had been as a correspondent for *PM*, and visited me at the *New Yorker* office in October.

It was only the second day after Boyer's return, and he still looked at people with astonishment, because they did not seem worried enough. I, who knew the symptoms, understood the way Boyer felt as soon as I saw him come into the office. We were to have lunch together and talk about Europe and Boyer's experiences as a war correspondent. Boyer was bigger and blonder than ever; he walked with chin and nose pointed upward and talked with wide gestures. He would have a noble and stupid face if it were not for his malicious and intelligent little eyes, which redeem it. Boyer still talked a little too loud, as people do in a foreign country where they assume nobody around understands them. He had arrived by Clipper and so had not had time to change back from his foreign to his domestic personality. When we got into the elevator to go down to lunch, Boyer began talking about the bombings he had been in. "The first time they bombed Berlin," he said, "they didn't do enough damage." The office girls who were jammed into the elevator all about him, some with their shoulder blades against his belly and others with their chins against his shoulder blades, looked up with interest. "The second time they bombed it, they were really getting somewhere," he said. "It made me feel good down in my air-raid shelter. Those bastards in Berlin don't like it." When he said "bastards" the girls looked confused, because he had no right to say that to them, but they had no right to be listening, either.

I said in a perfunctory way, "The only bombardment I was in was at Paris." I had said it so often that it didn't even interest me any longer, and June 3, 1940, seemed as long ago as the Battle of Hastings. All the girls continued looking at Boyer as if I had not said anything at all.

The elevator reached the street floor, and Boyer said, "What I want is a really good meal. With wine. I am used to drinking wine with my meals." We headed toward Fifth Avenue. Boyer suddenly stopped and said, "What are we doing about our defenses? I mean, have we really started or are we still futzing around?" His voice sounded very anxious.

I remembered when I had felt the same way, coming back from Lis-

bon, but just before meeting Boyer for lunch I had been thinking principally about the heavy overlay against a race horse named Hash, on which
I had failed to bet. Understanding Boyer's anxiety, I tried to formulate in
my mind what I truly believed about defense, canceling out wishful
thinking. "Yeah," I said, "I think we've started."

Boyer began walking again, looking over the heads of the people in the
street, who were so unworried and foolish. "Well, maybe we'll be all right
then," he said.

We walked uptown without any precise destination, until we came to
the sunken roller-skating rink at Rockefeller Plaza. As usual, there were a
good many people hanging over the railings, watching the skaters. We
joined them. Two professional skaters were putting on an exhibition. The
man wore a blue uniform like a moving-picture usher's, and the girl short
skirts which showed chunky, chapped legs. They were going through a
complicated sort of waltz to music relayed by a loud-speaker. The trouble
was, however, that while they skated well, they would have danced badly
under any circumstances. Several times the girl threw herself sideways
through the air, the man holding onto her wrists, and when she landed on
her skates with a clacking, mechanical noise, she looked around for approval. There were restaurant tables at either end of the rink and on a
level with it.

"This is a pretty good place to eat," I said. "It's nice outdoors today."
Boyer thought the place looked all right, too, so we walked down the
steps and a maître d'hôtel showed us to a table.

After we had ordered oysters, lobster Thermidor, and a bottle of Pouilly, I asked whether the Germans seemed much bucked up by their victories. Boyer said the army Germans did but the civilians didn't. "But the
civilians have nothing to say anyway," he said. "It's just the Army and the
Party. The country will never crack until somebody cracks the Army."

"Who?" said I.

We both knew the only possible answer.

Boyer looked gloomily at the people hanging over the railing above the
rink and at the skaters. They didn't seem potentially formidable. "It's a
wonderful country," he said, "but I think everybody is crazy."

I tried to be funny. "That's just a European frame of mind," I said,
imitating the voice of a normal, unfrightened American, like Harold Ross.
"You forget about the three thousand miles of ocean and the time Hitler
will need to digest all the countries he has already taken."

"People who talk like that give me a pain in the butt," Boyer said.

"I used to be like you myself, old man," I continued, "but now, after a
couple of months in a sane atmosphere compounded of Lindbergh's
speeches and editorials in the *New Masses*, I see how things really are."

Boyer said, "When you begin to think that sort of stupidity is even
funny, you are beginning to go crazy yourself. The first batch of French
prisoners I saw, I cried."

I was not listening very intently, because I had said the same things until I had noticed people didn't like to listen to me. Boyer was right, and nobody cared, I thought, and after a while Boyer would understand that without anybody telling him. A waiter served the oysters and poured two glasses of wine, and we began to eat. The beginning of a meal demands concentration, and while we were appraising the oysters and ranking the wine in the scale of all oysters and wine that had gone down our gullets, a tall girl came out of the little skate room under the stairs and began to move about the rink. There is nothing finer to watch than a graceful animal on legs a bit too long for symmetry—a two-year-old thoroughbred, a kudu, or a heron. The girl was leggy, and I thought she was brave to put on skates at all, because her little scut was such a long way from the ground in case she fell. There didn't seem much risk of that, though, the way she moved around. She seldom lifted her skates far off the surface, and she didn't jump up or squat on her haunches and revolve with one foot in the air like the instructress. She just moved well, and her hands made slight, disarticulated motions from the wrist, as if to call attention to the lovely, slow turns she was making.

Boyer had finished his oysters—he always ate with the speed of a small dog consuming meat in the presence of larger dogs of whose forbearance it is not sure—and was beginning to talk of the gray, tasteless fish in Germany and the gray, tasteless people who endured it when he noticed the girl. He said, "It's funny, but when you're terribly worried you're not interested in food. I didn't mind the taste of the stuff. But I wouldn't eat a piece of it now for a buck." The girl was wearing a black skirt and a thin shirtwaist through which the men could see the white, clean straps of her underwear. Boyer's nostrils flared, as if he could smell the faint aroma of laundry soap and ironing board that such underwear should have. If the girl had spoiled this bouquet with a perfume, as she probably had, nobody at that distance could know it.

"I know," I said. "Then, when you're a little less worried, you take an interest in food again, but not in women. When you take an interest in women, you're not worried."

Boyer said, "I don't feel like a man from Mars but like a man from earth who has landed on another planet. Don't the damn fools know what is happening on earth?" But his voice was milder than before, and he watched the girl's thin hips.

The girl summoned a male instructor with one of her small motions, and the two of them skated hand in hand. She was very blonde, with fine, threadlike hair that wouldn't stay up, and she had dark eyebrows and a small, turned-up nose that gave her a silly, friendly look. Boyer and I followed her with our eyes, and both felt angry when she placed the instructor's arm around her, under her right armpit. We were glad she held his hand firmly in hers, so it did not touch her breast.

"That girl skates as if thousands of other girls weren't cold and hungry, or cowering from bombs," Boyer said with a last, feeble effort to appear outraged. But he was obviously more interested in her than in his talk.

"He's beginning to be comfortable," I thought, "and he's ashamed of it." Just then the waiter arrived with the lobster Thermidor. I said, tactfully, "Oh, what the hell! Why don't you tell me all about Europe some other time?"

Boyer looked relieved. "Sure," he said. "That girl looks like somebody I used to know."

15 / Rape Is Impossible

THAT KIND OF FEELING was involuntary. It was due to the mental climate. Even actions directly connected with war had an unreal quality when they took place here; I remember the curious feeling I had when I went to register for compulsory service on October 16, 1940, in a schoolhouse where I had to squeeze 215 pounds of me into a child's seat, behind a child's desk, to fill out a blank. The associations evoked were of learning long division and looking forward to recess, rather than of bombed cities. Yet I had seen bombed cities, which none of the other men registering had. After sitting in the small seat for a couple of minutes I began to be overawed by the schoolteacher who was issuing the registration cards. I hoped she wouldn't ask me anything I did not know. I just got into the draft by two days; on October 18 I was going to be thirty-six years old and officially middle-aged. The psychological benefit was not slight; I have thought of myself ever since as a mere kid. I never was destined to fight, though—just get shot at.

Remoteness from the war affected everybody, but there were at least two groups in the country that tried consciously to minimize our danger. They were precisely these that had worked to the same end in France—a strong faction of men of wealth and the Communist party. The money people wanted to prove fascism more efficient than democracy, the Communists that democracy offered no protection against fascism. A military victory for the democracies would shatter the pretensions of both.

Pierre-Etienne Flandin, a former premier who has never been rated a revolutionary, gave me last winter a concise account of the way in which the French industrialists arrived at their policy of collaboration. Retrospectively it clarifies for me a great deal of what went on here in 1940–41.

"The great industrialists had never contributed so largely to a national campaign as they did to André Tardieu's group in the general elections of 1932," Flandin said. "Tardieu was badly beaten. So they said, 'What has the Republic come to when you can't even buy an election? Evidently it is time to change the system of government.' Being French, they felt particularly bad because they had wasted so much money. So they began to back the French fascist movements—De la Rocque, Doriot, all that, with Chiappe of course running the show. They mounted the riots of February 1934, expecting to take power by a *coup d'état*. The coup didn't come off. Then they gave up on accomplishing anything from inside France and decided to wait for the arrival of the Germans. The Front Populaire Government, elected in 1936" (of which Flandin had been an active parliamentary opponent), "had nothing to do with their decision. They had made up their minds two years earlier."

The American opposite numbers of the men of the *grands cartels* had been too badly panicked in 1932 to get together then. It was not until after the Roosevelt-Landon campaign of 1936 that they began to despair of democracy and to get vocal about it. The little men in Statler Hotel bars and golf-club locker rooms echoed the official line. What good was a system under which the majority of people voted to protect their own interests? It was damn selfish of working people to vote that way. "As a matter of fact this country was never meant to be a democracy anyway," they would say with the same knowing air with which they knocked a competing line of scrapple when they were out peddling pork products, "it was meant to be a republic. Get it?" And suffrage in a republic could be as limited as it was in a stockholders' meeting of Republic Steel. Money had never articulated its dislike of democracy during the years when it had been possible to elect McKinleys and Hardings and Coolidges and Hoovers.

I do not think that the money men who were to turn isolationists ever backed an American fascist movement on a large scale as the cartels had in France in 1934; they were not so conscious of what they wanted or perhaps so cynical as their European counterparts, and besides they had not completely given up on the ballot box. In 1940 they applied not only money but advertising techniques. When the advertising men failed to elect a President, they had to regretfully inform their clientele that the jig was up. There was no time to mount a nationalist authoritarian movement. The money by-passed that step and went in for isolationism, which was a form of passive aid for the Axis.

I stayed in the United States from July 1940 until July 1941. An important phase of the war was being waged all around me. It went well for the ultimate good of the country, but a trifle slowly. The election in the United States was a defeat for Germany; newspapers there and in Great Britain treated it as such. I had never been worried about it; the confidence expressed up to the last minute by my little friends who were identified with big business showed they lacked all sense of reality. The advertising manager of the *Herald Tribune* took five to four from me on the eve of the election. The beating did Willkie good too; it served as a disinfectant bath to rid him of parasites. He came out of the race minus the most antisocial elements of his support. When I met him for the first time, in the following January, he was still astonished by their desertion. I had imagined him a knave. I found him a naïf.

My most nightmarish memory of the year is of a trip I made to Chicago to interview the leaders of America First for an article I had been engaged to write for *McCall's Magazine* on propaganda in the United States. I was to cover all varieties of propaganda in two thousand words and make the subject as clear as a dress pattern. I hit Chicago during the debate on the Lease-Lend Bill. The Chicago *Tribune* carried on its editorial page the day I arrived a cartoon showing Liberty loaded with chains and being beaten with a spiked club by a sort of ape-man. The ape-man was labeled not "Nazism" or "Fascism" but "New Deal." The president of America First, an ecclesiastical-looking white-haired man rather like Warren Harding or Samuel Seabury, told me in a paternal, authoritative tone that Great Britain was in no danger but that it was no use trying to help her because she was doomed. It would be dangerous to help her while she was still in the war, he continued, but if we permitted her to get knocked out of the war we would be well able to take care of ourselves against any combination of powers that could have whipped her and us combined. I detected a certain confusion, but I was there to report and not to argue, and besides a reedy young man who was publicity-directing for the committee told me that the president knew all about modern war because he had been a Quartermaster General in 1917 and sold several million dollars' worth of sundries by mail catalogue every week. I am not sure yet whether all these people desired an Axis victory consciously, but the irrational stubbornness with which they denied its possibility made you think of certain women who continually and compulsively talk about the impossibility of rape. The subject fascinates them. It was a successful article, the editors of *McCall's* said, except that I had mentioned one America Firster's business connection with the Quaker Oats Company, which was an advertiser. They fixed it to read he was "an official of a cereal company."

Although I believed that in the United States, as in France, the para-Fascists were more dangerous than the Communists, the latter caused me considerably more personal annoyance, because a number of my friends had listened to them. I never expect to see eye to eye with a Ford personnel manager or the vice-president of an advertising agency, and it causes me no anguish at all to find myself in disagreement with a newspaper publisher. But I did hate to drop in on a perfectly good reporter or physician and find myself howling and banging the table because he thought that there was no choice between Churchill and Hitler and demanded who were we to object to the slaughter of a couple of million Jews in Poland when there were resort hotels right here that wouldn't take Jewish guests? Unpeculiarly enough, the two propaganda groups had taken the same line on perfecting the United States before we opposed the Nazis—Robert Maynard Hutchins of the University of Chicago, who was the accredited intellect of the money people, hit exactly the same note on that as *New Masses*.

I think I must say here what I believe myself, because if you are going to see a war through a man's eyes you ought to know what there is behind them. I think democracy a most precious thing, not because any democratic state is perfect, but because it is perfectible. It sounds heartbreakingly banal, but I believe that you cannot even fool most of the people most of the time. They are quite likely to vote in their own interest. I also believe that since a democracy is made up of individual electors, the electors will protect the rights of the individual. A democracy may sometimes grant too little power to its government and at others allow government to infringe on the rights of the individual—Prohibition is example enough—but the vote always offers the means of correcting imbalance, and the repeal of Prohibition is an example of that. Any system that is run by a few, whether they sit in a Fascist Grand Council or at the pinnacle of a pyramid of holding companies, is a damned bad system, and Italy is a fine example of that, but unfortunately we didn't have its finish to point to in 1940–41. And so much for my ideology.

I had thought all along that the Germans would invade Great Britain in the spring or summer of 1941 and that that was the place to be for a *New Yorker* man who wanted to see the war, but I had gotten to fiddle-fluting around with the State Department Passport Bureau about giving me permission to travel on a belligerent ship. I also fiddle-fluted with the British Ministry of Information about getting me a passage either on a freighter in convoy or a bomber, and before I got under way Germany had invaded Russia. That slimmed the prospects of an invasion of England, but I choked back my disappointment and decided to go anyway. June 22, when the news of the invasion of Russia got around in New York, was a hot Sunday. I walked up through Union Square, where the freestyle catch-as-catch-can Marxist arguers hang out, and all the boys who two days earlier had been howling for Churchill's blood were now screaming for us to get right into the war. "Well," I thought, "we are on the same side of a question for once, anyway." Somehow, I remembered my old French general who had said to his estranged friend, "I will shake hands, if you have arrived at better sentiments." The reason I had thought all year that we should declare war on the Axis immediately was that I didn't think either the training of our Army or war production could attain even half-speed until the Government had war powers.

16 / Destination: United Kingdom

ALONG IN JULY I got my passport and my means of transportation straightened out. I was to go by bomber.

Since fairly early in the war the British had been flying American-built bombers from Canada for immediate incorporation into the R.A.F. The bombers which made these one-way trips were the light types, like Lockheed Hudsons, and after they had been fitted with extra fuel tanks for the long hop, they had little space for freight or passengers. However, during the past few weeks the British Air Ministry had been using a number of the big, long-range, four-engined Consolidated bombers, which had been christened Liberators, in a regular two-way service. On westward trips they brought over groups of small-bomber pilots and occasional voyagers like the Duke of Kent and Prince Bernhard of Lippe. Going east, they carried not only passengers, mostly British subjects on official business, but also light freight, such as engine parts.

The division of the Air Ministry which managed this transatlantic service then was known as Atfero, which stood for Atlantic Ferry. An Atfero man at a Montreal airport put a tag on my suitcase which read "Destination: United Kingdom," and in approximately sixteen hours, which included four hours of loafing at an air base in Newfoundland, I reached my destination. The actual flying time was less than half that of the Pan American Clippers between New York and Lisbon. A loaded Liberator is only about half as heavy as a Clipper, but it has four fifths as much power in its engines. Its published top speed is three hundred miles an hour and a Clipper's is a hundred and ninety, but the published top speed of a military airplane is likely to be an underestimate. A secondary advantage of travel by Atfero was that it spared you from the bleak scorn of the Lisbon hotelkeepers, all of whose rooms, I heard, had been full since the fall of France. The principal reason more Americans did not go by Atfero is that passengers had to wangle both an invitation from the British authorities and permission from our own State Department.

On the morning before my plane was scheduled to leave Montreal, I reported to the Atfero office in a large office building in the city. The manager, a Mr. Jackson, received me with all the excitement a Long Island Railroad conductor displays at the sight of a commuter. After looking at my credentials, he turned me over to a Mr. Hart, who gave me a slip of pink paper which said, in effect, that I had been accorded a trip to the United Kingdom in a bomber but if I broke my neck it was my own fault. Hart assured me that this was just a matter of form. He gave me, in addition to my ticket, two pages of mimeographed instructions to passengers. One instruction read, "The following subjects should not be referred to within the hearing of any unauthorized persons: airports of departure and arrival; departure and arrival times of aircraft; details of armament, supply, storage, and the performance of aircraft, engines, and other war material. Particular discretion should be exercised in speaking with representatives of the press, whose object it is to extract the maximum amount of information and who often collaborate and piece together the scraps of information they collect individually." There were also instructions for the use of oxygen equipment. For example: "On the flight it may be necessary to use oxygen owing to the height at which the aircraft may have to fly. Oxygen masks are provided for each person on board. They will be found already connected to the oxygen supply. Please use great care in the handling of the masks, as they are quite fragile and will break easily if mishandled."

"It gets pretty cold above twenty thousand feet," Hart told me, "and I advise you to buy one of the flying suits that Atfero sells for seventeen dollars. I'll bring the suit to the field for you." I gave him seventeen dollars and then went out to stroll around the grounds of McGill University, where I had once taken a summer course shortly after the other great war, when Canadians and Americans were still slapping each other on the back because Those People had been put in their places forever. The grounds were full of Royal Canadian Air Force cadets, marching smartly and self-consciously between classrooms, where they were studying the theory of flight. I then went into the quiet tavern of the Prince of Wales Hotel, on McGill Street, the place where I had first tasted ale, and polished off a couple of reminiscent pints. Then I walked back to the Mount Royal, where I was stopping. A car was to pick me up in front of the hotel early the next morning and take me to the airport.

As I stepped into the elevator with my bag the next morning, I met Jackson, the Atfero man. He said he usually stayed at the hotel when he had a batch of planes to send off. Four more men with bags, a couple of them carrying flying suits, were already standing outside the hotel when we got to the sidewalk, and I judged, correctly, that they were to be my shipmates. Jackson introduced me to two of the men, a brisk, sandy-haired Lancashireman named Steadman, evidently in his forties, who had been in the United States on some business for the British Government, and a tall, sallow young Hollander named Van Der Schrieck, who carried a small canvas sack in his left hand. It was a diplomatic pouch, he explained. He had been out in the East Indies for the Dutch Government. The other two fellows stood a little apart. They were both very young, perhaps eighteen or nineteen, and they wore Texas-style sombreros and fancy, high-heeled cowboy boots. "They are a couple of kids who are going out as transport pilots to fly planes from factories to flying fields in England," Jackson said. "They haven't had enough experience to take bombers across, so they are going over as passengers."

Steadman, Van Der Schrieck, and I got into an automobile with Jackson, and the two kids got into another car, along with most of the baggage. When they climbed out at the airport, they looked more at home than they had at the hotel. They began walking about the nearest plane and talking like a couple of horse fanciers around a nag. I guess they liked the plane all right. It was the four-engined one in which we were to make the journey, and it was a mottled tan and green. The silvery Pan American Clippers have always looked to me like something a giant built with a Meccano set. This thing looked like a big, ill-tempered insect. I went over and introduced myself to the two kids in the cowboy hats. They shook my hand with fervor. "It certainly is mighty good to meet someone from the States," one of them said. "We been up here nearly a week." "You from Texas?" I asked, looking right at the hats. "How did you guess?" the other kid asked with obvious admiration. "Yes, sir, and it's far away now."

While we waited beside our plane, one of its sister ships came in from England. The kids were frankly critical of the pilot's landing. "Landed with his brakes on," one of them said. Jackson came over with two men wearing blue uniforms and visored caps. Each wore three rings of gold braid on his sleeve, indicating that he was a captain of a British air line. Jackson introduced the older of the two men as the captain of our plane and the other as Jimmy, a colleague who was going to cross as co-pilot with us because he felt a bit under the weather and didn't want the full responsibility of a ship this trip. Our captain was a round-faced, pink-fleshed man of about forty with a voice something like Charles Laughton's. Jimmy, who might have been about thirty-five, was tall, broad-shouldered, and apologetic. "Tonsillitis, you know," he whispered. "Going up to London and have my tonsils out. Do you suppose it's frightfully painful?"

Hart, Jackson's assistant, delivered my flying suit. It was a big brown affair, like a sleeping suit, and had a hood. "You won't need it until you leave Newfoundland," Hart told me. "He won't really go up until then." By this time somebody had let down a flap in the Liberator's belly. There were a couple of steps on the upper surface of this flap, and one by one we boosted ourselves inside. Our captain and Jimmy went up into the insect's head, where they could look out, but the rest of us remained, undigested, in its windowless thorax. The forward end of this thorax, the deepest part of the ship, was divided into two decks. A radio man, facing his instruments, had the upper deck all to himself. A big, red-haired chap, munching an apple, he sat there like a professor on a dais. The aft end of the thorax was not decked, but had two fairly wide shelves along the sides, and a passageway about the width of one of the shelves between them.

The engines began to turn over, and a man who we had been told was our flight engineer appeared from up forward. He was a tow-haired, wild-eyed young man who galloped about the ship as if he had passed his boyhood running on the tops of picket fences. He motioned us to get down into the bomb bay, under the radio man's feet; the captain, it turned out, wanted our weight in that part of the ship. We scuttled obediently into the bomb bay, a dark and miniature hold, where packing cases were stowed. The cargo was heavy rather than bulky, so we had plenty of room, and the Atfero people had spread mattresses over the crates. The engine noise increased, and we could feel the plane start to move in a series of quick, gentle lifts, as if somebody were pushing against our diaphragms with the heel of his hand. Then she steadied and we knew we were up. One of the kids from Texas waved both hands, palms upward, and grinned.

The flight engineer, who had disappeared forward, came tearing back again and made signs that we could come out from under, so we moved into the space aft of the radio man. A glorious and welcome light was coming through eight little windows and a sort of skylight known as an astrodome. We could move still farther aft into the tail of the ship, clear back to the glass-enclosed perch that the rear gunner occupies when the plane is on a bombing mission. In a short while we distributed ourselves about the ship according to our various temperaments. The two kids scrambled all over like monkeys. Steadman went back to the rear gunner's seat and looked out, perhaps trying to identify landmarks. Van Der Schrieck stretched out on one of the shelves under the astrodome and started to read *Berlin Diary*. I lay down on the other shelf and did nothing at all. It was possible to talk above the noise of the four 1,200-horsepower engines, but sustained conversation would have been difficult. If you yield to the noise, the way a fighter rolls with a punch, it is soothing. The plane rode more smoothly than any other I had ever been in. Once I made motions with my lips at the radio man: "How high?" He understood and held up ten fingers, then waved his hands and held up two fingers more—twelve thousand feet. The sky, through the astrodome, was blue, and the sun was brilliant.

We had a couple of dozen thermos bottles of hot tea, coffee, and cocoa aboard, stowed in the forward part of the tail, and a stack of lunchboxes from the Mount Royal, but as we were going to make a stop in Newfoundland for lunch there was not much reason to eat now. Jackson had told us that we would arrive at the base there in four hours; it was approximately nine hundred miles from Montreal. My reflections, as I lay on my shelf, were not entirely happy, despite the ideal flying conditions. I began to worry about my oxygen mask and how I should use it. I noticed several petcocks marked "Oxygen" at intervals along the side walls. Still, I felt like a city fellow who sees a cow but doesn't know how to get milk from it. Besides, I had read somewhere that at thirty-five thousand feet there is a constant temperature of sixty-seven degrees below zero, and I hoped that the captain would not go *too* high even though I had a flying suit. These thoughts were interrupted when the plane began to descend toward the Newfoundland airport. Looking out through the windows, we could see what appeared to be an enormous bare spot in the middle of an infinite green forest. As we circled lower we could make out a great airfield, its runways dotted with planes and protected by machine-gun pillboxes. The captain put the big Liberator on the ground as lightly as a dragon fly alighting on a leaf. I looked at the two boys from Texas. Their faces were ecstatic. When the plane came to a stop, the boys opened the hole in her belly and we all crawled out.

A slender, grinning young officer in some sort of khaki uniform was waiting beside the plane to greet us. We couldn't hear what he said, but when he turned and marched off across the runways we followed him. We learned afterward that he was a member of the Newfoundland Ranger Force, which polices the airport. He led us to a big, square frame building which bore a sign saying "Eastbound Inn." It was like a very large and unpretentious summer resort hotel. It houses the airport personnel and aviators and passengers who for one reason or another are lying over at this way station. We had lunch there: steak-and-kidney pie, stewed pears, and tea. As our deafness wore off, we began to talk a bit. Presently the radio man came in and sat down at our table. He was a Lowland Scot named Mitchell, and he said that this was his eleventh ferry crossing. Nothing serious had ever happened to him, he told us. "This is one of the largest military airfields in the world," he added, "and it's all been hacked out of the scrub since the beginning of the war. It's many hours' travel by land to a railroad or a town." He said he had been grounded there by a blizzard last March and had not been able to get away for three weeks. "It was very quiet," he remarked.

Our captain and Jimmy had stayed inside the plane. Now they came in to lunch, and the captain stopped by our table to say that we would have a four-hour wait. "I don't want to get in before dawn," he said. "Nothing to be gained by it." I went for a long walk in the sun with Steadman. Then I came back to the inn and sat around with Van Der Schrieck. We talked about the ninth-century Middle Kingdom of Lothaire, which had included the Low Countries, Alsace-Lorraine, and what is now Switzerland. Finally I went into the recreation room and watched the Texas boys play table tennis. By the time a Ranger came to summon us to our plane, we were bored with Newfoundland.

When we got aboard the Liberator again we put on our flying suits and ate a large number of sandwiches, although it was only a few hours after lunchtime. The two shelves along the sides of the part of the ship we passengers chose had hinged longitudinal leaves, which, when raised and fastened together, formed a continuous deck on which to spread our sleeping things. We decided we would be better off there than down in the bomb bay, which was very drafty and where there were no windows from which to watch the sunset or dawn, so we dragged three mattresses up from the bay and spread them athwartship on our newly created deck.

Our deck was slightly lower than the radio man's. We had a few light blankets, and we hung one over the aperture between us and the bay to shut off any draft. The radio man stayed at his instruments, wearing his headphones and munching another of what appeared to be an endless series of apples. He would be up all night, of course. We closed the door that led into the tail of the ship, and then the five of us lay down on the mattresses across-ship, forming an intricate mosaic of legs and arms. My feet were at the right of the Hollander's head, and his were next to my right ear. The arrangement proved fairly comfortable, but whenever somebody had to go out to make use of the toilet facilities, which were aft, it meant untying the human knot, opening the door, banging it several times to close it, and then reversing the whole operation on the return trip. The larder was also in the tail of the ship, and it seemed that as the air grew colder we thought more of food, so there were constant trips for thermos bottles and sandwiches. I realized after a few minutes that the plane had been badly tailored for me. It was about three inches too narrow. In order to lie down I had to bend either my neck or my knees just enough to develop a kink. Van Der Schrieck was a couple of inches taller, and the taller of the Texan boys was in as bad a plight. Steadman and the smaller Texan fitted all right. It was cold, but not as cold as I had expected, and to my great satisfaction I was breathing easily at the altitude, whatever it was. I dozed, for exactly how long I did not know, and saw a raspberry-pink glow through the windows when I awoke. I wondered whether it was the late American sunset or the early European dawn, but soon the sky grew dark and I knew.

I awoke again in the night, chilled and stiff. All of us seemed to awake at about the same time. Maybe one of us, in turning, had joggled the others. Mitchell sat there unblinking, the dimmed bulb on his table the only illumination in the place. The small Texan stumbled out to the larder and came back with three lunchboxes and a thermos of hot tea. We all shared the tea and grabbed things out of the lunchboxes. I got a ham sandwich as stiff and chilly as a slab of ice cream. I took a cold, rigid piece of ham out of the sandwich and held it in my palm, inside my flying suit, until it got at least as warm as I was. Then I ate it and went to sleep again. The next time I opened my eyes it was to a new quality of twilight. I knew it must be daybreak. We all got up and began to stretch, stamp, and look out of the windows, but we could as yet see only clouds. After a short while we sighted land far under us—Scotland or Ireland, I guessed. We grew restless. It's like getting into Grand Central on a train; the minutes after 125th Street seem the longest. We packed our mattresses back into the bomb bay, climbed out of our flying suits, and began to exchange our English addresses. The captain made another good landing, and we crawled out of the plane for the second time. We saw, rather than heard, a brisk R.A.F. officer, waiting outside, say, "Good morning." A friendly bull terrier with one pink eye thrust his muzzle against my hand.

Then we got into a couple of ancient Rolls-Royces and were trundled over to the officers' club at the edge of the flying field for a wash and breakfast. There was an immigration man with a couple of perfunctory questions to ask the aliens on the plane, who of course included me. By the time I got to the dining room for breakfast, our captain and Jimmy had established themselves at a table with Van Der Schrieck. I sat down with them, and we all had bacon, tomato, and sausage. The bacon was excellent, but the sausage contained, I was told, sixty-five per cent bread, which made it taste like a hot dog with the roll inside the frankfurter casing.

I complimented the captain on our fine crossing and then said, because I was a little curious, "We didn't have to use oxygen at all. Don't you usually fly higher than that?"

"Oh yes," the captain replied brightly, as he poured milk in his tea. "But I just kept her at thirteen thousand last night. Didn't want to aggravate Jimmy's tonsillitis."

17 / Non Angeli Sed Angli

I SPENT THE NIGHT of my arrival in Britain at the Central Hotel in Glasgow. The Central has an indefinite number of rooms, alcoves, and lounges, all meant to drink in, spread along the sides of a corridor on the first floor. At that date it was still easy to get whisky in any of them early in the evening (by 1942 there was very little of it). At eleven o'clock service ceased except in a lounge marked "For use of residents only." This was in deference to the eleven-o'clock closing law in public drinking places. If you are living in a hotel it counts as your home. Everybody from the other rooms moved into this lounge and continued to drink, but at midnight a lame waiter whom any ex-Walter Scott fan could identify instantly as a crusty old servitor, announced that drinks would be sold only to *actual* residents of the hotel. After he had weeded out small tippers and Englishmen whose faces he did not like he waved the survivors, mostly Scotsmen, Norwegians, Americans, and trulls, into another, more exclusive lounge. He applied the fine comb again at one o'clock and again we moved, to a lounge for *bona-fide* residents of the hotel. At four in the morning I found myself in what I thought was my eleventh drinking nook of the night, together with a major in kilts, a lieutenant in kilts, and a merchant-navy skipper. The major spoke a trifle brusquely to the waiter, and the waiter said, "Major, you've had enough. Go to bed now." The major sulked for a couple of minutes and then went, for he knew the waiter was the only man in Glasgow who could give him a drink. The merchant-navy man had been glaring at the lieutenant disapprovingly, and now he said, "It amuses me to see you wearing the kilt when I have better Highland blood than you." This sounded like a quotation from a Waverly novel, but I could not identify it.

The lieutenant said, "I have just come from a place called Crrete. Have you heard of it? I am a MacInnes of Skye." The merchant-navy man said, "I never cared for Skye." The lieutenant said, "That is no' imporrtant." The seafarer said, "I am a MacNeill of Barra." The lieutenant said, "You lie. You have not the faceel appearrance of a MacNeill of Barra." The crusty old servitor got between them and said, "Gentlemen, you've a wee thingie on both. There'll be no more drink tonight." I went to bed still trying to figure whether they had framed me with some amateur theatricals. But it had all been on the level. The first fact one must accept about Britain is that all British literature, no matter how improbably it reads, is realistic. You meet its most outrageous models everywhere you turn, because Britain is full of improbable people, behaving in what an American or a Frenchman wrongly suspects is a fictitious manner. Before coming to Britain I had intended to write about it from an American point of view, but the project reminded me of one Sam Langford once described. "It would be like a man who only understand Italian trying to teach French to a man who do not understand Italian either." The essential point in writing about Britain is never to try to explain it, and, in talking to Britons, never to try to make them explain themselves.

When I went down to my train the next day I was pleasurably impressed to find nearly all the seats in the first-class carriages occupied by private soldiers and aircraftsmen. The head porter of the hotel had sent a lad along half an hour ahead of time to get a place for me. I decided that the British social revolution, of which we had heard a good deal in America, had at last arrived. One minute before train time all the "other ranks" yielded their seats to officers and got out. They were batmen who had been sent to hold the places. "Obviously," I thought to myself, "in this country it is unwise to jump to conclusions."

The young man who had taken the seat opposite me in my compartment was a subaltern in a regiment identified for initiates but not for me by a pair of bronze pretzels on his lapels. They were, I was to learn later, representations of Staffordshire knots, and his regiment was the South Staffords. He was about six feet tall and rugged, but apparently suffering from concussion of the brain or an extraordinary hangover. I had a Penguin book that I had bought at a station newsstand in a hurry; it was the second volume of Robert Graves's *I, Claudius*. I had meant to buy the first volume. The subaltern slept for a while with mouth open; after we had ridden for half an hour he began to stir. In another half-hour he said, "Intrsting?" I said, "Yes, but I got the second volume by mistake and I haven't read the first volume." Half an hour later he said, "I think it's prefrable to begin reading early on in a book. Don't you agree?" I asked him if he cared to read a newspaper, and he declined on the grounds of ill-health. "Just finished a physical-training course, you know," he said, "and I felt so nauseously fit I went on a frightful beano." I suggested that we might get a drink in the restaurant car, and a little color came back into his face, elevating the tint to a dead white. "Would've never have had the courage to go of my own accord," he said. "Thanks immensely for moral support." We got the drink—that was the golden age when there were still restaurant cars and they still had a bit of drink to sell on British railways—and then we got another. Peter, the name the subaltern answered to when he had drunk himself back to semi-consciousness, said the waitress looked *enfilable;* a part of his boyhood had been spent at a school in France. He had been tossed out of Oxford during his first year, he said—not the intellectual type. He regretted it, because he had hoped for a boxing blue if he had remained. What really "intrsted" him was driving racing automobiles. He had enlisted as a private in the Brigade of Guards at the beginning of the war and had worked his way up to a commission in the less exalted South Staffords. "I attribute my success to working jolly hard," he said. He was such a congenial type that I consulted him about setting up my London life. I said I didn't want to go to the Savoy, which had from reports become a transatlantic *succursale* of the Stork Club, and which was the only London hotel I had ever heard of. Peter said he knew three really British hotels, one in St. James's Place, one on Dover Street—"that's where my parents always put up when they come up to town," he said—and a third on Half Moon Street. The parents put me off the Dover Street place. When we got to Euston Station, Peter led me out into London to find a lodging. We got in a taxi and had the cabbie drive us to St. James's Place, but that hotel had been blitzed. "Awfully sorry," Peter said, "I haven't been up to London in a couple of months, you know." We tried the one on Half Moon Street next. By that time our drunk was beginning to run down on us and we were in desperate need of drinks to keep it going, so I hardly looked around me before I registered. As I rushed out into the London blackout with Peter, I retained only a vague impression of a room with heavy yellow damask draperies. We got into a place called the Lansdowne soon after that and had some drinks with a boxer named Jackie Kid Berg whom Ray Arcel in New York used to train, and then into the Hungaria, where we were told we had to order dinner with our drinks because it was after eleven o'clock. "We have an extension until half-past twelve," they said, "but only for diners." So we ordered up a couple of redundant meals, which would have seemed to me curious in a country where food was rationed if I had not quite resigned myself to being Through the Looking Glass. After the Hungaria closed we went to a thing Peter knew called a bottle club, which was exactly like a 1924 New York clip joint with a cockney accent. For all I could tell they had imported it stone by stone, as Hearst used to buy himself knocked-down monasteries. This place had a dance floor as big as a copy desk, four colored musicians, a social secretary who was under indictment for crimes against nature, and the most terrible liquor in the world. It also had hostesses to help you drink this stuff. Everything was on a membership basis, cards and all; I wept joyous tears of recognition.

A couple of girls came over and sat with us; one was not making too much sense. "They laid the bodies on the dance floor," she would say. She'd had a lot. I gathered at last that a bomb had dropped next door during a blitz and the rescue people had really brought the dead and nearly-dead into the club and laid them out there. "Why don't you get out of this bloody awful London?" she said encouragingly. "Every time the blitz came I'd get blind drunk," she said, "and then I wouldn't mind it so, but next afternoon when I got up I'd have an awful hangover. Then the blitz would begin again and I'd get blind again. I thought I'd go mad." There hadn't been a blitz for nearly two months, but people were still edgy. I paid for one bottle of whisky—the legal theory was that it was your whisky and you just came there to drink it and bought chasers, so you couldn't ever order less than a bottle at a time. Peter paid for another and then, when I began to think of going home, I looked around and he wasn't there. I ran out into Denman Street, which was as black as deep mourning, and shouted "Peter! Peter!" but I never saw him again. Pamela, the blitz-batty hostess, got a cab and saw me home.

I put up at the hotel in Half Moon Street for six months following that and came back to it when I returned to England in 1942.

The hotel when I came there was governed by a board of directors largely composed of marquises, viscounts, and bart.'s—their names were printed on the stationery, which left so little room for correspondence that it was necessary to use two sheets of notepaper where one would ordinarily serve. None of these notables came in to operate the lift or the telephone switchboard, however, and the hotel, which has about forty rooms, was as short of help as it was long on directors. The rooms, even those that are technically on the same floors, are all on slightly different levels, as in the country houses most prized by Englishmen, and are always entered by falling down one step, tripping over three steps, or marching up a hall with a floor at a twenty-five-degree angle. The concierge by day was a magnificently pink, pompous, and sly Devon man known as Roberts either because that was his name or because he used to refer to the days when he had been Lord Roberts' batman. He wore a beautiful red-and-green-striped waistcoat that made his belly look like a beetle's back, with wide gold buttons and a watch chain over his paunch that you could have hung an anchor on, and he used to have a fairly good thing of pressing my trousers on an ironing board that he had rigged behind the desk. There was no valet *en titre*, but I always felt that a crease good enough for Lord Roberts was good enough for me. The concierge was respectful, pleasant-spoken, a man who had obviously understood how to limit his ambitions and adjust to his world.

The night porter, whom I knew only as Mac, was gaunt, yellow-toothed, limber, and rebellious. He was part Irish, part Canadian, and all cockney; he played the races, horse and dog, every day and usually came on duty tight but conscious and self-controlled. He had been a noncom in India and had a cigarette case that the Duke of Windsor, then Prince of Wales, had sent him for being one of a guard of honor at New Delhi, of which he took an un-Kiplingesque view. The clientele of the hotel alternately irritated and amused him, but he could put on as soldierly a show of respect to an arriving leftenant-colonel as would merit a half-crown from any decent lush. Once he had graded the tipping proclivities of the colonel he would cool off. Mac played darts on the team representing the Rule Britannia pub, Allen Street, Kensington, in the "News of the World" tournament. The team had got to the finals one year, but the cup had been dashed from the lip, as in most of Mac's enterprises. He swam in the Serpentine every morning before going home from work. Mac's domestic affairs, from the fragmentary references that he made to them in our conversations, which usually occurred in the early morning before I went to bed, must have been fairly involved. He was finally sacked for threatening to bash the French chef in the nose; he said he could never stomach bloody foreigners.

The clientele of the hotel in the summer of 1941, when London was just beginning to fill up again after the blitz, consisted partly of people, mostly old, whom Roberts liked to refer to as "county." The typical dinner party in the restaurant—where the hors d'oeuvre invariably consisted of vegetable marrow, beetroot, celery, and one sardine—was made up of an old deaf gentleman, three deaf old ladies (presumably his wife and two of her or his sisters), four girls with buck teeth and large feet, and one elegant subaltern or sublieutenant, the heir and pride of the family. The dowdy girls would look adoringly at the young man, who had come up to London on leave; the family had come up to meet him. His problem was to be sufficiently agreeable to the old people to borrow money, without spending so much time in their company that the leave and the borrowed money would do him no good. After he had left, the old people would converse in well-bred howls, because of their deafness, their comments on their acquaintances resounding to the furthest corner of what they always called the "restaraw." I remember one old Galsworthy type shouting that "Lady Viola must be eighty." "EIGHTY!" his *commère* shrieked back to him, "Why, she's older than I am!"

The cellar then was one of the best that survived in London, because young people never came to the place if they could help it, and the old people's doctors did not allow them to drink much. Cerutti, the old Italian wine waiter, one of Thackeray's own illustrations, was a shabby but a proud man then. A year later, when the restaurant had become one of the gayest and most constantly crowded-out in London, I was to see him resplendent in a new long-tailed coat and a sommelier's glittering chain, but cringing because he knew that there was nothing left in the house fit to drink.

Outside the window drapes that veiled this inner nodule of British propriety there resounded pretty continually the cheerful click of the Piccadilly tarts' high heels. Half Moon and Clarges streets, which are traverses between Piccadilly and Curzon Street, are important trade routes of summer evenings. The Piccadilly packets, having picked up cargoes, convey them back to their Curzon Street and Shepherds' Market home ports. They come back up Clarges Street light, chattering happily. The police, except for enforcing certain trade agreements, deal with the girls in the same spirit of comradely venality as cops in any other country. The fine aroma of larceny in the air makes a New Yorker feel at home. If the British were half as stuffy as they like to think they are, nobody could live with them.

They are, for example, the only nation in the world that habitually boasts of its own modesty. It is commonplace to read in a London leader or letter to the editor, "It is perhaps our fault as a nation that we do not speak sufficiently often of our own achievements." Really, it is one fault of which not even the Irish would accuse them. The Noel Coward kind of underemphasis is as glaring an affectation as a Von Stroheim strut, but happily no Briton can maintain it beyond the second drink. Drink, by the way, may have represented the difference in the resistant qualities of British and French statesmen. Hitler, whenever he denounces the British Prime Minister as "that drunkard," betrays his puzzlement at something Sam Langford understood. "You can sweat oat beer," Sam used to say, "and you can sweat oat whisky. But you can't sweat oat women."

On my second evening in London, just at the official blackout time, I saw a light showing through the interstice between a window shade and sash in a basement window. A man in front of a house diagonally across the street from it shouted, "Put out that bloody light!" and then walked over and kicked in the windowpane. There were still a good many people sleeping in bunks in the tube stations, and blitz reminiscences were not entirely out of fashion. In the early morning hours of July 27 there was a raid, which I waited out in my hotel bedroom. I thought that when it got really bad I would go downstairs, but it never got as bad as I expected, and then the all-clear sounded. When the guns first awoke me I thought for a minute that I was a fool for not having stayed home, but the feeling soon wore off. A couple of days later I was at the great plant of the London Gas, Light and Coke Company, talking to some workmen, because I had brought from America the idea of writing a profile of a typical British workingman. I never found one who was typical of all; it was presumptuous of me to have supposed I would. But at the gas works that day I met a mechanic from Poplar, a district in the East End of London, who told me that in his immediate neighborhood the July raid had been one of the worst ever. A heavy bomb had fallen in a court in the center of three or four old riverside warehouses belonging to a dog-biscuit manufacturer that served the people as shelters. The warehouses had caved in, and about seventy persons had been killed and a couple of hundred injured. "Lucky as 'ow less and less is sleepin' in the shelters every night," the Poplar man said. "A month ago a big one in the sime spot would 'ave killed five 'undred. But they cawn't beat Poplar. One old woman about itey-one years of ige, when they dug 'er out of the debbris, she let out a cry, 'Bloody 'itler cawn't kill me!' Why, when the moanin' Lizzies started up that night it was like old times, and the barridges and all. But what was unfortunate, the pubs, what we could a done with that time of night, was closed, so we couldn't get the old darlin' a bottle of Guinness."

The mechanic, a "welder and burner," who earned between seven and eight pounds a week—twenty-eight to thirty-two dollars, and excellent pay by English standards—was not much like an American workman of the same grade. He was dressed like a caricature of a coster, with cap and neckerchief—again that disquieting resemblance to a "literary" concept— and he was apparently quite willing to live in a slum, because he had long possessed enough money to move out of it if he had wished. But he had a heart as big as a melon. "In Poplar we're cool, calm, and collective," he said. "And we're determined to defeat this bloody 'itler and 'e *will* be defeated and all, there's no doubt about that, because we're not 'aving any."

"Any what?" I asked.

"Any dictytor," he said, and with a sudden burst of eloquence, as if to make it all clear:

"Once a Britisher 'as put 'is back to the wall and 'e says, 'I am not going to 'ave it'—then 'e's not going to 'ave it. Because 'e's *determined* not to 'ave it. And consequently—'E WILL NOT 'AVE IT."

Poplar and a thousand places like it, I understood, formed the wall against which Churchill had put *his* back. They also, quite without enthusiasm on their own part, form a protective wall around Mayfair.

18 / It Showed Nice Instincts

THE WAR, IN THE SUMMER OF 1941, had hit a dead level. All through 1940 and the first half of 1941 the Germans had knocked the world about. They had occupied France and western Europe and then bombed England and after that taken over the Balkans, but now to a fellow in London it looked like anybody's fight, or a deadlock. The Germans had gone into Russia and taken their bombers with them; Britain was getting stronger by the minute, with the German grip off her collar. It already began to be plain that the German victories in Russia had less significance than victories in western Europe. No way was apparent for Great Britain and Russia to win the war unless the United States came in, but it began to seem improbable they could lose it. And since American entry into the war was a good possibility, while Germany had no equal good fortune to antici- pate, a betting man would have had to lay slight odds against the Axis. I tried to fight off undue optimism, but I couldn't help thinking that any side which had come so near winning and failed was not going to win at all. It was so irresistibly reminiscent of the first time Germany had tried. The Punic Wars were not decided by a rubber, best two out of three. The same side won the First, Second, *and* Third, and I had a hunch that the German Wars would be the same, except that no Third might be neces- sary. Cannae, of which the Germans had always talked so much, had been the winning battle of a losing army. In their souls they identified themselves with Carthage that had been beaten and Siegfried that had been murdered. Behind their arrogance they were full of self-pity. Poplar had a better ticker than Potsdam, but I didn't see how you could make a man quit by putting your own back to a wall. It was better to push him up to a wall and then knock his head against it. The power for the push would have to come from the United States, as it had the last time. In the meantime the only active warfare based on Britain was being carried on by the R.A.F., which had gained a distinct edge on the Luftwaffe. So I asked permission to visit a fighter field.

I could not help thinking that morning of the trip I had made to St. Dizier in June 1940, when the French pilots were outnumbered twenty to one by the enemy. Now, a year and a bit later, I was riding in an English train to an English flying field, and the offensive in the air war in the West had passed to the British. As in 1940, belligerent pilots were flying over France, but now it was the Germans, operating from French air- ports, who had to maintain the unending patrol against an enemy who could strike at the point and moment he chose.

The road to St. Dizier that June day had been filled with troop-carrying lorries and French tanks and anti-tank guns going up to reinforce the hinge in the new line that Weygand had set himself to defend without any faith in his chances. Moroccan troops stood along the village streets, watching the tanks go by. The Moroccans had been scattered through the countryside to deal with the parachutists, whom, it turned out later, the Germans were not to use in that phase of the war. The weather was beautiful, and there was a feel of death in the air. You wanted to get off the road and lie down under a big oak tree by a canal and forget what was going to happen, but you couldn't. To console yourself, you said, "There are only ninety-nine chances out of a hundred it will happen." That had been optimism.

There was nothing beautiful about the English weather on the morning of the second journey; just a sun the color of lard trying to burn a mist away. During the invasion scare railroad-station signs giving the names of places had been taken down, but not advertising signs, and from the car window I could view a succession of mildly pretty semisuburban towns, all apparently called Mazawattee Tea or Bovril. The names of towns in 1941 were usually marked in small letters on the backs of station benches, and a stranger traveled in a constant state of fear that he had passed his destination.

I had picked this particular field for my visit because there were Polish fighter squadrons there. Poles are not only good fighter pilots but hyper-demonstrative. Underemphasis is probably a sterling virtue, but I some-times think the English overdo it. An officer I knew who commanded the ground defenses at another English airport had told me, "The Poles knock the Germans out of the air by the dozens, and when they come in from a good fight they land like a swarm of wasps, upwind, downwind, across-wind, and all over the place. They jump out of their cockpits and kiss one another and they hold up their fingers to show how many Germans they have shot down." It had seemed to me that that would be a cheerful thing to see.

I succeeded in getting off at the right town and walked about half a mile through the streets of a neat, quiet community to the airport. An infantryman and an airman on sentry duty together at the gate inspected my pass from the Air Ministry and waved me on to the station adjutant's office. Soldiers are posted at all British flying fields to guard them against ground-strafing and parachutists, so that the airmen can concentrate on keeping the planes flying. The troops at this field belonged to the Irish Guards. The atmosphere of the place was relaxed. Men were raking and burning leaves along the tree-lined road that led to the administration building, and I suppose it was the smell and the season and the comfort-able red-brick architecture which combined to remind me of the opening of a semester at an American university—a co-ed university at that, be-cause there were plenty of girls about. These were Waafs, wearing the gray uniform of the Women's Auxiliary Air Force, with flat, visored caps and commendably short skirts. Naturally enough, few girls with un-shapely legs volunteered for this branch of the service, although conscrip-tion of women has since brought the standard down, and I never saw more than two together without half expecting them to put their arms on one another's shoulders and dance off into the wings, but what the Waafs really did at the field was the clerical work and a good deal of just plain scrubbing-up around the place.

The station adjutant had been expecting me and had assigned a flying officer, an Irishman with a wide acquaintance among the Poles, to show me around. My guide's regular duty was to work with the Polish intelli-gence officers, piecing together their accounts of each day's operations. He and I got into a small car and started off toward what he called a squadron dispersal hut. There were three squadrons at the field, and their dispersal huts were widely separated, as were the hangars, workshops, and fuel tanks. Because of this, the flying officer said, the field had made a disappointing target for the Germans, who had never been able to do more than flatten one or two buildings and put a few holes in the runways.

Since a fighter plane has a limited fuel capacity, a sweep seldom lasts more than two hours, including getting out and back. Fliers taking part in the day's operations change into their battle clothes in the dispersal huts and wait there until they go off on their jobs. When they return, they report results at the huts, change to slacks, go over to the mess for tea, and are quite likely to show up for cocktails and dinner in the nearest big town.

As we drove along a road winding among the hangars, the flying officer waved toward a group of Hurricanes whose mottled camouflage was being painted solid black. "The good old Hurricanes are a little slow for day fighting now," he said, "but with some changes in equipment and a new coat of paint they make very useful night fighters." I could not help remembering how a French pilot had said to me in the previous summer, "Ah, if I only had a Hurricane!" We drove a couple of hundred yards farther and then stopped beside a field where half a dozen Spitfires were drawn up in front of a hangar. A man was tinkering under the cowl of one of them. We got out of the car and walked over toward him, and as we did so he straightened up to greet us. He was a blond chap, with a complete set of gold front teeth, and my guide introduced him to me as a Polish officer, an engineer charged with the maintenance of planes. I noticed that the fuselage of the Spitfire he had been working on bore not only the usual emblems but a drawing of the hind end of a kitten with a coquettish red heart on it, and I asked the Pole what that stood for. "Is design peculiar to pilot," he replied. "Without official significance. He is very original *esprit*." I asked if the original *esprit* was also a successful pilot, and the engineer said, "Moderately, yes. Here he has shot down two, three, *quatre*—yes, I think five *avions*. In Poland, two, I think, or three." The engineer flashed a golden grin. "We move so very much between countries," he said, "I have my Polish forgot, my French forgot, and English I have not yet ever arrived to learn, so sometimes I mix all together."

The engineer said that he, like ninety per cent of the Poles in the R.A.F., had been in the Polish Air Force, in which they all had flown crude Polish-built fighters with French engines. They had started the war with only a couple of hundred such planes and had managed to fly a few to Rumania when it was all over, but most of the pilots had crossed the border on foot. It took some of them months to reach France. There they had been incorporated in the Armée de l'Air and assigned to planes that were inferior even by French standards. "Squadron leader, who is our

high man here, flew Caudron 406 in France," the engineer said, with his
usual aureate display. "Took half an hour to climb ten thousand feet."
He insisted on showing me over the Spitfire, one of the newest types, with
two machine guns and a cannon in each wing. "Guns fire individually or
all together," he said. "Just press button." He sounded like a very persuasive Manhattan radio salesman. Since arriving at this airfield early
last summer, he told me, the three squadrons had shot down forty-five
German planes and lost eighteen pilots. "Now, when a pilot is descended,"
he said, "is usually over France, so is captured. Last year we had many
pilots shot down over Britain. They make forced landing or bail out, and
next morning they report back to station for another plane."

We took our leave of the engineer and drove on down to the dispersal
hut we had set out for, a one-story frame building, with a red-and-white
Polish flag drooping from a staff in front of it. The mist had begun to
clear, and the flying officer said to me, "I was afraid you had picked a bad
day, but it looks as if they'll go up all right. It'll probably be just a sweep
over the Channel, maybe over Cherbourg or Le Havre. I don't think
they'll find much opposition." When the pilots on a sweep can't get a
fight, he said, they sometimes drop low and "beat up" gun positions,
airdromes, and anything that looks as if it might be a military objective.
"Those two cannons can do real damage," he said, "but the most important thing about ground-strafing is that it keeps our fellows happy. Makes
them think they're doing something, you know. The risk isn't great. I've
known of only one plane from this station to be lost that way."

The hut was furnished with a double row of cots for the men to rest on
and a set of metal lockers for their flying gear. The most prominent
decoration was a very large poster of a slinky and altogether attractive
female—obviously a spy, if you know your poster types. It bore the
legend, "Keep mum. She's not dumb." There was also a chart showing
how to inflate and make use of the pneumatic doughnut-shaped dinghies
which airmen carry on flights over the Channel. It was like a cartoon
strip, with drawings of an airman descending by parachute, landing on
the water, climbing into his dinghy, and finally comfortably sitting in it,
smiling happily. Someone had cut a cheesecake picture of a Hollywood
girl out of a magazine and fitted her into the dinghy beside the airman.
"Happy landing!" a young Pole said when he saw me looking at it. There
were half a dozen pilots in the place, wearing their battle dress, smoking
cigarettes, and chattering in Polish. They illustrated their words with
great, full-arm gestures, imitating swoops and sudden banks and climbs;
you could follow three or four dogfights at once by watching them. Occasionally some flier would make a clucking noise suggestive of a machine
gun, and laugh as if he had told a good joke. Their battle dress had a
distinctly Slavic look, consisting of a sort of Russian blouse pulled tight at
the waist and baggy, gray woolen trousers stuffed into black boots.

They were all boys in their twenties, except one tall, hawk-nosed man, who, I was told, used to be a great landowner in Poland. He had been in the Polish Air Force Reserve long before the war began and had returned to the service as a fighter pilot. "He could have a ground job if he wanted it," the flying officer said, "but he prefers to go on sweeps. He's very old for a fighter pilot—thirty-eight."

The hawk-nosed man offered to explain one of the hut's most important features—a large-scale map of the southeast coast of England, the Channel, and the French shore. He pointed to a number of pins stuck into the map here and there within the limits of the Channel and said, "Boats to pick us up if we fall in. If a pilot knows he can't reach the coast—maybe petrol tank punctured—he makes for nearest boat. We carry this map in our heads. Very useful." Next he showed me his Mae West—one of those partially inflated jackets airmen wear, which look like an umpire's chest protector except that there is a rear as well as a front panel. Each Mae West has a pocket with a small container of compressed air in it, so arranged that the pilot can release the air as he bails out, thus fully inflating the contrivance in a few seconds. Another accessory in each jacket is a phial of yellow fluid. The phial breaks as the jacket hits the water, and the yellow stuff forms a large floating patch around the flier, making his whereabouts easy to spot from the air. Still another part of the equipment is a powerful flashlight, with which to attract the attention of passing planes if the flier is unlucky enough to be still in the water after sundown. The Mae West is practically unsinkable, but it will not, of course, protect a man from the Channel's cold waters. That's where the pneumatic dinghy helps; it is attached to the pilot's parachute, and if he can swim to it and get aboard, he probably has a much longer lease on life. One Polish pilot lasted seventy-two hours in a dinghy in mid-Channel, then was picked up, and returned to duty within a week.

The flying officer suggested that we start for the mess, since the pilots would be going out to their planes in a few minutes. "We can have a sherry and then stand on the terrace in front of the mess and see all three squadrons take off," he said. "After that we'll have a spot of lunch, and by the time we're through coffee they'll be back. Then we can stop by here again and see what they did. I don't expect there'll be much, though. A number of bombers from other fields will be going over, and our fellows are supposed to get to the coast just as the bombers reach it on their way back. If there are any Messerschmitts following the bombers, our crowd will tackle them. But I don't expect there'll be any Messerschmitts to get; they seldom come across any more. If the bombers aren't being followed, our fellows will continue on and make a sweep over the Channel, with maybe a look over a corner of France."

We got into the car again and drove to the mess, which was in a large Georgian brick building with a portico. The social room, where we went for our sherry, was full of faded black leather armchairs and settees that reminded me of the lobby of a Y.M.C.A. There were portrait photographs of the royal family scattered about the vaguely green walls, and there were files of half a dozen London newspapers, including the Polish daily and the Polish weekly now published here and *France*, the French-language daily. Most of the men in the place wore either the R.A.F. gray or the khaki battle dress of the Irish Guards, with its neat green-and-white shoulder badge. Irish and Poles were mingling as convivially as if they were all attending Notre Dame. "It is wonderful to have a Pole in our party when we're drinking," my companion observed. "Then, if we have any trouble with a policeman, we all pretend to be Poles. The real Pole says to the constable, 'I am sorry, officer, my friends don't understand good English. Perhaps you speak also Polish, no?' The copper just waves helplessly and says, 'Oh, go away!' "

When we had finished our sherry we went out onto the terrace. From there we could look down on a wide field where a row of Spitfires was lined up at either end, facing the center, as if for a quadrille. "This station was only built to accommodate two squadrons, or twenty-four planes," the flying officer explained, "and there isn't room for our three squadrons to taxi to the same side of the field and take off; there would be a lag of ten minutes or so. The first two squadrons would be out of sight before the third got into the air, or else they would be circling about, wasting petrol. So we divide the three squadrons into two sets and send them off in opposite directions. First set takes off over the second set's heads, second set takes off almost as the first gets into the air."

A good many of the officers in the mess hall had straggled outside to watch the take-off. I gathered that it was a fixture in their day, like the arrival of the noon train at a rural railroad station. A short, bull-necked pilot wearing flying clothes spoke to my companion. "I was going," he said, "but at eleven o'clock squadron leader changed plan. Where they go today?" "Le Havre, probably," the Irishman said. The Pole looked relieved. "Oh boy, I miss a beautiful useless trip!" he said. "They won't find anything. I was over there the other day—not one little Messerschmitt for shooting down."

A big officer with the chest, the shoulders, and the cheerful pink face of a New York police captain stopped directly in front of me and asked how I liked the place. His sleeves were ringed with the four stripes of a group captain, which is the R.A.F. equivalent of a colonel. "I heard you were coming," he said with a slow wink. "I have my sources of information." The enunciation was old-school-tie, but the tone and the manner were unmistakably Irish. "I am the group captain," he said, "and I have the misfortune to command this odd collection of mad people."

By now the noise of the Spitfires' motors was urgent and impatient, and the line of planes at our left began to move toward the center of the field. They picked up speed and soared like racing pigeons simultaneously released, and they were hardly in the air before the planes on the other side of the field began to advance. By the time the first set was a few hundred feet from the ground, the second had taken off. For a moment there seemed to be a single spiral of planes in the air; then the machines split up neatly into three groups and were off.

The planes disappeared in the direction of the Channel, and the group captain and I were turning to go back into the mess when a lone Spitfire started to tear across the field. "And who may that be?" the group captain demanded as the plane left the ground. He sounded startled. "It is the wing commander, sir," said a Pole at his side. "He decided to go too." The group captain kept a straight face until his informant moved away, and then he turned to me with a grin. "You see," he said, "the discipline is not what one would expect of a purely British wing. Only yesterday I was telling that wing commander that he must impress on his men the necessity of sticking to their formations. They leave formation and go out looking for individual fights. Well, if he goes off on his own, what is one to expect of the others?" I could tell by the group captain's tone that he thought the Poles were all right. "Last year, during the battle, we ran a little short of Spitfires at this base," he went on. "That wing commander was a squadron leader then, and his squadron lacked one Spitfire. He was certainly entitled to a fast plane for himself, but he chose to lead that squadron in a Hurricane and let his juniors have the Spitfires. He used to take off a quarter of an hour before the others and tell them to catch up to him over Brest or St. Omer or some such place. When they got there, they would find him in the middle of a dogfight. It was horribly irregular, but it showed nice instincts."

My flying-officer friend having faded discreetly away, the group captain and I lunched together in rather impressive solitude at the head table in the dining hall. The food was depressingly British—thick soup, joint and two veg, and suet pudding—but the group captain's spirits were immune to it. He told me that Poles from this field had brought down a hundred and thirty German planes during the Battle of Britain. At the start there had been some linguistic difficulties. "The most terrifying moment of my life came right out on that terrace last summer," the group captain said. "The first Polish squadron we ever had in the R.A.F. was making its first operational take-off. We had a New Zealand and a Canadian squadron at the field at the same time, and the whole lot were to take off just as you saw it done today. The New Zealanders and Canadians were on one side of the field and the Poles on the other. The officer at the control-room radio said to the Canadian flight leader, 'Lead and go first.' He said to the Pole, 'Lead and go last.' The Pole only understood 'lead,' and the two lines of planes started at the same second. There they were, rushing across the field at each other head on. I couldn't bear to look. Do you know, sir, those planes took off simultaneously, all thirty-six of them, without a single collision. It was just like putting the fingers of one hand between the fingers of the other. The Poles must have thought it was a particularly flashy maneuver."

By the time we had finished lunch and had coffee in the social hall, the group captain said he thought I had better be getting back to the dispersal hut to see the pilots come in, and sent for the flying officer, who again drove me to it. There we found only the squadron intelligence officer, a self-effacing man who had been in the old Polish Air Force since its formation. The three of us talked for a bit, and then we heard the planes and went out in front of the hut to watch them come in. Again they reminded me of pigeons, but this time of pigeons circling and swooping down to their loft as the owner signals with a white cloth on a pole. In a moment they were on the ground, and those from our squadron were jogging along toward the hut, their idly turning propellers high in the air and their noses hiding the pilots in the cockpits. As each plane neared the hut, a dozen Polish aircraftsmen rushed to greet it. Even before the pilots spoke, the men on the field knew there had been no fighting, because the rubber nipples on the muzzles of the planes' guns were unbroken. These nipples are put on to keep dust out of the gun barrels, and when the guns have been fired the rubber hangs in shreds about their mouths.

The Poles climbed out of their planes and walked toward the hut, lighting cigarettes. They were cheerful but not exuberant, because nothing much had happened. They crowded into the hut and gathered around the intelligence officer, who had spread a large map on a table. The squadron leader, a stocky, pugnacious little Slav with light gray eyes and a dented nose, pointed out the course his men had taken, and the intelligence officer marked it on the map with a pencil. The line crossed the English coast southeast of the airfield, zigzagged northeast over the Channel, crossed a corner of France, and came back to England again. One of the pilots said to me, "Nothing. No good. We saw three Messerschmitts, but too high, too far away. They beat it."

As the flying officer and I were taking our leave of the squadron, the tall, hawk-nosed pilot—the "old" one—said to me, "Is funny, no? In two summers, in two countries, we have only couple old planes. Then there come thousands Germans to hunt us from the sky. Now we have very many beautiful planes and we cannot find any Germans to fight with us."

19/The Long Name for the Lifeboat

LONDON, DURING THAT SUMMER OF 1941 when the tide of war stood still at lowest ebb, just before it started to flow in, was the official capital of eight countries and the unofficial one of France; there were besides the gov-

ernments of Great Britain, Norway, Poland, Holland, Belgium, Czechoslovakia, Yugoslavia, and Greece, and the Free French, a half-dozen
semirecognized national movements, free Danish, free Rumanian, free
Bulgarian, and free Austrian. His Royal Highness Prince Hassan, legitimate heir to the throne of Persia—he was a brother of the last shah of the
old line and had been acting as regent when Reza Khan took over the
power—lived in the room next to mine at the hotel on Half Moon Street
and would have been popped back onto a throne when the British and
Russians ran Reza Khan out that summer, I think, if Reza's son, the
present shah, had not been married to the sister of King Fuad of Egypt.
His Highness was a cheerful ovoid little man who touched his heart and
brow when he talked and was rather better in French than English. The
town was full of intrigue over postwar Europe that began to assume some
relation to reality as it became plain that the Reich would not win decisively. As yet, however, the cabals resembled deals in Imperial Russian
bonds; even Balkan statesmen felt it silly to become really heated about
remote possibilities. The acerbity among the exiled governments increased in proportion to their chances of getting home. In 1941 they
resembled cabin passengers on a raft. They got on fairly well together,
but as soon as they were rescued they would start jockeying for a stateroom with a bath, and by the time the rescuing ship reached land they
would all be scrambling for the same taxicab.

All the governments had their own intelligence services. The prime
ministers received exhaustive reports not only on what was happening in
their German-occupied countries, where their sources supplemented and
sometimes scooped the British Intelligence Service, but on what was happening in London. Ministers got reports on their opposite numbers in half
a dozen other governments, and operatives shadowed each other, until
lunch at Claridge's or the Ritz Grill resembled a traffic jam of characters
out of an Alfred Hitchcock film. Operatives of lower categories and corresponding expense accounts shadowed *their* opposite numbers at the
White Tower, the Greek restaurant on Percy Street. Every twenty-four
hours there was a general pooling and interchange of information, probably held in Albert Hall or Piccadilly tube station, and then everybody
heard the secret information that everybody else had been compiling.
London, since Pepys's day and before, has been a gossiping city. The
coffeehouses of the eighteenth century flourished with talk as the main
attraction; the Englishman in his club is sometimes a marvel of malicious
veiled curiosity. There is a fair argument for the thesis that all the careful
barriers the Briton builds around privacy—the blackball, the no-trespass,
the truth-increases, the libel principle in newspaper law, the mannered
reserve, and the choked voice—began simply as precautions against the
national weakness for talking too much. The flood of refugee gossip adding to the normal high stream of British indiscretions, the torrent of

confidential conversation overflowed its banks and London became the gabbiest city in the world.

My favorites in Babel were the Norwegians and the Poles, I suppose because I am a sucker for extremes. The Norwegians listened and never talked. The Poles talked and never listened.

"Why did Mr. Murrow" (Ed Murrow, the Columbia Broadcasting System announcer) "talk for two hours with Dr. Beneš yesterday?" a member of the Polish Government once asked me at lunch, after receiving a report from one of his agents. The Poles are always worried about the Czechs. "Why he don't talk to me?" my Polish friend insisted. "Why nobody take us seriously? Because we laugh, my God?" The Czechs seem to the Poles solid heavy people like liver dumplings. They used to go about in 1941 impressing visiting members of the Foreign Policy Association and the like. I tried to reassure my Pole by telling him the bravura of the Polish pilots had a greater effect on public opinion than any amount of ponderous talk, but he remained unhappy. "After the war all the Poles so brave will be dead and the Czechs will own Europe," he said. A moment later he began to laugh. "The Ministry of Shipping is giving to Polish Government new merchant ship to replace one we lost," he said. "We are thinking of name for it. I would like to call *Alma Mater Cracoviensis*, Holy Virgin of Cracow. But this name is too long to paint on one lifeboat." He emptied his wineglass, swallowed a mouthful of vegetable marrow, grimaced, and then said, in a discouraged tone, "Nobody take us seriously."

I suppose that on a strictly ideological basis I should not have favored the Poles. A Polish diplomat whom we all called Prince Tommy once said to me, with a delightful smile, "Poland was a democracy before the war, but without popular representation." That sounds like a National Association of Manufacturers' program for America, but whereas I might have bellowed with rage and started throwing beer glasses if a Republican had said it in the Artists' and Writers' Saloon, when Prince Tommy said the same thing it just sounded amiably ridiculous. Since I didn't work for the Chicago *Tribune* I wasn't bound to an ideological line anyway.

There was an extravagance about the gestures of the Poles I knew that would have repelled me if I had encountered it in a work of fiction, where I can always recognize an implausibility. What could be more trite than the story of the impoverished nobleman who borrows his arrears of room rent to save himself from being dispossessed and who stops on his way home and buys a bottle of champagne with the money? It sounds like the theme of an inferior *Lettre de Mon Moulin*. Except that I knew the protagonist. He was the Pole who once told me that he had been faithful all his life to one woman: "Any fragile blond with a morbid expression."

There was also the story of Radomski. Radomski was a fighter pilot. On a sweep over France he broke formation, yielding to the bad Polish habit, and pursued three Messerschmitts, which when they had got him away from his comrades turned on him, according to the sensible German custom. "Radomski dive to get away," one of his colleagues told me, recounting the adventure, "and then he reach for the clutch to pull out. 'Funny,' he say to himself, 'cannot find clutch.' He reach again. Still cannot find clutch. He say, '*Curieux*,' and he look. Clutch was there, all right, but Radomski's left arm was shot away. He brought plane back across Channel and landed."

One Pole I knew in the Ministry of Finance had remained in Warsaw, where he had been a factory owner, until December of 1940 before he had been able to escape. "Four Schutzstaffel men came to my house a few weeks before Christmas," he said. "They came to pick out presents for their wives. They went through the house, opening closets, dressers, cabinets, to find nice things to steal. I understand German well, naturally, and I could hear what they said to each other. There was one man, the tallest of the four, who was ashamed of himself, but he did not dare say so. Everything that the others proposed to him to steal for his wife, he made an excuse for not accepting. 'These sheets would not fit our bed,' he would say, or, 'Trude does not like that color.' The others got angry with him. One, who was as a corporal, said at last, 'Take these handkerchiefs anyway. I command you.' The tall man took the handkerchiefs. I saw his face when he went out. He looked very crushed, very guilty. Now he was one of the gang. He had shared in the loot. This is the policy all through Germany. The furnishings, the clothes from Polish homes are transported there and distributed among the German civilians. Not to accept marks a family as anti-Nazi, so all accept. Then they are *participes criminis*. 'Stand fast,' the Government tells them, 'because if the Allies come and find the loot, the noose will be about your necks. Stand fast, now we are all gangsters together.' It will not matter, really," he said, smiling, "because we will kill them all." As a British friend once remarked to me, the Poles are great cards.

The points of view that the Allies brought to London were not easy to reconcile, although a number of nice old retired naval officers and brewers' widows were always trying to do it by promoting Allied circles and forums. I remember one gathering at the Hyde Park Hotel where a member of the Polish Government who had resigned because of the 1941 treaty of friendship with the Soviets spoke, not on Russia, which would have been too controversial, but on what should be done with Germany after the war. As might be expected, his project resembled a blueprint for an ax murder. Then a Dutch economist got up and said that the future prosperity of Europe depended on the survival of an economically sound Germany. The Pole shouted, "That is the way your countrymen always were at Geneva—on the German side. Traitors!" There is nothing like free discussion for promoting good will. My friend who likes fragile blondes said to me after the row:

"It was so disgusting, so human, so deplorable."

20 / Rosie, You Be'ave Yourself

WHILE STILL HOPEFUL of finding the typical British workingman I walked one summer day down to Bermondsey, where there is at least a homogeneous type known as the Bermondsey man. Bermondsey, across the Thames from the proper East End, is the oldest transpontine borough of London. It is the only district on that side of the river named among the twenty-six wards of London in Thomas Stow's "Survey," where it is called Bridge Ward Without. It is named, according to Stow again, for the monks of the Abbey of St. Bermond's Eye, a redoubtable relic. Despite these Elizabethan and medieval associations, and the street names like Tooley Street and the Old Kent Road that suggest a pleasant antiquity, Bermondsey doesn't look any older than a grim part of Pittsburgh. The architecture is divided between early-nineteenth-century slum residential and late-nineteenth-century ghastly industrial. It was not apparent to me why anybody should love the place, and I don't think that any American workingman could.

But I knew from friends that Bermondsey people bred Bermondsey people who in turn lived and died in Bermondsey. They worked on the Bermondsey docks or in the great jam and pickle factories within the borough—the factories, of course, got all the women—and they had their fun in the Bermondsey pubs and cinemas. "Over the water" in Bermondsey means, not America, but Stepney, the East End Borough across the river that you can nearly spit across. For Bermondsey it is a foreign land. "Stepney's full of Irish and Chinks and Jews," one of the first Bermondsey men I met said to me. "Here we've only our own people." A moment later he was telling me how Sir Oswald Mosley and his blackshirts had once tried to march through Bermondsey before the war. "We gave them a proper bloody 'iding," he said with pleasure. Bermondsey's thinking is Left Labor, its feeling dominated by xenophobia. In its emotional quality it sometimes reminds me of a compact Brooklyn. Bermondsey constantly sends up to Parliament a local physician who is an avowed pacifist and a prohibitionist, being in direct disagreement with all his constituents on both counts. But he is a Bermondsey man. If the Government should send Anthony Eden down into the borough to contest the seat, I am convinced Eden would get licked. The only non-Bermondsey men with whom Bermondsey people have anything essential to do are owners of housing estates, owners of factories, and German airmen, and they don't like any of them.

Walking down to the Bermondsey Town Hall, I passed the blitz ruins of a great jam, pickle, chutney, and vinegar factory. A rescue worker of the Bermondsey civil defense told me how that had gone. "It was at night," he said, "so fortunately there was nobody in it but the watchmen and nine people in a shelter in the bisement. You should've seen the flimes—and the streets knee-deep in strawberry jam. We went in to dig the people out of the shelter, we could 'ear 'em shouting. We broke through a wall, but we couldn't put in the props to keep it open while we went on. The place was all over jam, sir. The props slipped away in the jam, and one of our chaps was crushed. It was bloody awful to think of, sir, and the smell of vinegar. We 'ad better luck some other times, o' course. Once we got a girl and 'er mother that was buried under twenty feet of debbris. It took sixteen hours. The girl was on top of 'er mother, and after we'd worked a few hours I got to where I could reach the girl's 'and. I 'eld it for hours to give 'er 'eart, and the old lady underneath was cheerful as a lark. ''Old on, Rosie,' I'd say to the girl. Most of us knows one another in Bermondsey. When we got 'em out the old woman, that 'ad been so plucky, went out like that. Dead. And the girl became quite 'ighsterical. 'You be'ave yourself, Rosie,' I said. 'It won't do, my girl.' It's criminal to lose one after you've dug for 'er so long, sir."

There was another, rougher type of rescue worker there who had more cheerful memories. "It would surprise you 'ow much people can stand, sir," he said. "Once we dug all night and got out a couple of old women weighing sixteen stone apiece. Then there was the old cove a warden found sitting on the kerbstone in front of where a lodging'ouse 'ad been a little before that, only now there was nothing left except a lonely criter. 'Come along with me,' the warden says. 'No,' says the old bloke, 'I've paid my tanner and I want my kip.' 'E meant to say," the rescue worker translated at my request, "that 'e 'ad paid sixpence for 'is bed and 'e was going to stay there until 'e got one or the other. It was like the chap who was in the Dundee Arms when it was 'it and they brought 'im into a first-aid stition with 'is chin split open. 'What 'appened to you?' the doctor says, just to mike converstion, and the chap says, 'What 'appened to me? I was standing at the bar and I 'ad just put down a florin and the guvnor 'ad just put a pint of bitter in front o' me and wallop! I found myself in the cellar without the beer, and I've lost the chinge o' me florin.'"

A mild man, an ambulance driver, told me how he and his mates went into ruins to collect the injured that the rescue men had dug out. "When there's nobody to 'elp sometimes, we go about collectin' the pieces what's left," he said shyly. "I once scriped most of an old lydy off a wall. It does sound a bit ghouly, doesn't it, now? But it 'as to be done."

A still milder man, the chief of the borough mortuary service, said, "We wash every bit with soap, no matter 'ow small, and it would please you to see them, sir. Not a speck of dust on 'em. And they 'ave a coffin and all the rites. Only we can't save their clothes for the relatives. You'll agree with me that when a person gets bombed their clothes is not much good afterward."

I went into the garage that served as headquarters for the civil-defense men and talked to a lot of them, after that. There were twenty-five or thirty about, and they had nothing much to do until the next raid, which, incidentally, was not to come until the spring of 1943, although none of us would have been sufficiently optimistic to suppose so. I had been talking to Joe Blake, the town clerk, who is an intellectual. Joe had been bitter about the lack of free secondary education, or at least the great difficulty of obtaining it. That automatically prevented working-class boys from getting any higher degrees, he said. "Bermondsey has just short of a hundred thousand people in normal times," Joe had said. "Do you know how many Bermondsey boys have gone up to the universities in the last twenty years? Three." But none of the defense workers were indignant about that. In civil life they had been dockers, mechanics' mates, shop assistants, and the like. "I once knew a chap 'oo 'ad been to Oxford," one fellow said. " 'E was a 'surance igent." That evidently settled the question for him.

I asked them what they expected to get out of the war, and most of them said with a puzzled air that they didn't expect to get anything except their old jobs, a vague something that they referred to as "better working conditions," and perhaps better housing, all in Bermondsey. "Of course we *should* get something out of it, shouldn't we?" one fellow said. "If we'd lost, we'd have lost something, wouldn't we? It's like putting up a bet." This seemed to strike most of the others as a heterodox and perhaps dangerous thought. Of the whole group only one had ever considered going to the colonies or America, having as a boy even obtained some free literature put out by a Canadian government bureau in London. But he had given up the thought. Curiously, for me, not one in the lot, although they were all under thirty-five, expected that he as an individual would ever earn twice as much as his best previous salary. Since none of them had ever earned better than six pounds, or $24, before, that meant that out of the thirty men none ever expected to make $48 a week. It seemed to me that of thirty New Yorkers in the same age range at least fifteen would have had surefire private schemes to get up in the world and make a lot of money, and most of the rest would have trusted to luck to bring them money too. At least twenty-five of the thirty New Yorkers would have been fooling themselves, I imagined.

21 / Dev's Double

THE FRENCH IN LONDON had their full share of humanity.

I had first heard the voice of Charles de Gaulle in the lounge of the Grand Hotel do Mont Estoril in Portugal in June 1940. It came over the radio from London: "I, the General de Gaulle" . . . "France has lost a battle, not a war" . . . "I invite to join me" . . . "*Vive la France*." The voice spoke of resistance and hope; it was strong and manly. The half-dozen weeping Frenchwomen huddled about the radio cabinet where they had been listening to the bulletins of defeat and surrender ceased for a moment in their sobbing. Someone had spoken for France; Pétain always seemed to speak *against* her, reproachful with the cruelty of the impotent. When I arrived in London in the following summer I wanted to see General de Gaulle as soon as possible and write a whacking profile about a modern Bertrand du Guesclin. Du Guesclin was the great fourteenth-century guerrilla knight who, anxious only to rid France of the invader (in that war the English), fought tirelessly until he had righted what appeared a hopeless military situation. Like most of my preconceptions, this one was on the romantic side. General de Gaulle, when I met him, was to remind me rather of another tall man whom I had encountered in Redmen's Hall over a cigar store in a shabby quarter of Providence, R.I., in about 1928. That man had been named Eamon de Valera, and at the time I had met him his party had been out of power in Eire and Dev had been barnstorming the United States to get Irish-Americans to sign away their claims to money from Irish Republican bonds. De Gaulle and De Valera both are tall and long-legged and long-nosed and narrow-boned, with long upper lips and the faces of a pair of hidalgos that El Greco might have painted on either side of the crucified Christ. They share the quality of being so long and narrow they appear out of drawing. They share also an Iberian pride, stubbornness, and suspicion of the people around them; there may be actual consanguinity, since De Valera's father was Spanish and De Gaulle comes from the part of France that Spaniards occupied repeatedly during the wars of the sixteenth and seventeenth centuries. Both are great patriots and have had to maintain their faith in causes of which more practical men would have despaired. But neither is easy to live with.

I learned from friends when I first got to London that I could not interview General de Gaulle at once. He was walking about in the streets contiguous to Carlton Gardens, his headquarters, but he was by official decree out of town. De Gaulle had displeased Winston Churchill by something he had said in Brazzaville, where the General had recently been, so neither the French nor British press was allowed to allude to his return to London. Naturally American correspondents couldn't allude to it either. "As soon as he makes it up with the P.M. it will be all right," my British friends told me, "but he has been a very naughty boy."

General de Gaulle's naughtiness in that instance had consisted of giving an interview to George Weller of the Chicago *Daily News* syndicate, in which he had put out a feeler for direct American support. Weller had quoted De Gaulle as offering to the United States bases in the African territories and Pacific islands under Free French control "without demanding destroyers in return." The Free French were keen to get Lend-Lease materials directly, instead of through the British Government. His Majesty's Gov. construed the talk about destroyers as a reflection on His Majesty's Gov. General de Gaulle repudiated the interview, although Weller is a reliable reporter. And shortly after this public expiation the British press acknowledged the General's return from Africa, sometimes spelled Coventry.

This sort of thing contributed to what one of my best-informed and most British friends called De Gaulle's "justified anglophobia," but it did nothing to encourage him in further gestures toward America. De Gaulle is intolerant of restraint, as he proved in the famous armored-division row in the French Army, and his London irritation was increased by the knowledge that Vichy propaganda in France accused him of being under Churchill's thumb. It was natural that he should try to bite a piece out of the thumb occasionally. But Churchill was stuck with De Gaulle almost as firmly as De Gaulle was stuck with Churchill.

If the Prime Minister had forced De Gaulle's permanent retirement to private life he would have confirmed the charge that Great Britain controlled the Free French. He would also have wasted a whole year of advertising De Gaulle's name. De Gaulle had to stay on.

Among the thirty or forty thousand Frenchmen and Frenchwomen in England, the General had no great personal support. They consisted of French citizens who had been in England before the fall of France, of refugees who had crossed on the last boats from French ports primarily to get away from the Germans, and only in small minority of young men who had escaped from occupied France with the specific purpose of joining De Gaulle. Members of the first group, the "French of England," found difficulty in comprehending the extent of the French disaster even in 1941. For them France had never ceased to be a great power, French law had never ceased to operate, and De Gaulle was a fantastic, unauthorized intruder on their schizoid dream. Many of the June 1940 refugees, hard fighters themselves, resented De Gaulle's claim to one-man leadership. They said that he had no right to claim a copyright on France, that nobody had elected him, and that even in accordance with military rank he was junior to several other officers who had escaped the debacle, like Catroux, a five-star general, and Vice-Admiral Muselier. These critics included the men of the Left, who doubted De Gaulle's republicanism, and some others whose Gallic irreverence was outraged by the man's mere aspect. "He looks as if he had swallowed his saber," these latter said. There were very few white men in the Free French "Empire" of Equatorial Africa. André Labarthe, the founder of the revue *La France Libre*, once referred to De Gaulle as *"le roi des nègres."* The *mot* made its instant round of the limited French world in London; De Gaulle, who is as serious as a saint, never forgave Labarthe. Labarthe, a scientist, military critic, and editor, whose republicanism, unlike De Gaulle's, dated from long before the war, had demonstrated his practical patriotism by kidnaping a ship loaded with copper from Bordeaux and forcing the skipper to take it to England in the last days before the Armistice of Compiègne. He had also made *La France Libre* the best of anti-collaborationist publications outside France. Labarthe came down to Algiers in the spring of 1943 and was made Minister of Information for the Government of North Africa. But De Gaulle refused to enter into the new combination government later that year until Labarthe had been dismissed. He preferred as Minister of Information a Frenchman of restrained bellicosity, Bonnet, whose name has unfortunate associations, and who had passed his time since the Armistice lecturing in America. It was a similar story with Vice-Admiral Muselier, whom General de Gaulle eliminated first from the Free or Fighting French Committee in London and then from any role in Algiers. Muselier had seized St. Pierre and Miquelon to permit a plebiscite by which the Free French gained those islands; he was perhaps the one man most hated by Vichy admirals like Darlan. Collaborationism was scarcely the basis of De Gaulle's trouble with him.

De Gaulle, however, protected with great obstinacy all through 1941, and may still be protecting, for all I know, a Colonel P———, who was considered a Fascist by every Frenchman and Englishman at all acquainted with the Free French setup whom I ever met. P——— carried stories against other Free Frenchmen; any attack upon him therefore aroused De Gaulle's suspicion—"the others" were trying to deprive him of his faithful watchdog! I was to see General Giraud go through a similar routine in defense of General Bergeret, in Algiers more than a year later. Most reactions of French generals are interchangeable. Again, in the summer of 1942 when I was in London a putty-colored little man of archetypical Mussolini-Mosley mien, one Charles Vallin, who for years had been second in command of the Croix de Feu organization in France, appeared mysteriously in London. This little man, composed entirely of stomach and eyebrows, announced that although he had not changed any of his anti-democratic views he had seen the light (i.e., decided Hitler would lose) and was promptly accepted by De Gaulle as a great anti-German. The General did not proclaim that Vichyites were irredeemable, but that only he had the right to give absolution. A hint of papal infallibility was implicit in his pretension.

De Gaulle's enthusiasm for democracy required considerable prodding during his first year of exile. I can remember the struggle of the British Political Warfare people to induce him to say, "*Liberté, Egalité, Fraternité*," during the course of a broadcast to France; he balked like a zebra and finally yielded with the air of Henri IV saying "Paris is worth a Mass." His imposition of the Cross of Lorraine on the Free French version of the tricolor never went down well with the anti-clericals among his compatriots. It left an opening for criticism which not even General Giraud in 1942 was to miss, although Giraud is no adept at controversy.

The politics of "the movement" furnished the subject for endless arguments over the wine-stained tablecloths of the "French pub," the York Minster in Dean Street, where the commonalty crowded in, as over the elegant napery of L'Ecu de France and Prunier's in the West End, where the immediate entourage of the General and the wealthy refugees made *langouste* and partridge serve in place of rationed meat and kept unquivering chins in spite of having to drink minor vintages. It was at the Ecu that the truly chic Free French of London gave a public farewell party for the young bloods leaving on the "secret" expedition to surprise Dakar in September 1940. Madame Prunier has carried on the London restaurant of the firm throughout the war, while Monsieur has continued to conduct the business in Paris. There were Frenchmen in London who were willing to be called "Free French" but not "De Gaullistes," and others who said that just "French" was enough, that a Frenchman was by definition free. One of the great weaknesses of the French community in Britain, considered as a microcosm of France, was that few representatives of labor and none of the peasantry had escaped the debacle. The two largest classes of French society were without expression in the plans for the future of their country. I had a good many friends among the soldiers and intellectuals who had come on to London after the fall of France, and I had, moreover, in a manner that it would be perhaps indiscreet to detail, rediscovered a number of old acquaintances in the British services concerned with work in occupied Europe, so that I found myself in the thick of the arguments. I always maintained the thesis, against Frenchmen who deprecated De Gaulle and Britons who complained of his crankiness, that since he was the only horse they had entered in the race they had better try hard with him. I thought him valuable as a trade-mark and as a person. For stubbornness and a lack of objectivity, in the leader of a forlorn hope, are rather qualities than defects. And I would quote Reynaud, with the addition of a softening *peut-être*, "He has perhaps the character of a stubborn pig—but he *has* character." It is, believe it or not, a great asset.

The consequence of this overelaborate discussion of every facet of De Gaulle's character was that by the time I interviewed him I was completely insulated against fresh impressions. I was in the frame of mind of a soldier entering a house that he has reason to believe booby-trapped. The General, suspicious by nature, had been made more so by numerous and probably conflicting reports on me, and my first innocent question, designed to stimulate conversation, was a disaster. "When are you coming to America, my general?" I asked him. He immediately had to decide whether I was a scout for the Foreign Office or whether Anthony J. Drexel Biddle, Jr., whom he knew I knew, had sent me over to feel him out with a view to a later official bid from the State Department. "I have not yet been invited," he said after a pause of a couple of minutes, and settled back in his chair as I have seen witnesses in a murder trial momentarily relax after turning a tough question from a cross-examiner.

De Gaulle is decidedly less imposing sitting down than standing up, because the part of him showing above a desk does not suggest a man of extraordinary stature. He is small-boned, with fine, slender hands and no great depth of chest or breadth of shoulder. His height folds up under his desk with his legs. He is consistently pale rather than sallow. It is as difficult to carry on a sequential conversation with De Gaulle as with De Valera. He reacts, but does not respond, to a question by delivering a speech on a tangential subject.

The General said that he was convinced the little people of France, the sailors, the peasants, the factory hands, the barbers, were for him and the rich were for Vichy and against him. I noticed, perhaps frivolously, that he did not say the little were against the rich or the rich against the little, but that he made of the breach between classes a question of reaction to De Gaulle. After the war, he said, a government with "bold ideas," "*des idées hardies*," would be necessary in France. He said that the people of France must determine their own future form of government, under a plebiscite to be called after the reconquest.

I left him without any idea that in the spring of 1942 he was to be canonized alive by the stay-at-home seers of the American press. It is nice to learn, however late, that one has talked with an angel.

22 / They Are Not Gone

THE WORKMAN AND SAILORS of Great Britain made great war in 1941. Opportunities for fighting were limited by circumstance, but the need for war material was limitless, especially after Germany attacked Russia. Not only the great forges and shipyards turned out the stuff; there were hundreds of peacetime plants converted to war industry along the network of roads that radiate from Manchester to the scores of smaller factory towns around, places with names we never hear in America, like Blackburn and Bury and Ramsbottom and Rawtenstall and Eccleston and Rochdale and Warrington. The bare hills north of the city were full of them; the flatlands that stretch westward to Liverpool and south into Cheshire bristled with smoking chimneys. That was where the war was. A Lancashireman working for the Ministry of Labour said to me, "Lancashire people have co-operation in their blood. It's here the trade unions, as well as the factories, started. And the Co-operative Stores, which are the largest medium of distribution in all England now, began at Rochdale, a bit north of Manchester. Why, even the troupes of girls who dance in unison —precision dancers, I think you call them—originated here. The original Tiller Girls were recruited from Manchester."

The engineers were as good as the workpeople they directed, and they used every bit of equipment they had. I remember coming into one Lancashire village and seeing two meticulously beautiful new Bofors gun barrels on a wagon drawn by an aged white horse on the high street, en route from a machinery plant to the railway station. The animal looked as if it might have pulled a field piece at Waterloo. The plant was a hundred and ten years old, with flagstone paving. Most of the lathes dated from the last century. The strong, beefy old man who ran it was boring gun barrels with a tolerance of two ten thousandths of an inch of error with an arrangement of machinery he had improvised himself. Before the war he had made textile printing presses for coloring calicoes. The power for his pet ordnance machine came from a dismounted motorcycle engine; the Archimedes lever with which he met all engineering problems was a bicycle chain. "Anything for war," he told me. "Ah'm 'eart and soul in it." He said, with a juvenile pride, "Ah'm number one wi' Admiralty. They tell me send goon tubes to London by passenger coach, not goods train." Men like him had held the breach while Britain modernized its industrial plant with machine tools from America, but now production had already reached the turn.

The Lancashire lads and the Lancashire ladies were, in their northern phrase, "champion." My favorite town in all England, however, was and is Grimsby, Lincs., which rhymes with "drinks."

In the men's bar of the Ship Hotel at Grimsby, Englishmen speak to other Englishmen after less than five drinks. This is a tribute to Grimsby's genius, which is bacchic and maritime in equal parts. Grimsby sent ships to the fleet of King John and still sends its ships to the wars with Grimsby skippers and Grimsby crews, eked out, it is true, by a supplement of fellows from other parts of England, whom Grimsby men refer to impartially as "they dommed farmers." The farmers drown like the Grimsby men, but they cause them a lot of vexation in the interim. In the Ship bar one may meet fifty-year-old sublieutenants of the Royal Navy (Reserve, naturally) who have tattooed fists and unbutton their uniform jackets to allow room for beer. They are not quite gentlemen, of course, any more than middle-aged Lieutenant James Cook was a gentleman when he sailed to find a continent. The gentlemen lose the continents. The sub-lieutenants come ashore from the mine sweepers and patrol boats that used to be trawlers. Only the very old boats with maimed or ancient skippers fish now. As for the convivial part of the Grimsby tradition, Sir Fretcheville Hollis, a Parliament man for Grimsby, told Samuel Pepys in 1667 that to win an election there he had to spend £352 for beer. Pepys set this down as a "develish lie," but Pepys was no Grimsby man. Under the combined influence of Grimsby beer and Grimsby informality, even pink-cheeked and well-turned-out young officers off destroyers become relatively effusive. They say "Beastly weathah we ah having" to men to whom they have never been introduced. Since ships bigger than destroy-ers seldom come to Grimsby, the town is relaxingly free of officers of senior grade.

The highest-ranking officer in the bar as I entered one evening was a lieutenant commander named Armstrong, whom I had met at the naval base, where I had been getting material for a story. He was a big man who looked to be about forty but must have been a good deal older than that, because he had once told me that he had been in sail in 1904. He had fought in the other war and then been a captain in the merchant marine and then retired, and now he was in service again. Armstrong was a kind of patrol-boat admiral. He had under his command at least a dozen converted fishing boats, of about two hundred tons each, carrying crews of thirty men.

Most of the patrons of the Ship get their drinks at the bar and then carry them to the long wooden tables. Armstrong was at a table with a pint of the local brew in front of him, and he motioned me to come and sit beside him. I got my beer and joined him. "One of my fellows had a do with a German plane," he said, by way of beginning. "Plane was attacking some fishing boats, and my fellow went to help. Between all of them they shot the plane down, but they're rowing about who did it. Fishermen say they did; my chaps say they did, naturally. One fishing boat sank. A bomb dropped close to her and she just came apart. My fellow said that the bomb hit the water, and the next thing he thought he heard was a burst of machine-gun fire. 'But it wasn't machine-gun fire,' he said. 'It was her rivets popping out so fast it just sounded like machine-gun fire.' All of her crew were saved. I thought you'd like that description. Same chap once told me he'd seen a trawler bombed, and she went so high he could see the top of a near-by lighthouse under her keel. And two sea gulls over the lighthouse, he said." I said something about wishing the fellow would write a book. Armstrong said, "I once had one chap who did. Well, it wasn't a book exactly, but a diary, anyway." I got up and brought another round of beer.

"You know how it is in our boats," Armstrong said when I had sat down again. "The chap in command gets lonely. When the ship is fishing, most of the space in her hull is used for a fish hold. The men all muck in together, eating and sleeping in the smallest possible space, and the skipper mucks in with everyone else. They don't mind that, because they're on shares, and the more fish they carry the more money they get. But when we take the boat over for the Navy we convert the fish hold into quarters for the crew. The skipper has a cabin forward, and since he's the only commissioned officer aboard, he can't eat with the rest. He has to take his meals alone, and the others say 'Sir' to him. That makes him moody and sometimes inclines him to drink. Spirits are tax-free in the Navy, as you probably know, and that is a temptation. Then he begins to brood about the new chaps in the crew. It would be splendid if we could man our boats a hundred per cent with fishermen, but it's impossible. A fishing boat carries a crew of thirteen, but when she goes to the Navy she needs thirty—gunners and fellows to handle mines and all that. And some of the new men have never been to sea. This chap who wrote the diary didn't drink heavily. The writing was his outlet. I came across it when I was going through his effects, poor chap. He copped it in a fight with some motor torpedo boats. A one-pound shell took half of his head off. I sent the diary, along with the rest of his things, to the widow, but I couldn't help copying a few entries."

Armstrong reached inside his jacket and brought out a typewritten page, which he passed to me. These were the entries:

Dec. 11. Coventry, London. Manchester. Ow I wish I could come up with a Jerry plane. I would show them. Today my steward put my knife spoon and fork in bucket of water to wash then forgot they were there chooked water overboard with them in it. I could of chooked im overboard too.

Dec. 16. I of a fine crew. One chap that worked in sweetshop. One bus conductor. One building workman. Two married men that of never been to sea.

What a bloody sample.

Dec. 21. I told cook to make rice pud. Late in day rice floating on galley floor he put about ½ a stone of rice in boiling water nice pud.

January 6. Today men grappled German mine were bringing it over side but not fast enough. I leaned over side and seized cable to help. Opened my mouth to give order and upper and lower plates fell out.

They are not gone. I know where they are.

"Do you know," Armstrong said, "something about that last entry makes me rather sad. So many Grimsby lads, you know."

"Yes," I said. "I get it. We know where they are."

In November I began to feel more curious about the front in the United States than anxious about Britain. In the United States there was still a great decision to be taken; Britain could do nothing but wait. It seemed to me that the old British official propaganda line, "Give us the tools and we will finish the job," had begun to boomerang. I was certain that the British alone could not do all the fighting that would be required away from the Russian front, and I knew that we would never produce weapons in quantity commensurate with our industrial strength until we were in the war. I was afraid that people at home might be taken in by the official British optimism as they had been by the French. I went home by sea because I wanted to experience what the British press liked to call the Battle of the Atlantic.

23 / Westbound Tanker

A TANKER IS A KIND OF SHIP that inspires small affection. It is an oilcan with a Diesel motor to push it through the water, and it looks painfully functional. Its silhouette suggests a monster submarine with two conning towers. A destroyer's clipper-ship ancestry is patent in the lines of its hull, but neither tankers nor submarines betray any origin. They seem to have been improvised simultaneously by some rudely practical person and then put in the water to fight each other. A tanker scores a point when it completes a voyage. When the oil reservoirs of the Allied bases are full, the tankers are beating the submarines. They have been doing that since the beginning of this war, but few people think of a tanker as a fighting ship. When a tanker gets sunk you read about it in the paper, but when it docks safely nobody hangs any flags in the streets.

The *Regnbue*, on which I came home from England to the United States, is a Norwegian tanker. It is not remarkable in any way. Norway had a tanker fleet second only to that of the United States, and Norwegian tankers in 1941 carried fifty per cent of the oil that had gone to Britain since the war began. The *Regnbue*—the name means "Rainbow," as you may have surmised—was built at Gothenburg, Sweden, in 1930. She displaces nine thousand tons, a good, middling tanker size, and can do eleven knots loaded, a fair, medium speed. Her lead-gray hull was streaked with rust, and her masts and funnel and deckhouses showed only a trace of paint the first time I saw her. A grimy Norwegian flag, ragged at the edges, flapped from her mizzenmast, and there was a cowled four-inch gun on a platform raised above her poop. I was joining her as a passenger, but I didn't learn her name until I got close enough to read it on a small sign on the side of her bridge. This was because the Norwegian Trade Mission in London, through which I had booked my passage, believes in secrecy about ship movements. Since the German invasion of

Norway, the Norwegian Government-in-exile has chartered most of the Norwegian ships in the world to the British Ministry of War Transport. The ships still fly Norway's flag, have predominantly Norwegian crews, and are, for the duration, in the custody of the Trade Mission.

An official at the Trade Mission, knowing I was ready to leave on short notice, had called me up at my hotel in London one Saturday morning and said that if I didn't mind sailing from London instead of a west-coast port, they had a ship for me. I said I didn't mind, although this would add several days to the voyage. Next morning I took a taxi to the Mission offices on Leadenhall Street and there handed over my passage money. The man who had telephoned me said that the ship was bound for New York in water ballast to take on cargo there. He gave me a sealed envelope addressed to one Captain W. Petersen and a slip of paper bearing written instructions for getting to the ship. I was to take a certain train at Fenchurch Street Station early Monday morning and travel to a small station near the Essex shore, a ride of an hour and a half. A taximan would meet me at the station and drive me to a pier, where I would find a boatman named Mace. Mace would put me aboard Captain Petersen's ship.

Shortly after eleven o'clock on Monday, December 1, I found myself in Mace's launch, moving through the water of the Thames Estuary toward the tanker, which lay about a mile offshore. The only other passenger in the launch was a Norwegian port engineer who was going out to examine the ship's motors. "Look at that paintwork!" the engineer said as we neared the *Regnbue*. "Tankers make such quick turn-arounds the crews have no chance to paint. Discharge in twenty-four hours or less, take bunker and water, and out to sea again. Oil docks are always in some place like *this*, too—miles from the center of the city. The men don't get a chance to see the town. I know. I was in tankers in the last war." Before he had time to tell me more about them, we were under the rope ladder leading to the *Regnbue*'s main deck. It was an extremely uninviting ladder, but the engineer went up it as if it were an escalator. A seaman dropped a line to Mace, who made a loop through the handles of my suitcase and portable typewriter, which then rose through the air like Little Eva going to heaven. I went up the ladder in my turn with neither grace nor relish. My style must have amused one of the several men who were leaning over the rail, because he looked down at me, then turned to the man next to him and said, "Commando."

This fellow, who was wearing a white jacket, was obviously a steward. He was of medium size but had long arms, so the jacket sleeves ended midway between elbow and wrist, baring the tattooing on his wide forearms. On the right arm he had a sailor and his lass above the legend, in English, "True Love." The design on the left arm was a full-rigged ship with the inscription "Hilse fra Yokohama," which means "Greetings from Yokohama." His head was large and bald except for two tufts of red hair at the temples, looking like a circus clown's wig. He had a bulging forehead and a flat face with small eyes, a turned-up nose, and a wide mouth. As soon as I got my breath, I said, "Passenger," and he took me in charge with a professional steward's manner, which, I afterward learned, he had acquired while working for a fleet of bauxite freighters that often carried tourists. The bauxite freighters had operated out of a port the steward called Noolians, and most of the tourists had been vacationing school-teachers from the Middle West. Fearing emotional involvement with a schoolteacher, he had switched to tankers. "Tankers is safe," he said. "No schoolteachers." His name was Harry Larsen.

The steward led me along the rust-stained steel deck to the ship's forward deckhouse. The main deck of a tanker is simply the steel cara-pace over the tanks. In rough weather the seas break over this deck. The human activities of the ship are concentrated in two deckhouses, fore and aft. The forward one is like a four-story house rising from the main deck and contains the bridge and the captain's and deck officers' quarters. A long catwalk ten feet above the main deck serves as the highroad between the deckhouses, and even on the catwalk you are likely to get doused when there is a sea running. The engine room and the galley, the ship's one funnel, the cannon, the refrigerator, the crew's quarters, and the cat's sandbox are all jammed in and around the stern deckhouse. The steward showed me to my cabin, which was the one called the owner's, although the owner had never used it. It was next to the captain's office. His bedroom was on the other side of the office, and we were to share a bathroom. It was a fairly good cabin, with two portholes, a bed, a divan, and a desk. The steward said that the captain was still ashore but I should make myself at home.

I went out on deck to look around and was pleased to see one of the British Navy's barrage-balloon boats alongside. A balloon boat is a lighter with a half-dozen or so bright, silvery balloons floating above it, each attached to a slender wire. The *Regnbue* dropped a wire cable aboard the lighter, and a couple of naval ratings rove the end of a balloon cable to ours. They let go the cable and the balloon rose above our foremast, securely attached, as we thought, to the *Regnbue*. It wasn't, though. It blew away two nights later, but it was a pretty embellishment as long as we had it. While I was watching the transfer, a little man in a blue uni-form came over and stood next to me. I asked him when he thought we would get under way. He said that he was the pilot and was going to take the ship a short distance farther down the river that afternoon. The cap-tain was coming aboard after we got down river. The pilot was a black-haired, red-faced Londoner with a habit of laughing nervously after practically everything he said. "Good thing about a tanker in water bal-last," he said. "She's just a box of air, what? Tanks half full of sea water, all the rest air—wants a long time to sink if she's torpedoed. Much as forty minutes, perhaps, eh?" He laughed. I said that I thought this was very nice, and he said that now you take a loaded tanker, it was just the opposite—the very worst sort of ship to be torpedoed aboard. "Flaming oil all about. Rather depressing, what?" he said. I agreed.

The steward came along and told us that dinner was on the table in the saloon, so the pilot and I followed him down a flight of stairs into a large, rectangular room with paneled walls and a dark green carpet. The most impressive feature of the saloon was a portrait, nearly life-size, of an old gentleman with a face the color of a Killarney rose and a bifurcated beard that looked like two blobs of whipped cream. The artist had used plenty of paint of the best quality. I could imagine a jury of boatswains giving the picture grand prize at a *salon*. "The founder of the line that owned this ship," the pilot said.

"Capitalist!" the steward said, simply and with distaste.

"Rum thing on Norwegian ships," the pilot said, "the captain doesn't eat with the other officers. As a passenger you'll mess down here in the saloon with the captain, and there'll be just the two of you at every meal. But in every other respect they're more democratic than our ships. Odd, what?"

The pilot had been at Dunkirk, he told me a bit later on. "I was in command of seven motorboats," he said, with his laugh, "transferring troops from the beach to destroyers. I lost the boats one by one. A motorboat doesn't take much smashing, does it? When the last one foundered, my two ratings and I swam to a destroyer's boat. What I shan't forget," he said, after a pause, "is the motorbike races on Dunkirk beach. Chaps waiting to be taken off, you know. Never saw better sport. There were soldiers making book on the races. Couldn't leave the beach until all bets were settled or they'd be known as welshers."

The dinner of pea soup, corned beef, and baked beans, ending with a double-size can of California peaches for the pilot and me, was big by London standards. The portions were on a scale I had almost forgotten, and there was a lot of butter. The steward said the food had been loaded at Corpus Christi, Texas, in October. "We don't take any food in England," he said. "I hope we get to New York for Christmas. I got nothing to make Christmas at sea—no newts, no frewts, no yin for drinking."

"We ought to make it," I said, with the confidence of inexperience.

"It depends what kind commodore we get," the steward said. "If we get slow commodore, old man retire from Navy fifty year and only come back for the war, we lucky to get New York for New Year's. I don't care much for New York anyhow," he added loftily. "Too much noise, too many Norweeyans in Brooklyn, argue, argue, argue! I like better Camden, New Yersey, go with the Polish girls."

The ship moved slowly down the estuary during the afternoon. We dropped anchor again before dark at a point where the Thames had definitely ceased to seem like a river and where half a dozen other ships already rode at anchor. Our men looked at them curiously, as one surveys the other occupants of the lounge car at the beginning of a long railroad journey. There were a couple of British tankers with fancy Spanish names, a gray, medium-sized Dutch freighter, and a big, boxlike Elder Dempster boat that had once been in the West African service. I have seen the Dutch freighter's name in a newspaper since. She had shot down a German plane. There was also a stubby, soot-black Norwegian steamer of not more than three thousand tons, which had a single funnel so narrow and long that it reminded me of an American river boat. The third officer, a husky blond chap who wore an orange turtle-neck sweater, pointed to the stubby ship and said to me, "That is the slowest ship in the world. Once she made one trip from Cape Town in four convooeys. They started two weeks apart, and she kept on losing one convooey and getting into the next. She was going full speed the whole time." All the ships were, like ourselves, light and bound for America to get a cargo.

The pilot came down from the bridge and joined me when the ship was at anchor. I asked him when he thought we should get to New York, and he said that with luck we ought to make it in about twenty days. It depended a lot on what connections we made at the assembly ports, he said. The *Regnbue* was going all the way around Scotland to get to the west coast of Britain. We would spend the first few days of our voyage in a small convoy sailing up the east coast of England to our first assembly port. From there, we would go to the west coast in a larger convoy, but we might have to wait a couple of days while this larger convoy was being assembled. Then we would proceed to the second assembly port and go through the same business there. We might be just in time to leave with a transatlantic convoy or we might have to wait a week. There was no way of telling. "The most ticklish bit in the trip begins about twelve hours above here," the pilot added consolingly. "If we get off tomorrow morning, you'll be in it by night."

Captain Petersen came aboard shortly before nightfall. He was a small, stoop-shouldered man. His brown shoregoing suit was carefully pressed. He had a long, curved nose and lank, sandy hair, and he spoke English slowly but accurately, using American idioms. He had lived in Philadelphia, where he worked in an oil refinery, during part of the last war, he told me, and then had moved to Hoboken, where he had roomed in the house of an Irish policeman. After the war he had gone back to Norway to enter navigation school with the money he had earned in America. All the reminiscences of the United States that he politely introduced into our conversation dated from before 1919. He gave detailed accounts of several Chaplin comedies, like *The Count* and *The Cure*, which he had seen then. We went down to supper with the pilot, and Captain Petersen, pointing to the whiskered portrait, said to me, "That is a man who once owned eighty sailing ships. Even when he was ninety-two he combed his beard for one hour every morning. I remember seeing him in my home town when I was a boy. The company owns only a couple of ships now. It belongs to an old lady, who lives in my town also."

His town is a sleepy little city in southern Norway which in the nineteenth century was a great port for sailing ships. The *Regnbue*, the captain explained to me, is emphatically a ship from his town. Not only is she owned there—although, as he explained, owners captive in Norway had no control over their ships for the duration of the war—but skipper, chief officer, and second officer all came from there and had known each other as schoolboys. Both the captain and the chief officer, a man named Gjertsen, had even been married aboard the *Regnbue*. Their brides had joined them on the ship at Antwerp and Constanta, Rumania, respectively. Petersen had been second officer and Gjertsen third officer then, and they had honeymooned in turn in the captain's suite. The wives were at home now. "The second and third officers have wives in Norway, too," he said, "and so has the chief engineer. I was lucky enough to have a vacation in December 1939, so I saw my wife and boy only a little while before the Germans came."

Petersen told me that when the Germans invaded Norway the Norwegian Government had commandeered Norwegian ships all over the world, ordering those at sea to put into neutral or Allied ports. A radio message had been sufficient to accomplish this. Only a small part of the merchant marine had been caught at home. Now the exiled government's income from ship hire not only supported it but provided a surplus, which is to be used for the nation's reconstruction after the Germans are driven out. He didn't show any doubt that they would be driven out, nor did anyone I talked to on the *Regnbue*. The boatswain, a weathered gnome of a man, once said to me, "I couldn't sleep at night if I didn't believe on it." The owners of the ships were nearly all caught in the invasion. The Government had promised that after the war they would receive compensation for the use of their ships, provided they paid allotments to the sailors' families in the meanwhile. So the captive families had been receiving small amounts of money, but even with money there isn't much food.

There was a door at each side of the saloon. One led to the pantry and steward's cabin, the other to the deck officers' quarters. The officers had their mess aft, in the other deckhouse. After supper on a normal evening aboard the *Regnbue*, I was to learn, the captain and the steward visited the deck officers. Then, at about eight o'clock, everybody visited the steward and drank coffee, made in a big electric percolator which the steward brought in from the pantry. I suppose a torpedo would have disrupted this routine, but nothing less could have. This evening marked my initiation into the ship's social life. Since we were still in port, it was a *soirée de gala;* none of the officers had to stand watch, and it was all right to use the short-wave radio in Gjertsen's cabin. Such sets are sealed at sea because they cause a radiation which can betray a ship's position. For news of the outside world you depend on what the wireless operator picks up on long-wave.

Around seven o'clock the captain, the pilot, the steward, and I marched into Gjertsen's cabin, where the other officers already were gathered.

Gjertsen, a tall, dark man who looked something like Lincoln, was stretched out on his berth halfway between floor and ceiling. His wedding picture hung just above the berth. Gjertsen had not been home since 1937. Haraldsen, the second officer, who was small and jolly, turned the dials of the radio, with occasional professional counsel from Grung, the wireless operator, a serious young fellow whom the others considered something of a dandy. He came from Bergen, which is almost a big city. Bull, the third officer, the big fellow in the orange sweater, sat on the divan looking at a picture of the backsides of thirty-two bathing girls in *Life*. He didn't turn the page all evening. Nilsen, the gunner, sat on the floor and said nothing. He hardly ever said anything to anybody. The captain explained to me later that it was because Nilsen was a whaler. Whalers talk themselves out on their first voyage, the captain said. They exhaust all possible topics of conversation, then fall silent for life. "It isn't like a lighthouse-keeper," Petersen said. "He hasn't had a chance to talk in months, so he is bursting with it. But a whaling man is talked out." Gjertsen hated the radio, but he insisted on keeping the set in his cabin because he liked company. No matter what kind of music Haraldsen got, Gjertsen said it was rotten and Haraldsen should turn to something else. Whenever they got a news program he just fell asleep. He said there was enough trouble on the ocean without dialing for it. They were all low that evening because of a broadcast by the Norwegian radio of the news that the Germans were planning to cut off the money for their families. "I wonder how long people in the old country will be able to keep from starving," Haraldsen said helplessly. "Why don't the British start the invasion?" Grung demanded, looking sternly at the English pilot. "All the fellows who escape from Norway say there are only a few thousand Germans there."

"Full moon tomorrow night," the pilot said pleasantly, by way of changing the subject.

"Yes, fine moon for dive bombers," the radioman said resentfully. "We'll be right in the middle of E-boat Alley then."

"Maybe there'll be fog," the pilot suggested helpfully. "Fog is no good for bombers."

"Fog is fine for E-boats," Grung said. "Can't see them coming." Grung, I was to learn, liked to have something to complain about; actually, he worried little about enemy action. Danger at sea is like having a jumpy appendix: men can live with it for years, knowing in an academic way that it may cause trouble but forgetting about it most of the time. Haraldsen said that the *Regnbue* had always been a lucky ship—fourteen crossings since the war began and never a conning tower sighted. Everybody banged on wood. "The *Meddelfjord* always was a lucky ship, too, before the last time," Grung said, insisting on his right to grumble. "I lost a good pal on her, the second engineer. Burned to death in the sea. The oil was blazing on top of the water, and the fellows had to swim in it. That was a nice joke!"

"We didn't miss that by much ourselves," the captain said to me. "We were together with the *Meddelfjord* at Newcastle, both bound for London. We stayed to discharge some of our oil. The *Meddelfjord* and eight other ships went on. Three of them were sunk by planes and motor torpedo boats."

Bull put down his magazine and said in a matter-of-fact tone, "I like to catch a Yerman. Bile him in ile."

Unexpectedly, Nilsen, the silent, spoke up. "I have no respect for them," he said.

Before coming aboard I had calculated roughly that the chances are at least ninety to one against being torpedoed on any one crossing. Incidentally, the American marine-insurance companies then charged a premium of one per cent to insure tanker cargo, which indicated that they thought the odds are considerably longer than a hundred to one. It is not a great risk to take, once. The men in the *Regnbue* lived continually with this risk, which is quite a different thing. They seldom talked of danger except when they were angry about something else, like no shore leave or the British failure to invade the Continent.

Bull started turning the dials of the radio set again and got a program of jazz music from Stockholm. A woman was singing something that sounded like "Klop, klop, klop! Sving, sving, sving!" Bull and Haraldsen laughed so hard they could barely stand it. "I can't explain it to you," Haraldsen said to me, "but to a Norwegian the Swedish language sounds always very funny." We had three or four cups of strong coffee apiece in the pantry and then went to our cabins. Norwegians use coffee as a sedative.

Long before I got up next morning I could hear the anchor chain coming in, and when I got out on deck we were moving along in a column of eight ships. The strings of signal flags looked like holiday bunting, and each ship had its own bright new balloon. Half a dozen sloops and corvettes in pink-and-green camouflage milled around our column. The convoy was probably not moving better than eight knots, so the corvettes looked lightning fast. Machine guns were being tested on all the ships, and the intermittent bursts of gunfire added to the gaiety. The tracer bullets from the machine guns are fun to watch as they skitter over the water; they seem a superior kind of flying fish, with electric light and central heating. We had a pair of Hotchkisses mounted, one on each side of the bridge. If we were attacked they would be manned by the two seamen on lookout. We also had two British machine gunners, who manned a small fort on the poop deck, where they had a couple of Lewis guns. There was not enough open space around for our gun crew to try out our four-inch gun, but an anti-aircraft battery on shore was practicing. Its guns went off at one-minute intervals, and the shells made a straight line of white smoke puffs across the sky, like pearls on a string. A couple of mine sweepers dragging magnetized floats went ahead of us, in case the Luftwaffe had planted any magnetics during the night.

We dropped the pilot at noon. Life on the ship picked up its sea rhythm. The crew consisted of the usual three watches, each of which was on duty four hours and then rested eight. Haraldsen, the second officer, was on the bridge from twelve to four, Gjertsen, the chief, from four to eight, and Bull, the third officer, from eight to twelve, when Haraldsen relieved him. I had a chance to get to know some of the sailors, because they came forward to stand their watches on the bridge. However, the engineer officers and the rest of the crew, down at the other end of the ship, remained relative strangers.

When the men came forward they wore life jackets. The officers, when they went up to the bridge, carried their life jackets with them and tied them to a stanchion. I had bought a kapok-lined reefer from Gieves, the naval outfitter in Piccadilly, a swank garment that purported to double as an overcoat and life jacket. It was supposed to close with a zipper, and each clash with the zipper presented a completely new tactical problem. The zipper changed its defensive arrangements to meet my attacks; I could never throw it twice with the same hold. Sometimes I could close it in a couple of minutes, but on other occasions it beat me. I was sure that if a torpedo ever struck us, I would go down in a death grapple with my zipper. I had an ordinary life jacket in my cabin, of course, but I had paid good money for the reefer. I was also given a huge, one-piece rubber suit, so stiff that it stood up in a corner of my cabin like a suit of armor. It was a Norwegian invention, Captain Petersen said, and everybody on the ship had one. The idea was to climb into its legs and tie yourself into the rest of it, so only your face showed. The air in the folds of the suit would both hold you up and insulate you from the cold of the water. This consoled me until Grung, the radioman, told me that a crew had once demonstrated the invention for the Norwegian Minister of Shipping and that while all of them had floated for hours, a couple of fellows who went in head first had floated upside down. Grung was a man of few enthusiasms. For example, we had a large escort for such a small convoy, and this made him unhappy. "There must be trouble expected or there wouldn't be so many," he said.

Late in the afternoon we reached the bad spot about which the pilot had told me. This is a lane along the East Anglian coast that London newspapers have named E-boat Alley. The commodore of the convoy was in the ship ahead of us, a British tanker. Commodores are usually commanders in His Majesty's Navy; they carry a pair of aides and a squad of signalmen with them and communicate their orders by flag signal or flash lamp. This commodore would go with us only as far as the first assembly port; he was an east-coast specialist.

I was in the saloon just before suppertime, reading Hakluyt's *Principall*

Navigations, Voiages and Discoveries of the English Nation, when I
heard a noise that sounded exactly like a very emphatic blast during the
excavation of a building site. The ship quivered, as if she had taken a big
sea. Larsen, the steward, was the only other man around; he was laying
out a few plates of salami and ham and herring salad as table decorations.
I took it for granted that the noise was a depth charge and said "My, my!"
to show how calm I was. Larsen winked and said, "Mak raddy der
bahding suit!" Both of us, I imagine, wanted to run out on deck and see
what had happened, but since we had only recently met, we tried to
impress each other. Captain Petersen came down to supper ten minutes
later and said that a mine had gone off a hundred feet from the commodore's ship and almost knocked her out of the water. "Gjertsen was on the
bridge and saw it," he said. "He says it threw a column of water higher
than the ship's masts. She was hidden completely. Then, when the water
settled, Gjertsen could see the ship was still there, but she had only a little
way on. Then she hoisted two red lights to signal she was out of control.
The blast must have damaged her rudder. So she has to go back to
port."

"Good-by, Commodore," Larsen said unfeelingly.

"It must have been one of those acoustic mines," the captain said, "but
it didn't work well. It went off too soon." There was a certain wonder in
his tone, as if he felt that the Germans must be overrated.

The explosion of the mine was the only evidence of enemy action we
were to encounter during the whole trip.

Larsen, the steward, had it figured out that in order to get to New York
by Christmas we would have to leave the west coast of England by
December 7. "We get off with lucky seven and in seventeen days we come
to New York," he said. "Get there Christmas Eve, the immigration officers
ain't working, and we stay on the ship until December 26." This was a
sample of what I got to know as Scandinavian optimism. We didn't reach
even the first of our two assembly ports until December 5, so it looked
certain that we would spend Christmas at sea. We were seventy-two
hours going up the east coast from London, anchoring each night because
of heavy fog. The second time we anchored, Larsen began getting out
and repairing the green-and-red paper Christmas decorations that formed
part of the tanker's stores. He went about his work during the day muttering a sad little refrain that I sometimes caught myself repeating: "No
newts, no frewts, no yin for drinking."

The crew looked forward to spending its shore leave in Brooklyn, even
if we got to New York after Christmas. To a Norwegian the finest part of
the United States is Brooklyn. For the duration of the war it is the
Norwegian fatherland. When a Norwegian seaman meets an American,
he usually begins the conversation with, "I got a cousin in Brooklyn."
Haraldsen, the second officer, had two brothers there. Larsen pretended
to be supercilious about Brooklyn, but he fooled nobody on the *Regnbue.*

The *Regnbue* had been in the Thames for only a couple of days, and few of her men had gone into London. The ship had been anchored at such an awkward distance from the city that it had hardly seemed worth the journey. Some men had got drunk at a hotel not far from the oil dock. Others had not even set foot on land. Corpus Christi, Texas, the ship's last American port of call, had not been exactly a Brooklyn, either.

Olsen the carpenter, Grung the radioman, and I were visiting the steward and drinking coffee on one of the foggy nights, and Olsen said, "The last time I was in Brooklyn I didn't take my shoes off for three weeks. My feet was so swollen I had to cut my shoes off." Olsen was a man who liked to startle people. "It must have been good liquor you were drinking," I said. This was just the kind of opening Olsen wanted. He put his head on one side and looked at me fixedly for a full half-minute, as if I were a dangerous lunatic. "Good liquor!" he finally said, contemptuously. "A man is a fool to drink good liquor. I never drink liquor that tastes good." He stared at me again, as if expecting me to leap at his throat, and then said, "Because why? I get drinking it too fast. Then I get drunk too quick. The best thing is whisky that tastes bad. Then you stop between drinks about ten minutes, until you need another one. Then you can keep on drinking for a month." The carpenter was a solid, rectangular fellow of fifty, with blue eyes set wide apart in a boiled-ham face. He could with equal competence make a davit out of iron pipe or reseat a rattan chair. He was the ship's delegate of the Norwegian Seamen's Union, to which all the men belonged.

The steward lay in his berth at the summit of a stack of drawers. There was no other place for him, because the rest of us occupied all the chairs. He said, "In Brooklyn I live in Hotel St. Yorge. Yentlemen! I don't go on Court Street in Eyetalian saloons. I yust buy good old bottle aquavit and go to my room and drink like yentleman. Go to Norweeyan church Sunday and put five dollars in collection. Brooklyn women too smart. Better leave 'em alone."

The radioman said that once he and some shipmates had been in a taxi-dance hall near Borough Hall and had asked a couple of hostesses to sit down and have a drink. The hostesses had charged them four dollars apiece for their time. "You got more for your money in Constanta," he said. Constanta, in Rumania, used to be a great port for Norwegian tankers before the war. "We had a man on one ship going down to Constanta," the carpenter said, "and he wouldn't believe all we told him about it. He said he had been in every other port in the world, and he wouldn't lose his head in Constanta. So he went ashore one night, and two days later we seen a man walking down on the dock with nothing on but his socks, and it was him. Always lots of fun in Constanta."

The steward found this so amusing that he reared up on the back of his neck and kicked the ceiling. He had been a leading light of the gymnastic society in a small town in southern Norway, and he liked to use the edge of his berth as a gymnastic bar. He spent a good deal of time composing to English and American girls on a portable typewriter he had in his cabin, and when he was at a loss for an English phrase he would get up, face his berth, and jump high in the air, twisting in time to land in a sitting position. Usually three or four jumps would bring him the phrase he wanted, and he would return to his typewriter. The steward called his cabin Larsen's Club, and the atmosphere was congenially ribald except when Captain Petersen was there. The skipper came in every night for his three cups of coffee. Captain Petersen was a friendly man who did not stand on formality, but he was a Methodist and a teetotaler. He didn't try to deter anybody else from drinking or talking randy, but Larsen seldom kicked the ceiling when the skipper was around. All the men were cut off from their home country and lonely, and the captain was the loneliest of all. Once he said to me, "It isn't so bad for a man who drinks and——" He stopped suddenly, as if just understanding what he had said, and went off to his cabin looking miserable.

At meals with Captain Petersen I had plenty of time for eating, because there was not much conversation. Once he said, as he began on his first plate of cabbage soup, "I have an uncle in New York who has been fifty-two years with the Methodist Book Concern." Twenty minutes later, having finished his second helping of farina pudding, he said, "He came over in a windjammer." On another occasion he said, "We had a China-man on the ship once. When we came to Shanghai he couldn't talk to the other Chinamen." After an interlude during which he ate three plates of lobscouse, a stew made of left-over meats and vegetables, he explained, "He came from another part of China." And once, taking a long look at the shipowner's portrait, he said, "I went to see an art gallery near Bordeaux." After eating a large quantity of dried codfish cooked with raisins, cabbage, and onions, he added, "Some of the frames were that wide," indicating with his hands how impressively wide they were. Once, in an effort to make talk, I asked him, "How would you say, 'Please pass me the butter, Mr. Petersen,' in Norwegian?" He said, "We don't use 'please' or 'mister.' It sounds too polite. And you never have to say 'pass me' something in a Norwegian house, because the people *force* food on you, so if you said 'pass' they would think they forgot something and their feelings would be hurt. The word for butter is *smor*."

It was morning when we reached our first assembly port, and the captain went ashore to see the naval authorities. He returned with word that we would sail next evening. In the afternoon a boat came out from shore and a naval officer climbed aboard to tell the captain that our destination had been changed from New York to Port Arthur, Texas. Luckily, the *Regnbue* had enough fuel for the longer journey or we would have lost more time taking bunker. The captain told me of the change and said he was sorry I would be carried so far from New York, but things like that happened all the time. The changes weren't made for strategic reasons, because no one could tell three weeks or a month in advance how the U-boats would be distributed off the American coast. It was just that there probably weren't enough "dirty" tankers to handle all the heavy oils from the Gulf of Mexico. A "clean" tanker handles only gasoline. A "dirty" tanker has tanks equipped with heating coils to keep heavy oils liquid. The *Regnbue*, the captain said with pride, was a first-class dirty tanker.

News of the change of destination quickly got about among the crew. There isn't much point in secrecy aboard a ship if none of the men are allowed to go ashore. Port Arthur is a dismal place compared to Brooklyn, and the seamen were disappointed. There are no Norwegians in Port Arthur, and no taxi-dance halls. Mikkelsen, the electrician, said that you couldn't even buy whisky in a saloon in Port Arthur; you had to buy a bottle at a package store and take it into a soft-drink joint to get a setup. Perhaps the most disappointed men on the ship were the British machine gunners, Ramsay and Robinson. They had been out to India and Australia with other ships but never to America. "Where is Texas?" Robinson asked me. "Will I be able to get up to New York for a week end?" Ramsay, who was a lance bombardier, laughed derisively. "You haven't got money enough to get that far," he said. "It's all of two hundred miles." Robinson earned three shillings and three-pence a day, of which the War Office sent one and three to his mother in Salford, slap up against Manchester. Ramsay drew nine-pence more for his single chevron, and he was always boasting to Robinson about his opulence.

The Britishers belonged to the Maritime Anti-Aircraft Regiment, generally called the Sea Soldiers at home. The Sea Soldiers ride on merchant ships in the manner of old-time American stagecoach guards. They have had more training with automatic arms than the seamen who man machine guns and are supposed to steady the seamen in a fight. Robinson and Ramsay had been partners on other ships and had been in a long running battle with some Axis submarines off the west coast of Africa just before they joined the *Regnbue*. Convoys were nearly always attacked off the African coast, they said. There was a belief among seamen that the Germans had a submarine base at Dakar, no matter what Pétain said. Robinson was a quiet lad who said, "A odn't been sottisfied i' infantry, so thought A'd try summat else, and this was fair champion—nowt to do." Ramsay was a Glaswegian, a hyperenergetic type who was always shadow-boxing on deck and shouting "Pooh!" or "Coo!" for no apparent reason. He used to brag about how many German planes he had shot down, although it is hard to apportion credit for bringing down a plane when a whole convoy is blazing away at it. One day he said that if we captured a German submarine—not a likely prospect—he would personally kill all the prisoners. Gjertsen, the chief officer, said to him seriously, "You can't kill anybody on this ship without the captain say so." This made Ramsay sulk. There were three other Britishers on the ship—a man in the engine room, a seaman, and a messboy. English seamen like to get on Norwegian ships when there is an opportunity, because the pay is better than the British scale. Nearly all seafaring Norwegians speak English, so there is no trouble about understanding orders. The only fellows on the *Regnbue* who knew no English were five youths who recently, and separately, had escaped from Norway by crossing the North Sea in small boats. They were all studying a textbook on Basic English. They had received word that after they had escaped their parents had been put in prison. News from Norway reaches England quite regularly by boat. There are even motorboats that smuggle mail between the two coasts.

Most of the men grew thoughtful when we cleared the first assembly port. We were within three hundred miles of Norway now, and they could not help thinking about it. Otherwise the tension, which had never been great, seemed to have completely vanished. There was no further danger from motor torpedo boats and not much from dive bombers. The big Focke-Wulf Kuriers and the submarine packs generally operated farther to the west, where the large convoys form, so we felt relatively safe. We had parted company with a couple of ships at the assembly port and picked up a couple of others. What bothered me was the weather. Captain Petersen advised me to chew on dry crackers and drink no water. The steward said, "Don't use nothing yuicy. Yust dry stuff."

The prescription of "a brisk walk around the deck," classic on passenger liners, is not much good on a tanker, because deck space is so limited. You can take a few steps on the bridge or make a circuit of the forward deckhouse, picking your way among ropes, slings, boats, and the entrances to two companionways. If you go aft you have a slightly longer promenade around the after deckhouse, although you have to crawl under the gun platform once on each lap to complete the circuit. The main deck, between the two deckhouses and forward of the bridge, is low and lashed by spray. There is a catwalk, an elevated pathway between the two deckhouses, but men with work to do are constantly passing back and forth on it, so there is no room for a *flâneur*.

At the beginning of the voyage I had decided to let my beard grow until I got home again. The boatswain, who came from a port in the far north of Norway, counseled me to shave my beard, on the ground that it would bring fine weather and then the ship wouldn't rock. The boatswain was a small man who looked as dry and tough as jerked meat. He had ice-blue eyes and a long, drooping, ginger-colored mustache, and he repeated his joke about the beard every morning. Then, later in the day, he would manage to ask me the time and say, "I had two gold watches but they're on the bottom now." His last ship had been bombed and sunk at her dock in Liverpool, and he had lost all his gear on board. Fortunately, he had been spending the night on shore with a respectable lady friend—the widow of an old shipmate, he was always careful to explain when he told the story. He had a French wife in Caen, but he had not seen her in seven years, because big ships seldom went there. I once tried to talk French with him, but he said with a sigh, "*Ya goobliay toute.*" The boatswain was aware that he said the same things every day, but he said them to be friendly. After all, nobody can think of something new to say when he sees the same shipmates daily for weeks on end. The quip about the beard contented the boatswain, and he laughed every time he said it. His laugh sounded like cakes of ice knocking together.

On December 7 we were in a gale. I turned in early and put my watch and fountain pen in the desk drawer, where they rattled like dice in a nervous crapshooter's hand. There is a difference of thirteen and a half hours between the time in Hawaii and Great Britain, and I was asleep before Grung, the radioman, picked up the first bulletin about the attack on Pearl Harbor. I heard the news when I went up on the bridge next morning. Bull, the third officer, pumped my hand and said, "We both allies now!" It felt more natural to be a belligerent on a belligerent ship than that anomalous creature, a neutral among belligerent friends. I tried to visualize New York. People at home must be frightfully angry, I imagined. I kept telling the Norwegians, "Americans aren't like the English. They get mad much quicker, and they stay mad." (I was to feel pretty silly about that after I got back to New York.) We all wondered why the fleet had been in Pearl Harbor and how the Japs had got there. The B.B.C. bulletins received by the radioman were skimpy. We were actually near the base of the British Home Fleet, but suddenly we felt far from the war. The ship had sailed with two neutrals aboard, and now it had none. The other neutral had been an ordinary seaman named Sandor, who was a Rumanian. Great Britain had declared war on Rumania a few days after we cleared, so Sandor had become an enemy alien. He took the news calmly. "Can't send me back now," he said. He had stowed away on the *Regnbue* at Constanta in the early summer of 1939 and had stayed with her ever since. He had learned Norwegian and English on the ship.

We were glad to get to our second assembly port, where we were permitted to turn on the short-wave radio in the chief officer's cabin. We sat around it for hours, listening to the B.B.C., the Norwegian broadcasts from London and Boston, and even Radio Paris, the Quisling station in Oslo, and Lord Hawhaw. We got some of our best laughs from an Italian English-language announcer who used to sink Allied shipping in astronomical quantities twice a day. It was a Norwegian broadcast from Boston, I remember, that told us Lindbergh had endorsed the war and a Free French announcer in London who said Senator Wheeler had done the same thing. The steward was amused. "Next thing, Quisling against Yermans!" he shouted.

As soon as we arrived at the second assembly port, the captain went ashore. When he came back he said that we were starting for America early the next morning. The port was at the head of a deep and narrow bay. The *Regnbue* and nine other ships were to start just before dawn and go to sea to meet vessels that would simultaneously leave other assembly ports. There would be from fifty to a hundred in the combined convoy, which was to be a very slow one. It would make only eight knots, because it included a lot of ships like the Norwegian steamer that Bull, the third officer, had pointed out to me some days before as the slowest ship in the world. We had lost her in the gale on December 7, but she had steamed into the second assembly port twelve hours behind us. She was called the *Blaskjell*, which means "mussel." An eight-knot convoy takes a long time to get across the ocean, Captain Petersen said, but going that way was better than hanging about waiting for a ten-knotter. Fast ships go alone, on the theory that they can run away from any submarine they sight, but the *Regnbue* was not nearly that fast.

It was about seven o'clock when we hove anchor next morning, but the moon was still high in the sky. The other ships that were going out showed one light apiece, and a corvette was talking to us in Morse code squawked out on a whistle that sounded like Donald Duck. A westerly wind was howling, and I remembered that we had received a gale warning the evening before. The moon slipped into a cloud abruptly, like a watch going into a fat man's vest pocket, and didn't come out again. When it is as dark as it was that morning it is hard for a landsman to tell if a ship is moving, because he can't see her position in relation to anything else. But after a while I was sure. When it began to get light I went up on the bridge and looked at the ships in front of us and astern. They were already plunging about. When you look at other ships in a heavy sea the extravagance of their contortions surprises you. Your own ship is going through the same motions, but you wouldn't believe they were so extreme unless you saw the other ships. The farther we got down the bay, the worse the weather grew. The commodore's ship, about a mile ahead of us, sent up a string of flags; the ships between us repeated the signal. Bull, who was on the bridge, said, "Commodore wants us slow down, says he can't hold his position." He threw the engine-room telegraph to "Half Speed." In heavy weather the *Regnbue* steered well only at full speed, and the men at the wheel had an unhappy time from then on. Now and then her bow came clear out of the water—from watching other tankers I could see exactly how it happened—and the sea gave her a ringing slap on the bottom. I felt that this was an impertinence, precisely the sort of thing a German would do if he were running the ocean.

By noon we were getting away from land. I went down to the saloon to have dinner with Captain Petersen and found him already ladling his third plate of milk soup out of the tureen. Milk soup is made of condensed milk and water, heavily sugared and full of rice, raisins, dried apricots, canned peaches, and anything else sweet the cook can find about the galley. It is served hot at the beginning of a meal, and only a Norwegian can see any sense in it. It appeared on the table regularly twice a week, and at each appearance the steward said, "Fawny soup today,

Liebling." At the beginning of every meal, without exception, he would say to me, "*Vaer so god*" ("Be so good"), and bow. I would say the same thing to him and bow, and we would both laugh. It was like the boatswain's joke about the beard.

On the bridge that afternoon the captain was preoccupied. He said that unless we could go at full speed, he didn't see how we could get to the rendezvous before dark, but only about one other ship in our lot could keep up with us at full speed. Our entire escort was one 800-ton corvette, and if we left the convoy, we left the escort. Sometimes you have a big escort and sometimes you have a small one. It's like going into a shop in England: you get what they have in stock. Haraldsen, the second officer, who was also on the bridge, was as jolly as usual. "By and by Florida!" he would shout when water whipped across the front of the wheelhouse and splashed in our faces. That was *his* standard joke. The corvette seemed to stand on its head every time it went into a wave, and Haraldsen got a lot of fun watching it. "The little feller is doing good," he would say. "I hope they got a good belly." By three o'clock we had lost the *Blaskjell* and two of the others, and a half-hour later we could see the commodore's ship turning. The commodore was signaling us to return to port. He had judged that there was no chance of reaching the rendezvous before night-fall, and he didn't want us to be out on the ocean alone when morning came. "We made about thirty miles in nine hours," Captain Petersen said. We turned, and on the way back to the assembly port we picked up the *Blaskjell* and passed her. At nine o'clock we were again at anchor in our old berth.

The boatswain was not the only one who looked suspiciously at my beard after the return. "This has always been a lucky ship," the carpenter said. "I think we got a Rasmus on board now." A Rasmus is the Nor-wegian equivalent of a Jonah. The next day the weather was fine. The carpenter said that this was just what you might expect now that we had missed the convoy. Captain Petersen put on his brown suit and went ashore. He came back with word that we were stuck for at least a week. We had already been at sea for a fortnight. It was not entirely bad news to the boatswain and the steward. The boatswain could now put the men to work painting the ship. When a ship's paint gets streaky, a boatswain becomes melancholy and embarrassed, like a housewife who has not had time to wash the curtains. Griffin, the English seaman on board, once said to me, "If the bos'n ain't a bastard, the ship's no good." He added that the *Regnbue* was quite a good ship. The steward saw a chance to get the supplies he needed for Christmas. About all that the captain and I had been hearing lately at our meals was a monologue by Larsen about the horrors of Christmas at sea without newts or frewts or yin. Once a ship has left the port of origin, navy people permit only the captain and the radioman to go ashore—the radioman for a single conference before a convoy leaves—so Larsen gave the captain a list to take to a ship chandler. The captain found no nuts or fruits, but in a couple of days a lighter brought out a case of gin and two cases of whisky, which the steward put away in the pantry closet. Ordinarily, I was told, no liquor was served on the ship except to pilots and immigration officers, but Christmas was always an exception.

The days at anchor were tranquil. Every morning the captain went ashore and the rest of us painted and theorized about our false start for America. The officers worked alongside the men, and I daubed a bit for company. Some of the men argued that we should have started for our rendezvous at midnight instead of just before dawn, and others said that with a wind like that against us we shouldn't have started at all. Haraldsen said why complain, maybe the convoy we had missed would be attacked anyway. (A couple of days later we heard that all but fourteen ships out of seventy had had to turn back because of the weather.) Evenings, we listened to the radio and talked about the war. The men talked a lot about what they were going to do with Quislings in Norway after the war. They used Quisling as a generic term, just as we do. Some of the men wanted to put them on Bear Island, up north of Norway. Others just wanted to kill them. Even the messboys were angry at Knut Hamsun and Johan Bojer for having betrayed Norwegian culture. The ship had a library of four hundred volumes. None of the seamen would read Hamsun or Bojer now. Norwegians seem more interested in books than music, and the captain was the only one who mentioned Kirsten Flagstad to me. He said Wagner had gone to her head.

Often, when Captain Petersen sat down to a meal, he would look at the customary plates of cold meat on the table and say, "I wonder what they have to eat in the old country now," or "I wonder what my wife has to eat." When we had fish he would say, "My wife never liked fish. Her father was a butcher," or else "My father-in-law always said, 'Fish is fish, but meat is nourishment.'" Once he heard me humming that old barroom favorite, "M-O-T-H-E-R." He said, "I heard a fellow sing that in vaudeville in Philadelphia. He had his wife on the stage and their six children. When he sang it one kid held up a card with 'M' on it. The next kid held up 'O' and so on until the smallest one held up 'R.' It was the cleverest thing I ever saw on the stage." Often he showed me photographs of his wife and their little boy.

We put to sea again a few days before Christmas. Just before we left, a naval man came out to say that our destination was now Baton Rouge. Nobody even speculated about the reason for this second change. We took it for granted that there was some kind of a muddle. Despite my beard and the carpenter's forebodings, we had normal North Atlantic winter weather this time. Early in the afternoon we sighted a huge fleet of ships on the horizon. This was to be a ten-knot convoy, so we had left the *Blaskjell* and a couple of other tubs behind. "Now we'll have something to look at," Haraldsen, the second officer, said as the courses of the large group and our small one converged. Every ship in a convoy has a number. Number forty-four had been assigned to us at the assembly port, and as we joined the others we hoisted the four flag and the pennon that corresponds to a ditto mark. All we had to do was find the forty-three ship and fall in behind her.

The small convoys we had traveled in along the coasts had gone in either single file or a column of twos. This one was in a column of eights. We had ships to port and starboard as well as ahead but only an escorting corvette behind us, as we were a file-closer. This tickled Haraldsen, because we wouldn't have to repeat any of the commodore's signals. A signal is passed down a file of ships, each repeating it for the benefit of the one behind. All the file-closer has to do is run up the answering pennon to acknowledge the message. Grung, the radioman, came out of his shack to look at the escort. There were only four corvettes for fifty-six large ships. "It's a bad yoke," he said bitterly. "Those English lords are sitting with girls behind drawn curtains on large estates and we can go to hell." When we had had a large escort on the east coast, Grung had said that was a bad sign. Haraldsen said, "Oh boy, I wish I had one of them girls here! Some fun." He had worked as a carpenter in New York during the building boom from 1924 to 1929 and talked of this as the romantic period of his life. "I got fifteen dollars a day," he said. "Fellows would wait for you in front of your yob—Yews, you know—and say, 'Listen, come with me. I give you a dollar more.' I like Yews." He had been on sailing ships during the last war, but he did not recall them with the same affection as, for example, John Masefield or Lincoln Colcord. "A sailing ship is hell in cold weather," he once told me.

It takes a combination of keen eyes and accurate navigation to keep a ship in its proper position in a convoy during the night, and the fleet is usually rather jumbled in the morning. This situation helped to kill time aboard the *Regnbue*. In the morning everybody was eager to see how badly the convoy had broken ranks. Bull, the third officer, was always on watch at dawn, and every morning he would say, with a sort of pride, "Dis der vorst convooey I ever see. Every morning all over der Atlahntic." The *Regnbue* nearly always held its position in relation to the commodore; either we kept to our course accurately or there was a telepathy which made him and us commit the same errors. Some of the other ships, however, would be far off on the horizon. This would always amuse Bull and the lookouts. The forty-three ship, which was supposed to stay just ahead of us, was nearly always miles to starboard, and when she tried to get back into her place we would, for the fun of it, speed up so that she couldn't edge in. She was an old tanker and slower than the *Regnbue*. Her skipper must have been a rather fussy sort; she would break into an angry rash of signal flags, and her radioman would bring out his signal flash lamp and deliver a harangue in Morse. Finally we would let her ease into the column. It usually took an hour or so to get everybody aligned.

The ships always reminded me of numbered liberty horses forming sequences in a circus.

After the convoy was re-formed we could kill another half-hour trying to count the ships. There were a few less every day. Ships drop out with engine trouble or get so far off the course during the night that they lose sight of the convoy. These run a bigger risk than the ones that keep pace, but most of them turn up in port eventually. Two ships carried catafighters; that is, Hurricane fighters that could be shot into the air from catapults if a Focke-Wulf appeared. In profile, the catapults looked like cocked pistols. We used to find comfort in looking at them, even though Grung said that the pilots were probably seasick and the planes would break away from their lashings in a storm just before we were attacked by an air fleet. Sometimes ships in convoy talk to each other out of boredom, like prisoners tapping on cell walls. One morning I found Bull, signal lamp in hand, carrying on a parley with a British tanker in the column to starboard. When at last he put the lamp down I asked what it was all about, and he said, "Oh, they invite us to come aboard for lunch."

"What did you tell them?" I asked.

"Oh," Bull replied, "I say, 'If you got a drop of yin, I wouldn't say no.'"

When you are in convoy it is sometimes impossible to remember whether a thing happened yesterday or the day before yesterday or the day before that. You watch the other ships and you read whatever there is to read and you play jokes on the ship's cat. You go to the pantry and slam the refrigerator door, and the cat runs in, thinking you are going to give him something to eat. Then you pretend to ignore him. Finally, when his whining becomes unbearable, you throw him a few bits of crabmeat. I had brought three books along with me on the *Regnbue*, but I had finished them in the three weeks we spent idling off the British coast. After that I read several ninepenny thrillers by Agatha Christie and Valentine Williams that happened to be aboard, and then a copy of *Pilgrim's Progress*, donated to the ship by the Glasgow Y.M.C.A. Eventually I was reduced to looking at September numbers of *Life*. Once I found an early 1939 issue of *Redbook*. I read every page of it gratefully, though it contained six stories about husbands who strayed but found that they liked their wives best after all. There was a strict black-out every evening, but I didn't mind it as much as I had in London, because on the ship there was no place to go anyhow. One of the lifeboats had a fashion of working loose from its fastenings in heavy weather, and then the boatswain would summon a gang to heave on the ropes until he could make it fast again. I used to look forward to the chance of pulling on one of the ropes. Whenever the crew had to make the boat fast while I was napping in my cabin, I felt slighted.

Some of the men were always speculating about our destination, Baton Rouge. It didn't show on any of the maps on the ship. If it had, they figured, the size of the print might have given them an idea of how big the town was. My own guess was that it was a city of a hundred thousand. Actually, the population is thirty-four thousand. American cities weren't listed in *Hvem, Hvad, Hvor*, the Norwegian equivalent of the *World Almanac*, and the favorite reference work on board. *Hvem, Hvad, Hvor* means "Who, What, Where." The book contains street plans of every city in Norway, even places of as few as five thousand inhabitants. The men used to mark the locations of their houses and show them to each other and to me. Once, Gjertsen, the chief officer, showed me where he lived in his home town. The next day he came into my cabin looking for me, with *Hvem, Hvad, Hvor* in his hand. "I made a mistake," he said, pointing to the plan of the place. "*Here* is where I live," and he showed me a dot about a quarter of an inch from the one he had made before.

As Christmas drew near, Larsen, the steward, was often missing from his cabin during the evenings. He was aft in the galley with the cook, constructing great quantities of "fat things" and "poor men," the Norwegian terms for doughnuts and crullers, respectively. On his journeys aft he carried with him a thick, calf-bound Norwegian cookbook. Larsen had formerly been a cook; he sometimes regretted his change-over from creative to executive catering. The cook was a tall, thin young man who looked as if he were built of candle wax. Together they elaborated on the plans for the Christmas Eve dinner. Rumors were spread by one of the British machine gunners, who had talked to the third engineer, who had it straight from a messboy, that there would be turkey. While the convoy moved along at its steady ten knots, nobody aboard the *Regnbue* talked of anything but the coming dinner.

On the great night the table was laid for a dozen persons in the saloon, where ordinarily the captain and I dined alone. We were lucky; the sea was reasonably calm. The steward and the boy who helped him in the saloon, which was forward, would have had a hard time in a gale, for the galley was in the after deckhouse and they had to carry all the food over the long catwalk between. Promptly at six o'clock the engineer officers came forward to dine with us. Larsen, the chief engineer, who was not related to Larsen the steward, was a girthy, middle-aged man who resembled Hendrik Willem van Loon. If I looked aft on a fair day I could generally see him standing by a door of the engine room with his hands in his pockets. He was a fixture in the seascape, like Nilsen, the gunner and ex-whaler, who silently paced the deck near the four-inch gun. Equally immutable was the British machine gunner on duty, wearing a pointed hood and sitting inside a little concrete breastwork on the poop deck, looking like a jack-in-the-box. Chief Engineer Larsen and his officers seldom came forward to visit us. To mark the occasion on this night, they were wearing collars and neckties. They looked scrubbed and solemn, and so did Captain Petersen and the three deck officers and the gunner and the radioman, all of whom were at the table.

Steward Larsen had set three glasses at each place—one, he told me, for port, one for whisky, and a third for gin. He had no aquavit for the Christmas dinner, and gin was supposed to replace it. To get the meal started, the steward brought in some porridge called *jul grot*, which is traditional and practically tasteless. Engineer Larsen said "Skoal" and emptied a glass of gin. We all said "Skoal" and did likewise. Then Steward Larsen served a thick soup with canned shrimp and crabmeat and chicken in it. We all drank again. The steward next served fish pudding, and there was more drinking of skoals. Then he brought in the turkey with the pride of a Soviet explorer presenting a hunk of frozen mammoth excavated from a glacier. The turkey had been in the ship's cold room since the September equinox, and the ship chandler's turkeys are presumed to have been dead for quite a while before they come aboard. We had plenty of canned vegetables and, above all, plenty of gin. The teetotaler Methodist captain, who stuck to his principles and didn't drink, brought out a couple of songbooks that he had got from a Norwegian church and suggested we sing some Christmas hymns. His guests sang them, without much pleasure, it seemed to me, and we ate a lot of jello covered with vanilla sauce and drank some more gin. All the men's faces remained rigid and solemn. Engineer Larsen said, in English, "Merry Christmas to our American friend." The captain whispered to me, "You can tell he's from Oslo. He talks too much." The steward then brought in mounds of doughnuts and crullers, and some fancy drinks in tall glasses. He called the tall drinks Larsen's Spezials. They were triple portions of gin with lump sugar and canned cherries. Everyone said, "Thank you, Steward. Very good." The whisky was served straight, as a dessert liqueur. We all began drinking it out of jiggers and saying "Skoal" some more. The singing got fairly continuous and the choice of numbers gradually grew more secular. Most Norwegian songs, I noticed, have many verses, and the men who are not singing pay no attention to the one who is. They look as if they are trying to recall the innumerable verses they are going to sing in their turn. We all got together on one patriotic number, though. The last line, translated into English, was "If Norway goes under, I want to go too." We clasped hands on that one.

The captain asked me to sing "My Old Kentucky Home," which I couldn't remember many words of, but fortunately three other fellows started to sing three other songs at the same time. The steward, considering his official duties over, drew up a chair to the table and received congratulations. The cook, looking taller and more solemn than ever, came in and was hailed as a great man. The drinkers still made intermittent efforts to remain grave. They yielded slowly, as if they were trying to protect their pleasure. Now the dignitaries of the crew, who had finished a dinner with exactly the same menu in their own quarters, began to appear in the saloon and take seats at the table—first the argumentative carpenter, then the boatswain with the cackle, and finally the pumpman, a tall fellow who looked like a Hapsburg and spent his life shooting compressed air into clogged oil tanks. The carpenter arose to sing a song. He had the same argumentative, deliberate delivery that he had in conversation, and he paused so long between verses that the chief officer, who had come down off the bridge and entered the saloon just after the carpenter had finished a verse, thought the all-clear had sounded and began a song of his own. The usually timid cook, buoyed up by one of Larsen's Spezials, thundered, "Shut up, Chief Officer! Let the carpenter sing!" As the chief officer and the fourth engineer joined the party, the third officer and another of the engineers left to stand their watches. The machine gunner from Glasgow arrived to wish the captain a merry Christmas and snitch a bottle of whisky. Two seamen, lads of about eighteen, came in to convey the respects of the crew. They had, I imagine, thought of this mission themselves. One, a small, neat boy with a straw-blond mustache, sang a long song with the refrain "Farvel, farvel" ("Farewell, farewell"). It appeared to make him very unhappy. Nearly all the seamen on the *Regnbue* were youngsters, which would have been true on a Norwegian ship even before the war. After three and a half years at sea they are eligible to take a course at a mates' school if they can save or borrow the price. Boys who don't like the sea quit before then.

Presently Steward Larsen pulled me by the arm and took me off with him to visit the rest of the crew. Before leaving the saloon, he had handed out a bottle of whisky to each four men, and on the whole they were doing all right with it. "I am a Commoonist," he kept saying to me on our way aft, "so I want you to love these fellers." Everybody on the ship had received as a Christmas greeting from the Norwegian Government a facsimile letter signed "Haakon, Rex." The letters, which had been put aboard at London for the captain to hand out, told Norwegian seamen that they were their country's mainstay. The "Commoonist" read this letter over and over again and cried every time. The Government had also sent the crew a set of phonograph records of patriotic songs. The favorite was called "Du Gamle Mor" ("Thou Old Mother"), which means Norway. The boys aft were all wearing blue stocking caps, which had come in a Christmas-gift bundle with a card saying they had been knitted by a Miss Georgie Gunn, of 1035 Park Avenue, New York City.

By the time Larsen and I staggered back over the catwalk to the saloon, everybody but Captain Petersen was unashamedly happy. It was very close in the blacked-out saloon with all the ports shut, and I went up to the bridge for air. Bull, the third officer, was on watch up there. He had been moderately dizzy when he had gone on watch at eight o'clock after eating his dinner, he told me, but now he felt only a sense of sober well-being. "I see ships all around," he said, "so ve must be in de meddel de convooey." Sandor, the Rumanian seaman who had stowed away on the ship in 1939 and remained aboard ever since, was on lookout duty. He said, "This makes three Christmas on ship since I left home. No good. On ship you see thirty, thirty-five peoples. On shore you see hoondreds peoples. I like to get one Christmas ashore." Sandor's chances were not bright. The British immigration officers at our second assembly port had told him that, since he was now an enemy alien, he would not be allowed on shore in Britain for the remainder of the war. They had added that the Americans would probably also refuse to let him land, so he might have to remain afloat indefinitely. Griffin, the English seaman, was at the wheel. When Sandor spelled him, Griffin came out of the wheelhouse and we wished each other Merry Christmas. I had heard so much talk about home towns and traditions that night that I asked Griffin where he was from. "Blowed if I know," he said cheerfully. "Sandor don't know where 'e's going and I don't know where I come from."

When I went down to my cabin, a row that would have done credit to an early convention of the American Legion was going on in the saloon. I looked in, but everybody was shouting in Norwegian and no one looked sufficiently detached to translate for me, so I didn't hear what it was all about until the next day, when I was told that someone had been trying to get subscriptions to the Norwegian Air Force Spitfire Fund and that Grung, the radioman, had protested that the Norwegian Government, even in exile, was giving $300,000 a year to missionaries in China and Africa. "Let them spend the missionary money for Spitfires before they bother workingmen," he had said. The steward had called Grung a bad name and Grung had pushed him over a case of empty whisky bottles. Later, when I happened to see Grung coming out of the radio shack, I asked him what Larsen had called him. "He called me a Commoonist," Grung said.

The party gave us something to talk about for a couple of days afterward. The carpenter went around repeating a line he had memorized from the label of an Old Angus whisky bottle: "Yentle as a lamb." He would say it and roll his eyes and then exclaim, "Yeezis!" On Christmas morning an English ship signaled to us, "Merry Christmas. Keep your chins and thumbs up." Grung and Bull had a consultation and then, not being able to think of anything witty, just ran up the answering flag meaning "Message noted."

One morning, when we were about halfway across the Atlantic, I found Bull in a particularly good humor. "Look around," he said, handing me a glass. "Vare is escort?" I had a good look around and there wasn't any. The corvettes had disappeared during the night. "Does that mean we've reached the safe part of the Atlantic?" I asked. "Safe yust so long ve see no submarine," Bull said. Captain Petersen, who came up a half-hour later to look around, said, "Maybe the escort from America was supposed to meet us here, and it didn't, and the British Corvettes had a date to meet an eastbound convoy off Iceland. We don't count as much as east-bound ships, because they're loaded." We went on all day without an escort. Grung came out of his shack and stared at three hundred and fifty thousand tons of valuable shipping moving placidly on, unprotected and unattacked. "Admiral Raeder must be lousy," he said at last.

Next morning a force of Canadian destroyers met us. No harm had been done. It wasn't the only time the *Regnbue* had traveled in an un-convoyed convoy, Bull said. Once she had left Halifax in a convoy es-corted by a battleship that was returning from an American dockyard. A couple of hundred miles out, the battleship had been summoned to help hunt the *Bismarck*, so she had moved off at thirty knots and left the merchantmen to push on by themselves to England. There were never enough vessels for convoy duty, Bull said, but luckily there never seemed to be enough submarines, either. The Battle of the Atlantic sounded imposing, but it was rather like a football game with five men on a side.

A few days after we met the Canadians, the ships bound for Gulf ports split off from the convoy. We were one of them. Each ship was to proceed as an individual, the theory at that time being that waters within a few hundred miles of the American coast were fairly safe. We had always cherished a notion that we were one of the fastest ships in our convoy. When dispersal day came, however, most of the others bound for the south quickly left us behind. Twenty-four hours after the split we were alone in the ocean, without another ship in sight. We steered southwest within a couple of hundred miles of the coast for nearly two weeks and saw only two vessels, neither of them a warship. Nor did we sight a single patrol plane. We hoped that no hostile aircraft carrier would ever have the same luck. The *Regnbue*, now that she was alone, zigzagged in a constant series of tangents to her course. This lost a mile an hour, which still further delayed my home-coming.

The weather stayed seasonably rough. We never ran into the kind of storm that sends smashed ships to port to make pictures for the news-paper photographers, but for days on end we couldn't see the sun long enough to get a position, and on New Year's Eve, when we were thirty-one days out of London, we had a sixty-mile gale, which made a second holiday party impossible. The day before we left the convoy I had been standing at the wheelhouse window watching the extraordinary antics of the tankers around us. A tanker in water ballast is a good sea boat but not a comfortable one. It rides the waves like a canoe, but it has a tendency to twist from side to side as it comes down. As I have already noted, this is even more disconcerting to watch than to endure. I was thinking about this when Mikkelsen, the electrician, a big, snaggle-toothed West Nor-wegian, came up and stood next to me. He looked at the ships for a while, then said quietly, "Fine weather." According to his lights it probably was.

After you leave your convoy you may have no other ships to watch and discuss, but you have a chance to fire your gun. That is an event to look forward to for days. Admiralty regulations require a ship to fire at least two shots on each trip. The captain gave Nilsen, the gunner, the order to prepare to fire these ritual shots. A day was set for the performance—not too soon, because, on account of scarcity of ammunition, we couldn't afford such pleasures more than once and we wanted to prolong the period of anticipation. The ordinarily silent Nilsen became the embodiment of the busy-executive type. The other members of the gun crew were the Hapsburg pumpman, two Diesel motormen, the fourth engineer, and the little sailor who had sung "*Farvel.*" They assumed new dignity among their fellows during the days before the gun practice. Everybody on the *Regnbue* told jokes about the last time the gun had been fired. Some said that Larsen, the chief engineer, had been asleep in his cabin when the gun went off and had been knocked off his divan. Others told the same story about the cook, the steward, or the second officer. All of this was invention, because nobody on a merchant ship sleeps when the gun is to be fired. One might as well expect a small boy to sleep late on Christmas morning.

On the big day the raised gun platform served as an excellent stage for the gun crew and the protagonist, the gun. The boatswain had distributed pounds of cotton batting, and we had stuffed our ears with wads of the stuff. The little sailor, a romantic chap, had carefully smudged his forehead with black grease so that he would look like one of Admiral Tordenskjold's powder monkeys. An empty oil drum would serve as target. A couple of sailors threw it off the stern. Nilsen's crew loaded the gun. Then, after the ship had gone an estimated two thousand meters, they fired. There was a great spat of flame from the gun's muzzle, a satisfactory roar, and something splashed in the water a long distance away. I could not see the oil drum, but Haraldsen, the second officer, who had once been an ensign in the Norwegian Navy, said that the shell had not missed by much. We all shouted "Hurrah!" It was better than the Fourth of July. The gun was reloaded and fired again. After the second shot we all felt much safer, because we knew that the gun would not burst until the next trip.

The days continued alike as we went on, but they had a different feeling. After we had passed Hatteras even the carpenter and the radioman, the ship's leading grousers, began to admit it was probable we would make port. And all through the ship men made plans for whatever shore leave they might get. Larsen, the steward, who had once worked out of the port of "Noolians," proposed to the cook and a couple of others that they hire a taxi at Baton Rouge and drive straight to the French quarter in New Orleans. "I always say I'm going to save money," he told me, "but when I get near land I can't keep my temper." Captain Petersen looked forward to renewing acquaintance with the pastor of the Norwegian church in New Orleans, where he planned to go by train. A few of the men owned electric flatirons, and these were in heavy demand by shipmates who wanted to press their pants. Grung, the radioman, was in charge of the pay list. All of the men had fairly large sums coming to them, and each signified to Grung the amount he wanted to draw at Baton Rouge. Usually a man changed his mind several times, raising the ante each time. The cook and the steward held long conferences about stores, occasionally asking me how to spell "bitterscots pewding" or "tomates cetseps." The steward said that he would send the list ashore to a ship chandler in "Noolians" when we went through customs and have the stuff trucked up to Baton Rouge.

The ship had not taken stores for more than three months now, and the eggs caused a daily argument between the steward and me. For several mornings he had served them hard-boiled, a sign he had no real confidence in them. Each morning I would open my first egg and say, "*Darlig*," which is Norwegian for "Bad."

The steward would protest, "*Naj, naj.*"

"But this one has green spots inside the shell," I would say.

"Ex like dot sometimes," he would maintain.

The captain always ate his eggs without any remark; his silence accused me of finicking. At last, one morning toward the end of the voyage, he opened an egg and looked at the steward. "*Darlig*," he said. The steward looked embarrassed. Then the captain ate the egg; a bad hard-boiled egg is probably as nourishing as a good one.

Next morning the steward brought me an amorphous yellow mass on a plate. It tasted mostly of sugar, but he offered me a jug of maple- and cane-sugar syrup to pour on it. I took a spoonful, fancying it some Norse confection, and said, "Not bad. What do you call it?" The steward said, "I call it ummelet. Same ex." Once the captain opened up a bit more than usual and talked about the Oxford Movement. The Movement had been strong in Norway, he said, and had frequently coincided with Quislingism. "A shipowner in my town," he once said to me, "got crazy about the Oxford Movement. He took his wife and children to a public meeting, and then he got up in the meeting and said that when he went to Antwerp on business he used to use bad women. His wife fainted. I don't call that a Christian." Several times the captain talked about his native town. "It has two fine hotels, and the harbor is full of beautiful little islands," he said once. "You can take your family in a boat fishing and then have a picnic on an island. In the winter we go skiing. My boy is three years old, and he has his second pair of skis. In the summer we used to have lobster parties, or dumpling-and-buttermilk parties. But it probably isn't like that now."

"By and by Florida" had been a gag line with Haraldsen, the second officer, throughout the voyage, but one day we really got there. It was the first land we had sighted since leaving Britain, and it looked exactly like the newsreels, with fine, white hotels and palm trees and scores of spick-

and-span motorboats in the blue water offshore, fishing for whatever people fish for in Florida. The weather was clear but cold. When we got close to shore we were permitted to use the radio receiving set in the chief officer's cabin again, and one of the first things I heard was an announcer saying, "There is no frost in Florida. This morning's temperature was thirty-seven." I tried to get some war news and heard another announcer saying, "The slant-eyed specialists in treachery continue their advance toward Singapore." One, two, three, four, five seconds. "You could not employ them better than by making a lather of creamy Sweetheart soap." We sailed along the shore. There were plenty of airplanes overhead now. They swooped almost to our masthead and looked us over every five minutes. It made all the men happy just to see the coast. From the bridge we kept looking through our glasses for bathing girls, but the weather was too cold for them. We wondered what the people in the Palm Beach and Miami hotels thought of our rusty ship, with its wheelhouse fortified with concrete slabs and its ragged red flag with the blue cross. Fellows kept making attempts at jokes, like "There's the dog track; let's go" or "Grung, get out the flash lamp and signal women that want a date yust wait on the beach. I going to swim in."

That afternoon the steward came into my cabin and said that the captain and the officers were giving me a farewell supper that evening. As on Christmas Eve, it was formal dress—collars and neckties. The occasion itself was solemn; Norwegians are not effusive. My companions just sat there, talking Norwegian among themselves and ignoring me. Nobody made a speech, but at the end of the meal the cook carried in a cake about the size and shape of an Aztec calendar stone. It was encrusted with slightly damp sugar. He held it out to me, and I stood up and reached for it. It nearly pulled me forward on my face, and as I looked down on the top, I saw, written in icing, "*Farvel.*"

A few nights later we were at the mouth of the Mississippi, waiting for a pilot. A northerly gale howled down at us straight from Lake Michigan. There were plenty of lights visible on the shore, more than I had seen at a comparable hour since leaving New York in the summer. Somehow I had expected our lights to go out when we entered the war. It seemed strange coming in our blacked-out ship to a country that was neither neutral *nor* dark. A boy in a rowboat brought out the pilot, a heavy-set, shivering man in a leatherette jacket who announced as soon as he came aboard that it was the coldest damn winter he had ever known in Louisiana. He brought aboard a copy of the New Orleans *Times-Picayune*, containing a lot of basketball scores and society notes and a few stories about a war that seemed to be on some remote sphere. A naval party came aboard and sealed the radio shack. The pilot took us seventeen miles up the river and then was relieved by a second pilot, who was going to take us the eighty remaining miles to New Orleans. I turned in.

We dropped anchor off quarantine in New Orleans at about ten o'clock on the morning of the forty-second day out of London. It was Sunday. We had to pass the immigration and public-health officers' inspections before the *Regnbue* could continue up the river. I had my suitcase packed before the government officers arrived, hoping that I would be able to go back to shore with them. It was the sort of day we had had off Florida, chilly but bright, and the city looked good in the sunlight. The *Regnbue's* men, lining the rails, talked about how fine it would be to be going ashore again. I had been at sea for only six weeks, but few of them had set foot ashore in four months. The immigration-and-health boat came out soon after ten with a party including a doctor and a rat inspector. The immigration men brought five armed guards to post about the ship to see that none of our allies would try to land too soon. Soon a customs officer came aboard and asked the captain if any man on the ship had more than three hundred cigarettes. Seamen buy their cigarettes in America, and our men had started to run short a fortnight before. Captain Petersen did not seem astonished by the question. He sent Grung to take a census of the cigarettes on board. Grung came back after a half-hour with word that only the second engineer had more than three hundred cigarettes. He had three hundred and twenty-five. The customs man asked if the twenty-five were loose, and Grung said that five of them were. The customs man said he thought he could let the second engineer keep the other twenty, although, he pointed out, he was making an exception. I pictured a large convoy missing a tide while the United States Customs counted cigarettes. Then the customs man asked about liquor, because he would have to seal up what we had on board. Grung went on a search for liquor and reported back that we had had two bottles of whisky and one of gin but that one of the public-health men had drunk about half of one of the bottles of whisky.

Next the immigration men came to the consideration of me. They said that since I had a good passport and had apparently been born in New York, I probably had a right to land in the United States, but not until my baggage had been passed by a customs appraiser. Unfortunately, they said, no appraisers had come along. "The last thing I expected to find on this ship was a passenger," the head immigration man said, giving me a rat inspector's look. He said that unless I wanted to stay on the ship for twenty-four hours longer I would have to pay two days' wages for the appraiser myself. Double pay for Sunday work. I said that would be all right, and they sent for an appraiser. It cost me $13.33. While waiting for the appraiser, I went out on deck. Captain Petersen came out too, and we stood looking at the shore. He was quiet, as usual, but he seemed to be struggling with an unusual emotion. At last he said, "Say, is it true the Hippodrome has been torn down?"

I said, "Yes, and the Sixth Avenue El, too."

Again he looked troubled, and I thought he was going to say he would miss me, but he said, "*The Big Show* were a wonderful play." That was an extravaganza that had played at the Hipp in 1917, when the captain had lived in Hoboken.

I said, "Yes, with Joe Jackson."

"A very funny man," Captain Petersen said.

A shabby motorboat came toward us from the left bank of the river. Captain Petersen said, "It must be a ship chandler after our business." There was a man on the forward deck with a megaphone, and as the boat came under our bow he called up inquiringly, "Captain, Captain?" Petersen pointed to his peaked cap, his emblem of office. The fellow shouted, "We got orders to send you on to Curaçao! You got enough bunker?" Curaçao is nine days from New Orleans for a ten-knot boat. Petersen showed no sign of surprise or disappointment. "We need bunker," he shouted back, "but we can get out in twenty-four hours!"

An hour later, when I was in a boat going ashore, I could see most of the *Regnbue* fellows on deck, leaning over the rail. There was the carpenter, with his square head and his obstinate shoulders, and the tall pumpman, and the electrician, and the two British gunners in their khaki uniforms. I could make out the bearish form of Sandor, the Rumanian, who would not have to stay on board alone now, because the others would stay with him. And there was Larsen, the steward, in a belted, horizon-blue overcoat and a bright green hat, his shoregoing uniform. He wouldn't go ashore, after all.

BOOK III

The World
Gets Up

24 / Toward a Happy Ending

PEARL HARBOR had left slight trace on the public mind, it seemed to a man coming off a boat in mid-January of 1942, but it had closed the second phase of the war. The first had ended with the disaster of the Pétain armistice. The second had been a negative success because our side had avoided collapse. The third, however unpromisingly it might start, however long it might last, was bound to end in the defeat of the avowedly fascist powers, because the combination of peoples they had attacked was too big, too strong, and too game for them. Hitler's chance to own the world had depended on a successful bluff. If, with the aid of the French industrialists and their counterparts in Great Britain and the United States, he could have secured a dominance of the West without war, isolating Russia, he might have brought it off. He still had had a chance as long as he could keep Russia and the United States neutral. But with all the holders of high cards in the game he was in the position of a poker player who has tried to steal a pot with no pair. He could keep on raising until he ran out of chips in order to delay the showdown; that would be an insane card player's reaction. His situation made me, personally, extremely and perhaps unreasonably happy. Millions of men meriting better than I have lived and died in humiliating periods of history. Free men and free thinking always get a return match with the forces of sadism and anti-reason sometimes. But I had wanted to see a win, I had wanted my era to be one of those that read well in the books. Some people like to live in a good neighborhood; I like to live in a good age. I am a sucker for a happy ending—the villain kicked in the teeth, the stepchildren released from the dark basement, the hero in bed with the heroine. Maybe the curtain will go up on the same first act tomorrow night, but I won't be in the audience.

By 1942 I had my personal hurts as well. I had Suzette's letter, which had taken nearly a year to reach me, telling of her father's death, cold, undernourished and humiliated, in the Montmartre flat where we had so often broken bread. Jean, the son, had won a Croix de Guerre and had been demobilized, Suzette had written—I could imagine him dodging about France to avoid conscription for German factory labor. Sauvageon, living in the *zone interdite* between occupied and unoccupied France, had managed to get a letter out to me too, through Switzerland. He had written of the mass emigration of the Alsatians and Lorrainers who had chosen to retain their French nationality.

The third round would be the good one, I thought, and I didn't stay long at home waiting for it to begin. I made the return trip to England by another Norwegian ship, this time a fast one that traveled without escort. The chief excitement of this trip was a long series of after-dinner checker games between me and the chief engineer, Johansen, who referred to himself as "some of the oldest engineers afloat." I once beat him with a quadruple jump, in a game for three bottles of beer.

London had changed more than New York since our entry into the war. It was full of Americans now, and one more attracted about as much attention as an extra clam at a shore dinner. I felt like an until recently only child whose mother has just given birth to quintuplets. And I was more of a stranger to the American news sources with whom I now had to deal, the Army and Navy Public Relations offices, than correspondents who had been in London for only three months, because the organizations had been set up since the time I had left.

I had a high idea of what the American Army in the European theater of operations would eventually be, and my first clues to it did not disappoint me. There were few ground combat troops in Great Britain as yet and many less Air Corps people than I had expected to find, but the preparations of the Services of Supply indicated how great the fighting force would soon be. The S.O.S. was building, for example, a depot in the South of England for the repair of American Army motor vehicles, and from its size one could get a fair idea of how many vehicles would be in operation and how big an army they would serve. It was like estimating an elephant's size from the print of one foot. The dimensions of the A.E.F. would certainly be elephantine, which pleased me because it indicated that the Government had not been impressed by the Sunday-supplement strategists who talked about an exclusively air war.

I knew that the quality of American troops would be good, once they had paid their entry fee with a couple of bobbles, because Americans are the best competitors on earth. A basketball game between two high-school teams at home will call forth enough hardness of soul and flexibility of ethic to win a minor war; the will to win in Americans is so strong it is painful, and it is unfettered by any of the polite flummery that goes with cricket. This ruthlessness always in stock is one of our great national resources. It is better than the synthetic fascist kind, because the American kid wears it naturally, like his skin, and not self-consciously, like a Brown Shirt. Through long habit he has gained control over it, so that he turns it on for games, politics, and business and usually turns it off in intimacy. He doesn't have to be angry to compete well.

While I had been away from London, Manetta, the manager of the Savoy Grille, had taken over the restaurant in my old hotel in Half Moon Street, and it was now one of the busiest and noisiest pubs in London, with a British version of a swing band, no tables available on less than three days' notice, American colonels crowding the members of refugee governments away from the ringside, and Jack, the cockney bartender who during my first visit had drooped disconsolately in front of a fine assortment of whiskies, now overworked and understocked, like the wine waiter. The hotel portion of the establishment looked much as it always had, although because of the Americans if was harder to get a room. Some of the old county women, having booked weeks in advance, would arrive there and in time descend from their rooms, leading either a spaniel or a small grandniece wearing a blue hair ribbon. They would march stiffly toward the once tranquil dining room, hear the first blast of the swing band, enter the gabble of the cocktail lounge where the new clientele waited for tables, and then turn and hobble desperately away, dragging dog or child after them.

London had the atmosphere of a town where people are gathering for a gold rush or an opera festival; everybody felt that something good was going to begin soon. Psychologically we had already passed to the attack. The correspondents, while they waited to be let in on the time and place, wrote stories about the growing American forces in Britain. After three years of going out to French, British, and Polish troops for stories, I enjoyed the novelty of being with Americans, although the uniform I now had to wear when I went out to troops made me feel that I was playacting. I had passed through British railway stations so often and so unremarked in mufti that the salutes of British noncoms now took me by surprise and I was generally well past the saluter before I realized I had left him with a poor view of American military courtesy. It would have been hopeless to explain each time that a correspondent didn't rate a salute—I was bald enough and old enough to be a field officer and was wearing an officer's uniform.

The Air Corps, which was just beginning to take over a few British fields, reminded me of a football squad beginning its training for the season. It would win a lot of games if it was not rushed into heavy competition too soon. My favorite unit in the first weeks was a Flying Fortress bombardment group that resembled a football squad physically too. There is an official maximum size for fighter and medium bombardment pilots, but the really big boys in the Air Corps get into the big ships, where there is relatively a lot of head room. The commander of one squadron of the group had been All-Southern at Mississippi State; one of his pilots had played tackle for Alabama in the Rose Bowl, and another had understudied an All-American halfback at Duke; Tommy Lohr, a rugged little lightweight back from Brown, was another pilot in the group, and altogether they would have made a good squad for any coach in a normal season. But this time they had other business.

The original public-relations crew in London, being for the most part newspapermen who had recently acquired uniforms and lived in deadly fear of irritating real soldiers, were not of much help in getting out to see troops. According to them the C.O. of any unit a correspondent wanted to see was sure to be busy, and anyway there were no living accommodations for newspapermen at the flying field. I arranged all that with my Fortress fellows by always occupying the bed of a man who had gone on forty-eight-hour leave to London. While the man was in London he would sleep in my room at the hotel. When the regular occupant of the bed at the field returned there was always somebody else going up to town and I would move into his bed while he took mine in London. I never really interviewed anybody, just lived around the place and learned by osmosis, until I sometimes thought of myself as a redundant member of the group, a goldbricker nobody had yet caught up with. We were living in hutments and sleeping on cots; there were toilets that flushed and showers; between meals and after dinner we would sit in the lounge of the officers' club, where there were deep chairs and a bar. In retrospect, after we all got to Africa, it seemed a most luxurious period.

The Fortresses made their first flights over France while I was living with this group. The accuracy of their bombing, even in their first raids, astonished officers of British Bomber Command and the Ministry of Economic Warfare, who had selected the targets. The British thought at first that these were selected crews of veterans and that the accuracy couldn't be retained in large-scale operations. But I knew that they were boys who had had at most a year and a half in the Air Corps, and that there were thousands more like them at home. The factories would furnish the planes, the American system of public education would furnish the crews; it couldn't be anything but a win. And the ground forces, I felt confident, would be up to the air people in efficiency. The factories and the schools would work for them, too. And the good American food that the boys had eaten had given them the bone and lungs and recuperative power that no Nazi state system of physical education could superimpose on rickety frames.

The boys themselves, I thought, were the best proof they had something to fight for. Four officers fly in each Fortress, and every one of them at that time had to be a college man. You could look around the lounge in the evening and see 250 officers, all giving a common impression of fitness and good humor. There wasn't a raddled, vicious face in the lot. They had come from state universities and technical schools and little denominational colleges all through the country, where tuition fees were nominal or nonexistent. This brazen public defiance of the profit system had resulted in the creation of our greatest national asset. They hadn't had to spend their elementary-school days getting up competitive examinations which would admit them to secondary school, or their secondary-school days preparing competitive examinations for college. They had had time to play. Some of them were sons of rich men, a few were sons of mechanics, and most were in between, but there was no trace of class accent to distinguish one from another. There were regional accents, of course. And the standard of training in all those schools that to me had for years been just names in columns of football scores must have been pretty good, because the kids could all do their stuff as well as the few members of the group who had been to Ivy colleges.

I hadn't been with so many Americans so young in twenty years, and I thought they had an edge on my own college generation, although maybe I was less than fair in retrospect because I had been an insecure, intolerant undergraduate myself. All the boys had to do, I thought, was to look around at each other and they would understand that democracy was worth defending. The noncoms they flew with, six sergeants to a Fortress, were just as different from products of other regimes as the officers. They were all high-school men, even though in civil life they had clerked in grocery stores or driven laundry trucks. They had no idea that they were bound down in any social class, and they thought for themselves about everything they saw and did. They were good stuff.

The officers of the different ships wore no insignia to show which Fortress they belonged to, but it was easy to pick out crewmates in the lounge of the club. They were the men who usually occupied adjacent chairs, engaged in long sessions of insulting one another, and lent one another money in crap games. One of my favorites, a boy named Jones from Memphis, used to sit next to the phonograph, changing the records. The songs they liked were full of sobs: "I'll Be Around When He Is Gone," or "Someone's Rocking My Dream Boat," or "This Is the Story of a Starry Night." A psychiatrist has since told me that he considers such fare extremely depressing for men about to go out on bombing missions, but there were no suicides. I never hear those songs now without seeing the faces of the kids in the lounge, and sometimes I forget which of them are dead.

There was one Fortress pilot whom his colleagues called the Baron, who once told me that his only ambition for after the war was to sit in the grandstand at the Yankee Stadium every afternoon and watch the ball game. He was known as the Baron because once when he had been doing some drinking in the club he had said, "When we get to Germany I will be a baron if I feel like it because my family has a castle on the Rhine and I can walk in and claim it any time." His father had been an officer in the German Army in the war previous to this one, but that did not prevent the Baron from being the kind of suburban boy who shoots a good game of pool, plays semipro baseball on Sunday while he is still in college and officially an amateur, and is perennially worried about a pending charge of driving while under the influence of alcohol. When the home-town papers began to arrive at the station after the first few Fortress raids the fellows from small cities had a lot of fun reading each other their clippings. One town had had a Joe Snodgrass Day in honor of a navigator from there who had been in a raid, and it had raised a fund of $62 to buy candy and chewing gum for him, but not cigarettes because some of the subscribers objected to smoking. The Baron said to me, "In the town I come from the people think I am a bum, and I guess they would be surprised I am here at all." He had played varsity baseball at three colleges, none of them tough academically, and you could deduce that he had not been exactly a studying type from the fact that he had been thrown out of two of them. He was a good pilot, and he flew in a careless, easy-looking way. "Flying is the hardest thing in the world to learn," he once said to me, "and the easiest thing to do after you've learned it." He had met a co-ed at the third college where he had played ball, and married her. He was always showing new acquaintances a picture of his wife, tall and dark, and she was very pretty. The Baron had a hard time emotionally in England. He didn't like anything he had heard about Hitler, but it used to make him angry when Englishmen referred to Germans as Huns. "My old man is all right," he used to say.

Quite a while afterward I met a bomber crew from that group in Africa, and they told me they thought the Baron had been killed over Lorient. "At least, when we last saw that ship it was blazing and only five hundred feet off the ground, and nobody had bailed out," the bombardier said. "It wasn't the Baron's regular crew. There was something the matter with a supercharger in his own ship that morning, and the pilot of the ship he was lost in had a heavy cold and the co-pilot was green, so the Baron volunteered to fly them. That was a raid when we had to come down lower than usual to get through cloud over the target. We don't know whether flak or fighters got the Baron's ship, but just as it made the turn after bombing, smoke and flames began pouring out of it and it began losing altitude. They could have bailed out all right, but they were heading into a group of German fighters, so they kept the guns going and they blew two 109's to bits on the way down. They were too goddam busy to jump."

I used to sometimes try to get fliers talking about what they wanted after the war, but most of them had ambitions rather like the Baron's. One fellow wanted to stay on his honeymoon until all his bonus money ran out, another wanted to play golf all day and poker all night every night and drink whisky constantly, and a lot of them wanted to stay in the Air Corps or get jobs in commercial aviation. They didn't have very much to say about the future of the world, if they thought about it. They weren't vindictive, either. They liked to hear me talk about my Polish friends. "I guess those boys are really bloodthirsty," they would say with objective astonishment. "It's better for us not to get mad," one of them said to me. "The type of precision bombing we do you've got enough to do without being angry."

25 / Birds of My Country

I SAILED FOR AFRICA from England on the night of November 9, twenty-four hours after the first African landings had been announced in London. For nearly two weeks before I left I had been subject to call at my hotel on twelve-hour notice. I had known there must be colleagues waiting for the same call, but I had never admitted that I was one of the elect, and none of the others had said anything to me. The secret of our destination had been well kept until November 8, but after the news of the first landings we who were still in London knew where we were going. We also knew that we had been only second-grade elect, having been left out of the first wave. Personally I felt all right about that, since I had never wanted to see a fight between Americans and Frenchmen. Our party, the second echelon of prose masters, left London late in the evening from a spur railroad station used only for troop movements, in an atmosphere thick with fog and mystery. It included Ernie Pyle, of Scripps-Howard, Bill Lang of *Time, Life,* etc., Red Mueller of *Newsweek,* Gault Mac-Gowan of the New York *Sun,* Ollie Stewart of the Baltimore *Afro-American,* and Sergeant, now First Lieutenant, Bob Neville, whom I had known when he was on the *Herald Tribune* and *PM* and who was now going to Africa as a correspondent for the army magazine, *Yank.* I recognized a kindred spirit in Ollie the moment I saw him. "Where do you hope we land at?" he asked me. "Someplace where resistance has ceased," I told him. That established a perfect rapport.

I had had an attack of the gout in my right foot two days before pulling out, and I went limping off to the war instead of coming limping back from it. I had always previously felt a bit of pride in the recurrences of this fine eighteenth-century disease, a tribute to the high standard of living I had attained at a relatively early age, but this time I was peeved with it. I figured that someone might think it was psychogenic. It made me feel worse to find the Roosevelt Hospital unit from New York on the transport we boarded for the voyage; there were fifty-two nurses who got a first impression of decrepitude that I never consequently had a chance to overcome, because each was immediately appropriated by three Air Corps officers. Lieutenant Colonel Gurney Taylor, who was, I think, second in command of the unit, then turned traitor to his class by telling me about a ten-cent specific for the malady, a breach of confidence which will cost the civilian medical profession several hundred dollars a year for the rest of my life expectancy. I had to go to war to get a gout remedy. Except for the gout and the nurses the trip was without event; we docked at Mers-el-Kebir on November 21 without having seen any more enemy action than I had experienced in my two other sea passages.

There was a light air raid at Oran on the night of our arrival. The reaction to it of the local population seemed to me exaggerated; then I realized that there were still French-speaking people to whom an air raid was a novelty. I spent the next four weeks in and around Oran, making one excursion into eastern Morocco with the reconnaissance troop of the First Infantry Division when it seemed that the frontier of Spanish Morocco might become a war front. The fighting in Tunisia, as we heard about it from officers and correspondents who passed through Oran after visits to the front, was on a small scale, and few American troops were engaged. I used my time getting the feel of North Africa and gaining a gradual and unforced familiarity with the First Infantry Division, which had captured Oran, and remained in the Department. The First had many enlisted men from the sidewalks of the Bronx and Brooklyn, and a rich New York accent had new charms for me in Africa. There is an analogical sentiment in a chanson of Gace Brule, the thirteenth-century Champenois poet:

> "The little birds of my country
> Have sung to me in Brittany,"

where he was in exile, I think.

"Give da passwoy," I once heard a First Division sentinel challenge.

"Nobody told me nuttin," the challenged soldier replied.

"What outfitchas outuv?"

"Foy Signals."

"Whynchas get on da ball? Da passwoy is 'tatched roof.' "

"What is it mean?"

"How do I know? Whaddaya tink I yam, da Quiz Kids?"

It looked and acted and talked like a good division even then, making you know it could do the fine things it has since done. I got the same feeling from it that I had had the first time I had seen my Fortress group in England, before the Fortresses had been on a single operation.

26 / What Do You Think That Bugle's Blowing For?

ORAN WAS THE FIRST PART of metropolitan France I had been in since June 1940. I thought I might be able to gauge from it the effects of all the events since then upon the French. I knew how strong the anti-British sentiment had been at the armistice time, how guilty the French must have felt because of the Armistice nonetheless, and how greatly a sensation of guilt increases bitterness. A corresponding sense of guilt toward France underlies the most extreme instances of British francophobia. So I did not expect to find undiluted enthusiasm for the Allied cause. But Oran disappointed even me, and I was astonished by the American policy of coddling the most obviously disaffected Oranais. These were the high civil and military officials and the large landowners.

The Prefect, a M. Boujard, had come in during the Popular Front government of Léon Blum in 1936 and had performed a star turn in political contortionism by remaining at the head of the Department ever since. He had carried out economic collaboration with the resident German and Italian commissions, enforcing the Nuremberg-patterned anti-Jewish laws and exalting the rest of the Vichy program. No one had held a pistol at his head to compel him to stay. The General of Division, one Boisseau, a furtive gray fox of a man, had insisted on the determined defense of Oran that had lasted sixty hours and cost several hundred American and perhaps a thousand French lives. This resistance had been inspired by his belief that the Allies would be chased out of Africa and he would then lose his promotion and pension rights if he had not fought against them. I had the pleasure of hearing him address some of his officers on the firing range at near-by Arzeu when American soldiers were demonstrating material that was to be turned over to the French. An American mortar put in a couple of bad shots. "I had no illusions about the American Army!" the general announced with loud satisfaction. Officers suspected of having favored the Americans even in thought, like a Zouave major I met (who had, by the way, fought like a lion against us), were practically ostracized. Liaison officers assigned to American units were scolded for "fraternizing" with the Americans—nearly two months after we had officially become allies. Most of the officers above the grade of battalion commander were a sad lot; those not definitely hostile, because they owed their promotions to Vichy, were apathetic because in their hearts they had never expected to fight again and hated the prospect.

"They are selfish!" my friend the Zouave major said, "they are in love with their pensions. Let it pass! But the blasphemy is that they do not want to fight!" He was a Basque who had escaped from Occupied France and then asked for service in Africa in the spring of 1941 when he had become convinced that Great Britain would not be conquered. "I have been suspect here," he told me, "so that it was more necessary for me than for the others to fight well against the Americans. Else the higher officers would have said, 'His sentiments were dictated by cowardice.' I could not have remained in the army."

The higher civil servants were in the same category as the higher officers. The minor functionaries, like postmen and cops, were in the main decent enough, but had had to conform.

The great landed proprietors of the Department, grandsons of immigrant French peasants, had piled up huge fortunes in paper francs during the armistice period by exporting to Germany their grain, their fruit, and the alcohol made from their brandy. They were the most implacable enemies we had. The poor Oranais noticed a slight improvement in nutrition soon after we landed, because dates and oranges could no longer be exported and were sold for home consumption. But this was of no benefit to the big farmers. They had never suffered personally and would have preferred to continue exporting their fruit. The money that they had been piling up would have been eventually worthless, for the Reichsbank, turning out unbacked francs by the trillion, would have inevitably forced a howling inflation. We, by pegging their franc at seventy-five to the dollar, had turned their paper into real money, and a good many of them into real millionaires. But they were angry because we had not given them a better rate. When, a couple of months later, we hiked the franc up to fifty to the dollar, we pushed a lot more money their way, still without gaining their gratitude. The leading stevedoring firm, to which the American port authorities threw the army business, was Italian-Fascist. The harbor was wide open for sabotage. A few of the ships that the American naval salvage crew had raised with great difficulty after they had been sunk by the French naval authorities were "accidentally" rammed and resunk by towboats. The French naval people retained their posts. In the first days after our arrival, I learned, some of the business had been given to a smaller competing stevedore firm. The Prefect had made representations to the American command that the owner of this smaller firm was suspected of being a British sympathizer! So the business went to the Italian.

The great landowners of the Department are of a distinct species, French only in the sense that the pre-Revolutionary Carolina rice planters were English. They are African-born; they visit France only to make a splurge in Paris or to treat their obesity at Vichy, and they are reactionary to an extent only possible in a country where a few white men live by the exploitation of a large native population. The miserable Arabized Berbers who work their great estates get almost nothing. The planters say that if you give a native anything above the lowest subsistence level he will quit work; he would not really like adequate food or clothes. They talk exactly like Mississippians. Naturally they are not in favor of manhood suffrage, labor unions, or any talk about the equality of races. They had not really collaborated with the Nazis: the Nazis had come along belatedly and collaborated with them. While they had been included in one of the ninety-odd departments of a democratic nation they had been restrained from complete self-expression. The apparent German victory had started them saying, "I told you so, democracy couldn't last." Our arrival desolated them.

These landowners, and the Prefect and the general, were the solid people who entertained Major General Lloyd R. Fredendall, the local ranking American general officer, at their homes. He let them think they were translating public opinion for him and apparently accepted what they said. He was a soldierly man who may have felt that his position had been eased by the decision of the Vichy people and the local big shots to retain all their old perquisites and keep on running the Department. He received masses of alarming reports every day from his own counterintelligence service, the intelligence officer of the battalion of American infantry in the town, and the intelligence section of First Division, but these were filed away. One point the solid people were always careful to impress upon the general was the depth and fervor of anti-Semitic feeling in Oran. The solid people and their henchmen were administering Jewish real estate and cafés; their friends and relatives of the professional class were enjoying the practices Jewish doctors and lawyers had been forced to abandon. But they even got the American military administration to discharge French-English interpreters on the docks because the interpreters were Jewish (and of course pro-Ally). They said the Arab dockworkers would resent having Jews placed over them.

There was in truth a violent anti-Semitism in the city of Oran, but it was of the same kind as the anti-Semitism of Harlem, the result of deliberately inciting one exploited race against another. The Algerian-born French citizens of Spanish descent, colloquially called Néos, together with immigrants from Spain make up about a third of Oran's population. Another third is Moslem, and the two groups furnish practically all the manual labor of the city. About fifteen per cent of the population is composed of Algerian Jews. These Jews, Europeanized in varying degrees, had enjoyed French citizenship until Vichy adopted the German anti-racial laws. They had been neither great landlords nor important bankers, but shopkeepers, small moneylenders, renting agents or owners of a poor type of housing, craftsmen, chafferers, and professional people. The Oranais of French origin, a small minority, are mostly functionaries, skilled workmen or money people. A French physician, the official leader of the anti-Semitic movement in Oran, told me that there was a disproportionate number of Jewish doctors and lawyers, the classic complaint.

The number of French physicians and lawyers in relation to the total Arab-Néo-Jew-French population was more disproportionate still, however. There were neither physicians, lawyers, nor men of property among the Arabs and Néos, the two most numerous groups of the population. But Arabs and Néos, as helpless against their major exploiters as a Harlem rioter against his, had been encouraged to hate the convenient Jew.

Oran is as odd as its ruling class. It has between 150,000 and 200,000 inhabitants and looks like a cross between Miami Beach and Washington Heights, although it is dirtier than either. The harbor lies in the shape of a crescent, with a continuous ridge of hills rising behind it, and the city is built on their slopes and crests.

Along the boulevards that offer good sea views there are *style-moderne* apartment houses with rounded corners, lots of glass, and balconies in the European manner of 1929. The older buildings are dingy but equally un-Oriental, and the climate is so cold in winter that the scattered palm trees look like a real-estate man's importation. A third of the population is *indigène*, which is the French term for the commingled Arabized Berbers and Berberized Arabs, but in weeks of walking about town I never saw a mosque. The only indigène who looked even faintly picturesque was an old fellow employed by a tintype photographer to pose with American soldiers in the Place du Maréchal Foch. The French say that Oran is the least French city in Africa, but it is at the same time the least African. Néos, Jews, native Oranais with French grandparents, and even the few indigènes who adopt European clothes and vocations seem to merge into the same vague Mediterranean type.

But since the Department of Oran, like the two other Algerian departments, was technically a part of metropolitan France, every action of the French and American authorities there might set a precedent for the reconquest, and I was shocked by the mess things were in. It was as if continental United States had extended statehood to Puerto Rico and Hawaii and had then itself been occupied by an enemy power, leaving the untypical new states to carry on pro tem as the United States of America, and the sugar companies had then been left free to run Puerto Rico and Hawaii.

Members of uniformed fascist organizations had left the city or at least hidden their *sturm* duds when the Americans marched in. They had sniped at our people all through the battle and might legitimately have expected to be backed against a wall and shot. But within a couple of weeks they reappeared in the cafés wearing their capes, monocles, and high boots and talking loudly about the day of revenge, not against the Germans, but us. The Légion des Anciens Combattants, the opposite number of the Sturm-Abteilung, paraded, the Service d'Ordre de la Légion, which corresponded to the Schutzstaffel, strutted; the Compagnons de France, facsimile of the Hitlerjugend, made early morning hideous with their marching song, *"Maréchal, Nous Violà."* The civil servant who had been the local head of the Légion Tricolore, the battalion being recruited to fight against our Russian ally on the eastern front, was mobilized as a major in the French Army to fight by our side against the Germans. I had a faint suspicion he would not fight too hard. The Darlan government refused to mobilize Jews with their regiments. The Falange operated openly among the Néos, its leaders telling them that the Germans would soon appear in Oran and hand it over to Franco. Spain had held the city for two hundred and fifty years, until the Barbary Pirates had driven the Spanish garrison out in 1790. The French had moved in about forty years later.

The greed and violence of the ruling clique in Oran had provoked a more articulate reaction there than in any other African city. Long before 1939 Oran had been known as a city where political passions were strong. The Left Republicans, who drew their main strength from among the skilled workers and small functionaries born in France, had somehow managed to keep up a daily newspaper, l'Oran Républicain, even during the Pétain regime. It had had occasional issues suppressed and had appeared many times with large blank spaces created by the censor; its plant had been searched dozens of times for weapons or communist propaganda, but it had survived. Perhaps the Prefect, that pluperfect trimmer, had not wanted to neglect any possible hedge. The editors of l'Oran Républicain were by the time of my advent among the angriest and most disappointed people in North Africa. We had even left the old Vichy censorship undisturbed, so that when the Républicain's leader writer prepared a pro-American editorial, the censors blue-penciled it. All through the Department Jews and Frenchmen who had publicly expressed satisfaction at our landing were now serving jail sentences for their bad taste. Post-office clerks and railway conductors who had been discharged for suspected pro-Ally sympathies were still out of jobs, and those who belonged to the uniformed fascist groups were being given more responsible jobs than ever. I asked a profound-appearing major in the British Political Warfare office at Oran about this, and he said, "People should not expect to profit from their patriotism." The slogan of the occupation was, "Keep the rascals in."

General Fredendall obviously did not formulate our policy for the North African theater. He got his directives from Algiers, where General Eisenhower and Robert Murphy of the State Department were running the show, and it was of course impossible to know whether they themselves were making policy or receiving it from Washington. But Fredendall's complacency in matters of detail jarred me. I spent part of one Sunday afternoon talking to him about the Service d'Ordre de la Légion, commonly spoken of as the S.O.L., the members of which had formed an elite guard of uniformed fascism, like the German SS after which they were patterned. The next time he saw me, in the lobby of the town's principal hotel, which had been requisitioned by the Army, he graciously approached me and said, "You don't have to worry about those S.O.L.'s anymore. Their secret intelligence section is working with us now." Within a few days they had probably turned in the name of every De Gaullist in Oran as a candidate for a concentration camp. There was a general understanding that the policy of leaving the Vichy people in power was in accord with the famous agreement with Admiral Darlan signed by Eisenhower or Murphy or both, but Fredendall said he had never seen a copy of the agreement. I would have liked to know its exact terms.

State Department special agents had done the undercover work of preparation for the Oran landing and had studied the local political situation for two years while they had the German and Italian commissions living in the same hotel with them. These agents were as surprised and nearly as angry as the Allied sympathizers in Oran at the turn political affairs had taken. Their attempt to organize a militant fifth column to aid the landing had not come off, but they had furnished the landing force with excellent intelligence, and the people who had risked their lives to secure this intelligence were now being openly threatened by the S.O.L. A very beautiful Scandinavian woman, married to a Frenchman, who had been one of our most effective agents, told me that she had received repeated menaces through the mail and that Fascists regularly scrawled insults on her door.

Toward the middle of December I began to think I had used up the material that interested me in Oran, but it was not until the day before Christmas that I actually got started toward Algiers. I went down to the airfield, about fifteen miles from the city, to get on a transport plane, but was stranded by a combination of low priority and bad weather. The field was deep in a quality of mud worse than Mississippi gumbo, or so Southern soldiers informed me. One plane got out loaded with lieutenant colonels and high-priority freight, which I subsequently discovered at Algiers was toilet tissue and laundry soap, both rated ahead of correspondents. Then the base operations officer announced that the weather had closed down and there would be nothing more that day. I was in the operations shack, madder than hell, when Lieutenant Colonel Joe Crawford, commander of the second battalion of the Sixteenth Infantry, wandered in and invited me home with him for a quiet infantry Christmas. His battalion was stationed about three miles from the airport, and he said he could bring me in again next day if the weather improved and get me on a plane. I liked the battalion, and I was so tired of Oran that I didn't want to go back to it even for one night, so I thanked Crawford and came along.

Headquarters company was billeted in the buildings and courtyard of a wealthy colonist's farm; the other companies were in tents on the slopes of a couple of hills. I had just pulled off one gumboot and broken a thumbnail doing it when the bugle began to blow assembly in the farmyard.

The first note had hardly sounded, it seemed, when the top sergeant began to yell. The top sergeant of headquarters company was a New Yorker with a frozen movie-gangster smile and a hard mind, and he yelled, "C'mon, get goin'! Whaddaya tink dat bugle's blowin' for?" I looked out of a window and he was handing out bandoliers of rifle ammunition, spieling all the while like a peddler pitching popcorn at Coney Island, "C'mon, get your ammunition. Da mora dis we use da shorter it'll be!" He turned his head toward me and added, "We hope!" I didn't know what the bugle was blowing for, until Don Kellett, the battalion intelligence officer, came in and said that the radio had announced a state of alert ordered for American forces all over North Africa. The battalion was to get ready to move and fight on five minutes' notice, but the reason for the alert had not been stated. He surmised that the Spaniards had let the Germans through Spanish Morocco. Crawford thought there might be an outbreak of sabotage organized by the Fascists throughout North Africa, and Chuck Horner, the executive officer, bet on a plague of parachutists. Night was falling, and our Christmas carol was "What do you think that bugle's blowing for?"

It was a good battalion of a good regiment. In an unbelievably short time the company officers reported that their outfits were ready to go. No further orders came to the battalion, and the soldiers waited under arms, packs on backs. Then a rocket appeared over the airfield. It was a green one followed by half a dozen whites and some reds and blues. Kellett said he didn't know what the signal meant, but it looked like trouble. "Maybe parachutists have landed and those mugs are too excited to get off regular signals!" he said. The wind was toward us, and we could hear machine-gun fire. We tried to raise the airfield on the telephone and couldn't. "Get a couple of patrols over there," Crawford ordered.

The tough top sergeant went out himself with one patrol. They walked out into the dark, and Crawford and Horner and Kellett and I awaited their return in the command post, the nerve center of the area. Every couple of minutes Kellett would walk to the door and come back, saying, "More rockets. Blue and green now," or "More shooting." Horner said, "It's a tough one to sweat." The sergeant returned after three quarters of an hour.

"We had to work our way onto the field to find out what all the shooting was for, sir," he said, "and their patrols fired at us. It was lucky it was the Air Corps that was shooting, because they can't hit nothing. When we got over on the field we found it was just a lot of drunks shooting off rockets and machine guns because it was Christmas Eve. They never heard of no alert." Crawford was pretty mad. He said, "That Air Corps mentality again!" He finally got the executive officer at the field on the telephone and said, "I have a lot of men with itchy trigger fingers here and your people are pretty lucky they didn't get brassed off." Crawford was so conscientious that he had even kept me sober, and we were all angrier about the Air Corps having such a good time than about anything else. The battalion slept in its clothes and on its weapons that night.

The first thing I heard in the morning was Kellett coming into the big sleeping room and saying to Crawford, "We got a flash that Darlan's been assassinated."

Crawford said, "Merry Christmas!"

27 / The Hat of M. Murphy

ALGIERS ON CHRISTMAS DAY, when a C-47 transport plane got me there from Oran, was calmer than any city had a right to be after having witnessed within the space of eight weeks a partially successful *coup d'état*, the landing of an army from another hemisphere and the assassination of an equivocal admiral. It was hard to determine whether the calm was due to apathy or to the Algerois' fear of expressing any anti-Axis sentiment when we might be looking for another Darlan to take the defunct cheat's place. Certainly the average European or Moslem inhabitant of the city seemed more preoccupied with alimentation than with war.

The driver of the army car that brought me into town from the airfield told me that good billets were scarce, but that I might as well try my luck at the best hotel in the city first. Allied Headquarters had set aside six double rooms for correspondents, he said, and since there were departures and arrivals every day I might find a bed. I recognized the hotel from the motion picture *Pepe le Moko*. It was the one where Pepe's mistress stayed with her rich protector while Pepe pined in the Casbah.

My luck was in. As I started into the revolving door I met a fellow named Dave Brown whom I had known in New York for years. He said he had a room with one vacant bed in it. Dave, an American, had worked in the financial department of the New York bureau of Reuters, Ltd., the British news agency, for twelve years without ever being sent out of the office to cover a story. At last Reuters had sent him with the American force that landed in Morocco, as a trial assignment, I suppose, and he was doing a fine job of it. In New York Dave had long lived above an Armenian restaurant near Radio City and played the horses in partnership with the proprietor. I had always suspected the Armenian of giving Dave good tips when the rent was due and bad ones when it looked as if Dave were getting prosperous enough to move. Living with a spot-news man during a busy news period is a great luxury for a magazine correspondent, because the spot-news fellow has to keep up with the hour-to-hour situation and file frequent news bulletins. The magazine writer keeps posted without any exertion. For a week after the Darlan assassination Dave would be summoned from his bed two or three times a night to go up to General Eisenhower's headquarters for handouts, sometimes during air raids. I could lie snug beneath my Berber blanket and snore.

I found it difficult to distinguish at first, on walking through the climbing streets of the city, whether I was in a friendly place or an occupied enemy town. One could walk interminably without seeing a single caricature of Hitler in a shop window or an Allied newsreel advertised by a theater. The windows of the bookstores near the University of Algiers were crammed with Germanophile apologetics—testimony, perhaps, to Anglo-Saxon belief in freedom of the press. There were no signs of patriotic street demonstrations, such as one occasionally saw even in the Paris of 1939–40. I gathered from café conversations that there had been a few immediately after the debarkation of the Allies, but that the local officials had discouraged them as examples of Jewish bad taste. The place had a restful, neutral surface quality like Dublin.

Perhaps the mysterious agreement with Darlan had included a clause barring pro-Ally propaganda; I could think of no other reason why up-to-date films presenting the best aspects of American life had not been rushed in almost with the first assault wave. As it was, the leading American film attraction in the city was a 1935 film featuring Victor Moore as a henpecked husband, a role peculiarly difficult for Moslems to sympathize with. Even Darlan's death had not cleared the air of the heavy smudge of ambiguity that had hung over Africa since the deal with him. On one of my first walks I went into a crowded restaurant for a change from army food. There was less nourishment but more flavor in civilian cooking, and you could afford the change once in a while if you had the solid army rations to fall back on when you got hungry. The only vacant chair was at a table with a small blond man who soon told me that he was a Syrian-born Jew, owned the best jewelry shop in town, had been educated at the American University at Beirut, and knew Arabic so well he composed poems in it. He said that he didn't know what to make of the Allies' "desertion" of their pre-landing "friends," exactly the same turn of words I had heard many times in Oran. Here, however, the desertion seemed even more weird, because the friends had come out with arms in their hands and risked their lives for us on the night of our landing. The jeweler offered to introduce me to some of the men who had led the *coup* which had paralyzed the defense forces for several hours, and I accepted. We took a rendezvous for five o'clock that afternoon, at the apartment of Dr. Henri Aboulker, of the faculty of medicine of the university. It had been an uncommonly good lunch for a within-the-law restaurant in Algiers: some indistinguishable kind of stew meat cooked with a reddish sauce and olives.

You can hope for lucky encounters only if you walk around a lot. A distinguished blackface comic once told George Lyon, a former city editor of mine, that there are only three kinds of people in the world worth talking to, whores, newspapermen, and actors, and they all need sturdy legs in their business. After a roundabout stroll I got back to Dr. Aboulker's apartment on the Rue Michelet in time for my appointment.

Dr. Aboulker was seventy-eight years old. He was permitted to continue his practice and remain on the faculty of medicine, although a Jew, because citizens who had been wounded or received military decorations in the last World War were as yet exempt from the provisions of the racial laws. The stage in which they too would be barred would undoubtedly have been reached later, but even Vichy had hesitated to do it. It would have looked awkward for that professional war veteran, the Marshal.

The Pétainist African regime which had remained in under Darlan and had now apparently survived him had taken measures to avoid any future repetition of this awkward situation by excluding Jews from the new mobilization, however. No Jew would be able to say twenty-five years after *this* war that he had deserved well of his country, the Darlanois were determined. They had left one loophole, at the insistence of General Giraud, who was as stubborn in military affairs as he was politically indifferent. Jews, Moslems, foreigners held in concentration camps, former soldiers of the Foreign Legion, and anybody not formally enrolled with a regular class of the Army Reserve could volunteer in a new catch-all organization called the Corps Franc d'Afrique, which was promised immediate service in the front line. "If they want to fight, let them fight," Giraud said. "Nobody stops them." He was constitutionally impervious to the argument that segregation impaired their rights as Frenchmen. He meant it when he said that the only right that counted was the right to kill Germans. But the Pétainist civil officials considered the Corps Franc a beautiful invention for silencing obstreperous fellows of all creeds. "If you are such a patriot, join the Corps Franc," they said. Meanwhile they remained in their grandiose offices five hundred miles from the firing line, scheming to requisition all the most comfortable villas in Algiers and move into them before British or American bigwigs did. The competition for palaces was keen and absorbed a deal of the war energy of all three allies.

Dr. Aboulker had both wounds and decorations in profusion. His right leg had been shattered by machine-gun bullets and then ingeniously patched together again, but he could walk only with the aid of a cane, a detail the humorous significance of which will become apparent shortly to the reader. His apartment, a collection of large high-ceilinged rooms on the second or third floor of a fine *immeuble* dating from about 1900, reminded me irresistibly of that of Dr. Perrot, the anti-Semitic physician I had visited in Oran. A man's taste is formed more by his culture, his profession, and the period in which he is young than by his race or politics. The two apartments contained the same mixture of pretentious nineteenth-century furniture, which looked archaic, and of painting which had been revolutionary in the two physicians' youth and still seemed fresh, from the late impressionists through *les fauves*. The doctor was a somber old man who kept his hat on in the house for fear of drafts. One of his sons, a straight, slender lad in his early twenties, was in the group that received me. The others, all, I think, Jews, included my jeweler friend, a philosopher, a couturier, and several others whose callings I do not remember, a paradoxical group of putschists. Two of the younger men there, they told me, had been at the by-now famous conference between General Mark Clark, Murphy, and the two French officers who had prepared the plan for our Algiers landing, when Clark had been brought by submarine to a beach villa owned by one of the group. One of the young men had waded into surf up to his chest to steady the kayak in which the general had made his way back to the submarine. They said that Murphy had used the Aboulker apartment as his headquarters during the months of preparation for the putsch and even on the night when the landing was expected. According to the original plans for that night, they said, the Americans were supposed to land in the harbor of the city at one o'clock. At eleven the putschists, 540 young men of whom 450 were Jews, went out with arms which the United States Government had furnished to them and seized the telegraph office, the municipal power plant, the Préfecture of Police, and other nerve centers, and arrested the ranking army officers who were not in on the plot and Admiral Darlan himself. Some of them said they were sorry they had not killed Darlan then. He had temporized, saying he would join them, and they had only held him prisoner. "It would have been easy to finish him if killing had been part of our plan," one man said, "but we lacked the habit of ruthlessness." The Americans had not appeared on schedule, some of the officials whom the putschists had missed at their first swoop had alerted the troops stationed in the suburbs, and by two o'clock in the morning the putschists themselves had been besieged in the various buildings they had taken. The troops outnumbered them and had artillery. After a resistance during which several of their number had been killed, the pro-Allied civilians had surrendered. They had held Darlan for four hours, and it is easy to understand how much their attack had served to distract attention from our landing. By eight o'clock the next morning the Americans were in possession of the city. During the course of the day they freed the men who, if our attack had been a failure, would certainly have been tried and executed by Darlan's gang. "It is now almost impossible for one of us to see Mr. Murphy," the old doctor said. "He shuns us like a case of an extremely contagious disease."

"The army brass hats and the people of the Préfecture whom we arrested hate us," one of the younger men said. "They hate us because we know what cowards they are. You should have seen how miserably they

acted when they saw the tommy guns, the brave Jew-baiters. The chief of
the secret police, who has been of course restored to his position, kneeled
on the floor and wept, begging one of my friends to spare his life. Imagine his feeling toward the man who spared him! Another friend, a doctor,
is to be mobilized—in a labor camp, of course—under the military jurisdiction of a general whom *he* arrested." After a good deal more talk and
the consumption of a couple of glasses of white wine—too sweet, exactly
like that the anti-Semite had offered me—a couple of the younger men
drove me home to my hotel in an automobile. I was too late to eat at the
officers' mess, so I had dinner at a black-market restaurant that had been
recommended to me. I had mushroom soup, *rouget de la Méditerranée
meunière*, a couple of grilled thrushes, chicken en casserole, rum cake
with cream, oranges, coffee, and a bottle of Veuve Clicquot of a year I
hadn't heard of but which did well enough to wash down campaign fare.
I was happy in the possession of a great deal of information which could
do me no professional good because I couldn't have got it through the
censor. But useless possessions are always the ones we revel in. I was also
happy that night because I thought I knew that the pessimism of the
Aboulker circle was exaggerated. "Be patient," I had told them, "the heart
of the State Department is in the right place. It has only been temporarily
mislaid—perhaps under a lettuce seed."

The telephone in our room summoned Dave Brown fairly early next
morning to the downtown office building where the Allied Forces had
set up their public-relations headquarters. I fancied it had something to
do with politics but didn't worry much about it. At about eleven I had my
breakfast of black imitation coffee, a dry piece of bread, and watery
confiture and my cold bath. I could have had a good breakfast at the mess
up until eighteen-fifteen, and there was hot water at the hotel until nine,
but I never got up that early. I dressed and walked down to public
relations myself to see if I had received any money. When I entered the
correspondents' room there Dave told me that the French government of
North Africa had announced the arrests of fifteen persons for plotting to
assassinate General Giraud. Their names had not been announced, but
anti-collaborationists had already supplied half a dozen correspondents
with tentative lists. "You hadn't been out of Dr. Aboulker's apartment half
an hour," Dave said, "when they arrested everybody there. They picked
up the fellows who drove you home, too." It occurred to me immediately
that the secret police whom our sympathizers had arrested on the landing
night now were back in power, and that opportunities for a frame-up
were excellent. The boy who had killed Darlan had been executed without any public hearing; the men of the Préfecture could attribute any
statement they wished to him. Infallibly they would say he had impli-
cated every prominent De Gaullist in town in a double murder plot, of
which he had carried out the first half. That is what they did say.

A few days later—this incident is out of precise sequence, but it seems to belong here—a small, dapper young man called on me at the hotel and told me that the married daughter of Dr. Aboulker wanted to see me to relate the circumstances of his arrest, and that she and her husband would meet me in her father's apartment that afternoon. I went up there with Dave, whose superiors in London were continually bombarding him with requests for information on the political story that he couldn't send out. The daughter, whose married name I forget, was an extraordinarily pretty and spirited brunette. The political police, armed with tommy guns, had arrived soon after my departure, she said, when she was alone in the apartment with her father and her two children, aged three and eight. Her father was in an electric cabinet, treating the leg that had been shattered in the World War and that still bothered him. She had answered the door and a plain-clothes man had pushed a tommy gun into her stomach while another had pointed his submachine gun at her eight-year-old boy and ordered him to put his hands up. The brave Fascists were taking no chances. Then a dozen detectives had searched the apartment for weapons. "There weren't any, luckily," she said, "because we had got rid of those M. Murphy had furnished to us." They had dragged her father from his cabinet, not allowed him to dress, and hauled him off to jail without his trousers. "They would not let him take his cane," she said, "and without it he cannot stand upright, which amused them. They dragged him down the stairs. I haven't been allowed to see him in prison. By the way," she said, "I have something here that will amuse *you*."

She walked off into another room and came back carrying a black Homburg hat. She handed it to me. It was quite a good hat, made by Christy's of London, the kind that anybody who wanted to be mistaken for a Foreign Office man might be glad to wear.

"The hat of M. Murphy!" she said. "He left it here that evening of the landing. He said, 'I will be right back' and went out. He hasn't been here since!"

28 / Giraud Is Just a General

THE WEEK THAT FOLLOWED the arrest of our former agents in Algiers restored all the esteem I had had for newspapermen when I was twenty years old. After enough years newspapermen begin to pall on other newspapermen; they begin to take their good qualities for granted and wince at their shortcomings, of which the most common are a vanity that sometimes borders on the thespian and a sort of perpetual mental adolescence that I think stems from starting work on a fresh story every day or every week or month and never having time to get to the bottom of anything.

They forget that newspapermen as a class have a yearning for truth as involuntary as a hophead's addiction to junk. The question of whether the junkie really loves hop is academic; he can't get along without it. A newspaperman may write a lie to hold his job, but he won't believe it, and the necessity outrages him so that he craves truth all the more thereafter. A few newspapermen lie to get on in the world, but it outrages them, too, and I have never known a dishonest journalist who wasn't patently an unhappy bastard.

There were about thirty journalists in Algiers at the time, including radio reporters, and not one of them accepted the official French version of the arrests—that the motive had really been the safety of General Giraud—or the far more disturbing official American efforts to play down the whole affair. The journalists, like my cockney in Poplar, weren't 'aving any. It made me all the happier that not only the professing liberals, but the representatives of conservative papers, and the plain routine second- and third-string representatives of press associations all got the idea. I think it even impressed the Army and State Department people running the North African show. They could stop us from sending our stuff out, and they did, but they saw in us an articulate, tangible cross section of the opinion they would have to face at home. There was no division on national lines; British and American correspondents were in complete accord.

Largely, I think, because of the row we raised, General Bergeret, who had come to Africa as Darlan's personal assistant and had remained with Giraud, virtually running the civil side of the administration, and Rigault, a character in charge of public relations, became aware that people of the Allied powers would not accept so crude a return to Gestapo government. The Anglo-American press of Algiers was therefore summoned to an interview with General Henri Honoré Giraud himself. The general thought our protest an unwarranted intrusion into a routine administrative affair. He had not checked on the affair personally because he was too busy with his army. Giraud believed, as a military principle, in standing by one's subordinates. All his principles are military. He was therefore going to put us in our places.

The office where he received us was in a secondary school for boys, and we were herded into his presence much as if we were going before the headmaster. After we had stumbled forward one by one to have our hands crushed in his psychologically steely grip, we stood back and waited, in our habitual civilian postures. The general's eye wandered over us moodily, and I imagined that he had expected us to hold *"Fixe!"* until he had said *"Repos!"* Brigadier General Robert McClure of the United States Army, who was in charge of Allied public relations and censorship in the theater of war, was to attend the mass interview, but his automobile had been delayed in the blackout. I could see Giraud getting angrier by the second at having to wait for a general four stars down to him.

Giraud wears five. A few wispy hairs which stood apart from the main body of his moustache and got in the path of his breath quivered like shreds of paper in front of a powerful electric fan. He sat down at his desk, and his aide ordered us all out of the room until McClure arrived. We went into one of the classrooms and sat on some benches, hoping we would not be expelled from school.

Giraud is as straight and nearly as tall as De Gaulle, but he is better-proportioned, more in drawing. Also he has been a general for so much longer that he has settled into the role more comfortably. De Gaulle's expression is occasionally irascible, as if he anticipated that somebody might challenge his authority. The thought has not occurred to Giraud for years. The painter he suggests is not El Greco, but Meissonier. He is, as I had known ever since the Battle of France, a good general.

When General McClure arrived at the schoolhouse, we all filed into the Giraud presence again. McClure is happily ignorant of French; Giraud could not say anything to him except through the intermediary of an officer far junior to a brigadier general. One cannot say to a captain, "Ask the brigadier general, in English, where the hell he has been." According to military protocol the situation was impossible. All Giraud's actions are limited by military conceptions. He therefore said nothing to McClure.

He began his discourse to us by saying that he was happy to be making war by the side of an ally so rich in the most modern material. When his army had marched through Belgium and into Holland to engage the Germans in 1940 he had had only seven airplanes for a quarter of a million men. Now he had 50,000 men fighting in Tunisia, and fighting well, and he had hoped to have modern equipment for them. He had been promised modern equipment, but it was not here. He looked accusingly at us, as if some correspondent might be wearing a $2\frac{1}{2}$-ton truck in a shoulder holster. He could not for the life of him, he said, see why there was so much fuss about a dozen civilians, who might or might not be guilty, when hundreds of his people were being killed every week because they were fighting with only rifle ammunition and little of that. A British captain named Hyphensmith translated for the benefit of those who could not understand French.

"I am not interested in politics," the general said, "I make war."

One of the correspondents said that since this was a war for democracy, a word which brought no change in the general's expression, it was important that the people of occupied countries should not get the idea that if they helped us we would after our arrival permit them to be put in jail. I said that many of the current North African officials who remained in power had been put in by Vichy as selected watchdogs who could be depended upon. The general said he did not know of one such official. Since he had been a prisoner of war through most of the Armistice and had arrived in Africa only after our landing, he may not have known much, but he had certainly heard a lot.

Frank Kluckhohn of the New York *Times*, through the intermediary of Captain Hyphensmith, passed up a list of the reported prisoners to the general and asked him to verify it. There were about a dozen names on the list, including those of a couple of men high in the political police who had known about the plot to aid the Allied landing and helped conceal it. There were Dr. Aboulker and two of his sons, a man named Brunel who was the son of a former mayor of Algiers, and some others. Giraud said, triumphantly, "See how accurate your information is!" and crossed off a couple of names, including that of Aboulker, who we all knew quite well was in jail. Giraud's manner recalled Napoleon calling a grenadier by name, after having just received the information from the grenadier's corporal. I was sure he had been misinformed by his Gestapo, even to the identity of the men arrested. When he came to the extremely Corsican names of the two police officials—one of whom he later appointed Prefect of Algiers—he said, "These men withheld information from their superiors. A good policeman does not withhold information from his superior!" He himself had been in a submarine on his way to Africa when the policemen had "withheld," and if these men had informed their superiors the landing would have been opposed and Giraud perhaps captured. But it was hard for him to pardon a breach of discipline, even in the enemy's camp. He said that no trials of the accused men were contemplated. He seemed genuinely puzzled by our exaggerated interest in the affair.

Giraud, although entitled to dozens of decorations, wore none. His unribboned, khaki chest would have been conspicuous even on a French captain. As we were about to leave, one of the British correspondents asked him why he wore no decorations.

"Because I have taken an oath not to wear any until I enter Metz at the head of a victorious army," Giraud said. I thought that his choice of an objective made the man clear. A politician would have said Paris, a sentimentalist would have named his own native province. But Metz is a garrison town, the most important strategically on the Franco-German frontier. The soldier wanted to get back to his barracks.

Giraud, I felt, would react to any attack on Bergeret and Rigault as De Gaulle had to reflections on his precious Colonel P——— in London a year or so earlier, by suspecting the detractors of his subordinates. But more than anything else he wanted to fight and beat the Germans, and he was as susceptible to a gift of matériel as a little child to candy. I had known civilian intellectuals incapable of visualizing the reality of war; Giraud was the reverse of the medal. He had no civilian imagination. Freudians would be astonished by a human 100 per cent masculine or 100 per cent feminine. Giraud is even more astonishing in his way. He is 100 per cent a general.

The dressing down of the correspondent corps by General Giraud having produced no carminative results, we were invited to the villa of M. Murphy for cocktails and a conference on New Year's Eve. This was a parallel to the hard and soft method employed by New York detectives in reducing a prisoner to reason. M. Murphy lived in a fine villa high on the fashionable hill. The cocktails were good, there was a fire on the great hearth, a dog wandered among the guests to soften their hearts toward its master, after the English manner. Everything was *très gentleman*. M. Murphy deprecated the importance of the arrests, regretted that the strict censorship of political despatches would have to stay on, implied that Darlan had not been such a bad fellow after all, and in general tried to pour gin on the troubled waters. He got so many arguments from correspondents that one of the headquarters colonels who was there for the free drinks became quite petulant about us. Military petulance is usually in proportion to the distance from the firing line and in inverse ratio to the probability of the officer who is being petulant ever getting there. "We have war to get on with!" this colonel said, fiercely biting the olive out of a martini. M. Murphy introduced the name of Marcel Peyrouton and asked us what we thought of him. Everybody who had been in France thought he was terrible, so Murphy decided to bring him on anyway. Personally, I think now that it was a good idea. Peyrouton had decided that we were going to win the war, and he made an excellent ferret for us, bringing numerous collaborationist rats out of the administrative sewers they were hiding in.

Within the next few months the political situation in Algeria got much better. The suspected "assassins" were released. Peyrouton replaced Chatel, the left-over governor general, and then got rid of the prefects of Algiers and Oran, who were replaced by anti-Axis men; Brunel, the former mayor, a De Gaullist, got an important place in the Government; the curious Rigault disappeared from the office of information and was replaced by General René Chambe, an aviator and man of letters who had recently escaped from France and a really topnotch sort; Bergeret lost his importance and was posted to an unimportant command in West Africa. The S.O.L. and the Légion were dissolved, although the Compagnons de France were not, De Gaullist publications from London were allowed into North Africa, the racial laws were abolished and General Giraud went on record in favor of a republican form of government for a redeemed France. I imagine that he did so after the same kind of an educational course that had preceded De Gaulle's "*Liberté, Egalité, Fraternité*" speech from London, but he said it. Critics of the regime complained of the slowness with which reforms were put into effect, but with the diminishing flagrancy of the things they objected to they began to seem merely querulous.

Along with this improvement in political matters, State Department officials in Africa tried to sell the idea that they had intended things thus all the time, and that the stand of the press at home and of the correspondents on the spot had had nothing to do with the change. If so they had certainly concealed their sentiments as expertly as their intentions. I do not think that anything would have changed if we had not got up on our hind legs and yelled. The thesis that the department goes serenely on its way, indifferent to the press, does not always accord with developments.

The trouble was that—

African political affairs had been in a frightful mess while Darlan lived and for about a month thereafter—what would have happened had he survived will always be a subject for unpleasant speculation. A bungling censorship had prevented the British and American publics from getting any exact information, and afterward the public would not believe reports of improvement even when they were true. Ken Crawford, of *PM* and the Chicago *Sun*, arrived in Algiers in February or March and found little to get indignant about. When he told his employers so they decided he had gone over to the enemy. But he hadn't been there in the bad time. Remembering the Darlan days, the liberal press refused to accept *anything* that Washington said about North Africa thereafter. I strongly suspect that the Free French publicity organization here—it sounds a bit absurd to call people on Fifth Avenue Fighting French, to distinguish them from Giraud's troops in Tunisia—took advantage of this opening in their smear-Giraud campaign last spring. They even invented a "Giraudist" movement which they said had been set up by the State Department against De Gaulle. The term *Giraudiste* simply doesn't exist in Africa, any more than "Eisenhoweriste" or "Pattoniste," or "Montgomeryiste." Giraud, by his own fervent wish, is just a general.

The time between January 1 and January 23, 1942, was from a military point of view the most ticklish of the whole North African campaign. In November and December the British force with American attached fragments in Tunisia had been small and the Americans along the Algerian coast few and extremely preoccupied with the possibilities in Spanish Morocco. But the German army at Tunis had been even more limited. It had been brought in by troop carrier, glider, and an occasional furtive steamer from Sicily, and it lacked heavy equipment, although it had a short line of supply to the land forces from numerous African ports. Rommel was too far to the east to help the Tunis force, and the supplies pouring into Tripoli went to him. When in January he fell back clear to Tripoli, however, he was in a position where he could shift troops up to Tunisia at will. A force that would not be important in the Libyan theater, where the armies were relatively large, might be strong enough to upset the whole balance of strength in Tunisia, where battalions were still considered important units. Then too there was always the chance that Rommel might pull all his troops out of Tripoli and race for Constantine and Algiers with his whole army.

The problem was eased when the British secured the port of Tripoli on January 23 before Rommel had acquired too much of a head start in the race north. With the short supply line they now had they could keep on his heels all the way, which they did, while the British First Army and the Americans were steadily adding strength in the west. After that he was cooked. Action, if it came at all during January, was bound to begin in southern and central Tunisia, where the Rommel territory overlapped that of Von Arnim, the northern commander. Northern Tunisia was bogged down in mud. Early in January I decided that I had stalled Ross long enough without contributing a story on the shooting war, so I started for the advanced area. I was fed up with the political atmosphere in Algiers anyway.

The easiest way to get into the war was to ride a transport plane out to an advanced airfield, where we had a fighter group, and then if there was not enough to write about there arrange to go by truck or jeep up to one of the two or three detachments of American ground troops in the area. It turned out that the transports were booked full for the morning I had chosen for my departure. An Air Corps major whom I had known in England and reencountered at Algiers said he could fix that by reserving a place for me on the French courier plane which made a circuit of British and American airports east of Algiers every day, carrying mail and local passengers.

This plane, which was of a type that the French had been allowed to use for courier service even after the Armistice, because it used so little gasoline, did not look as if it could fly into a strong wind. When I first saw it I was conscious of a lack that I could not define. At last it came to me. It was like an illustration from a 1922 magazine and there should have been a Coles Phillips girl in the foreground. A little man in a long over-coat and a soft gray hat came up to me while I stood gazing and asked me where I was going. I told him, thinking he was some kind of a ticket collector, and he opened the door of the plane, climbed in, and said, "Come along, you're the only passenger." He was the pilot. Before he sat down at the controls he pulled a Guide Michelin out of his pocket, looked at it, put it back and said, "Ça, va." Then he took off.

We made our first landing at Telergma, south of Constantine, where we picked up a technical sergeant and a box of dates addressed to a lieutenant in a fighter squadron. The man in the long overcoat said to me, "Up to here it's all right, but I've never been to your field, and it's said to be difficult to find, in between some mountains." We carried the tech sergeant to Canrobert and got two British aircraftsmen who said they were on pass and were going back to Algiers with the little man, clean around the circuit via Biskra.

When I had first asked my friend the major about means of flying into the advanced field he had said, "First you get a transport, and then you get about a dozen Spits to act as escort, and then you go in." The man in the long overcoat dropped into the field very nicely, begged me to be so good as to speed the box of dates on its way, tipped his soft hat and flew away, leaving me in the middle of the war.

29 / The Foamy Fields

"The Foamy Fields" was collected in two different volumes of Liebling's work: first in *The Road Back to Paris* and then in *Mollie and Other War Pieces*. It was written and originally published during World War II. After the war, Liebling revealed in footnotes and postscript some identities, locations, and additions that had to remain secret or were unknown when the piece first appeared. Here we print the full postwar text.—*Editor*

IF there is any way you can get colder than you do when you sleep in a bedding roll on the ground in a tent in southern Tunisia two hours before dawn, I don't know about it. The particular tent I remember was at an airfield in a Tunisian valley. The surface of the terrain was mostly limestone. If you put all the blankets on top of you and just slept on the canvas cover of the roll, you ached all over, and if you divided the blankets and put some of them under you, you froze on top. The tent was a large, circular one with a French stencil on the outside saying it had been rented from a firm in Marseilles and not to fold it wet, but it belonged to the United States Army now. It had been set up over a pit four feet deep, so men sleeping in it were safe from flying bomb fragments. The tall tent pole, even if severed, would probably straddle the pit and not hit anybody. It was too wide a hole to be good during a strafing, but then strafings come in the daytime and in the daytime nobody lived in it. I had thrown my roll into the tent because I thought it was vacant and it seemed as good a spot as any other when I arrived at the field as a war correspondent. I later discovered that I was sharing it with two enlisted men.

I never saw my tentmates clearly, because they were always in the tent by the time I turned in at night, when we were not allowed to have lights on, and they got up a few minutes before I did in the morning, when it was still dark. I used to hear them moving around, however, and sometimes talk to them. One was from Mississippi and the other from North Carolina, and both were airplane mechanics. The first night I stumbled through the darkness into the tent, they heard me and one them said, "I hope you don't mind, but the tent we were sleeping in got all tore to pieces with shrapnel last night, so we just moved our stuff in here." I had been hearing about the events of the previous evening from everybody I met on the field. "You can thank God you wasn't here last night," the other man said earnestly. The field is so skillfully hidden in the mountains that it is hard to find by night, and usually the Germans just wander around overhead, dropping their stuff on the wrong hillsides, but for once they had found the right place and some of the light anti-aircraft on the field had started shooting tracers. "It was these guns that gave away where we was," the first soldier said. "Only for that they would have gone away and never knowed the first bomb had hit the field. But after that they knew they was on the beam and they come back and the next bomb set some gasoline on fire and then they really did go to town. Ruined a P-38 that tore herself up in a belly landing a week ago and I had just got her about fixed up again, and now she's got shrapnel holes just about everywhere and she's hopeless. All that work wasted. Killed three fellows that was sleeping in a B-26 on the field and woke up and thought that was no safe place, so they started to run across the field to a slit trench and a bomb got them. Never got the B-26 at all. If they'd stayed there, they'd been alive today, but who the hell would have stayed there?"*

"That shrapnel has a lot of force behind it," the other voice in the tent said. "There was a three-quarter-ton truck down on the field and a jaggedy piece of shrapnel went right through one of the tires and spang through the chassix. You could see the holes both sides where she went in and come out. We was in our tent when the shooting started, but not for long. We run up into the hills so far in fifteen minutes it took us four hours to walk back next morning. When we got back we found we didn't have no tent." There was a pause, and then the first soldier said, "Good night, sir," and I fell asleep.

When the cold woke me up, I put my flashlight under the blankets so I could look at my watch. It was five o'clock. Some Arab dogs, or perhaps jackals, were barking in the hills, and I lay uncomfortably dozing until I heard one of the soldiers blowing his nose. He blew a few times and said, "It's funny that as cold as it gets up here nobody seems to get a real cold. My nose runs like a spring branch, but it don't never develop."

When the night turned gray in the entrance to the tent, I woke again, looked at my watch, and saw that it was seven. I got up and found that the soldiers had already gone. Like everyone else at the field, I had been sleeping in my clothes. The only water obtainable was so cold that I did not bother to wash my face. I got my mess kit and walked toward the place, next to the kitchen, where they were starting fires under two great caldrons to heat dish water. One contained soapy water and the other rinsing water. The fires shot up from a deep hole underneath them, and a group of soldiers had gathered around and were holding the palms of

---

* The B-26 was Lieutenant-General James Doolittle's personal plane. He was on a tour of inspection, and the three soldiers were members of his crew.

their hands toward the flames, trying to get warm. The men belonged to a maintenance detachment of mechanics picked from a number of service squadrons that had been sent to new advanced airdromes, where planes have to be repaired practically without equipment for the job. That morning most of the men seemed pretty cheerful because nothing had happened during the night, but one fellow with a lot of beard on his face was critical. "This location was all right as long as we had all the planes on one side of us, so we was sort of off the runway," he said, "but now that they moved in those planes on the other side of us, we're just like a piece of meat between two slices of bread. A fine ham sandwich for Jerry. If he misses either side, he hits us. I guess that is how you get to be an officer, thinking up a location for a camp like this. I never washed out of Yale so I could be an officer, but I got more sense than that."

"Cheer up, pal," another soldier said. "All you got to do is dig. I got my dugout down so deep already it reminds me of the Borough Hall station. Some night I'll give myself a shave and climb on board a Woodlawn express." Most of the men in camp, I had already noticed, were taking up excavation as a hobby and some of them had worked up elaborate private trench systems. "You couldn't get any guy in camp to dig three days ago," the Brooklyn soldier said, "and now you can't lay down a shovel for a minute without somebody sucks it up."   .

Another soldier, who wore a white silk scarf loosely knotted around his extremely dirty neck, a style generally affected by fliers, said, "What kills me is my girl's brother is in the horse cavalry, probably deep in the heart of Texas, and he used to razz me because I wasn't a combat soldier."

The Brooklyn man said to him, "Ah, here's Mac with a parachute tied around his neck just like a dashing pilot. Mac, you look like a page out of *Esquire*."

When my hands began to feel warm, I joined the line which had formed in front of the mess tent. As we passed through, we got bacon, rice, apple butter, margarine, and hard biscuits in our mess tins and tea in our canteen cups. The outfit was on partly British rations, but it was a fairly good breakfast anyway, except for the tea, which came to the cooks with sugar and powdered milk already mixed in it. "I guess that's why they're rationing coffee at home, so we can have tea all the time," the soldier ahead of me said. I recognized the bacon as the fat kind the English get from America. By some miracle of lend-lease they had now succeeded in delivering it back to us; the background of bookkeeping staggered the imagination. After we had got our food, we collected a pile of empty gasoline cans to use for chairs and tables. The five-gallon can, known as a flimsy, is one of the two most protean articles in the Army. You can build houses out of it, use it as furniture, or, with slight structural alterations, make a stove or a locker. Its only rival for versatility is the metal shell of the Army helmet, which can be used as an entrenching tool, a shaving bowl, a wash basin, or a cooking utensil, at the discretion of the owner. The helmet may also serve on occasion as a bathtub. The bather fills it with water, removes one article of clothing at a time, rubs the water hastily over the surface thus exposed, and replaces the garment before taking off another one.*

There was no officers' mess. I had noticed Major George Lehmann, the commanding officer of the base, and First Lieutenant McCreedy, the chaplain, in the line not far behind me. Major Lehmann is a tall, fair, stolid man who told me that he had lived in Pittsfield, Massachusetts, where he had a job with the General Electric Company. When I had reported, on my arrival at the field, at his dugout the evening before, he had hospitably suggested that I stow my blanket roll wherever I could find a hole in the ground, eat at the general mess shack, and stay as long as I pleased. "There are fighter squadrons and some bombers and some engineers and anti-aircraft here, and you can wander around and talk to anybody that interests you," he had said.

Father McCreedy is a short, chubby priest who came from Bethlehem, Pennsylvania, and had been assigned to a parish in Philadelphia. He always referred to the pastor of this parish, a Father McGinley, as "my boss," and asked me several times if I knew George Jean Nathan, who he said was a friend of Father McGinley. Father McCreedy had been offici- ating at the interment of the fellows killed in the raid the evening before, and that was all he would talk about during breakfast. He had induced a mechanic to engrave the men's names on metal plates with an electric needle. These plates would serve as enduring grave markers. It is part of a. chaplain's duty to see that the dead are buried and to dispose of their effects. Father McCreedy was also special-services officer of the camp, in charge of recreation and the issue of athletic equipment. "So what with one thing and another, they keep me busy here," he said. He told me he did not like New York. "Outside of Madison Square Garden and the Yankee Stadium, you can have it." He wore an outsize tin hat all the time. "I know a chaplain is not supposed to be a combatant," he said, "but if parachute troops came to my tent by night, they'd shoot at me because they wouldn't know I was a chaplain, and I want something solid on my head." He had had a deep hole dug in front of his tent and sometimes, toward dusk, when German planes were expected, he would stand in it waiting and smoking a cigar, with the glowing end of it just clearing the hole.

When I had finished breakfast and scrubbed up my mess kit, I strolled around the post to see what it was like. As the sun rose higher, the air grew warm and the great, reddish mountains looked friendly. Some of them had table tops, and the landscape reminded me of

* This is known as a whore's bath. The impelling reason for exposing only one surface at a time was cold, not modesty.

Western movies in Technicolor.* I got talking to a soldier named Bill Phelps, who came from the town of Twenty-nine Palms, California. He was working on a bomber that had something the matter with its insides. He confirmed my notion that the country looked like the American West. "This is exactly the way it is around home," he said, "only we got no Ayrabs." A French writer has described the valley bottoms in southern Tunisia as foamy seas of white sand and green alfa grass. They are good, natural airfields, wide and level and fast-drying, but there is always plenty of dust in the air. I walked to a part of the field where there were a lot of P-38's, those double-bodied planes that look so very futuristic, and started to talk to a couple of sergeants who were working on one. "This is Lieutenant Hoelle's plane," one of them said, "and we just finished putting a new wing on it. That counts as just a little repair job out here. Holy God, at home, if a plane was hurt like that, they would send it back to the factory or take it apart for salvage. All we do here is drive a two-and-a-half-ton truck up under the damaged wing and lift it off, and then we put the new wing on the truck and run it alongside the plane again and fix up that eighty-thousand-dollar airplane like we was sticking together a radio set. We think nothing of it. It's a great ship, the 38. Rugged. You know how this one got hurt? Lieutenant Hoelle was strafing some trucks and he come in to attack so low he hit his right wing against a telephone pole. Any other plane, that wing would have come off right there. Hitting the pole that way flipped him over on his back, and he was flying upside down ten feet off the ground. He gripped that stick so hard the inside of his hand was black and blue for a week afterward, and she come right side up and he flew her home. Any one-engine plane would have slipped and crashed into the ground, but those two counter-rotating props eliminate torque." I tried to look as though I understood. "Lieutenant Hoelle is a real man," the sergeant said.**

I asked him where Hoelle and the other P-38 pilots were, and he directed me to the P-38 squadron's operations room, a rectangular structure mostly below ground, with walls made out of the sides of gasoline cans and a canvas roof camouflaged with earth. A length of stovepipe stuck out through the roof, making it definitely the most ambitious structure on the field.

Hoelle was the nearest man to the door when I stepped down into the operations shack. He was a big, square-shouldered youngster with heavy

---

* This use of the familiar false as touchstone of the unfamiliar real recurred often both in writing and conversation during World War II. "Just like a movie!" was a standard reaction. It assured the speaker of the authenticity of what he had just experienced.

** These praises of the Lightning now look as old-fashioned as a cavalryman's praise of the Anglo-Arab charger, and the mechanic's talk about an eighty-thousand-dollar airplane, sounds like a reference to the good nickel cigar.

eyebrows and a slightly aquiline nose. I explained who I was and asked him who was in charge, and he said, "I am. I'm the squadron C.O. My name's Hoelle." He pronounced it "Holly." There was a fire in a stove, and the shack was warm. Two tiny black puppies lay on a pilot's red scarf in a helmet in the middle of the dirt floor, and they seemed to be the centre of attention. Six or eight lieutenants, in flying togs that ranged from overalls to British Army battle dress, were sitting on gasoline cans or sprawled on a couple of cots. They were all looking at the puppies and talking either to them or their mother, a small Irish setter over in one corner, whom they addressed as Red. "One of the boys brought Red along with him from England," Hoelle said. "We think that the dog that got her in trouble is a big, long-legged black one at the airport we were quartered at there."

"These are going to be real beautiful dogs, just like Irish setters, only with black hair," one of the pilots said in a defensive tone. He was obviously Red's master.

"This is a correspondent," Hoelle said to the group, and one of the boys on a cot moved over and made room for me. I sat down, and the fellow who had moved over said his name was Larry Adler but he wasn't the harmonica player and when he was home he lived on Ocean Parkway in Brooklyn. "I wouldn't mind being there right now," he added.

There was not much in the shack except the cots, the tin cans, a packing case, the stove, a phonograph, a portable typewriter, a telephone, and a sort of bulletin board that showed which pilots were on mission, which were due to go on patrol, and which were on alert call, but it was a cheerful place. It reminded me of one of those secret-society shacks that small boys are always building out of pickup materials in vacant lots. Adler got up and said he would have to go on patrol. "It's pretty monotonous," he said, "like driving a fast car thirty miles an hour along a big, smooth road where there's no traffic. We just stooge around near the field and at this time of day nothing ever happens."

Another lieutenant came over and said he was the intelligence officer of the squadron. Intelligence and armament officers, who do not fly, take a more aggressive pride in their squadron's accomplishments than the pilots, who don't like to be suspected of bragging. "We've been out here for a month," the intelligence officer said, "and we have been doing everything—escorting bombers over places like Sfax and Sousse, shooting up vehicles and puncturing tanks, going on fighter sweeps to scare up a fight, and flying high looking for a target and then plunging straight down on it and shooting hell out of it. We've got twenty-nine German planes, including bombers and transports with troops in them and fighters, and the boys have flown an average of forty combat missions apiece. That's more than one a day. Maybe you'd like to see some of the boys' own reports on what they have been doing."

I said that this sounded fine, and he handed me a sheaf of the simple statements pilots write out when they put in a claim for shooting down a German plane. I copied part of a report by a pilot named Earnhart, who I thought showed a sense of literary style. He had had, according to the intelligence officer, about the same kind of experience as everybody else in the squadron. Earnhart had shot down a Junkers 52, which is a troop-carrier, in the episode he was describing, and then he had been attacked by several enemy fighters. "As I was climbing away from them," he wrote, "a 20-millimetre explosive shell hit the windshield and deflected through the top of the canopy and down on the instrument panel. Three pieces of shell hit me, in the left chest, left arm, and left knee. I dropped my belly tank and, having the ship under control, headed for my home base. On the way I applied a tourniquet to my leg, administered a hypodermic, and took sulfanilamide tablets. I landed the ship at my own base one hour after I had been hit by the shell. The plane was repaired. Claim, one Ju 52 destroyed." The intelligence officer introduced Earnhart to me. He was a calm, slender, dark-haired boy and he persisted in addressing me as sir. He said he came from Lebanon, Ohio, and had gone to Ohio State.

Still another lieutenant I met was named Gustke. He came from Detroit. Gustke had been shot down behind the German lines and had made his way back to the field. He was a tall, gangling type, with a long nose and a prominent Adam's apple. "I crash-landed the plane and stepped out of it wearing my parachute," he told me, "and the first thing I met was some Arabs who looked hostile to me, and as luck would have it I had forgotten to bring along my .45, so I tripped my parachute and threw it to them, and you know how crazy Arabs are about cloth or anything like that. They all got fighting among themselves for the parachute, and while they were doing that I ran like hell and got away from them. I got to a place where there were some Frenchmen, and they hid me overnight and the next day put me on a horse and gave me a guide, who brought me back over some mountains to inside the French lines. I had a pretty sore ass from riding the horse."

A pilot from Texas named Ribb, who stood nearby as Gustke and I talked, broke in to tell me that they had a fine bunch of fellows and that when they were in the air they took care of each other and did not leave anybody alone at the end of the formation to be picked off by the enemy. "In this gang we have no ass-end Charlies," he said feelingly.

I asked Lieutenant Hoelle what was in the cards for the afternoon, and he said that eight of the boys, including himself, were going out to strafe some German tanks that had been reported working up into French territory. "We carry a cannon, which the P-40's don't, so we can really puncture a tank the size they use around here," he said. "We expect to meet some P-40's over the target, and they will stay up high and give us cover against any German fighters while we do a job on the tanks. Maybe I had better call the boys together and talk it over."

A couple of pilots had begun a game of blackjack on the top of the packing case, and he told them to quit, so he could spread a map on it. At that moment an enlisted man came in with a lot of mail and some Christmas packages that had been deposited by a courier plane. It was long after Christmas, but that made the things even more welcome, and all the pilots made a rush for their packages and started tearing them open. Earnhart, who was going on the strafe job, got some National Biscuit crackers and some butterscotch candy and a couple of tubes of shaving cream that he said he couldn't use because he had an electric razor, and the operations officer, a lieutenant named Lusk, got some very rich home-made cookies that an aunt and uncle had sent him from Denver. We were all gobbling butterscotch and cookies as we gathered round the map Hoelle had spread. It was about as formal an affair as looking at a road map to find your way to Washington, Connecticut, from New Milford. "We used to make more fuss over briefings in England," the intelligence officer said, "but when you're flying two or three times a day, what the hell?" He pointed out the place on the map where the tanks were supposed to be, and all the fellows said they knew where it was, having been there before. Hoelle said they would take off at noon. After a while he and the seven other boys went out onto the field to get ready, and I went with them. On the way there was more talk about P-38's and how some Italian prisoners had told their captors that the Italian army could win the war easy if it wasn't for those fork-tailed airplanes coming over and shooting them up, a notion that seemed particularly to amuse the pilots. Then I went to the P-38 squadron mess with Adler, who had just returned from patrol duty and wasn't going out on the strafe job, and Gustke, who was also remaining behind. This mess was relatively luxurious. They had tables with plates and knives and forks on them, so they had no mess tins to wash after every meal. "We live well here," Adler said. "Everything high-class."

"The place the planes are going is not very far away," Gustke said, "so they ought to be back around half past two."

When we had finished lunch, I took another stroll around the post. I was walking toward the P-38 squadron's operations shack when I saw the planes begin to return from the mission. The first that came in had only the nose wheel of its landing gear down. There was evidently something the matter with the two other wheels. The plane slid in on its belly and stopped in a cloud of dust. Another plane was hovering over the field. I noticed, just after I spotted this one, that a little ambulance was tearing out onto the field. Only one of the two propellers of this plane was turning, but it landed all right, and then I counted one, two, three others, which landed in good shape. Five out of eight. I broke into a jog toward the operations shack. Gustke was standing before the door looking across the field with binoculars. I asked him if he knew whose plane had belly-landed, and he said it was a Lieutenant Moffat's and that a big, rough Texas pilot the other fellows called Wolf had been in the plane that had come in with one engine out. "I see Earnhart and Keith and Carlton, too," he said, "but Hoelle and the other two are missing."

A jeep was coming from the field toward the operations shack, and when it got nearer we could see Wolf in it. He looked excited. He was holding his right forearm with his left hand, and when the jeep got up to the shack he jumped out, still holding his arm.

"Is it a bullet hole?" Gustke asked.

"You're a sonofabitch it's a bullet hole!" Wolf shouted. "The sonofabitching P-40's sonofabitching around! As we came in, we saw four fighters coming in the opposite direction and Moffat and I went up to look at them and they were P-40's, coming away. The other fellows was on the deck and we started to get down nearer them, to about five thousand, and these sonofabitching 190's came out of the sun and hit Moffat and me the first burst and then went down after the others. There was ground fire coming up at us, too, and the sonofabitches said we was going to be over friendly territory. I'm goddam lucky not to be killed."*

"Did we get any of them?" Gustke asked.

"I know I didn't get any," Wolf said, "but I saw at least four planes burning on the ground. I don't know who the hell they were."

By that time another jeep had arrived with Earnhart, looking utterly calm, and one of the mechanics from the field. "My plane is all right," Earnhart told Gustke. "All gassed up and ready to go. They can use that for patrol."

The telephone inside the shack rang. It was the post first-aid station calling to say that Moffat was badly cut up by glass from his windshield but would be all right. The mechanic said that the cockpit of Moffat's plane was knee-deep in hydraulic fluid and oil and gas. "No wonder the hydraulic system wouldn't work when he tried to get the wheels down," the mechanic said. The phone rang again. This time it was group operations, calling for Earnhart, Keith, and Carlton, all three of them unwounded, to go over there and tell them what had happened. The three pilots went away, and a couple of the men got Wolf back into a jeep and took him off to the first-aid station. Hoelle and the two other pilots were still missing. That left only Gustke and me, and he said in a sad young voice, like a boy whose chum has moved to another city, "Now we have lost our buddies."

A couple of days later I learned that Hoelle had bailed out in disputed territory and made his way back to our lines, but the two other boys are either dead or prisoners.

* Normal confusion.

* * *

NOT many Mondays ago I was standing in a chow line with my mess tins at an airfield* in southern Tunisia, waiting to get into a dugout where some mess attendants were ladling out a breakfast of stew and coffee. The field is enormous, a naturally flat airdrome of white sand and alfa grass that doesn't hold rainwater long enough to spoil the runways—terrain of the kind a French writer once said looked like foamy seas. All around the field there are bulky, reddish mountains. To the east, the sun was just coming up over one of them, and the air was very cold. The mess shack was covered on top and three sides by a mound of earth. It served officers and men of a squadron of P-40 fighters, and on that particular Monday morning I stood between a corporal named Jake Goldstein, who in civilian life had been a Broadway songwriter, and a private named John Smith, of New Hope, Pennsylvania, who used to help his father, a contractor, build houses. Goldstein told me about a lyric he had just written for a song to be called "Bombs." "The music that I think of when it goes through my head now," he said, "is kind of a little like the old tune called 'Smiles,' but maybe I can change it around later. The lyric goes:

> There are bombs that sound so snappy,
> There are bombs that leave folks sad,
> There are bombs that fell on dear old Dover,
> But those bombs are not so bad.

The idea is that the real bad bomb is when this girl quit me and blew up my heart."

"It sounds great," I told the Corporal.

"It will be even bigger than a number I wrote called 'What Do You Hear from Your Heart?'" Goldstein said. "Probably you remember it. Bing Crosby sang it once on the Kraft Cheese Hour. If you happen to give me a little writeup, remember that my name in the songwriting business is Jack Gould." Private Smith started to tell me that he had once installed some plumbing for a friend of mine, Sam Spewack, the writer, in New Hope. "His wife, Bella, couldn't make up her mind where she wanted the can," Smith said, "so I said—"

I never heard any more about Bella Spewack's plumbing, because Major Robert Christman, the commanding officer of the squadron, came up to me and said, "Well, it's a nice, quiet morning." He had his back to the east. I didn't get a chance to answer him, because I started to run like hell to get to the west side of the mound. A number of soldiers who had been scattered about eating their breakfast off the tops of empty gasoline cans had already started running and dropping their mess things. They always faced eastward while they ate in the morning so that they could

---

* This time it was Thélepte, in Tunisia.

see the Messerschmitts come over the mountains in the sunrise. This morning there were nine Messerschmitts. By the time I hit the ground on the lee side of the mound, slender airplanes were twisting above us in a sky crisscrossed by tracer bullets—a whole planetarium of angry worlds and meteors. Behind our shelter we watched and sweated it out. It is nearly impossible to tell Messerschmitts from P-40's when they are maneuvering in a fight, except when one plane breaks off action and leaves its opponent hopelessly behind. Then you know that the one which is distanced is a P-40. You can't help yelling encouragement as you watch a fight, even though no one can hear you and you cannot tell the combatants apart. The Messerschmitts, which were there to strafe us, flew right over the mess shack and began giving the runways and the planes on the field a going-over.

We had sent up four planes on patrol that morning and they tried to engage the strafing planes, but other Germans, flying high to protect the strafers, engaged the patrol. Some "alert" planes that we had in readiness on the perimeter of the field took off in the middle of the scrap, and that was a pretty thing to watch. I saw one of our patrol planes come in and belly-land on the field, smoking. Then I saw another plane twisting out of the sky in a spin that had the soldiers yelling. We all felt that the spinning plane was a Messerschmitt, and it looked like a sure thing to crash into one of the mountains north of us. When the plane pulled out and disappeared over the summit, the yell died like the howl at Ebbets Field when the ball looks as if it's going into the bleachers and then is snagged by a visiting outfielder. It was a Messerschmitt, all right. A couple of minutes later every one of the German planes had disappeared, with our ships after them like a squad of heavy-footed comedy cops chasing small boys.

The fellows who had ducked for cover hoisted themselves off the ground and looked around for the mess things they had dropped. They were excited and sheepish, as they always are after a strafe party. It is humiliating to have someone run you away, so you make a joke about it. One soldier yelled to another, "When you said 'Flop!' I was there already!" Another, who spoke with a Brooklyn accent, shouted, "Jeez, those tracers looked just like Luna Park!"*

We formed the chow line again and one fellow yelled to a friend, "What would you recommend as a good, safe place to eat?"

"Lindy's, at Fifty-first Street," the other soldier answered.

"The way the guys ran, it was like a Christmas rush at Macy's," somebody else said.

Everybody tried hard to be casual. Our appetites were even better than they had been before, the excitement having joggled up our internal

---

* See note on p. 202. Luna was an amusement park at Coney Island, so famous that it gave its name to imitations all over Europe. Fireworks were a nightly feature, but they were pretty pallid compared to any respectable anti-aircraft barrage. Luna is no more.

secretions. There were arguments about whether the plane that had escaped over the mountain would crash before reaching the German lines. I was scraping the last bits of stew from my mess tin with a sliver of hard biscuit when a soldier came up and told me that Major——,* whom I had never met, had been killed on the field, that five men had been wounded, and that one A-20 bomber had been ruined on the ground.

After I had washed up my tins, I walked over to the P-40 squadron operations shack, because I wanted to talk to a pilot familiarly known as Horse about a fight he had been in two days before. The day it had happened I had been visiting a P-38 squadron's headquarters on the field. I had seen eight P-38's go out to attack some German tanks and only five come back, two of them badly damaged. A lot of Focke-Wulf 190's had attacked the P-38's over the target, and Horse and three other P-40 pilots, who were protecting the 38's, had been up above the 190's. Horse was a big fellow with a square, tan face and a blond beard. He came from a town called Quanah, in Texas, and he was always showing his friends a tinted picture of his girl, who was in the Waves. Horse was twenty-five, which made him practically a patriarch in that squadron, and everybody knew that he was being groomed to command a squadron of his own when he got his captaincy. He was something of a wit. Once I heard one of the other boys say that now that the field had been in operation for six weeks, he thought it was time the men should build a sit-down latrine. "The next thing we know," Horse said, "you'll be wanting to send home for your wife."

I found Horse and asked him about the fight. He said he was sorry that the 38's had had such a bad knock. "I guess maybe it was partly our fault," he said. "Four of our ships had been sent out to be high cover for the 38's. They didn't see any 38's or Jerries either, so when their gas was beginning to run low they started for home.** Myself and three other fellows had started out to relieve them and we passed them as they came back. The 38's must have arrived over the tanks just then, and the 190's must have been hiding at the base of a cloud bank above the 38's but far below us. When we got directly over the area, we could see tracers flying way down on the deck. The 190's had dived from the cloud and bounced the 38's, who never had a chance, and the 38's were streaking for home. We started down toward the 190's, but it takes a P-40 a long time to get anywhere and we couldn't help. Then four more 190's dived from way up top and bounced us. I looped up behind one of them as he dived. My two wing men were right with me. I put a good burst into the sonofabitch and

---

* We were not allowed by the censor to mention names of casualties until they had appeared in the lists published at home. Now I cannot fill in this blank, because I forget the poor gentleman's name.
** See note p. 206 on confusion.

he started to burn, and I followed him down. I must have fired a hundred and twenty-five rounds from each gun. It was more fun than a county fair. Gray, my fourth man, put a lot of lead into another 190, and I doubt if it ever got home. The other two Jerries just kept on going."

The P-40 operations shack was set deep in the ground and had a double tier of bunks along three of its walls. Sand and grass were heaped over the top of the shack, and the pilots said that even when they flew right over it, it was hard to see, which cheered them considerably. The pilots were flying at least two missions a day and spent most of the rest of the time lying in the bunks in their flying clothes, under as many coats and blankets as they could find. The atmosphere in the shack was a thick porridge of dust diluted by thin trickles of cold air. Major Christman, the squadron leader, once said in a pleased tone, "This joint always reminds me of a scene in 'Journey's End.' "* The pilots, most of whom were in their earliest twenties, took a certain perverse satisfaction in their surroundings. "Here we know we're at war," one of them said to me. "Not that I wouldn't change for a room and bath at a good hotel."

During most of my stay at the field I lived not in the Journey's End shack but in one known as the Hotel Léon because technically it belonged to a French lieutenant named Léon,** a liaison officer between the French forces and our fliers. It was the newest and finest dugout on the field, with wooden walls and a wooden floor and a partition dividing it down the middle, and the floor was sunk about five feet below ground level. When I arrived at the field, there were plans to cover the part of the shack that projected above ground with sand, in which Léon intended to plant alfa. I was travelling with an Associated Press correspondent named Norgaard, and soon after our arrival Léon, a slender man with a thin, intelligent face and round, brown eyes, welcomed us to his palace. We put our stuff into the shack and emerged to find Léon throwing a modest shovelful of sand against one of the walls. Norgaard offered to help him. "There is only one shovel," Léon said with relief, pressing it into Norgaard's hands. "It is highly interesting for our comfort and safety that the house be covered entirely with sand. I am very occupied." Then he walked rapidly away, and Norgaard and I took turns piling sand around the Hotel Léon for endless hours afterward. Léon always referred to a telephone switchboard as a switching board, oil paper as oily paper, a pup tent as a puppy tent, and a bedding roll as a rolling bed.

After my talk with Horse, I walked over to the Hotel Léon and found it

---

* See note p. 202 on citations of the fictitious as criteria of reality.
** I suppressed his last name, Caplan, because he might have had relatives in France, who, if my piece in the *New Yorker* had reached France (highly unlikely), might have been made to suffer. Léon, when I saw him long after the war, was the number two man in the French Shell Oil Company—a *potentat petrolier*.

crowded, as it usually was. Only Léon and Norgaard and I, together with Major Philip Cochran and Captain Robert Wylie, lived in the hotel, but during the day Cochran and Léon used it as an office, and that was why it was crowded. When I first came to the field, it had been operating for six weeks practically as an outpost, for there was just a unit of American infantry, fifty miles to the southeast, between it and the region occupied by Rommel's army. Cochran, though only a major, had run the field for almost the entire period, but by the time I arrived he had reverted to the status of operations officer. The shack had telephone lines to detachments of French troops scattered thinly through the hills to our east, and they called up at all hours to tell Léon where German tanks were moving or to ask our people to do some air reconnaissance or drop bags of food to a platoon somewhere on a mountain. The French had no trucks to transport food. Sometimes Cochran flew with American transport planes to tell them where to drop parachute troops and sometimes he flew with bombers to tell them where to drop bombs. Because of Cochran's and Léon's range of activities, they always had a lot of visitors.

Attached to the partition in the shack were two field telephones, one of which answered you in French and the other in English. Two soldier clerks, who were usually pounding typewriters, sat on a bench in front of a shelf along one wall. One of them was Corporal Goldstein, the songwriter. The other was a private first class named Otto, who wore metal-rimmed spectacles with round lenses and belonged to the Pentecostal brethren, an evangelical sect which is against fighting and profanity. Otto owned some barber tools, and he cut officers' hair during office hours and enlisted men's at night. That morning he was cutting the hair of Kostia Rozanoff,* the commandant of the Lafayette Escadrille, a French P-40 outfit that was stationed at the field. Rozanoff was a blond, round-headed Parisian whose great-grandfather was Russian. Otto, perhaps taking a cue from the shape of Rozanoff's skull, had clipped him until he looked like Erich Von Stroheim, but there was no mirror, so Rozanoff was happy anyway. Cochran, dressed in a dirty old leather flying jacket, had just come back from a mission in the course of which he thought he had destroyed a 190, and was trying to tell about that while nearly everybody else in the shack was trying to tell him about the morning's strafing. Also in the shack was Colonel Edson D. Raff, the well-known parachutist, who had once unexpectedly found himself in command of all the American ground forces in southern Tunisia and for weeks had successfully bluffed enemy forces many times larger. He had flown in from his post in Gafsa in a small plane which he used as his personal transport. He was crowded in behind Otto's barbering elbow and was trying to talk to Cochran over Rozanoff's head. Raff is short and always wears a short carbine slung over his left shoulder, even indoors. He invariably flies very low in his plane

---

* Rozanoff survived to fly jets. He will recur.

to minimize the risk of being potted by a Messerschmitt. "I have one foot trailing on the ground," he says.

Lieutenant Colonel William Momyer, the commanding officer of the field, was sitting between Rozanoff and Corporal Goldstein, telling about a mission he had been on himself that morning, escorting a lot of A-20's over Kebili, a town where the Italians had begun to repair a dynamited causeway across the Chott Djerid. "I bet the wops will never get any workmen to go back to that place," Momyer said. "We scared hell out of them." Momyer had shot down a Junkers 88 and a Messerschmitt within a week. He was hot.

Among the others in the shack that morning were Norgaard, the Associated Press man, and a tall P-40 pilot named Harris, who kept asking Léon whether any French unit had telephoned to report finding the Messerschmitt he had been shooting at during the strafing episode, because he was sure it must have crashed. It was the Messerschmitt we had seen pull out of the spin over the mountain. The English-speaking telephone rang and Captain Wylie answered it. He has the kind of telephone voice that goes with a large, expensive office, which he probably had in civilian life. It was somebody up the line asking for Major ——, the officer who had just been machine-gunned in the strafing. "Major —— has been killed," Wylie said. "Is there anything I can do for you?"

There was a variety of stuff on the field when I was there. In addition to Christman's P-40 squadron and the Lafayette Escadrille, there was a second American P-40 squadron commanded by a Major Hubbard, which had a full set of pilots but only five ships. This was because the powers that be had taken away the other ships and given them to the Lafayettes in the interest of international good will. Hubbard's pilots were not sore at the Lafayettes, but they didn't think much of the powers that be. There was also a bomber squadron. The people on our field were not by any means sitting targets. They constantly annoyed the Germans, and that is why the Germans were so keen on "neutralizing" the field. But they didn't come back that day, and neither lunch nor dinner was disturbed.

The guests of the Hotel Léon often didn't go to the mess shack for dinner, because Léon would prepare dinner for them on the premises. He was a talented cook who needed the stimulation of a public, which was, that Monday evening, us. He also needed Wylie to keep the fire in the stove going, Cochran to wash dishes, and me and Norgaard to perform assorted chores. He got eggs from the Arabs and wine from a nearby French engineer unit, and he had gathered a choice assortment of canned goods from the quartermaster's stores. He also bought sheep and pigs from farmers. Léon's idea of a campaign supper was a *soufflé de poisson*, a *gigot*, and an *omelette brûlée à l'armagnac*. He made the *soufflé* out of canned salmon. The only trouble with dining at Léon's was that dinner was seldom ready before half past eight and it took until nearly midnight to clean up afterward.

During that Monday dinner we speculated on what the enemy would do next day. Norgaard said it was hell to have to get up early to catch the Germans' morning performance, but Cochran, the airfield's official prophet, and a successful one, said, "They'll want to make this one a big one tomorrow, so you can sleep late. They won't be over until two-thirty in the afternoon." Momyer, who was having dinner at the hotel that night, agreed that there would be something doing, but he didn't predict the time of day. Léon said, "I think also that there is something cooking in." Momyer decided to maintain a patrol of eight planes over the field all day. "Of course, maybe that's just what they want us to do, use our planes defensively, so we will fly less missions," he said, "but I think this time we ought to do it."

I had such faith in Cochran that it never occurred to me that the Germans would attack us before the hour he had named, and they didn't. The only enemy over the field the following morning was Photo Freddie, a German reconnaissance pilot who had become a local character. He came every morning at about forty thousand feet, flying a special Junkers 86 job so lightened that it could outclimb any fighter. The anti-aircraft guns would fire, putting a row of neat, white smoke puffs a couple of miles below the seat of Freddie's pants, the patrol planes would lift languidly in his direction, like the hand of a fat man waving away a fly, and Photo Freddie would scoot off toward Sicily, or wherever he came from, to develop his pictures, thus discovering where all the planes on the field were placed. The planes were always moved around after he left, and we used to wonder what the general of the Luftwaffe said to poor Freddie when the bombers failed to find the planes where he had photographed them. Now and then some pilot tried to catch Photo Freddie by getting an early start, climbing high above the field, and then stooging around until he appeared. Freddie, however, varied the hour of his matutinal visits, and since a P-40 cannot fly indefinitely, the pilot would get disgusted and come down. I do not think anybody really wanted to hurt Freddie anyway. He was part of the local fauna, like the pet hens that wandered about the field and popped into slit trenches when bombs began to fall.

At about twenty minutes past two that afternoon Norgaard and I returned to the Hotel Léon to do some writing. An Alsatian corporal in the French army was working in front of the shack, making a door for the entrance. The corporal had been assigned by the French command to build Léon's house, and he was a hard worker. He always kept his rifle by him while he was working. He had a long brown beard, which he said he was going to let grow until the Germans were driven out of Tunisia. Only Goldstein and Otto were inside the hut this time. I said to Goldstein,

"Why don't you write a new number called 'One-Ninety, I Love You'?" Otto, who had been reading the *Pentecostal Herald*, said, "I do not think that would be a good title. It would not be popular." At that precise moment all of us heard the deep woomp of heavy ack-ack. It came from one of the British batteries in the mountains around the field. We grabbed our tin hats and started for the doorway. By the time we got there, the usual anti-aircraft show was on. In the din we could easily distinguish the sound of our Bofors guns, which were making their peculiar seasick noises —not so much a succession of reports as one continuous retch. The floor of the shack, as I have said, was five feet below ground level and the Alsatian had not yet got around to building steps down to the entrance, so we had a nice, rectangular hole just outside from which to watch developments. The Germans were bombing now, and every time a bomb exploded, some of the sand heaped against the wooden walls was driven into the shack through the knotholes. The only trouble was that whenever a bomb went off we pulled in our heads and stopped observing. Then we looked out again until the next thump. After several of these thumps there was a straight row of columns of black smoke a couple of hundred yards to our right. I poked my head above ground level and discovered the Alsatian corporal kneeling and firing his rifle, presumably at an airplane which I could not see. The smoke began to clear and we hoisted ourselves out of the hole to try and find out what had happened. "I do not think I touched," the Alsatian said. A number of dogfights were still going on over the mountains. Scattered about the field, men, dragging themselves out of slit trenches, were pointing to the side of a mountain to the north, where there was smoke above a downed plane.

Léon had a little and old Citroën car, which he said had become, through constant association with the United States Army, "one naturalized small jeeps." He had left it parked behind the shack, and as Norgaard and I stood gawping about, Léon came running and shouted that he was going out to the fallen plane. We climbed into the naturalized jeeps and started across the field toward the mountainside. At one of the runways, we met a group of P-40 pilots, including Horse, and I yelled to them, "Was it theirs or ours?" "Ours, I think," Horse said. We kept on going. When we reached the other side of the field, we cut across country, and Léon could not make much speed. A couple of soldiers with rifles thumbed a ride and jumped on the running boards. As we went out across plowed fields and up the mountain toward the plane, we passed dozens of soldiers hurrying in the same direction.

When we arrived where the plane had fallen, we found three trucks and at least fifty men already there. The plane had been a Messerschmitt 109 belonging to the bombers' fighter escort. Flames were roaring above the portion deepest in the earth, which I judged was the engine. Screws, bolts, rings, and unidentifiable bits of metal were scattered over an area at least seventy-five yards square. Intermingled with all this were widely scattered red threads, like the bits left in a butcher's grinder when he has finished preparing an order of chopped steak. "He never even tried to pull out," a soldier said. "He must have been shot through the brain. I seen the whole thing. The plane fell five thousand feet like a hunk of lead." There was a sour smell over everything—not intolerable, just sour. "Where is the pilot?" Norgaard asked. The soldier waved his hand with a gesture that included the whole area. Norgaard, apparently for the first time, noticed the red threads. Most of the soldiers were rummaging amid the wreckage, searching for souvenirs. Somebody said that the pilot's automatic pistol, always the keepsake most eagerly sought, had already been found and appropriated. Another soldier had picked up some French and Italian money. How these things had survived the pilot's disintegration I do not know. While the soldiers walked about, turning over bits of the plane with their feet, looking for some object which could serve as a memento, an American plane came over and everybody began to run before someone recognized it for what it was. Just as we came back, a soldier started kicking at something on the ground and screaming. He was one of the fellows who had ridden out on our running boards. He yelled, "There's the sonofabitch's God-damn guts! He wanted my guts! He nearly had my guts, God damn him!" Another soldier went up to him and bellowed, "Shut up! It ain't nice to talk that way!" A lot of other men began to gather around. For a minute or so the soldier who had screamed stood there silently, his shoulders pumping up and down, and then he began to blubber.

Léon picked up a large swatch of the Messerschmitt's tail fabric as a trophy, and as the soldiers walked away from the wreck most of them carried either similar fragments or pieces of metal. After a while Norgaard and I climbed into Léon's car and the three of us started back toward the field. When we arrived, we learned that a lieutenant named Walter Scholl, who had never been in a fight before, had shot down the Messerschmitt. He was the fellow who, in the Cornell-Dartmouth football game of 1940, threw the famous fifth-down touchdown pass for Cornell, the one that was completed for what was considered a Cornell victory until movies of the game showed that it shouldn't have been Cornell's ball at all and the decision had to be reversed. But this was one win that they couldn't take away from him. Two other pilots had shot down two Junkers 88 bombers. One of our planes on the ground had been destroyed, and a slit trench had caved in on two fellows, nearly frightening them to death before they could be dug out.

NORGAARD often said that the country reminded him of New Mexico, and with plenty of reason. Both are desert countries of mountains and mesas, and in both there are sunsets that owe their beauty to the dust in the air. The white, rectangular Arab houses, with their blue doors, are like the houses certain Indians build in New Mexico, and the Arabs' saddle blankets and pottery and even the women's silver bracelets are like Navajo things. The horses, which look like famished mustangs, have the same lope and are similarly bridlewise; burros are all over the place, and so is cactus. These resemblances are something less than a coincidence, because the Moors carried their ways of house-building and their handicraft patterns and even their breed of horses and method of breaking them to Spain, and the Spaniards carried them to New Mexico eight hundred years later.[*] All these things go to make up a culture that belongs to a high plateau country where there are sheep to furnish wool for blankets and where people have too little cash to buy dishes in a store, where the soil is so poor that people have no use for heavy plow horses but want a breed that they can ride for long distances and that will live on nearly nothing.

"This horse is young," an Arab once said to Norgaard and me as he showed us a runty bay colt tied in front of a combined general store and barbershop in a village about a mile from the airfield. "If I had had a little barley to feed him, he would be bigger, but what barley we had we have ourselves eaten. It is a poor country."

We used to go down to this village to get eggs when we were too lazy to make the chow line for breakfast or when we felt hungry at any time of day. We'd take them back to the shack and cook them. Solitary Arabs squat along the roadside all over North Africa, waiting for military vehicles. When one comes into sight, the Arab pulls an egg out from under his rags and holds it up between thumb and forefinger like a magician at a night club. The price of eggs—always high, of course—varies in inverse ratio to the distance from a military post. Near big towns that are a long way from any post the Arabs get only five francs (ten cents at the new rate of exchange) for an egg, but in villages close to garrisons eggs are sometimes hard to find at any price. Norgaard and I followed a standard protocol to get them. First we went into the general store and barbershop, which was just a couple of almost empty rooms that were part of a mud house, and shook hands with all the male members of the establishment. Naturally, we never saw any of the females. Then we presented a box of matches to the head of the house, an ex-soldier who spoke French, and he invited us to drink coffee. The Arabs have better coffee and more sugar than the Europeans in North Africa. While we drank the coffee, we sat with the patriarch of the family on a white iron bed of European manufacture. The patriarch had a white beard and was always knitting socks; he stopped only to scratch himself. Once, as we were drinking coffee, we watched our French-speaking friend shave a customer's head. He simply started each stroke at the top of the cranium and scraped downward. He used no lather; the customer moistened his own poll with spittle

---

[*] The cactus, though, was imported *from* Latin America into North Africa, where it is considered a prime fodder plant, particularly appreciated by camels.

after each stroke of the razor. Once, when the customer made a particularly awful face, all the other Arabs sitting around the room laughed. During the coffee-drinking stage of the negotiations we presented the Arabs with a can of fifty English cigarettes. After that they presented us with ten to fifteen eggs. Soldiers who were not such good friends of theirs usually got twenty eggs for fifty cigarettes, but it always costs something to maintain one's social life. One day I asked the barber why the old man scratched himself, and he said, laughing, "Because of the black spots. We all have them, and they itch." With much hilarity the Arabs showed us the hard, black spots, apparently under their skins, from which they were suffering. I judged the trouble to be a degenerate form of the Black Death, tamed during the centuries by the rugged constitutions of our hosts. Norgaard thought that the spots were just chiggers.

The Germans had come over our airfield on a Monday morning and strafed it and they had come back on Tuesday afternoon and bombed the place. They were going to start an offensive in southern Tunisia, we later learned, so they wanted to knock out this, the most advanced American field. On Wednesday morning the Germans made no attack. That afternoon Norgaard and I decided that we needed some eggs, so we walked down to the Arab village. I carried the eggs home in my field hat, a visored cap which has long flaps to cover your neck and ears when it is cold and which makes a good egg bag. We got back to the Hotel Léon between five and six o'clock. Major Cochran was out flying, and Léon was out foraging. Jake and Otto had gone to chow. There was less than an hour of daylight left.

Cochran, with his fine instinct for divining what the Germans were likely to do, had been sure that they would come over for the third day in succession, and Lieutenant Colonel William Momyer, the commanding officer of the field, had maintained a patrol of P-40's over the field all day. Cochran was among those taking their turns on patrol duty now. In forty minutes more all the planes would have to come down, because the field had no landing lights. And nothing had happened yet.

The walk had made Norgaard and me hungry and we decided to have our eggs immediately. We threw some kindling wood in the stove to stir the fire up and I put some olive oil in the mess tin in which I was going to scramble the eggs. The olive oil belonged to Léon. I took the lid off the hole in the top of the stove, put the mess tin over the hole, and broke all the eggs into the oil. I think there were eleven of them. They floated around half submerged, and although I stirred them with a fork, they didn't scramble. We decided that I had used too much oil, so we added some cheese to act as a cement. Before the cheese had time to take effect, we heard a loud explosion outside—plainly a bomb—and felt the shack rock. Norgaard grabbed his tin hat and ran out the door to look, and I was just going to follow him when I reflected that if I left this horrible brew on the stove hole a spark might ignite the oil and thus set fire to the shack. I carefully put the mess on a bench and replaced the lid on the stove. I put on my helmet and followed Norgaard out into a kind of foxhole outside our door. More bombs exploded and then all we could hear was the racket of the Bofors cannon and .50 calibre machine guns defending the field. I went back inside, removed the stove lid, and put the eggs on again. Just as some warmth began to return to the chill mess, another stick of bombs went off. In the course of the next minute or so, I repeated my entire routine. Before I finished cooking dinner, I had to repeat it three times more. Finally the eggs and the cheese stuck together after a fashion and I drained the oil off. Then, since no bombs had dropped for a couple of minutes, I poured half the concoction into Norgaard's canteen cup, I put what was left in my mess tin, and we ate.

After we had eaten, we left the shack and started toward the large, round pit, some fifty yards away, which served as a control room for the field. Night had closed in. There had been no firing now for ten minutes, but as we approached the pit, our anti-aircraft opened up again, firing from all around the field simultaneously. The Bofors tracer shells, which look like roseate Roman candles, reminded me of the fireworks on the lagoon at the World's Fair in Flushing. The burst ended as abruptly as it had begun, except that one battery of .50's kept on for an extra second or two and then stopped in an embarrassed manner.

We saw a lot of our pilots clustered around the pit. A corporal named Dick usually stood in the pit talking to our planes in the air by radio telephone, but Major Robert Christman, the C.O. of one of the post's fighter squadrons, was in Dick's place. I recognized Christman's voice as he spoke into the telephone, asking, "Did you see the gunfire? Did you see the gunfire?" You wouldn't ask a Jerry that if you were shooting at him, so I knew they were firing the anti-aircraft guns to light one or more of our planes home. Christman asked again, "Did you see the gunfire? Did you see the gunfire?" Then he said to somebody else in the pit, probably Dick, "Hold this a minute." He stuck his head up over the side of the pit and shouted in the direction of a nearby dugout, "They say they saw the fire! Cochran's going to lead in and land to show the other ship the way! Lord, how that Cochran swears when he's excited! Tell the ack-ack to hold everything!" The switchboard through which the control room communicated with all the ack-ack batteries was in the dugout. Nothing was convenient on that field. It sometimes seemed that one of the pilots had scratched the whole thing out of the ground with a broken propeller blade after a forced landing.

We could see a plane showing red and green lights slowly circling over the field, descending gradually in long, deliberate spirals, as if the pilot wanted somebody to follow him. Then there was a blast of machine-gun fire and a fountain of tracers sprayed up from a distant edge of the field. "God damn them!" Christman yelled. "Tell them to hold that fire! What do they want to do—shoot Phil down?" The plane coasted slowly, imperturbably lower. It was Cochran's firm belief, I knew, that the ack-ack on the field had never hit anything, so he probably wasn't worried. The plane skimmed over the surface of the field. There was one pitiful red light on the field for it to land by. "He'll never make it that way," a pilot near me said. "What the hell is he doing? He'll overshoot. No, there he goes up again."

In a minute Christman, back at the phone once more, said, "Cochran went up because the other fellow couldn't see him. The other ship says he saw the gunfire, though. Now he wants a burst on the southern edge of the field only." Somebody in the switchboard dugout yelled, "Come on now! Battery C only, Battery C only! Everybody else *hold* it!" All the guns on the field immediately fired together. I could hear Momyer's voice yelling in the dugout, "God damn it, I'll have them all court-martialled!" Christman shouted, "He says he saw it and now he can see Cochran! He's coming in!" Cochran was again circling in the blackness above the field. The pilot next to me said, "This is sure sweating it out." I recognized him, partly by his voice and partly by the height of his shoulders, as Horse, the big Texan who wore a square beard.

"Did we get any of theirs?" I asked Horse.

"Yes, sir," Horse said. "Bent got one for sure. He's in already. And a French post has telephoned that another one is down near there in flames and that pilot out there with Cochran had one smoking. He must have chased it so far he couldn't get back before dark. Must have forgot himself. I don't rightly know who he is."

The ack-ack batteries fired again. They apparently did what was wanted this time, because nobody cursed. Christman called up from the pit, "They want one more burst, all together, and then they're coming in!" The message was relayed and the ack-ack fired another salvo. Now there were two planes, both showing lights, moving in the sky above the field, one high and one low. "Cochran's coming in," Horse said. "Look at him. Just like it was day and he could see everything." The lower pair of lights drifted downward, straightened out and ran forward along the field, and stopped. The other lights slowly followed them down, seemed to hesitate a moment, then slanted toward the ground, and coasted into a horizontal. "Good landing," Horse said. "We sure sweated that one." The second pilot to land turned out to be a lieutenant named Thomas, who had become too absorbed in the pursuit of a Junkers 88 to turn back until he had shot it down. That made three Junkers for us, each carrying a crew of four men. I learned that the German bombs had spoiled, to use the airmen's term, two of our planes on the field. A couple of minutes later a jeep that had gone out to meet Cochran's plane brought him to where the rest of us were standing. He is a short, box-chested man, and the two or three flying jackets he was wearing made him look shorter and stockier than he really is. He was feeling good. "I'm sorry I cursed you out, Bob! I was excited!" he yelled down into the control pit to Christman. Momyer, who had come out of the dugout, made as if to grab Cochran and hug him, but stopped in astonishment when he heard Cochran being so polite. It seemed to remind him of something. Looking rather thoughtful, he went back into the dugout and called up the lieutenant colonel in command of the ack-ack, which he had been abusing. "Thank you very much, Colonel," I heard him say. "Your boys certainly saved the day."

That evening was a happy one. Léon's shack was crowded with pilots talking about the successful fight and scrambling eggs and eating them out of mess tins. Cochran felt so good that he decided to have his first haircut since he had left New York three months before, so he sent over to the enlisted men's quarters for Otto to do the job. Otto is a young man with reddish hair and white eyebrows and a long nose, and he had a habit of getting interested in a conversation between two senior officers and breaking into it. Once, hearing Colonel Edson D. Raff, the parachute-troop commander, telling Lieutenant Colonel Momyer that he could take Tunis with no more than four hundred and fifty men, Otto blurted out, "How can you be so sure?" Aside from this failing he is a good soldier and when he gives a haircut he really cuts off hair, so nobody can say he is looking for a return engagement in the near future.

It was well after dark when Léon came in from his foraging, which had been a success too. "I have bought three small peegs," he announced triumphantly, "and when they are theek enough we shall eat them." He had left them in the care of a *hôtelier* in a town a few miles away. They were subsequently taken, and presumably eaten, by the Germans. At the time, however, Léon thought it a safe *logement* for the pigs. "I have also talked with the aide of General Koeltz," Léon said to Cochran and Momyer, "and he says that in the case any pilot sees any trucks moving on the road of which we have spoken yesterday, he is allowed to shoot without permission." While Otto cut Cochran's hair, we added up the box score of the three-day German attack on the field. The home team felt that it had done pretty well. During the Monday strafing the Germans had spoiled one of our planes on the field and another in the air and had killed one officer, a major, with machine-gun bullets. We had merely damaged one of their fighters. On Tuesday, while they had spoiled two more of our planes on the ground with bombs, we had shot down a Messerschmitt 109 and two Junkers 88's. That meant that we had lost a total of three planes but only one life while they had lost three planes and nine lives. One of our missions had also destroyed a Focke-Wulf 190 on Monday morning and a Messerschmitt had been badly damaged in the dogfight that had accompanied the strafing of our field. Wednesday evening we had destroyed three more planes and twelve men, and the Germans had succeeded only in damaging two planes on the ground, which gave us an imposing lead. "They won't be over tomorrow morning," Cochran said. "Maybe not all day. They'll want to think things over and try something big to make up for their losses and get the lead back. They'll be like a guy doubling his bet in a crap game."

That field had been fought over many times before in the course of history and a corner of it had been the site of a Numidian city. Bent, a pilot who talked with a British accent and had once done some digging among old ruins in England, said that every time he flew over that corner he could plainly see the gridiron pattern of the ancient streets on the ground. Horse, the bearded pilot, was irreverent about Bent's claims. "Maybe a couple of thousand years from now," he said, "people will dig around this same field and find a lot of C-ration cans that we've left and attribute them to archeology. They'll say, 'Those Americans must surely have been a pygmy race to wear such small helmets. It scarcely seems possible they had much brains. No wonder they rode around in such funny airplanes as the P-40.' "*

Another officer who turned up in Léon's shack that evening was Major (afterward Lieutenant Colonel) Vincent Sheean, who always points out these days that he was once a correspondent himself. He said he had been driving in a jeep on a road near the field when the bombing started, so he had stopped and jumped into a ditch. Sheean had come down from the second highest headquarters of the African Air Forces to see that the French pilots of the Lafayette Escadrille, which had recently arrived at our field, received understanding and kind treatment from their American comrades. A couple of the Lafayette pilots happened to be in the shack when he arrived; they had received so much kind treatment that they could hardly remember the words of "Auprès de Ma Blonde," which they were trying to teach to Momyer on a purely phonetic basis.

The next day, Thursday, was as quiet as Cochran had said it would be. The Germans left us completely alone. In the morning the Lafayette Escadrille fellows went on their first mission, covering a French local offensive in a mountain pass, and returned without meeting any enemy aircraft.

The exposed position of our mess shack had begun to worry Major Christman's men after the strafing we had received the Monday before, and he had ordered the chow line transferred to a place called the Ravine, a deep, winding gulch on the other side of the high road along one end of the field. Most of the men lived in the Ravine and felt safe there. They had scooped out caves in its sides and used their shelter halves to make doors. One stretch of the gully was marked by a sign that said "Park

---

* I was back in 1956, but even the C-ration cans are gone. The natives of those parts are extremely poor, and may have thought even tin cans worth salvaging.

Avenue." Sheean and I stood in the chow line for lunch and then took an afternoon stroll along Park Avenue. Afterward I went back to Léon's shack to write a letter and found it crowded, as usual. An engineer officer who had been at the field a couple of days was asking Cochran how he could be expected to get on with the construction job he had been sent there to do if new bomb holes appeared on the field every day and his detachment had to fill them up. "We've been filling up bomb holes ever since we been here, and it looks like we won't get a chance to do anything else," the engineer said. "My colonel sent me down here to build revetments for airplanes and he's going to expect me back soon." Another visitor, a captain in the Royal Engineers, asked him if there were any unexploded bombs on the runways. Men on the field always referred to this British captain as the booby-trap man, the planting of fiendish traps for the enemy being his specialty, and added with respect, "Even the parachute troops say he's crazy." He had made several jumps with Colonel Raff's parachutists to install his humorous devices in places where he thought German soldiers would later get involved with them. The American officer told him that there were several unexploded bombs on the runways and that he had marked off their positions with empty oil drums.

"But haven't you removed the fuses?" the booby-trap man asked with obvious astonishment.

"To hell with that!" his American colleague said with feeling. "They won't do any harm if they do go off. It's a big field."

"Oh, but they'll make quite a lot of noise," the booby-trap man said, still vaguely unhappy.

The American officer looked at the booby-trap man and Cochran as if they were both lunatics and went out of the hut without saying anything more. "How *extraordinary!*" the booby-trap man said. "He didn't even seem interested." He sounded hurt, like a young mother who has just learned that a visitor does not care for babies.

The booby-trap man looked like a conventional sort of Englishman, with a fair, boyish face and a shy smile. He spoke with the careful accent of the north countryman who has been to a university and he did not himself use the term "booby trap." He preferred to call his darlings, variously, trip mechanisms, push mechanisms, pull mechanisms, and anti-personnel switches. Trip mechanisms, for instance, are the ones soldiers inadvertently set off by stumbling over a concealed wire, and pull mechanisms are those they explode by picking up some innocent-seeming object like a corned-beef tin. The captain was an amateur botanist and seldom went out without a couple of pocketfuls of small devices to set about the countryside in likely spots as he ambled along collecting specimens of Tunisian grasses. I asked him that afternoon how he had started on what was to become his military career, and he said with his shy smile, "I expect it was at public school, when I used to put hedgehogs in the other boys' beds. After a while the hedgehogs began to pall and I invented a system for detuning the school piano, so that when the music master sat down to play 'God Save the King' it sounded god-awful."

"I sometimes try to imagine what your married life will be like, Captain," Cochran said. "Someday the baby will be in the crib and your wife will go to pick it up and the whole house will blow up because you've wired the baby to a booby trap."

"I trust I shall be able to restrain my professional instincts to fit the circumstances of domestic life," the booby-trap man said rather stiffly. He was a man who really took his branch of warfare seriously.

SLEEP in the Hotel Léon was usually interrupted in the gray hour before dawn by the jangle of a field telephone that spoke French. Then Léon would sit up and pull the telephone from the holster in which it hung at the foot of his bed. He slept wearing all the clothes he possessed, which included several sweaters, a long military overcoat, and a muffler. When he grabbed the phone, he would say, "Allo! Oui?" (The rest of us sometimes would sing "Sweet Allo, Oui" to the tune of "Sweet Eloise.") The French voice at the other end of the phone was almost always audible, and, so that the half-awake American officers in the shack would get the idea of what was going on, Léon would reply in a hybrid jargon. He would say, for example, "One *ennemi appareil* flying sousewest over point 106? *Merci, mon capitaine.*" Then he would hang up and fall back into bed, muttering, "*Imbécile*, why he don't fly west? He will be losted."

A partition divided Léon's shack into a bedroom, in which four of us slept side by side, and an office, in which only two slept. In the bedroom were Léon, Major Cochran, Norgaard, and myself. Captain Robert Wylie and Vincent Sheean slept in the office. We would try to ignore Léon's first morning call, but before long there would be another; Cochran would be asking what was going on, and we would hear the roar of the motors down on the field being warmed up for the dawn patrol and the morning missions. Then we would hear Wylie clattering around our stove in his G.I. shoes and there would be a glow in the shack when he put the match to the paper with which he started the fire. Wylie, who wasn't a flying officer, always tried to have the shack warm by the time Cochran got up, and he wanted the Major to stay in bed until the last minute. He was as solicitous as a trainer with a favorite colt, and the rest of us benefited from the care he took of Cochran, because we didn't get up early, either. Wylie is a wiry man with a high forehead and a pepper-and-salt mustache. He wears glasses and looks like an advertising artist's conception of an executive who is in good humor because he has had an excellent night's sleep owing to Sanka. He is a highly adaptable man. After Wylie had puttered around for a while, we would sit up one by one and stretch and complain about being disturbed or about the cold and then go outside to wash. Mornings on which the anti-aircraft opened up against early visitors, the tempo was accelerated. Cochran undressed at night by loosening the knot in his tie and drew it tight again in the morning as a sign that he was dressed. These were symbolic gestures he never omitted.

On the morning of the fifth and last day of our small private war, it was the anti-aircraft that brought us out of bed. We scrambled for the door, lugging our tin hats, our toothbrushes, and our canteens. The Germans were already almost over our field, but they were quite high, since our patrol planes had engaged them on the way in and they could not break off the fight to strafe us. The German planes were single-engined fighters, which sometimes carry wing or belly bombs, but this time they were not bombing. Some of the defending planes were marked with the tricolor *cocarde* of the French Army. It was, I suppose, a historic combat, because the pilots of the Lafayette Escadrille, which was stationed at the field, were making the first French air fight against the Germans since the armistice of 1940. The Escadrille, which had been equipped with a number of our Curtiss P-40's in Morocco, had been with us only a few days.

As we watched, a plane fell, apparently far on the other side of a ridge of mountains near the field, and we yelled happily, thinking it was a Messerschmitt. After the fight we were to learn that it had been a P-40 with a French sergeant pilot. Cochran kept up an expert running commentary on what all the pilots were trying to do, but he frequently didn't know which were French and which German. During the battle we simultaneously watched and brushed our teeth. A couple of the French planes landed on the field while the others were still fighting, so we knew that they must have been shot up. Finally, one group of planes above the field started away and the others chased them, but the first planes simply outclimbed their pursuers and left them behind; then there was no longer any doubt about which were Messerschmitts and which were Curtisses. One German plane remained over the field, at perhaps thirty thousand feet, even after the rest of the invaders had disappeared. "That's what kills me," Cochran said, pointing to the lone plane. "There's that sucker stooging around and casing the joint for a future job and he's so high nobody can bother him." Finally the stooge, evidently having found out all he wanted to know, took his leisurely departure.

A group of P-40's rose to relieve the Lafayettes, and the French planes came buzzing in like bees settling on a sugared stick. In a few minutes Kostia Rozanoff, commandant of the Escadrille, and his pilots had gathered in Léon's shack to discuss the fight. All of them had had combat experience in 1939 and 1940, but the engagement this morning had been the *rentrée*, and they were as excited as if they had never seen a Messerschmitt before. Despite the fact that they were old hands, Cochran said, they had fought recklessly, climbing up to meet the Messerschmitts instead of waiting until the Germans dived. "If they don't dive," Cochran had frequently warned his own pilots, "you just don't fight." The French

pilots' ardor had got them a beating, for besides the pilot whom we had
seen fall and who, Rozanoff said, had not bailed out and was quite certainly killed, the two planes that had landed during the combat were
riddled and would be of no use except for salvage, and one of their pilots
had been wounded. The Germans apparently had suffered no damage
at all. Rozanoff, a chunky, blond man who gets his name, as well as his
coloring and his high cheekbones, from his Russian ancestry, is thirty-
seven and has a deep voice, like Chaliapin's. He said that the pilot who
had been killed was his wing man and he could not understand how he
had failed to see the Messerschmitt that had attacked him from the rear.
"I cry him turn," Rozanoff kept saying. "I turn. He turns not. Poor little
one."

It was extremely sad that the first Escadrille combat had not been a
victory; it would have been such a fine story to bolster French morale all
over the world. I remembered the sergeant pilot, who had been a likable
fellow. An officer of the district gendarmerie brought the sergeant's wedding ring back to the field later in the morning.

My friend Norgaard and I had chosen that Friday for our departure
from the field. We were going in to the big city, where the censors and
the cable offices were, to write some stuff and get it off. There was air
transportation between our field and the more settled places to the west,
where staff officers and diplomats lived, but the service did not run on a
formal schedule. Big Douglas transports skimmed in over the mountains
once and sometimes twice a day, carrying mail and supplies, and they
usually had room for passengers going back. They came at a different
hour each day to make it as hard as possible for the Germans to waylay
them. When they came, they stayed merely as long as was necessary, and
the only way to be sure of a ride was to have your bedding roll made up
and to stay near the landing field waiting for the transports to appear.
When they did, an officer would drive you and your luggage out to them
in a jeep and you would get your stuff aboard. Norgaard and I hung
around in front of our shack that morning, waiting. As the day wore on, a
strong wind came up and blew great clouds of sand. At about eleven
o'clock two transports arrived, escorted by some Spitfires. Cochran had
planned to drive us down to the transports, but he was called to the
telephone, and Christman said that he would drive us instead.

When we arrived where the transports were standing on the runway,
the transport captain, whose name, I noted from the leather strip on the
breast of his flying jacket, was Lively, came over to the jeep and asked
where his Spits could get gas. His ship was named the Scarlett O'Hara.
He and Christman started discussing what was the quickest way to get
the gas. Christman and Norgaard and I stayed in the jeep. Dust was

blowing over the field a mile a minute. Suddenly Christman looked over his shoulder, called on God, and vanished. Within a moment Lively was also gone. I turned around to speak to Norgaard, and discovered that he too had evaporated. I hate to sit in an empty jeep when I don't know why the other passengers have jumped. I do not remember actually getting out myself, but I know that I was already running when I heard somebody yell, "Hit the dirt!" Under the circumstances, this sounded so sensible that I bellyflopped to the ground, and I landed so hard that I skinned my knees and elbows. No surface in the world offers less cover than a runway. I regretted that my body, which is thick, was not thinner. I could guess what had happened: German strafers had ridden in on the dust storm and nobody had seen them until they opened fire. I knew that the very nasty noises above me were being made by airplane cannon and that the even nastier ones close to me came from the detonation of the small explosive shells they fire. The strafers, I figured, were heading for the transports—large, expensive, unarmored jobs that you could punch holes in with a beer-can opener. I was therefore in line with the target and was very sorry to be where I was.

As soon as there was a lull in the noises overhead, I got up and ran toward the edge of the runway to get away from the transports, but more noises came before I made it, so I flopped again. After they had passed, I got up and ran off the runway. I saw a soldier in a fine, large hole nearly six feet deep. He shouted, "Come right in, sir!" You can have Oscar of the Waldorf any time; I will always remember that soldier as my favorite host. I jumped in and squeezed up against him. Almost immediately the noises came a third time and two transport pilots jumped down on my back. I was astonished that I had been able to outrun such relatively young men. I was 38.

By this time all of our machine guns along the edges of the field were firing away, and there was a fourth pass, as the fliers say, and a loud crash, as if one of the Germans had dropped a bomb. A minute or two later the noise began to die down. Looking up from the bottom of the hole, we could see a man descending in a parachute. The big, white chute was swaying this way and that in the wind. The man had an awful time landing. We could see that even from a distance. The chute dragged him and bounced hell out of him after he landed. Afterward, word got around the field that he was an American. I didn't find out until a couple of days later, though, that the man with the chute had been Horse. In landing, he hit his head against the ground and suffered a concussion of the brain. They put him in an ambulance and started for the nearest hospital, which was forty miles by road, but he had bad luck. The Germans had been strafing that road, too, that morning, and when the ambulance got within five miles of the hospital, it was blocked by two burning ammunition trucks. The shells on the trucks were exploding. The squadron surgeon and the ambulance-driver put Horse on a stretcher and carried him around the trucks to a safe point on the other side, and an ambulance from the hospital came out to pick him up, but by the time it got there he was dead.*

When the shooting at the field was over, the pilots and the soldier and I got out of the hole and walked back toward the transports, which were still there. Norgaard climbed out of another hole not far away. He said that when he had jumped out of the jeep he had crawled under it, and there he had found a transport lieutenant who had had the same idea. They had given up the jeep after the first pass and run for it, just as I had already done. We stared at the parallel furrows the Messerschmitt cannon had plowed down the runway, as if they had been the teeth of a rake, and ourselves the field mice between them. The transport boys borrowed our jeep to get gas for the Spits, which had been immobilized during the raid because their tanks were empty. When the boys came back, we climbed into one of the transports. The big planes took off almost immediately. "Leave them laughing," Norgaard said to me when he recovered sufficient breath to say anything.

We learned later that the strafing had been done by eight Messerschmitts flying in four loose pairs, and that was why there had been four passes. Another Messerschmitt, making a run by itself, had dropped one bomb, ineffectually. There had also been a high cover of Messerschmitts; one of them had accounted for Horse. We were told that Cochran had said, with a hint of admiration in his voice, "It is getting so that the Germans patrol our field for us." A lot of Air Force generals who were on a tour of inspection visited the field shortly after we left, said that the situation was very grave, and left, too. This point in the war over the field may be compared to the one in a Western movie at which the villain has kicked hell out of the heroine and just about wrestled her to the brink of ruin in a locked room.**

At about two-thirty that same afternoon the Lafayette Escadrille was patrolling the field, in the company of two pilots from the American P-40 squadron commanded by Major Hubbard. This squadron had its full complement of pilots but only five planes. The pilots took turns flying the five ships, so they were not getting a great deal of practice. Nevertheless, Hubbard's squadron had already scored two victories that week. The two American pilots in the air were Hubbard and a man named Beggs. Two of their mates, Boone and Smith, were on the ground on alert call, sitting in their planes ready to reinforce the patrol if they were called.

* Horse's square name was Alton B. Watkins, but hardly anybody at Thélepte knew. Father McCreedy buried him under a metal plate marked "Horace."
** See note on p. 202.

This field didn't have one of those elaborate radio airplane-detectors that warn swank airdromes of the approach of enemy aircraft. It had to rely on its patrol system and on tips that watchers telephoned in. The tipsters were not infallible, as Norgaard and I had noticed that morning, and in the afternoon they slipped up again. Ten Junkers 88 bombers unexpectedly appeared, flying toward the field at three thousand feet. There was an escort of four fighters, unusually small for so many bombers, flying high above them and, as someone described it to me, acting oddly uninterested. The Frenchmen on patrol, also flying high, made one swipe at the escort and it disappeared, not to be seen again. Nine of the bombers were flying in three loose V's and one ship was trailing the third V. Hubbard took the bomber on the right of the first V and shot it down. Beggs got the middle one and a Frenchman knocked down the one on the left. The other Junkers had begun to drop their bombs. Boone and Smith came up off the field through the falling bombs to join the battle. Hubbard shot down another plane, and Boone, who had never fired a shot at a man or a plane before, came up behind one Junkers and blasted it out of the sky; it caromed against another Junkers on the way down, which gave Boone two planes with one burst of fire. He went on to destroy two more. Smith, opening fire at extreme range for fear that he would be shut out, blew the rudder off another Junkers, which also crashed. The tenth Junkers headed for home, but it never got there; the French picked off that one. It was the jack pot, ten out of ten. It was also the end of the five-day war over our airfield. No producer of Westerns ever wound up a film more satisfactorily.* The Germans stayed away, in fact, for nineteen days and then came back only once, for a quick sneak raid.

Of the ten German bomber crews, only four men came out of the fight alive and two of these died in the hospital. The two others said that the ten bombers had been escorted by four Italian Macchi C. 202 fighters, which had deserted them. Why the Luftwaffe should have entrusted four Macchis with the protection of ten Junkers 88's is harder to explain than the result. The Germans, fortunately for our side, sometimes vary their extreme guile with extreme stupidity.

I didn't have a chance to return to the airfield for about ten days, and then I stopped in on my way down to Gafsa, where the Americans were supposed to be launching a ground offensive. Captain Wylie, who told me about the big day at the field, said that Boone had come into the operations shack looking rather incredulous himself. "Probably I'm crazy," he had said to Wylie, "but I think I just shot down four planes."** The Frenchmen thought up a gag. They said it was a victory for three nations

---

* See note on p. 202. From here on, I will cease to call attention to this phenomenon.
** His luck did not last. He was killed a couple of weeks later.

—"The Americans shot down seven planes, we shot down two, and the Italians shot down the tenth so the crew couldn't tell on them."

The Americans left the field undefeated, for the two P-40 squadrons were relieved not long afterward by other outfits and sent back from the fighting zone to rest. Christman's squadron had been fighting there steadily for two months. I met the fellows from Christman's bunch again while I was trying to get a ride into civilization from another airfield, a bit west of the one where they had been stationed. A lot of trucks drove up and deposited the officers and men of the squadron on the field, with their weapons, their barracks bags, and their bedding rolls. Christman was there, and Private Otto, the squadron barber, and Corporal Jake Goldstein, the reformed songwriter. I renewed my acquaintance with a pilot named Fackler, whom I remembered especially because he had once, finding himself flying formation with two Messerschmitts who thought he was another Messerschmitt, shot one of them down, and I again met Thomas, the Oklahoma boy who had been lost in the air one night and had been lighted home by the fire of the field's anti-aircraft guns, and a non-flying lieutenant named Lamb, who used to practice law in New York, and a dozen others. I felt as if I had known them all for a long time.

Eleven transports came in to take the squadron west, and I arranged to travel in one of them. I was in the lead ship of the flight, and the transport major who commanded it told me that his orders were to drop the squadron at a field only about an hour's flight away. Then the transports would go on to their base, taking me along with them. It was pleasant to see the faces of the P-40 boys aboard my transport when it took off. They didn't know anything about the field they were going to, but they knew that they were going for a rest, so they expected that there would at least be huts and showers there. They looked somewhat astonished when the transports settled down in a vast field of stubble without a sign of a building anywhere around it. There were a few B-25 bombers on the field and in the distance some tents. A transport sergeant came out of the pilot's compartment forward in our plane and worked his way toward the tail of our ship, climbing over the barracks bags heaped in the space between the seats. "I guess this is where you get out," he told the P-40 fellows.

A couple of soldiers jumped out and the rest began passing out bags and rifles to them. Pretty soon all the stuff was piled outside the plane and the soldiers were standing on the field, turning their backs to a sharp wind and audibly wondering where the hell the barracks were. A jeep with an officer in it drove out from among the tents and made its way among the transports until it arrived at our ship. The transport major talked to the officer in the jeep, and then they both drove over to the transport Christman was travelling in and picked him up, and the three of them drove back to the tents. Some soldiers who had been near the jeep had heard the field's officer say that nobody there had been notified that they were coming. The transport major had replied that all he knew was that he had orders to leave them there. The soldiers who had heard the conversation communicated the news to the others by Army telegraphy. "Situation normal!"* one soldier called out, and everybody laughed. Soldiers are fatalistic about such situations.

Some time before a report had circulated among the men that the squadron was to go back to the United States. Now I heard one soldier say, "This don't look like no United States to me."

Another one said, "When we get back there, Freddie Bartholomew will be running for President." He didn't seem sore.

Somebody said, "I hear they're going to start us here and let us hack our way through to South Africa."

Somebody else began a descant on a favorite Army fantasy: what civilian life will be like after the war. "I bet if my wife gives me a piece of steak," he said, "I'll say to her, 'What the hell is this? Give me stew.' "

Another one said, "I bet she'll be surprised when you jump into bed with all your clothes on."

The delicacy of their speculations diminished from there on.

After a while the jeep came back. The transport major got out and said, "There seems to be some mistake. You'd better put your stuff back in the ship." We all got back into the planes, and the major told me that this obviously wasn't the place to leave the men but that he would have to wait until base operations could get headquarters on the telephone and find out their destination. We sat in the planes for an hour; then another officer came out in a jeep and said that nobody at headquarters knew anything about the squadron, so the major had better not take it any place else. The major told his sergeant to instruct the men to take their luggage off the planes. "We enjoy doing this. It's no trouble at all," one of the soldiers in my plane said. The transports took off and left them standing there. I learned later that they eventually got straightened out. After two or three days someone at headquarters remembered them; the pilots were sent to western Morocco and the ground echelon was moved to another field.

All this happened what seems now to be long ago, in the pioneer days of the American Army in Tunisia. The old field, from which I had watched the five-day war, was never knocked out from the air, but it was taken by German ground troops with tanks, and then the Americans took it back and went on. The Hotel Léon, if the Germans hadn't burned it, was certainly full of booby traps for the Americans when they got there. I shouldn't like to have slept in it. Léon is now in a large Algerian city, where he has been assigned to a calmer liaison job. Cochran was promoted and decorated and posted to a new command.**

* See note on confusion p. 206.
** He is now back in Erie, Pa.

P. S. on Rozanoff in 1954

There are lines you pick up from a particular person that become parts of your habitual repertory. They have associations that keep them bright for you, but they sound so flat you feel called upon to explain what once made them seem funny. For example, I sometimes say between drinks: "It is better as a kick in za pants, so say my grandmozaire."

This expression never tickles anybody else, but it evokes the image of a round, pink Slavic face with a roof of yellow hair like the down on an Easter chick—the face of Kostya, le Commandant Rozanoff—and a conversational voice precisely like the old basso Chaliapin's.

Rozanoff would knock off three ounces of straight whiskey in a gulp. He was what old bartenders call a lip drinker: When he had got the edge of the vessel against his lower lip, he would throw his head back and the drink over his tongue and down. Then he would intone his cherished line of what he believed to be American, and hold out his canteen cup for more whiskey. The rest of his English was negligible. I forget how the alternation began—with the jest or the gesture—but it usually continued until the pink face blurred before my eyes. He was invincible.

Rozanoff fondled the illusion that all Americans drank their whiskey straight and in the manner he practiced. Like the grandmozaire gag, it was part of the tradition of his squadron in the Armée de l'Air, les Sioux, pronounced, under another misapprehension, "Syukes." (They assumed, apparently, that Americans would sound the "x," and they wanted to say it the American way.) The original members of the squadron, in World War I, had been American volunteers, and after they went, the squadron had kept the name, the insigne, and its concepts of American customs. The insigne, an Indian head in full war bonnet, was painted on the American P-40 that Rozanoff got out of when I first met him—at Thélepte, in January, 1943. "Rozanoff," he said, shaking hands, and then, before even declaring himself conventionally enchanted: "These machines respond to the controls too slowly, and then react too violently." He had been a test pilot before the war, and the habit stuck. When I met Rozanoff, he commanded a group of nine French pilots who had been assigned new P-40s at Casablanca. From Casa, they had flown toward the front, with a stop at Algiers to refuel. But only seven arrived at Thélepte.

Rozanoff told me that evening that he was thirty-eight, and when I relayed the information to some of our young pilots, they were gloomy, because we were short of planes at that field and they thought it wasteful to let a man so old fly a new fighter. "His reflexes are just too slow for three hundred miles an hour," they said. (They were flattering the P-40 slightly.) Ten years later, I read in a French magazine that Rozanoff, the leading test pilot of France, had hit eight hundred and thirty-seven in a Mystère IV, the new French jet. He had pierced the sound barrier—

horizontally, not diving—five times in a single flight. Most of the young pilots who had survived the war considered themselves middle-aged by that time. It cheered me no end, especially considering the training regime of the Commandant, who had in the intervening years become the Colonel.

A few weeks ago, I saw on page 6 of the Sunday New York *Times* a headline that puzzled me for a moment:

FRENCH JET CRASH
PERILS MINISTERS

I don't like "perils" as a verb, although as I have ascertained it is in Webster's Unabridged. What was more important, I couldn't understand at first glance how a jet crash could "peril" a passenger. It would kill him. This was a momentary obtuseness. The Ministers had not been in the plane. The bank of the head explained:

PLANE PARTS FALL NEAR PLEVEN
AND BRITISH SUPPLY CHIEF—
NOTED PILOT IS KILLED

The lead said parts of the plane had fallen "about fifty yards" from the statesmen, which didn't excite me unduly. But the second paragraph began, "Col. Constantin Rozanoff, 49 years old, who was at the controls of the Mystère IV, France's latest jet, met instant death." Kostya is the diminutive for Constantin. I remembered Kostya had told me his grandparents were Russian and he was French. The *Times* said he was a native of Poland; his birth may have occurred during the family's westward migration.

Kostya had been showing off the plane before the visiting officials, including a British air marshal. I imagine he had wanted the R.A.F. to be stunned with admiration. Skimming the ground, he would have allowed a clearance of about one centimetre, if I knew him. I was happy to see he had not been at fault personally. "The plane encountered a strong gust of wind, one wing touched the ground, and the craft crashed, exploded, and burst into flames. Parts were hurled in all directions." It would have pained Kostya to think he was losing his touch, but winds at an altitude of almost nothing are unpredictable. From an air-mail copy of *Le Monde* that I saw a couple of days later, I learned that the French had been showing the British their jets with a view to selling them some. Kostya had been doing eleven hundred kilometres—six hundred and eighty-four miles—an hour.

While I was still reading the *Times* story, however, I didn't know about Kostya's added incentive. There was a picture that showed him wearing one of the enormous helmets that make all jet pilots look like hydrocephalics. The Indian head, his old talisman, was clearly visible on its front. Kostya was sitting in a cockpit, reaching down over the side, and some joker was handing him up a building brick, to celebrate his first crash through the "wall" of sound.

The joke was in Rozanoff's own vein. I remembered the time in Africa when a French division commander, General Welvert, fifty miles away, learned of the presence of Kostya and his pilots at the American field, and decided this gave him a private air force. The General telephoned an order for le Commandant Rozanoff to wait on him immediately. Rozanoff was too busy, fighting two or three times a day; besides, he had no idea of putting himself under the orders of a ground-force general. When Rozanoff didn't show up, the General sent over a message, by hand, ordering him to consider himself under arrest. Kostya got down into his hole so that only his head showed above ground at the entrance. He held two sticks vertically in front of his face and made a horrendous grimace. One of his pilots took a photograph of him that way, and they sent it over to the *divisionnaire* with the message "The Commandant Rozanoff in prison, at the orders of General Welvert." Old Welvert had had no right to send for him, of course. It was a time when all French generals were trying to accumulate as much authority as possible against the day when Giraud's people and de Gaulle's people would have to share the marbles. That was a day Welvert never lived to see; he was killed by a mine in the spring offensive. (An Algerian infantryman in one of his battalions was named Ahmed Ben Bella.)

Nobody could say Kostya didn't have a sense of humor. During the winter of the war that turned out not to be phony, he once told me, the French shot down a Messerschmitt of a new mark in the area between the two armies in Lorraine. The pilot had bailed out before the plane hit. By a lucky chance, it was not a complete wreck. The Army of the Air had a curiosity to examine a Messerschmitt of this latest edition; Rozanoff therefore went out into the disputed land to repair the plane. He worked at night under a tarpaulin, to hide his light, and slept under the wings by day. After several nights, he had repaired the engine, and one dawn he took off for France. But as he prepared to land on the airfield at Toul, the French ack-ack opened up and shot the unannounced Messerschmitt full of holes. He had to bail out, like the German pilot before him, and the plane crashed "in much worse state than before"—an irretrievable mess. He thought it very funny. "It is better as a kick in za pants," he said, and we had a drink on his adventure.

Kostya lived through a difficult time at Thélepte, until the victory over the ten bombers made everybody happy. He and his brother pilots had been, as I've said, members of the old Armée de l'Air. They had flown their planes to Africa after the debacle of 1940 in the belief the French government would continue the war. But when Pétain surrendered the empire, they had not skipped out to join de Gaulle. So their will to fight the Germans was still in question when I first met them. The seven out of nine who arrived at the field with the P-40s must have suspected the reason for the non-appearance of the two others, but they dared not admit their suspicion, even to themselves. Consequently, Rozanoff made constant inquiries about the two men, unreported since Algiers. Was it possible, he would ask, that there had been an unobserved air action deep in Allied territory in which they had been shot down, or that they had made a forced landing in the mountains and nobody had found them? "They were experienced pilots," he would say. "They had plenty of fuel. It is inconceivable that they lost their way." In fact, as we learned later, the two men had flown their planes to Vichy France and delivered them to the Pétainists.

I gather my memories of Rozanoff as the infantrymen gathered up the pilot's ring and papers. He was a barrel-chested man, and even in 1943 the barrel had begun to slip. The piece in *Le Monde* said that with the years he had developed *"une certaine corpulence."* He wore a dirty leather flying jacket, like everybody else at Thélepte, but he topped it with a visored blue cap circled with gold braid. His movements were brusque, his forms of speech were vigorous rather than graceful. *"Il manque d'élégance,"* the French liaison officer at the field complained, and I was constrained to agree.

In the early spring of 1944, I was coming out of a newsreel theatre in Piccadilly when I saw a French aviator in a bus queue. I was with a pretty girl in a becoming blue uniform, and this type in the bus queue made her the eye. I regarded him with resentment, and then I saw it was Kostya, in a blue uniform storm coat, blue trousers, black shoes—completely regulation. He was a lieutenant colonel. He told me that after the African campaign he had been promoted and attached to the staff of the new French Air Force, which incorporated both de Gaullist and Giraudist elements. De Gaulle had by that time solidly established his leadership. Kostya said that he was testing planes again, and was happy. We made a date to have lunch at the *popote* of the staff, which was in South Kensington.

The lunch was gay. We drank a fair amount of cognac, and then I invited Kostya and some other officers, one of whom was the novelist Joseph Kessel, to accompany me to a remarkable club of which I was a member. The club was called Frisco's; it was in Sackville Street, in a bomb-damaged retail shop whose glassless windows were masked with heavy cardboard. The secretary and proprietor was Frisco, an American Negro legally named Bingham. Like hundreds of other such clubs in London, it was licensed to sell to members and guests during the afternoon hours, when ordinary pubs were shut. Its remarkable feature was the amount of whiskey Frisco was able to lay hands on in a period when even the best hotel bars gave clients a grim choice between gin and sobriety. In 1944, Frisco's was usually full of colored American soldiers, who ran a continuous jam session on an old piano. The secretary took on all comers at darts, and since he had the advantage of thirty years' expatriate practice, he cleaned up.

Kostya, rendered ecstatic by the presence of so much whiskey, shouted, "It is better as a kick in za pants, so say my grandmozaire!" as soon as he got his hand around a glass. Then he emptied the glass. His war cry rang out again, above the notes of "Don't Get Around Much Any More" in intricate syncopation from the old piano. At first, his cries were intermittent but regular, like the call of the bobwhite. Then they became more rapid and, finally, just about continuous. Kessel and I tried to fly on his wings, but he lost us. After the fourth drink, Kessel was flying blind, and I, a mere groundling, was in a spin. "Better as a kick, better as a say, better as my grandmozaire's pants." It was all a blur.

There was a crash. I had preceded Kostya through the sound barrier by eight years.

I never saw him again, and now I never will.

30 / First Act at Gafsa

GAFSA, the Capsa of the Numidians, is a very ancient town on a very slight hill. Warm springs gush from the foot of the hill under a fifteenth-century Arab citadel, which was wrecked by our engineers last February. The citadel was still intact when I first saw the place. There is an oasis around the town, which used to be an important knot in the cord of caravan routes between the Sahara and the Mediterranean. Gafsa had last winter, and by now probably has again, about ten thousand inhabitants, of whom five or six hundred are Europeans, eight hundred are native Jews, and the rest Arabs. The male Europeans, some of whom have their families with them, are government functionaries or employees of the railroad; the Jews, whose ancestors came there not a great while after the Destruction of the Temple, are traders and traditionally middlemen between the Christians and Moslems.

The climate there even at the end of January, when Norgaard and I reached the place, was warm and dry. A battalion of the Twenty-sixth Infantry was stationed in the town, with some batteries of French 75's, a battalion of Senegalese, and some Algerians, Zouaves, or Tirailleurs. The

Americans, who were out of the First Division, were the only ground troops we had south of Sbeitla, which was about fifty miles away. They had been there for a month and were quite at home in the place, which, as almost every enlisted man you talked to was sure to say, looked like a set in a *Beau Geste* movie of the Foreign Legion. Old Jews sold surprisingly good native pastries, and Arabs peddled dates in the square in front of the American barracks. The soldiers had adopted Arab kids as mascots and clothed them in G.I. shirts and shoes. There was a great outdoor Roman swimming pool, filled by running warm water from the spring, which had a good deal of sulphur in it but was still pleasant to bathe in, and the Americans spent a lot of time swimming in it. The French soldiers preferred to dangle fishlines into the stream near its source and catch small blue fish, extremely voracious, which apparently were used to living in hot water. There was also a clean Arab bath, in a narrow *Arabian Nights* alley, where the attendants would stretch you on the floor and twist your arms and legs out of joint and then pound you with a hot brick before allowing you to steam yourself in peace. I remember seeing the English booby-trap man, pink and jolly from the steam, in the Arab bath, wearing a towel around his loins. People leave you with curious last pictures of them, in a war.

The men of the Twenty-sixth had carried out numerous raids against Italian detachments that occasionally appeared in the no man's land to the east, between Gafsa and Maknassy. Neither adversary had any fixed garrison in this flat, desolate stretch of about seventy miles. Once the fellows from Gafsa had bagged eighty-four prisoners—that was reckoned a big haul for southern Tunisia in January. But during the entire night that followed the arrival of Norgaard and myself the sound of armored vehicles moving into and through the town never ceased; morning found most of the First Armored Division in readiness for the big thrust to the sea we had heard about.

Here, in the words of the old Yorkshire song, is where we get our own again. Earlier in the book I have described the fight that Norgaard and I saw between Gafsa and Sened, and I can continue here from the end of it. After we returned from the battlefield and heard that the offensive had been countermanded and our 200-odd casualties would apparently have to be written off to training, we went over to the mess of a French battery to have dinner. The battery was commanded by a captain named O'Neill, whose family had emigrated to France from Ireland in the seventeenth century. He looked like a conventional O'Neill, blue-eyed and florid and saddle-nosed, but he spoke English to Norgaard with a heavy French accent. Captain O'Neill had a battery of three guns, one of the original four having been found useless, and he had as prime mover for the three guns one old motor truck that burned alcohol, so the battery moved in installments, one gun at a time. Their shooting, he said, was very good, but they never arrived at any place in time to shoot. We showed up at the mess before O'Neill and his officers, who were accustomed to dining late, whereas American Army chow is usually dished up early. A young native Jew who wore a blue beret and a European business suit invited us into his house for an *apéritif* while we waited. He had delicate Arab features and eyes as blue as O'Neill's, and he spoke excellent French.

The Jew's one-story house was large and square, with thick mud walls to insulate it from the summer sun. It was built around a small circular court that let in air and daylight. The house looked ageless, like most of the others in town; the Numidians had probably built in exactly the same fashion—but the rooms leading off the court were wired for electric light and filled with heavy gaudy contemporary furniture from some factory in Europe. The Jew's ancient bearded father, who spoke no French, and his small, comely brunette wife and gray-eyed daughter kissed our hands. He poured sweet wine for us and gave us olives and sliced turnips pickled in lemon. His name was Chemouni. When a servant who had been left on watch outside came in and told us that O'Neill had arrived, we left the Chemounis, feeling faintly embarrassed by their fervor. I remembered them a few weeks later, when I heard that we had abandoned Gafsa to the advancing Germans and Italians.

At Gafsa, Norgaard and I slept without blankets on the concrete floor of a former French barracks. A captain in a regiment of armored infantry had spread his bedding roll in a corner of the same building. His regiment was not in the fighting; he had been sent up by his colonel as some sort of observer. The captain was a Virginian; he and Norgaard got to talking about a book by Douglas Freeman, called *Lee's Lieutenants,* that they had both read. The captain, like us, had been out on the battlefield, observing. He seemed pretty tired. He said that he knew old Freeman well; the author was a friend of the captain's family, and as a boy the captain had accompanied the already adult writer on long rambles over the Virginia battlefields. The captain told us he had a house at Yellow Tavern, where Jeb Stuart had been killed. There were Yankee musketballs imbedded in the stair rails, he said. "People down in my part of the country talk about battles as if they were some kind of fine antique, like old lace," he said. "I always used to daydream about them as a kid. But, my God, if I'd known a battle was like this——"

It reminded me of Stendhal writing in his diary: "All my life I have longed to be loved by a woman who was melancholy, thin, and an actress. Now I have been, and I am not happy."

Next morning every soldier in town knew that the offensive had been called off. A part of the armor had already pulled out during the night, roaring north on the road to Feriana and Sbeitla. But the troops who had taken Sened Station held it firmly. We heard that there were captured enemy guns and tanks there, and since captured matériel, like

prisoners in quantity, was still a novelty at that stage of the campaign, Norgaard wanted to drive out to have a look. As soon as we had got out on
the naked road between Gafsa and Sened both of us, I think, were again
sorry we had quit the shade of the palm trees and anti-aircraft guns. The
hot metallic sky that it hurt your eyes to look into hung over the road and
weighed down on your brain with its implicit Messerschmitts; every
group of tanks or guns you met parked off the road seemed an invitation
to air attack, and you hurried to get away from it. Then, until you
reached the next collection of armor, you felt lonely. Signs along the road
warned drivers to keep a 300-yard interval and look out for strafers.
Sometimes as we passed an outfit we would see a man off by himself
squatting on his hunkers and looking up into the sun, his right hand
shielding his eyes, afraid to concentrate entirely on his most personal
functions.

There was no temptation to drive across fields as we got close to Sened,
for the fields had almost certainly been mined by the retreating enemy.
Sened Station was sinister—a wooden *gare* full of wasps' nests, a *buffet,*
in a separate building, which two of our booby-trap captain's noncoms
were busily rigging with their trip wires, as happy as parents decorating a
Christmas tree, three or four buildings, a water tower, and a church, all
shattered by shellfire. The booby-trap men at work meant that we in our
turn were going to abandon the place almost immediately. You don't
booby-trap where you are going to stay. We talked to the trappers, both
Royal Engineers, one of whom was carrying so many one-pound cakes of
dynamite under one arm that they seemed always on the point of wriggling loose. It looked like coarse white laundry soap. "Lord love you, sir,
it wouldn't explode if it did fall, not without a deetonyter, it wouldn't," he
said. They wore a fixed, slightly fatuous smile which seemed a mark of
their curious vocation. "We 'ad some nasty ones to tike up before we put
ours in," the man with the dynamite said. "We've rearrynged them so
Jerry will 'ave a time with them, when 'e comes back. 'E won't be surprised, not 'alf."

There were three American medium tanks in a triangle where the main
road went by the station, looking as if they had been punched clean
through and then ripped with a giant can opener. Armor-piercing shot
from German 88's had gone into them, bounced around inside like
buckshot in a rattle, and then gone out the other side, leaving something
to be grilled by the flames as the fuel burned. The broken bits had been
extracted that morning and buried; a soldier's web belt, stiff with blood,
remained outside the hole through which they had drawn the crew of one
tank. A couple other soldiers were looking at this tank and the belt. One
of them seemed to feel the same blood excitement as the fellow we had
seen go wild at the fallen German plane by the airfield. He was saying,
over and over again, "I'll never take no more prisoners, the bastards, I'll

never take no more prisoners!" A couple of 88's had laid doggo and caught the tanks with crossfire as they entered the town.

The artillery was still firing in the hill ridge about five miles away.

We asked a bearded, wild-looking soldier who was sitting in a parked jeep what the guns were pounding at. "We got a lot of Germans trapped up there on the mountain," he said. "How many?" Norgaard wanted to know. "About a division, I guess," the soldier said. "I don't see how you could hide a whole division on that hill," Norgaard said calmly, and the soldier answered, "They got the mountain all hollowed out, and that's where they're hiding." A couple of days later, when we had got back to Second Corps headquarters, we asked the G-2 what had happened to the Germans trapped on the hill, and he said, "Oh, you mean those last nine Heinies? They surrendered." We got back to town fast. There was an uncomfortable feeling about Sened, a tacit menace that made me feel worse than actually being bombed or shot at. Norgaard said he had exactly the same reaction.

The reason why none of our early operations in this area could amount to anything was that we had no infantry available to occupy the tactically important hills and stay on them. A war conducted almost exclusively with planes and armor is in its essence a medieval conception. The armored knights ride out, the armored knights ride back again, but they would become helpless if they dismounted, so war is resolved into a series of raids. And the strategic air-force scheme of destroying the enemy's factories is strangely like the medieval one of burning his crops.

I did not get back to Gafsa for six weeks after the affair at Sened Station. In the meanwhile we had executed in rather ragged fashion a previously determined withdrawal from Gafsa, Feriana, Sbeitla, and the old airfield on which Norgaard and I had lived during the private war. We had lost almost all of two battalions of armor and two battalions of infantry, and for the moment at least all our prestige with the French and Arabs. The Germans, pushing on our heels, had tried to get through to Tebessa, but they had failed. I had missed all this unpleasantness by going off on a frivolous trip in another direction, which has nothing to do with the story of the war, and I was rather glad I had missed it. I had had my bellyful of retreat in France.

When we prepared to go back to Gafsa it was in a substantial, intelligent manner, with plenty of infantry. It was more than just infantry, it was the First Division. I didn't have to file a daily dispatch, like the newspaper correspondents, so I decided to travel into action with the division and live with it. Major General Terry Allen, the division commander, whom I had met at Oran and again in Algiers, said it was all right with him as long as I kept out of his way, so I brought my bedroll down to division headquarters at Bou-Chebka, on the Algerian-Tunisian frontier, on the night of March 16. The division was moving to Gafsa that night, fifty miles across territory occupied neither by us nor the enemy, where we might bump into anything or nothing. It turned out to be nothing.

31 / Gafsa Revisited

THE TENTS OF DIVISION HEADQUARTERS at Bou-Chebka stood on a hill covered with cedar trees. They were still standing when I arrived, but by the time I had had supper at the headquarters mess almost all the tents had been struck and loaded on trucks for the advance, and it was raining. The G-2, chief of the intelligence section of the divisional staff, a 34-year-old West Pointer with a high forehead and an almost prim manner, was worried during supper because he said a reconnaissance party had reported seven Italian tanks moving around on the very site which he had chosen in advance for the divisional command post, and whither the headquarters vehicles would be heading. The colonel commanding the tank-destroyer battalion had wanted to go down and get the Italian tanks while there was still light, the G-2 said, but the appearance of the tank destroyers down there might have given the show away. So General Allen had decided that the tanks should be left alone. "They'll probably go away anyway," he had said. The divisional chief of staff, who takes life seriously, let off a bit of steam by "eating out" the headquarters mess officer for serving C-rations at the last meal before the jump-off. "You know we have a limited quantity of C-rations, and it's the only form of ration the men can carry with them when they're fighting," he said. He did not say that we would have preferred a tastier meal ourselves because we did not know when we would get another. Brigadier General Teddy Roosevelt, the assistant division commander, was as restless and wriggly as a little boy whose family is taking him to a circus and who wants to get started early. Allen was in good enough humor but preoccupied. He had the responsibility.

I was to travel with a lieutenant named Ted Liese, who had once been in the display-advertising business in New York. He was now in charge of the liaison officers attached to division. A division is divided into three combat teams, each made up of a regiment of infantry and a battalion of artillery. Each team has a liaison officer, generally a young lieutenant, at headquarters. He travels back and forth between the CT command post and division, maintaining direct connection between the two. The division reconnaissance, or "recon" troop, the tank-destroyer battalion, the French, the British, and division artillery also maintain liaison men at division. Liese was a kind of housekeeper for the entire group. I permitted myself to be separated from my bedroll and typewriter, which were loaded on a truck that would follow us into Gafsa after the division had captured it, and retained only my musette bag with my mess kit in it and my rifle belt and canteen. I had no rifle, but I preferred a rifleman's belt to the usual pistol belt officers wear, because the cartridge pockets are ideal receptacles for ration chocolate and chewing gum.

The first echelons of the division started moving at dark, but we were not to get off until one o'clock in the morning. We waited in the rain. The jeeps assigned to us were being used on various errands in the early evening, but they got back in plenty of time. We climbed in and, after waiting around awhile, moved into the procession of vehicles of all kinds that now filled the Gafsa road. I had been over the main road a dozen times; it would have been of no interest to me even if I could have seen. The sensation of being in a great caravan of vehicles moving forward through the night is soporific; I had the comfortable certainty for once that if shooting started it would be well up ahead of me in the early echelons, and not from a plane diving out of the sky directly over my head. I slept. I woke up when we turned off the road somewhere south of Feriana. The tracks through the semidesert had been marked out with white tape, and there were M.P.'s everywhere to guide us. The parking spaces for the various units were marked with signs illuminated by blackout lights; I had the feeling I was being driven into the parking area around the Yankee Stadium on the night of a prize fight. We reached divisional-headquarters area at a little after four o'clock. I got out of Liese's jeep and then could not find it again in the dark, so I threw my mackinaw coat on the ground and flopped on it and went to sleep. The rain had stopped.

When I awoke it was daylight and the divisional artillery was making a loud, comforting noise. I find nothing objectionable in the sound of artillery fire when I know it is going out. I got up and looked around for my jeep, but somebody said Liese had already been sent on a mission to one of the combat teams. Our jeeps and trucks were widely dispersed on the plain, and as soon as the men awoke they picked themselves off the ground and started digging themselves foxholes. I would like to say someplace that foxhole is a widely misused term, being applied freely to deep, carefully constructed slit trenches as well as hasty burrows. The kind men make when they are out in the open in fear of imminent attack really are foxholes. But the German planes which had dived-bombed or strafed even single vehicles in the small-scale Sened thing six weeks earlier never put in an appearance to bother this divisional attack. It was a tipoff that the enemy had not awaited us in Gafsa but had already pulled out. We could not see the town from our first CP of the day, but at about eight o'clock we heard an explosion heavier than any of the artillery and saw a mighty column of gray-black smoke on the horizon toward Gafsa. The last elements of the enemy had blown a great munition dump.

I strolled over by Allen's tent and heard him successively telephoning his combat-team commanders, asking, "How you doing, kid?" The infantry were closing in on Gafsa through the hills. "It's all going like a maneuver," Allen would say at the conclusion of each call, "too good to be true."

Sergeant Jimmy Mimms, the general's driver, and an M.P. named Cawthorne, who acts as bodyguard, were frying Deerfoot sausage and making coffee by the gasoline-burner process, and every time Mimms got an especially fine color on a sausage he would send it over to the general, to tempt him to eat. "He's just got to eat, Cawthorne," he would say. Allen paid no attention to the first six or seven burnt offerings. Finally he accepted one and sent Cawthorne back for more. "The battle must be going all right," Mimms said. "I guess we're in now."

We were. That afternoon the First Division moved into Gafsa, which had been deserted by the Arabs during the bombardment. The Arabs came back very slowly, as if they had bad consciences. Rain had begun again at noon. A waddy between division headquarters and the town appeared so swollen that headquarters decided to stay where it was for the night.

General Allen's aide, Major Kenneth Downs, had been a war correspondent for International News Service when I first knew him, and he now invited me to share his jeep and tag around with him for the rest of the offensive. Downs and his jeep driver and I charred some Spam and heated some soluble coffee in the shelter of a tarpaulin held against the side of a hill, and after the meal Downs and I pitched a pup tent. The driver decided to sleep under the tarp in what he thought was a sheltered nook in the hillside. We crawled under cover at seven o'clock. I never slept sooner or harder in my life. It must have been about two in the morning when Downs banged me on the head to awaken me, which he did. I said, "What's the matter?" and he said, "The tent has blown away." By that time my blankets were soaked through, but I was not concerned about that, because I had borrowed them anyway. I sat up in the jeep for the rest of the night. The driver, who had been rained out of his burrow, was in the jeep already. Downs, I think, managed to scrouge into the general's tent. Next morning we moved into Gafsa.

The French inhabitants of Gafsa had been evacuated in American Army trucks before the arrival of the Germans, so there were more good billets available in town than when I had been there before. Division headquarters moved into the Gendarmerie Nationale, a fine modern place. Gafsa was the capital of an administrative area with a population of about 150,000 natives, so the government buildings were out of proportion to the size of the town alone. It was the first town I had ever been in that our side had recaptured from the enemy, and was in its small way a symbol that this particular breed of bug could be dislodged like any other. But the science of booby-trapping has taken a good deal of fun out of following hot on an enemy's heels. Our engineers had been through the lower floors of the gendarmerie already, looking for booby traps, but they hadn't had time to do the living quarters in which Downs and I were billeted. It caused me acute distress to turn a doorknob or draw a shutter. In the end the division engineers decided that the Italians who had last been in Gafsa had lacked the time or possibly the skill to put any booby traps in the buildings. They had mined the roads and shoulders of the roads leading into and out of town, however, and protected most of their heavy mines with things the engineers called "bouncing babies." The babies were metal containers that were blown into the air by a charge of black powder when a soldier stepped on a hidden trip wire. They were packed with high explosives and steel ball bearings, and were timed to explode when about chest high in the air. The steel balls did the killing. Knowledge that there are bouncing babies about is disconcerting when you are in a jeep during a road strafing. You hesitate to dive for a road-side ditch.

Soon after we pulled into Gafsa I went for a walk about town to see how it had been affected by the occupation. The old Moorish citadel had been partially wrecked by an explosion. The engineers had used it as a storehouse for explosives and had blown it to save the stuff from the enemy. The destructions had not been well carried out; it had been planned, for example, to run a number of locomotives north over the railroad and then blow a railroad bridge north of town so that the use of the road would be barred to the enemy, but somebody had blown the bridge first, so that the locomotives were trapped in Gafsa. Then, since no preparations had been made to destroy them, they were abandoned and fell into German hands.

I met an Arab in the market place in front of the old citadel who said he had been some sort of a government employee, a police-court interpreter, I think, and had remained through the occupation. He was frightened, because the French notion of justice for Arabs is summary. The houses of all the Frenchmen had been thoroughly pillaged. So he was eager to talk and to convince me that his heart at least had been with the Allies. Most of the Moslems of Gafsa had fled to join their kin in the hills during the occupation, he said, because they wanted to escape the exactions of the Italians and because a great force of American bombers had come over shortly after the evacuation and flattened a lot of Arab houses. The bombers had killed about four hundred Arabs who were in a bread-line on the market place, he said. "The people were much impressed, and those who had gone about talking of the victory of the Germans as certain were discredited," he said, indicating that there are several kinds of propaganda. "They realized that the Americans must have mistaken them for Italian troops.

"When the Germans and Italians first came here they encouraged the people to rob the houses of the French and Jews," he said, "and some of the more ignorant elements of the population complied with their wishes. The Germans did not stay here long, but went on, leaving an Italian garrison. The Italians were revoltingly poor. They pulled up even the young onions out of the gardens in the oasis and ate them as if famished. They broke into Arab houses and stole carpets off the floors and sold them to other Arabs living in the surrounding country, to get a few *sous*. They are a people without shame." The German words, *Araber Laden,* or *Araber Geschäft* had been scrawled in chalk on the doors of a great number of shops, and the Arab said this had been done immediately after the evacuation, according to instructions from the Axis Arabic-language radio in Tunis, to protect Arab-owned businesses from pillage by invading troops. "I never listened to that radio, of course," he said, "but so I have heard it related." I had never imagined that so many Arabs knew even a couple of German words, but he said that a number in Gafsa had been prisoners of war in Germany in 1914–18 and had learned the language there. It was easy to guess that the place had been full of Arab Axis agents during our previous stay there; some of them were probably still wearing the G.I. shirts compassionate doughboys had given them.

I walked out to the house of the Chemounis, near the roadblock where the Feriana road entered town. It was still standing, but when I looked inside it seemed that nobody had lived there for years. There was nothing in the place but a few pages of Hebrew printing on the hard earth floor and a chandelier that swung crazily from the roof of the room where Norgaard and I had drunk wine. I wondered whether the family had escaped from Gafsa or been destroyed. I asked a lad I met on the road near by what had happened to them, and he said that they were in town, living in the old Jewish quarter, a couple of fetid alleys where only the poorest and least Europeanized Jews had lived in January. The boy was Jewish himself. He guided me to the house where the Chemounis lived. A scarecrow of a man, wearing a beret and a long blue robe, precipitated himself upon me, blubbering and trying to kiss me. "They have stolen even my trousers," Chemouni sobbed, pressing his face against the front of my field jacket. Other Jews, those who had recently been outwardly European now like my friend indistinguishable from the most Oriental, flocked about with their stories of the occupation. The Germans had come to the houses of the leading Jews on the first night, but had taken worthwhile things like money, jewelry, and stocks of raw wool, leaving furniture and minor personal possessions alone. Then they had gone on, but not before inviting the Arabs to help themselves to the leavings. There had been a wild competition between Arabs and Italians to gut the Jewish houses. The Italian commandant of the place had ordered all the Jews into a few houses in the old quarter and had put them on a ration even smaller than that accorded to the Arabs, which had been minuscule. No Jews had been killed, although two young men had almost gone before a firing squad because an Arab accused them of having betrayed an Axis parachutist to the Americans in December. The two young men had escaped to the desert. The caïd of Gafsa, the chief Moslem official, had remained on the job through the occupation, and so had the spahis, the French-trained native police. The caïd had fled with the Italians, fearing the returning French would shoot him, but the spahis were still on the job, again under the orders of their original French superiors. They were recovering stolen Jewish and French property from Arab houses, but what they found was ruined or of slight original value.

Israel had been spoiled again, but naked as they had been the members of the community had apparently hoarded a few hens and roosters against the day of their deliverance. The *shochet*, the ritual slaughterer with his matted beard, was killing these chickens for the family feasts of celebration, holding the blade in his lips between strokes while he smoothed back the neck feathers of the chicken he was going to slit next. A couple of big Jewish soldiers from the Bronx, with tremendous hands that could palm a basketball and great feet that could kick a football sixty yards, had their arms comfortingly on the shoulders of ancient, tiny matriarchs with whom they had no means of communication except signs, because the Tunisian Jews speak no Yiddish. The Bronx Jews and the Tunisian Jews looked as different as a Percheron and an Eohippus.

"The Arabs are very bad," Chemouni said to me. "They have always been bad." "How long has your family lived in Gafsa?" I asked him. "I think for two thousand years," he said. His little girl, who spoke French as easily as any child in the Parc Monceau, looked at me with large frightened gray eyes. I asked him if she would go to live in France after we had won the war. He said no, of course not, she would marry and live in Gafsa. "Not a single bomb touched a Jewish house," he said. "God protects his people."

The *controleur civile*, the chief French administrative official for the district, had returned, and I went to talk to him. The Axis radio, he agreed, had had an important effect on the *indigenes*. Also the attitude of the Bey of Tunis had had an important effect. The Bey, Moncef Pasha, of the old Beylical Hoceinite family, had allowed the Germans to put him at the head of an "autonomous" Tunisian government in Tunis. It would be necessary to install another bey as soon as the Allies got to Tunis. Since the beylicate was not hereditary from father to son as long as it remained within the Hoceinite clan, that would be easy. Moncef Pasha had dozens of cousins. The *controleur* was much concerned with the problem of bringing the wives of himself and the half-dozen other leading French officials back to Gafsa. "There are so many soldiers in the streets," he said, "I am afraid it will be very embarrassing for them." We moved out a couple of days later, to spare their blushes.

32 / Under the Acacias

GENERAL ALLEN HAD BEEN PLEASED with the smoothness of the Gafsa operation, but he was uneasy, too, because he could not believe that the enemy would relinquish the region without a fight. The First Division had been ordered to capture and hold Gafsa as a railhead for the supplies of the British Eighth Army when the Eighth made its junction with the forces in our part of Tunisia, but you cannot hold a town unless you hold its approaches. There are two or three ranges of hills around the oasis of El Guettar, which is twelve miles southeast of Gafsa, and Allen thought of them as a dentist thinks about the possibly infected roots of a tooth. So the division slipped out of Gafsa with the same noiseless ease it had achieved in the other night move and attacked two of the ridges south of El Guettar.

Downs and his jeep moved with the division headquarters, and naturally so did I. This night ride was a short one. The headquarters vehicles turned off the main road at a point where hundreds of palm trees were silhouetted against the night sky, the oasis proper. I had recovered my bedroll after the first advance and had it in the jeep with me. After the driver had stowed the jeep under a tree, Downs and I dragged out our rolls and spread them near the side of the road, on the highest ground we could find. The oasis was on low ground, and we knew there must be a lot of mosquitoes in the grass. The Numidian frogs, which make a noise like parrots, sang from the shallow irrigation ditches that intersected the fertile land. When I awoke, to the accustomed thunder of the guns, I found myself in a Josef Urban stage set, appropriate to the last act of a musical comedy but not a war play. There were hundreds of acacia and almond trees in blossom under the palms. The white acacia blossoms and the pink ones of almond dripped down on us all through the battle.

A Ranger battalion attached to the division had attacked at four in the morning at one spot, and at six the infantry attacked at another. They found the enemy forces in strong positions, but these troops were sleepy, half-starved Italians who surrendered in droves and wept for joy when presented with C-rations, to our men the most despised form of army nourishment. First Lieutenant, now Captain, Ralph Ingersoll, the former editor of *PM*, was with the Ranger battalion which executed the first attack, and made of it the central episode of his book, *The Battle Is the Payoff*. Our men made more than a thousand prisoners, but there was not one German in the lot.

Allen, who at first meeting appears to be a slapdash, reckless sort of

fellow, perhaps because of his old-line cavalry personality and mannerisms, is in fact a worrier. He felt that things had been going too well to be
on the level. He ordered an advance on Djebel Berda, the only ridge left
unexplored, for the next morning.

Brigadier General Teddy Roosevelt, the assistant division commander,
likes to circulate among the units in action during a battle. He invited me
to make the circuit with him in his jeep on the day when the Djebel
Berda attack was scheduled. Just as we were leaving the oasis a couple
of the division engineer officers came up with Ingersoll in tow. One of
them said, "General Roosevelt, I would like to have you meet Lieutenant
Ingersoll." Roosevelt, who hadn't been thinking of the *PM* Ingersoll, said,
"How do you do, Lieutenant?" and we walked away. I said, "That was
Ralph Ingersoll, the *PM* editor." The general likes to descant on the thesis
that all the prominent interventionists stayed safe at home while he, a
hard-shell America Firster, went to war. He stopped sharply. "Hell," he
said, "I always thought that man was a sonofabitch."

I had got to know Roosevelt pretty well at Sainte Barbe, near Oran,
where the First Division headquarters had been when I first arrived in
Africa. As assistant division commander he spends much of his time between battles visiting battalions and reporting back to division on their
needs. His staccato, gamecock walk serves to identify him as long as he is
within field-glass range. He always carries a short cane, head down, in the
pocket of his field jacket, and he always makes a point of speaking to the
mess sergeant of each outfit he visits. He asks the sergeant, for instance, if
the company has enough baking powder. The sergeant invariably says no,
and Roosevelt leaves him with the impression that if he, Roosevelt, were
Secretary of War, there would be enough baking powder. Simple as this
device is, it makes men feel that the divisional command is on their side.
Roosevelt has a special way of saluting across his face, a little like Dave
Chasen's celebrated gesture, and when he is on one of his tours of the
division he goes out of his way to get saluted by as many soldiers as
possible. He says that saluting is a criterion of division morale. He was in
the First Division in the last war, in which he earned several wound
stripes and decorations. After holding a reserve commission in the tranquil years between wars, he came back to the Army and his division in
April 1941. He speaks of himself as an old First Division soldier, and
when he visits regimental headquarters in back areas, bands play "Old
Soldiers Never Die, They Simply Fade Away" for him. He has a memory
for the first names of the veteran First Division noncoms he encounters.
He is at his best, however, in battle; his gamecock strut and his slightly
corny humor take on a new and attractive quality when they are being
exhibited under fire. The men consider Roosevelt an intellectual because
he carries a considerable stock of books in his blanket roll. His library
includes anthologies of verse, which he memorizes in vast chunks; works
on anthropology, a subject which he discusses on any provocation; and a

large number of detective stories, with which he reads himself to sleep.

Roosevelt's aide, Lieutenant Mike Stevenson, drove the jeep for us on the Djebel Berda morning. The German ground troops had not appeared on the previous day, but their planes had put in some energetic dive-bombings of American gun positions in the late afternoon. The Stukas had destroyed two field pieces and killed their crews, by far the heaviest loss of the day. The skies were full of German planes on the Djebel Berda morning, too, and the general, the lieutenant, and I spent considerable time clambering out of and into our jeep. I wedged myself so hard into the interstice between a parked truck and a bank of earth on one occasion, I remember, that when the planes disappeared I could hardly get out. I seemed to have contracted with fear, and when I expanded to normal size again I was stuck. I went in so hard that both pockets of my field jacket were completely filled with pebbles, as if I had been a human steam shovel. The general didn't seem to mind. The command post of the Eighteenth Infantry Combat Team was at the foot of a high hill which had an observation post on top of it. When we had got that far Roosevelt, who changes his mind as quickly as another man, decided that he wanted to stay at the observation post and watch the attack, which the Eighteenth was going to make. This was all right with me, and we all climbed up to the O.P.

This action took place on two ridges of hills which form an amphitheater that is open at both ends. The Americans, who already held the ridge which forms the northern side of the amphitheater, moved infantry by truck to both ends of the arc opposite them. The infantry detachments at the two ends then worked inward toward each other, for the enemy was supposed to be, if he was in the neighborhood at all, on the southern ridge at the center of the arc, at the point where the amphitheater was widest. If the battlefield had been a football stadium, the enemy would have had a seat on the fifty-yard line. The O.P. was in a correspondingly advantageous position on the American ridge. American artillery fired over our heads, blasting a spot on the hills across the way, where the enemy was supposed to be. G-2, the intelligence section of the divisional staff, had reported that two thousand Italian troops with three batteries of artillery were on Djebel Berda, but some skeptics still insisted that they must have pulled out. A force that size could not hope to hold out against a division, they argued, so it had probably vanished toward the coast.

Our infantry detachments, using ground cover and visible from the observation post only occasionally, and then just for a moment or two at a time, carried out their slow advance for four hours without a sign of enemy activity, as our guns continued to pound his ridge. The situation was beginning to get slightly embarrassing for General Allen, and ad-herents of the no-enemy theory, who had ordered the attack, were starting to speak up when puffs of white smoke broke out on the opposite ridge at points in front of the advancing infantry. The enemy was firing on our men with mortars, and our infantry was temporarily pinned down. Our artillery searched for the mortar positions and evidently found them, for the mortar fire ceased and our infantry moved on again. Allen, in the O.P. with us, looked pleased with himself, like a dentist whose probe has at last hit the sensitive spot. He had found trouble.

By nightfall our infantry reported that the enemy apparently was caught in our pincers, where he could be finished off by a night or dawn attack. The Americans were now on both ridges, and our artillery was comfortably tucked in behind our infantry—like a fighter's chin behind his left shoulder.

We drove back to the oasis well pleased with the day's results, but I still sensed a lack, and I think in their hearts the others did too. American troops had not yet beaten German troops in battle in this war. The forces in Tunisia had won a few skirmishes against Germans and had a few hard knocks, but hadn't won an action on a large scale. The First Division had been broken into its component units and fed into the fighting a battalion at a time during the winter, and the individual battalions had fought well. As a division it had a success against the French at Oran, and now it had a victory over Italians. It is safe to say that all its officers felt it could hold its own against a German division, but it had never had a chance to try. Until American troops had beaten German troops in a fair fight, there would always remain a doubt in the back of the minds of the people at home. It was all right to demonstrate mathematically that we had enough men and enough factory capacity to make victory sure, but the Germans had done such a job of self-advertising that even Americans wondered whether they weren't a bit superhuman. The First Division was scheduled to furnish the answer, and other American divisions as they gained experience would amplify it.

At five o'clock next morning, as I slept in the oasis, a peremptory voice broke into my dream, which I have now forgotten. Half awake, I realized that it was no dream voice; then as I became fully conscious I knew that it came from inside a half-track equipped with radio which was parked about ten yards from me. This half-track belonged to the liaison officer of a tank-destroyer battalion. The battalion communicated with division headquarters through the radio set in the half-track. And now I could hear the voice on the radio saying, "Baker reports German tanks threatening to overrun ——— Field Artillery." Lieutenant Colonel Herschel Baker was the commander of the tank destroyers. A moment later I heard, "Baker recommends infantry on lower slope ground fall back toward soft ground and resist tanks with rocket guns." I rubbed my eyes, spat, and walked over to G-2 to find out what was happening. It was the test match.

When I could find a G-2 man who had time to talk to me I learned that some tanks of the Tenth German Panzer Division had appeared on the plain between the two ridges that morning. They had entered the stadium through gullies in a part of the ridge still held by the Italian infantry, and they had begun the day by trying to climb a slope and overrun the batteries of American artillery which had been posted below our ridge. Our infantry and gunners stood firm, and our artillery had shot through several of the tanks. The T.D. outfit, coming to the rescue of the artillery, engaged the tanks, which moved off and started to make their way down the center of the field toward the western exit, which meant, incidentally, toward us at headquarters. The only combat troops in the oasis were the men of the headquarters defense platoon, which had four 37-millimeter cannon. The universal belief in the division was that these cannon would puncture nothing more heavily armored than a Kiddiekar.

Apparently the German intention was to come around the rear of the American position in the north stands and cut the main road back to Gafsa, then retake that town and thus leave the First Division stranded. If the maneuver succeeded, the entire disposition of Allied forces designated to contain the German Army in Tunisia while the Eighth Army smashed its way through the Mareth Line would be upset. We would have to retreat from them while they retreated before the Eighth Army. The German commander also probably hoped to cause panic among the cut-off American troops and get a lot of equipment and prisoners. "They think they can push us over and laugh at us because Americans can't stand up to German armor," my G-2 man said in a hard tone. Since the tanks were coming in our direction I decided that the oasis was as good an observation post as any.

The oasis was cut up into the small holdings of individual Arabs by crumbling mud walls and irrigation ditches. The Arabs had used the earth from the ditches to make the walls. There were red earthen water jugs nested in the tops of some of the palm trees—I suppose the owners, who climb like gibbons, carry water from the ditches up to the tops of the trees in dry spells and sprinkle the choice dates. In some of the others there were whitened bovine skulls, to frighten the birds from the ripe fruit. Under the palms were the acacias and almonds with their blossoms, and at ground level there were the thin green blades of spring onions and the flowers of black-eyed peas. The sun filtered through the blossoms; the drone of bees was so strong that it was hard to distinguish at once an approaching airplane motor.

A young liaison officer named Troup Howard Matthews, who was on call to carry messages to the First Armored Division, but who had nothing to do for hours at a stretch, suggested that we move to the outer edge of the oasis and observe. We strolled over there and sat on a mud wall. Matthews was twenty-five years old and one of the few mildly intellectual young officers I had met, a low-voiced New Orleans boy. He had worked for the National Broadcasting Company in New York before entering the Army, and as we sat on the wall waiting we tried to enumerate the bars in Rockefeller Center. We had had about one drink apiece in the previous month. Italian troops had occupied the oasis before us, and I tried to piece together a couple of torn Italian letters to see what their folks at home had been writing to them about. There was a low plain between the oasis and the ridges we had watched on the previous day, and I hoped our engineers had put out some mines beyond the oasis' edge. There was a small salt lake in the middle of the plain, but the tanks would not have to cross it to get to us.

Matthews looked through his binoculars and saw a couple of small dots creeping hesitantly toward us like lice across a panhandler's shirt front. He said they were tanks. They came nearer, very indirectly and with frequent halts, until they got as big as bedbugs on a wall, and then geysers of black smoke and dirt began to appear near them. There were about a dozen dots now. Matthews said he could see twenty. They would stop sometimes when the geysers spouted up, and then I would think they had been hit, but soon they would come crawling on again. The geysers were shellbursts; our howitzers, firing from their position back of the ridge we held, were shooting at them. The foremost tanks got within two miles of us, which is close for motorized battle, but I do not think they knew that the palm trees concealed the C.P., or they would have made a more determined effort to overrun it. Then the howitzers got to them. Four tanks were shot through. Their clumsy black bodies, belching dark smoke, remained on the field right below the command post now. You could see them with the naked eye, and they had outgrown the bedbug stage. They were about as big as caramels. The American 105 and 155 mortars are not ideal anti-tank weapons, because of their high arching trajectory. But they had served. Matthews and I went to breakfast.

All day long, that day of the stadium battle, the German tanks toddled about the field and in the first rows of our hill grandstand while the artillery potted at them and the tank destroyers, waddling into action like bull pups, drew their fire and returned it. Finally, all eighteen tank destroyers were knocked out, but only after they had wrecked thirty-one tanks. By the time this tank-destroyer battalion was finished, another had arrived from the rear, so our position was not weakened. Old Baker, the tank-destroyer commander, came rolling into the oasis late in the afternoon to say good-by to General Allen. He said he had had surprisingly few casualties and was loading his men into trucks and taking them back to Feriana to get some new guns. Baker, with white hair, apple-red cheeks, and bright blue eyes, looks like Father Christmas minus the whiskers and is always full of bounce. He had been riding around among the tanks in a jeep and had somehow captured a German who had a lot of pornographic postcards in his wallet. Baker was as happy as a lark.

During all the fighting our infantry held firmly to the hills. Without it, the artillery, which was in this battle the striking arm, would have been overrun. G-2 had somehow picked up the information that the Germans would make their big attack at 4:45 in the afternoon. I went out to the edge of the oasis with some other idlers to wait for it, repeating to myself idly,

"The Spartans on the sea-wet rock, sat down and combed their hair,"

and understanding for the first time that they had sat down not because they were heroes but because there was nothing else to do. Promptly at 4:45 twenty Stukas flew over the oasis, paying us no heed, and dived on our gun positions. The only American plane in sight all day had been a Piper Cub used by the artillery spotters. The echo of the Stukas' bombs and of the whistling devices between their front wheels had hardly died down before the enemy began his attack, but it was out of our sight. We could hear the guns and see the German shellbursts on our ridge. This time, as I learned a little later, the Germans sent forward some armored infantry, known as Panzer Grenadiers, whose mission apparently was to climb through our infantry lines and reach our guns. German tanks followed the grenadiers. The guns killed all but nine of the two hundred grenadiers of the leading platoons, and the rest of the attacking party stopped and went away. The American guns fired time shells, and the divisional artillery commander, a calm, professorial kind of brigadier general, told me afterward that he was highly pleased with their effect. As it turned out, that particular battle ended at that particular instant, because the Tenth Panzer Division never resumed the attack. It had lost forty or fifty tanks, most of which remained in our hands and were blown up by our engineers so that they would be beyond repair. What was more important, it was licked.

If one American division could beat one German division, I thought then, a hundred American divisions could beat a hundred German divisions. Only the time was already past when Germany had a hundred divisions to spare from the Russian front, plus God knows how many more to fight the British, plus garrison troops for all the occupied countries. I knew deep down inside me after that that the road back to Paris was clear.

MOLLIE &
OTHER
WAR PIECES

To many men who would now be in their forties

Contents

FOREWORD

ALL THE PIECES in this book are about things that happened between the beginning of 1943 and the end of 1944; most were written from the field, but some in 1945, when I was just home. The latest in date is the pseudo-short-story *Day of Victory*, which was written in the summer of 1946, in celebration of the second anniversary of the Liberation of Paris, of part of which it is an unofficial report. A pseudo-short-story is one in which fact is turned to fiction by changing the names of the actors and perhaps juggling a bit with details. I have no compunctions in including two such stories with the rest of the reports.

I covered bits of the war in 1939–40 in France, and in 1941 in Britain and on the high seas, but those seem in retrospect not merely previous but different wars, with a different feeling, and so I have not included them. Collectively, the wars were the central theme of my life from October, 1939, until the end of 1944, and I sometimes feel a deplorable nostalgia for them—as my friend the Count Rzewski once said about something else: "So disgusting, so deplorable, so human." The times were full of certainties: we could be certain we were right—and we were—and that certainty made us certain that anything we did was right, too. I have seldom been sure I was right since. It had attractive uncertainties, too; you never had to think about the future, because you didn't know if you would have one. Yet the risk was so disseminated over time that you seldom felt that *this* was the moment when the future might end.

I know that it is socially acceptable to write about war as an unmitigated horror, but subjectively at least, it was not true, and you can feel its pull on men's memories at the maudlin reunions of war divisions. They mourn for their dead, but also for war.

A. J. LIEBLING

1

Confusion Is Normal in Combat

First Servant—Let me have war, say I, it exceeds peace as far as day does night......

Second Servant—'Tis so, and as wars in some sort may be said to be a ravisher, so it cannot be denied but peace is a great maker of cuckolds.

First Servant—Ay, and it makes men hate one another.

Third Servant—Reason, because they then less need one another.

—*Coriolanus*

(The Third Servant then says: "The war's for my money," but I feared some reader might mistake the appearance of this line unsoftened by parentheses for an indorsement of his declaration.)

For Hal Boyle

Quest for Mollie

MOLLIE is a part of the history of La Piste Forestière, and La Piste Forestière is perhaps the most important part of the history of Mollie. La Piste Forestière, or the Foresters' Track, is a dirt road that connects Cap Serrat, on the northern coast of western Tunisia, with Sedjenane, a town twenty miles inland. The country it runs through is covered with small hills, and almost all the hills are coated with a ten-foot growth of tall bushes and short trees, so close together that once you leave the road you can't see fifty feet in front of you. From the top of any hill you can see the top of another hill, but, because of the growth, you can't tell whether there are men on it. This made the country hard to fight in. The hillsides that have no trees are bright with wild flowers in the spring, and when some other war correspondents and I travelled back and forth along the Foresters' Track in jeeps, we sometimes used to measure our slow progress by reference to the almost geometrical patterns of color on such slopes. There was, for example, the hill with a rough yellow triangle of buttercups against a reddish-purple background of other blooms; it indicated that you were five miles from the road's junction with the main highway at Sedjenane. With luck you might reach the junction in two hours, but this was extremely unlikely, for the road was just wide enough for one truck—not for a truck and a jeep or even for a truck and a motorcycle. Only a man on foot or on a horse could progress along the margin of the road when there was a vehicle on it, and the horse would often have to scramble by with two feet off the road, like the sidehill bear of eastern Tennessee. When a jeep met a convoy, it sometimes had to back up for hundreds of yards to where there was room to get off the road and wait. Then, when all the heavy vehicles had passed, the jeep would resume its journey, perhaps to meet another convoy before it had recovered the lost yardage. Even when you got in behind trucks going your way, they were packed so closely together that they advanced at a crawl, so you did too. Bits of the war were threaded along the Foresters' Track like beads on a string, and the opportunity to become familiar with them was forced upon you. Mollie, for me, was the gaudiest bead.

The reason the Foresters' Track is such a miserable excuse for a road is that in normal times there is little need for it. There is a lighthouse at Cap Serrat and a forest warden's house about halfway between that and Sedjenane. The few Berbers in the district, who live in brush shelters in the bush, have no vehicles or need of a road. But in late April and early May of 1943, La Piste Forestière was an important military thoroughfare. The Allied armies, here facing east, lay in a great arc with their right flank at Sousse, on the Gulf of Tunis, and this little road was the only supply line for twenty miles of front; that is, the extreme left flank of the Allied line. The actual front line ran parallel to the road and only a few hundred yards east of it during the first days of the offensive that was to end the Allies' North African campaign, but because of the hills and the brush, people on the road couldn't see the fighting. However, American artillery placed just west of the road—it would have been an engineering feat to get it any considerable distance into the brush—constantly fired over our heads as our jeeps piddled along. The gunners hoped that some of their shells were falling on the Germans and Italians who were trying to halt our infantry's advance with fire from hidden mortars and machine guns. The Luftwaffe in Africa had predeceased the enemy ground forces; the budget of planes allotted it for the African adventure was exhausted, I suppose, and the German High Command sent no more. This was lucky for us, because one good strafing, at any hour, would have jammed the road with burned-out vehicles and Allied dead. By repeating the strafing once a day, the Germans could have kept the road permanently out of commission. The potential danger from the air did not worry us for long, however. You soon become accustomed to immunity, even when you cannot understand the reason for it.

Trucks left ammunition along the side of the road to be carried up to the fighting lines on the backs of requisitioned mules and horses and little Arab donkeys, a strangely assorted herd conducted by an equally scratch lot of soldiers. The Washington army had decided years before that the war was now one-hundred-per-cent mechanized, so the field army, quite a different organization, had to improvise its animal transport as it went along. The wounded were carried down to the road by stretcher bearers. Ambulances, moving with the same disheartening slowness as everything else, picked up the casualties and took them out to a clearing station near the yellow-triangle hill I have mentioned, where some of the viable ones were patched up for the further slow haul out. Cruder surgical units, strung out along the road, took such cases as they were equipped to handle. These units were always right by the side of the road, since in that claustrophobe's nightmare of a country there was no other place for them to be. The advanced units were French and had women nurses with them. A French doctor I knew used to say that it helped the men bear pain if nurses were looking at them. "Since we have so little anesthesia," he said, "we rely upon vanity." Sometimes I would sit in my jeep and watch that doctor work. He had broken down a few saplings and bushes by the side of the road to clear a space for his ambulance, and next to the ambulance he had set up a camp stool and a folding table with some instruments on it. Once a traffic jam stopped my jeep near his post when he had a tanned giant perched on the camp stool, a second lieutenant in the Corps Franc d'Afrique. The man's breasts were hanging off his chest in a kind of bloody ruff. "A bit of courage now, my son, will save you a great deal of trouble later on," the doctor said as he prepared to do something or other. I assumed, perhaps pessimistically, that he was going to hack off the bits of flesh as you would trim the ragged edges of an ill-cut page. "Go easy, Doctor," the young man said. "I'm such a softie." Then the traffic started to move, so I don't know what the doctor did to him.

The Corps Franc d'Afrique was a unit that had a short and glorious history. Soon after the Allied landings in North Africa, in October, 1942, the Corps Franc organized itself, literally, out of the elements the Darlanists in control of the North African government distrusted too much to incorporate into the regular French Army—Jews, anti-Nazis from concentration camps, de Gaullists, and other Allied sympathizers. A French general named Joseph de Goislard de Montsabert, who had helped plan the landings, had been thrown out by his collaborationist superiors, who, even after Darlan's agreement to play ball with the forces of democracy, had remained his superiors. De Montsabert, because he had a red face and snowy hair, was known to his troops as Strawberry in Cream. There had been, among the French in North Africa, a number of other professional officers and many reservists who, like the General, were apparently left out of the war because they were suspected of favoring de Gaulle or merely of being hostile to Germany. The Darlan regime had refused to mobilize the Jews because it clung to the Vichy thesis that they were not full citizens, and it did not want them to establish a claim to future consideration, and it was holding thousands of Spanish and German refugees and French Communists in concentration camps.

De Montsabert and a few of his officer friends, talking on the street in Algiers one rainy November day of that year, decided to start a "Free Corps" of men who wanted to fight but whom the government would not allow to. They took over a room in a schoolhouse on the Rue Mogador as headquarters and advertised in the *Echo d'Alger* for volunteers. The ad appeared once and then the Darlanist censorship, which was still operating under the Americans, like every other element of Vichy rule, suppressed it. But scores of volunteers had already appeared at the schoolhouse and de Montsabert sent them out with pieces of schoolroom chalk to write "Join the Corps Franc" on walls all over the city. Hundreds of new volunteers came in. General Giraud, who had arrived in Africa to command all the French but had subsequently accepted a rôle secondary to Darlan's, heard of the movement and interceded for it. Giraud, whatever his limitations, considered it natural that anybody in his right mind should want to fight the Germans. Darlan and his Fascist friends began to think of the Corps Franc as a means of getting undesirables out of the way, so the government recognized it but at the same time refused it any equipment. The Corps began life with a miscellany of matériel begged from the British and Americans. Its men wore British battle dress and French insignia of rank, lived on American C rations, and carried any sort of weapons they could lay their hands on. The most characteristic feature of their appearance was a long beard, but even this was not universal, because some of the soldiers were too young to grow one. After the Corps Franc's arrival in Tunisia, it added to its heterogeneous equipment a great deal more stuff it captured from the enemy. The Corps went into the line in February of 1943, in the zone north of Sedjenane, and it remained there into the spring.

Late April in Tunisia is like late June in New York, and heat and dust were great nuisances to our men when they were attacking. In February and March, however, coastal Tunisia is drenched with a cold and constant downpour. The Foresters' Track was two feet deep in water when the Corps Franc began to fight along it. There were two battalions to start with—about twelve hundred men—to cover a sector twenty miles long. A third and fourth battalion had been added by the time the Americans began their offensive. The Corps, in the beginning, had only two ambulances, converted farm trucks owned by a Belgian colonist in Morocco. The Belgian and his son had driven the trucks across North Africa to join the Corps. But the trucks were unable to negotiate the flooded Track, so the men of the Corps carried their wounded out to Sedjenane on their shoulders. I once asked my doctor friend why they had not used mules. "The mules rolled over in the water and crushed the wounded men," he said. "We know. We tried it with wounded prisoners."

Now that the great attack was on, there were other troops along the Track with the Corps—the Sixtieth Infantry of the American Ninth Division, part of the American Ninth Division's artillery, an American tank-destroyer battalion, some Moroccan units, and some American motor-truck and medical outfits. The medics and the artillery made the French feel pampered and their morale got very high. One hot morning, I passed a lean, elderly soldier of the Corps Franc who was burying two of his comrades. He looked about sixty—there was no age limit in the Corps—and had a long, drooping mustache of a faded biscuit color. He had finished one grave and was sitting down to rest and cool off before beginning the other. The two dead men lay with their feet to the road. Blueflies had settled on their faces. I told my jeep driver to stop and asked the gravedigger what men these were. "One stiff was an Arab from Biskra," the old soldier said, "and the other a Spaniard, a nihilist from Oran." I asked him how his work was going. He wiped the sweat from his forehead and said happily, "Monsieur, like on roller skates."

A quarter of the men in the Corps Franc were Jews. A Jewish lieutenant named Rosenberg was its posthumous hero by the time I arrived in the Foresters' Track country. He had commanded a detachment of twenty men covering the retreat of his battalion during a German counterattack in early March. This was a sequel to the counterattack against the Americans at Kasserine Pass in late February, and both assaults were prototypes, on a small scale, of the counteroffensive the Germans were to launch in Belgium at the end of 1944—the last flurry of the hooked and dying fish. Rosenberg, holding one of the innumerable little hills with his men, had decided that it was not fitting for a Jew to retire, even when the Germans looked as though they had surrounded his position. He and his men held on until the rest of the battalion had made its escape. Then he rose, and, intoning the "Marseillaise," led his men in an attack with hand grenades. He and most of his men were, of course, killed.

Besides the Jews, the Corps had hundreds of political prisoners from labor camps in southern Algeria—Spanish Republicans who had fled to Africa in 1939, anti-Nazi Germans who had come even before that, and French "Communists and de Gaullists," to employ the usual Vichy designation for dissidents. The political prisoners had been released upon agreeing to enter the Corps Franc, which they did not consider an onerous condition. There were also hundreds of Frenchmen who had joined because they distrusted the Vichy officers in the regular Army, or because they were "hard heads" who detested any species of regularity, or because they were too old or ill for more conventional fighting units. In the Corps Franc, they were at liberty to march and fight until they dropped. There were also a fair number of Mohammedans, good soldiers who had joined to earn the princely wage of twenty-three francs a day, ten times what they would have got if they had waited to be mobilized in their regular units. Whenever I had a chance, I asked Corps Franc soldiers who they had been in civilian life and why they had enlisted. I remember a former *carabiñero* who had fought in the Spanish Loyalist Army, and a baker of Italian parentage from Bône, in Algeria, who said, "I am a Communist. Rich people are poison to me."

Other members of the Corps who made a special impression on me were a former admiral in the Spanish Republican Navy, who was now a company commander and would not allow junior officers to shout at soldiers; a Hungarian poet who had been studying medicine at the University of Algiers; a sixteen-year-old Alsatian from Strasbourg who had run away from home to avoid having to become a German citizen; and a French captain, a shipping broker in civil life, who proclaimed himself a Royalist. The captain's sixteen-year-old son was also in the Corps; the boy was a motorcycle dispatch rider. I also remember two tough Parisians who had not seen each other since one had escaped from jail in Dakar, where they had both been imprisoned for trying to join the Free French in Brazzaville. The other had escaped later. "Say, it's you, old pimp!" one of the men shouted joyously. "And how did you get out of the jug, old rottenness?" the second man shouted back. Once I shared a luncheon of C-ration vegetable hash, scallions, and medlars with a little fifty-three-year-old second lieutenant, one of those Frenchmen with a face like a parakeet, who until 1942 had been vice-president of the Paris Municipal Council, in which he represented the *arrondissement* of the Opéra. He had got out a clandestine paper and had helped Jewish friends smuggle millions of francs out of France. Betrayed to the Gestapo, he had been arrested and put in Cherche-Midi Prison; he had escaped with the aid of a jailer and come to Africa and the Corps Franc. The middle-aged soldier who waited on us spoke French with a farce-comedy Russian accent; he had been a waiter at the Scheherazade, a night club in Montmartre, and had often served the lieutenant when he was a civilian. A handsome young Viennese half-Jew, who had been on the Austrian track team in the last Olympic Games, once asked me for some sulfanilamide. He had been in a labor camp for six months without seeing a woman but had been allowed one night's leave in Oran before being sent on to the front. He wanted the sulfanilamide, he said, so that he could treat himself; he was afraid that a doctor might order him away from the firing line. And in a hospital tent at the clearing station I came across a man with a French flag wrapped around his waist; the medics discovered it when they cut his shirt away. He was a hard-looking, blondish chap with a mouthful of gold teeth and a face adorned by a cross-shaped knife scar—the *croix de vache* with which procurers sometimes mark business rivals. An interesting collection of obscene tattooing showed on the parts of him that the flag did not cover. Outwardly he was not a sentimental type.

"Where are you from?" I asked him.

"Belleville," he said. Belleville is a part of Paris not distinguished for its elegance.

"What did you do in civilian life?" I inquired.

That made him grin. "I lived on my income," he said.

"Why did you choose the Corps Franc?"

"Because I understood," he said.

The American soldiers interspersed with the men of the Corps Franc along the Foresters' Track found them a fantastic lot. Most of the men then in the Ninth Division came from New York, New Jersey, or New England, and their ideas of North Africa and Frenchmen had been acquired from films with Ronald Colman as Beau Geste or Charles Boyer as Charles Boyer. They thought the Frenchmen very reckless. The Ninth had had its first experience in battle on the road to Maknassy, in southern Tunisia, only a few weeks earlier, and it was not yet a polished division. The men of the Ninth in Germany later took risks as nonchalantly as any Corps Franc soldier used to, but at the time I am speaking of they would sometimes call the Frenchmen "those crazy headhunters." This term reflected a tendency to confuse the Corps Franc with the Moroccans in the same zone; the Moroccans are not headhunters, either, but there is a popular American belief that they are paid according to how many enemy ears they bring in.

There were two tabors, or battalions, of Moroccans in the zone; a tabor consists of several goums, or companies, and each soldier who is a member of a company is called a goumier. For the sake of simplicity and euphony, Americans called the Moroccan soldiers themselves goums. The goums used to ride along the side of the road on bay mules or gray horses—sure-footed, mountain-bred animals—until they got near the place where they were going to fight. Then they would dismount and go off into the brush on bare feet, and return with their booty when they had finished their business. The goum's sole outer garment is the *djellabah*, which looks like a long brown bathrobe with a hood. It is made of cotton, wool, linen, goats' hair, or camels' hair and usually has vertical black stripes. It sheds water, insulates against heat and cold, is a substitute for a pup tent at night, and serves as a repository for everything the goum gloms, like the capacious garment of a professional shoplifter. In their Moroccan homeland the goums live with their wives and children in their own villages and are supposed to pay themselves with the spoils of tribes that resist the French government. In Tunisia the spoils were pretty well confined to soldiers' gear. As a goum killed or captured more and more enemies, he would put on layer after layer of tunics and trousers, always wearing the *djellabah* over everything. The girth of the goums increased as the campaign wore on. This swollen effect gave a goum an air of prosperity and importance, in his opinion; his standing as a warrior, he thought, was in direct ratio to his circumference. A goum who was doing well often wore, between sorties, one German and one Italian boot and carried a string of extra boots over his saddlebow. The funny part of it was that a goum wearing six men's clothing could slip noiselessly through a thicket that was impassable to a skinny American. The French officers commanding the goums assured me that their men were not paid by the ear; if a goum occasionally had a few dried ears concealed in a fold of his *djellabah*, one officer explained, it was because goums had discovered that such souvenirs had a trade value in G.I. cigarettes and chewing gum. "Far from paying for ears," this officer said, "we have recently been offering a small reward for live prisoners for interrogation. It is evident that a prisoner without ears is not a good subject for interrogation, because he does not hear the questions plainly." To hold the goums' respect, the officers had to be able to march, climb, and fight with them, and a goum is as inexhaustible as a mountain sheep and about as fastidious as a hyena. Most goums come from the Atlas Mountains and few of them speak Arabic, much less French, so the officers have to be fluent in the southern Berber dialects, which are all that the men know. The goums are trying companions in minefields, because, as one officer remarked, "They say, 'If it is the will of God, we go up,' and then they just push forward." Neither they nor the Corps Franc had mine detectors. An American captain named Yankauer, who was the surgeon at the clearing station near the yellow-triangle hill, was once digging scraps of steel out of a goum who had stepped on a mine. The man let out one short squeal—there was no anesthetic—and then began a steady chant. Yankauer asked a goum officer, who was waiting his turn on the table, what the goum was saying. The officer translated, "He chants, 'God forgive me, I am a woman. God forgive me, I am a woman,' because, you see, he has cried aloud, so he is ashamed." The goums' chief weapons were curved knives and long rifles of the vintage of 1871, and one of the supply problems of the campaign for the American G-4 was finding ammunition for these antediluvian small arms. Colonel Pierre Magnan, who had succeeded de Montsabert in command of the Corps Franc, was the senior French officer in the zone. I was with him one day when the commander of a newly arrived tabor presented himself for orders. "How are you fixed for automatic weapons, Major?" Magnan asked. "We have two old machine guns," the goum officer said. Then, when he saw Magnan's glum look, he added cheerily, "But don't worry, my Colonel, we use them only on maneuvers."

Magnan was a trim, rather elegant officer who, before the Allied landings, had commanded a crack infantry regiment in Morocco. On the morning of the American landings, he had arrested General Noguès, the Governor General of Morocco, and then asked him to prevent any fighting between the French and Americans by welcoming the invading forces. Noguès had telephoned to a tank regiment to come and arrest Magnan. Magnan, unwilling to shed French blood, had surrendered to the tankmen and become a prisoner in his turn. The liberated Noguès had then ordered a resistance which cost hundreds of French and American lives. Magnan was kept in prison for several days after Noguès, who was backed by our State Department, had consented to be agreeable to the Allies. Magnan had then been released, but he was deprived of his command and consigned to the Corps Franc. He now commands a division in France, and de Montsabert has a *corps d'armée*, so the scheme to keep them down has not been precisely a success.

The Axis forces north of Sedjenane must have been as hard put to it for supply routes as we were. I don't remember the roads the Intelligence maps showed behind the enemy's lines, but they could not have been numerous or elaborate. The Germans did not seem to have a great deal of artillery, but they occasionally landed shells on our road. Once, I remember, they shot up a couple of tank destroyers shortly after the jeep I was in had pulled out to let them pass. Throughout, it was a stubborn, nasty sort of fighting in the brush, and casualties arrived in a steady trickle rather than any great spurt, because large-scale attacks were impossible.

Our men fought their way a few hundred yards further east each day, toward Ferryville and Bizerte. Eventually, when Rommel's forces crumpled, men of the Corps Franc, in trucks driven by American soldiers, got to Bizerte before any other Allied troops.

On Easter Sunday, which came late in April, I was out along the Track all day, riding in a jeep with Hal Boyle, a correspondent for the Associated Press. At the end of the afternoon we headed home, hoping to get back to the press camp before night so that we wouldn't have to buck a stream of two-and-a-half-ton trucks and armored vehicles in the blackout. Traffic seemed, if anything, heavier than usual along the Foresters' Track, as it always did when you were in a hurry. The jeep stopped for minutes at a time, which gave Boyle the opportunity to climb out and get the names and home addresses of American soldiers for his stories. Sometimes he would stay behind, talking, and catch up with the jeep the next time it was snagged. We could have walked along the Track faster than we rode. Finally we came to a dip in the road. Fifty yards below and to our right there was a shallow stream, and there was almost no brush on the slope from the road down to the water. This, for the Foresters' Track country, was a considerable clearing, and it was being used for a number of activities. Some goums were watering their mounts in the stream, some French and American soldiers were heating rations over brush fires, a number of vehicles were parked there, and Colonel Magnan and some officers were holding a staff meeting. As we approached the clearing, we were stopped again for a moment by the traffic. A dismal American soldier came out of the brush on our left, tugging a gaunt, reluctant white horse. "Come along, Horrible," the soldier said in a tone of intensest loathing. "This goddam horse got me lost three times today," he said to us, looking over his shoulder at the sneering, wall-eyed beast. He evidently thought the horse was supposed to guide him.

We moved downhill a bit and stopped again, this time behind an ambulance that was loading wounded. There was a group of soldiers around the ambulance. Boyle and I got out to look. There were four wounded men, all badly hit. They were breathing hard and probably didn't know what was going on. Shock and heavy doses of morphia were making their move easy, or at least quiet. The four men were all from the Sixtieth Infantry of the Ninth Division. A soldier by the road said that they had been on a patrol and had exchanged shots with a couple of Germans; the Germans had popped up waving white handkerchiefs, the Americans had stood up to take them prisoners, and another German, lying concealed, had opened on them with a machine gun. It was the sort of thing that had happened dozens of times to other units, and that undoubtedly has happened hundreds of times since. Such casualties, a Polish officer once said to me, are an entry fee to battle. That doesn't make them easy to take, however. The soldiers had been told about this particular trick in their training courses, but they had probably thought it was a fable invented to make them hate the enemy. Now the men around the ambulance had really begun to hate the enemy.

While Boyle was getting the names and addresses of the men, I saw another American soldier by the side of the road. This one was dead. A soldier nearby said that the dead man had been a private known as Mollie. A blanket covered his face, so I surmised that it had been shattered, but there was no blood on the ground, so I judged that he had been killed in the brush and carried down to the road to await transport. A big, wild-looking sergeant was standing alongside him—a hawk-nosed, red-necked man with a couple of front teeth missing—and I asked him if the dead man had been in the patrol with the four wounded ones. "Jeez, no!" the sergeant said, looking at me as if I ought to know about the man with the blanket over his face. "That's Mollie. Comrade Molotov. The Mayor of Broadway. Didn't you ever hear of him? Jeez, Mac, he once captured six hundred Eyetalians by himself and brought them all back along with him. Sniper got him, I guess. I don't know, because he went out with the French, and he was found dead up there in the hills. He always liked to do crazy things—go off by himself with a pair of big field glasses he had and watch the enemy put in minefields, or take off and be an artillery spotter for a while, or drive a tank. From the minute he seen those frogs, he was bound to go off with them."

"Was his name really Molotov?" I asked.

"No," said the sergeant, "he just called himself that. The boys mostly shortened it to Mollie. I don't even know what his real name was—Warren, I think. Carl Warren. He used to say he was a Broadway big shot. 'Just ask anybody around Forty-fourth Street,' he used to say. 'They all know me.' Me, I'm from White Plains—I never heard of him before he joined up."

"I had him with me on a patrol that was to contact the French when the regiment was moving into this zone last Thursday," a stocky blond corporal said. "The first French patrol we met, Mollie says to me, 'This is too far back for me. I'm going up in the hills with these frogs and get me some Lugers.' He was always collecting things he captured off Germans and Italians, but the one thing he didn't have yet was a Luger. I knew if I didn't let him go he would take off anyway and get into more trouble with the C.O. He was always in trouble. So I said, 'All right, but the frogs got to give me a receipt for you, so I can prove you didn't go A.W.O.L.' One of the soldiers with me could speak French, so he explained it and the frog noncom give me a receipt on a piece of toilet paper and Mollie went off with them." The corporal fished in one of the pockets of his field jacket and brought out a sheet of tissue. On it, the French noncom had written, in pencil, "*Pris avec moi le soldat américain Molotov, 23 avril, '43, Namin, caporal chef.*"

"Mollie couldn't speak French," the American corporal went on, "but he always got on good with the frogs. It's funny where those big field glasses went, though. He used to always have them around his neck, but some-body must have figured they were no more good to him after he was dead, so they sucked them up. He used to always say that he was a big-shot gambler and that he used to watch the horse races with those glasses."

By now the four wounded men had been loaded into the ambulance. It moved off. Obviously, there was a good story in Mollie, but he was not available for an interview. The driver of the truck behind our jeep was giving us the horn, so I pulled Boyle toward the jeep. He got in, still looking back at Mollie, who said nothing to keep him, and we drove away. When we had gone a little way, at our customary slow pace, a tall lieutenant signalled to us from the roadside that he wanted a hitch and we stopped and indicated that he should hop aboard. He told us his name was Carl Ruff. He was from New York. Ruff was dog-tired from scram-bling through the bush. I said something about Mollie, and Ruff said that he had not known him alive but had been the first American to see his body, on Good Friday morning. The French had led him to it. "He was on the slope of a hill," Ruff said, "and slugs from an automatic rifle had hit him in the right eye and chest. He must have been working his way up the hill, crouching, when the German opened on him and hit him in the chest, and then as he fell, the other bullet probably got him in the eye. He couldn't have lived a minute."

It was a month later, aboard the United States War Shipping Adminis-tration steamer Monterey, a luxury liner that had been converted to war service without any needless suppression of comfort, that I next heard of Molotov, the Mayor of Broadway. The Monterey was on her way from Casablanca to New York. On the passenger list were four correspondents besides myself, a thousand German prisoners, five hundred wounded Americans, all of whom would need long hospitalization, and a couple of hundred officers and men who were being transferred or were on various errands. It was one of the advantages of being a correspondent that one could go to America without being a German or wounded, or without being phenomenally lucky, which the unwounded soldiers on our boat considered that they were. The crossing had almost a holiday atmosphere. We were homeward bound after a great victory in the North African campaign, the first the Allies had scored over Germany in a war nearly four years old. The weather was perfect and the Monterey, which was not overcrowded and had wide decks and comfortable lounges, had the aspect and feeling of a cruise ship. The wounded were glad, in their sad way, to be going home. The prisoners were in good spirits, too; they seemed to regard the journey as a Nazi Strength through Joy excursion. They orga-nized vaudeville shows, boxing matches, and art exhibitions, with the ener-getic coöperation of the ship's chaplain, who found much to admire in the

Christian cheerfulness with which they endured their increased rations. A couple of anti-Nazi prisoners had announced themselves on the first day out, but the German noncoms had knocked them about and set them to cleaning latrines, so order had soon been restored. "That's an army where they really have some discipline!" one of the American officers on board told me enviously. The prisoners had to put up with some hardships, of course. They complained one evening when ice cream was served to the wounded but not to them, and another time they didn't think the transport surgeon, a Jew, was "sympathetic" enough to a German officer with a stomach ache.

The hospital orderlies would wheel the legless wounded out on the promenade deck in wheelchairs to see the German boxing bouts, and the other wounded would follow them, some swinging along on crutches or hopping on one foot, some with their arms in slings or casts, some with their broken necks held stiffly in casts and harnesses. They had mixed reactions to the bouts. An arm case named Sanderson, a private who wore the Ninth Division shoulder patch, told me one day that he wished he could be turned loose on the prisoners with a tommygun, because he didn't like to see them jumping about in front of his legless pals. Another arm case, named Shapiro, from the same division, always got a lot of amusement out of the show. Shapiro was a rugged-looking boy from the Brownsville part of Brooklyn. He explained how he felt one day after two Afrika Korps heavy-weights had gone through a couple of rounds of grunting, posturing, and slapping. "Every time I see them box, I know we can't lose the war," he said. "The Master Race—phooey! Any kid off the street could of took the both of them."

Shapiro and Sanderson, I learned during one ringside conversation with them, had both been in the Sixtieth Infantry, Molotov's old regiment. They had been wounded in the fighting around Maknassy, in southern Tunisia, early in April, the first serious action the regiment had been in. Molotov had been killed late in April, during the drive on Bizerte, and until I told them, the boys hadn't heard he was dead. I asked them if they had known him.

"How could you help it?" Shapiro said. "There will never be anybody in the division as well known as him. In the first place, you couldn't help noticing him on account of his clothes. He looked like a soldier out of some other army, always wearing them twenty-dollar green tailor-made officers' shirts and sometimes riding boots, with a French berrit with a long rooster feather that he got off an Italian prisoner's hat, and a long black-and-red cape that he got off another prisoner for a can of C ration."

"And the officers let him get away with it?" I asked.

"Not in the rear areas, they didn't," Shapiro said. "But in combat, Mollie was an asset. Major Kauffman, his battalion commander, knew it, so he would kind of go along with him. But he would never have him made even a pfc. Mollie couldn't of stood the responsibility. He was the greatest natural-born foul-up* in the Army," Shapiro added reverently. "He was court-martialled twenty or thirty times, but the Major always got him out of it. He had the biggest blanket roll in the Ninth Division, with a wall tent inside it and some Arabian carpets and bronze lamps and a folding washstand and about five changes of uniform, none of them regulation, and he would always manage to get it on a truck when we moved. When he pitched his tent, it looked like a concession at Coney Island. I was with him when he got his first issue of clothing at Camp Dix in 1941. 'I've threw better stuff than this away,' he said. He never liked to wear issue. He was up for court-martial for deserting his post when he was on guard duty at Fort Bragg, but the regiment sailed for Morocco before they could try him, and he did so good in the landing at Port Lyautey that they kind of forgave him. Then he went over the hill again when he was guarding a dock at Oran in the winter, but they moved us up into the combat zone before they could try him then, so he beat that rap, too. He was a very lucky fellow. I can hardly think of him being dead."

"Well, what was so good about him?" I asked.

Sanderson, who was a thin, sharp-faced boy from Michigan, answered me with the embarrassed frankness of a modern mother explaining the facts of life to her offspring. "Sir," he said, "it may not sound nice to say it, and I do not want to knock anyone, but in battle almost everybody is frightened, especially the first couple of times. Once in a while you find a fellow who isn't frightened at all. He goes forward and the other fellows go along with him. So he is very important. Probably he is a popoff, and he kids the other guys, and they all feel better. Mostly those quiet, determined fellows crack up before the popoffs. Mollie was the biggest popoff and the biggest screwball and the biggest foul-up I ever saw, and he wasn't afraid of nothing. Some fellows get brave with experience, I guess, but Mollie never had any fear to begin with. Like one time on the road to Maknassy, the battalion was trying to take some hills and we were getting no place. They were just Italians in front of us, but they had plenty of stuff and they were in cover and we were in the open. Mollie stands right up, wearing the cape and the berrit with the feather, and he says, 'I bet those Italians would surrender if somebody asked them to. What the hell do they want to fight for?' he says. So he walks across the minefield and up the hill to the Italians, waving his arms and making funny motions, and they shoot at him for a while and then stop, thinking he is crazy. He goes up there yelling '*Veni qua!*,' which he says afterward is New York Italian for 'Come here!,' and '*Feeneesh la guerre!*,' which is French, and when he gets to the Italians he finds a soldier who was a barber in Astoria but went home on a visit and got drafted in the Italian Army, so the barber translates for him and the Italians say sure, they would like to

---

* A euphemism, of course.

surrender, and Mollie comes back to the lines with five hundred and sixty-eight prisoners. He had about ten Italian automatics strapped to his belt and fifteen field glasses hung over his shoulders. So instead of being stopped, we took the position and cleaned up on the enemy. That was good for the morale of the battalion. The next time we got in a fight, we said to ourselves, 'Those guys are just looking for an easy out,' so we got up and chased them the hell away from there. A disciplined soldier would never have did what Mollie done. He was a very unusual guy. He gave the battalion confidence and the battalion gave the regiment confidence, because the other battalions said, 'If the Second can take all those prisoners, we can, too.' And the Thirty-ninth and the Forty-seventh Regiments probably said to themselves, 'If the Sixtieth is winning all them fights, we can also.' So you might say that Mollie made the whole division." I found out afterward that Sanderson had oversimplified the story, but it was essentially true and the tradition endures in the Ninth Division.

"What kind of a looking fellow was Mollie?" I asked.

"He was a good-looking kid," Shapiro said. "Medium-sized, around a hundred and sixty pounds, with long, curly blond hair. They could almost never get him to have his hair cut. Once, when it got too bad, Major Kauffman took him by the hand and said, 'Come along with me. We'll get a haircut together.' So he sat him down and held onto him while the G.I. barber cut both their hair. And everything he wore had to be sharp. I remember that after the French surrendered to us at Port Lyautey, a lot of French officers gave a party and invited a couple of officers from the battalion to it, and when the officers got there they found Mollie was there, and the Frenchmen were all bowing to him and saluting him. He was dressed so sharp they thought he was an officer, too—maybe a colonel."

Another boy, a badly wounded one in a wheelchair, heard us talking about Mollie and rolled his chair over to us. "It was the field glasses I'll always remember," he said. "From the first day we landed on the beach in Morocco, Mollie had those glasses. He told some fellows once he captured them from a French general, but he told some others he brought them all the way from New York. He told them he used to watch horse races with the glasses; he was fit to be tied when he got to Morocco and found there was no scratch sheets. 'Ain't there no way to telegraph a bet on a race?' he said, and then he let out a howl. 'Vot a schvindle!' That was his favorite saying—'Vot a schvindle!' He was always bitching about something. He used to go out scouting with the glasses, all alone, and find the enemy and tip Major Kauffman off where they were. He had a lot of curiosity. He always had plenty of money, but he would never tell where he got it from. He just let people understand he was a big shot—maybe in some racket. When we was down at Fort Bragg, he and another fellow, a sergeant, had a big Buick that he kept outside the camp, and they used to go riding all around the country. They used to get some swell stuff."

"He never shot crap for less than fifty dollars a roll when he had the dice," Shapiro said, "and he never slept with any woman under an actress." The way Shapiro said it, it was as if he had said, "He never saluted anybody under the rank of brigadier general."

During the rest of the voyage, I heard more about Mollie. I found nobody who was sure of his real name, but the majority opinion was that it was something like Carl Warren. "But he wasn't American stock or Irish," Sanderson said one day in a group discussion. "He seemed to me more German-American." Another boy in the conversation said that Mollie had told him he was of Russian descent. Sanderson was sure that Molotov wasn't Russian. "Somebody just called him that because he was a radical, I guess," he said. "He was always hollering he was framed." "He used to have a big map of the eastern front in his tent in Morocco," another soldier said, "and every time the Russians advanced he would mark it with pins and holler, 'Hey, Comrade, howdya like that!' " One boy remembered that Mollie had won fifteen hundred dollars in a crap game at Fort Bragg. "He had it for about three days," he said, "and then lost it to a civilian. When he got cleaned in a game, he would never borrow a buck to play on with. He would just leave. Then the next time he played, he would have a new roll. Right after we landed in Morocco, he was awful flush, even for him, and he told a couple of guys he'd climbed over the wall of an old fort the French had just surrendered and there, in some office, he found a briefcase with fifty thousand francs in it. The next thing he done was hire twelve Arabs to cook and clean and wash dishes for him."

"I was inducted the same time with him, at Grand Central Palace," an armless youngster said, "and him and me and the bunch was marched down to Penn Station to take the train. That was way back in January, 1941," he added, as if referring to a prehistoric event. "He was wearing a blue double-breasted jacket and a dark-blue sport shirt open at the neck and gray flannel trousers and a camel's-hair overcoat. They took us into a restaurant on Thirty-fourth Street to buy us a feed and Mollie started buying beers for the whole crowd. 'Come on, Comrades,' he says. 'Plenty more where this comes from.' Then he led the singing on the train all the way down to Dix. But as soon as he got down there and they took all his fancy clothes away from him, he was licked. 'Vot a schvindle!' he says. He drew K.P. a lot at Dix, but he always paid some other guy to do it for him. The only thing he could ever do good outside of combat was D.R.O. —that's dining-room orderly at the officers' mess. I've seen him carry three stacks of dishes on each arm."

When I told them how Mollie had been killed, Shapiro said that that was just what you'd have expected of Mollie. "He never liked to stay with his own unit," he said. "You could hardly even tell what battalion he was in."

I was not to see the Army's official version of what Mollie had done in the fight against the six hundred Italians until the next summer, when I caught up with the Second Battalion of the Sixtieth Infantry near Marigny, in Normandy. Mollie's protector, Major Michael S. Kauffman, by then a lieutenant colonel, was still commanding officer. "Mollie didn't capture the lot by himself," Kauffman said, "but he was instrumental in getting them, and there were about six hundred of them all right. The battalion S-2 got out a mimeographed training pamphlet about that fight, because there were some points in it that we thought instructive. I'll get you a copy." The pamphlet he gave me bears the slightly ambitious title "The Battle of Sened, 23 March, '43, G Co. 60th Infantry Dawn Attack on Sened, Tunisia." The Sened of the title was the village of Sened, in the high *djebel* a couple of miles south of the Sened railroad station. It was country I remembered well: a bare plain with occasional bunch grass, with naked red-rock hills rising above it. The Americans had fought there several times; I had seen the taking of the railroad station by another regiment at the beginning of February, 1943, and it had been lost and retaken between then and March 23rd.

On the first page of the pamphlet there was a map showing the Italian position, on two hills separated by a narrow gorge, and the jump-off position of the Americans, two much smaller hills a couple of miles to the north. Then there was a list of "combat lessons to be learned," some of which were: "A small aggressive force can knock out a large group by determined action," "Individuals, soldiers with initiative, aggressiveness, and courage, can influence a large battle," and "Confusion is normal in combat." I have often since thought that this last would make a fine title for a book on war. The pamphlet told how an Italian force estimated at from thirty men to three thousand, according to the various persons interviewed in advance of the fight by S-2 ("Question civilians," the pamphlet said. "Don't rely on one estimate of enemy strength. Weigh all information in the light of its source."), had taken refuge in the village of Sened. G Company, about a hundred and fifty men, had been ordered to clean out the Italians. It had artillery support from some guns of the First Armored Division; in fact, a Lieutenant Colonel MacPherson, an artillery battalion commander, was actually the senior American officer in the action. This colonel, acting as his own forward observer, had looked over the situation and at four in the afternoon of March 22nd had ordered the first platoon of the company to attack. It was soon apparent, judging by the defenders' fire, that the lowest estimate of the enemy's strength was very wrong and that there were at least several hundred Italians on the two hills. Then, in the words of the pamphlet, "Private Molotov"—even his officers had long since forgotten his civilian name—"crawls to enemy position with Pfc. De Marco (both are volunteers) and arranges surrender conference. C.O. refuses to surrender and fire fight continues. Individual enemy riflemen begin to throw down their arms. First platoon returns to Sened Station at dark with 147 prisoners, including 3 officers."

"De Marco was a friend of Molotov's," Colonel Kauffman told me. "It was Mollie's idea to go up to the enemy position, and De Marco did the talking. It must have been pretty effective, because all those Italians came back with them."

"G Company," the pamphlet continued, "attacks again at dawn, first and third platoons attacking. Entrance to town is deep narrow gorge between two long ridges. Town lies in continuation of gorge, surrounded on all sides by 1,000–2,000 foot *djebels* as shown in sketch. (Possible enemy escape route was used by Ancient Romans as park for wild animals used in gladiatorial matches.) Approach to gorge entrance is terraced and well concealed by a large olive-tree grove; five (5) or six (6) field pieces in grove have been knocked out by previous day's artillery fire."

Although the pamphlet didn't say so, the olive groves had once covered all the plain. That plain is now given over to bunch grass, but it was carefully irrigated in the days of the Roman Empire. The "wild animals used in gladiatorial matches" were for the arena at the splendid stone city of Capsa, now the sprawling, dried-mud Arab town of Gafsa, fifteen miles from Sened.

"Company attacks as shown on sketch," the pamphlet continued, "third platoon making steep rocky climb around right, first platoon (Molotov's) around left. Light machine guns and mortars follow close behind by bounds, grenadiers move well to front with mission of flushing enemy out of numerous caves where he has taken up defensive positions. Left platoon, commanded by Sergeant Vernon Mugerditchian, moves slowly over ground devoid of concealment, and finally comes to rest. Molotov goes out alone, keeping abreast of faster moving platoon on right, and assists Lt. Col. MacPherson in artillery direction by shouting."

The combined artillery and infantry fire made the Italians quit. The pamphlet says, in closing, "Italian captain leads column of prisoners out of hills, bringing total of 537 (including officers). Total booty includes 2 large trucks, 3 small trucks, several personnel carrier motorcycles, 200 pistols, machine guns, rifles, and ammunition."

"Mollie liked to go out ahead and feel he was running the show," Colonel Kauffman said. "We put him in for a D.S.C. for what he did, but it was turned down. Then we put in for a Silver Star, and that was granted, but he was killed before he ever heard about it. He was a terrible soldier. He and another fellow were to be tried by a general court-martial for quitting their guard posts on the docks at Oran, but we had to go into action before court could be held. The other fellow had his court after the end of the campaign and got five years."

The officers of the battalion, and those at division headquarters, knew that I was going to write a story about Mollie sometime. Whenever I would encounter one of them, in a country tavern or at a corps or Army headquarters, or on a dusty road behind the lines, during our final campaign before Germany's surrender, he would ask me when I was going to "do Mollie." I am doing him now.

Even after I had been back in the States for a while that summer of 1943, I had an intermittent interest in Mollie, although La Piste Forestière assumed a curious unreality after I had been living on lower Fifth Avenue a couple of weeks. I asked a fellow I knew at the *Times* to check back through the casualty lists and see if the death of a soldier with a name like "Carl Warren" had been reported, since I knew the lists gave the addresses of the next of kin and I thought I might be able to find out more about Mollie. The *Times* man found out that there hadn't been any such name but that there was often a long interval between casualties and publication. I took to turning mechanically to the new lists as they came out and looking through the "W"s. One day I saw listed, among the Army dead, "Karl C. Warner, sister Mrs. Ulidjak, 230 E. Eightieth Street, Manhattan." The juxtaposition of "a name like Warren" with one that I took to be Russian or Ukrainian made me suspect that Warner was Molotov, and it turned out that I was right.

A couple of days later, I went uptown to look for Mrs. Ulidjak. No. 230 is between Second and Third Avenues, in a block overshadowed by the great, brute mass of the Manhattan Storage & Warehouse Company's building at the corner of Eightieth. Along the block there were a crumbling, red-brick elementary school of the type Fusion administrations like to keep going so that they can hold the tax rate down, a yellowish, old-fashioned Baptist church, some boys playing ball in the street, and a banner, bearing a number of service stars, hung on a line stretched across the street. As yet, it had no gold stars. No. 230 is what is still called a "new-law tenement," although the law governing this type of construction is fifty years old: a six-story walkup with the apartments built around air shafts. Ulidjak was one of the names on the mailboxes in the vestibule. I pushed the button beside it, and in a minute there was an answering buzz and I walked upstairs. A thin, pale woman with a long, bony face and straight blond hair pulled back into a bun came to the apartment door. She looked under thirty and wore silver-rimmed spectacles. This was Mrs. Ulidjak, Private Warner's sister. Her husband is in the Merchant Marine. She didn't seem startled when I said I was a correspondent; every American expects to be interviewed by a reporter sometime. Mrs. Ulidjak had been notified of her brother's death by the War Department over a week before, but she had no idea how it had happened or where. She said he had been in the Sixtieth Infantry, all right, so I was sure Warner had been Mollie. "Was he fighting the Japs?" she asked me. When I told her no, she seemed slightly disappointed. "And you were there?" she asked. I said I had been. Then, apparently trying to visualize me in the context of war, she asked, "Did you wear a helmet, like Ernie Pyle? Gee, they must be heavy to wear. Did it hurt your head much?" When I had reassured her on this point, she led me into a small sitting room with a window opening on a dark air shaft. A young man and a young woman, who Mrs. Ulidjak said were neighbors, were in the room, but they went into the adjoining kitchen, apparently so that they would not feel obliged to look solemn.

"Was your name Warner, too, before you were married?" I asked Mrs. Ulidjak.

"No," she said, "Karl and I were named Petuskia—that's Russian—but he changed to Warner when he came to New York because he thought it sounded sweller. We were from a little place called Cokesburg, in western Pennsylvania. He hardly ever came up here. He had his own friends."

"Did he go to high school in Cokesburg?" I asked.

The idea amused Mrs. Ulidjak. "No, just grammar school," she said. "He was a pit boy in the coal mines until we came to New York. But he always liked to dress nice. You can ask any of the cops around the Mall in Central Park about him. Curly, they used to call him, or Blondy. He was quite a lady's man."

Then I asked her the question that had puzzled Mollie's Army friends: "What did he do for a living before he went into the Army?"

"He was a bartender down to Jimmy Kelly's, the night club in the Village," Mrs. Ulidjak said.

She then told me that her brother's Christian name really was Karl and that he was twenty-six when he was killed, although he had looked several years younger. Both parents are dead. The parents had never told her, as far as she could remember, what part of Russia they came from. When I said that Mollie had been a hero, she was pleased, and said he had always had an awful crust. She called the young neighbors, who seemed to be of Italian descent, back into the sitting room and made me repeat the story of how Mollie captured the six hundred Italians (I hadn't seen the official version of his exploit yet and naturally I gave him full credit in mine). "Six hundred wops!" Mrs. Ulidjak exclaimed gaily. She got a lot of fun out of Mollie's "big shot" stories, too. She showed me a large, expensive-looking photograph of him "addressing" a golf ball. He was wearing light-colored plus-fours, white stockings, and brogues with tassels, and there was a big, happy grin on his face that made it plain that he was not going to hit the ball but was just posing. He had a wide, plump face with high cheekbones and square white teeth, and the hair about which I had so often heard looked at least six inches long. "He had a room at 456 West Forty-fourth Street, and a little Jewish tailor down in that neighborhood made all those nice things for him special," she said admiringly. She had never heard him called Molotov.

I went over to West Forty-fourth Street a few days later. The 400 block, between Ninth and Tenth Avenues, looks more depressing than the one the Ulidjaks live on. It is mostly shops dealing in the cheap merchandise that is used as premiums, and stores that sell waiters' supplies, and lodging houses favored by waiters and cooks. It was evident from the look of the house at No. 456 that though Mollie had spent a disproportionate share of his income on clothes, he had wasted nothing on his living quarters. No one at No. 456 remembered Mollie. The tenants and the janitor had all come there since his time. I couldn't find the little tailor. But on the north side of Forty-fourth Street, near Ninth Avenue, there is a building occupied by the Warner Brothers' Eastern offices, and I was sure that this had given Mollie the idea of calling himself Warner.

That evening I went down to Jimmy Kelly's, on Sullivan Street. Kelly's is the kind of club that never changes much but that you seldom remember anything specific about unless you have had a fight there. I had been there a few times in the late thirties, but I couldn't remember the bartender's face. Kelly's has a dance floor a little bigger than two tablecloths, and there is always a show with young, sometimes pretty girls imitating the specialties that more famous and experienced performers are doing at clubs uptown, and a master of ceremonies making cracks so old that they have been used in Hollywood musicals. The man behind the bar the night I showed up said he had been there several years and had known his predecessor, whose name was not Molotov. He had never heard of a bartender named Molotov or Warner or Mollie or Karl at Kelly's. After I had had a couple of Scotches and had told him the story, he said he wondered if the fellow I meant hadn't been a busboy. The description seemed to fit one who had worked there. "We all used to call this kid Curly," he said, "but Ray, the waiter who is the union delegate, might remember his real name."

Ray was a scholarly-looking man with a high, narrow forehead and shell-rimmed spectacles. "Curly's name *was* Karl C. Warner," he said after he had been told what I wanted to know. "I remember it from his union card. He was a man who would always stand up for his fellow-worker. Waiters and Waitresses Local No. 1 sent him down here in the summer of 1940 and he worked until late the next fall. He was outspoken but a hard worker and strong—he could carry three stacks of dishes on each arm. A busboy has a lot to do in a place like this when there is a rush on—clearing away dishes, setting up for new parties, bringing the waiters their orders—and a stupid boy can spoil the waiters' lives for them. We had another boy here at the same time, an Irish boy, who kidded Curly about the fancy clothes he wore, so they went down in the basement and fought for a couple of hours one afternoon. Nobody won the fight. They just fought until they were tired and then stopped. Curly had wide interests for a busboy," Ray continued. "When there was no rush on, he would sometimes stop by a customer's table, particularly if it was some man who looked important, and talk to him for ten minutes or so. The customers didn't seem to mind. He had a nice way about him. He had a kind of curiosity."

The Army stories about Mollie's wealth made Ray and the bartender laugh. "He used to come back here now and then during the first year he was in the Army," Ray said, "and always he would borrow ten or twenty dollars from one of us waiters. We would lend it to him because we liked him, without expecting to get it back." A busboy at Kelly's is paid only nominal wages, Ray told me—just about enough to cover his laundry bill—but the waiters chip in a percentage of their tips for the boys. "I guess Curly averaged about forty a week here," he said. "If he was anxious to get extra money, he might have had a lunch job someplace else at the same time, but I never heard about it. A tailor like he had probably made those suits for about twenty-five per. What else did he have to spend money on? His night life was here. He used to tell us he had worked at El Morocco, but we used to say, 'What's the difference? Dirty dishes are the same all over.'"

At the union headquarters, which are on the twelfth floor of a loft building on West Fortieth Street, Mollie was also remembered. The serious, chunky young woman in the union secretary's office said, "Warner was always a dissident. He would speak up at every meeting and object to everything. But we all liked him. He stopped paying dues a few months before he went into the Army, but at Christmastime in 1941 he came back here and said he heard that union members in the services were getting a present from the local, so he wanted one, too. So we gave it to him, of course. The secretary will be interested to know he is dead."

The young woman called the secretary, a plump, olive-complexioned man, from his desk in an inner room and said to him, "You remember Karl Warner, the blond boy with curly hair? He has been killed in Africa. He was a hero."

"Is that so?" the secretary said. "Well, get a man to put up a gold paper star on the flag in the members' hall right away and draw up a notice to put on the bulletin board. He is the first member of Local No. 1 to die in this war."

I thought how pleased Mollie would have been to be restored to good standing in the union, without even having paid up his dues. Then I thought of how much fun he would have had on the Mall in Central Park, in the summertime, if he could only have gone up there with his Silver Star ribbon on, and a lot of enemy souvenirs. I also thought of how far La Piste Forestière was from the kitchen in Jimmy Kelly's.

When I walk through the West Side borderland between Times Square and the slums, where Mollie once lived, I often think of him and his big talk and his golf-suit grin. It cheers me to think there may be more like him all around me—a notion I would have dismissed as sheer romanticism before World War II. Cynicism is often the shamefaced product of inexperience.

He has become a posthumous pal, though I never knew him when he was alive. He was full of curiosity—he would have made a great explorer —and fond of high living, which is the only legitimate incentive for liking money. He had faith in the reason of his fellow-man, as when he sensed that the Italians at Sened were no more eager to fight than he was. The action that earned him his Silver Star cost no lives. It saved them. He bragged, but when challenged he would not back off. The brag was like the line a deckhand throws over a bollard—it pulled performance after it. I lived with him so long that I once half-convinced myself he was not dead. This was when I began to write a play about him, and was reminded by more experienced hands that it is customary for the protagonist of a work of that nature to remain alive until the last act.

"Suppose," I said, "that the corpse with the face shot away that I saw by La Piste was not Mollie at all, but that Mollie had put his uniform and dog-tags on a dead goumier and gone over the hill wearing a Moroccan *djellabah*, to wage a less restricted kind of war, accumulating swag as he went? And suppose he was living in Morocco now, with a harem, a racing stable, and a couple of Saharan oil wells? And suppose he returned to New York as a member of the Moroccan, or the Mauretanian, Delegation to the United Nations, or, better yet, a Delegate from the Touareg state that is sure to be formed sooner or later? The last would afford him the advantage of a veil covering his face below the eyes, to conceal his grin.

Mollie would like the fancy togs, and if any old rival, perhaps the Irish busboy, recognized him in the last scene and twitted him with his defection, he could pull out from his flowing sleeves hundreds of dried Nazi ears to prove he had waged war effectually to the last. If Allah has so willed it, the thing is.

Or suppose he had switched uniforms with a dead German, and thereafter, as a secret agent, confounded all the Wehrmacht's plans? He liked to operate in disguise, as he proved when he fooled the French officers at Casablanca, and superior officers of foreign powers confided in him on sight. I like him better as a Touareg, and I think he would have liked

Touaregs better as company. I dropped the play because that was all the plot I could think of.

Long after I abandoned thought of writing about Mollie again, I had a letter from a lady in Mechanicsburg, Pennsylvania, that cleared up the question of how Mollie transmuted his last name. It had nothing to do with Warner Brothers—a warning, this, against adopting mere plausibility in place of valid evidence. She wrote that her brother, a Mr. Karl Warner, had come to Cokesburg as boss of a construction job in about 1932, and had given the Petuskia boy a job as watchman, in defiance of all local counsel. Young Petuskia was considered a bad risk. The boy proved honest, and afterward wanted to pull up stakes and follow the construction gang when it left town. Warner told him he was too young. The Mechanicsburg lady was sure the boy had subsequently taken the Warner name in honor of her brother.

I am sure she is right, but it sounds like a detail out of an old-fashioned boys' book.

The air vendetta that is described in the next set of pieces took place in an earlier phase of the war in North Africa—all, in fact, during the month of January, 1943. I wrote the stories in my room at the Hotel Aletti, in Algiers, in early February. There were no facilities for sending despatches from the rudimentary air fields, several hundred miles away, where the fighting happened. This was one of the good points of being a correspondent—you could leave the discomfort of the scene of combat without being wounded.

Headquarters were so far from our war that the censor officers read our despatches like notes on an unknown world. For the staff it was rather like running a war in Ohio from a hotel in Washington, except that their hotel was better. It was the Saint George, up on the hill. But the Aletti was a fine place too—you could have a bath, though seldom a hot one, in a bathtub, and receive female visitors if they stood in well with the concierge. In town there was a great deal of Algerian wine, which is maligned in France by the very blenders who import it in vast quantities to give body to their thin vintages, and there was excellent food to be had if you knew where to look for it, in the Street of the Gate of Weeping, in the establishment of a Swiss who considered himself, as a neutral, immune from wartime food regulations. The fish and the small birds were almost literally beyond price, and there was a wine so kind that if I had a daughter, I would give her its name—Miliana.

In the twilight, as we walked to our dinners, German planes would come like swallows out of Sicily, far away, and jettison their bombs before reaching the center of our magnificent anti-aircraft display, like a beehive drawn in lines of orange tracer. If Headquarters hadn't been there, we wouldn't have had such a pretty beehive, and the pilots wouldn't have flinched so soon. My debts to the Supreme Command are therefore double—it stayed in a safe place and it kept it safer.

Then, in the dark after the third armagnac, we would steal away to a place of enchantment called the Sphinx, where girls would act charades that graying members of the American Legion still dream of with nostalgia in Terre Haute. It was a schizoid existence: in Tunisia, with your belly pressed to the ground, the Hotel Aletti seemed a mirage, but when you were in Algiers, you wondered whether you had lived on the Foamy Fields or imagined them.

2

For
Boots
Norgaard

The next pieces are about ground fighting, or what passed for it, in the first month of our maiden effort in Africa. The troops, pacific by nature, eased themselves into it like an old man with chilblains getting into a hot bath.

Gafsa, the center of these operations, is one of the oldest continuously inhabited places on earth, which is a reflection on human selectivity, because it is a desolation; it was the seat of a prehistoric culture called by archaeologists the Gafsan, which has left stone artifacts as evidence of the near-idiocy of the first inhabitants. Norman Douglas, who visited it in 1911, quoted an Arab song about it that begins:

"Gafsa is miserable; its water is blood . . ."

During all its long, ignoble history this has been so. Sallust tells how Marius, the Roman general, took it by night marches across the desertic steppe to the north, followed by a surprise attack. The steppe offered a formidable barrier to large bodies of troops, because camels had not been introduced into North Africa, and water supply was a problem. Marius solved it by having his soldiers drive cattle before them to the last spring. There he had them slaughter the beasts, skin them, fill the hides with water, and begin their march burdened only with these and meat, a concentrated ration, travelling across the high steppe in the cold nights and laying up in the heat of the day. There was no air observation and they cut the throats of the few travellers they met. He achieved complete surprise, and when the Gafsans came out to work their gardens in their oasis, the Romans rushed them so fast they had no chance to shut the city gates behind them.

Marius, following a colonialist tradition already old, denounced the Gafsans as treacherous and uncivilized, before putting the men to the sword and selling the women and children into slavery. But the city grew up again as a Roman garrison and colony, and was fought over by Moslem princelings all through the Middle Ages because by then the camels had come to North Africa, and it lay across a great caravan route. And in time Major-General Terry Allen of the First Division captured the city by the same maneuver—a night march across the desert, this time in trucks and jeeps, to avert annoyance by the *Luftwaffe*. He did this, however, before the third episode in the following narration, when the First Division, which was precocious compared to all others, had already found its stride. Gafsa is about 50 miles southeast of Cochran's old field at Thélepte.

Gafsa

THE Anglo-American North African campaign is sure to furnish a lot of historical controversy sooner or later, so there is no harm in correcting the record on one point immediately. The junction of the American Second Corps and the British Eighth Army, fighting its way north from Mareth, was copiously reported in newspapers in this country last April. Most of the reporters said that the meeting took place on the Gafsa-Gabès road. According to their stories, the historic moment came when an American motorized patrol met a British motorized patrol. Actually, the Eighth Army and the Second Corps joined up more than two months before the motorized incident, in the hall of the Hôtel de France, a two-story palace in Gafsa. I know, because I was there. In fact, I might say that I introduced them.

Gafsa, called Capsa by the Numidians, is a very ancient town on a very slight hill in south-central Tunisia. Warm springs gush from the foot of the hill, below a fifteenth-century Arab citadel, which was wrecked by our engineers during the fighting last February. The citadel was still intact when I first saw the place. The climate of Gafsa, even in late January, when Norgaard and I reached it, is warm and dry. There is an oasis around the town, which used to be an important knot in the web of caravan routes between the Sahara and the Mediterranean. Last winter Gafsa had, and by now probably has again, ten thousand inhabitants, of whom five or six hundred are Europeans, eight hundred are native Jews, and the rest Moslems who call themselves Arabs but are predominantly of Berber stock, like most North Africans. The Europeans are administrators or railroad workers. The Jews, whose ancestors came there not long after the Destruction of the Temple, are traders and traditionally middlemen between the Christians and the Moslems.

When Norgaard and I arrived in Gafsa, a battalion of American infantry was stationed there, together with several batteries of French seventy-fives, a battalion of Senegalese, and some Algerian *tirailleurs*. The

Americans, who belonged to the First Division, were the only ground troops we had south of the town of Sbeitla, which was sixty miles away. They had been there for a month and were quite at home in the place, which, as almost every enlisted man you talked to was certain to say, looked like a set in a Beau Geste movie. Old Jews sold surprisingly good native pastries and Arabs peddled dates in the square in front of the American barracks. The soldiers had adopted Arab kids as mascots and clothed them in G.I. shirts and shoes. There was a great outdoor Roman swimming pool, filled by warm running water from the springs. The water contained a good deal of sulphur, but it was nevertheless pleasant to bathe in, and the Americans spent a lot of time swimming in it. The French soldiers preferred to dangle fishing lines in a nearby spring-fed stream and catch little, extremely voracious blue fish,* which apparently were used to living in hot, sulphurous water.

There was also a clean Arab bath, in a narrow Arabian Nights alley, where the attendants would stretch you on the floor and twist your arms and legs out of joint and then pound you with a hot brick before allowing you to steam yourself in peace. I remember seeing, at the bath, an English captain I knew, a booby-trap expert, pink and jolly in the steam, wearing a towel around his loins. A couple of weeks later he accidentally blew himself up with an extremely special mine he had just devised. He simply vanished. Somehow I always think of him flying toward heaven draped in a towel and deeply embarrassed.** Gafsa also had a bordello offering a dozen girls whom a friend of mine described as "sort of French" and a madam who was a de Gaulliste. When a British lieutenant general came to town for a look around, the much-junior American officer who was his host wanted to give him a touch of real luxury—sheets to sleep between. He borrowed a pair from the madam.

Norgaard and I had gone to Gafsa because it was the American-held point nearest to Montgomery's advancing army and it seemed a likely place to witness the joining of the two forces. We expected the Americans either to hold on to the town until Montgomery arrived or else to launch an offensive from it in order to join him. The latter course presupposed heavy reinforcements, and we thought that we sensed their coming.

The Americans in Gafsa had carried out numerous raids against the Italian detachments that occasionally appeared in the no man's land to the east, between Gafsa and Maknassy. Neither adversary had any fixed garrison in this flat, desolate stretch of about seventy miles between the two towns. Once the fellows from Gafsa had bagged eighty-four prisoners. That was reckoned a big haul for southern Tunisia in January.

* Tilapia.
** This never happened, although when I wrote this piece, I fully believed it had. One more instance of confusion—I had the story from a "reliable source" who knew us both.

Captured Italian carbines and automatic pistols, if you had a chance to get them back to Algiers, attracted much attention. Even the stars which Italian soldiers wear on their lapels had a certain curiosity value. If you gave one to an Army nurse at an evacuation hospital, she would be quite happy, for which reason few stars ever got back as far as Algiers, and nurses at base hospitals to the west didn't get to see any until April or May. But by then there were so many Italian prisoners that the stars were no longer chic.

Norgaard and I had been told, by Léon Caplan, to look up a friend of his at Gafsa, a French captain named O'Neill. O'Neill, whose family had emigrated to France from Ireland in the seventeenth century, pronounced his name "Onay." He looked like a conventional O'Neill—blue-eyed, florid, and saddle-nosed—but he spoke English, which he had learned at a *lycée*, with a heavy French accent. Captain O'Neill commanded a battery of three guns which had been buried in a cache after the fall of France and thus concealed from the German Armistice Commission. All three guns had to be hauled by one old motor truck that burned alcohol, so the battery travelled in installments, one gun at a time. They could shoot well enough, O'Neill said, but they never arrived anywhere in time to shoot at an enemy. O'Neill invited us to dine at the battery mess with him, his two lieutenants, and a chaplain attached to the unit.

We showed up at the mess, which was in a shed built onto the side of a one-story house, ahead of O'Neill and his officers, who were accustomed to dining late. American Army chow is usually dished up early. The owner of the house, a young native Jew who wore a European business suit and a blue beret, invited us in for an apéritif while we waited. He had delicate Arabian features, and eyes as blue as O'Neill's, and he spoke excellent French. The Jew's house was large and square, with thick, mud walls to insulate it from the summer sun. It was built around a small circular court that let in air and daylight. The house looked ageless, like most of the others in town—the Numidians had probably built in exactly the same fashion—but the rooms leading off the court were wired for electric light and filled with heavy, gaudy contemporary furniture from some factory in Europe. The Jew's ancient, bearded father, who spoke no French, and the younger man's small, comely, brunette wife and their gray-eyed daughter kissed our hands. The French took over Tunisia in 1881, and in the old man's youth there had been no French-language schools in the country, but in the son's there had been. The younger man poured sweet wine for us and gave us olives and sliced turnips pickled in lemon juice. The family name, he told us, was Chemouni. When a servant who had been left on watch outside came in and told us that O'Neill had arrived, we left the Chemounis, feeling faintly embarrassed by their fervor. I remembered them a few weeks later, when I heard that we had abandoned Gafsa to the advancing Germans and Italians.

O'Neill's mess was the most exiguous I have encountered in the French

Army. We had a thin soup and a few scraps of breast of lamb, finishing off with some black imitation coffee sweetened with gray Arab loaf sugar. There was a bottle of rough red wine, and Norgaard and I had brought over three cans of American fruit for dessert. One of O'Neill's lieutenants was a hawk-nosed, Assyrian-bearded man who walked with a pronounced limp, assisting himself with a spiked cane. He was a French colonist who had farmed an oasis on the edge of the Sahara. The other was a handsome, wavy-haired young Parisian, a Regular Army officer who had escaped from the Occupied Zone in France and made his way to Africa in 1941. He spoke most nostalgically of Fouquet's, a restaurant which I had never admired but which, I had to agree, would have looked good in Africa. The chaplain, a young man with scraggly whiskers, was merely shy and hungry.

After dinner, Norgaard and I walked to the office of the American signals officer, in the Hôtel de France, to get the dope on how to send messages out of Gafsa. (They would have to go first by Army courier to where the censors were.) The hotel was a rectangular, flat-topped, yellow stucco building two stories high. It was neater and more modern than, I think, most Americans would imagine a hotel in Gafsa to be. There was running water in all the rooms and there were at least two bathtubs in the house. The American commandant, Lieutenant Colonel (now Colonel) Bowen,* had taken it over as a headquarters and lived upstairs. The signals officer presided over his telephones on the street floor, in what had once been the hall and dining room. We were talking to him when a French officer appeared in the doorway leading from the street and asked for Colonel Bowen. Apparently the signals man couldn't understand French, so when the officer asked for Bowen again, I took it upon myself to say, "He is upstairs. What do you want him for?"

"It is the British officers from the Eighth Army at Gabès," the Frenchman said. "Those he requested to see."

"The Eighth Army at Gabès?" I said, startled, because two days before I had heard that the Eighth was still a hundred miles south of there. I took this to mean that Montgomery had moved north that hundred miles in forty-eight hours, breaking the Mareth Line en route. That would have been a record even for him.**

"They are officers, three of them, from the Eighth Army, and they come from Gabès," the Frenchman said, "but the Army itself is not there. They say they come from a patrol that got up there somehow. They came into our lines at Kriz, on the Chott Djerid." His voice was quite matter-of-fact. "If you will show them to Colonel Bowen, I will leave them with you," he

* And now (1962) Major-General.
** Our image of Montgomery then was of a dashing fellow. That was before we had to work with him.

said, and ducked out into the dark without waiting for an answer. That was how I came to introduce the Eighth Army to the Second Corps.

A moment after the Frenchman disappeared, the three British officers came through the doorway. They walked with mincing steps, lifting each foot quickly as if they were glad to get it off the floor and putting it back reluctantly. Their shoes were wrapped in rags, and I deduced that their feet must be masses of blisters. Two of the men wore long beards and one, whose head was wrapped in a blood-soaked bandage, looked as if he badly needed a shave. All three were wearing khaki battle-dress pants and shirts, from which great swatches of material were missing, evidently torn off to make bandages. One of the men with beards carried a goatskin water sack, with the long hair outside; it reminded me of Robinson Crusoe. Their faces were sunken and their eyes seemed preternaturally large, and in one case really protuberant. The eyes of this fellow were round and sky-blue and his hair and whiskers were very fair. His beard began well under his chin, giving him the air of an emaciated and slightly dotty Paul Verlaine. "We walked forty miles farther than we should have," he said to me apologetically, "because some Arabs told us the Germans had taken Gafsa and that two thousand Americans were prisoners. But we knew that the French were at Kriz and Tozeur, so we went around that way. We've been walking for five nights and five days." Some soldiers who had drifted into the room brought in chairs for them and they sat down, looking about them a trifle incredulously, as if they had not really expected to get out of whatever awful scrape they had been in. A sergeant went upstairs to inform Bowen of their arrival. The soldiers gave the British officers cigarettes and offered to bring them food and water. The officers said that the French at Kriz and Tozeur had already given them as much as they could handle for a while, and they were no longer thirsty or hungry. The least bearded man passed his hand over his head, and Norgaard asked him, "Grazed by a bullet?"

The man shook his head slowly—you could almost hear it ring—and said, "No. An Arab hit me with a stone. They tried to strip us of our clothes, and when we fought they tried to kill us. We ran. We had no weapons, you see."

"Have any others come in?" the fair man asked us. "Have you heard anything about Big Dave?"

The signals officer said, "No, you're the first British who've come into our lines."

· The man with the bandaged head said, in a discouraged voice, "Big Dave must have been killed. There was all that shooting back in the wadi." He looked on the verge of falling asleep.

The fair man said, in a tone of sudden energy, as if he were trying to carry out a duty before he too caved in, "It's very important that we put out a radio warning to all our people behind the German lines that the enemy may have got our code. We must change the code."

"Are you *really* from the Eighth Army?" I asked the man with the goatskin sack.

He said they were.

"When did you leave the Eighth?" I asked.

"November seventeenth," he said. This was January twenty-eighth. "We've been living behind the enemy lines ever since. We were supposed to stay out four weeks longer, but we had a bit of hard luck."

A lieutenant came down the stairs and said that Colonel Bowen wanted to see the men, and they climbed up, holding on to the banister and resting as much weight on their hands as possible. I could hear the fair man saying, "We've got to put out that warning immediately." After a few minutes the lieutenant came down again and sent one of the men out to get the medics' ambulance. "The Colonel doesn't know quite what to make of them," he said. "They seem to be all right, but he says they might be spies. So he wants to send them up to G-2 at Corps tonight. They'll be comfortable in the ambulance."

Corps, as Norgaard and I knew, was near Tebessa, in Algeria, a hundred miles away. Driving over the narrow road, partly through rocky hills, without lights, an ambulance would be lucky to make it in six hours. Norgaard and I had one jeep, with an Army driver, between us. We decided that we ought to follow the ambulance to Tebessa. We hurried over to barracks to get our bedrolls and our driver, whose name was Eddie. He was a good-natured pfc from Queens who had been impressed by the tales of war he had heard in Algiers and was now being stuffed with horror stories by the infantrymen with whom he had taken up quarters in Gafsa. He looked relieved when we told him we were getting out of there, even though it meant a cold night drive. It didn't take long to roll our bedding and get it into the rear seat of the jeep. When three men carry three bedrolls in a jeep, it means that the men all ride in the front seat.

When we got back to the Hôtel de France, we learned that the ambulance had not yet arrived. We found the three officers from the Eighth Army in the kitchen, drinking hot coffee and surrounded by officers and men who were asking them about the desert. I spoke to the man with the bandaged head, and he told me that the fair-haired chap, Sadler, was the only commissioned officer of the three, a lieutenant. The two others were sergeants. They all belonged to an organization known as the SAS, which stood for Special Air Service. I asked him if it had anything to do with the RAF and he said no, it was an air service in a negative way. "You see, when we were first formed, we used to specialize in destroying German airplanes on the ground," he said. "Get back of their lines, get onto an airfield at night—do in a sentry, you know, or something of that sort; it's easy—and then attach pencil bombs to as many planes as we could get to. The bombs are timed to go off in a short time. We do a bunk, the bombs go off, and all the planes burn. Quite a good idea. Colonel Stirling, the one we call Big Dave, really thought of it first. Bright chap.

"They used to drop us by parachute behind the lines and let us find our way back," he continued, gravely sipping his coffee. "Worked well in places like Crete and Greece, but no future in it in Africa. Distances too great, you know. Easy to drop your men near an airport but impossible for them to walk back. So Colonel Stirling thought of using jeeps. Wonderful things, jeeps, absolutely fine. They go anywhere in desert country. Our fellows swing wide of the actual fighting area, come in behind the enemy lines, and then simply live in the desert for weeks, annoying them. One chap in SAS has got a hundred and twenty planes with his own hands. Big Dave must have got nearly a hundred. But Jerry got onto that airport dodge. Now there are too many guards and too many booby traps. So on this last trip out we stayed away from airfields and did just mines, traffic disruption, and general confusion. Sometimes we made Jerry and the Eye-ties think that they had been flanked in force and that a whole motorized column was operating in their rear. We made a whole Italian division pull out of one area, frightened stiff. Glorious fun, really."

I asked the sergeant where he was from and he said Nottingham. He told me that his name was Cooper and that he was twenty years old. He said he had been at school when war broke out and had enlisted in the Scots Guards. "I didn't like that," he said, "drill and spit and polish, all that. Big Dave was an officer in the Scots Guards himself, and he mustn't have liked it either. Then I went into the Commandos when they were started, and they were quite good at first, but they got formalized. Became too smart, you know—show yourself in London bars, Captain Lord Thisandthat, meet Leftenant the Right Hon., Lady Ursula's brother. So I became a parachutist and then I went into this thing. This is heaven," he said, absent-mindedly touching his bandaged head and then looking at his fingers to see if any blood had soaked through. "Extra pay and no drill or any of that foolishness." Cooper said he was a gunner and land navigator. He and his companions took their bearings in the desert just as if they were aboard ship, he said.

The other sergeant, the one with the goatskin sack, was a Free Frenchman who had been in the French Legation at Cairo when France fell. He was a navigator and an expert in Arabic. He told me his name was Taxis and that he was the old man of the group—thirty-one. He said that the disposition of the Tunisian Arabs was very bad. "You must never drive out in the desert without a gun," he said, "and the pilots must never forget to carry their pistols when they fly over the desert, in case they are forced to land." The Arabs who had tried to rob the men of their clothes had not acted like the Arabs in storybooks, who respect the laws of hospitality. They had invited the three ragged men to eat and then had pointed out a place in a wadi that they had said was safe to sleep in. When the men were dozing off, they had attacked them with stones.

"Our particular SAS lot started out with thirty men and a dozen jeeps," Cooper said. "It's wonderful what you can get on a jeep. We mount a heavy and a light machine gun on each one, besides radio equipment, and then we tie supplies and tins of extra petrol onto them until the springs barely clear the ground. They're the finest combat vehicle developed in this war. When you come to a deep wadi, where you can't progress farther, you can lower them into the wadi by ropes and get them out the same way on the other side. When a jeep breaks down seriously, we take the best of its tires and motor parts and use them as replacements on other jeeps, and the petrol helps too. So you have fewer and fewer jeeps as you go along. When your own petrol begins to run out, you raid an enemy petrol dump or shoot up some enemy trucks and take what they have. You lose all sense of strangeness, really, after a while. It seems as normal to go to an Eye-tie dump for your petrol as to one of our own places.

"We went along for weeks without any trouble. Big Dave himself commanded the party. When we started, the Eighth was still near Alamein and we operated for a while in true desert. We would always hide out in the daytime and sleep, and then do all our moves by night. When we got up into this semi-hill country, we would find deep wadis or crevices to hide away in. We would come out onto the roads by night and shoot up the enemy convoys. We weren't the only party out, of course. There were dozens of others, mostly LRDP, but all doing the same sort of thing, approximately. LRDP means Long Range Desert Patrol. They're very similar to us, but there are more of them. Altogether, we made a shambles of the enemy's line of supply. Their convoys became afraid to move by night at all, and when they used the roads by day, our fighter planes shot them up, so they had trouble both ways. One of our best tricks was to come onto a road and move along it *toward* the front, so they would never suspect us of being intruders. A string of empty lorries would come back from the front, having unloaded, and we would flash our lights at them for the right of way. They would flash back and then we would open fire with our machine guns, right at the lights. We got thirty-seven lorries that way one evening, left them flaming on the road. Once we had a battle with some Italian armored cars. We chased them with our jeeps. I suppose they thought we were at least light tanks, in the dark. We never had a casualty in six weeks, until the thing in the wadi north of Gabès."

"One of the most amusing bits was the mines," Sadler said.

"Yes, I nearly forgot," Cooper said. "Naturally, Jerry was preparing his retreat, and as our people got nearer, the German sappers would lay mines along the shoulders of the roads and in fields that columns would be likely to take a cut through. Their own people could keep on using the roads until the last minute because the engineers had marked the lanes through the mines. We used to go out sometimes to places where they had been working and take up their mines and then replace them in a slightly altered pattern. It must have been disconcerting when their lorries hit their own stuff.

"But we got to feeling too safe. We had gone so long unobserved that we thought it would last forever. Our party split up a couple of times and toward the end there were just fifteen in our particular group, travelling with four jeeps. We were lying up in a deep wadi about ten miles north of Gabès, a place with cliff walls four hundred feet high. I was fast asleep under my blankets when I heard the first shots. Germans with tommy guns were coming up both ends of the wadi. Some Arabs must have spotted us going in there and told Jerry. There wasn't a chance to fight our way out of that position. I managed to climb up a cliff, but I had no chance to get a weapon or a heavy coat. Sadler and Taxis got away by the same method, and we joined after we got to the top of the cliff. We waited around to see if any of the others would get away, but nobody did. There was a lot of shooting in the wadi and then silence. After a time, we began to walk."

The ambulance had finally pulled up in front of the Hôtel de France. A captain who had been deputed to escort the three suspicious characters to Corps was waiting at the kitchen door, and the three men got up and hobbled out to their conveyance. Norgaard and I went out after them and climbed into our jeep with Eddie and followed them up to Tebessa. It was the coldest, and it seemed the longest, ride I have ever had. We rode with our windshield down, on the theory that this would make it a trifle easier to see through the blackness, and we had a wind in our faces all the way. Norgaard and Eddie alternated driving, and I was always in the middle, with my arms stretched out behind them. I felt like a figurehead on a ship, driving chest first into a gale. The fellows lying inside the ambulance were of course more comfortable. Occasionally, when one of them sat up to smoke a cigarette and used a cigarette lighter, we could see a bearded face gleam through a rear window. Otherwise the ambulance was just a patch of blackness slightly more solid than the dark around it.

We got to Corps, which was eight miles outside of Tebessa, at two o'clock in the morning. A G-2 officer came out of the staff tent and climbed into the ambulance to talk to the Eighth Army officers. He had a bottle of whiskey with him, which was an excellent idea, because they were pretty well done in by that time. After half an hour he climbed out and told us that he thought they were all right.

WITH DR. FREEMAN IN AFRICA

NORGAARD and I went back to Gafsa within a week, and by the time we got there a big military action for that stage of the war was already going on. It was an offensive in the direction of Maknassy, the first all-American venture of the Tunisian campaign.

Sened, thirty miles east of Gafsa, was the first objective. The bulk of Rommel's army was only a little west of Tripoli, and there was nothing but a long, thinly held, tempting corridor between him and von Arnim. The Americans making the attack believed that they could go on from Sened to Maknassy and from Maknassy to the coast of the Gulf of Gabès, cutting Rommel's line of supply and retreat. The major general in command* told the war correspondents that he was going on to Maknassy, at least, and "draw the pucker string tight." We understood from his manner that he meant to go farther than that if he got the chance.

Norgaard and I had an Army jeep, and we drove out from Gafsa to see the battle. We had formerly had an Army driver, but on this trip Norgaard himself drove. The battle was in its second day. A battle, in the sort of open, desert warfare that was going on then, is not an easy thing to find, and we often had to stop to ask directions. We made our first stop beside two American Negro soldiers, sitting with their legs dangling into two parallel slit trenches cut in the dead-looking terrain. Each man was eating a mixture of cold meat and beans out of a small, shiny tin can which reflected the sun's rays a distance of several miles in that flat country** and each turned his face upward periodically, with mouth full, to stare into the hot, aluminum-colored sky. I got out of the jeep and walked up to the end of one trench, and its proprietor, a tan man, looked at me, but the other soldier continued to stare at the sky. Then the tan man looked up at the sky and his companion looked at me. "We was dive-bummed yesterday," this second soldier, a very dark man, said to me. "Driving the infantry up to the line in two-and-a-half-ton trucks. Dive-bumming makes me sick to my stomach."

I tried to sound hearty and casual as I asked, "What outfit you men out of?"

"The Rolling Umpty-seventh," the tan man said, while the dark man took his turn looking at the sky. The Umpties are a motor-truck regiment which I had already met under happier circumstances, in England.

"How you doing?" I asked, for want of a better question.

"Really, sir, I don't belong on this battlefield at all," the tan soldier answered. "I'm strictly a non-combat man."

I thought to myself that we were two of a kind.

I asked the men how far ahead the front was. I put into my voice the implication that I wanted to rush right into the middle of things. The men didn't know exactly where the battle was. Soldiers seldom do.

I walked back from the twin slit trenches to the jeep. "They don't know where the battle is," I said to Norgaard. "Maybe we had better go farther ahead." He said all right, so we started off across the sand again. We took

---

* General Lloyd Fredendall.
** A khaki C-ration can came in later. Nobody in the Source of Supplies, apparently, had had the imagination to foresee the tactical disadvantages of the bright ones.

to the desert, keeping away from the main road between Gafsa and Sened, because there were trucks on it and trucks attract strafers. The line of telephone poles beside the road gave us our direction. When we had gone a short way, we saw a pair of jeeps coming toward us over the sand, and we stopped. There were a couple of American officers and eight men in the jeeps, all belonging to a tank-destroyer battalion that had lost its equipment earlier in the campaign. They were serving as battlefield military police, guiding traffic and waiting for prisoners to take charge of.

The officers didn't know exactly where the front was either. They invited us to have a can of coffee beside a mud house, a mile or so away, where the M.P.'s had set up headquarters, and we all drove there together. There were a few scraggly olive trees around the house and a low mud wall around the trees, presumably to prevent the sand's blowing away from their roots. One of the soldiers poured some gasoline into a couple of empty ration cans and lighted it. He laid two strips of metal across the top of each can, then filled two smaller ration cans with water from his canteen and placed them on the burners. When the water came to a boil, he divided a packet of soluble coffee between the two improvised coffee pots. "The Statler people would give a million dollars to get hold of this process," he said. When we had drunk the coffee, he started another batch.

While I was waiting for more coffee, I stood on the mud wall with one of the M.P. officers and looked over the country. A railroad paralleled the highway and we could see a station, with some trees around it, about five miles away. It was a stop between Gafsa and Sened, needed God knows why. "Our guns were out behind there early this morning and Jerry dropped a few shells in among those trees," the officer said. "Then our guns moved forward, way up toward Sened. I think you can go ahead eight or ten miles at least before you have to start to look around. You missed a good show this morning, though. About twenty Stukas came over and a dozen P-40's bounced them and shot down eight. Boy, they were falling all over the place! They'll be back, though," he added cheerily.*

After Norgaard and I had finished our coffee, we climbed back into the jeep and started forward again. Almost immediately the mud-house grove seemed in retrospect a pretty nice place to spend the day. Sened lies in a gap between two bare, east-west ridges. As we moved toward it, we spotted a number of dispersed scout cars and wireless-equipped jeeps, the vehicles characteristic of a reconnaissance troop. "A recon outfit," Norgaard said knowingly. "Aren't they usually fairly well out in front of

---

* Later that day the Stukas did come back with a strong escort of fighters, thirty-one planes in all. Six P-40s from Thélepte attacked them and five of our planes were shot down. They attacked to protect an infantry advance that had been canceled, which is the way things go. I saw the planes still smoking on the hills next day; the pilots, now ashes, had been among the victors of January 15.

everybody?" We drove to within fifty yards of one of the scout cars and climbed out. A couple of soldiers were sitting on the ground with their backs against the wheels of the car, reading books. They had their slit trenches already dug beside them. Norgaard and I walked up to them and asked them what outfit this was. One of the men, a corporal, looked up and said, "Sorry, sir, but you got any identification?" He reminded me of a stage-door man. We showed him our identification cards and he explained that the scout cars, which were, as Norgaard had surmised, a recon outfit, had been all the way around the enemy's position during the previous day and night and had come back to report and await another assignment. "We could have took the place, I guess," he said, probably without much justification.

My companion, like a good Associated Press man, started making the rounds of the scout cars and taking down the names and home towns of the recon soldiers. This is always a fruitful procedure for a press-association man, because he can load up his dispatches with the names, and the papers in the home towns are glad to use them. Every soldier, when he named his home town, said, "And I wish I was there now" or "Boy, how I wish I was there this minute!" The corporal I had spoken to asked me if it was true that Bing Crosby was dead. I said I didn't know. He asked me if Groucho Marx was dead. He said he had heard that they were and that Fred Allen was dead, too. The Army in Tunisia was always full of rumors about well-known people who were supposed to have died. When my companion had written down the names of enough towns like Owensboro, Kentucky, and Central Falls, Rhode Island, we moved on again.

As we drove along, we had a clear view of the ridge north of Sened, and after we had driven a mile or so we saw a number of tanks coming around the western end, just below the crest, and snaking down the southern side of the ridge toward the town. There were occasional puffs of gray smoke on the slope above them, where the enemy was dropping shells. We began to hear our own guns up ahead, quite loud. Then we came upon the ammunition half-tracks of an artillery outfit. The soldiers told us, confidently, that the reconnaissance troop we had just left had been annihilated on the day before and that a tank-destroyer outfit had just lost all its vehicles. This was the tank-destroyer battalion the M.P.'s belonged to. The fact was that the vehicles had been lost in a quagmire in northern Tunisia a month before, but an artilleryman, garbling a conversation with one of the M.P.'s, had brought back the more fascinating report that the tank-busters had been ambushed during the current action. The soldiers said that two batteries out of their battalion were a mile or two ahead of us. The guns were armored 105's, six to a battery.

We drove on across the plain and eventually came upon a tall captain with a Red Cross brassard, standing between two jeeps, both of which were flying Red Cross flags. We stopped to talk to him. The guns we had been told about were now in sight, four hundred yards further on. The captain, whose name was Bradbury, said he was battalion surgeon. Each of the jeeps had two litters slung to its sides, and when dive bombers or German artillery caused a casualty among the gunners, Bradbury would run forward in one of the jeeps and get the wounded man. He stood there looking at the guns like a spaniel watching for a ball to retrieve. "Yesterday I had seventeen," he said, "including several from the infantry that happened to be hit near us. Only three so far today. None in this position so far. We've moved half a dozen times since daybreak." All the shots we heard were going out (boom-scream) and none were coming in (scream-boom), so we weren't worried. I opened a can of Spam and we ate it cold. "Maybe they have pulled their stuff out of Sened already," Norgaard said optimistically. I had been watching the sky all day while he drove, sometimes looking straight up for Stukas and sometimes into the sun for strafers, but nothing had happened, and I began to hope that the P-40's had polished the local Luftwaffe off for the day.

After we had finished the Spam and said so long to Bradbury, Norgaard and I drove on up to the guns and stopped behind them. They were in the open, because there was no cover anywhere around. They had stopped shooting for the moment, probably to change range or target, and we walked up to one gun crew, who were smoking cigarettes beside their piece. As soon as we reached them, an officer shouted over to them from an armored half-track to their rear, telling them to check on our identifications. "I'm sorry, sir," one soldier said, "but after all, how do we know who you are? We got no time for Ayrabs or casual strollers." We showed our identification cards and the soldier, looking at mine, said, "Huh, a *Landsmann!* I'm from New York, too. Fourteent' Street and Avenue A. I wish I was dere now. At a movie, wit' my shoes off."

Then they had to start shooting again. We walked back toward the half-track, which we knew, because of its high radio antenna, was a command vehicle. The officer who had shouted to the gunners was a square-faced, fair-haired major named Burba. He was executive officer of the battalion and had been in command of the two batteries since his C.O., a lieutenant colonel, had been wounded. He was from McAlester, Oklahoma. He was a cool, methodical officer who looked as if he had definite information about everything, so I asked him what his battery was shooting at.

"Enemy guns in a grove of trees back of Sened," he said. "We think their infantry has pulled out of the town already."

I asked him what range he was firing at and he said five thousand yards. "I have one battery here," he said, "and another over about a mile to the right and slightly forward—you can see them over there," and he pointed. "Every fifth shell we fire is a smoke shell, so we can see where we're hitting, and the fire of the two batteries is converging on the grove of trees. When we get all our fire together and just right, we'll come down on them and that will be the end of the battle."

"Where's our infantry?" I asked in a careless tone. I could not see any troops out in front of us.

"There are two battalions in echelon in those two olive groves to the right and forward of the other battery," Burba said, pointing again. "When we've knocked out all resistance, they will go forward and occupy the town. Or maybe the tanks will get there first."

The tanks, as a matter of fact, were in the process of trying to get to the town before the infantry. They were crawling down from the southern side of the ridge, where my colleague and I had already seen them, and moving out in front of the 105's, looking like a file of mechanical toys that a street peddler winds up and sets down on a sidewalk. When they had deployed before us, they turned left and moved on toward the town. They must have been a couple of thousand yards ahead of us when something began kicking up dust and smoke, sometimes in front of them and sometimes behind. "It's those Jerry 88's," Burba said. "They've got the tanks under a crossfire. We'll fix that in a few minutes." The tanks were now coming back toward us, all except one, which remained motionless on the plain. "That's the way the infantry was yesterday," one of Burba's junior officers, who had joined us, said. "They went up toward the firing line in trucks and three or four of the trucks got dive-bombed before the fellows could get away from them. It was a mess. After that they couldn't get anybody back into the trucks for a while. After *we* knock out the opposition, they'll all be heroes."

"That 88 is a great gun," Burba said admiringly, looking at the motionless tank through his binoculars. "Ripped that thing just like a G.I. knife does a tin can. Flat trajectory. High muzzle velocity."

"Pretty long range, hasn't it?" I asked.

"Thirteen thousand five hundred yards," Burba said heartily, as if he were a salesman pushing the German gun to a reluctant prospect.

At this point the six guns in Burba's battery let off as one, and the other battery followed. Then there was a prolonged shrieking noise and something monstrous landed a hundred yards behind us and ricochetted off to our left. It kicked up a lot of dust. It must have been an armor-piercing solid shot, because there was no explosion. "Let's get behind the half-track," Burba said, in the same tone in which he might have said, "Let's get out of this wind." We all moved over behind the vehicle. Something else shrieked past, through the interval between the two guns on the right flank of the battery, it seemed to me, and I couldn't help thinking that while Burba had been explaining to us what we intended to do to the Germans, some equally competent, equally stolid German artillery officer had been outlining his plans of what he intended to do to us.

Norgaard and I had the embarrassing feeling that we were not helping the battery by our presence and that if we got hit we would cause them a lot of extra trouble. We were also embarrassed by the thought that if we left too abruptly, Burba and the others might think we were fair-weather friends. My colleague reminded me that he really had to get back to headquarters at Gafsa by five in order to file a bulletin. I wasn't working for a press association and so I had no bulletin to file, but we had only one jeep between us and I decided that I couldn't expect my companion to wait. I said, "I guess we may as well go, Major. See you some other time." Norgaard said something to the same effect, and we walked away, feeling as sheepish as we ever have in our lives.

We got into our jeep and drove to the rear, past the patient Captain Bradbury. We paused for a moment to say goodbye again. I looked back and saw a column of black smoke rising from one of our gun positions. The enemy had evidently scored a hit.

Each knot of soldiers we passed on the way to the front had seemed a friendly island inviting a prolonged stay. We were not tempted to stop to talk to any of them on the way back. We reached Gafsa, and were about to park our jeep opposite the Hôtel de France, which was serving as American headquarters, when we saw in the street the major general who was in command of the American operation based on Gafsa. We stopped to ask him if the infantry had got to Sened—we had been two hours on the way home—and he said they had and that Sened was now in our hands. "The only damned trouble," he said, "is that the British First Army has called off the whole offensive because there has been some kind of threat in the north. I guess we're going to play it safe and wait for Montgomery." The bigger part of an American armored division which had been held in reserve just outside Gafsa to exploit our initial gains was sent north that night without having fought, and the great projected offensive went into the record as only a raid.

The American forces in the field were under the direct control of Lieutenant General Kenneth Anderson, who was commanding the British First Army at that stage of the campaign. Anderson himself was officially under the command of General Eisenhower, in Algiers. This occasioned considerable confusion of viewpoint among the men in the field, but things got a lot better later when the British Eighth Army, the British First Army, and the American Second Corps were all placed directly, and with equal status, under the command of General Alexander. The aborted offensive cost us a couple of hundred casualties, but we took a hundred and fifty prisoners, which in that period of the campaign seemed a lot. The battle had never developed into a really big affair, but at moments it had seemed about as big as Norgaard or I or anybody we saw between Gafsa and Sened had wanted.

This impression was confirmed when Norgaard and I got ready to turn in after dinner. When we were at Gafsa, we slept on the concrete floor of a small French barracks, which was used as a catch-all hostel for transient officers. In one corner of the barracks, a captain from an American armored-infantry regiment had spread his bedding roll. His outfit had not been involved in the day's action and he had been out in the field in a jeep as an observer of fighting methods. He was a florid, pleasant-faced blond of twenty-seven, and he was reading by the light of a candle he had placed next to one elbow on the floor. We said hello and walked over to talk to him. He was reading Douglas Southall Freeman's "Lee's Lieutenants," which Norgaard had also read, and they got to talking about it. The captain told us that he came from the battlefield region of Virginia, where children save Minié balls instead of Indian arrowheads, and that he knew old Dr. Freeman well. "I own a house at Yellow Tavern, where Jeb Stuart was killed," he said, "and there are some Yankee musket balls in the stair rail. When I was a boy, I used to walk over the battlefields with Dr. Freeman, and he would tell me where the different regiments had stood and where they had charged or retreated and who had been killed and where. I often used to dream of battles when I was a boy. I thought of them like an illustration in a book, all blue and gray and orange and blood-red, and not very noisy." He closed his book and lay down, ready to go to sleep. "My God!" he said. "If I had known they were like this!" I thought of a line in Stendhal's diary: "All my life I have longed to be loved by a woman who was melancholy, thin, and an actress. Now I have been, and I am not happy."

THE CHEMOUNIS REVISITED

On the next day, the High Command decided to call off the offensive of which the Sened action was to have been merely the first stage. The Command's decision was supposed to be a secret, but when tank units which had not yet been committed to the fight began pulling out of Gafsa and heading north, the troops remaining there understood what had happened. There was a feeling among the men that as soon as enough tanks had been withdrawn from the region the enemy might come back and counterattack at Sened, but he didn't until a while later, and in the meantime the men who had taken Sened sat tight.

Norgaard and I heard that there were captured enemy guns and tanks at Sened. Since captured material, like prisoners in quantity, was still a novelty at that stage of the North African campaign, we thought we would get into the jeep the Army had lent us and drive out from Gafsa, where we were quartered, to have a look. As soon as we had got out on the naked main road to Sened, both of us were sorry we had left the shade of the palm trees and anti-aircraft guns. The hot, metallic sky, which it hurt your eyes to look into, hung over the road and weighed down on your brain with its implicit Messerschmitts. Every group of tanks or guns you met, parked off the road, seemed an invitation to air attack, and you hurried to get past it. Then, until you reached the next collection of armor, you felt lonely. Signs along the road warned drivers to keep at three-hundred-yard intervals and look out for strafers.

There was no temptation to get off the road and drive across the fields to avoid strafing as we got close to Sened, for the fields had almost certainly been mined by the retreating enemy. Sened was sinister—a wooden *gare* full of wasps' nests; a *buffet*, in a separate building, which two British booby-trap noncoms were busily rigging with their trip wires, as happy as parents decorating a Christmas tree; three or four dwellings, a water tower, and a church, all shattered by shellfire. The fact that the booby-trap men were at work meant that we in our turn were getting ready to abandon the place. You don't booby-trap a place you are going to stay in. We talked to the trappers, both Royal Engineers, one of whom was carrying so many one-pound cakes of TNT under his left arm that they seemed always on the point of wriggling loose. It looks like coarse white laundry soap. When I expressed concern, he said, "Lord love you, sir, it wouldn't explode if it did fall, not without a deetonyter, it wouldn't." The two men wore the fixed, slightly fatuous smile which seems to be a mark of their curious vocation. "We 'ad some nasty ones to tike up before we put ours in," the man with the TNT said. "We've rearranged them so Jerry will 'ave a time with them when 'e comes back. 'E won't be surprised, not 'alf."

There were three torn American medium tanks in a cluster where the main road went by the depot, looking as if they had been punched clean through. Armor-piercing shot from German 88's had gone into them, had bounced around inside like buckshot in a rattle, and then had gone out the other side, leaving the crew to be grilled by the flames as the fuel burned. The charred bodies had been extracted that morning and buried. A soldier's web belt, stiff with blood, lay on the ground outside the hole through which the bodies in one tank had been withdrawn. A couple of soldiers were looking at the belt. One of them was saying, over and over again, "I'll never take no more prisoners! The bastards! I'll never take no more prisoners!" A couple of 88's had lain doggo and caught the tanks with crossfire as they entered the town.

Our artillery was still firing at the ridge of a hill about five miles away. We asked a bearded, wild-looking soldier who was sitting in a parked jeep what the guns were pounding at.

"We got a lot of Germans trapped up there on the mountain," he said.

"How many?" Norgaard wanted to know.

"About a division, I guess," the soldier said.

"I don't see how you could hide a whole division on that hill," Norgaard said calmly.

"They got the mountain all hollowed out and that's where they're hiding," the soldier answered. (A couple of days later, at the American Second Corps headquarters, we asked a G-2 officer what had happened to the Germans trapped on the hill and he said, "Oh, you mean those last nine Heinies? They surrendered.")*

Norgaard and I got back to Gafsa fast. There was an uncomfortable feeling about Sened, a tacit menace that made us feel worse than actually being bombed or shot at.

That night I left the Gafsa region, and I didn't return for six weeks. Meanwhile, the American forces executed, in a rather ragged fashion, a withdrawal from Gafsa and several other towns. We lost almost all of two battalions of armor and two battalions of infantry, and, for the moment at least, all our prestige with the French and Arabs. When the Army recaptured Gafsa, in March, it was in a substantial, intelligent manner, with the entire First Division of infantry. During the operation, I was permitted to tag along with the headquarters of the division. Our troops got back into Gafsa almost without fighting, for the enemy had pulled out before our obviously superior force. The hard fight of the campaign came about a week later, at El Guettar, but that has nothing to do with my memories of Gafsa.

Gafsa was the first town I saw after our side had recaptured it from the enemy, and to me it was, in its small way, a symbol of the fact that this particular breed of bug could be dislodged, like any other. Gafsa is the capital of an administrative district with a population of a hundred and fifty thousand, so the government buildings are far larger than the size of the town itself warrants. Division headquarters, and I with it, moved into the building of the Gendarmerie Nationale, a fine, modern place with sleeping rooms on the upper floors. But the science of booby-trapping has taken a good deal of the fun out of following hot on an enemy's heels. Our engineers had already been through the lower floors of the Gendarmerie looking for booby traps, but they hadn't had time to do the living quarters, in a corner of which I was billeted. It acutely distressed me to turn a doorknob or draw a shutter. Eventually the division engineers decided that the Italians, the last of the enemy to withdraw from Gafsa, had lacked the time, or possibly the skill, to put any booby traps in the buildings. On that first day of my third visit to Gafsa, though, I didn't know what they were going to decide.

Soon after we pulled into town, I went for a walk to see how it had been affected by the occupation, which had lasted four weeks. The sixteenth-century Arab citadel had been partly wrecked by an explosion. Our engineers had used it as a storehouse for explosives during our oc-

---

* This was approximately the place where Mollie, seven weeks later, was to help persuade the Italians to surrender. At the moment of which I now write, he was in Oran, facing charges for leaving his post.

cupancy and, before our withdrawal, had blown it up to keep the enemy from getting the stuff. Our destruction in Gafsa had not, on the whole, been well done. It had been planned, for example, to move a number of locomotives north over the railroad that ran through the town and, after they had gone by, to blow up a railroad bridge to the north, so that we would have the locomotives and the enemy couldn't use the line, but somebody had blown up the bridge first, so the locomotives had to be left in Gafsa. Then, since no preparations had been made to destroy them, they fell into German hands. There was another oversight: the French civilian population of about five hundred had been evacuated by truck, but the native Jews had been left behind.

I met a French-speaking Arab in the market place in front of the old citadel who said he had been some sort of government employee—a police-court interpreter, I think—and had remained through the German occupation. He was frightened, because the houses of all the Frenchmen had been thoroughly pillaged by Arabs and the French notion of justice for Arabs is summary. He was consequently eager to talk and to convince me that his heart, at least, had been with the Allies. Most of the Gafsa Moslems had fled to join their kin in the hills during the German occupation, he said, because they wanted to escape the levies of the Italians and also because a great force of American bombers had come over shortly after the evacuation and flattened a lot of Arab houses. The bombers had killed four hundred Arabs on a breadline in the market place, he said. "The people were much impressed, and those who had gone about talking of the victory of the Germans as certain were discredited," he said, indicating that there are several kinds of propaganda. "They realized that the Americans must have mistaken them for Italian troops," he added adroitly.

I asked him to tell me more about the occupation. "When the Germans and Italians first came here," he said, "they encouraged the people to rob the houses of the French and Jews and some of the more ignorant elements of the population complied with their wishes. The Germans did not stay here long, but went on, leaving an Italian garrison. The Italians were very poor. They pulled up even the young onions out of the gardens in the oasis and ate them as if famished. They broke into Arab houses and stole carpets off the floors and sold them to other Arabs living in the surrounding country, to get a few *sous*. They are a people without shame." The German words *"Araber Geschäft"* had been scrawled in chalk by the Arabs on the doors of a great number of shops, and the Arab told me that this had been done immediately after our evacuation, under instructions given over the Axis Arabic-language radio in Tunis, to protect these Arab establishments from pillage by the incoming Axis troops. "I never listened to that radio, of course," he said, "but so I have heard it related." I said I was surprised that so many Arabs knew even a couple of German words, and he explained that a number of them in Gafsa had been prisoners in Germany during the last war and had learned the language. It was easy to guess that the town had been full of Arab Axis agents during our first stay there. Some of them had probably been wearing the G.I. shirts compassionate Yanks had given them.

Presently I walked to the house of the Chemounis, the Tunisian Jewish family which, on my first visit to Gafsa in January, had entertained Norgaard and me. There had been young Chemouni himself, dressed in a European business suit, and his old, bearded father, and his attractive wife, and little, gray-eyed daughter. The house was still standing, but when I peered in through the open door, it looked as if nobody had lived there for years. There was nothing left in the place but a few pages of some Hebrew book scattered on the hard earth floor and a chandelier that hung crookedly from the roof of the once comfortable room in which Norgaard and I had drunk sweet wine and eaten olives and sliced pickled turnips. I wondered whether the family had escaped from Gafsa or been murdered. I asked a lad who came along the road what had happened to them and he said that they were all alive and had moved to the old Jewish quarter of the town, a couple of fetid alleys in which only the poorest and least Europeanized Jews had lived. The boy, who was Jewish himself, guided me to the house where the Chemounis were now. A scarecrow of a young man, wearing a beret and a long blue robe, precipitated himself upon me, sobbing and trying to kiss me. I knew it was Chemouni, though I could hardly recognize him. "They have stolen even my trousers," he said, pressing his face against the front of my field jacket.

Other Jews—many who, like my friend, had a few weeks before been outwardly European and were now indistinguishable from the most Oriental of Jews—flocked about me with their stories of the occupation. The Germans had come to the houses of the leading Jews on the first night and had taken worth-while things like money, jewelry, and stocks of raw wool, but had not touched their furniture and clothing. They then had left town, but not before they had invited the Arabs to help themselves to the leavings. As it turned out, there had been a wild competition between Arabs and Italians to gut the Jewish houses. The Italian commandant of the place had ordered all the Jews into a few houses in the old quarter and had put them on a ration even smaller than that accorded the Arabs, which had been minuscular. No Jews had been killed, but two young ones had come close to going before a firing squad because an Arab accused them of having betrayed an Axis parachutist to the Americans in December. The two had saved their lives by escaping to the desert. The Caïd of Gafsa, the town's chief Moslem official, had remained on the job through the occupation, and so had the spahis, the French-trained native police. The Caïd had fled with the Italians, fearing that the returning French would shoot him, but the spahis were still at their posts, once more under the orders of their French superiors. They were recovering stolen Jewish and French property from Arab houses, but what they found was now either completely ruined or almost valueless. The Caïd had left a large house containing, as part of the harem, a private movie theatre supplied with an extensive assortment of pornographic films.

Israel had been despoiled again, but it had apparently managed to hoard a few hens and roosters against the day of its deliverance. Near where I was standing, the *shochet*, the ritual slaughterer, an old man with a matted beard, was killing these chickens for family feasts of celebration, holding the blade in his lips between strokes while he smoothed back the neck feathers of the chicken whose throat he was going to slit next. A couple of big Jewish soldiers from the Bronx, with hands huge enough to palm a basketball and great feet that could kick a football sixty yards, placed their arms comfortingly on the shoulders of ancient, tiny matriarchs with whom, because the Tunisian Jews speak neither English nor Yiddish, they had no means of communication except signs. The Bronx Jews and the Tunisian Jews looked as different as a Percheron and an Eohippus.

"The Arabs are very bad," Chemouni said to me. "They have always been bad."

"How long has your family lived in Gafsa?" I asked him.

"I think for two thousand years," he said.

Chemouni's little girl, who spoke French as easily as any child in the Parc Monceau, looked at me with large, frightened, gray eyes. I asked Chemouni if his daughter would go to live in France after we had won the war. He said no, of course not; she would marry and live in Gafsa.

GAFSA REVISITED

The girl did not stay in Gafsa, nor did my Monsieur Chemouni. When I returned there in the spring of 1956, I learned that both were in Israel, but Chemouni's brother remained—a military tailor for the French garrison.

The "dissidence" in Algeria had brought new trade to Gafsa, this Chemouni explained. There was the biggest French garrison ever, both of ground and air troops, to stop the traffic in munitions across technically neutral Tunisia, which had just regained its independence, to technically French Algeria, which was in full rebellion.

The French still maintained troops in Tunisia—they were withdrawn in subsequent months, except from the naval base of Bizerte. While they were not officially allowed to attack the gun-runners on Tunisian soil, they could follow them and break up their operations as soon as they crossed the line. Airplanes and helicopters were particularly useful for this job. Meanwhile guerillas, all for official purposes Algerians, operated on both sides of the border against the French, while Tunisian troops supposedly operated against the guerillas to preserve Tunisian neutrality.

The French military said that some of the guerillas were themselves

Tunisians, and that the army of the new neutral state merely cooperated with them. The situation was somewhat clarified when the French pulled out and moved across the line into Algeria, where they set up electric barriers along the frontier to keep the gun-runners out. When that happened the military-tailoring business must have fallen off drastically.

The tailor Chemouni told me that much of his work consisted in removing badges of rank from uniforms, because the military believed that the snipers, whether in fact Tunisian or Algerian, picked targets according to grade. Since the snipers had presumably served in the French Army themselves, they presumably recognized the insignia.

There had been a great change since 1943. Tunisians had taken over the civil administration, and French civilians no longer lived among the Moslems in the old town, around the fort and baths. They had removed to the military quarter, around the railroad station on the other side of the oasis, where they felt safer at night. There had been an incident on the road near town a week or two before, when guerillas of some sort had burned a truck and a bus, and cut the throats of the truck-driver, an Italian, and of a European couple traveling in the bus. The husband was a White Russian, employed at a phosphate mine.

Because of this I had had to pay a taxi driver in Tunis extra fare to drive me down to Gafsa, a hundred and fifty miles or so, but we had had a tranquil journey. We had paused only briefly, however, at the old airfield in Thélepte. It felt lonely there; we got the wind up.

The Hotel de France was out of business in Gafsa; its only successors were two very dirty *pensions* near the depot. A young French fighter pilot who talked to me after dinner at one of them thought I was a spy for an American oil company. After I reassured him, he told me that we had been mad to come by road—the country was in a state of anarchy. This was, of course, normal.

At Tunis, the Armée de l'Air had offered to send me in a military plane because they could not guarantee the safety of the roads. The young man at Gafsa seemed overwrought—the dissidents, he said, had taken to shooting at planes with rifles when the planes strafed them. This made him nervous. I did not think he compared well with Rozanoff.

My taxi-driver, a naturalized French citizen of Sicilian birth, spent the night with a friend down the road, a Frenchman who continued to run the municipal electric plant, and whose throat nobody had cut, perhaps because that would have cut the current along with it.

The remaining Jews continued to live in the old town, as they had for a great many centuries before Mohammed was born. I visited another Chemouni there, chief, I was told, of the name. He was a swollen old man with dropsical legs, a merchant who kept a general store, and who lived in a second-floor flat with an electric refrigerator, an index of great wealth. He treated me to sweet liqueur, and said business could be better, but he wasn't thinking of moving, just yet.

There was an old Tunisian proverb, he said: "The worst of those we know is better than the best of those we don't know." So he was going to stay on a while.

Next day my driver, who was named Daniel Portanova, and I drove over to the coast of the Gulf of Gabès, and returned to Tunis by the shore road, uneventfully. I haven't been back to Gafsa since.

Those first few months of intimate, warm, confused war in northwest Africa were made for ad lib fighters like Mollie and Major Cochran. But the campaign reached the age of reason with a lecture which I attended without great expectations.

The first meeting of General Omar Nelson Bradley with the international public, as represented by British and American newspaper and radio correspondents, occurred on the crest of a brush-covered hill at a place called Béja, in northern Tunisia, on April 22, 1943. The American phase of the Allied offensive against the Axis forces in Africa was about to begin. Bradley, who was fifty years old, held the temporary wartime rank of major general, and had no combat record in the First World War and no idiosyncrasies that could be expanded into a legend, had been named to succeed Lieutenant General George S. Patton as commander of the American II Corps, which was the whole American ground force engaged in the African fighting. Since even Patton, for all his pistol-slapping and advance publicity, had failed to make the II Corps work as an offensive unit, correspondents took his replacement by an unknown to mean that the Americans would have a minor role in the final battle against the Axis on the African continent. Press briefings at Patton's headquarters, conducted by an intelligence officer, had been like formal audiences, with all present required to buckle the chin straps of their tin hats, in token of instant readiness to face the moderately distant foe. Before the offensive began, the press-relations officer at Béja had announced with some little embarrassment (the P.R.O. had been commissioned straight out of the publicity department of a movie company, so he was naturally mindful of military dignity) that the new man had decided that he would brief the correspondents in person, and, as there were at least thirty of them and only one of him, he would come to the press camp for this purpose. The new man arrived in a jeep, carrying a map under his arm and attended by his aide, a captain of almost juvenile appearance, who carried an easel and a pointer. The General wore a tin hat—not buckled under the chin, probably because his reconnaissances sometimes took him into shelling and he didn't want his head jerked off. He also wore a canvas field jacket, G.I. pants, and canvas leggings, thus qualifying as the least dressed-up commander of an American army in the field since Zachary Taylor, who wore a straw hat. He had a long jaw and a high, notably convex forehead, and he was wearing spectacles. After the Green Hornet, with his ruddy, truculent face and his beefy, leather-sheathed calves, the new general, lanky and diffidently amiable, seemed a man of milk.

The aide set up the easel in press headquarters; then the General hung the map, took the pointer, and, in a high, not loud voice, as Missourian as the Truman voice that later became familiar to radio listeners, began to demonstrate how the II Corps intended to progress in an eleven-day drive to Mateur, the key to Bizerte, through enemy positions that had stopped the best troops of the British First Army for five months. Some people think a general should have a voice like a recorded bugle call played over a loudspeaker. But the Bradley delivery is really an asset—hesitant, slightly rustic, compelling the hearer to listen hard for the next phrase and at the same time convincing him of the General's candor. At Béja, he laid down his schedule with no more panache than a teacher outlining the curriculum for the new semester. The Americans, he said, had been moved from the south-central to the extreme northwest arc of the Allied semicircle facing the Axis redoubt—because, the correspondents had suspected up to this point, they were to make merely a holding attack, in country so rugged that they could switch quickly to the defensive if the Germans came at them. Meanwhile, the British First and Eighth Armies were to crash through at more promising points on the Axis perimeter. When a correspondent who had been with the British in this zone through the bitter months of frustration asked how the inexperienced 9th Division was going to get Green and Bald Hills, two notoriously nasty positions that had stopped the Guards, General Bradley said that that was up to General Manton Eddy, the division commander, but that he didn't expect any undue delay. All parts of the inquiring correspondent visible above his battle dress turned purple.

Only two American infantry divisions, the 1st and the 9th, appeared on the General's map. The absence of the corps's other infantry outfit, the 34th Division, was interpreted by some to mean that it was being held in defensive reserve and by others that it had been sent home as useless. Either supposition, if confirmed, would bear out the notion that the American attack was not too banefully intended. There was, however, a gap half as wide as a divisional front between the 9th and the 1st. "What are you going to have in there, sir?" a knowing fellow asked. The new general looked at him with a gratified, pedagogical smile, as at a pupil who had asked a bright question. "I'm going to patrol that with a troop of motorized cavalry," he said. (A couple of days later, when General Eddy expressed his own disquiet about the gap, Bradley told him reassuringly, "If they come through there, Bill Kean and I will go in with a couple of BARs." BARs are Browning automatic rifles. Kean, who later commanded the 25th Division in Korea, was then the II Corps's chief of staff.) The new general didn't have much more to say. It was a historic début, although nobody knew it at the time. Had any programs been printed, they would sell at a big premium today.

Bradley had been in Tunisia two months without a command when he took over the II Corps. General George Catlett Marshall, then Chief of Staff of the Army, had, General Marshall later said, sent Bradley there "to be Eisenhower's legs and wisdom." He spent most of his time at the front, returning to Algiers to tell the Commander-in-Chief what was going on. General Eisenhower was not only several hundred miles away; he was— nominally, at least—in command of the British First and Eighth Armies and the French XIX Corps, in addition to the Americans, and was also supreme political arbiter of North Africa, which left him only limited time for tactical details. This had been Bradley's first experience in a real war, and he had been looking at it closely—going up into forward observation posts, and talking to company and platoon leaders and to riflemen to check on what he had learned and taught in the previous thirty-two years. So he was bringing to his first recital what a music critic unafraid of clichés would call a ripened technique and a mature understanding of the content of the music. Into the gap in his offensive alignment, when the time came, he slipped the fresh 34th Division, and, pushing it forward in depth on a rather narrow front, he sent it against Hill 609, the highest eminence of the first range he had to fight across. The 1st had already reached the flanks of 609 and could put artillery fire on it to help the attackers. So employed, the 34th, which so far in this campaign had known only defeat and was considered a liability, took 609 and came out believing itself a division *d'élite*, which was most of what it needed to be one. This made the new general's military gifts manifest to his first audi- ence, and they have never had cause to change their opinion of him. Many generals, in the course of history, have taken a hill at the cost of a division, and as many have lost a division without taking a hill. Bradley took a key hill and gained a division. His troops reached each of their objectives almost exactly in accordance with the schedule he had laid down. "There was one time when Matt Eddy was a few hours behind, up on the left flank," General Bradley said a couple of years later, during the campaign in western France, "but I told him to step on it."

Bradley explained that small bit of virtuosity seven years later, over a drink.

"All hills, with narrow draws between them—a country just laid out for defense," he said of northern Tunisia. "They'd get up in the hills, and when you went down in the draws to get around them, they'd put fire on you." He had thought he knew what to do about the hills, he said—go straight up them, as you would when hunting wild goats in the mountains of Hawaii. It had also occurred to him that the German 88, though its flat trajectory made it wonderful for shooting across valleys at vehicles in the open, would not be much good at firing over hills at close range to hit hidden soldiers on the reverse slopes. "I remember that gap between the Ninth and the First," he said. "What I was thinking was that if the suckers did come in over those hills, they wouldn't have any good road they could get far on, and we could round 'em up before they got far into our rear. It was about nine miles from where they were over to the Djebel Abiod road, and by the time they had climbed down there we could have armor to meet them."

The Chairman sipped at his drink and looked across at the staircase as if he could see the Djebel Abiod road, in the shadow of hills covered with purple wild flowers and separated by narrow black gorges in which dwarf cows found water. Then he smiled. "I wanted that gap for the Thirty-fourth," he said. "Alexander [General, now Viscount, Alexander, the field commander of the joint Allied forces in Africa] and Bedell Smith [Eisenhower's Chief of Staff] had wanted to send the Thirty-fourth home for retraining, they thought it was so bad. It had its tail down between its legs. I said, 'Leave it to me and I'll guarantee that it carries its first important objective, if I have to give it every gun in the Corps.' It's good for troops to feel they have an important objective. You may have to move them up and move them back once or twice when they're green, just to give them the habit of fighting, but if you do it too often they get the feeling they're being thrown away. That treatment had spoiled the Thirty-fourth. So I didn't want it in at the start, when they might think they were getting more of the same. Then I put them at 609. You remember it. It was almost a cliff. But the Thirty-fourth went up it. The suckers got down in the crevices when we put fire on it, and then after our fellows had passed over they came out and took them in the rear. But our fellows cleaned them up. After that, the Thirty-fourth had its tail over the dashboard. You couldn't hold it."

The Thirty-fourth was the division components of which had been so messed around with in the fighting between Sened and Maknassy, while other components had subsequently been set out on hills near Kasserine like goats set out to lure a tiger. Then, when the tiger, in the form of German armor, came, the American armored division that had been cast in the role of big-game hunter lost its nerve and let the Germans scoop up the infantry goats, along with about 100 of our tanks. The residue of the Thirty-fourth was left with a goat mentality, which it imparted to the replacements. Old Dr. Bradley's psychotherapy fixed it up. Confusion, though normal, is not inevitable.

3

Entr'acte

I WAS LUCKY enough to get back to New York at the end of the African campaign, as I have told in the first piece in the book, and had five months at home before I came to the wars again, this time as a passenger on a Norwegian fruit ship that was considered fast enough to run without escort—seventeen knots. She certainly was that time, although I heard she copped it later. You were always hearing that ships you had just been on were sunk, and sometimes it was true. This reefer was of 3,000 tons, very clean and yacht-like, and she landed me in the Adelphi Hotel at Liverpool on November 6, 1943, my fourth and last eastward crossing during the war. My notion was to get to England early in order to be sure of a good spot in the invasion. I did not want to get caught up in some ancillary theatre and then not be able to transfer out in time for the main event, and as the lone correspondent of *The New Yorker* I had to fight my own campaign against red tape and the stuffy lay bureaucrats of the large press organizations, who wanted to make the battle an exclusive feature for their employers, like *Gasoline Alley* or Arthur Krock. When not engaged in this sordid guerilla, I tried various activities to kill time. "Run, Run, Run, Run," arose out of one of them, or out of two of them if you like. It was such an unsettling experience that I didn't write about it at the time; it was hardly a news story, being about something that happened when I wasn't there and then didn't happen when I was. I wrote it in the fall of 1945, at home, but it is all true, except that I made the chief character a more obvious fraud than I am, by lending him some of the characteristics of correspondents I disliked.

Run, Run, Run, Run

WHEN Allardyce Meecham heard that the boys were dead, he felt that he should have flown with them. Meecham was a war correspondent, but he had not yet had a chance to see much of the war. He had come to England in February, 1944, straight from the Hotel Algonquin, where he had had only four or five days to wear his uniform in the lobby, and he did not feel natural wearing it even after a fortnight in London. His nearest approach to action so far had been a visit to an American bomber station in Essex, where he had arranged to go on a bombing mission with a Marauder crew. Now he felt guilty because he had not gone. If he had he would have been dead, too, and that had not been part of his plan, but he felt somehow that this was an ignoble consideration. At the field, a squadron intelligence officer named Kobold had told him the mediums had been having very small losses, an average of one in two hundred sorties. "I wanted to fly one mission and write a story about it, and pretend to myself that I was a big man," Meecham thought self-accusingly, "but if I had expected they would be killed I wouldn't have gone with them." This may or may not have been true. There was no way now of proving it. But Meecham never gave himself the benefit of the doubt because he was afraid that if he did it once he would take advantage of the precedent. "What could you have done, anyway," he asked himself, "if you had known they were going to be killed? Would you have made some excuse and left? Or would you have tried to get them not to go? They would have wanted to know how you could be sure. They would have said you were crazy. They would have gone anyway." But he continued to feel as if he had done something wrong. Meecham had left the airfield because he had tired of hanging about waiting for flying weather. Three days' missions had been washed out and there was no sign it would open up, and he had a date with a British woman officer in London for Friday evening.

This was Sunday. Meecham was standing at the bar of his hotel in Piccadilly, and next to him was Kobold, the intelligence officer he had met at the bomber base. Kobold had come into London on a weekend pass, and he had just told Meecham the bad news. "I wasn't frightened," Meecham thought. "I really wasn't. I told them I was coming back to fly with them next week. They expected to be there. They had flown forty missions. They didn't think the weather would clear off during the weekend. They said I would be a sucker to stay." The weather had cleared on Friday afternoon, after he had left. Saturday morning the bomber crew had been killed. At what precise minute, Meecham wondered, but he felt almost sure he knew. It was March, and dawn came medium late. They would not have been fairly on their way before eight. Over Beauvais, in the north of France, at nine, nine-thirty, maybe. Perhaps at the moment he had picked up the telephone by his bed to order breakfast. "Two teas, sausage and tomato. Darling, do you want sausage and tomato or sausage and mushroom? There's bacon, but it's usually like eating a candle." That must have been the minute. "Two sausage and tomato, then. And lots of toast. Thank you."

"They had all their bombs aboard," Kobold was saying. He was an oldish lieutenant who felt that he should have been a captain months ago. "One big hell of a cloud of smoke, and then parts of the plane falling out of it. No chutes—no time for them. The other boys brought back wonderful pictures of it. Poor bastards." The intelligence officer talked loudly, a little truculently, because he wanted a couple of B-17 pilots at the other end of the bar to hear him. The heavy-bomber people sometimes talked as if they had all the losses; the lieutenant wanted to impress this pair. He never flew on operations himself.

Meecham stood just six feet in shoes, but because of his thin, long legs and short, beanlike torso he seemed longer than that when he stood up and shorter than that when he sat down. He had a white face, wide at the cheekbones and covered with faint, rusty blotches, and carroty hair that for the last five years had just failed to cover the top of his head. People seeing him at a bar thought of him as tall and red-headed, but others, who had looked at him seated at a restaurant table, remembered him as bald and middle-sized. His eyelashes were almost white. In New York he was a dramatic critic, but as the war entered its fifth year and all his acquaintances—book reviewers, editorial writers, political columnists, racing handicappers, and publishers' assistants—became war correspondents and went overseas, he had felt lonely. There must be something in the war that none of these people were fine enough to perceive, he had told his wife, who had a responsible job in the promotion department of a women's magazine and always referred to herself as a "gal." She had agreed with him. She was a good gal. "Besides," she had said, "I think it would be a professional disadvantage for a dramatic critic after the war not to have been a war correspondent. No one would want to hear you lecture." She was having an affair with a Rumanian fashion photographer, who worked her for assignments. Meecham had been disappointed that even his own wife misread his motives. But, fighting down this disappointment, he had gone to his managing editor and asked to be sent to Europe. The editor had sent him because he rather thought there would be a lull before the invasion of the Continent. Meecham would spell one of the paper's regular correspondents accredited to the Army, who would come home for a short vacation before the big show began. "But, of course, if it should start suddenly, you'll be there," the editor had said. "Yes, sir," Meecham had said in a voice from which he had tried to exclude excitement. He had felt exalted as he walked over to Abercrombie & Fitch to be measured for his uniform. But, as he now reflected, he had not thought that he really might be killed. "I wanted something for nothing," he thought unmercifully. He was on the point of admiring how hard on himself he could be, and then he remembered that that would constitute self-approval, so he stopped.

Meecham remembered the interior of the Nissen hut he had slept in at the Marauder field. There had been cots and a table and a stove, hooks on the walls to hang clothes on, and even coat hangers, but to him it had been a Spartan place, where he had been more conscious of the war than in his room in London, which contained a good deal of inlaid furniture and a double bed with a yellow damask cover. There were electric-light bulbs in the hut, but they were not shaded, and you had to go outdoors to get to the latrine. There were six cots in the hut. A Marauder carries a complement of three officers and three enlisted men; the hut accommodated the officers of two planes. One set of three had gone to town on pass; men who flew together took their passes at the same time. This gave Meecham his choice of three cots. The boys of the other Marauder crew had just come back from forty-eight hours in London. Meecham found them in the hut when Kobold brought him there in the evening. He had stayed at the officers' club drinking gin and Italian vermouth with the C.O. and a couple of non-flying intelligence officers until the bar closed, at ten o'clock. Then Kobold had guided him to the hut. It would have been hard to find in the blackout if he had been alone. Kobold had introduced Meecham to the three crewmates. One of them, a large, hairy, blond young man, was in bed already. He was Captain Barry, the pilot. Barry was smoking a last cigarette before going to sleep. One bare, powerful arm lay outside the blankets as he puffed. A B-26, romantically known as a Marauder, is not an easy plane to fly, and old pilots get big forearms and biceps. Barry reached out a big hand to shake Meecham's. "Make yourself at home," he said. Brownlea, the co-pilot, a wiry young man with a crew haircut, sat at the table with his back to the stove, reading what Meecham observed wonderingly was a book by Robert Briffault, an author Meecham associated vaguely with Granville Hicks and Ouida. "I hope you don't mind loud noises," Brownlea said. "Barry is about to go to sleep. Luckily they have radar here or somebody would have shot him down before this. When he snores he sounds exactly like a four-motor job. He has the Air Force sack medal with so many clusters it looks like a bunch of grapes." "Brownlea is an intellectual," Barry said. "He is a wizard intellectual, they would say in the R.A.F. He is very cheesed with life. He thinks life is a ruddy pantomime. Someday when he is at the controls he will be thinking of an ideology and he will prang the crate. A wizard prang." Elkan, the bombardier-navigator, was sitting on a cot, looking over a set of shiny photographer's prints; he had interrupted the examination only long enough to nod at Meecham when Kobold introduced them. He was a thin young man who in civilian clothes could have been mistaken for a high-school junior. He could not weigh more than a hundred and fifteen pounds and he had a long, pointed nose and large ears. He was still wearing the Class A uniform blouse and pinks in which he had come back from London, and the garrison cap was still on his head. The left breast of his blouse was pretty well loaded with ribbons— even Meecham could recognize the Silver Star, the Distinguished Flying Cross, the Air Medal nutmegged with oak-leaf clusters, the E.T.O. ribbon dotted with stars, and a couple of the innocuous red-and-yellow ones that make good background even though they don't mean anything much.

Kobold went away and Meecham settled down on a cot. "I'm glad to have you here, sir," Brownlea said to Meecham. "Barry and Elkan are good joes, but Elkan is emotional and Barry is inclined to pure escapism. I have been wanting a chance to talk to someone who has really been around a lot."

Meecham was ashamed to tell him that his travels, until this trip, had been limited to a tourist-class vacation in France when he was in college and four trips to the Central City, Colorado, annual dramatic festivals, so he said nothing.

"Don't give Brownlea any encouragement, sir," Elkan said, "or he will read you the first ten chapters of his book."

"I wouldn't think of it," Brownlea said. "Anyway, they're only in a kind of outline form. I really don't know anything about writing. What I want to know is what you think of the Russians."

Meecham considered himself an untrammelled liberal—during the Spanish Civil War he had attended several cocktail parties for the benefit of the Loyalists—but he had heard talk at home about the Fascist mind of the Air Corps, so he was careful in answering. He liked these boys so much already that he didn't want to alarm or antagonize them. He said merely, "I know the Russians are our Allies. I mean, I believe they're sincere, and they're certainly fighting hard."

"Is that all?" Brownlea said. "Why, they're absolutely wonderful. They're the only hope I see for civilization. Surely, sir, you don't think capitalist society can survive all this? Say, have you ever read this man Briffault?"

"Brownie got a brushoff from a society dame at a bottle club in London," Barry said. "She said she was going to spend a penny and she never came back. He's been a militant proletarian ever since."

Meecham said that, of course, the rôle Russia would be called upon to play in the future should not be underestimated.

"Well, I don't worry much about that," Barry said, "although I still have a card in the typographical union, so it burns my ass when I read in the *Reader's Digest* that organized labor is to blame for about everything that gets screwed up. I worked my way through the University of California that way, setting type at night on a paper in Oakland. Where the hell does the *Reader's Digest* think I am, and where is the bird who is writing that stuff? Sitting on his can, I bet. But being from the Coast, I mean, I don't think very much about this war. I'd like to be out smacking those Japs around. I haven't got anything too much against the Germans, except Hitler is a son of a bitch."

"I have," Elkan said. "I'm a Jew, and they've been killing millions of Jews who didn't do a goddam thing to them. I hate the bastards. I like to think of what the bombs will do to them when we make our run."

"You see?" Brownlea said. "Pure emotion. Barry and Elkan don't know anything about the economic bases of imperialism. They reduce everything to personal relationships."

"She said she had to spend a penny," Barry said to nobody in particular. "Brownie offered to lend her a shilling. She gave him a look that said, 'Anybody that dumb . . .' And the brush."

Elkan said, "To change the subject, which of these pictures do you like the best?"

"Are they of a broad?" Barry asked.

"No, you wolf—me," Elkan answered severely. "I went down to see the Tower of London yesterday, and then I walked around and had some pictures taken at a photographer's. I want to pick out the best one and have some copies made from it to send home. I want to send them to my mother and my girl and people like that." Meecham had already learned that Elkan's parents lived in Bayonne, New Jersey, where his father had a dry-cleaning store. He had gone two years to Rutgers but hadn't had enough money to continue, and for a year or so before he enlisted he had helped in the store. He hadn't as much assurance as some of the bigger, louder boys, who gave the impression that the whole Air Force came from Texas, but the fellows in his squadron had a lot of respect for him. Barry, Brownlea, and Meecham began passing the photographer's proofs from one to another. Meecham could see that the two pilots were considering them very seriously. In all but one of the proofs, Elkan had the visor of his cap pulled well down and was scowling and puffing out his chest. The photographer had got a good, clear picture of the ribbons. But the thin, triangular face and the frail, bony neck still looked like a little boy's. Only one of the proofs showed Elkan smiling. The wide smile made him look younger and more ingenuous than ever, but the picture was the only one of the lot that wasn't absurd. All three of the consultants agreed it was the best.

"That's the only one that looks like the real Ernie," Barry said.

"That's the one your mother would like to have," said Brownlea.

And Meecham said, "That's the best." He could sense that Ernie was disappointed and that if he had not been there the little bombardier-navigator might have tried to argue with the others.

But Elkan accepted the reinforced verdict. "Christ," he said sadly, "I guess I'll never look like a hero." Meecham could see that he was worrying about his girl back home.

They had talked a while longer and then turned in. Meecham had felt unexpectedly ashamed because his body looked so white and old compared to theirs. He was forty-three and the last exercise he could remember had been a fight with the juvenile of a show he had panned in 1937, but the bartender and the home-and-garden editor had stopped it after the first swing, when the juvenile's pince-nez fell on the floor.

There had been no mission the next morning, on account of the weather. Meecham had got up at seven and gone dutifully to mess, but the boys had chosen to sleep until nearly noon.

"It must be awfully slow for you here, sir," Barry had said the next time Meecham saw him. "I suppose you wanted to go over with us and see some fun."

"It isn't dull at all," Meecham had said, and meant it. "It's very interesting." He had not added, "It's all new to me," because he felt a childish reluctance to let the boys know he was so green. He hadn't really thought of flying a mission on his first visit to the field, either. But Barry looked so competent and unworried that Meecham had found himself saying, "I sure would like to go with you. Do you think the C.O. would let me?"

Barry had grinned and said, "Sure. We've flew lots of correspondents in our ship. It breaks the monotony." And they had shaken hands on it.[*]

Meecham had slept in the hut a second and third night and each had been followed by a day of bad weather. Even in this brief time he had begun to think of himself as a member of the crew of the Typographical Error, the name Barry had given his B-26. He had gone through the preliminary processes of a Marauder mission, which at that time he had thought piquant rather than grim. The squadron intelligence officer had told him what to do if he had to bail out over France. He was to hide his parachute and then take cover and lie still until somebody found him. The French underground people would be pretty sure to find him, the intelligence officer said, and they would smuggle him across France and

[*] Harold Ross, the great editor of The New Yorker, said when he read this in manuscript that Barry, a college man and a linotyper, would not have said, "flew." My only answer was that the prototype of Barry in real life *had* said "flew." Since I was pretending to write fiction, this was not a valid argument, but I had my way. I can see now that "we've flew" looks unconvincing. But I hear the pseudonymous Barry's voice in my head sometimes, and he still says it.

into a neutral country, although it might take months. The prospect had sounded alluring as the intelligence officer described it, and Meecham had been unable to stop daydreaming about adventures with admiring and sympathetic Frenchwomen. The one thing the officer had not said anything about was what to do if you were dead. So Meecham had not thought about it.

On the third bad morning he had begun to feel bored and had remembered the date with the woman officer in London. There was a train at noon and he had decided to leave by it. When he began packing his bag the boys were still in bed, and when he finished he went around to each cot and shook hands before he started for the jeep that was to take him to the railway station. Meecham could remember Barry's strong grip and Elkan's slender hand and Brownlea grinning and waving his clenched left fist. Brownlea's father, Meecham had learned, was president of a savings bank in Boston.

Remembering, Meecham felt that the date with them was more binding than if they had survived and that he could never be pleased with himself if he did not fly a mission now. But there was no exhilaration in the thought. He returned to Essex three days later. He found it easy to arrange, at Ninth Air Force Headquarters, for permission to go along on a bombardment. "The story has been done a lot of times before," a public-relations officer warned him. "There's nothing much to it." Meecham explained that he just wanted to see what it was like. He didn't say anything about the crew of the Typographical Error. It seemed to him for a moment, after they had said he could go, that he was doing a causeless thing. It isn't being brave, he told himself, because the mathematical chance of getting hurt is no greater now than it was last week, and then it was very small. Barry and his ship just had bad luck. And there won't be any story in it either. But he was afraid, and that was precisely what he could not afford to admit to himself. Nobody at the field seemed astonished that he wanted to do it. The boys at the officers' club made him welcome with gin and Italian vermouth, and he was introduced to the officers he was now assigned to fly with. Their ship was named the Roll Me Over,* and they were nice boys enough, Meecham thought, but it was like a widower's marriage; he could not get as interested in them as in the dead crew. Schifferdecker, the pilot, was a squat, broad-shouldered boy who had played football at Cornell, where he had taken a course in hotel manage-

---

* From that great song:
    "Roll me over, in the clover,
    Roll me over, lay me down, and do it again—"
which was the pre-invasion "Battle Hymn of the Republic." It was frequently asserted, during World War II, that "this is not a singing war." It was—people always sing when they are frightened—but the songs did not lend themselves to community performance.

ment. He kept telling Meecham that after the war the British would have to build modern hotels all over England if they expected any Americans ever to come back there. Thurman, the co-pilot, a tall, handsome young man from someplace in Wisconsin, did not have much to say for himself. He had a girl in a show in London, his crewmates said, and he considered every hour he had to spend at the field time wasted. "Missions are the only chance he has to catch up on his sleep," Schifferdecker said. Muldowney, the bombardier-navigator, was a pale, gray-eyed young man who looked like a very youthful Franchot Tone and knew it, and who had played in a dance band in St. Paul before enlisting in the Air Corps. "It's a good deal, having a correspondent along," he told Meecham. "We'll be in a soft spot, right in the center of one of the middle elements, where nothing ever happens. Those flak gunners loose off at the first ships, and then, when the first elements drop their bombs, the gunners run like hell. We'll have a breeze. Same thing for fighters. We haven't been getting much fighter opposition. The Heinies keep most of that in Germany to use against the heavy bombers. But what we have been getting usually lays for the rear element, on the way home, hoping to knock off stragglers. We lost a ship that way yesterday. The boys in the middle have a soft touch." Muldowney had a wide, white grin. "An easy one is always all right with me," he went on. "I've had twenty-eight missions so far, and every easy one means that much better a chance to finish the fifty."

There was no cot for Meecham in the hutment where the Roll Me Overs slept, so he spent the night in a hut in another part of the field, about half a mile from the mess hall. The men in the hut with him were armament and engineering officers. Only two were in bed when Meecham got there. The rest were up most of the night preparing planes for the takeoff. They got in so late that they had just begun to snore when an orderly turned on the lights before dawn next morning. They stayed in bed, the blankets over their heads, while Meecham and the two men who had been in bed early began to dress. Meecham hated to get up early in the morning for any reason at all, and on this particular day he felt worse than usual. He dressed fast, for him, but he was not yet familiar with lace boots, and he had to fumble around in his musette bag to find toothpaste and a towel. Then he felt colicky and went out to look for a latrine. By the time he returned the two other men had gone to the mess hall, and he began to fear that he would lose his way in the dark. The buildings were, of course, blacked out, so he would have no lighted windows to guide him. It would sound like an implausible excuse for missing the raid. He went out of the hut and saw the silhouette of a jeep moving up the road past the hut. There were at least a dozen men on it, some sitting on the hood. He yelled, "Going up to mess?" Someone shouted to him to jump on. Awkwardly he ran along beside the slowly moving jeep, not knowing quite how to get aboard without knocking some other rider off his perch. The jeep stopped and somebody said, "Come along, Pop. You can sit in the back." One of the youngsters in the back seat scrambled out and found a few inches of space on a mudguard, and half a dozen hands grabbed Meecham and hoisted him into the place just vacated. He rode along to the mess hall oblivious of everything except his humiliation. At table he found Schifferdecker and Thurman. Muldowney came along a couple of minutes later, carrying a shiny brown quilted flying suit which he had drawn for Meecham. The breakfast was poor—an omelet badly made of powdered egg and bacon that was all rind and grease. The fruit juice was all gone and the coffee tasted metallic. He wondered if the breakfast was really that bad or if he was frightened. "This is pisspoor chow," Thurman said, and Meecham was reassured. The men in the mess hall straggled out in little groups, crewmates and fellows who knew each other, and climbed into weapons carriers for the ride out to the dispersal building for the briefing. Meecham, of course, rode with the Roll Me Overs.

The briefing reminded him of a lecture in a compulsory course at college. The hall was filled with fellows in flying gear who talked to each other and did not seem too attentive. The intelligence officer stood on a dais at one end of the hall and waved a pointer at various spots on a large map that was projected on a screen behind him. Meecham learned later that all the fliers had been to these particular targets several times and that the lecture had about the same interest for them as an explanation of how to reach New Rochelle. "Our primary target today will be the Montdidier airfield," the officer said. "There is a battery of six mediums on the approach to the Montdidier field. Six mediums." Somebody whistled. "All of you can go now except the bombardiers. Bombardiers stay a minute after the others leave."

Meecham went out with Schifferdecker and Thurman and three sergeants who had joined them in the briefing hall. The sergeants were the rest of the Roll Me Over's crew—radio-gunner, flight engineer, and tail gunner. They were named Mickiewicz, Klopstock, and Leopardi. Muldowney had to stay to get his detailed bombing map. When he came out they all got into a weapons carrier with perhaps twenty other fliers. The carrier rolled along on the cinder path that circled the field, stopping at each plane to let off the men who were going to fly in it. So Meecham found himself eventually standing under the shadow of the Roll Me Over. It was daylight now, but the sky was still pink with the embers of dawn. In the truck the boys had been singing a song of which Meecham had been able to distinguish only the first line, "How's your love life?"* He put on the flying suit over his G.I. pants, his sweater, and his combat jacket. Muldowney was brisk and happy, although cold. He rubbed his gloved hands together furiously and stamped about in his flying boots. Schifferdecker was serious and conscientious, conferring with the ser-

---

* This was not a classic, like "Roll Me Over," and I never heard it again. It sounded like something they would get off the other side of a hit record in the officers' lounge.

geants. Thurman leaned against the fuselage and Meecham noticed that he looked sleepy. He wondered if Thurman could have got down to London on a late train and back in time to fly. Meecham nodded toward the ship and asked Muldowney if it was all right to get aboard. Muldowney said sure, and went ahead to show the way. This was a moment Meecham had anticipated with distaste, because he didn't know how to get into a B-26 and had a feeling it might call for some display of acrobacy. It was not so hard as he had feared. There were two metal stirrups no higher than those on an English saddle, and when you got one foot up you reached up with your hands and caught two metal handles in the interior of the plane. Then you swung yourself up and in. He could see that it would be easy to get out when they returned—he would only have to swing himself out by the handles and drop. Somehow this was a major satisfaction. Muldowney motioned him into a compartment behind the nose of the plane. There was no need to kneel or crawl. "There's a hell of a lot of room in these things," Muldowney said. "More than in a Fort. You just sit over there at the side on that pile of chutes." The others came aboard one by one. Schifferdecker and Thurman went past Meecham and into the pilots' compartment, in the nose. The sergeants joined Meecham and Muldowney in the compartment behind the pilots' because Schifferdecker would want their weight up forward for the takeoff. "This is a place for the navigator to work," Muldowney told Meecham, "but there isn't any real navigating to do when we follow the leader in a big formation like today. Of course, if we got crippled or had to beat it off by ourselves for any reason, it would be different. I just wander around the ship when we get going, sometimes here and sometimes in the bomb bay. We're carrying frag bombs today, by the way. Thirty one-hundred-pound frag bombs. We drop them on the runway and dispersal area to take care of planes and personnel. Sometimes we carry a couple of big ones, but today frags." The motors were turning over. Other planes taxied by them on their way to the runway. Then the Roll Me Over began to roll, too. The motors made such a noise that conversation became impractical, although it was still possible to understand a shouted monosyllable. The compartment in which Meecham rode was comfortable, but there was only a view straight out to either side. There was nothing to see in either direction except other B-26s. The plane was swaying and slipping about and he could see Thurman turn and swear. Schifferdecker was running the ship. The pilots sat next to each other. The backs of their seats were armor-plated, as a protection against pieces of flak. Meecham could see there was room for a man to crouch behind them, and he looked forward enviously because there was more to see from the nose of the plane. Thurman, as if reading his thoughts, waved to him to come forward, and he did, scrunching his torso and hams down behind Thurman's seat, while his legs extended over behind Schifferdecker's.

Now the sky was as blue as the Bay of Naples on the wall of a spaghetti joint, and it was full of B-26s. They flew in "loose fives," their favorite formation. Meecham started to count all those in sight; he made it sixty-seven, including the planes on the Roll Me Over's wings, but more appeared constantly and he stopped counting. He deduced that the B-26s were just circling while the groups assembled and that the serious part of the expedition had not begun yet. Then the course began to seem to him more purposeful. Almost before he was sure of this, Thurman was plucking at his elbow, waving an arm downward. They were over the coast, heading out over the Channel, which looked not blue but had, at its English edge, the color of a puddle of rain water glistening in sunlight. Then it became lead color. Meecham noticed for the first time that the motors were saying words. They were saying words, groaning, rather, "No, no, no, no." He had ridden in planes before but he had never recognized the words. When they got over the French coast, he thought, "I should be curious. I haven't seen France in twenty years." He looked and it seemed quite like England. He leaned close to Thurman's ear and shouted, "How long to over target?" Thurman howled back, "Twenty minutes." Meecham went back to the pile of parachutes in the navigator's cabin and Muldowney appeared, probably from the bomb bay, and seemed to be saying something about "fighters." Meecham returned to his place behind the pilots and looked down. He saw a midget plane far below them. It was a Spitfire, but he did not know it; he could not tell Allied fighters from Germans. All the attention began to embarrass Meecham. He felt that Muldowney was treating him like a grandfather on a Sunday auto ride. Muldowney reached through the doorway to the pilots' compartment and tapped Meecham on the shoulder. He wanted to show him something dead ahead, a series of specks in the sky. Then Muldowney grinned and started back to the bomb bay. The specks were not fighters, Meecham saw as the plane drew up on them, but puffs of black smoke. They multiplied, as he watched, and hung in the air, little black balls of grime. He knew what they were from his sporadic attendance at newsreel theatres. The planes of the forward elements were flying through them now. The flak was at very nearly the right altitude, and Meecham began to hear a new sound over the motors—a sharp "Pak!" like a champagne cork popping and then "S-s-s" like half the wine in the bottle fizzing out. The "Pak!" was the shell bursting, and the fizz was the flight of the fragments. Once Thurman threw up a hand in front of his face and flattened himself against the back of his seat, but nothing happened. Meecham wondered if it had been a close one or if Thurman was just jumpy from too much tomcatting. The co-pilot was waving his hand now and Meecham, following his gesture, could see the bombs falling away from the planes up ahead of them, like chewing-gum nuggets out of a vending machine. Then there were no more puffs in the sky. He felt Muldowney's hand on his shoulder again. The boy had been away only an instant, it seemed. Muldowney was laughing and waving his hands palm upward. Thurman took off his earphones and put them on Meecham, so Meecham could listen to the intercom. Schifferdecker said to Meecham through the intercom, "How'd you like it?" Meecham tried to smile, and for all he knew succeeded. Then Schifferdecker made Thurman take the ship. Meecham understood from that that they were on the way home. He gave Thurman the earphones again. The motors said now, "Run, run, run, run." He said to himself, "I am not making this up, that is what they are saying." He listened again and they were indeed saying, "Run, run," instead of "No, no." Meecham looked at the air speed indicator and it said "330," which pleased him. Then he went back to Muldowney's compartment and relaxed on the parachutes. Muldowney was grinning and waving his hands and shouting into Meecham's ear, and finally Meecham could understand what he was saying: "I told you that flak would stop as soon as the first planes got their bombs away!" Meecham succeeded in asking whether *he* had got his bombs away and Muldowney joined a thumb and forefinger in a circle to show he had put his bombs right on the bull's-eye. Sergeant Mickiewicz, a bulky blond with a red face, appeared in the compartment and grinned at Meecham. Nothing happened on the way back, but it seemed five times as long as it had going out.

When they got out of the plane, Schifferdecker started swearing. "The goddam wash nearly made me airsick," he said. "Those goddam cowboys in the ships on our wings must think they're driving taxicabs. Whoever checked them out in a bomber ought to have his head examined. What a ratfuck!" He explained that a ratfuck was "a rat race, but all bollixed up."

Thurman said, "If they don't keep us too long at the goddam interrogation I can catch the twelve-o'clock train to London."

Muldowney said, "Twenty-nine down and twenty-one to go. I hope they send us a correspondent on every trip! I wonder if any of those leading planes got flak in them."

Meecham felt unreasonably exalted. After all, he told himself reprovingly, he had only escaped from a danger that he had got himself into. And not a great danger, either, he thought. I didn't see one plane shot down. Still, he couldn't help thinking, pretty good for a dramatic critic. He had forgotten Barry and Elkan and Brownlea.

Meecham was still in the midst of his euphoria when he boarded the London train at Chelmsford in midafternoon. He had not been in as much haste to get away as Thurman, and had remained to eat a pretty good lunch of pork chops and canned pineapple at the field. The train was crowded, and although he had a first-class ticket, he had to stand in the corridor outside a compartment filled with American enlisted men who had got on further up the line. When they saw his war-correspondent shoulder flash they tapped on the glass and asked him in. They were all

Fortress men who, it appeared, had been on dozens of twelve-hour missions over Germany, from almost all of which they had returned with their ships aflame and three engines out. Meecham was ashamed to tell them he had been only as far as France that morning. By the time the train arrived at Liverpool Street station his exuberance was waning. Coming out into Broad Street, he felt hungry again. He had had what for him was a phenomenally long day. He stopped in at a place called Gow's, a combination fishmonger's and restaurant, and ordered a dozen oysters at the counter. He ordered a second dozen, but the man behind the counter said that the Ministry of Food did not allow them to sell more than eight bob worth to a customer and he had had it. Meecham felt a certain resentment; he had half a mind to tell the man where he had been that morning. That would show him. But perhaps the man had a son in the R.A.F., so he would not be impressed. Or three R.A.F. sons, all killed in the Battle of Britain, so he would be pained by any reference to flying. The thought recalled Barry and Brownlea and Elkan for the first time that day. Meecham wondered why it had seemed essential that, because of them, he go on a mission after they were dead. He paid for his oysters and went out into the street to look for a taxi. He hoped his girl was in town and had no date for the evening. After all, this ought to impress her.

Another time-killing expedient of mine was to try to construct from information what life in occupied France must be, and in this I had great assistance from friends in the British Political Warfare Board and with the Free French Government in London, who supplied me with hundreds of clandestine newspapers published in France and smuggled out by their agents. The next piece is one of a series I wrote that winter under the same generic title—the newspapers reminded me that another kind of war was going on across the Channel while we waited for spring. Looking at this sample now, I think it should help the people who have grown up since to understand a lot about current French attitudes.

Notes from the Kidnap House—1944

THE secret newspapers of France do not give French people much news of the outside world. That is left to the British radio and the Algiers radio, which do not have the paper and distribution problems of the journals in enemy-occupied territory. Since most of the resistance newspapers are no larger than a sheet of typewriter paper and have only four pages, they concentrate on local news and editorial comment. The three largest groups of publications—those in each group are loosely affiliated—are Communist, Socialist, and Mur, this last name being short for Mouvements Unis de Résistance. Mur is an organization of "new men," men who are not connected with the old political parties, and is strongly de Gaullist. The masthead of all Mur papers carries the slogan "One chief, de Gaulle; one struggle, for our liberties." Mur is for "social as well as political democracy," by which it means the nationalization of banks and probably of heavy industry, ruthless punishment of the rich men and Vichy politicians who collaborated openly or tacitly, and the guidance of France by a "new élite" of men who have made their way up through the resistance movements. The editorials in its papers maintain that "the shame of Vichy does not excuse the shortcomings of preceding governments." Some editorials in the Mur papers oppose the presence in Algiers of men like Pierre Cot, Vincent Auriol, and other pre-Vichy government figures, although conceding that in the interest of unity they must be tolerated for a brief while. Mur is nationalistic, occasionally to the point of xenophobia, whereas the Socialist and the Communist newspaper groups place more emphasis on the class struggle and less on the personal leadership of de Gaulle and new élites. Yet these, too, endorse de Gaulle and the Algiers government, and Mur endorses in some degree the class struggle. The difference lies in the importance each faction gives the different aspects of the fight. The Socialists, the largest single party in France before the armistice, defend most of their party record, and the heroic attitude of Léon Blum since his arrest, especially at the Riom trial, has added weight to this defense. Blum, like Edouard Herriot, has become a martyr in his own lifetime. *Populaire*, Blum's old newspaper, has seven regional editions, all clandestine, and reaches at least a million readers. Its preoccupation with the party record sometimes makes it seem to look backward too much. Recently it published a noble but nostalgic appeal to President Roosevelt to vindicate the New Deal by disregarding the demands of American capitalists. The editorialist, in his hideout, apparently had not heard that the term "New Deal" is now in the same limbo as "Popular Front." In almost every issue, *Populaire* runs, under the heading of "Our Martyrs," a list of Socialist resistants shot by the Gestapo or murdered by the Vichy militia, as if to emphasize the fact that the Socialists have at last become a party of action. The Communist press, headed by the several editions of *L'Humanité* and comprising a number of newspapers for various vocational groups of intellectuals and workers, benefits not only from the present prestige of Russia but from the name that Communist resistants have won for courage and austerity.

There are dozens of other resistance papers, of political shades more difficult to classify, ranging from *L'Aurore*, the organ of conservative Republican resistance, to a little sheet called *Le Soviet*, which carries at its masthead the line "Long live Trotsky and Lenin! Down with Stalin, grave-digger of the Third International!" All, however, agree on at least two points. *The first of these is the French refusal to be patronized or treated as a decadent nation, especially by the English-speaking nations, whom the French blame for rebuilding Germany between the two great wars, before leaving France to fend for herself in 1939. The resistants look forward to liberation not as a favor but as the first small installment due them on a debt of blood.* Smuts'* speech last November served to intensify this feeling, which crystalized in the streamer headline of one clandestine paper, *Libération*: "Pétain, Badoglio, Smuts Examples of Intelligence of Marshalls." "Great Britain three years ago carried all the hopes of our people; these are things one does not forget, in spite of the Smutses," an editorialist, in hiding from the Gestapo, wrote in *Libération*. "*France decadent? Really? Well, if all France were in ruins, if there survived of all her decimated people only a few women and old men, the representative of France, whoever he might be, would have the right to sit with Churchill, Roosevelt, and Stalin and be treated with the most profound respect*, because, if there hadn't been a certain nation called France and a certain battle called Verdun, Monsieur Smuts might now, with a little luck, be a junior native customs official in South Africa. . . . *With or without Smuts, the European resistance movement is going to remake the Continent into a free Europe of free citizens.* Taught by our common experience of slavery, we have more in common with the men of Free Belgium, of Tito or Ribar, than with most Francophile diplomats. Who knows if the greatest service Smuts could render us is not to awaken our compatriots to the true mission of France: to remake Europe and open Africa?" Another clandestine paper, *Franc-Tireur*, says, "*The countries that hoped to save themselves the horrors of war by neutrality and those who could organize for victory out of the reach of the enemy while for nine months we held the line—haven't they also their responsibilities? Didn't they count too much on France and her Army, on the military qualities of her people, to conquer a force they had allowed to develop?* This war, in which we were the sacrificed advance guard, has been waged against a racial dictatorship which intended to hold the world underfoot. It is unthinkable that it should end in another dictatorship, nationalistic or plutocratic. France, even defeated, remains great enough and has enough claims to gratitude not to merit the treatment of a vassal or a servant." This feeling was also revealed in a statement Daladier made to the German police who a year ago came to the prison of Bourrassol to remove him to the Reich. "I congratulate myself," he said, "for having declared war in 1939. A year later you would have won the war. Today I have the pleasure of telling you that you are irretrievably lost."

The second point of universal agreement is that France remains intrinsically great. These two basic sentiments make the resistance press

---

* I forget what Smuts said, but they didn't like it. I almost forget who Smuts was. That was before South Africa made the headlines.

*hypersensitive to any hint of infringement on French sovereignty. A re-
cent report from Washington that General Eisenhower would choose the
Frenchmen with whom the Allies would treat meant to many resistants
that the Americans would attempt to choose the rulers of France. Since,
in the minds of French workingmen, America has always stood for big
business and since the de Gaullists feel that the State Department has
always worked against them,* there is an almost universal fear that the
English-speaking powers will try to impose a Kolchak government in
striped pants, headed by a shifty *type* like Georges Bonnet. Bonnet was
not allowed to participate officially in the Vichy regime because of his
association with the Jewish bank of Lazard Frères, and therefore he could
now be presented as being free of the Vichy taint. Camile Chautemps,
who has been in Washington long enough to be able to disclaim any
connection with the "later excesses" of the Vichy regime, is another bogey
of the resistance men. The recollection of the high favor Bonnet and his
friends enjoyed, back in the Munich days, with men still prominent in the
British government, such as Halifax, Hoare, and Simon, does not dispose
resistants to look forward to receiving British support against the tendency they think they see in American policy. An extreme statement of
the frame of mind that has resulted from the refusal of the Allied governments to commit themselves is the following, in *Combat: "We think it
would be criminal and absurd to have complete confidence in foreign
military staffs, in foreign military representatives, or in officers of the
French Army of the colonial type to set up a republic and let the citizens
of France express themselves.* To say everything—if a choice has to be
made one day between 'terrorism' and AMG, our choice is made. Of
ourselves we are sure, of 'practical men' we are not."

More interesting to me than the editorial opinion of these journalists—
who, since they live in constant danger of being captured, tortured to
make them give information about their colleagues (usually by having
their fingernails torn out), and then shot, lack the calm detachment of,
say, Arthur Krock—are the pictures of French life presented, at least by
implication, in such publications as *Bulletin des Chemins de Fer,* the
clandestine organ of the railroad workers. Railroad men have perhaps
the hardest rôle in the resistance movement. A factory saboteur faces the
danger of detection and arrest, but when a railroad worker wrecks a train
he may not survive to be arrested. Furthermore, trains and freight yards
are constant targets of bombing attacks; a railroader takes the same risks
as the German troops among whom he finds himself. There are no air-raid
shelters in freight trains as there are in factories. Moreover, railroaders
furnish much of the information about troop and ammunition movements
that leads to air attacks, and thus they call down the lightning on themselves. These dangers are superimposed upon conditions which are diffi-

cult enough in themselves—"overwork, long hours, pathetic remnants of rolling stock left by the Boche, coal dust that hardly burns in place of the good fuel of other days"—and upon the psychological strain of having to work for the Germans. "I know your suffering at feeling yourselves unarmed executioners of your countrymen when you drive trains toward Germany heavy with conscripted French workmen," one writer in *Bulletin* tells his comrades. (Many times, it may be noted, train crews have managed to stop somewhere and give the deportees a chance to escape through the windows of the cars.) "I know how you feel when you drive toward Germany freight trains loaded with all the substance that the Boche has drained from our rich land," the writer continues, "but you must endure, because you alone can on the great day, you eight hundred thousand rail workers, prevent the German from applying his strategy, paralyze his troop movements, isolate his units, immobilize his supplies, break his power, and precipitate his defeat."

The remainder of the same issue of *Bulletin* is more matter-of-fact. There is a prescription for getting rid of a fellow-employee who appears to be spying on resistance activities (accidentally drop a packing case on his toes), a list of the past month's railroad wrecks, and a note on a low *type*, an assistant stationmaster at the Perrache station, in Lyons, who curries favor with the German police. This *type* was present when political prisoners in a train passing through were throwing notes to friends on the platform. He saw a man on the platform cover a note with his foot. "The swine pointed the man out to a cop," *Bulletin* records. "He will not be overlooked." There is also the story of the wrecking of three civilian express passenger trains, with a heavy loss of life. These wrecks were the work not of any resistance group, readers are informed, but of *agents provocateurs* trying to twist public opinion against patriots. Patriot saboteurs do not molest trains of no military importance, especially passenger trains.

Another publication I always like to find in a packet that a friend in the underground movement now and then brings to my flat in London is *La Terre*, which calls itself "the organ of peasant resistance." Farmers, as a group, have always had the temperament and the facilities for resisting official pressure. Readers of *La Terre* are continually enjoined to delay threshing, to hide their harvests until they can be turned over to the *Maquis*, or at least to sell their crops privately to other Frenchmen, since any food delivered to Vichy authorities will be siphoned off to the Germans and sent out of the country. The government has inspectors to check up on agricultural production and delivery. Some of the inspectors, of course, are "reasonable," shutting their eyes to all discrepancies, since they are at heart as anti-Boche as anybody else. Others, not "reasonable," are mobbed or ambushed and beaten up with farm implements. In a Breton village, my latest *La Terre* informs me, three hundred people gathered around an inspector who had complained of the light weight of some pigs delivered by a farmer, and chased him into the mayor's office, from which the gendarmes had to rescue him. In another village, also in Brittany, an officious gendarme tried to make the farm wives stop baking, because the farmers are supposed to deliver all their flour to the government. Enraged women dumped him into a horse trough. In the Yonne department, farmers hide requisitioned horses and cows; in Loir-et-Cher, the farmers deliver no eggs, insisting that the hens stopped laying in 1940. In Seine-et-Oise, the peasants have formed committees to demand high grain prices. Everywhere the peasants unite to hunt informers, just as farmers in Iowa, not long ago, used to chase process servers. *La Terre* holds up the example of the scorched earth set by the Russian peasants. Incidentally, "Le Père Milon," de Maupassant's story of a Norman peasant who spent his nights killing German soldiers during the 1871 occupation, has been republished, according to *La Terre*, as a resistance pamphlet.

There are labor papers of all political shades. One, *Les Informations Sociales*, analyzes for French workers, in the tone of the *New Republic*, the Beveridge Plan and the differences between the C.I.O. and the A.F.L. *Les Informations* describes itself as "the bulletin of information for militant unionists." In addition to publishing informative articles, it has reprinted, without comment, Stalin's decree dissolving the Third International. It reports feelingly the arrest and deportation to Germany of Léon Jouhaux, president of the Confédération Général du Travail, for a time a fellow-prisoner of Herriot in the fortress of Bourrassol, and it denounces several prewar labor leaders who had accepted posts in fake labor unions set up by Vichy and are now trying to hedge against the defeat of Germany. It gives a long list of leaders of miners' unions sentenced for starting a strike against the Germans and it praises miners for bearing so much of labor's struggle against the enemy.

C.G.T., clandestine journal of the now submerged but still powerful Confédération, argues the necessity of beginning at once to rebuild a world labor movement and cites an index of prices which have made life almost impossible for French workmen in the last few years. In October, 1942, bread was up, over prewar prices, a hundred and forty per cent, potatoes two hundred per cent, wine two hundred and thirty per cent, and shoes three hundred and twenty-five per cent. *Mouvement Ouvrier Français*, another labor publication, says that the working class is the main object of German attack: the employers continue to eat well, even though they must pay high prices, but workers have the choice of producing goods for the conqueror at starvation wages in France or of being deported to Germany, where, on rations almost as scanty, they will be killed by Allied bombers. *Combat*, the most widely circulated Mur paper, notes, apropos of the deaths of French workmen in air raids in the Reich, that the French censor forbids the phrase "Died in Germany" in the death notices that relatives insert in French papers, although the German papers, with their usual maudlin bad taste, carry long accounts of ceremonies held over the graves of French workers killed in the Reich. Germans put pansies on the graves of Frenchmen they have brought to Germany for forced labor, a proof, *Combat* says, of the well-known Boche sensibility.

One of the leading publications in the resistance press is *Cahiers du Témoignage Chrétien*, an excellently printed monthly which sets forth the Catholic arguments in favor of resistance. One issue, discussing whether collaboration is permissible for a Christian, decides that "collaboration with Nazism, perverse in itself, is against the interests and soul of France. Conclusion: *non possumus*." *Cahiers*, which reaches a large portion of the clergy and Catholic intellectuals, presents religious arguments against racism and anti-Semitism. It is interesting to observe the parallel reactions to Nazism in publications of sections of the clandestine press representing widely divergent groups. *Lettres Françaises*, the underground organ of French writers, charges that "a high proportion of pederasts among the collaborationists is to be expected, for to be against one's own country is against nature." The same sort of thought on the depravity of collaboration occurs in one of the regional clandestine publications, *Combat du Languedoc*. "That the Boche tortures and massacres accords with his business of being a Boche, but that a Frenchman sells other Frenchmen to the enemy, that is the ultimate depth of abjection. On the day of liberation, patriots . . . will sweep away the obscure rabble of informers for the Gestapo. Not even the memory of their crimes must survive in free France."

The regional publications have the strongest and most acrid odor of conflict. One issue of *Combat du Languedoc*, for example, contains a long blacklist of the traitors in surrounding towns and departments. There is in one town an ex-Republican priest who now informs against other clergymen who harbor Jews and *Maquis*; in another there is a Negro doctor, "forgetful of Nazi doctrines," who spies, and "a woman who sent her husband to forced labor and remained with a German soldier." There is a man who took money to betray the place where patriots had hidden the Strasbourg Cathedral's bells, removed to southwest France in 1939. Another man listed was a gunrunner for the Spanish Republicans in the civil war who has now turned coat and informs against refugees escaping across the Pyrenees. There is the president of a chamber of commerce who toasted a German victory, the Germanophile prefect kept by the widow of a former president of the Republic, the French colonel who sent his son to a Schutzstaffel cadet camp. Collaborators are named in print, even down to a man who was seen to tear a Lorraine cross from the neck of a young girl. From another regional publication I cite this excerpt: "Clermont-Ferrand—Our comrade ——— was arrested at sixteen-thirty, October 26th. He was brought to the morgue at two o'clock the next afternoon. His face was swollen almost beyond recognition; his neck bore marks of strangulation. All his fingernails had been torn out. One foot was swollen, enormous. He had two bullet holes in his temple. The executioners are known. They will not be tortured. They will be shot like dogs."

"*La Voix du Nord*," the oldest and most powerful regional underground publication in the north of France, which has been occupied by the Germans since 1940, begins the latest issue I have received with a eulogy of Cardinal Lienart, Archbishop of Lille, who in a sermon defended the refusal of labor to work for Germans. This, in strongly Catholic Flanders, is news of the greatest importance. *Le Patriote de l'Oise*, another regional paper, thanks the Bishop of Beauvais for his steadfastness, and *La France Unie*, published in Brittany, praises the leading Catholic preacher of Rennes for his sermons on resistance; he has, the paper says, proved that deportation contradicts the doctrines of Christ. The first two of these publications have a strong Communist tinge, which indicates that the Germans and Laval have brought the French church and the French Communist Party into agreement for the first time in history. *La Voix du Nord* cites as a less appetizing example the local Catholic official of Secours National, a Pétain version of *Winterhilfe*, who takes, for his nephews and nieces, the best shoes and clothes donated to this charity. His sister, *La Voix* declares, then distributes the remainder to the needy, but only to the needy who attend mass regularly. Another local petty grafter it names is a police adjutant who stops people carrying small parcels of food in the streets and confiscates them unless the people can prove that they have been bought legally but who himself levies an illegal tribute of a pound of butter every week from each farm wife. It notifies people living on the coast that Germans billeted in coastal villages have been provided with civilian clothing in which to escape if a surprise landing is made by the Allies. *La Voix* urges its readers to memorize the faces of these Germans, so that they will be able to point them out to Allied troops.

Le Patriote de l'Oise, which appears to be Communist, tells of police raids on "our de Gaullist friends" in the district in which it is published. It warns of the presence of Vichy state police in the town of Creil and advises readers to "leave cafés when these *types* enter." *La Voix* tells how gendarmes surrounded a house in which they knew a Communist was hiding, in a village in Flanders; it was his own house, in the town of his birth, and it was a public secret that he had returned there. The man tried to escape by an attic window and the gendarmes shot him off the roof. "We know them," *La Voix* concludes simply. Until some assurance to the contrary is received, many writers in the resistance papers seem to fear that the Allies are coming to rescue the gendarmes.

4

And So
to Victory

WE did get to France, as you must know if you have seen the Cinemepic called *The Longest Day*, in which with swashbuckling magnificence tricked out with little homely touches a glittering team Eisenhowered by Darryl Zanuck storms the Hun-infested shores, and with John Wayne and Robert Mitchum alternately carrying the ball sweeps on, over the hills, to the unforgettable refrain of a theme song that I keep getting mixed up with

"Ballocks, and the same to you,"

which has been bowdlerized into the "River Kwai March." The original words fit in perfectly with the Wayne-Zanuck-Mitchum version.

Everybody, of course, had his own D-Day.

For Bunny Rigg—

Cross-Channel Trip

THREE days after the first Allied landing in France, I was in the wardroom of an LCIL (Landing Craft, Infantry, Large) that was bobbing in the lee of the French cruiser Montcalm off the Normandy coast. The word "large" in landing-craft designation is purely relative; the wardroom of the one I was on is seven by seven feet and contains two officers' bunks and a table with four places at it. She carries a complement of four officers, but since one of them must always be on watch there is room for a guest at the wardroom table, which is how I fitted in. The Montcalm was loosing salvos, each of which rocked our ship; she was firing at a German pocket of resistance a couple of miles from the shoreline. The suave voice of a B.B.C. announcer came over the wardroom radio: "Next in our series of impressions from the front will be a recording of an artillery barrage." The French ship loosed off again, drowning out the recording. It was this same announcer, I think—I'm not sure, because all B.B.C. announcers sound alike—who said, a little while later, "We are now in a position to say the landings came off with surprising ease. The Air Force and the big guns of the Navy smashed coastal defenses, and the Army occupied them." Lieutenant Henry Rigg, United States Coast Guard Reserve, the skipper of our landing craft, looked at Long, her engineering officer, and they both began to laugh. Kavanaugh, the ship's communications officer, said, "Now what do you think of that?" I called briefly upon God. Aboard the LCIL, D Day hadn't seemed like that to us. There is nothing like a broadcasting studio in London to give a chap perspective.

I went aboard our LCIL on Thursday evening, June 1st. The little ship was one of a long double file that lay along the dock in a certain British port.* She was fast to the dock, with another LCIL lashed to her on the other side. An LCIL is a hundred and fifty-five feet long and about three hundred dead-weight tons. A destroyer is a big ship indeed by comparison; an LST (Landing Ship, Tanks) looms over an LCIL like a monster. The LCIL has a flat bottom and draws only five feet of water, so she can go right up on a beach. Her hull is a box for carrying men; she can sleep two hundred soldiers belowdecks or can carry five hundred on a short

* Weymouth.

ferrying trip, when men stand both below and topside. An LCIL has a stern anchor which she drops just before she goes aground and two forward ramps which she runs out as she touches bottom. As troops go down the ramps, the ship naturally lightens, and she rises a few inches in the water; she then winches herself off by the stern anchor, in much the same way a monkey pulls himself back on a limb by his tail. Troop space is about all there is to an LCIL, except for a compact engine room and a few indispensable sundries like navigation instruments and anti-aircraft guns. LCILs are the smallest ocean-crossing landing craft, and all those now in the European theatre arrived under their own power. The crews probably would have found it more comfortable sailing on the Santa María. Most LCILs are operated by the Navy, but several score of them have Coast Guard crews. Ours was one of the latter. The name "Coast Guard" has always reminded me of little cutters plying out to ocean liners from the barge office at the Battery in New York, and the association gave me a definite pleasure. Before boarding the landing craft, I had been briefed, along with twenty other correspondents, on the flagship of Rear Admiral John L. Hall, Jr., who commanded the task force of which our craft formed a minute part, so I knew where we were going and approximately when. Since that morning I had been sealed off from the civilian world, in the marshalling area, and when I went aboard our landing craft I knew that I would not be permitted even to set foot on the dock except in the company of a commissioned officer.

It was warm and the air felt soporific when I arrived. The scene somehow reminded me more of the Sheepshead Bay channel, with its fishing boats, than of the jumping-off place for an invasion. A young naval officer who had brought me ashore from the flagship took me over the gangplank of the landing craft and introduced me to Lieutenant Rigg. Rigg, familiarly known as Bunny, was a big man, thirty-three years old, with clear, light-blue eyes and a fleshy, good-tempered face. He was a yacht broker in civilian life and often wrote articles about boats. Rigg welcomed me aboard as if we were going for a cruise to Block Island, and invited me into the wardroom to have a cup of coffee. There was standing room only, because Rigg's three junior officers and a Navy commander were already drinking coffee at the table. The junior officers—Long, Kavanaugh. and Williams—were all lieutenants (j.g.). Long, a small, jolly man with an upturned nose, was a Coast Guard regular with twenty years' service, mostly as a chief petty officer. He came from Baltimore. Kavanaugh, tall and straight-featured, was from Crary, North Dakota, and Williams, a very polite, blond boy, came from White Deer, Texas. Kavanaugh and Williams were both in their extremely early twenties. The three-striper, a handsome, slender man with prematurely white hair and black eyebrows, was introduced to me by Rigg as the C.O. of a naval beach battalion which would go in to organize boat traffic on a stretch of beach as soon as

the first waves of infantry had taken it over.* He was going to travel to
the invasion coast aboard our landing craft, and since he disliked life
ashore in the marshalling area, he had come aboard ship early. The commander, who had a drawl hard to match north of Georgia, was in fact a
Washingtonian. He was an Annapolis man, he soon told me, but had left
the Navy for several years to practice law in the District of Columbia and
then returned to it for the war. His battalion was divided for the crossing
among six LCILs, which would go in in pairs on adjacent beaches, so
naturally he had much more detailed dope on the coming operation than
normally would come to, say, the skipper of a landing craft, and this was
to make conversations in the tiny wardroom more interesting than they
otherwise would have been.

Even before I had finished my second cup of coffee, I realized that I
had been assigned to a prize LCIL; our ship was to beach at H Hour plus
sixty-five, which means one hour and five minutes after the first assault
soldier gets ashore. "This ship and No. X will be the first LCILs on the
beach," Rigg said complacently. "The first men will go in in small boats,
because of mines and underwater obstacles, and Navy demolition men
with them will blow us a lane through element C—that's sunken concrete
and iron obstacles. They will also sweep the lane of mines, we hope. We
just have to stay in the lane."

"These things move pretty fast and they make a fairly small target bow
on," Long added cheerfully.

The others had eaten, but I had not, so Williams went out to tell the
cook to get me up some chow. While it was being prepared, I went out on
deck to look around.

Our landing craft, built in 1942, is one of the first class of LCILs, which
have a rectangular superstructure and a narrow strip of open deck on
each side of it.** Painted on one side of the superstructure I noted a neat
Italian flag, with the legend "Italy" underneath so that there would be no
mistake, and beside the flag a blue shield with white vertical stripes and
the word "Sicily." There was also a swastika and the outline of an airplane, which could only mean that the ship had shot down a German
plane in a landing either in Sicily or Italy. Under Britain's double summer
time, it was still light, and there were several groups of sailors on deck,
most of them rubbing "impregnating grease" into shoes to make them
impervious to mustard gas. There had been a great last-minute furore
about the possibility that the Germans might use gas against the invasion,
and everybody had been fitted with impregnated gear and two kinds of

---

* This officer's name could not be used then, either because he commanded a unit in
the invasion, or because he was wounded in the course of this operation. He was
Eugene Carusi, again an attorney in Washington.
** It was the LCIL-88.

protective ointment. Our ship's rails were topped with rows of drying shoes.

"This is the first time I ever tried to get a pair of shoes pregnant, sir," one of the sailors called out sociably as I was watching him.

"No doubt you tried it on about everything else, I guess," another sailor yelled as he, too, worked on his shoes.

I could see I would not be troubled by any of that formality which has occasionally oppressed me aboard flagships. Most of the sailors had their names stencilled in white on the backs of their jumpers, so there was no need for introductions. One sailor I encountered was in the middle of a complaint about a shore officer who had "eaten him out" because of the way he was dressed on the dock, and he continued after I arrived. "They treat us like children," he said. "You'd think we was the pea-jacket navy instead of the ambiguous farce." The first term is one that landing-craft sailors apply to those on big ships, who keep so dry that they can afford to dress the part. "The ambiguous farce" is their pet name for the amphibious forces. A chief petty officer, who wore a khaki cap with his blue coveralls, said, "You don't want to mind them, sir. This isn't a regular ship and doesn't ever pretend to be. But it's a good working ship. You ought to see our engine room."

A little sailor with a Levantine face asked me where I came from. When I told him New York, he said, "Me too—Hundred twenty-second and First." The name stencilled on his back was Landini. "I made up a song about this deal," he said, breaking into a kind of Off to Buffalo. "I'm going over to France and I'm making in my pants."

Through the open door of the galley I could watch the cook, a fattish man with wavy hair and a narrow mustache, getting my supper ready. His name was Fassy, and he was the commissary steward. He appeared to have a prejudice against utensils; he slapped frankfurters and beans down on the hot stove top, rolled them around, and flipped them onto the plate with a spatula. I thought the routine looked familiar and I found out later that in his civilian days Fassy had worked in Shanty restaurants in New York.

While I was standing there, a young seaman stencilled Sitnitsky popped his head into the galley to ask for some soap powder so he could wash his clothes. Fassy poured some out of a vast carton into a pail of hot water the boy held. " 'Not recommended for delicate fabrics,' " the steward read for the infantry to gather up on their way through to positions inland.

Since the frankfurters and beans were ready, I returned to the wardroom. There the board of strategy was again in session. The beach we were headed for was near the American line, only a mile or two from Port-en-Bessin, where the British area began. Eighteen years before I had walked along the tops of the same cliffs the Americans would be fighting under. In those days I had thought of it as holiday country, not sufficiently spectacular to attract *le grand tourisme* but beautiful in a reasonable, Norman way. This illogically made the whole operation seem less sinister to me. Two pillboxes showed plainly on photographs we had, and, in addition, there were two houses that looked suspiciously like shells built around other pillboxes. Our intelligence people had furnished us with extraordinarily detailed charts of gradients in the beach and correlated tide tables. The charts later proved to be extraordinarily accurate, too.

"What worries me about landing is the bomb holes the Air Forces may leave in the beach before we hit," the commander was saying when I entered. "The chart may show three feet of water, but the men may step into a ten-foot hole anywhere. I'd rather the Air Forces left the beach alone and just let the naval guns knock out the beach defenses. They're accurate."

The general plan, I knew, was for planes and big guns of the fleet to put on an intensive bombardment before the landing. A couple of weeks earlier I had heard a Marine colonel on the planning staff tell how the guns would hammer the pillboxes, leaving only a few stunned defenders for the infantry to gather up on their way through to positions inland.

"We're lucky," the commander said. "This beach looks like a soft one."

His opinion, in conjunction with frankfurters and beans, made me happy.

We didn't get our passengers aboard until Saturday. On Friday I spent my time in alternate stretches of talk with the men on deck and the officers in the wardroom. Back in Sicily, the ship had been unable to get off after grounding at Licata, a boatswain's mate named Pendleton told me. "She got hit so bad we had to leave her," he said, "and for three days we had to live in foxholes just like infantrymen. Didn't feel safe a minute. We was sure glad to get back on the ship. Guess she had all her bad luck that trip."

Pendleton, a large, fair-haired fellow who was known to his shipmates as the Little Admiral, came from Neodesha, Kansas. "They never heard of the Coast Guard out there," he said. "Nobody but me. I knew I would have to go in some kind of service and I was reading in a Kansas City paper one day that the Coast Guard would send a station wagon to your house to get you if it was within a day's drive of their recruiting station. So I wrote 'em. Never did like to walk."

Sitnitsky was washing underclothes at a sink aft of the galley once when I came upon him. When he saw me, he said, "The fois' ting I'm gonna do when I get home is buy my mudder a washing machine. I never realize what the old lady was up against."

Our neighbor LCIL, tied alongside us, got her soldier passengers late

Friday night. The tide was low and the plank leading down to our ship from the dock was at a steep angle as men came aboard grumbling and filed across our deck to the other LCIL. "Didjever see a goddam gangplank in the right place?" one man called over his shoulder as he eased himself down with his load. I could identify a part of a mortar on his back, in addition to a full pack. "All aboard for the second Oran," another soldier yelled, and a third man, passing by the emblems painted on the bridge, as he crossed our ship, yelled, "Sicily! *They* been there, too." So I knew these men were part of the First Division, which landed at Oran in Africa in 1942 and later fought in Sicily. I think I would have known anyway by the beefing. The First Division is always beefing about something, which adds to its effectiveness as a fighting unit.

The next day the soldiers were spread all over the LCIL next door, most of them reading paper-cover, armed-services editions of books. They were just going on one more trip, and they didn't seem excited about it. I overheard a bit of technical conversation when I leaned over the rail to visit with a few of them. "Me, I like a bar [Browning automatic rifle]," a sergeant was saying to a private. "You can punch a lot of tickets with one of them."

The private, a rangy middleweight with a small, close-cropped head and a rectangular profile, said, "I'm going into this one with a pickaxe and a block of TNT. It's an interesting assignment. I'm going to work on each pillbox individually," he added, carefully pronouncing each syllable.

When I spoke to them, the sergeant said, "Huh! A correspondent! Why don't they give the First Division some credit?"

"I guess you don't read much if you say that, Sarge," a tall blond boy with a Southern accent said. "There's a whole book of funnies called 'Terry Allen and the First Division at El Guettar.' "

All three men were part of an infantry regiment. The soldier who was going to work on pillboxes asked if I was from New York, and said that he was from the Bensonhurst section of Brooklyn. "I am only sorry my brother-in-law is not here," he said. "My brother-in-law is an M.P. He is six inches bigger than me. He gets an assignment in New York. I would like to see him here. He would be apprehensive." He went on to say that the company he was with had been captured near the end of the African campaign, when, after being cut off by the Germans, it had expended all its ammunition. He had been a prisoner in Tunis for a few hours, until the British arrived and set him free. "There are some nice broads in Tunis," he said. "I had a hell of a time." He nodded toward the book he was holding. "These little books are a great thing," he said. "They take you away. I remember when my battalion was cut off on top of a hill at El Guettar, I read a whole book in one day. It was called 'Knight Without Armor.' This one I am reading now is called 'Candide.' It is kind of unusual, but I like it. I think the fellow who wrote it, Voltaire, used the same gag too often, though. The characters are always getting killed and then turning out not to have been killed after all, and they tell their friends what happened to them in the meantime. I like the character in it called Pangloss."*

Fassy was lounging near the rail and I called him over to meet a brother Brooklynite. "Brooklyn is a beautiful place to live in," Fassy said. "I have bush Number Three at Prospect Park."

"I used to have bush Number Four," the soldier said.

"You remind me of a fellow named Sidney Wetzelbaum," Fassy said. "Are you by any chance related?"

I left them talking.

Our own passengers came aboard later in the day. There were two groups—a platoon of the commander's beach battalion and a platoon of amphibious engineers. The beach-battalion men were sailors dressed like soldiers, except that they wore black jerseys under their field jackets; among them were a medical unit and a hydrographic unit. The engineers included an M.P. detachment, a chemical-warfare unit, and some demolition men. A beach battalion is a part of the Navy that goes ashore; amphibious engineers are a part of the Army that seldom has its feet dry. Together they form a link between the land and sea forces. These two detachments had rehearsed together in landing exercises, during which they had travelled aboard our LCIL. Unlike the Coastguardsmen or the infantry on the next boat, they had never been in the real thing before and were not so offhand about it. Among them were a fair number of men in their thirties. I noticed one chief petty officer with the Navy crowd who looked about fifty. It was hard to realize that these older men had important and potentially dangerous assignments which called for a good deal of specialized skill; they seemed to me more out of place than the infantry kids. Some sailors carried carbines and most of the engineers had rifles packed in oilskin cases. There were about a hundred and forty men in all. The old chief, Joe Smith, who was the first of the lot I got to know, said he had been on battleships in the last war and had been recalled from the fleet reserves at the beginning of this. He took considerable comfort from the fact that several aged battleships would lay down a barrage for us before we went in. You could see that he was glad to be aboard a ship again, even if it was a small one and he would be on it for only a couple of days. He was a stout, red-faced, merry man whose home town was Spring Lake, New Jersey. "I'm a tomato squeezer," he told me. "Just a country boy."

Cases of rations had been stacked against the superstructure for the passengers' use. The galley wasn't big enough to provide complete hot meals for them but it did provide coffee, and their own cook warmed up

---

* He and I were having a Voltairean reunion right there. I had been at El Guettar too, and had never heard what happened to the battalion.

canned stew and corned beef for them for one meal. The rest of the time they seemed simply to rummage among the cans until they found something they liked and then ate it. They ate pretty steadily, because there wasn't much else for them to do.

Our landing craft had four sleeping compartments belowdecks. The two forward ones, which were given over to passengers, contained about eighty bunks apiece. Most of the crew slept in the third compartment, amidships, and a number of petty officers and noncoms slept in the fourth, the smallest one, aft. I had been sleeping in this last one myself since coming aboard, because there was only one extra bunk for an officer and the commander had that. Four officers who came aboard with the troops joined me in this compartment. There were two sittings at the wardroom table for meals, but we managed to wedge eight men in there at one time for a poker game.

There was no sign of a move Saturday night, and on Sunday morning everybody aboard began asking when we were going to shove off. The morning sun was strong and the crew mingled with the beach-battalion men and the soldiers on deck. It was the same on board every other LCIL in the long double row. The port didn't look like Sheepshead Bay now, for every narrow boat was covered with men in drab-green field jackets, many of them wearing tin hats, because the easiest way not to lose a tin hat in a crowd is to wear it. The small ships and helmets pointed up the analogy to a crusade and made the term seem less threadbare than it usually does. We were waiting for weather, as many times the crusaders, too, had waited, but nobody thought of praying for it, not even the chaplain who came aboard in mid-morning to conduct services. He was a captain attached to the amphibious engineers, a husky man I had noticed throwing a football around on the dock the previous day. He took his text from Romans: "If God be for us, who can be against us?" He didn't seem to want the men to get the idea that we were depending entirely on faith, however. "Give us that dynamic, that drive, which, coupled with our matchless super-modern weapons, will ensure victory," he prayed. After that, he read aloud General Eisenhower's message to the Allied Expeditionary Force.

After the services, printed copies of Eisenhower's message were distributed to all hands on board. Members of our ship's crew went about getting autographs of their shipmates on their "Eisenhowers," which they apparently intended to keep as souvenirs of the invasion. Among the fellows who came to me for my signature was the ship's coxswain, a long-legged, serious-looking young man, from a little town in Mississippi, who had talked to me several times before because he wanted to be a newspaperman after the war. He had had one year at Tulane, in New Orleans, before joining up with the Coast Guard, and he hoped he could finish up later. The coxswain, I knew, would be the first man out of the ship when she grounded, even though he was a member of the crew. It was his task to run a guideline ashore in front of the disembarking soldiers. Then, when he had arrived in water only a foot or two deep, he would pull on the line and bring an anchor floating in after him, the anchor being a light one tied in a life jacket. He would then fix the anchor—without the life jacket, of course—and return to the ship. This procedure had been worked out after a number of soldiers had been drowned on landing exercises by stepping into unexpected depressions in the beach after they had left the landing craft. Soldiers, loaded down with gear, had simply disappeared. With a guideline to hold onto, they could have struggled past bad spots. I asked the boy what he was going to wear when he went into the water with the line and he said just swimming trunks and a tin hat. He said he was a fair swimmer.

The rumor got about that we would sail that evening, but late in the afternoon the skipper told me we weren't going to. I learned that the first elements of the invasion fleet, the slowest ones, had gone out but had met rough weather in the Channel and had returned, because they couldn't have arrived at their destination in time. Admiral Hall had told correspondents that there would be three successive days when tide conditions on the Norman beaches would be right and that if we missed them the expedition might have to be put off, so I knew that we now had one strike on us, with only two more chances.

That evening, in the wardroom, we had a long session of a wild, distant derivative of poker called "high low rollem." Some young officers who had come aboard with the troops introduced it. We used what they called "funny money" for chips—five-franc notes printed in America and issued to the troops for use after they got ashore. It was the first time I had seen these notes, which reminded me of old-time cigar-store coupons. There was nothing on them to indicate who authorized them or would pay off on them—just *"Emis en France"* on one side and on the other side the tricolor and *"Liberté, Egalité, Fraternité."* In the game were three beach-battalion officers, a medical lieutenant (j.g.) named Davey, from Philadelphia, and two ensigns—a big, ham-handed college football player from Danbury, Connecticut, named Vaghi, and a blocky, placid youngster from Chicago named Reich. The commander of the engineer detachment, the only Army officer aboard, was a first lieutenant named Miller, a sallow, apparently nervous boy who had started to grow an ambitious black beard.

Next morning the first copy of the *Stars and Stripes* to arrive on board gave us something new to talk about. It carried the story of the premature invasion report by the Associated Press in America. In an atmosphere heavy with unavowed anxiety, the story hit a sour note. "Maybe they let out more than *Stars and Stripes* says," somebody in the wardroom said. "Maybe they not only announced the invasion but told where we had landed. I mean, where we *planned* to land. Maybe the whole deal will be called off now." The commander, who had spent so much time pondering element C, said, "Add obstacles—element A.P." A report got about among the more pessimistic crew members that the Germans had been tipped off and would be ready for us. The Allied high command evidently did not read the *Stars and Stripes*, however, for Rigg, after going ashore for a brief conference, returned with the information that we were shoving off at five o'clock. I said to myself, in the great cliché of the second World War, "This is it," and so, I suppose, did every other man in our fleet of little ships when he heard the news.

II

PEACE or war, the boat trip across the English Channel always begins with the passengers in the same mood: everybody hopes he won't get seasick. On the whole, this is a favorable morale factor at the outset of an invasion. A soldier cannot fret about possible attacks by the Luftwaffe or E-boats while he is preoccupied with himself, and the vague fear of secret weapons on the far shore is balanced by the fervent desire to get the far shore under his feet. Few of the hundred and forty passengers on the LCIL I was on were actively sick the night before D Day, but they were all busy thinking about it. The four officers and twenty-nine men of the United States Coast Guard who made up her complement were not even queasy, but they had work to do, which was just as good. The rough weather, about which the papers have talked so much since D Day and which in fact interfered with the landing, was not the kind that tosses about transatlantic liners or even Channel packets; it was just a bit too rough for the smaller types of landing craft we employed. An LCIL, as its name implies, is not one of the smallest, but it's small enough, and aboard our flat-bottomed, three-hundred-ton job the Channel didn't seem especially bad that night. There was a ground swell for an hour after we left port, but then the going became better than I had anticipated. LCTs (Landing Craft, Tanks), built like open troughs a hundred feet long, to carry armored vehicles, had a much worse time, particularly since, being slow, they had had to start hours before us. Fifty-foot LCMs (Landing Craft, Mechanized) and fifty-foot and thirty-six-foot LCVPs (Landing Craft, Vehicles and Personnel), swarms of which crossed the Channel under their own power, had still more trouble. The setting out of our group of LCILs was unimpressive—just a double file of ships, each a hundred and fifty-five feet long, bound for a rendezvous with a great many other ships at three in the morning ten or fifteen miles off a spot on the coast of lower Normandy. Most of the troops travelled in large transports, from which the smaller craft transferred them to shore. The LCILs carried specially packaged units for early delivery on the Continent doorstep.

Rigg turned in early that evening because he wanted to be fresh for a hard day's work by the time we arrived at the rendezvous, which was to take place in what was known as the transport area. So did the commander of the naval beach battalion who was riding with us. I stood on deck for a while. As soon as I felt sleepy, I went down into the small compartment in which I had a bunk and went to sleep—with my clothes on, naturally. There didn't seem to be anything else to do. That was at about eight. I woke three hours later and saw a fellow next to me being sick in a paper bag and I went up to the galley and had a cup of coffee. Then I went back to my bunk and slept until a change in motion and in the noise of the motors woke me again.

The ship was wallowing slowly now, and I judged that we had arrived at the transport area and were loafing about. I looked at my wristwatch and saw that we were on time. It was about three. So we hadn't been torpedoed by an E-boat. A good thing. Drowsily, I wondered a little at the fact that the enemy had made no attempt to intercept the fleet and hoped there would be good air cover, because I felt sure that the Luftwaffe couldn't possibly pass up the biggest target of history. My opinion of the Luftwaffe was still strongly influenced by what I remembered from June, 1940, in France, and even from January and February, 1943, in Tunisia. I decided to stay in my bunk until daylight, dozed, woke again, and then decided I couldn't make it. I went up on deck in the gray pre-dawn light sometime before five. I drew myself a cup of coffee from an electric urn in the galley and stood by the door drinking it and looking at the big ships around us. They made me feel proletarian. They would stay out in the Channel and send in their troops in small craft, while working-class vessels like us went right up on the beach. I pictured them inhabited by officers in dress blues and shiny brass buttons, all scented like the World's Most Distinguished After-Shave Club.* The admiral's command ship lay nearby. I imagined it to be gaffed with ingenious gimmicks that would record the developments of the operation. I could imagine a terse report coming in of the annihilation of a flotilla of LCILs, including us, and hear some Annapolis man saying, "After all, that sort of thing is to be expected." Then I felt that everything was going to be all right, because it always had been. A boatswain's mate, second class, named Barrett, from Rich Square, North Carolina, stopped next to me to drink his coffee and said, "I bet Findley a pound that we'd be hit this time. We most always is. Even money."

We wouldn't start to move, I knew, until about six-thirty, the time

* An allusion to an advertisement then widely familiar, but which I now forget.

when the very first man was scheduled to walk onto the beach. Then we would leave the transport area so that we could beach and perform our particular chore—landing one platoon of the naval beach battalion and a platoon of Army amphibious engineers—at seven-thirty-five. A preliminary bombardment of the beach defenses by the Navy was due to begin at dawn. "Ought to be hearing the guns soon," I said to Barrett, and climbed the ladder to the upper deck. Rigg was on the bridge drinking coffee, and with him was Long, the ship's engineering officer. It grew lighter and the guns began between us and the shore. The sound made us all cheerful and Long said, "I'd hate to be in under that." Before dawn the transports had begun putting men into small craft that headed for the line of departure, a line nearer shore from which the first assault wave would be launched.

Time didn't drag now. We got under way sooner than I had somehow expected. The first troops were on the beaches. The battleship Arkansas and the French cruisers Montcalm and Georges Leygues were pounding away on our starboard as we moved in. They were firing over the heads of troops, at targets farther inland. Clouds of yellow cordite smoke billowed up. There was something leonine in their tint as well as in the roar that followed, after that lapse of time which never fails to disconcert me. We went on past the big ships, like a little boy with the paternal blessing. In this region the Germans evidently had no long-range coastal guns, like the ones near Calais, for the warships' fire was not returned. This made me feel good. The absence of resistance always increases my confidence. The commander of the naval beach battalion had now come on deck, accoutred like a soldier, in greenish coveralls and tin hat. I said to him cheerfully, "Well, it looks as though the biggest difficulty you're going to have is getting your feet in cold water."

He stood there for a minute and said, "What are you thinking of?"

I said, "I don't know why, but I'm thinking of the garden restaurant behind the Museum of Modern Art in New York."* He laughed, and I gave him a pair of binoculars I had, because I knew he didn't have any and that he had important use for them.

Our passengers—the beach-battalion platoon and the amphibious engineers—were now forming two single lines on the main deck, each group facing the ramp by which it would leave the ship. Vaghi and Reich, beach-battalion ensigns, were lining up their men on the port side and Miller, an Army lieutenant with a new beard, was arranging his men on the starboard side. I wished the commander good luck and went up on the bridge, which was small and crowded but afforded the best view.

An LCIL has two ramps, one on each side of her bow, which she lowers and thrusts out ahead of her when she beaches. Each ramp is handled by means of a winch worked by two men; the two winches stand

---

* I liked a woman who lived across the street from there.

side by side deep in an open-well deck just aft of the bow. If the ramps don't work, the whole operation is fouled up, so an LCIL skipper always assigns reliable men to operate them. Two seamen named Findley and Lechich were on the port winch, and two whom I knew as Rocky and Bill were on the other. Williams, the ship's executive officer, was down in the well deck with the four of them.

We had been in sight of shore for a long while, and now I could recognize our strip of beach from our intelligence photographs. There was the house with the tower on top of the cliff on our starboard as we went in. We had been warned that preliminary bombardment might remove it, so we should not count too much upon it as a landmark; however, there it was and it gave me the pleasure of recognition. A path was to have been blasted and swept for us through element C (underwater concrete and iron obstacles) and mines, and the entrance to it was to have been marked with colored buoys. The buoys were there, so evidently the operation was going all right. Our LCIL made a turn and headed for the opening like a halfback going into a hole in the line. I don't know whether Rigg suddenly became solicitous for my safety or whether he simply didn't want me underfoot on the bridge, where two officers and two signalmen had trouble getting around even without me. He said, "Mr. Liebling will take his station on the upper deck during action." This was formal language from the young man I had learned to call Bunny, especially since the action did not seem violent as yet, but I climbed down the short ladder from the bridge to the deck, a move which put the wheelhouse between me and the bow. The upper deck was also the station for a pharmacist's mate named Kallam, who was our reserve first-aid man. A landing craft carries no doctor, the theory being that a pharmacist's mate will make temporary repairs until the patient can be transferred to a larger ship. We had two men with this rating aboard. The other, a fellow named Barry, was up in the bow. Kallam was a sallow, long-faced North Carolinian who once told me he had gone into the peacetime Navy as a youth and had never been good for anything else since. This was his first action, except for a couple of landings in Nicaragua around 1930.

The shore curved out toward us on the port side of the ship and when I looked out in that direction I could see a lot of smoke from what appeared to be shells bursting on the beach. There was also an LCT, grounded and burning. "Looks as if there's opposition," I said to Kallam, without much originality. At about the same time something splashed in the water off our starboard quarter, sending up a high spray. We were moving in fast now. I could visualize, from the plan I had seen so often in the last few days, the straight, narrow lane in which we had to stay. "On a straight line—like a rope ferry," I thought. The view on both sides changed rapidly. The LCT which had been on our port bow was now on our port quarter, and another LCT, also grounded, was now visible. A number of men, who had evidently just left her, were in the water, some up to their necks and others up to their armpits, and they didn't look as if they were trying to get ashore. Tracer bullets were skipping around them and they seemed perplexed. What I hate most about tracers is that every time you see one, you know there are four more bullets that you don't see, because only one tracer to five bullets is loaded in a machine-gun belt. Just about then, it seems in retrospect, I felt the ship ground.

I looked down at the main deck, and the beach-battalion men were already moving ahead, so I knew that the ramps must be down. I could hear Long shouting, "Move along now! Move along!," as if he were un-loading an excursion boat at Coney Island. But the men needed no urg-ing; they were moving without a sign of flinching. You didn't have to look far for tracers now, and Kallam and I flattened our backs against the pilot house and pulled in our stomachs, as if to give a possible bullet an extra couple of inches clearance. Something tickled the back of my neck. I slapped at it and discovered that I had most of the ship's rigging draped around my neck and shoulders, like a character in an old slapstick movie about a spaghetti factory. The rigging had been cut away by bullets. As Kallam and I looked toward the stern, we could see a tableau that was like a recruiting poster. There was a twenty-millimetre rapid-firing gun on the upper deck. Since it couldn't bear forward because of the pilot house and since there was nothing to shoot at on either side, it was pointed straight up at the sky in readiness for a possible dive-bombing attack. It had a crew of three men, and they were kneeling about it, one on each side and one behind the gun barrel, all looking up at the sky in an extremely earnest manner, and getting all the protection they could out of the gunshield. As a background to the men's heads, an American flag at the ship's stern streamed across the field of vision. It was a new flag, which Rigg had ordered hoisted for the first time for the invasion, and its colors were brilliant in the sun. To make the poster motif perfect, one of the three men was a Negro, William Jackson, from New Orleans, a wardroom steward, who, like everybody else on the LCIL, had multiple duties.

The last passenger was off the ship now, and I could hear the stern anchor cable rattling on the drum as it came up. An LCIL drops a stern anchor just before it grounds, and pays out fifty to a hundred fathoms of chain cable as it slowly slides the last couple of ship's lengths toward shore. To get under way again, it takes up the cable, pulling itself afloat. I had not known until that minute how eager I was to hear the sound of the cable that follows the order "Take in on stern anchor." Almost as the cable began to come in, something hit the ship with the solid clunk of metal against metal—not as hard as a collision or a bomb blast; just "clink." Long yelled down, "Pharmacist's mate go forward. Somebody's hurt." Kallam scrambled down the ladder to the main deck with his kit. Then Long yelled to a man at the stern anchor winch, "Give it hell!" An LCIL has to pull itself out and get the anchor up before it can use its motors, because otherwise the propeller might foul in the cable. The little engine which supplies power for the winch is built by a farm-machinery company in Waukesha, Wisconsin, and every drop of gasoline that went into the one on our ship was filtered through chamois skin first. That engine is the ship's insurance policy. A sailor now came running up the stairway from the cabin. He grabbed me and shouted, "Two casualties in bow!" I passed this information on to the bridge for whatever good it might do; both pharmacist's mates were forward already and there was really nothing else to be done. Our craft had now swung clear, the anchor was up, and the engines went into play. She turned about and shot forward like a destroyer. The chief machinist's mate said afterward that the engines did seven hundred revolutions a minute instead of the six hundred that was normal top speed. Shells were kicking up waterspouts around us as we went; the water they raised looked black. Rigg said afterward, "Funny thing. When I was going in, I had my whole attention fixed on two mines attached to sunken concrete blocks on either side of the place where we went in. I knew they hadn't been cleared away—just a path between them. They were spider mines, those things with a lot of loose cables. Touch one cable and you detonate the mine. When I was going out, I was so excited that I forgot all about the damn mines and didn't think of them until I was two miles past them."

A sailor came by and Shorty, one of the men in the gun crew, said to him, "Who was it?" The sailor said, "Rocky and Bill. They're all tore up. A shell got the winch and ramps and all." I went forward to the well deck, which was sticky with a mixture of blood and condensed milk. Soldiers had left cases of rations lying all about the ship, and a fragment of the shell that hit the boys had torn into a carton of cans of milk. Rocky and Bill had been moved belowdecks into one of the large forward compartments. Rocky was dead beyond possible doubt, somebody told me, but the pharmacist's mates had given Bill blood plasma and thought he might still be alive. I remembered Bill, a big, baby-faced kid from the District of Columbia, built like a wrestler. He was about twenty, and the other boys used to kid him about a girl he was always writing letters to.* A third wounded man, a soldier dressed in khaki, lay on a stretcher on deck breathing hard through his mouth. His face looked like a dirty drumhead; his skin was white and drawn tight over his high cheekbones. He wasn't making much noise. There was a shooting-gallery smell over every-

---

* Every letter began: "Well, Hazel, here I am again."

thing, and when we passed close under the Arkansas and she let off a salvo, a couple of our men who had their backs to her quivered and had to be reassured. Long and Kavanaugh, the communications officer, were already going about the ship trying to get things ticking again, but they had little success at first.

Halfway out to the transport area, another LCIL hailed us and asked us to take a wounded man aboard. They had got him from some smaller craft, but they had to complete a mission before they could go back to the big ships. We went alongside and took him over the rail. He was wrapped in khaki blankets and strapped into a wire basket litter. After we had sheered away, a man aboard the other LCIL yelled at us to come back so that he could hand over a half-empty bottle of plasma with a long rubber tube attached. "This goes with him," he said. We went alongside again and he handed the bottle to one of our fellows. It was trouble for nothing, because the man by then had stopped breathing.

We made our way out to a transport called the Dorothea Dix that had a hospital ward fitted out. We went alongside and Rigg yelled that we had four casualties aboard. A young naval doctor climbed down the scramble net hanging on the Dix's side and came aboard. After he had looked at our soldier, he called for a breeches buoy and the soldier was hoisted up sitting in that. He had been hit in one shoulder and one leg, and the doctor said he had a good chance. The three others had to be sent up in wire baskets, vertically, like Indian papooses. A couple of Negroes on the upper deck of the Dix dropped a line which our men made fast to the top of one basket after another. Then the man would be jerked up in the air by the Negroes as if he were going to heaven. Now that we carried no passengers and were lighter, the sea seemed rough. We bobbed under the towering transport and the wounded men swung wildly on the end of the line, a few times almost striking against the ship. A Coastguardsman reached up for the bottom of one basket so that he could steady it on its way up. At least a quart of blood ran down on him, covering his tin hat, his upturned face, and his blue overalls. He stood motionless for an instant, as if he didn't know what had happened, seeing the world through a film of red, because he wore eyeglasses and blood had covered the lenses.* The basket, swaying eccentrically, went up the side. After a couple of seconds, the Coastguardsman turned and ran to a sink aft of the galley, where he turned on the water and began washing himself. A couple of minutes after the last litter had been hoisted aboard, an officer on the Dix leaned over her rail and shouted down, "Medical officer in charge says two of these men are dead! He says you should take them back to the beach and bury them." Out there, fifteen miles off shore, they

---

* This was me. It seemed more reserved at the time to do it this way—a news story in which the writer said *he* was bathed in blood would have made me distrust it, if I had been a reader.

evidently thought that this was just another landing exercise. A sailor on deck said, "The son of a bitch ought to see that beach."

Rigg explained to the officer that it would be impossible to return to the beach and ordered the men to cast off the lines, and we went away from the Dix. Now that the dead and wounded were gone, I saw Kallam sneak to the far rail and be sicker than I have ever seen a man at sea. We passed close by the command ship and signalled that we had completed our mission. We received a signal, "Wait for orders," and for the rest of the day we loafed, while we tried to reconstruct what had happened to us. Almost everybody on the ship had a headache.

"What hurts me worst," Lechich said, "is thinking what happened to those poor guys we landed. That beach was hot with Jerries. And they didn't have nothing to fight with—only carbines and rifles. They weren't even supposed to be combat troops."

"I don't think any of them could be alive now," another man said.

As the hours went by and we weren't ordered to do anything, it became evident that our bit of beach wasn't doing well, for we had expected, after delivering our first load on shore, to be employed in ferrying other troops from transports to the beach, which the beach-battalion boys and engineers would in the meantime have been helping to clear. Other LCILs of our flotilla were also lying idle. We saw one of them being towed, and then we saw her capsize. Three others, we heard, were lying up on one strip of beach, burned. Landing craft are reckoned expendable. Rigg came down from the bridge and, seeing me, said, "The beach is closed to LCILs now. Only small boats going in. Wish they'd thought of that earlier. We lost three good men."

"Which three?" I asked. "I know about Rocky and Bill."

"The coxswain is gone," Bunny said. I remembered the coxswain, the earnest young fellow who wanted to be a newspaperman, and who, dressed in swimming trunks, was going to go overboard ahead of everyone else and run a guideline into shore.

"Couldn't he get back?" I asked.

"He couldn't get anywhere," Rigg answered. "He had just stepped off the ramp when he disintegrated. He must have stepped right into an H. E. shell. Cox was a good lad. We'd recommended him for officers' school." Rigg walked away for the inevitable cup of coffee, shaking his big tawny head. I knew he had a headache, too.

A while afterward, I asked Rigg what he had been thinking as we neared the coast and he said he had been angry because the men we were going to put ashore hadn't had any coffee. "The poor guys had stayed in the sack as late as they could instead," he said. "Going ashore without any coffee!"

✻   ✻   ✻

Long was having a look at the damage the shell had done to our ship, and I joined him in tracing its course. It had entered the starboard bow well above the waterline, about the level of the ship's number, then had hit the forward anchor winch, had been deflected toward the stern of the boat, had torn through the bulkhead and up through the cover of the escape hatch, then had smashed the ramp winch and Rocky and Bill. It had been a seventy-five-millimetre anti-tank shell with a solid-armor-piercing head, which had broken into several pieces after it hit the ramp winch. The boys kept finding chunks of it around, but enough of it stayed in one piece to show what it had been. "They had us crisscrossed with guns in all those pillboxes that were supposed to have been knocked off," Long said. "Something must have gone wrong. We gave them a perfect landing, though," he added with professional pride. "I promised the commander we would land him dry ass and we did." Long has been in the Coast Guard twenty years and nothing surprises him; he has survived prohibition, Miami and Fire Island hurricanes, and three landings. He is a cheerful soul who has an original theory about fear. "I always tell my boys that fear is a passion like any other passion," he had once told me. "Now, if you see a beautiful dame walking down the street, you feel passion but you control it, don't you? Well, if you begin to get frightened, which is natural, just control yourself also, I tell them." Long said that he had seen the commander start off from the ship at a good clip, run well until he got up near the first line of sand dunes, then stagger. "The commander was at the head of the line about to leave the ship when young Vaghi, that big ensign, came up and must have asked him for the honor of going first," Long said. "They went off that way, Vaghi out ahead, running as if he was running out on a field with a football under his arm. Miller led the soldiers off the other ramp, and he stepped out like a little gentleman, too." The space where the starboard ramp had once been gave the same effect as an empty sleeve or eye socket.

It was Frankel, a signalman who had been on the bridge, who told me sometime that afternoon about how the wounded soldier came to be on board. Frankel, whose family lives on East Eighteenth Street in Brooklyn, was a slender, restless fellow who used to be a cutter in the garment centre. He played in dance bands before he got his garment-union card, he once told me, and on the ship he occasionally played hot licks on the bugle slung on the bridge. "A shell hit just as we were beginning to pull out," Frankel said, "and we had begun to raise the ramps. It cut all but about one strand of the cable that was holding the starboard ramp and the ramp was wobbling in the air when I saw a guy holding on to the end of it. I guess a lot of us saw him at the same time. He was just clutching the ramp with his left arm, because he had been shot in the other shoulder. I'll never forget his eyes. They seemed to say, 'Don't leave me behind.' He must have been hit just as he stepped off the ramp leaving the ship. It was this soldier. So Ryan and Landini went out and got him. Ryan worked along the rail inside the ramp and Landini worked along the outside edge of the ramp and they got him and carried him back into the ship. There was plenty of stuff flying around, too, and the ramp came away almost as soon as they got back. That's one guy saved, anyway." Ryan was a seaman cook who helped Fassy, the commissary steward, in the galley, and Landini was the little First Avenue Italian who had made up a special song for himself—"I'm going over to France and I'm making in my pants."

Along about noon, an LCVP, a troughlike fifty-footer, hailed us and asked if we could take care of five soldiers. Rigg said we could. The craft came alongside and passed over five drenched and shivering tank soldiers who had been found floating on a rubber raft. They were the crew of a tank that had been going in on a very small craft and they had been swamped by a wave.* The tank had gone to the bottom and the soldiers had just managed to make it to the raft. The pharmacist's mates covered them with piles of blankets and put them to bed in one of our large compartments. By evening they were in the galley drinking coffee with the rest of us. They were to stay on the ship for nearly a week, as it turned out, because nobody would tell us what to do with them. They got to be pretty amphibious themselves. The sergeant in command was a fellow from Cleveland named Angelatti. He was especially happy about being saved, apparently because he liked his wife. He would keep repeating, "Gee, to think it's my second anniversary—I guess it's my lucky day!" But when he heard about what we thought had happened to the men we put ashore, he grew gloomy. The tanks had been headed for that beach and should have helped knock out the pillboxes. It hadn't been the tankmen's fault that the waves had swamped them, but the sergeant said disconsolately, "If we hadn't fucked up, maybe those other guys wouldn't have been killed." He had a soldier's heart.

III

ON the morning of D Day-plus-one, the LCIL was like a ship with a hangover. Her deck was littered with cartons of tinned rations left behind by the land fighters she had carried to the Norman shore. There was a gap where the starboard ramp had been and there were various holes in the hull and hatches to mark the path of the anti-tank shell that had hit her while she had been on the beach. Everybody aboard was nursing a

* These were amphibious tanks, with inflated canvas "jackets," and they were self-propelled. The censor allowed no reference to them, since they were a novelty. Of 32 headed for our beach, 28 flooded out. Only the weather was to blame.

headache. The big fellows running the show had found nothing for us to do since our one run to the beach, which we had reached at 7:35 A.M. on D Day. The reason we hadn't been sent in again was that the German resistance was so strong that now the troops were being taken in only on smaller craft, which offered smaller targets. So we hung around in the Channel, waiting for orders and talking over the things that had happened to us. The men in the engine room, which was so clean that it looked like the model dairy exhibit at the World's Fair—all white paint and aluminum trim—had sweated it out at their posts during the excitement on deck and the engine-room log had been punctiliously kept. On the morning of D-plus-one, Cope, the chief machinist's mate, a tall, quiet chap from Philadelphia, told somebody that from the order "Drop stern anchor" to the order "Take in on stern anchor," which included all the time we had spent aground, exactly four minutes had elapsed. Most of us on deck would have put it at half an hour. During those four minutes all the hundred and forty passengers we carried had run off the ramps into three feet of water, three members of our Coast Guard complement of thirty-three had been killed, and two others had rescued a wounded soldier clinging to the end of the starboard ramp, which had been almost shot away and which fell away completely a few seconds later. The experience had left us without appetite. I remember, on the afternoon of D Day, sitting on a ration case on the pitching deck and being tempted by the rosy picture on the label of a roast-beef can. I opened it, but I could only pick at the jellied juice, which reminded me too much of the blood I had seen that morning, and I threw the tin over the rail.

By D-plus-one we were beginning to eat again. That morning I was on the upper deck talking to Barrett, a seaman from North Carolina, when we saw a German mine go off. It threw a column of water high into the air and sank a ship near it, a transport called the Susan B. Anthony. German planes had been fiddling around above our anchorage during the night, without bombing us; evidently they had been dropping mines. We had seen three of the planes shot down. Barrett looked at the waterspout and said, "If we ever hit a mine like that, we'll go up in the air like a arrow."

Susan B. put her nose in the air and slipped backward calmly, like a lady lowering herself into an armchair. In twenty minutes she was gone. It looked as if all her crew got off. Barrett had bet a pound, even money, that we would be hit during the action. I asked him if he had collected the bet and he said, "Sure. As long as we got hit whether I take the money or not, I might as well take it." In the wardroom, Kavanaugh, the communications officer, talked to me about Bill, one of the Coast Guard boys who had been hit. Long told me about a patch he had devised that would expand in water and would close up any underwater holes in the hull, and seemed rather to regret that he had had no chance to try it out. Lieutenant Rigg kept repeating a tag line he had picked up from Sid Fields, a

comedian in a London revue: "What a performance! What a performance!" But the most frequent subject of conversation among both officers and men was the fate of the fellows we had put on the beach, usually
referred to collectively as "those poor bastards." We had left them splash-
ing through shallow water, with tracer bullets flying around them and
only a nearly level, coverless beach immediately in front of them and with
a beach pillbox and more of the enemy on a cliff inshore blazing away
with everything they had. We had decided that hardly any of our men
could have survived.

Late that afternoon our landing craft got an order to help unload
soldiers from a big troopship several miles off the French shore. We were
to carry the men almost as far as the beach and then transfer them to
Higgins boats. One of our ramps was gone and the other one was not
usable, and it would have been superfluous cruelty to drop a soldier with
a full pack into five feet of water, our minimum draught. We gathered
from the order that the Germans were no longer shooting on the beach;
this, at least, represented progress.

The soldiers who lined the decks of the transport, all eager to get
ashore at once, belonged to the Second Division; they wore a white star
and an Indian head on their shoulder flashes. A scramble net hung down
the port side of the vessel, and soldiers with full equipment strapped to
their backs climbed down it one by one and stepped backward onto our
landing craft. As each man made the step, two seamen grabbed him and
helped him aboard. It often took as much time to unload the soldiers from
a big ship as it did for the ship itself to get from Britain to the Norman
coast, and it seemed to me that a small expenditure on gangplanks of
various lengths and furnished with grapples, like the ones used in boarding operations in ancient naval battles, would have sped these transfers
more than a comparable outlay for any other device could possibly have
done.

While we were loading the men, a thirty-six-foot craft approached us
on the other side. There were two other thirty-six-footers there side by
side already. The newest thirty-six-footer got alongside the outer one of
the pair of earlier arrivals and the crew boosted up a man who had been
standing in the stern of the boat and helped him on to the other craft. The
man made his way unsteadily across both of the intervening thirty-six-
footers to us, and men on the boats passed his gear, consisting of a
typewriter and a gas mask, along after him. He was in a field jacket and
long khaki trousers without leggings. The clothes were obviously fresh out
of a quartermaster's stores. He wore the war correspondent's green shoulder patch on his field jacket. His face and form indicated that he had led
a long and comfortable life, and his eyes betrayed astonishment that he
should be there at all, but he was smiling. Some of our Coastguardsmen
helped him over our rail. He said that he was Richard Stokes of the St.
Louis *Post-Dispatch*, that he had been a Washington correspondent and

a music critic for many years, that he had wanted to go overseas when we got into the war, and that he had finally induced his paper to send him over. He had got airplane passage to Britain, where he had arrived two weeks before, and had been sent to the invasion coast on a Liberty ship that was to land men on D-plus-one. "It seems just wonderful to be here," Stokes said. "I can hardly believe it." He had been very much disappointed when he found out that because of the violence of the German resistance, the Liberty ship was not going to land her passengers for a couple of days. The ship's captain had said to him, "There's another crowd going ashore. Why don't you go with them?" Then the skipper had hailed a boat for him. "And here I am," said Stokes. "It's too good to be true." He was sixty-one years old, and the world seemed marvellous to him. He said he had never been in a battle and he wanted to see what it was like.

We got all our soldiers—about four hundred of them—aboard and started in toward the same stretch of shore we had left in such haste thirty-six hours before. The way in looked familiar and yet devoid of the character it had once had for us, like the scene of an old assignation revisited. The house with the tower on top of the cliff was now gone, I noticed. The naval bombardment, although tardy, had been thorough. Scattered along the shore were the wrecked and burned-out landing craft that had been less lucky than ours. Several of our men told me they had seen the LCT that had been burning off our port quarter on D Day pull out, still aflame, and extinguish the fire as she put to sea, but plenty of others remained. Small craft came out to us from the shore that had so recently been hostile, and soldiers started climbing into them, a less complicated process than the transfer from the troopship because the highest points of the small craft were nearly on a level with our main deck. I could see occasional puffs of smoke well up on the beach. They looked as if they might be the bursts of German shells coming from behind the cliff, and I felt protective toward Stokes. "Mr. Stokes," I said, "it seems to be pretty rough in there." He didn't even have a blanket to sleep on, and he didn't have the slightest idea whom he was going to look for when he got in; he was just going ahead like a good city reporter on an ordinary assignment. He watched two boats load up with soldiers and then, as a third came alongside—I remember that the name painted inside her ramp was "Impatient Virgin"—he said, "Mr. Liebling, I have made up my mind," and went down and scrambled aboard, assisted by everybody who could get a hand on him. He got ashore all right and did some fine stories. A couple of weeks afterward he told me, "I couldn't stand being within sight of the promised land and then coming back."

There was nothing for us to do during the daylight hours of D-plus-two, but toward eight o'clock in the evening we got an order to go out to another troopship and unload more Second Division soldiers, who were to be taken to a beach next to the one where we had landed on D Day. The ship was an American Export liner. Several other LCILs were also assigned to the job of emptying her. I was on our bridge with Rigg when we came under her towering side, and the smell of fresh bread, which her cooks had evidently been baking, drove all other thoughts from our minds. Rigg hailed a young deck officer who was looking down at us and asked him if he could spare some bread. The officer said sure, and a few minutes later a steward pushed six long loaves across to our bridge from a porthole at approximately our level. They were an inestimable treasure to us. Everything is relative in an amphibious operation; to the four-man crews who operate the thirty-six-foot LCVPs, which are open to the weather and have no cooking facilities, an LCIL seems a floating palace. They would often come alongside us and beg tinned fruit, which they would receive with the same doglike gratitude we felt toward the merchantman for our bread.

The soldiers came aboard us along a single narrow plank, which was put over from the port side of the troopship to our rail, sloping at an angle of forty-five degrees. We pitched continuously in the rough water, and the soldiers, burdened with rifles and about fifty pounds of equipment apiece, slid rather than ran down the plank. Our crew had arranged a pile of ration cases at the rail, right where the gangplank was fastened, and the soldiers stepped from the end of the plank to the top case and then jumped down. We made two trips between the merchantman and the small boats that night, and only one soldier fell, and was lost, between the ships during the whole operation. That, I suppose, was a good percentage, but it still seemed to me an unnecessary loss. On our first trip from ship to shore, while we were unloading soldiers into small boats a couple of hundred yards off the beach, there was an air raid. The soldiers standing on our narrow deck, with their backs to the deckhouse walls, had never been under real fire before, but they remained impassive amid the cascade of Bofors shells that rose from hundreds of ships. Much of the barrage had a low trajectory and almost scraped the paint off our bridge. On one ship some gunners who knew their business would hit a plane, and then, as it fell, less intelligent gun crews would start after it and follow it down, forgetting that when a plane hits the water it is at the waterline. An anti-aircraft shell travelling upward at an angle of not more than twenty degrees wounded Commander Carusi sleeping in a dugout on the side of a cliff ashore a couple of nights later.*

A beach-battalion sailor came out to us on one of the first small boats from the shore. He was a big, smiling fellow we had brought from En-

---

* Carusi says that he was lying outside the dugout awaiting evacuation next morning, when one medical corpsman said to another, "No use taking that white-haired old sonofabitch. He won't make it." It made Gene so sore he *ordered* them to take him. They got him back to England and he survived.

gland on our first trip to the invasion coast, one of "those poor bastards" we had all assumed were dead. The cooks hauled him into the galley for sandwiches and coffee, and within a couple of minutes officers as well as men were crowding about him. Nearly everybody we asked him about turned out to be alive—the commander of the beach battalion; Miller, the Army lieutenant; little Dr. Davey; Vaghi and Reich, the poker-playing ensigns; Smith, the beach battalion's veteran chief petty officer; and others whom we had got to know on the ship. They had had a rough time, the sailor said. They had lain for five hours in holes they had scooped in the sand when they went ashore, while one or two American tanks which had landed shot at pillboxes and the pillboxes shot back. Then some infantrymen who had landed in small boats at H Hour worked their way up the beach and took the German positions, releasing our friends from the position in which they were pinned down. They were living on the side of a hill now and getting on with their work of organizing traffic between ship and shore. It was very pleasant news for us aboard the landing craft. We worked all night unloading soldiers, but the Coast Guard crew didn't mind; they were in a good mood.

Early the next day, D-plus-three, I thumbed a ride ashore to go visiting. I hailed a passing assault craft, a rocket-firing speedboat, which took me part of the way and then transferred me to an LCVP that was headed inshore. The LCVP ran up onto the beach, dropped her bow ramp, and I walked onto French soil without even wetting my feet. This was the moment I had looked forward to for four years minus nine days, since the day I had crossed the Spanish frontier at Irún after the fall of France. Then the words of de Gaulle—"France has lost a battle but not the war"—were ringing in my ears, for I had just heard his first radio speech from London, but I had not dared hope that the wheel would turn almost full circle so soon. There was the noise of cannonading a couple of miles or so beyond the cliffs, where the First Division was pushing on from the fingerhold it had made good on D Day, but on the beach everything was calm. Troops and sailors of the amphibious forces had cleared away much of the wreckage, so that landing craft coming in would not foul their hulls or anchor chains; metal road strips led up from the water's edge to the road parallel with the shore. Men were going about their work as if there were no enemy within a hundred miles, and this was understandable, because no German planes ever arrived to molest them as they unloaded vehicles and munitions for the troops up ahead. To men who had been in other campaigns, when a solitary jeep couldn't pass down a road without three Messerschmitts' having a pass at it, this lack of interference seemed eerie, but it was true all the same. During the first week after the invasion began, I didn't see one German plane by daylight. Almost in front of me, as I stepped off the boat, were the ruins of the concrete blockhouse that had fired at us as we ran in on D Day. The concrete had been masked by a simulated house, but the disguise had been shot away and the place gaped white and roofless. I had more a sense of coming home to the United States Army than to France, for the first M.P. of whom I inquired the way to the command post of the beach battalion said he didn't know. This is S.O.P., or standard operating procedure, because a soldier figures that if he tells you he knows, he will, at best, have trouble directing you, and if the directions turn out to be wrong you may come back and complain. He has nothing to lose by denying knowledge.

I walked along the beach and met a beach-battalion sailor. He was equally unknowledgeable until I convinced him that I was a friend of the commander. Then he led me two hundred yards up a cliff to the place I had asked about. The commander was not there, but a Lieutenant Commander Watts* and a Lieutenant Reardon, both New Yorkers, were. They had gone ashore on another landing craft, but I had met them both while we were in port in Britain awaiting sailing orders. They had landed five hundred yards up the beach from us and had, of course, got the same reception we got. The command post was installed in a row of burrows in the face of the cliff from which the Germans had fired down on the incoming boats and the beach on D Day; now it was we who overlooked the beach. In the side of another cliff, which was almost at a right angle to this one, the Germans had had two sunken concrete pillboxes enfilading the beach, and I realized that the crossfire had centred on our landing craft and the others nearby. Meeting these men reminded me of what the First Division soldier had said to me a few days earlier about "Candide": "Voltaire used the same gag too often. The characters are always getting killed and then turning out not to have been killed at all, and they tell their friends what happened to them in the meantime."

Watts said that after they had left their landing craft, they had run forward like hell and then had thrown themselves down on the beach because there was nothing else to do. The forepart of the beach was covered with large, round pebbles about the size, I imagine, of the one David used on Goliath, and when the German machine-gun bullets skittered among them the stones became a secondary form of ammunition themselves and went flying among the men. "We had infantry up ahead of us, but at first they were pinned down too," Watts said. "A couple of tanks had landed and one of them knocked out a seventy-five up on the side of the hill, but in a short while the Germans either replaced it or got it going again. Then, after a couple of hours, two destroyers came and worked close in to shore, although there were plenty of mines still in there, and really plastered the pillboxes. The infantry went up the hill in the face of machine-gun fire and drove the Germans out of the trench

* Henry B. Watts, Jr., now chairman of the Board of Governors of the New York Stock Exchange.

system they had on the crown of the hill. I'll show it to you in a couple of minutes. It's a regular young Maginot Line. By nightfall we felt fairly safe. We found out later from prisoners that the Three Hundred and Fifty-second German Field Division had been holding anti-invasion exercises here the day before we attacked. They had been scheduled to go back to their barracks D Day morning, but when scouts told them about the big fleet on the way in, they decided to stay and give us a good time. They did." It wasn't until a week later, in London, that I found out that because of this untoward circumstance our beach and those on either side of it had been the toughest spots encountered in the landings, and that the losses there had not been at all typical of the operation.

I was delighted to discover Smith, the old chief petty officer, reclining in a nearby slit trench. He was looking very fit. He was forty-seven, and I had wondered how he would do in the scramble to the beach. He had not only made it but had gathered a large new repertory of anecdotes on the way. "A guy in front of me got it through the throat," Smitty said. "Another guy in front of me got it through the heart. I run on. I heard a shell coming and I threw myself face down. There was an Army colonel on one side of me, a Navy captain on the other. The shell hit. I was all right. I looked up and the captain and the colonel was gone, blown to pieces. I grabbed for my tommy gun, which I had dropped next to me. It had been twisted into a complete circle. I was disarmed, so I just laid there."

While I was listening to Smitty, Reardon, talking over a field telephone, had located the commander somewhere on top of the cliff, along the German trench system, which had been taken over by the amphibious engineers as billets. Watts and I decided to walk up and find him. We made our way along the face of the cliff, on a narrow path that led past clusters of slit trenches in which soldiers were sleeping, and got up to the crest at a point where some Negro soldiers had made their bivouac in a thicket. We followed another path through a tangled, scrubby wood. The Germans had left numbers of wooden skull-and-crossbones signs on the tree trunks. These signs said *"Achtung Minen"* and *"Attention aux Mines."* Whether they indicated that we had taken the enemy by surprise and that he had not had time to remove the signs put up for the protection of his own and civilian personnel, or whether the signs were put there for psychological purposes, like dummy guns, was a question for the engineers to determine. Watts and I took care to stay in the path.

We found the commander, who was in good form. He said he had lost only a couple of the forty-five beach-battalion men who had been on the landing craft with us but that in the battalion as a whole the casualties had been fairly heavy. "Not nearly what I thought they would be when I left that boat, though," he said.

✿ ✿ ✿

The trench system was a fine monument to the infantrymen of the First Division who had taken it. I couldn't help thinking, as I looked it over, that the German soldiers of 1939–41 would not have been driven from it in one day, even by heroes, and the thought encouraged me. Maybe they were beginning to understand that they were beaten. There were no indications that the position had been under artillery fire and I could see only one trace of the use of a flamethrower. As I reconstructed the action, our fellows must have climbed the hill and outflanked the position, and the Germans, rather than fight it out in their holes, had cleared out to avoid being cut off. They had probably stayed in and continued firing just as long as they still had a chance to kill without taking losses. As the French say, they had not insisted. The trenches were deep, narrow, and so convoluted that an attacking force at any point could be fired on from several directions. Important knots in the system, like the command post and mortar emplacements, were of concrete. The command post was sunk at least twenty-five feet into the ground and was faced with brick on the inside. The garrison had slept in underground bombproofs, with timbered ceilings and wooden floors. In one of them, probably the officers' quarters, there was rustic furniture, a magnificent French radio, and flowers, still fresh, in vases. On the walls were cheap French prints of the innocuous sort one used to see in speakeasies: the little boy and the little girl, and the coyly equivocal captions.

An engineer sergeant who showed us through the place said that the Americans had found hairnets and hairpins in this bombproof. I could imagine an *Oberstleutnant* and his mistress, perhaps the daughter of a French collaborationist, living uneventfully here and waiting for something in which the *Oberstleutnant* had unconsciously ceased to believe, something that he wished so strongly would never happen that he had convinced himself it would happen, if anywhere, on some distant part of the coast. I thought of the Frenchmen I had known in 1939, waiting in a similar mood in the Maginot Line. The sergeant, a straight-featured Jewish fellow in his late thirties, said, "Those infantrymen were like angels. I tell you, I laid there on the beach and prayed for them while they went up that hill with nothing—with bayonets and hand grenades. They did it with nothing. It was a miracle." That made me feel good, because the infantry regiment involved had long been my favorite outfit.* The commander was sardonic about one thing. "You remember how I used to worry about how my men would fall into bomb holes and drown on the way in because the Air Forces had laid down such a terrific bombardment?" he asked. "Well, I defy you to find one bomb hole on this whole beach for a mile each way."

The commander and Watts accompanied me back to the shore. On the

* 16th Regiment, First Division.

way, we stopped at a field hospital that had been set up under canvas. There I talked to some Italian prisoners who were digging shelter trenches. They were fine, rugged specimens, as they should have been, because since the Italian surrender they had undoubtedly had plenty of exercise swinging pickaxes for the Todt organization. Their regiment of bridge-building engineers had been disarmed by the Germans in Greece and the men had been given the choice of enrolling in Fascist combat units or in labor service, they told me. They had all chosen labor service. They seemed to expect to be commended for their choice. They had built many of the trenches in the district. "We wouldn't fight for Hitler," they assured me. I thought that the point had been pretty well proved. Now they were digging for us. They said that all Germans were cowards.

We went down to the shore, and the commander, who, being beach-master, was in charge of all traffic alongshore, hailed a Duck for me. The Duck put me on an LCVP, which took me back to my ship. On the way out, I realized that I had not seen a single French civilian the entire time ashore.

When I came aboard our landing craft, Long, the engineering officer, grinned at me.

"Did you notice a slight list, sometimes on one side, sometimes on the other, the last two days?" he asked.

I said, "You mean the one you said must be on account of the crew's all turning over in their sleep at the same time?"

"Yes," he said. "Well, today we found an open seam down in the stern. She started to list that night the big bomb dropped next to us, but you were sleeping too sound to get up. So maybe we'll go back to port. She has no ramps, the forward anchor winch is sheared in half, and she may as well go into the yard for a couple of days."

The morning of D-plus-four, Rigg signalled the command ship for per-mission to put back to Britain. As soon as the signalman blinked out the message, every man on board knew there was a chance we would go back, and even fellows who had expressed a low opinion of Weymouth looked extremely happy. While we were waiting for an answer to our request, an LCIL that acted as a group leader, a kind of straw boss among the little ships, passed near us, and the lieutenant on her bridge ordered us over to help tow a barge of ammunition. We were to be paired with another LCIL on this job. The barge, a two-hundred-and-fifty-tonner, was loaded with TNT, and the idea was for one LCIL to make fast on each side of her and shove her in to shore. The Diesel motors of an LCIL, although they can move their craft along at a fair speed, haven't the towing power of a tug. The two LCILs bounced about in the choppy sea for quite a while as we tried to get towing lines aboard the big barge that would hold. Even after we finally got started, every now and then the lines would snap and we would bounce against the side of the barge, as we put more lines aboard her, with a crash that disquieted us, even though we had been told many times that the explosive was packed so carefully that no jouncing would possibly set it off. We were very happy when the barge grounded on the beach according to plan and we could cast off and leave her. Just before we had finished, the group leader came along again and an officer on her bridge shouted over to us through a megaphone, "Report to control-ship shuttle service!" This meant that we were going back to Britain; control ships organize cross-Channel convoys. We were not sorry to go.

By Sunday, D-plus-five, when we at last got started, the water had smoothed out so much that the Channel was like the Hyde Park Serpentine. The flat-bottomed LCIL will bounce about in the slightest sea, but today our craft moved along like a swanboat. The water was full of ration cartons, life jackets, and shell cases, and on the way over we picked up one corpse, of a soldier wearing a life jacket, which indicated that he had never got ashore. Since German planes were dropping mines every night, the lookout was instructed to keep a sharp watch for suspicious objects in the water, and this was almost the only thing it was necessary to think about as we loafed along. A seaman from Florida named Hurwitz was lookout on the bow in the early morning. "Suspicious object off port bow!" he would bawl, and then "Suspicious object off starboard quarter!" Most of the suspicious objects turned out to be shell cases. Finally, Hurwitz yelled "Bridge! The water is just full of suspicious objects!"

The main interest aboard now was whether we would get to port before the pubs closed, at ten o'clock in the evening. Long was getting unheard-of speed out of his motors and it seemed that we would make the pubs easily. Then we happened upon a British LCT that was all alone and was having engine trouble. She asked us to stand by in case her motors conked out altogether. We proceeded at four knots. When the British skipper signalled to us, "Doing my utmost, can make no more," which meant that our chance of beer had gone glimmering, Rigg made a gesture that for delicacy and regard for international relations must have few parallels in naval history. He ordered a signal that may someday be in schoolbooks along with Nelson's "England expects every man to do his duty." "Never mind," he signalled the crippled LCT. "We would have been too late for pub-closing time anyway."

I have left the story of *our* Longest Day—I did not stop to see Wayne and Mitchum lead their charge—in the form in which I wrote it and saw it through censorship and sent it on by wireless from London in parts, as fast as I could after getting ashore. The writing, naturally, took more than one day. While I was writing it the first of the doodlebugs, or V-1's, arrived in the London sky, and continued to pass overhead during the labor of composition.

They caused considerable confusion the first night because they came intermittently for hours, instead of in groups like normal bombers, and so the air raid sirens, controlled by radar, kept sounding alerts and all clears. The things though unmanned had motors. I had no right to pull aside my blackout curtain to see what was happening, and I did not want to interrupt my work to go down to the street—I had a twinge of gout, anyway—so I passed the night in a state of baffled curiosity and fell asleep toward morning. I was awakened by the waitress who brought my breakfast at the set hour, a big Irish girl, who had come to London to work for the good wartime wages. British girls of her age were subject to draft. She drew the curtains, and when I asked her what the hell had been going on, she said, without heat:

"It's them pilotless airplanes. I do hope they won't be a success."

I have left it that way because it is on the whole more accurate than I could make it today. A situation later assumes meanings that it did not have at the time, and you write them into it in retrospect and fool yourself. I have, however, reinserted a few details barred by the censor, like the loss of the Susan B. Anthony, the nature of the flooded tanks and Gene Carusi's name and what happened to him. I have been inconsistent even in this. I find I have not named the men killed; the coxswain was Moran, the men at the winch Rocky Simone and Bill Frere. Bill was the man whose blood got on me, although I had seen shreds, too, of what I afterward learned had been Moran, and I was impressed, when I reflected on Frere's name, to think that I had been drenched in a "brother's" blood. Afterward I re-reflected and have settled for coincidence.

Also, the instant of that day that recurs to me most often has been that when I sat with the roast-beef tin in my hand—the label said it had been packed in Uruguay—and couldn't eat, a most unusual difficulty for me. The meat in the opened tin had a jellied look, and the stuff sloshing on the forward deck, as the LCI-88 rolled, had a jellied look too—the shell had torn open dozens of the cans of rations the soldiers had left aboard, and the liquid on the deck was a mixture of blood and condensed milk, with Campbell's soup. It was an insult.

The rules of the censor also barred reporting that we had seen the LCI-85, another of our group, capsize and sink, riddled and abandoned, and there were other casualties we did not ourselves know at the time. Of the ten LCI's, including the 88, of LCI-flotilla 110, that went in at that hour, four were sunk, and all of the rest, I think, were hit. Those lost were, besides the 85, the 91, 92 and 93, all hit *before* they discharged their passengers, a high proportion of whom were killed. When it was all over, the planners decided that LCI's were too high and vulnerable for the work.

Altogether H plus 65 on Easy Red Beach, Omaha, was an even bloodier mess than we knew at the time, and I am glad we didn't. Anybody who thinks there was a theme song should have his head examined.

5

Direction: Paris

I CROSSED over into France again aboard a Landing Ship, Tanks, on June 24th. The Channel was criss-crossed by convoys, traveling without incident, and on Omaha there were new roads, and traffic M.P.'s to show you the way out. The five briefer stories that follow, all despatches, chronicle my advance on Paris, leaving out a few devious detours that I did not think would interest Harold Ross and Bill Shawn, my editors at *The New Yorker*. One was to Rennes, the first large French city we liberated after the breakout. I remembered Rennes from the pre-war past—1926—as a city whose warm ways belied its austere appearance, and early reports had the population, of both sexes, lavishing its gratitude on Americans. I had a particular memory of an establishment there called *La Feria* (the Fair) that had impressed me, in 1926, by its provincial elegance, as if a ring of the doorbell admitted you to the world of Maupassant's Maison Tellier. I remembered also that Rennes was the seat of an Archbishop, the primate of Brittany, who should be able to communicate a sharp insight into the relations between the devout Bretons and the Occupant during the invasion, a subject that suddenly interested me. I visited the Archbishop first, a splendid gentleman named Roques, who had been noble in the resistance, and who was promoted to Cardinal within a short time, along with two or three other resistance Archbishops, while a number of senior Pétainist Cardinals temporarily withdrew from public life. The Church never runs short of suitable spokesmen in a new situation. The Archbishop had taught, either French literature in Germany or German literature in France, I now forget which, for many years as a priest, and had a deep understanding of the German soul, which he found poorly cooked, like a runny *oeuf en gelee*, and so, likely to disintegrate at a slight shock, such as the vibration of a loud vulgar voice with an Austrian accent.

I proceeded later—not directly, for I have a sense of fitness—from the Archbishop's palace to La Feria, to which a cop was kind enough to direct me. It now stood alone, untouched, in a great expanse of bombing rubble around the railroad yards, which had received constant attention from our planes. I found only the Madame, who had been the *sous-maîtresse* in 1926, and two *pensionnaires* in residence, since the Boche had moved out, and La Feria's future under the new order was unclear. The decor had been modernized in a nasty way just before the war began. Madame was touched by my fidelity and long memory, but especially by my sense of what was proper in calling on the Archbishop first. She was, like all *Bretonnes*, pious, and told me she found it paid.

"Do you know," she said, "of all the buildings in the quarter of the railroad station, only the Cathedral and La Feria were spared by the bombardments."

Letters from France

JULY 14 (BY WIRELESS)

FOR a year before the Allied landings here, Germans occupied a large, moated, Norman farmhouse near which I now live. Sixty of them were billeted in it, sleeping in great, pine-panelled living rooms on mattresses they had stolen from a nearby summer hotel and in the fetid warmth which is a German soldier's ideal of comfort. This atmosphere is customarily maintained by keeping all windows and doors closed tight. The owners of the farmhouse, who moved into the kitchen wing when their guests took over, listened regularly to the B.B.C. broadcasts and always harbored from two to six young men who were evading forced labor in Germany. In the evening, Madame H.,* the matriarch who rules the family, clipped certain items bearing on the war from the German-controlled French newspapers, or, when there was nothing worth clipping, reread old items in the collection she was gathering. A couple of nights ago, while I was drinking warm milk in the kitchen, which, because Americans are billeted in the house now, is still the family living room, Madame showed me her clippings. The first one was dated August 17, 1941. Each of them had to do either with a proclamation by a German *Kommandantur* or with a Vichy official threatening reprisal for some act of sabotage committed in northwestern France or with an announcement of the execution of hostages, invariably described as "Jews and Communists."

Madame H., who had no direct contact with the resistance movement and knew nothing first-hand about the victims named in the newspapers, felt certain from the first that they were on the only decent side. Collaborationist cant never deceived her for a moment, and yet she is of the type most susceptible to Pétainolatry—rich, intensely Catholic, and in considerable fear of "Reds." Her son, a blond, broad-headed chap with a decided limp, was a prisoner of war in Germany for three years. He had served in Alsace in a French engineering regiment and right after his capture was set to work with other prisoners digging up French mines. A

* Hamel was the name.

mine exploded, killing six of his comrades and shattering one of his feet. Even after that, he was sent into forced labor, first in Alsace and then in Germany. Officials of the local *Kommandantur* approached Madame H. some time after the armistice with an offer to have her son sent home if she would persuade him to be an informer against farmers who were withholding cattle and fats from the Germans. She said she would prefer not to have her son home. Eventually the Germans released him anyway, along with a few thousand other crippled or tubercular prisoners, when, in 1943, Vichy put on a great drive to induce young Frenchmen to volunteer for labor in Germany to "relieve" prisoners of war who had been there since 1940. These incapacitated prisoners were supposed to be the advance guard of a great mass of returning Frenchmen; actually, they were the only ones ever released. Young H., as he will be known in the countryside as long as his mother lives, although he is now over forty, came home with a great admiration for the Alsatians, who, he says, are the most patriotic French he ever met, and with an almost patronizing view of Germans. "A German is either a bandit or a decent fellow," he says. "There are no in-between Germans. The bandits run the rest. I have seen the Germans in air raids, and individually they are shameless cowards, but fantastic discipline keeps them going." He says there was enough food, but it was all starchy, and that few German workmen, even at the time he left the country, seemed to believe that Germany could win the war, whereas most French prisoners were confident even in the worst days that Germany would lose.

When H. returned to Normandy and saw what the German Army had become by then, he grew optimistic, too, like most of the Normans who had stayed home. The athletes in uniform who had invaded western France in 1940 had given place to a mixed lot of Georgians, Russians, Poles, and adolescent and middle-aged Germans, and the motorized equipment that had amazed the French in the blitzkrieg days had been shipped away to active fronts and been supplanted in great part by horse-drawn vehicles. The soldiers of the polyglot regiments seemed resigned to defeat and stuffed themselves in quiet desperation, consuming Norman butter and milk as if they were trying to eat enough to last them through the black years they saw ahead of them. The arrogance of the invaders had given way to the alternate fits of meekness and ill manners of the garrison troops. The Germans were so short of motor vehicles that they commandeered farmers' carriages for their officers and sometimes drafted farmers to drive them. A substantial farmer, a neighbor of Madame H., tells about the time he drove a German major to a railroad station three miles from the officer's billet; he managed to take an hour getting to the station, pretending first that he didn't know the way and then that the horse had gone lame. The German missed his train and was furious about it, but the Norman pretended not to understand anything he said. This was the sort of thing that kept the Germans miserable; they had the feeling that they were constantly being tricked and laughed at. The German authorities knew that they were getting only a fraction of the cattle and dairy produce available, but they couldn't confiscate the herds without putting a stop to production, since they had no agricultural personnel of their own to put on the farms.

Few of the country people in Normandy expected a landing there. The majority, in fact, thought that there would be no landing at all but that the Allies would wear Germany down by bombing. They were perhaps persuaded to this way of thinking by a hope that their land would not be fought upon. But the landings, when they came, delighted them. The discomfiture of the Germans was particularly pleasing, and peasants, offering their best bottled cider to Americans, suddenly burst into laughter as they remember how the supermen scuttled off. During the first days of the invasion, there was a bit of foolish talk in British newspapers, and probably also in American papers, which I have not seen, about the Normans' lack of enthusiasm, stories evidently written by correspondents who acquired their ideas of Frenchmen from music-hall turns and comic drawings. One might as well expect public demonstrations of emotion in Contoocook, New Hampshire, or in Burrillville, Rhode Island, as in Normandy, where the people are more like New Englanders than they are like, for instance, Charles Boyer. Young men of the resistance groups did invaluable service both before and after the landing; they drew us plans of German fortifications before we landed and then went through the German lines repeatedly during the fighting in order to get information about enemy movements. Not one report of a French civilian's sniping at Allied troops has been authenticated, and relations between our soldiers and the country people are excellent everywhere, now that the inevitable misunderstandings of the early days have passed.

A common cause of misunderstanding was the farmers' habit of loitering about fields which had been requisitioned for Allied tank parks. One Armored Forces colonel was thinking of having the *maire* of a certain village shot as an obvious spy when a French-speaking American officer interrogated the *maire* and found that he was just waiting around for a chance to milk his cows. "There may perhaps be a war and you may perhaps be beating Boches," said the *maire*, with traditional Norman scepticism, raising his voice occasionally as the sound of guns threatened to drown his words, "but what I am sure of is that my horned beasts must be milked." Even the farmers who were happiest to see the Allied tanks arrive are now beginning to ask wistfully when they are going to get their pastures back again.

The French sometimes misinterpreted American actions, too. There was, for example, the *maire* of a small *commune* just outside Cherbourg who came into Army Civil Affairs headquarters there five days after we took the city and complained to a French liaison officer that American troops had put him out of the *mairie* and that now he had no place in which to carry on the affairs of the *commune*. The French liaison officer, Captain Gérard Lambert, an energetic Gaulliste, replied emphatically, "But that is against all the policy set on high levels! They have no right to commandeer a French Government building unless for extreme military necessity," and he and the *maire* immediately drove off to the *mairie*. There were no American troops there, but a sign on the door said, "Keep Out—U. S. Military Police." As Captain Lambert and the *maire*, who must have been around seventy-five, climbed the stairs to the first floor, the captain said, "This is curious. Why did they order you out?"

The old man answered indignantly, "Because they said there were mines in the cellar."

The captain said with dignity, "You are an idiot."

"However, my captain," the old man said, "it is not certain there are mines in the cellar." So he did remain.

All sorts of difficulties were referred to our Civil Affairs officers during the first few days following the liberation of any city. The manager of the Cherbourg branch of the Banque de France requested Lieutenant Colonel Frank Howley, Cherbourg Civil Affairs Chief, to have a guard posted over a certain heap of rubble in Valognes, a town which had been almost completely flattened by artillery fire. The bank manager explained that he had sent a hundred million francs to the Valognes branch for safekeeping, because he had expected the bombardment of Cherbourg. A shell had demolished the Valognes branch and two adjoining buildings had collapsed on top of it, so the hundred million francs were now buried under all three. The manager seemed to fear that some casual looter might shove the ruins out of the way and unearth the money, a feat which, actually, a steam shovel will probably accomplish in about two weeks.

Cherbourg, the nearest thing to a big city we have yet captured, was the first testing ground in France for the Allies' Army Civil Affairs Branch. When the Americans took over, on June 27th, the city had no water, electricity, gas, transportation, or government. The Vichy *sous-préfet* had fled and so had twenty-five thousand of Cherbourg's civilian population of forty thousand. The Civil Affairs team, headed by Colonel Howley, an American, and including both British and American officers, moved in before the street sniping had ended, and immediately started in on the job of resuscitation. The Civil Affairs men's task, as Howley saw it, was to get the city government functioning normally again. The Civil Affairs Branch had no enlisted personnel it could put to work policing the streets or making repairs. Cherbourg had had a fairly modern water system; water was pumped from the little Divette River to a purifying plant, from which it was distributed through mains. Bombs had broken the pipeline from the river to the plant. Major John C. Diggs, a former sanitary engineer for the State of Indiana, is Public-Works Officer in the Howley team. He got together the staff of the Cherbourg water system, who told him that the Germans had taken away all the reserve pipe. He got piping from the Army Engineers, the French installed it with their own workmen, and on July 1st the city had water again. "All they needed was a little encouragement," Major Diggs told me. "I've seen several floods and hurricanes in Indiana and the effect on local governments is always the same—they're a bit stunned, like a man suffering from battle shock. A little shove gets them going again." When it was time to turn the water on, a new problem presented itself, one that it is safe to say nobody in Washington or London had foreseen. There were hundreds of empty buildings in Cherbourg, many of them partly wrecked. The hastily departing owners had left the taps open. When the water was turned on, thousands of gallons would not only be wasted but would do further damage to the structures. Men with loudspeakers borrowed from the local American Psychological Warfare Unit were sent through the streets to warn people to turn off their taps. This expedient did not, of course, take care of the empty houses, so the British Major Palfrey, Police Officer of the team, the American Lieutenant Colonel Hensel, who is its Civil Defense expert, and the American Lieutenant Davis, who is a former battalion chief in the Columbus, Ohio, fire department, got in touch with the French police, the Défense Passive, and the local fire department, respectively, and members of all three services went, just to be sure, to every house in the city and turned off the open taps. Two other officers, Lieutenant Robertson and Captain Westervelt, who were utilities and telephone men in civilian life, got the electric-power and telephone system restored to service in much the same thorough-going fashion.

On June 29th, M. Coulet, General de Gaulle's Normandy delegate, installed in office, as the new *sous-préfet* of Cherbourg, M. Le Viander, who had been chief engineer of the municipality and active in the resistance movement. He had been absent from the city when the invasion came but had made his way to the Allied lines a couple of days after the landings. Police and civil servants fell into line and took orders from the new *sous-préfet*, who was, after all, a colleague who had been in civil service a long time, more readily, in most cases, than they had taken them from his Vichy predecessor. He knew precisely which of his subordinates had collaborated beyond absolute necessity, and he sacked them. They were not numerous. After that, the *sous-préfecture* and the Civil Affairs men worked smoothly together. The same thing had already happened in Bayeux, where M. Coulet had his headquarters and where he had installed another resistance *sous-préfet*. The Civil Affairs team in the much smaller but architecturally more interesting Bayeux is headed by a Britisher and includes both American and British officers.

Coulet, a tall, thin-lipped, smooth-shaven man of slightly sombre elegance, speaks English well. He has no army behind him, but he has the prestige, in a Norman's eyes, of representing the only French government the Normans recognize, the Gouvernement Provisoire, and he proceeds with complete assurance, making contact with the resistance group in each district as soon as the Allied forces enter it, and organizing the district with the assistance he receives from local resistance leaders. It is a program which up to now has worked smoothly and bloodlessly. So far, there have been neither legal nor unofficial executions.—

JULY 20 (BY WIRELESS)

The contrast which existed in the first World War between the front and behind the lines has returned with the present Allied campaign in Normandy. Staff officers drive toward the front along roads upon which the shadow of a strafing plane never falls and, leaving it, return to an area in which traffic and sanitation are as well organized as in Westchester. Nobody worries about the possibility of a flanking movement or a break-through by the enemy because our flanks rest on the sea and the enemy has shown no signs of real striking power. Even within a couple of miles of the front there is only slight danger, because the Germans have disclosed little artillery. The arrival of a shell on a road near a command post is something to talk about for the next three days. The last few hundred yards make all the difference; the fighting is a nasty business in which hedgerows, drainage ditches, and apple trees have assumed the same lethal associations as Tunisian *djebels*. This struggle for orchards and pastures is disheartening because it is so repetitious. There is, as Army men say, no observation in this country, which means that you can't see an enemy position until you have taken the one in front of it. Even then you don't know that it really is an enemy position until a machine gun opens fire on you from a hedge or a mortar in the next field ahead starts dropping stuff in the one you have just taken. It is not safe to assume that any corner of any field you are attacking is undefended. The property sense of the Norman is so strong that no bit of useful land is without its surrounding hedge and ditch. The Germans dig in behind the hedges like moles—moles with excellent eyesight—and the pattern of the fields frequently gives them a fine opportunity for crossfire, which happens to be one of their specialties. The business of rooting them out of these fields is both dangerous and tedious, and it is one phase of war in which airpower is of almost no help, because foliage conceals the defenders from strafing planes and because bombing entire fields on speculation is likely to pay extremely small dividends in dead Germans. Our artillery is useful in inducing machine gunners to keep their heads down, but foot soldiers have to make the actual kills.

After each few days of this hedgerow fighting, one of our divisions comes to a small town, which it takes. The towns, except for their names, are as much alike as the orchards: always the main street that is merely a stretch of the motor highway; the austere gray stone church that had survived eight centuries and then been shattered the week before; the trepanned, amputated houses with glassless windows; and, if there is one café still ungutted, the sign upon it that says "Off limits to military personnel." A unit takes a mild pride in the catalogue of the towns it has captured—such as St. Jean de Daye, known to the troops as Saint John D Day, and La Haye de Puits, called Hooey da Pooey—but that's about all. There are usually several dead Germans in the buildings of these towns, snipers left behind by their retreating comrades and killed by incoming Americans. Our soldiers, preoccupied with the possibility of surviving snipers and with the mortar fire that the enemy is sure to drop back into any town he has abandoned, hurry past the bodies with only perfunctory interest. There is more affinity between a wax dummy and a corpse than between a corpse and a live man. Some of the corpses wear fairly good gray-green uniforms, and others wear nondescript rags. The most impressive corpses seldom come from the best regiments; the most effective German troops here are the starveling adolescents of the new Nazi formations. Older, more fully developed men give up sooner. The Russians, Georgians, and Poles who were starved into enlisting in German coastal regiments are naturally the easiest game of all. Unfortunately, we have liquidated most of these "static" troops and are now meeting a higher percentage of Germans. For all their stubbornness in defense, the Germans have not been making any counterattacks in force. This has led to a certain optimism, particularly in the zone beginning a thousand yards to the rear of the line. Some officers are saying that the situation reminds them of Tunisia late in April, 1943, when the Germans, though still hanging on to good defensive positions, were about to collapse rather suddenly.

Many peasants remain in their homes in the battle areas, despite the efforts of both Germans and Americans to move them out. The Germans have been trying to evacuate people and their livestock before them as they retreat, but the peasants hide themselves and their beasts. When American troops start fighting around their farmhouses, our Civil Affairs officers attempt to get the peasants to move back of our lines, for their own protection, but they usually say that they won't go unless they can take their cattle with them, and since they can't take their pasture along with the cattle this is not practical. A crop farmer can leave his land for a time and find it there when he comes back, but herds will stray or starve or sicken or wander into machine-gun fire if left to themselves, and the Normans stick to their cows. Near St. Lô, a refugee camp has been established for people whose homes have been destroyed. It is an unusual refugee camp, because it does not receive any supplies from the Army; the French authorities provide the food and the farmers of the district donate clothing and furniture. The refugees have organized themselves into a self-governing community and have succeeded in making themselves more comfortable than the American soldiers of the local Civil Affairs detachment, who are now taking French lessons from the refugee children. Almost every family has deaths to mourn, but the tragic aspect of the situation is naturally not comprehended by the children, who consider the affair a sort of large-scale picnic and are not disturbed by the racket of the American medium artillery immediately behind their temporary home. The subway-train noise the shells make as they go over the children's heads merely provokes them to imitative whistles. Very old people are similarly unmoved by the war. A well-to-do farmer's widow, crippled with rheumatism, and her *bonne* were the only inhabitants left in the village of St. André de L'Epine after two days of heavy fighting. When our Civil Affairs detachment got there, it evacuated them in an ambulance. The mistress was seventy-seven and the maid seventy-two, and the thing that had made the greatest impression on them was the fact that they hadn't been able to get any milk or vegetables for several days and had had to eat their pet rabbit. Their house had been badly damaged and every other building in the village had been flattened.

The Fourteenth of July apparently found everybody in the liberated zone happy. Tricolors that had not seen the light since the Pétain armistice fluttered over houses and draped window sills everywhere, usually along with homemade American flags and often with signs saying "Vive l'Amérique" or "Merci à Nos Libérateurs." The understanding recently reached between de Gaulle and the United States Government seemed to have removed the last suspicion entertained by the French, and the crowds that gathered for the ceremonies in front of the *mairies* were unaffectedly joyous. As one thick-waisted old farmer, an ex-cuirassier, said, "An armored formation has cut up my best pasture, a promising heifer has gone up with a mine, and a bomb has removed most of the tiles from the roof of my house, but, *Monsieur*, I assure you, I was never so happy in my life." And Mme. Hamel said, as she put on her red-white-and-blue rosette (an extra-large one), "Last year I wore a blue dress, my daughter a white one, and my daughter-in-law a red one, and we walked down the street arm in arm, because it was forbidden to wear the tricolor. Now it is different." However, it would be a mistake to assume, because things have gone so smoothly in the part of France liberated up to now, that there will be no serious problems, especially of relief, in *départements* which are either less self-sufficient or which the Germans have had more time to loot. It is also too soon to be able to say that in the big cities the change of regime will be effected with as little violence as it has in the essentially reasonable, rural Normandy. Still, there is every justification for being satisfied with the way things have gone so far.

There was one ceremony on Bastille Day that had not been foreseen— the burial of Brigadier General Theodore Roosevelt, who had died of a heart attack after surviving more front-line perils than any other general officer in this theatre of operations. Nearly all of Roosevelt's scrapes were of his own seeking; he was as nearly fearless as it is given to man to be. The name "Rough Rider," in white letters on his jeep, was a familiar sight just behind the lines in four campaigns of this war. It had been painted out by the time of the funeral and the vehicle had been returned to the motor pool and anonymity, and there was no other charger to lead behind the scout car that carried this flamboyant little man's body to the grave. Nothing else was missing from the solemnities. The man who used to tell his friends in New York how as a small boy he had put on the shoes of his father, the former President, and walked ecstatically about his bedroom at Sagamore Hill was never a sufficiently acute politician to fill them, but he found his métier in 1940, when he took up his reserve commission in the Army. Old Teddy was a dilettante soldier and a first-class politician; his son was a dilettante politician and a first-class soldier. After serving with the First Division in Africa and Sicily and with the French in Italy, he was assigned to a new unit, as assistant division commander, a couple of months before D Day. It was the Fourth Division, which had never fought before, and, by his own example, he gave it much of the lift that took it across the beaches and all the way to Cherbourg. It is no longer a run-of-the-mill division but one of the best in the Army, and his death has endowed it with a tradition. In the circumstances, it was easy to condone his indiscriminate passion for reciting poems, which he rolled out with the large facility of a juke box full of quarters. He was a man you had to see fight to believe in.*

The taking of St. Lô was the climax of the hedgerow phase of our campaign. St. Lô, at the juncture of several major highways, is a larger version of the rural crossroads that are the prizes of smaller operations. The correspondents, going out every day in jeeps to the St. Lô sector of the front, got to know every turning in the lanes, bordered by the omnipresent hedges, that led to the suburbs where the final attack was to be made. Troops fanned out from these lanes to fight their way through the fields. Each day it was possible for vehicles to get past one or two more turnings in the lanes; one remembered these new turnings by the burned-out halftracks or by groups of dead cows. The jeeps that carried the correspondents breasted a seemingly regular stream of other jeeps

---

* Roosevelt and I had a date to meet at the Café de la Regence in Paris on the fourteenth. Instead, we kept it as described above.

with litters, each bearing two seriously wounded men, strapped to their hoods. The stream was regular because the casualties in this sort of war, though they vary from field to field, don't vary from day to day. You lose a few more men in one hedge-fenced pasture and one or two less in another; there is never a spate of casualties, but the stream never dries up, either. There were about as many German as American wounded on the litters, but we seemed to see many more German than American dead on the ground, probably because we were advancing over terrain that had been hammered by American artillery, whereas the enemy had employed comparatively little artillery. We also got to know every sizable gap in the ragged seven-to-ten-foot-high hedges along the lanes, for the gaps enabled enemy snipers and mortar crews to see and to shoot accurately. A rapidly moving jeep raised a cloud of dust that might bring down mortar fire even where there was no gap; a jeep creeping at the ten miles an hour that is prescribed in the area seemed to the occupants to be minutes getting past each gap. When, by the evening of July 18th, the Americans had fought themselves out of the turnings and hedgerows, they rushed into the town of St. Lô with all the joy of a band of claustrophobes released from a maze.

The Germans, as expected, broke out what artillery they had and bombarded St. Lô as soon as our troops came in, and our tired infantrymen, lying face down in the streets at the foot of the buildings, realized that life is just a succession of frying pans and fires. The correspondents, flat on their faces like the rest, wondered whether the Pulitzer Prize was worth all this trouble. They were further depressed by the magnificent aplomb of the brigadier general* who walked erect down the centre of the street, directing troop movements with a cane. When a sniper's bullet went through his right arm, he transferred the cane to his left hand. That gesture will be hard for us to match in our autobiographies.

AUGUST 4 (BY WIRELESS)

Riding, last week, down the road that led to Coutances, Avranches, and beyond evoked memories of the tragic June of 1940, when refugees streamed down the one route left open for civilians between Paris and Tours. Last week, as four years ago, the road was choked with vehicles moving as slowly as a trickle of water through dust, but this time, instead of autobuses and pitiful automobiles loaded with civilians, the traffic was halftracks, empty ambulances, tank destroyers, two-and-a-half-ton trucks, the small, tracked carriers (called weasels) that take ammunition across country, and, scattered through all the heavy stuff, jeeps. The procession

* Norman D. (Dutch) Cota, then of the 29th Division. He later got one of his own, the 28th. The victor of St. Lô was the C.O. of the 29th—Major-General Charles W. Gerhardt.

was heading toward the Germans instead of away from them. One would never have believed, in peacetime, that the mere act of riding slowly down a road in an uncomfortably crowded vehicle on two separate occasions could produce such antithetical emotions. In 1940, the unfortunates on the road stared apprehensively at the sky every time the procession stopped because of a jam. In 1944, soldiers in trucks grinned every time they heard an airplane motor. The Luftwaffe had lost its terror; the Ninth Air Force was patrolling the skies of France with absolute authority. The men moving forward had a hunch that no serious battle awaited them. It turned out that they were mostly right. There were some sharp local actions, which were less counterattacks than group attempts to escape, but in general the parallel with the end of the Tunisian campaign held good: German resistance, disconcertingly stiff in the earlier phase of the Normandy fighting, crumbled suddenly and swiftly, and American units heading toward their objectives unexpectedly found themselves racing other units that had progressed farther and faster than anyone had anticipated. It was a disturbing experience for the artillery officers, who soon found that there was no place that their shells would not be likely to fall among Americans advancing from other points of the compass.

I watched the air bombardment that preceded the breakthrough from an upstairs window of a Normandy farmhouse. The dwelling looked south, toward the area, five miles away, which was to be bombed. There were three ridges, the first two crowned with poplars, the third with pines, between the farmhouse and the target area. One stream of bombers came in to the left of the farmhouse, turned behind the third ridge, dropped its bombs, and came away to my right; another stream came in over my right, turned, and went off to the left. For two hours the air was filled with the hum of motors, and the concussions of the bombs, even though they were falling five miles away, kept my sleeves fluttering. I was living with a headquarters battery of divisional artillery, and some of the men in it, watching the bombardment from the sloping ground under my window, rolled on the grass with unsportsmanlike glee. Their emotion was crude but understandable. "The more bombs we drop, the less fight there'll be left in them," a soldier said, and, remembering the first bombs on Paris in 1940 and all the bombings I have seen decent people undergo since then, I could not feel ashamed of the men's reaction.

The only residents of the farm who seemed uncomfortable were a great, long-barreled sow and her litter of six shoats, who walked about uneasily, shaking their ears as if the concussions hurt them. At brief intervals, they would lie down in a circle, all their snouts pointing toward centre. Then they would get up again, perhaps because the earth quivering against their bellies frightened them. Puffs of black flak smoke dotted the sky under the first two waves of bombers; one plane came swirling down, on fire and trailing smoke, and crashed behind the second ridge of poplars. White parachutes flashed in the sun as the plane fell. A great cloud of slate-gray smoke rose from behind the trees where it had gone down. Soon after that the flak puffs disappeared; the German gunners either had been killed or, as one artillerist suggested, had simply run out of ammunition. The succeeding waves of planes did their bombing unopposed. It was rather horrifying, at that.

After the bombardment, we waited all afternoon for the order to advance. We had heard that the divisional artillery headquarters and the division's battalion of medium howitzers, which throw their shells about seven miles, were to be moved up that night to positions beyond the line the Germans had held that morning. As it happened, the breakthrough wasn't quite as abrupt as all that. We didn't move until the evening, and then we moved only a couple of miles, to a hollow behind the first ridge of poplars, territory that infantry of another division had won from the enemy a couple of days before. When night fell, neither our own infantry division,* which the Germans have been good enough to refer to as a *corps d'élite*, nor our armor had even gone into battle. The infantry divisions ahead of us** had been expected to move forward hard on the tail of the air bombardment and make an opening through which we and the armor would pass, but they had not advanced appreciably. Discouraging rumors, such as frequently attend the opening of offensives, cropped up in the small, exclusive mess of the divisional artillery that night. One was that the Germans had not been shaken by the bombardment, another that they had been annihilated but that bomb craters had made all the roads impassable. The favorite explanation of the delay, I am afraid, was that the divisions ahead of us had snarled things up as usual.†

Next morning, at seven o'clock, a combat team of infantry from the division I was with went into action. By nine o'clock, the news came that the men had advanced thousands of yards in the first hour, and all day they kept on moving forward, against slight opposition. Parts of two armored divisions, engaged at other points, also made rapid advances. The early discouragement around our headquarters disappeared. The mess even made generous allowances for the shortcomings of other infantry divisions. (It turned out afterward that they had run into an abortive German offensive just beyond the bombed area and had not done badly at all.) The artillery prepared to move up behind the infantry, in order to shoot it out of trouble when it ran up against the inevitable tough going. But the tough going that had developed at some point in every other

* The First, of course.
** Fourth, Ninth and Thirtieth.
† This was unjust. Many of those glorious bombs had fallen short *on* the Thirtieth, which suffered its top day of casualties.

operation the division had participated in, whether in the Mediterranean campaign or in France, did not develop in this curious advance.

"The dough," as officers of divisional artillery call the infantry, flowed forward for five days; the artillery followed, but it was hardly ever called upon to shoot. Whenever the Germans looked as though they might make a stand, some other American unit got behind them. By the fifth evening, the gunners found themselves in the impasse I have already described. It was an artillerist's nightmare: there was no place they *could* shoot without fear of hitting some of our own people. Army Corps headquarters had marked on a map what are called "no fire" lines; these lines completely hemmed our guns in. On that fifth night, the division stretched out toward Coutances like a long finger. There were—theoretically, at least—Germans in front of us and on both flanks, but there was part of an American armored division behind the Germans in front of us and there were other American troops behind the Germans on our right. Still other American troops were supposed to be getting around to the rear of the Germans on our left, too, and all the Germans in the area were trying to get out at once. The chief danger we faced was being trampled to death by escaping supermen while we slept.

Divarty, the familiar term for divisional artillery headquarters, is under ordinary conditions an ideal place to follow the progress of a battle, or at least one division's part in it, because Divarty controls the small spotter planes, usually Piper Cubs, which serve as the division's eyes. The pilots and observers in these craft, known to "the dough" as Maytag Messerschmitts, are not Air Forces men but artillery officers. They report not only on targets and the effect of the division's artillery fire but on all enemy troop and vehicle movements they observe. This information is channelized through Divarty to Division, which is short for division headquarters. When ground observation is available, Divarty has the best of that, too, for the artillery has its observers at points of vantage up in the line with advanced elements of the infantry. These observers have telephone lines to their battalions, and the battalions in turn have direct lines to Divarty. The infantry is served by a parallel but separate telephone network. Communications between the infantry and the artillery go through a division switchboard. The infantry and artillery of a division live like a sensible married couple—in the same house but in separate beds.

There is a detached, academic atmosphere about Divarty that is lacking in the larger, more bustling Division, and artillerists in general view war with the objectivity of men who seldom see their victims. The headquarters battery of Divarty has no guns; it merely has a switchboard, a set of maps, and a lot of telephone wires. Divarty is a small, itinerant brain trust which moves quietly with the front-line troops and calls down upon distant Germans the thunder of the division's battalions of artillery. It sets up its command post in a farmhouse or barn within the division area, lays its wires to the battalions, and blacks out windows and chinks through which light might escape. Then, after nightfall, when the Cubs come down, its higher officers sit around a long row of tables—in an atmosphere that recalls a newspaper copy desk during the slack hours—drinking strong coffee and playing cribbage while they wait for telephone calls. A call comes in, and an executive officer engages in a brief conversation, rings off, then remarks, "Infantry patrols report some sort of Jerry movement at that road junction at 4124. Mediums can reach it." He picks up the telephone again, makes a call, and returns to his cribbage game, and outside, in the night, twelve hundred pounds of high explosive scream toward the dark crossroad twenty-five times, at short, irregular intervals. In this particular engagement, however, we simply ran out of crossroads to shoot at.

My Dear Little Louise

DURING our breaking-out offensive in Normandy, the division artillery headquarters occupied four command posts in five days. A French family was living in one wing of the first house we used, although most of the roof was gone and a couple of the bedrooms had only three walls, but the farmhouses in which we had our second and third command posts were deserted. The Germans had forced all the inhabitants to leave. In our fourth one, we found civilians again. The Germans, not expecting so quick an advance, had not evacuated people from what they still considered the rear area. In the barnyard of that place, we found a dead Panzer Grenadier of a Schutzstaffel division. His paybook said that he had been born in Essen, and on his body there was a typewritten form which he had filled out but obviously had not had time to hand in to his company commander, asking for what we would call an emergency leave to go home. His reason was "Bombing deaths in family—urgent telegram from wife." He had been hit by a fragment of shell, but it had not torn him up much. A detail of our fellows buried him in back of the barn.

The dead cows were more of a problem. Now that we have moved on to Brittany, one of the things that make us happy is that we are out of dead-cattle country. The war moves more swiftly and it isn't necessary to drop artillery shells on every field and crossroad. Besides, the cattle in Brittany are fewer and more scattered than in Normandy, where every pasture was full of them. You need a bulldozer to bury cows properly, unless you are going to take all day about it, and nobody had men to spare for a large-scale interment detail. They lay in the fields with their four legs pointing stiffly in the air, like wooden cows discarded from a child's Noah's Ark, and their smell hung over the land as the dust hung over the roads. Men are smaller than cattle and they are always buried first; we lived in the stench of innocent death. At our fourth command post, there were more dead cows than usual, because, the people on the farm told us, eighteen extra cows had arrived with the Germans a couple of weeks before. There had been two sets of Germans in the farm buildings—ten paratroopers who had showed up driving eight cows, and forty S.S. men who had appeared driving ten cows. The paratroopers, one of whom was a captain, had got there first and taken up quarters in the farmhouse. The S.S. men, arriving later, had billeted themselves in the outbuildings, but only after a noisy argument, in which they had failed to get the paratroopers out of the big house. The captain had too much rank for them. The paratroopers had been fighting a long time and were very down in the mouth, the people of the house said. A soldier who served as interpreter had told the French family that the war was over, that Germany was beaten. But the S.S. fellows, who had come from soft berths in Warsaw and Brno, were still *gonflés en bloc* (blown up hard) and talked as if they owned the earth. That was less than two weeks ago, but even the S.S. men, to judge by those taken prisoner, have changed now. The S.S. soldiers had brought a refugee family with them, to milk the cows, the people on the farm said. Every day the paratroopers drank the cream from their eight cows and threw the milk away. Both sets of Germans had departed abruptly, but the S.S. had left one man to guard the cows, presumably in case the reports of the Allied attack proved exaggerated. A shell had killed the cowtender.

I am sure that I will remember our two deserted command posts longer and more vividly than the two that were inhabited. Perhaps that is because you think more about people when they aren't there, and because you can be your own Sherlock Holmes and reconstruct them in accordance with your own hypothesis. The first deserted farm was a solid rectangle of stone and stucco buildings with walls nearly a foot thick. The farmyard, on which all the buildings fronted, could be reached only by narrow lanes that pierced the solid row of buildings at the front and at the back. It would have been a tough defensive position to crack if there had been any tactical reason to defend it. The farmhouse was very old and must have belonged to an aged, rich, crippled, bigoted woman or to a crippled man who had a fat old woman for a housekeeper. There was a crutch in the farmyard, lying as if it had fallen off a departing wagon, and in two of the bedrooms there was a pair of old, mended crutches that must have been discarded for newer ones. In the kitchen, by the great open hearth, there was a reclining chair with an extension on which to rest your legs, and in one bedroom there were several old and dirty corsets, whose whalebones, despite the garments' immense girth, had all sprung because of the continual effort to encompass a bulging body. There was a tall Norman clock in every room. Clocks of this sort are made in little towns, like Périers and Colombières and Marigny, which nobody outside Normandy ever heard of before this summer. Every crossroads seems to have had its clockmaker as well as its baker and its harness maker. The wooden cases of these timepieces are generally rather austere, but the dials are framed by hammered gilt sculpture; sheaves, golden apples, plows, and peasants in donkey carts are favorite motifs. The pendulums are vast, and they too are encrusted with ornament. A bride, I imagine, although no one has told me so, brings a clock as part of her dowry, and a house where there are many clocks has been ruled in turn by many women. This house was full of hideous modern religious images and of wax fruits and flowers under glass bells. There were no books except devotional ones and those that gave quick ways of making the computations a farmer must make in doing business with wholesalers. There were many of each kind.

The farmsteaders had left the place in a great hurry, and some soldiers, either German or American, had been there afterward and rummaged through the house, littering the floors with things, useless to them, that they had pulled from the cupboards—women's high-collared blouses, skirt hoops, dingy photographs of family outings and one of a man in a cuirassier's uniform, with breastplate and horsetail helmet, and three or four parchment manuscripts. One, dated 1779, was the deed of sale of a farm, another was a marriage contract dated the Year 3 of the First Republic. The contract enumerated the items the bride was to bring in her dowry, which included six pillowcases, one canopy for a bed, and ten handkerchiefs; the whole thing was to come to a thousand and fifty-seven francs. If the husband died before the wife, she was to be allowed to withdraw that much from the estate in consideration of her dowry. If the wife died first, the widower was to keep the pillowcases, handkerchiefs, and all the rest, probably to bestow on his next choice. I wondered, naturally, which of them had survived the other. There were canopies over the beds in all the bedrooms; one must have been the canopy listed in the contract. The house had stone floors that did not shake even when some guns just across the road were being fired, which happened for one entire night we spent there.

The guns were only three thousand yards behind the front line, but they were firing at a target—a railroad station or road junction—eleven miles away. They belonged not to division artillery but to a remote, unfamiliar entity called Corps. The battery commander, a harassed captain, called on our artillery general as soon as we moved in and said he hoped the general did not mind guns; there were a lot of generals who couldn't sleep on account of the noise and he had had to move twice already. He was like a man apologizing to his new neighbors for having noisy children; he was sensitive. Our general said that the guns were music to his ears, and we all smiled mechanically and obediently. The captain said, "I'm sure glad to hear that, because I feel I have an ideal setup here."

Across the yard from the house, in a small storeroom, lived a donkey so old that he had a gray beard. His hoofs were long and misshapen, like the nails of an old dog who gets no exercise, and he stayed in his gloomy cell, blinking out at the world, without enough energy to walk into the adjoining barn and eat the hay, although he would accept cabbages if they were brought to him.

From the crippled woman's, or man's, house we moved into a region that had been heavily bombed on the first day of the offensive and was completely deserted except for the surviving animals. An officer who had done some reconnoitering had found a hamlet, Chapelle en Litige* (Chapel in Litigation), which was intact. Bombs had fallen into all the adjoining fields and bomb craters had made the roads into it almost impassable, but its half-dozen houses and the dependent barns stood untouched. One officer, who considers the Air Forces a form of artillery totally lacking in professional direction, said, "If they had dropped hundred-pound bombs instead of five-hundred, they'd have killed just as many cows without spoiling the roads."** The façade of the granite house in which we set up shop was hidden by pear trees *en espalier*, laden with fruit and lush with leaves. An old hen had made a nest in a branch under the hayloft window and was rearing her chicks there; they were hard to find, buried among the pears, and produced a noise that was inexplicable to us until we discovered them. Some of the soldiers with us took up quarters in smaller houses, and once they had found niches for themselves, we all strolled about the village looking over the interiors of the houses. The owners had evacuated them in an orderly fashion, taking most of their belongings with them. There was not much left except furniture.

I found a pile of letters, most of them old, a few recent, lying on a dressing table in one of the houses. In a nearby cupboard was a long row of schoolboys' notebooks filled with exercises in drawing, arithmetic, and composition. All the books bore the inscription, written in a hand which became progressively less slack, "Cahier d'Albert Hédouin." A couple of recent business letters were addressed to Veuve Hédouin, and I assumed that Albert was the widow's son. There were also in the cupboard a

---

* La Chapelle en Juger, which is an older synonym for the same thing, was the right name.
** Brigadier-General (then) Clift Andrus, the First Division artillery commander.

number of the usual breviaries and cheap books of devotion, including a pamphlet of prayers for prisoners of war. Idly, because as a camp follower I had nothing else at the moment to do, I took some of the letters and, sitting down on the threshold of the plain little house I was in, started to read them.

One was dated September 25, 1914. It began, "My dear little Louise: I utilize a little moment to send you news of me. I am in good health and hope my letter finds you the same. I'd rather be at Chapelle en Litige than where I am, for it isn't nice to sleep outdoors. If this thing ends soon, I won't be sorry. I am with Anatole and Désiré, and they are in good health, too. Probably the buckwheat has been harvested, if the weather is as good there as it is here. I'd like to help thresh it and drink a big bowl of cider instead of being here, but it's useless to think about it. When you wean the little colt, leave him in the barn for two days, then turn him into the fields of broom, where the donkey is. Put some branches on top of the gate, so he won't try to jump over it. When you get this letter, send me some news of what goes on at home. Have you made a barrel of cider for Pannel yet and have the cows turned out well? Excuse me for being brief, my dear little Louise and cherished babies. I write this letter in the open air, sitting on my knapsack, and now I must go. Your husband, who loves you and kisses you again and again, Louis Hédouin, 336th Infantry. P.S. Put the donkey in Fernand's field."

The next letter was dated in November, 1914, and began, "My dear little Louise: It is with great pleasure I learn that you are in good health. I too am in good health. Dear little Louise, I think you should make at least three barrels of cider, although I know it will give you a lot of trouble. Considering the price of apples and the price of cider, it pays better to make cider than to sell apples. And make a good barrel for us, so that we can have the pleasure of drinking it together when I come home." ("Come home," I thought. "That war had four years to go then.") "My dear little Louise, you tell me that you have planted some wheat. Good. Prices are going up. I hope you have sowed oats, dear one. Dear little Louise, I hope you are well. Also the cows and calves. Butter is selling at a pretty good price, if it can only continue. I was glad to hear you had someone help you thresh the buckwheat. Dear little Louise, I wish I could have been there, but it's useless to think about it. Here one is and here one stays—until when, nobody knows. Your husband, who loves and will never cease to love you and the dear little children, Louis."

Looking up, I saw that four or five cows, probably wanting to be milked, were staring hopefully at me, and I wondered how Louis Hédouin would have felt if he had known that in thirty years not even a woman would be left to care for the cattle in Chapelle en Litige. There was another letter, also written in 1914, in which he said he had been to mass and then eaten some ham dear little Louise had sent him; he would rather have attended mass at home, but it was "useless to think of it."

"Dear little Louise," he went on, "you say you have had a card from Aimable and he is in good health. So much the better, for you can't imagine how unhealthy it is where he finds himself. I couldn't either, unless I had been there, but don't worry, I'm all right. Dear little Louise, you say that Marie has had a letter from Pierre and he is a prisoner. So much the better. That way he is sure to survive. I know that threshing must be a lot of trouble to you. I am sorry you are alone and have so much work to do. Do you remember, on that evening before I went away, Enée said that this business wouldn't be over before Easter? I am afraid he was right. It is sad when I think of it. Days are indeed long. Louis."

And on March 15, 1915, he wrote that he was sorry to hear that Louise was suffering but hoped she would soon be delivered—the first indication I had had that he knew she was pregnant. "My dear little Louise," he continued, "I had a letter from Papa the same time as yours. He says he has sold the old cow for three hundred and forty-five francs. It's not bad, when you think that she only had four teeth left. What about the black cow you thought was going to calve March 8th and what are you doing with the Jersey? Tell me in your next letter. Dear little Louise, you say you have threshed the oats. Good. There must have been some loss, but you did the best you could. The worst of it is we probably won't be home in time for the haying this season. Excuse me for not having written. We were taking ammunition up to the front lines. Lately things go badly. The regiment has refused to march to an attack. Everybody is sick of this business, and we lose courage and ask for an end of this terrible war. A sweet kiss from your husband, Louis."

Then, on the twenty-second of March, the latest date I found on any of his letters, Hédouin wrote, "My dear little Louise: I have received with great pleasure your letter of the eighteenth. Your mother writes to me that you have had a nine-pound boy and are doing well, and the boy, too. My dear little Louise, you did well to have a midwife from Remilly, and she didn't charge much, either—eight francs. My dear little Louise, I'd like to be with you, but it's useless to think of it. Distance keeps us apart. I hope God will help you in your troubles. My parents write me that at home people are saying this will end soon. So much the better. Dear little Louise, the boy will be called Albert. Before telling you, I waited to see whether you would have a boy or a girl. Your husband, who loves you, Louis. P.S. What about the black cow?"

Nineteen-fifteen. I did a bit of subtraction. Albert would have been twenty-four in 1939—just the right age. I thought of the graded notebooks and the pamphlet of prayers for prisoners of war.

Letter from Paris

SEPTEMBER 1 (BY WIRELESS)

FOR the first time in my life and probably the last, I have lived for a week in a great city where everybody is happy. Moreover, since this city is Paris, everybody makes this euphoria manifest. To drive along the boulevards in a jeep is like walking into some as yet unmade René Clair film, with hundreds of bicyclists coming toward you in a stream that divides before the jeep just when you feel sure that a collision is imminent. Among the bicyclists there are pretty girls, their hair dressed high on their heads in what seems to be the current mode here. These girls show legs of a length and slimness and firmness and brownness never associated with French womanhood. Food restrictions and the amount of bicycling that is necessary in getting around in a big city without any other means of transportation have endowed these girls with the best figures in the world, which they will doubtless be glad to trade in for three square meals, plentiful supplies of chocolate, and a seat in the family Citroën as soon as the situation becomes more normal. There are handsome young matrons with children mounted behind them on their bikes, and there are husky young workmen, stubby little *employés de bureau* in striped pants, and old professors in wing collars and chin whiskers, all of them smiling and all of them lifting their right hands from the handlebars to wave as they go past. The most frequently repeated phrase of the week is *"Enfin on respire!"* (At last, one breathes!)

Happiest of all, in the French film manner, are the police, who stand at street intersections with their thumbs in their belts and beam paternally at everybody instead of looking stern and important, as they used to. Cyclists wave to them appreciatively. When, occasionally, a truck passes through a street, taking policemen to their beats, people standing on the café *terrasses* applaud and shout *"Vive la police!"* For Paris, where the street cry has always been *"A bas les flics!"* (Down with the cops!), this is behavior so unprecedented that the cops sometimes look as though they think it is all a dream. There is good reason for the change of heart; for the first time since Etienne Marcel led a street mob against the royal court in about 1350, the police and the people have been on the same side of the barricades. It was the police who, on August 15th, gave the signal for a mass disregard of the Germans by going on strike. It was also the police who, four days later, began the street fighting by seizing the Prefecture of the Seine, their headquarters, across the square from Notre Dame on the

Ile de la Cité. Three thousand of them, in plainclothes and armed with carbines, revolvers, and a few sub-machine guns, took the place over and defended it successfully for six days before being relieved by the arrival of the French armored division of General Leclerc. This was the largest centre of patriot resistance during the struggle. Because it is in the middle of the city, it was the knot that kept the network of patriot strongpoints together. The Germans held fortresses in the Place de la Concorde, the Place St. Michel, the Luxembourg Gardens, and along the Rue de Rivoli. Von Choltitz, the German military governor of the city, was finally captured by soldiers of the armored division in the Hôtel Meurice, and the Crillon was fought for as though it were a blockhouse. During the five days of fighting before the first elements of Allied troops began to penetrate the city, the Germans sallied from their strongpoints in tanks and systematically shot up the town. The Forces Françaises de l'Intérieur had erected barricades to stop the tanks, and boys fourteen or fifteen years old, with courage that was more than a riposte to the fanaticism of the Hitler Jugend, often destroyed tanks by throwing bottles of incendiary fluid through their ports. The bottles were usually filled with mixtures prepared by neighborhood druggists. The youngsters who did the fighting were not always of the type that is ordinarily on good terms with the police. They included the problem children of every neighborhood as well as students and factory workers. So the oldest of all Paris feuds has ended.

It has perhaps already been hinted in the New York press that our army had not expected to take Paris quite so soon. The city was to be bypassed and encircled to save it from street fighting, on the theory that the last elements of the German garrison would withdraw just before being cut off. Thus a certain amount of damage to the city's buildings would be prevented, unless, of course, the Germans mined them before departing. As it turned out, the Germans laid mines, all right, but they didn't set them off because they were caught sitting on them. There were ten tons of explosives in the vaults under the Senate alone. But none of this is so important for the future of the world as the fact that the French saved their selfrespect forever by going into the streets and fighting. The F.F.I.s were already in control of the city when the regular troops arrived, they like to tell you when you talk with them in the cafés. And, with a fine bit of military courtesy, the Allied Command, when it was informed that conditions in Paris called for an immediate move, sent in Leclerc's division first. Frenchmen had begun the liberation of Paris; other Frenchmen completed it. As a result, the Parisians are happy not only because of the liberation but because they feel they earned it.

The gratitude toward Americans is immense and sometimes embarrassing in its manifestations. People are always stopping one in the street, pumping one's hand, and saying "Thank you." It is useless to protest. To the Parisians, and especially to the children, all Americans are now *héros du cinéma*. This is particularly disconcerting to sensitive war correspondents, if any, aware, as they are, that these innocent thanks belong to those American combat troops who won the beachhead and then made the breakthrough. There are few such men in Paris. Young women, the first day or two after the Allies arrived, were as enthusiastic as children; they covered the cheeks of French and American soldiers alike with lipstick. This stage of Franco-American relations is approaching an end. Children, however, still follow the American soldiers everywhere, singing the "Marseillaise" and hopefully eyeing pockets from which they think gum might emerge. And it is still hard for an American who speaks French to pay for a drink in a bar.

The city is resuming normal life with a speed I would never have believed possible. The noise of battle has receded and the only visible reminders of the recent fighting are some damaged buildings, holes in a few streets, and a considerable number of captured German automobiles dashing about loaded with F.F.I.s and their girls, all wearing tricolor brassards and festooned with German machine pistols, Lugers, and grenades. French adolescents have for years been deprived of the simple pleasure of riding about on four wheels, and if they seem to find an excessive number of military missions for themselves, all of which involve riding down the boulevards and cheering, nobody can blame them. Until very recently they seemed to have great difficulty in resisting the equally natural temptation to shoot off their new weapons, and every day sounded like the Fourth of July, but the F.F.I., whose officers are serious soldiers, is now being absorbed into the French Army and the promiscuous shooting has come to an end. On a shattered concrete pillbox in the Place de la Concorde some playful fellow has printed, in chalk, "Liquidation. To rent, forty thousand francs." And, as I write, a painter is relettering "Guaranty Trust of New York" on the building next to the Crillon that the bank occupied before we went to war.

The physical conditions of life here are not too bad. Paris was spared the most uncomfortable experience a big modern city can have, for the water system has continued to work, a very important factor not only in sanitation but morale. Only a limited quantity of electricity is available; the power plants and distributing system are in good shape, but the hydroelectric power from central France is no longer coming in and there is a very small supply of fuel. Consequently, lights are on for only about two hours every evening, except in government offices. There is as yet no gas for cooking, but it has been promised that there soon will be. For that matter, there is not very much to cook; the city had no more than a two weeks' supply of strictly necessary foods when the liberators entered it, and though the American and French authorities have been steadily pumping food into the town, there is not yet enough for the reëstablishment of good eating at home, let alone good restaurant life. Only a few small black-market restaurants still exist. The price of *petit salé* (a kind of New England boiled dinner), one pear, and a half bottle of Bordeaux is seven hundred francs. This is the best fare you can get, and seven hundred francs, just to remind you, is fourteen dollars. Butter is four hundred francs a pound. However, the day of the black-market people is ending, because there are great quantities of butter, meat, and vegetables in Normandy, Brittany, and Anjou at about an eighth of Paris prices, and bringing them here is now simply a matter of transportation. Considering that all this food is only fifty to a hundred and fifty miles away, there is little reason to doubt that the problem will soon be solved. A decent pair of leather shoes cost a hundred dollars, a man's suit three hundred, and a portable typewriter five hundred and sixty. My advice to the Frenchman who wants any of these things is to do without for a few weeks, because such a situation can last only under the rule of the Germans, who drain a country dry of everything except grace, beauty, and good sense. The German occupation gave the black market a sort of moral sanction here. In Britain the feeling has been, ever since the blitz days, that a man who bought in the black market deprived other Britons of their share. Here people said, truthfully enough, that if you had money and didn't buy in the black market, what you wanted to buy would simply go to Germany. The black-market operators themselves are an unprepossessing lot, however, and a visit to a black-market restaurant will quickly convince anyone that a fair proportion of the patrons are engaged in other branches of the same racket.

The question of what is to be done with all this group is receiving considerable attention in the new French press. There are already eleven dailies in Paris, all almost direct offshoots of the clandestine resistance papers. Only three bear names well known before the war—the conservative *Figaro*, the Communist *L'Humanité*, and the Socialist *Le Populaire*. These three had been suppressed by Vichy, but *Populaire* and *Humanité* became as powerful as ever in their clandestine editions. Others, like *Combat*, *Libération*, and *Franc-Tireur*, are resistance papers appearing for the first time above ground and in full size. The editorial offices and printing plants of the big collaborationist papers have been handed over to the newcomers. *Populaire*, for example, is now published in the plant of *Le Matin*, on the Boulevard Poissonnière. The new papers have from the beginning taken divergent political lines; in the cases of *Figaro*, *Humanité*, and *Populaire*, it would perhaps be better to say that they have resumed them. They are in complete accord, however, on the prestige and position of General de Gaulle and his provisional government. So is every man, woman, and child I have heard speak of de Gaulle or his government in Paris. The man's prestige is so vast that it is slightly nauseating now to think of the "opposition" to him that rich Frenchmen were still telling credulous friends about in London and Washington only a few months ago. He put the seal on a personal legend last Saturday, when, on foot and towering above a couple of million compatriots, he led a parade down the Champs-Elysées and as far as Notre Dame, where he listened to the Te Deum while snipers and F.F.I.s exchanged shots around him. Such overwhelming popularity may in time prove to be a handicap to him; he must eventually disappoint some of the people who now expect irreconcilable things of him. His hold on the public could not possibly be greater. A united France has crystallized around him.

While de Gaulle led the march, a few Americans were otherwise engaged.

Day of Victory

AUGUST 26, 1944, the day after the official Liberation of Paris, was a brilliant, sunny Saturday. Allardyce Meecham, a war correspondent who had once been a dramatic critic in New York, descended the fifth, and last, flight of steps between the floor on which he had been billeted and the lobby of the Hotel Scribe. Meecham, an awkward, red-haired man of forty-three, felt himself an unimpressive representative of a victorious army, and his futile wait for the lift, which was apparently out of order, had accented his sensation of inadequacy. He had arrived in Paris early that morning. All of his colleagues he had encountered since getting to the Scribe had, by their telling, acted as advance scouts for motorized-cavalry units and infiltrated into the city on Tuesday, Wednesday, or Thursday, before the surrender of the German garrison, which had taken place on Friday. Meecham had missed even that. He had gone off on a side trip into lower Brittany early in the week and had not known that Paris was going to be liberated until it was too late for him to precede even the Public Relations officers. On his way into the freed capital, with some officers from a corps in Brittany who had no real business in Paris but wanted to see the fun, he had felt guilty because, although he complained in a loud tone about having missed the big moment, he knew in his heart that he was content to have the combat troops go first. Not once, in two months of war, had he arrived in a town alone in time to receive the surrender of an S.S. Panzer division, an experience apparently banal for Hearst correspondents. When, on a single occasion, at St.-Lô, he had inadvertently got into a bad spot, he had been so shaken that he had been unable to write the story.

Meecham was dressed in a tanker's combat jacket and a pair of dress-pink trousers, an incongruity caused by the circumstance that he had left his Class A uniform blouse hanging in the closet of a hotel in Angers, while the G.I. pants he generally wore with the combat jacket were in his estimation too dirty to wear in Paris. He had been a bit muddled with drink on leaving Angers and had forgotten the blouse. On his head he wore a helmet liner. His only overseas cap was in the pocket of the blouse in Angers.

When Meecham reached the lobby, which was crowded with victorious correspondents and Public Relations officers, he pretended to be preoccupied and in a hurry, since he didn't want to hear them make light of their thrilling experiences and had none of his own to depreciate. As he made for the revolving door to the street, however, he was blocked off by Wallaby Bates, an Australian correspondent for a London newspaper, who was wearing British battle dress fronted by a landing net of ribbons from the last war. Wallaby shouted, in a concerned voice, "I say, Meech, haven't seen Larry Boddlebaum, have you? Our jeeps were cracking along on the way in from Chartres last week. Heard there were only a couple of middle-drawer Hun divisions left in Paris, so we thought we'd disregard them, what? Larry's jeep was behind mine, and as I went past an intersection, I saw a lot of their chaps around a dinkum super Mark VI tank—p'raps a Mark VII or VIII. I didn't have a chance for a proper dinkum look-see, what? I heard a spot of machine-gun fire behind me, and I wonder if poor old Larry copped it."

Meecham mumbled apologetically that he hadn't seen Mr. Boddlebaum, and hurried on toward the door. Just outside, he stepped on the heels of an oldish man in a costume that included a floppy garrison cap, worn fighter-pilot style, parachutist's boots, the patches of two armored divisions, one on each shoulder, and a new bit of purple ribbon. This was Larry Boddlebaum, war correspondent for a magazine popularizing scientific research and for another devoted to homemaking, to each of which he contributed one article a month. He had worn the purple ribbon ever since, in a blackout in Normandy, he had fallen over a latrine made from a packing box.

Boddlebaum turned in some irritation, but on recognizing Allardyce Meecham, he put on an expression of hearty good humor. "Why, if it isn't old Meech!" he shouted. "Haven't seen old Wallaby Bates, by any chance, have you? Wallaby and I were hightailing along a road near Fountainblue a few days ago, meaning to get under a parachute drop that we heard the boys were going to make behind the kraut line, him in one jeep and me in another. Next thing I knew, I was looking into the muzzle of an eighty-eight, but I ducked into the brush just as the thing went off. Haven't heard of poor old Wallaby since."

"He's just inside the door, looking for you," Meecham said.

Boddlebaum did not seem as pleased as one might have expected. He waved his hand, with a gesture which Meecham interpreted as a dismissal, and turned to a group of three women correspondents, whom he halted with outflung arms and shouts of greeting. Meecham, as he walked away, heard him shout, "Haven't any of you girls seen old Wallaby Bates, have you?"

The sidewalk and street in front of the hotel were crowded with cheering, chattering, happy people who enthusiastically waved their hands with fingers spread in the V sign whenever they thought they saw a correspondent or a jeep driver look at them. They left no path for jeeps and command cars, barely parting before each arriving vehicle. "*Vive l'Amérique!*" a man wearing a tricolor brassard marked "F.F.I." shouted. "*Vive Roosevelt!*" He rushed at Meecham and seized him by the right hand, which he clasped fervently. From the strength of the man's clutch, Meecham deduced that he must once have been a weight-lifter. Meecham's wife, a woman of such strong character that he never audibly disagreed with her, detested Roosevelt, so now he answered simply, "*Vive la France!*" Then, perhaps because he, too, had begun to feel liberated, he said boldly, "*Vive Roosevelt pour moi aussi!*" The man, still crushing his hand, said, "He speaks French admirably!"

A young woman with bare brown legs and green wooden earrings threw her bare arms around Meecham and forcefully kissed him on the left side of his face. A taller young woman, on whose equally brown limbs blond hairs glinted delightfully, closed on Meecham from the right and kissed him on that side of his face, pressing so hard he could feel her teeth through her lips and letting her mouth stay against his cheek for an extra second. The F.F.I. man cried, "Honor to the liberators!" Meecham started to say, "I have done nothing. I am only a journalist," but he couldn't speak French fast enough. By the time he had said "nothing," the first young woman cried, "He is modest! He is adorable!," and kissed him again, this time on the left temple, knocking the helmet liner over his right eye.

"How tall they are!" exclaimed a third woman, throwing her arms about Meecham's neck and pulling his head forward, while the F.F.I. man and the barelegged girls still hung on. The woman kissed him firmly on the forehead. "Look! He has lipstick all over!" a female voice farther back in the crowd squealed.

Meecham, feeling the man's grip ease, managed to break away and straighten the helmet liner. He grabbed a handkerchief from his hip pocket and made a motion to wipe the lipstick from his face, but there was a chorus of protesting voices—"No, no, don't do that." To humor his admirers, Meecham dropped his hand and stumbled on, the handkerchief still in his fist. He was exhilarated in a way new to him. He had never before experienced a manifestation of public approval, except after a lecture at a women's club in Greenwich. That, since he had been paid for his services, had been relatively tepid. None of the clubwomen had offered to kiss him, and he could not recall having regretted this omission.

As he turned the corner into the Boulevard des Capucines, his insufficiency as a newspaperman no longer weighed upon him. The press services would have kept his paper covered on the spot news of the liberation of Paris, he knew. What his editor wanted of him, he reflected with satisfaction, was something more subtle. This was the sequel to a Greek drama—this was "Prometheus Unbound." Replacing the handkerchief in his pocket, he stopped, took out a pencil and a Press Wireless blank, and wrote down the phrase. A woman grabbed him and kissed him before he had finished. Another, looking up at him, could not find a free space to leave her mark—she had, he noticed, a rather large mouth with flaring lips—so she took a handkerchief out of her handbag, spat on it, and scrubbed away at his face until she had cleared a sufficient area. Then she, too, kissed him.

Feeling pleased but silly, Meecham moved on to the front of the Café de la Paix. It was not open for business officially, but a number of American officers and several correspondents were already seated at tables on the terrace, and when he went to the door and talked to the manager standing there, he obtained the privilege of buying a glass of white wine for thirty francs. A waiter brought it to him at a table, and he began to think out a lead for his story—something about how it was the beginning of a return to normal when an American could again sit at a table at the Café de la Paix and wait for everybody he knew in the world to come walking by. He wrote it down.

When he had finished the glass of wine, he had another. He called over a news vendor and bought a paper, one of the new Resistance ones he had never heard of. General de Gaulle, he read, was to lead a great procession that afternoon down the Champs-Elysées and through the center of Paris to Notre Dame, where there would be a solemn Te Deum of victory. His French was really not too bad, especially after this two-month refresher course, which had begun in Normandy in June. The Te Deum would be the symbolic highlight of the liberation, Meecham decided, and he would build his color story around it. He had a third glass of wine and thought the story might turn out better than Will Irwin's account of the San Francisco earthquake. "Will Irwin once wrote a great story and called it 'The City That Was,'" he would begin. "This is the story of a City That Once Again Is." He had always liked newspaper stories that began "This is the story of" and then went on to whatever they were stories of. Stark. The lead about sitting at the Café de la Paix was less stark, but too good to throw away, he decided, so he might just as well use it further down in the story. Two women war correspondents from the Midwest walked up and looked at his lipsticked face disapprovingly. "Having a good time?" one of them said. He didn't ask them to sit down because they reminded him of his wife, a magazine executive who always referred to herself as a gal.

One of Meecham's chief talking points, in persuading his editor to send him to Europe, had been his familiarity with France, a theme on which he had expanded until even he had begun to forget that it was based wholly on a summer-vacation trip taken between his freshman and sophomore years at college. But he had now begun to feel quite honestly at home. After one more glass of wine, he started into the complex of streets that begins in back of the Grand Hotel and that he thought he remembered led off in the general direction of the Champs-Elysées, where he intended to arrive in time for the procession. On the way, he thought, he might be able to find a restaurant at which to eat. He could also stop in some *bistros* and collect some good quaint quotes.

All the shops and all the restaurants that he passed were closed. The proprietors had lowered the shutters during the sporadic street fighting, which had ended only on the previous day, and had not yet opened them again. But a number of the little bars were doing business. Meecham went into one near the Rue Caumartin. On the customers' side of the short metal counter at the front of the place he saw a small Chinese and a bulky Frenchman with a mouth that stuck out like a doorknob. The Frenchman wore a jersey and beret, and when Meecham entered, he was showing something to the proprietor, a little snipe-nosed man who, on his side of the bar, was wiping glasses. When Meecham came closer, he could see that the man held out on an upturned palm a very small automatic pistol. "It was tough on the Place de la République," the man was saying. "*Ça ratatinait.*" The word sounded so much like machine-gun fire that Meecham got the idea immediately. "*Ça ratatinait,* my boy," the man repeated, "but the boys of the République, huh, the little old kids of the neighborhood—well, *Ça ratatinait.* I got one *Schleuh* myself, species of a *Fridolin,* what! He was coming out of the subway station and he tried to run away, but I got him! Of course, there has been some criticism among the neighbors because he was so old and, according to what they say, inoffensive. Evil tongues—ambushed enemies of the Resistance. Nearly seventy years old he was, a sort of clerk. He had been billeted in a hotel in the neighborhood, it appears, for four years. But a Boche, what? How could I know he wasn't preparing something nasty? He could have turned on me, if he had been armed, huh?"

"You were right," the proprietor said. "You killed him with that gun?"

"And how!" the bulky man said. The Chinese giggled.

When Meecham ordered a glass of wine, the proprietor said it was on the house. The Chinese said, "Next one is on me. All Allies." The bulky man was cool for a moment, as if he feared the arrival of an American might divert attention from his recital. Soon, however, he sensed the new tactical opportunity and began to tell Meecham the story from the beginning. The proprietor and the Chinese looked as if they were trying to think of something else while he talked. Probably they had already heard him through several times. "Ça ratatinait," the man said. And again, "Ça ratatinait." While he was talking, they drank the Chinaman's round, and when the story was finished, Meecham bought one. Then the big man and the Chinese went out.

"He wouldn't buy a round, that one," said the proprietor, looking after the big man. "A dirty type. I'll bet he was a police spy before the Germans surrendered. He probably killed the old man to create himself a character as a patriot."

Meecham and the proprietor had another drink together. Meecham was now feeling the heat. It was high noon.

"I say, you're well arranged," the proprietor said, making his first allusion to the marks on Meecham's face. "The girls have been kind to you, what? You look like a real Red Indian in war paint."

"Perhaps I'd better wash it off," Meecham said.

"Sure. Then they can begin again. There's a washbasin in the back there."

After Meecham had washed, he felt a bit fresher, and asked the proprietor if he knew where there was a good restaurant open.

"It would be difficult to say, today," the proprietor said judicially, "but there is a black-market joint not far from here that I think will not be closed. The prices are horrible, of course. Take your right to the next street and then your right again until the next street and then your left for a hundred metres, and there you are."

Meecham had no trouble finding the place. It was a small restaurant with threadbare vestiges of chic. The plush on the divans was worn and footpaths were frayed across the pile of the carpets. The maître d'hôtel showed a black bow tie and a yellowish dickey under his white summer jacket. One American had already found the place before Meecham got there. Seated on the divan at the rear of the room, which was rather wide than deep, was a colonel named Rushby, one of the officers who had driven up from Brittany with Meecham. He was with a very pretty girl, Meecham noticed at once. The restaurant was full, and the maître d'hôtel said, "I regret, but we are complete for the moment."

"I will wait," Meecham said. "I have not seen any other restaurant in the quarter." He hoped Rushby would see him standing, since he might then feel obliged to ask him over. He felt sure that the Colonel did not want to be interrupted.

Before Rushby did see Meecham, a sleek Frenchman sitting alone at a table near the door rose and approached him. "Perhaps the gentleman would not mind sitting with me," he said. "It is ironic that on the day of victory one of our liberators should not find a place in a restaurant." The well-fed man was the only customer who had paid any heed to Meecham's entrance; the others—women of expensive appearance and men who looked as if they spent much of their time in barbers' chairs— seemed to pretend not to see him. "Certainly, M. Philippe," the maître d'hôtel said to the well-fed man, and Meecham said he would be delighted. When the two sat down, M. Philippe asked Meecham to share a bottle of non-vintage champagne that had just been opened for him. "It's not what I would have had with my lunch before the war," he said with resignation, "but *à la guerre comme à la guerre.*" Meecham smiled politely, and his host said, "You understand French admirably." When M. Philippe had filled Meecham's glass, he said, as if he were enunciating something startling, "To tell the truth, I am very glad to see American uniforms here. At least, you will be able to defend us from the Communists. The French, you know, Monsieur, are a very undisciplined people. They need a firm hand over them. The Germans could have taught us some valuable lessons, if we had been willing to learn."

"But Hitler—" Meecham began.

"Oh, I do not say there were not some portions of the doctrine that were perhaps excessive," M. Philippe said, refilling the glass the correspondent had just emptied. "But it is necessary to be a civilized being. Have you observed the condition of the streets, Monsieur? Paving stones torn up for barricades, burned-out tanks, barbed wire? All totally unnecessary."

Just as Meecham began to feel uncomfortable, he heard his name called in a loud voice. It was Colonel Rushby, yelling, "Hi ya, Meech! Come over here and help me talk to Michèle. She don't savvy coochy avec mwah."

Meecham got up and said to M. Philippe, "I am sorry, but I must go and have lunch with my friends. I had not seen them before."

"It is a pity," M. Philippe said with a wave of his hand, and went on placing creamed mushrooms inside his face.

Meecham, who was not quite sober, recognized without difficulty that Rushby was quite drunk. Michèle was a brunette with a triangular Hispanic face and a Lupe Velez coiffure. Girls in Paris, like those in New York, often styled themselves after Hollywood stars, Meecham already had noticed, but since they had seen no American films for five years, they imitated stars of an older vintage. He ordered food for three. Rushby had wanted only drink, and the girl had been afraid to order food for fear that the Colonel might not pay for it. The luncheon—roast pork, creamed mushrooms, and chocolate éclairs—was not the sort of thing Meecham would have expected in a good French restaurant, but it seemed to fit the pomaded clientele.* Rushby did not refuse to eat, and the food seemed to

* Fats and sweets were the rarest and dearest forms of food in a rationed society and were accordingly the most chic among profiteers and racketeers of the Occupation.

sober him somewhat. "Suppose we both got a girl," he said to Meecham. "You got to stick to me. I can't talk to these frogs. Maybe this babe has a friend." Michèle said all the girls she knew had by this time probably gone to watch the parade. "But there will be plenty in the streets," she said. "All you have to do is ask. You must stay with us, else I am afraid. I do not understand what he says. I thought it would be amusing not to understand, but it is rather frightening." Meecham had by this time decided that it was not essential that he literally see the parade. The feel of the city is what counts for *my* story, he told himself. He took the check, since it turned out that Rushby had only a few hundred francs. It came to about three thousand francs, which was sixty dollars of his newspaper's money. "They are giving you a special discount," Michèle said, seriously. "They are very decent." After the bill had been paid, they had a round of brandies on the house and then went out into the street arm in arm, Michèle between the two men.

The sun streamed down, the streets were full of holiday-makers, and Meecham, for the first time since he had left the Place de l'Opéra, was certain where he was—he could see the Madeleine. However the customers in the restaurant may have felt about the Liberation, these crowds in the street—parents with their children, girls with arms intertwined, larking young men in their shirtsleeves marked with tricolor brassards— were unaffectedly happy. They flocked down the Rue Royale and all the transverse streets leading to de Gaulle's line of march. Meecham could have found plenty of color to write about if he had any longer been looking for it. But now he was looking for a girl. There were, of course, hundreds, but they all seemed to be escorted or to be travelling in groups. He hesitated to approach a band and try to cut out one individual. Ordinarily, he would have given up the idea, but the drink, the sun, and the feeling of being a hero in the eyes of these happy people made him a man his wife would have recognized with difficulty. Rushby urged him on. "Go on and get yourself a number," he kept saying. "I'm going nuts out here in the sun."

Meecham fixed his attention on two tall girls, a blonde and a redhead, who were staring at his little group and smiling. They looked, he thought, like two unusually nice stenographers just back from a holiday at the seashore, brown and summery. The redhead was being Joan Crawford; the blonde was being either just herself or an imitation of some star Meecham did not recognize. "Come here!" he said to the blonde abruptly, remembering to use the familiar form of the imperative verb. "Come with us. It is the day of victory." Unhesitantly, the girl came to them. The redhead walked away into the crowd.

The girl took Meecham's arm, and now the four proceeded two by two, with Michèle and Rushby in front. "I know a hotel near here," Michèle said. "Lead on," said Meecham, now authoritative. He translated Michèle's remark to Rushby, who said, "That's swell!" The blonde said nothing, but clasped Meecham's arm as if she wanted to convert herself into a tourniquet.

In the hotel, it was cool behind Venetian blinds that had been kept closed against the sun all day. Meecham and the blonde had a room that was draped and furnished in imitation of the interior of a sheik's tent, but had a modern bed. There was a silver-framed photograph of Rudolph Valentino on a wall. To Meecham, the place seemed unconventional.

"What do you do when there is no holiday?" Meecham asked the girl, when they had become a little used to each other. "Do you work in an office?"

"No," the girl said. "I work in a house on the Rue Pigalle, and my sister, the redhead, and I had looked forward to twenty-four hours without men. Besides, I very much wanted to see General de Gaulle. But on the day of victory, I cannot refuse anything to one of our liberators."

Meecham had already begun to think of seeing the girl often during his stay in Paris, but a mistress in a brothel did not sound practicable. Afterward, though, he began to think of what a fine anecdote this experience would make, and was pleased.

Meecham ordered a bottle of champagne. It was brought up to the room and served by the housekeeper, a stout woman who was dressed in a kind of operetta maid's costume. After they had drunk a couple of glasses, they were tranquil, almost as if the champagne had been a sleeping potion, until what seemed a great noise of small-arms fire broke out over in the direction of the line of march. The sound was repeated and unmistakable. Yet inside the factitious Arab tent, war seemed a dream of the night before last. It couldn't be the Germans coming back, Meecham thought, reasonably. Even if the military situation had not precluded such a return, there would have been much artillery fire before they could reach the heart of the city. "It's the Militia, the murderers," the girl said. "There are plenty of them disguised with Resistance brassards now. They are shooting at the crowd because it is happy. And the real F.F.I.s must be shooting back. Stay here." Meecham had made no move to go.

In a couple of moments there came a burst of knocks at the door, and the housekeeper precipitated herself into the room without even asking pardon. "Come quick!" she cried. "Your friend the Colonel has gone mad. He will get us all killed!" She pulled Meecham by the leg. He reached for his trousers, but the woman said quickly, "There is no time for that. Have you gone mad, too? He has a revolver and he is trying to fire out of the window of his room at some F.F.I. guards on a roof who he thinks are snipers."

The blonde understood. Parisians appeared to react quickly to such situations, Meecham thought afterward. "He has no uniform on!" the blonde wailed. "They will see a man shooting and they will turn a machine gun on the house! Madame is right! We shall all be killed." The women ran out through the door, and Meecham followed them.

They entered another door, and he followed them again. The room in which he now found himself, he at once noted, was lined with mirrors. The ceiling and all the walls reflected a sculpturelike group of struggling figures, most of them nude. Rushby's was dominant. The Colonel, a tall man and an extraordinarily hairy one, was holding his Colt .45 at arm's length over his head to keep it away from the four women who surrounded him. Michèle had grabbed him around the knees and the housekeeper had tackled him waist-high—to prevent his progress to the window, Meecham supposed—while the proprietress of the establishment, a rather elegant female in an evening gown, had slipped her arms around his chest from the rear, and the blonde girl, who was tall for a woman, jumped again and again at the revolver hand. As Meecham watched, the whole mass swayed and went down, and there was an explosion comparable to that a howitzer might make in a less confined space. The pistol, describing a high arc, soared toward him and fell near his feet. There was broken glass around, some of it powdered so fine it looked like synthetic Christmas-tree snow. The bullet had hit one of the wall mirrors. Meecham stumbled toward the recumbent group and started to pull women to their feet like a football referee endeavoring to find who has the ball at the bottom of the pile. When he got down to Rushby, the Colonel was snoring peacefully.* Meecham and the women picked him up and laid him out on the bed, and a couple of hours later he was able to walk out almost sober. That must have been at about five o'clock, which was eleven A.M., Eastern War Time.

At 10 P.M., Eastern War Time, a copy boy began to lay takes of Meecham's story on the desk of his cable editor in New York.

"Will Irwin once wrote story called citythatwas," the lead began. "This is story of city that is again period bullets militia disguised as efefeye failed mar this sequel greek drama which originally never had such happy ending period this was prometheus unbound period it was throbbing heartwarming day of victory period burnedout tanks lay scattered about streets in front cafe de la paix bits broken glass."

* His head had hit the bidet.

6

Massacre

I remained in Paris, to report on political things, while my young friend David Lardner, who had come over for the purpose, relieved me as correspondent of *The New Yorker* with the Armies. Dave, extremely nearsighted, had been rejected from service, but was desperately keen to risk his skin. He was killed at Aachen in Germany when the jeep in which he was riding ran on a mine. He was one of the best.

With a photographer of a newly set up French War Crimes Commission, I made a trip to the Côte-d'Or, a region that, like Rennes, I had known in happier days. After I returned to Paris and wrote the following despatch, I went home, and missed the Battle of the Bulge. I never came back to the war. Before I could feel sufficiently ashamed for that, it was over.

The Events at Comblanchien—

November, 1944

THE COMMUNE of Comblanchien, in the Department of the Côte-d'Or, lies on the stretch of the National Highway that runs between Lyon, to the south, and Dijon, to the north. Comblanchien is six miles north of Beaune and three miles south of Nuits-St. Georges, in the Burgundy wine country. The commune has an area of a thousand acres; most of them are on the eastern side of the highway, falling away gently toward the railway that parallels the road at a distance of half a mile and forms Comblanchien's eastern boundary. A narrower strip of the village lies west of the highway, and in this direction the ground slopes up and more abruptly. A hundred feet above the road on this side there is a big, box-like, gray-and-white building which the people of the countryside call a château but which looks more like an old-fashioned American summer-resort hotel. From a small cupola on the roof of this building there is an excellent view of the surrounding country. The thousand acres are, except for a few fields of cabbages and sugar beets and the open mouths of four or five granite quarries, fairly well covered with grapevines, as one might expect in this region. The Comblanchien granite has more than a local reputation and when transportation was available it was sent as far away as Paris. The wines of Comblanchien are classed among the Côte de Nuits, but they are a secondary *cru* and have no such fame as those of Vosne-Romanée and Vougeot, both nearby communes. The wines bring good prices but not the extravagant sums that make the heir to a few acres in one of those more favored communities a rich man by birth. The village had five hundred and twenty inhabitants according to the last census, but it has rather fewer now. None of them are what the French call "rich rich," but a few are comfortably off. The proprietors of the Comblanchien vineyards work with their hands, like their hired help. The stone quarries are owned by outside companies and worked by employees who get modest wages. What distinguishes Comblanchien from other communities in the region is the burned-out shells of its houses.

There are perhaps a hundred houses in Comblanchien. About fifty of them are strung out along the highway; the rest are either scattered or grouped in clumps of two or three among the vineyards and fields that extend from the highway down to the railroad. Forty of the fifty on the highway are now in ruins. One of the town's three cafés and one of its three general stores have survived. Its one church is burned out, and so is the post office. The part of the community back among the vines and fields has suffered less; there are about a dozen charred ruins here and there. At one side of the road, as you come into town from the north, you see a rude sign that says, "Honor to all our liberators, who will avenge the martyrs of our dear village. Long live Comblanchien. Long live France. Long live de Gaulle."

"The events at Comblanchien" or the "things that happened at Comblanchien," as they are usually called by the people of the countryside, have some of the elements of a mystery story. Around nine-thirty on the night of August 21, 1944, about two weeks before the liberation of the region, some German soldiers disembarked from a troop train that had halted in the village and, together with the Germans from other detachments in the vicinity, set fire to many of the houses, after killing all the miserable people they caught in them. Most of the other inhabitants of Comblanchien had hidden in the vineyards, and toward morning the Germans went away. The German authorities never offered any explanation of the attack, and the Mayor of Comblanchien, a timid man, never asked for any. There was nothing to stop the Germans from coming back and completing the massacre by daylight, but they didn't. The people of Comblanchien continued to work in the vineyards by day and sleep there at night until the region was liberated. Then M. Jordan, a sergeant of the gendarmes in Corgoloin, a village near Comblanchien, started an investigation to establish what had happened. Comblanchien has no *gendarmerie* of its own, because it is not large enough; it has only a *garde-champêtre*, or constable. Jordan, who was in the Maquis, had been hiding in the vineyards on the night of the attack. He came out of his hiding place when he saw the fires and, slipping around among the Germans, he heard them crying, *"Hunde! Schweine! Schweine! Terroristen! Hunde!"* "I think it was because they were so frightened," he said afterward. "It is unimaginable how frightened they were." He has not been able to discover any other motive for the massacre.

✿ ✿ ✿

Comblanchien, for four years after the Germans marched into Burgundy, in June, 1940, was without a history, but it was not happy. Like
thousands of other communities in France, it had an unending premoni-
tion of outrage. All through the land, fear was the most nearly intolerable
feature of the occupation. France was a kidnapped country; the kidnapper might let her live in a locked room, but when rescue seemed at
hand the kidnapper might try to kill her. Everyone had the feeling that
the Germans might arrest or kill anybody, at any time, for no reason that
would make sense to a civilized man. Materially, life was difficult. In
Comblanchien there was more food than in a big city, but only the
farmers really had enough. The quarry workers earned seven francs an
hour, but the purchasing power of the franc had almost vanished, so
textiles and matches and tools and clothing and tea and coffee, which
came from outside Comblanchien, cost incredible amounts. These workers, who had only little patches of ground in which to grow things, could
raise just a few vegetables and rabbits and chickens. They ate the vegetables and bartered their chickens and eggs and rabbits for such treasures
as spools of thread to repair their clothes, or bits of leather with which the
Comblanchien cobbler could patch their shoes. They seldom got meat
and, though they lived in a wine-growing district, they rarely could afford
to drink wine. The vineyard workers were in much the same predicament.
Many couples in Comblanchien serve both the regional industries; the
husband works in a quarry and the wife works in the vineyards. The
commune owns some woods, and on Sunday the laborers of Comblanchien would cut enough firewood to last them the week. The buses
which ran along the highway were infrequent and overcrowded; the men
and women who were employed in other villages of the region couldn't be
sure that they could ride to work. Only the relatively well-off owned
bicycles, so people often walked five or six miles to work every day and
back again at night, hurrying to get home before the nine-thirty curfew
the Germans had imposed. There was not much chance for the people of
Comblanchien to do any poaching; the Germans had attempted to confiscate all the sporting guns in the region, and the peasants who had defied
the order to disarm and had retained their weapons kept them carefully
hidden against the day they would have something more important than
partridges to shoot. Besides, the German soldiers, who were always
underfed, killed most of the game in the country. They shot at anything
edible and even dynamited streams and fish ponds.

There were, it is true, some residents of Comblanchien upon whom the
German occupation imposed no material privations. These were the
dozen or so well-to-do farmers who were getting such high prices in Dijon
that they were accumulating great wads of banknotes, although in a
currency that shrank in value every day. But even they felt the oppression
of something worse than want. The mere presence of Germans made
everyone feel subhuman. The sound of German voices filled the farmers

with a *malaise*, like the sound of rats scurrying within the walls of a house. The Mayor, M. Moron, was the wealthiest man of the commune. He owned a large pink building on the west side of the road, where he made and stored wine, and a good solid stone house on the east side of the road, where he lived. He was a tall, rather good-looking man, but no hero. *"Pas d'histoires"* was his motto, which might be freely interpreted to mean "For God's sake, no trouble." Moron is a common surname in Burgundy and has no pejorative connotation. The next wealthiest citizen was the deputy mayor and president of the communal council, M. Chopin. Chopin is also a Burgundian name. Chopin is a good solid chunk of a man with a bull neck and a strong, big-barrelled body like that of one of his prize plow horses. Both men regarded the Germans with a mixture of apprehension and dislike, the first sentiment dominating in M. Moron and the second in the more choleric Chopin.

One person in Comblanchien who did not seem to mind the presence of the Germans overmuch was Robert Ravigneaux, a café proprietor, whose bar was often filled with German soldiers who travelled the National Highway in convoys by night and stopped at Comblanchien to drink. Ravigneaux overcharged them for their drinks, and he told the townspeople that this was his form of resistance. The convoys didn't travel by day, because they were afraid of an Allied air attack. But even with their limited hours, they always seemed to have time to stop for refreshments, and there were no German equivalents of the "Off Limits" sign posted on the roadside cafés. Ravigneaux was a noisy, quarrelsome fellow who was not a native of the region—he had come to Comblanchien from the northeast of France five years before the war. He had an artificial left leg which was painted a pale flesh pink and on which he wore a sock and garter, just as he did on his other leg. When he got drunk, he would pull up the trouser of his amputated leg, slap the painted wood, and tell people that he had lost his leg in the last war, although everybody in Comblanchien knew that in 1944 he was only thirty-nine. Ravigneaux was drunk much of the time; it was his handsome, full-bosomed wife who watched the cash.

From time to time after the surrender of France, German soldiers were stationed in Comblanchien, in the Occupied Zone, and then withdrawn. In May, 1944, a new detachment arrived and moved into the château. This unit was known in Comblanchien as the Schoning Company, because it was commanded by Oberleutnant Schoning, a naval reservist who in civil life had been an architect in Kiel. The men under him were Marines. The Germans had found little for their Marine Corps to do aboard a portbound navy, so they had assigned detachments from it to various duties all over Europe. Schoning had about fifty men. Their job was to patrol the area, and chiefly the railroad, between Beaune and

Nuits-St. Georges, to guard against sabotage. The Oberleutnant was not much of a warrior. He was forty—just too young to have fought in the other war and just too old to have received any concentrated military training in the Nazi regime. He lived in fear that "terrorists" would attack the château, although the region is not really adapted to serious guerrilla warfare; it is too well cultivated and thickly inhabited. The vineyards would make excellent cover for a few snipers, but men cannot lie flat on their bellies for long. Schoning had been taken in by the Reich's propaganda. He saw terrorists everywhere. Soon after he arrived, he issued an order that every one of his men must learn to operate a field telephone so he could call the *Feld-gendarmerie* at Beaune immediately if the château were attacked. "The lives of each and all of us may depend on his comrades' presence of mind," Schoning's order read. What he lacked as a fighting man he made up for by abnormal arrogance, a phenomenon not confined to the German Army. He snarled and shouted constantly. Also, he never appeared outside the château without a machine pistol under his arm. As a joke, he invariably poked this weapon in Madame Ravigneaux's face when he visited the café. He was there often; he was an alcoholic, like Ravigneaux, himself a snarling man. There was something congenial to Schoning in the other disagreeable presence, although Schoning spoke no French and neither Ravigneaux nor his wife knew any German. The Oberleutnant's ignorance of French increased his suspicion of the citizenry. If anybody in Comblanchien laughed within his hearing, he was sure a joke had been made about him, and he would order the interpreter in his company, an Alsatian named Paul Zenses, to translate what had been said. Zenses had been drafted into the German Marines after the Nazis had "incorporated" Alsace and Lorraine into the Reich, in November, 1940. When Schoning was not with him, the Alsatian was on friendly terms with some of the local people. However, Schoning communicated his edginess to the rest of his men, and the groups that patrolled the railroad frequently fired at animals or shadows, thinking they were Maquis. People got used to hearing bursts of fire at night and thought nothing of them.

There had never been any special reason Schoning should fear an attack or the people of Comblanchien should have been subjected to any unusual repressive measures. There had been no acts of resistance in Comblanchien since the beginning of the occupation, although a number of the men there belonged to Maquis groups that operated elsewhere in the region. Some of these men had joined a group that had been established in a nearby district immediately after D Day, when General Koenig, in London, had called all the French Forces of the Interior to rise in active resistance, but after these orders had been countermanded, the Comblanchien men had returned to their homes, with the exception of two who had got themselves shot. Now the local Maquis affair had apparently blown over, and anyhow everybody was too busy in the vineyards and fields to worry about it. Protracted panic is a luxury beyond the means of working people. If the local Germans had wanted to make trouble, however, an opportunity lay at hand. All the men who had been in the Maquis could be distinguished by the new shoes that the resistance organization had distributed to them. The shoes were of Army issue and had been hidden from the Germans when the French military were officially disbanded, in 1942. The shoes were too good to give up, even if they did identify the wearers as men subject to the death penalty. Jordan used to go about telling the youths to stain their shoes and scuff them. But the Germans in the château were too stupid to notice such things, the men figured.

By late August the inhabitants of Comblanchien had almost forgotten the affair of the Maquis, except for the young blowhards, who sometimes drank and boasted about the feats they claimed they had brought off. The *garde-champêtre* of Comblanchien, who is not precisely Hercule Poirot, had been in the Maquis too, and he was soon going about telling people he had killed five Germans, which was, to put it mildly, inexact. Even M. Moron breathed easy. He had been summoned to the château to talk to Schoning three times, and each time he had gone in the fear that he would be held as a hostage. On the first occasion, Schoning had merely wanted to tell him that the water supply at the château was inadequate and that he would have to send a hogshead of water up the hill to him every day. The second time Schoning wanted to complain that the water had not been delivered promptly one morning. Schoning had been exceedingly nasty about it and had shouted even louder than usual. The third time Schoning was furious because a woman who had been doing housework for the Germans refused to come any more. She said she was sick, but the Mayor suspected that her husband, who worked in a quarry, had told her to give up her job at the château. The other workmen had probably threatened him. Schoning had ordered the Mayor to find a substitute, but he had been unable to find one. However, M. Moron had not been bothered again.

There was a great deal of work to do late in August. Most families, taking advantage of the double daylight-saving time, worked in their gardens right up to the nine-thirty curfew before going indoors to begin their suppers. A minute or two after curfew on the evening of Monday, August 21st, an hour easy to fix in the memory because the soup had just been put on everyone's table, a bell rang in the cottage of the watchman at the more southerly of the two grade crossings in the commune to warn of the approach of an unexpected train from the south. This crossing, No. 191 on the railway maps, is something less than a mile from the other, No. 190, and between them the rails run through a shallow cut. The passing of an unscheduled train was not unusual. The Germans had been using the railroad to move troops and matériel up toward Normandy. This sort of activity had increased since the Allied landings in the Midi on August 15th, because the Germans were systematically withdrawing from the south of France, evacuating base units as well as fighting troops. The watchman at No. 191 was, and is, Louis Maublanc, a youth of nineteen, who lives in the cottage with his widowed mother and a swarm of small brothers and sisters. A moment after the bell rang, Maublanc went out to close the swing gates of the crossing. He went over the track to close the farther gate and had just got back on his own side of the track when the train came along. It was a long train, he remembers—perhaps fifty cattle cars, filled with troops. French railroad cars are small, but even figuring only forty men in each, there were two thousand soldiers. They were carrying rifles, tommy-guns, and machine guns. The engine stopped on the crossing. Some officers got out of the cars, walked up to the locomotive, and spoke to the engineer. Maublanc says that he heard the man shout something about Comblanchien, so the officers had probably asked where they were.

There is a story in the countryside that the train was deliberately stopped at Comblanchien, but that is not true. The train stopped at Comblanchien because there was another train on the track at Nuits-St. Georges, three miles north. Many of the men in the cars were drunk and were singing and howling at each other. It is hard to tell when German soldiers are angry, the French say, because they are always howling anyway. The cars must have been well stocked with wine—the right of way where the train had stopped was littered with empty bottles next day— and the noncommissioned officers aboard were taking no notice of all the drunkenness. This did not seem unusual to Maublanc. German soldiers heading north were never happy; they undoubtedly sensed, despite their own propaganda, that things were going badly up there and that they might be killed. So they were generally drunk. Dusk was coming on, but there was still enough light, Maublanc noted regretfully, to work by in the gardens, if he hadn't had to go indoors because of the curfew. He was looking toward the west, where the sunset colors were fading in the sky. Suddenly he saw a burst of tracer bullets flying from the western slope. At once the Germans in the train started shouting much more loudly than they had done before. Some of them began firing machine guns in the general direction the bullets had come from. Others piled out of the cars and flung themselves flat along the tracks. Twenty of them poured into the Maublancs' cottage and pointed machine pistols at the widow Maublanc and her little children. Other soldiers grabbed Maublanc by his arms and throat. In all the things being shouted at him, he could distinguish one word again and again—"*Terroristen!*"—a word that even Frenchmen who speak no German understand. Meanwhile, somebody gave an order and the train moved past the crossing and into the cut, whose embankment offered some protection from the fire from the slope.

The train was so long that when it stopped the locomotive was almost at grade crossing No. 190. From the new position the machine gunners on the train laid down a real barrage. There was a volley of answering machine-gun fire from the west. Many villagers believe that the Germans attacked Comblanchien with malice aforethought and that they invented the story of the shots directed at the train. It has been established, however, that there actually was firing from the west. A few hundred yards west of the railroad line there is a poplar tree. When Jordan went over the ground, weeks later, he found bullets in both the east and west sides of the trunk and that many branches had been cut away from it. Lambert, the crossing watchman at No. 190, says that he saw five German soldiers on the train hit, but this testimony was impossible to check, because the train, when it did leave, carried away all the soldiers it had arrived with. Young Maublanc, who, like every other inhabitant of the region, knew that there was not a force of resistants within a hundred miles capable of attacking two thousand soldiers, was as puzzled as the Germans. The soldiers who had seized him finally flung him to the ground and left him there. Why they didn't kill him he doesn't know. As for his mother, she was so confused that she can recall almost nothing of what happened.

Nobody knows, and possibly nobody ever will know, who fired those first shots. Most probably, Jordan thinks, one of Oberleutnant Schoning's timorous, trigger-happy patrols let off a few rounds at a shadow in the vineyards, as the patrols often had before. It is known that two patrols were out when the shooting began. There is nothing to indicate that the first shots were aimed at the train or even came near it. The source of the heavier west-to-east fire which, a few minutes later, answered the barrage from the train is not mysterious. By what seems clearly to have been a coincidence, a German motor convoy had stopped on the National Highway in Comblanchien at the same time the train halted at the first grade crossing. It consisted of a dozen vehicles, each manned by a driver and a helper. There may have been in the group a couple of *Volkswagen* carrying officers, and perhaps some trucks had aboard a few hitch-hiking soldiers, but in all there could not have been more than fifty men. However, some of the trucks had machine guns mounted for use against strafing airplanes. The men in the convoy were scattered among the cafés of Comblanchien when the soldiers on the train began firing toward the highway. The convoy men, in their turn, shouted "*Terroristen!*" and ran to their machine guns. The fire was by now coming from two directions, most of it far overhead. Some of the convoy soldiers, therefore, fired to the east, toward the gun flashes they could see below them from the railroad; others fired west toward some flashes they saw.

Oberleutnant Schoning, who was finishing his dinner in the château when the firing from the train started, was immediately frightened. "Terrorists have begun their attack on the château!" he shouted to Zenses, who has since told Jordan what happened in the château that night. No one else had heard, or at any rate paid attention to, the first few shots from the slope. It was the shooting from the east that made the first impression. The machine guns at the château immediately began firing in the direction of the supposed attack. It is not known whether the fire from the château or from the trucks was responsible for the casualties—assuming there were any—on the train. The château was hit, but not many times. Jordan found a couple of bullet holes in it later, but it is not certain that Oberleutnant Schoning even knew the house had been struck. Zenses, who was sure that an attack on the château was beyond the means of the local resistance, felt that there was a horrible misunderstanding of some sort. The fire from the château, he feared, might hit the innocent people of Comblanchien, and he thought that perhaps Schoning could avert a massacre. After a couple of minutes of the firing, which did not seem to be directed at the château, Zenses suggested to the Oberleutnant that he be sent with a patrol down to the village to see what was happening. "I will take a patrol down there myself," Schoning said. "You will come with us." It was a heroic decision for the ex-architect; his pride had prevailed. The Oberleutnant and ten or fifteen of his men put on helmets, filled their belts with incendiary grenades, slung machine pistols over their shoulders, and went down to their usual destination, Ravigneaux's café.

Ravigneaux and his wife were in the café when the firing began. They heard the first burst and then the sustained fire. Some truck drivers from the convoy had been drinking there and they had run out without paying. That was all the Ravigneaux could tell Zenses. Schoning saw the convoy people firing from the trucks. There was still fire from the east, but it was going over their heads. Schoning said to Zenses, "There is some mistake, but I cannot do anything to stop it. You go back to the château. I have no more need for you." Zenses, before he went back to the château, paused in the village street and looked down toward the railroad, from which, he could readily see, many of the bullets were coming. It was now completely dark. As he looked across the vineyards, he saw a pillar of flame rise, halfway between the railroad and the highway, about where a peasant named Sergent lived. He realized even then that the Germans had begun to burn the village.

II

MAX HENRY was one of the most respected citizens of Comblanchien. However, he had a hard time bringing up his family after the German occupation began. He was not a farmer but a salaried man, one of the few white-collar workers in the village, and he owned only the bit of ground surrounding his house. All prices were high in occupied France, and a man on a fixed salary was in a bad position, especially if he had to maintain appearances. M. Henry had two grown children to educate—a twenty-year-old son, Claude, and a sixteen-year-old daughter, Denise. Both went to the college in Beaune, six miles south of Comblanchien, and they continued to go despite the occupation. By August last year, Claude had finished a course preparing him to be an officer in the merchant marine. He must have been an optimist to choose that career, as he did, shortly after the armistice with Germany, when the French merchant marine had almost ceased to exist. He was to go to Paris on September 20th to take his final examinations for a commission.

M. Henry was a bookkeeper at the Comblanchien quarry of Civet, Pommier & Company of Paris, dealers in cut stone. He had worked for the company for twenty-five years, the last thirteen of them in Comblanchien. He was in his early forties. During the first year of the war he had been acting superintendent of the quarry, for a brief period, after the superintendent had been mobilized, in September, 1939. Then, in the spring of 1940, M. Henry himself was mobilized and a rigger in the quarry was made temporary superintendent. After the demobilization, the company took M. Henry back, but only as a bookkeeper, and kept the rigger on as nominal superintendent. The original superintendent, who had got a higher salary than M. Henry had, was not rehired. M. Henry had to take over all the correspondence, because the ex-rigger was uneducated. So M. Henry was something more than bookkeeper, and his chief was something less than superintendent, and neither of them got a full superintendent's salary, which was probably the company's idea in the first place. M. Henry was paid twenty-eight hundred francs a month. This would not have been lavish for a man with two children in school even if the franc had had its prewar value, but the franc had lost almost all its purchasing power. Fortunately, the Henrys had their house and chicken yard and vegetable garden and enough vines to provide them with family table wine, and Mme. Henry was an excellent manager. She was a thin, worn-looking woman with high color in her cheeks and black hair drawn tight in a bun behind her head. She came from the Department of the Meuse, and her husband from Reims. Madame was decidedly better educated than the farm women of the community, but she worked as hard as any of them, and Claude and Denise worked too, when they were home. M. Henry was very tall and thin, so thin in proportion to his height that when he was a young man he had been excused from military service; in 1940 the Army was less particular and he was mobilized as a private.

Monday, August 21, 1944, was a hot day, and Claude and Denise, who were home from college, went swimming in a stream with friends. One of the friends took a picture of Claude posed on a diving board. Mme. Henry still has it. It shows a tall, long-legged boy with heavy eyebrows, a straight nose, and the French variant of the crew haircut. On the evening of August 21st, until nine-thirty, when the curfew imposed by the Germans compelled everybody in Comblanchien to go indoors, the whole Henry family picked string beans in the garden. Because of double daylight-saving time, it was still light at curfew, but they had to go into the house just the same. They washed up (there was a bathroom in the Henry house, which was one of the most modern in the village) and sat down to supper. Like many of the buildings in the commune, the house fronted on the National Highway, which ran through the village; it was on the east side of that thoroughfare. M. Henry had built it himself in 1931. The exterior was of simulated gray-stone, an unconvincing concretish substance, and the house had six rooms, four on the ground floor and two in a kind of turret above. The front door was in the middle of the house and opened into a hall. M. and Mme. Henry's bedroom was at the right on the ground floor as you went in. Denise's bedroom was behind theirs. The dining room was on the left side as you entered, and the kitchen and the bathroom were behind that. The staircase leading to the turret was in the hall, and a shorter flight of stairs in the back led down to the basement. Claude's bedroom was on the second floor, in back; at the front of the turret was a spare bedroom.

The family had begun supper in the dining room when, Mme. Henry told me several weeks ago, while I was in Comblanchien, they heard two shots which, she said, sounded "like a signal." The sounds did not alarm them, because the patrols from the company of German Marines frequently fired shots for trivial reasons; the idea that these shots were a "signal" is undoubtedly purely retrospective. Then there was a real outbreak of shooting. It seemed to come from the southeast and it was so loud that all the Henrys dropped to the floor. Mme. Henry remembers that as the family lay on the floor her husband pulled her away from the window. After a while there was a pause in the firing. M. Henry, perhaps to reassure the others, said that there was no accounting for Germans; he was going to bed. He went into his bedroom and began to undress. Mme. Henry followed him and sat down on the bed, but she was afraid to take her clothes off.

It happened that Claude Henry was a member of the Forces Françaises de l'Intérieur, and an effective one, but he had kept his activities so secret that not even his parents knew of them. He lived at home only during the college vacations and on weekends. He had helped in *coups de main* and acts of sabotage in parts of central France less accessible to the Germans than the Côte-d'Or, in which Comblanchien is situated, and had organized resistance groups in several villages. He had also tended a parachute strip on which Allied planes dropped arms for the Maquis. Claude, driving an old truck, would pick up the weapons and distribute them to comrades.

When, on the night of August 1st, his parents went to their bedroom,

Claude went upstairs to his room, which faced east and south. Denise followed him after a couple of minutes. Looking out a window, they saw, through the gathering darkness, gun flashes down along the railroad, which was half a mile away, and then Claude pointed out to her what he said were groups of Germans moving up along the two roads that wound through the Comblanchien vineyards toward the village. Some of the men had flashlights, which they swung about as if they were looking for something. They stuck pretty well to the roads; the Germans were always timid about going into the vineyards, where, they fancied, the broad leaves might conceal snipers. Then Claude and Denise saw a house, midway between the railroad and the highway, begin to burn. The flames rose very high in an instant; the Germans were undoubtedly using incendiary grenades, which are usually effective immediately. "They are coming this way!" Claude said, and he hurried Denise down into the basement, shouting to his parents to join them. Mme. Henry hastened downstairs, but M. Henry, the methodical, bookkeeping kind of man, stayed in his room to dress.

A moment later there was a great crash on the ground floor. Some of the Germans had hurled grenades through the window of the dining room, setting fire to the house, and others had fired machine pistols and automatic rifles through the front door, their favorite way of breaking a lock. The three in the cellar heard boots and gunstocks on the floor over their heads, and then they heard the soldiers shouting at Henry. Claude, who had had six years of German at school and college, knew that the intruders were questioning his father. Claude also knew that his father did not understand a word of the language, so he ran up from the basement. His sister went up the basement steps behind him, but ran out the back door into the garden, where she threw herself down among the vines. Mme. Henry remained in the basement, too frightened to move.

Before his son had appeared, Max Henry had come out into the hall from his bedroom, although he had not finished dressing. The Germans presumably pushed him back against the wall and poked the muzzles of their automatic weapons against his body. He must have waved his hands in protest; he must have heard again and again, without understanding, the German words for "concealed arms." Denise, lying in the garden, saw the window of her brother's room, on the second floor, light up and Claude appear, followed by three or four Germans. He was gesticulating, evidently trying to convince them that there were no weapons concealed there, and he was talking fast. "He was talking the entire time I could see him," Denise told me when I was in Comblanchien. "Then they all went out of the room."

The house was already burning, and a minute later the flames mounted high in the sky. A dozen Germans ran out the front door, shouting and laughing. The night should have been growing darker rapidly now, but there was still light in the village, because the Germans had set fire to a score of houses, and the highway was illuminated by the fires in the houses lining it. Neither Max nor Claude Henry came out of the house. Denise, cowering among the vines, heard her mother call her name. She called back, and Mme. Henry crawled through the garden to her daughter's side. She had come up from the basement and out the back door the moment the Germans left the house. Flames were roaring in both the dining room and the bedroom at the front of the house, but they had not got into the hall between them, Denise said. Mme. Henry, who earlier in the evening had been the most timid member of the family, now found a courage that still astonishes her. "Claude and Papa must be in there," she said to her daughter. "Let us go in and find them." The two women went into the house through the back door. Max Henry lay in front of the door to his bedroom. His head had been severed from his body, apparently by a burst of machine-gun bullets. His blood puddled the floor of the little house he had built for his family. Claude Henry was lying at the foot of the staircase, his feet resting on one of the lower steps. He lay with his once handsome face among his brains. The Germans had probably killed M. Henry while Claude was still frantically talking upstairs; Claude must still have hoped to save the elder Henry when Denise saw him in his room with the Germans. When Claude had reached a point on the stairs from which he could see his father's body, a German behind him had presumably shot him in the back of the neck with his revolver. Then another German, apparently, fired a redundant shot into the boy's head as he lay dead. "We must put the bodies in the basement, where they will be preserved from fire," the mother said. The slight woman and the strong girl picked up the butchered bodies of their men—first the father and then the son—and carried them down into the basement. One of them must have made a third trip for Max Henry's head. The bodies were not touched by the fire and later received a proper burial. The women went outside again, but Mme. Henry, acting as incomprehensibly as people often do in crises, said, "The fire hasn't caught upstairs yet; maybe we can save some bed coverings and a mattress. They will be almost impossible to replace." So they went in and got some blankets. The flames reached upstairs before they could make another trip for a mattress.

Mme. Henry and her daughter lay in the garden all night. Houses were burning everywhere and there were intermittent bursts of gunfire. German soldiers passed back and forth on the highway a few yards from the two women, carrying things they had stolen from wrecked houses—quilts and chandeliers and chamber pots. They loaded them onto the dozen or so trucks of the convoy that had halted in the village that night. The magpie compulsion of a German soldier is hard to believe unless one has seen German trucks overflowing with a ragman's treasure of miserable household wares, wrecked along a roadside after a strafing.

The Henry house was one of a row of four on the highway that stood a little apart from the rest of the village. A woman named Gabut was in the house next to the Henrys', with her four children, when the enemy came. The Henry women heard her shrieking to the Germans not to kill her after her house had been set afire. She said afterward that she thought she had been spared because she had a crippled, subnormal child that could not stand up. A German pulled the child from its crib, and when the child fell to the floor he became interested in it. The crisis of blood lust past, he ran out of the house without killing the woman.

On the other side of Mme. Gabut's house was the house of a man named Salomon, a Communist who had led an abortive Maquis uprising near Comblanchien in June. Salomon had left the village some time ago, but his wife and her sister had lived in the house during most of the summer. This night, however, they, too, were away. It is logical that if this outbreak of arson and murder had been a premeditated punitive expedition against Comblanchien the Germans would have gone immediately to Salomon's house, since he was a known "terrorist." But they did not. The fourth house in the row was inhabited by a sixty-three-year-old man named Joseph Blanc, a retired postal employee living on a pension, and his wife and daughter. The Blancs, like their neighbors, must have trembled when they saw the Gabut and Henry dwellings burning. They ran to the basement of their house, but the Germans left them alone, at least for the moment. Two widows, mother and daughter, who lived not far from the Henrys but on the other side of the highway, were less fortunate. One of these women, Mme. Chapuzot, the mother, was sixty-eight. She worked in the vineyards when there was work for her and made mattresses at home when there was none. Her daughter, Mme. Voye, was forty-six, a cheerful, hardworking woman who hoed in the vineyards, did housework, and washed bottles for the wine merchants whenever she had a chance. The Henry women heard these two widows shrieking and begging the Germans to spare them, but the soldiers killed them both. It is hard to imagine that the Germans thought the two women dangerous. They were killing now simply because they had had a taste of blood, like weasels loose in a chicken yard.

At a farm in the commune they killed a young farm laborer named Marcel Julien. He was a pleasant, uneducated boy of eighteen who, unlike many Frenchmen of his age, had never been in the Maquis or done anything untoward. The Germans spared the other men on the farm, however. Their choice of victims that night was entirely capricious. The men who saw Julien killed say that the German who shot him was wearing shorts and an undershirt, carried a carbine, and was "slobbering" with fury. This led the people who later tried to reconstruct the massacre to think that this particular murderer must have come from the German truck convoy and not the troop train. German Army truck drivers were known to discard their outer clothes in hot weather. After some of the soldiers from the train had reached the National Highway and encountered the men from the truck convoy, who numbered about fifty, both parties must have realized that they had been firing at each other and not at an attack of what they called *Terroristen*. At any rate, the exchange of shots between the two groups ceased. The killing and burning, however, went on uninterrupted. In fact, it was now on a partnership basis. Some of the inhabitants of Comblanchien say that they recognized, among the soldiers attacking the houses, several of the Marines in Oberleutnant Schoning's detachment, but identifications in such circumstances are undependable. It is certain, however, that at eleven-thirty, an hour and a half after the murder of the two Henrys and the two widows, a band of Germans went to the Salomon house and began shouting for the "terrorist women" to come out. They must have meant Salomon's wife and sister-in-law, and this indicates to the man who has made the most careful study of the massacre—M. Jordan, the sergeant of gendarmes from Corgoloin—that officers from the troop train must have made contact with Schoning sometime between ten and eleven-thirty and asked him to point out the houses of people he suspected of "terrorism." In the absence of the Salomon women, the Germans set fire to the house and then went on to Blanc's, next door. They demanded that Blanc hand over the women, whom they said he was sheltering. The old man shook his head helplessly, and they shot him to death. They also fired at and wounded his wife and daughter, but the women escaped and managed to hide in the vineyards.

M. and Mme. Blaise Lieutard were a couple of retired railroad employees who had built themselves a house not far from the Henrys', fifty yards back from the road. They had lived in Comblanchien nine years. They had both worked in the Gare de Lyon, in Paris, for thirty years, he as an electrician and she as a messenger in the railway offices, and they had a joint pension of a thousand francs a month. The Lieutards had come to Comblanchien after their retirement because Mme. Lieutard's sister, Mme. Gauthron, lived there and Mme. Lieutard wanted to be near her. Mme. Gauthron was the village dressmaker and was married to a stone-cutter in one of the quarries. M. Lieutard was a wiry little southern Frenchman of sixty, but, as his wife says when recounting her story of the dreadful night, "he looked older because he had had so much trouble." In Comblanchien the Lieutards had practiced severe economies, like all French couples of their type, who save throughout their working lives for the house they will build when they reach the pension age. Their pink stucco house—four rooms and a kitchen—might have seemed exiguous and jerry-built even to a promoter of Long Island building developments, but to Mme. Lieutard it was the fulfillment of a lifetime's hopes. She is a short woman with a broad, flat face and straggly, faded blond hair. Her eyes are blue-white and she has stubby little hands and feet; she could not have been pretty even when she was young, but her face, when she talks of the past glories of the little house, is radiant. On the ground floor there were two rooms and a storage "cellar." There was no inside stair-case; to get to the second floor you walked up stone stairs on the outside of the house. The Lieutards had what Mme. Lieutard called a Louis Quinze bedroom, on which they had spent twenty thousand francs. In a corner of this room, and in a corner of the living room, which adjoined it, there were green-enamelled fireplaces. In the kitchen was a magnificent green metal salamander for heating water and a sink into which water ran from a long, convoluted pipe about as thick as a strand of macaroni. They had fine curtains on all the windows, and two overstuffed chairs which would have attracted attention in the window of any furniture store on the outer boulevards of Paris. Madame is in despair when she thinks of it. They were very comfortably off before the war, when the franc still had some value. Besides their pension, they had the usual chicken yard and garden and cages of fat rabbits, which were a joy as well as an auxiliary source of nourishment. Like all rustic French workers who have had to live in the city for a long time, they took immense pleasure in their return to the country. They had but one cause for anxiety: their only daughter, a Mme. Pascal, was a widow, her husband having died shortly after the Lieutards retired. She had two children, a boy and a girl. Her husband had left her no money and she had had to go back to her old job in the material office in the Gare de Lyon. Her parents, however, were able to help her out now and then with a few hundred francs or a fine hamper of country *charcuterie*.

Living conditions did not become difficult for the Lieutards until after the armistice. Under the Germans, it was impossible for them to live on their pension and send anything to their daughter and her children, so M. Lieutard went back to work, as chief electrician at the railroad station in Beaune. His salary was seventeen hundred francs a month, but his pen-sion stopped, since he was now working again, so his income was only seven hundred francs a month more than it had been. M. Lieutard had no bicycle and could not afford to buy one, so he walked the six miles to Beaune and back every day. "And he had slightly flat feet," Mme. Lieutard recalls. Walking made him very hungry, but food was even more expensive in Beaune than in Comblanchien, so he had to eat in the workmen's restaurant there. It served nothing but vegetables and noodles, and all the cooking was *à l'eau*, which is repugnant to most Frenchmen, who believe that boiling takes all the nourishment out of food. When he got home at night, he was sometimes so hungry that there were tears in his eyes. He often ate bread with mustard on it, for lack of meat. When the chickens laid, the Lieutards had to barter the eggs for thread or salt or other necessities they could not afford to buy, and when they killed a chicken it went into the package they sent to Paris every week for their grandchildren. Sometimes M. Lieutard did not dare look at the rabbits, for fear he would be impelled to kill one and stew it, and thus enrage his wife. Cigarettes were of course beyond his means, so he planted a little tobacco in the garden. He had heard that it should be dried in the sun, but he never had the patience to wait; he would put the green leaves on the stove and try to toast them dry, so that he could smoke them immediately. Early in 1944, the Lieutards' daughter, who had saved up some money, decided that it would be easier to feed and lodge the children in the country than in Paris, even without her job, so she came to join her parents and brought the children with her. The girl was fifteen, the boy thirteen. She confided her savings—twenty-five thousand francs—to her mother for safekeeping. Mme. Lieutard hid the money in one of her overstuffed chairs, one that had cost three thousand francs. The Lieutards were happy to have their daughter and her children with them. Mme. Pascal helped her aunt, Mme. Gauthron, with the dressmaking, and the children went to school. It was no longer necessary to send packages to Paris, so M. Lieutard got a taste of meat once in a while now. During the summer the old electrician watched the German troop trains that passed through the station in Beaune and drew his own conclusions about how the war was going for *"ces messieurs."* He talked to the train crews, who told him about air bombardments and sabotage along the line. He became optimistic, and used to say to his wife, "When this is over, we will offer ourselves a nice faceful of food and then we will repaint the house."

When Lieutard heard the firing begin on the night of August 21st, he summoned his family into the storage "cellar," a windowless part of the ground floor. The women were in their slips—they slept together upstairs —while Lieutard, exiled from his Louis Quinze room, shared a room on the ground floor with his grandson. "It was a genteel little room with green walls and folding beds," Mme. Lieutard says with infinite regret. The Germans ran up to the house and entered it. The Lieutards and Pascals slipped unnoticed out the back door of the "cellar" and into the garden, but there they were trapped, for they were fenced in by chicken wire except at the front of the house, and if they went out that way, they would run into the Germans. M. Lieutard tried to tear his way through the wire at the side of the house. A German soldier, coming from Mme. Lieutard does not know where, turned a flashlight on him. Mme. Lieutard, Mme. Pascal, and the two children took refuge behind a hen coop and lay flat on their bellies. Mme. Pascal's legs are long and her feet extended beyond the shelter. It was mere chance that the German didn't see them. M. Lieutard turned toward the light and said, in a faint voice, *"Qu'est ce que c'est?"* "He sounded as if his throat was stopped up, my little man," Mme. Lieutard says. The German fired—an explosive bullet that went in at Lieutard's right collarbone and came out the middle of his back, leaving an opening as big as a saucer. The inoffensive little man crumpled on the bit of garden earth he had spaded up so many times in the past nine years. "He bled! he bled!" Mme. Lieutard says. "He had planted celery on that spot, but he bled so much the celery never came up. They killed him like a wild boar." Mme. Lieutard's comparison seemed to accentuate the difference rather than the similarity between poor Blaise Lieutard and a savage beast. The German leaned over the stricken man and put his weapon to the victim's head and blew it to bits. Then he went away, shouting for his companions, probably to show them what he had done.

The women, clawing at the fence behind the chicken coop with a strength they had never suspected they had, were able to make a small opening between the wire and a fence post, and through this the children and then the mother and grandmother succeeded in wriggling. They crawled on all fours through a field of wheat stubble, lacerating their hands and knees and tearing their light garments to shreds, before they reached the nearest vineyard, where they hid under the leaves like vermin. And from between the vines Mme. Lieutard saw her small house, her treasure, burn. The overstuffed chair with Mme. Pascal's twenty-five thousand francs in it burned, too. Some of the chickens and rabbits survived, and Mme. Lieutard, who now lives with her sister, visits the ruined house morning and evening to feed them. I discovered her there when I visited Comblanchien. "I found a fork among the ashes today," she said, "but it was all black and twisted. We had such pretty tableware! Oh, Monsieur, if they had not burned the house, I would have had a roof to shelter my head and I would have had all our things to remind me of my poor husband! Or if they had not killed him, we could have got along without the house; we would have had each other! But this way they have left me nothing."

The Germans also killed a seventy-two-year-old man named Simonot, a stonecutter, but no witness to the crime remains in Comblanchien. Simonot lived with a spinster sister even older than himself, and she has moved away from Comblanchien.

Not even the bar of the irascible Robert Ravigneaux escaped. When Schoning and his interpreter, Paul Zenses, visited the café early that evening, as the trouble was just beginning, Schoning advised Ravigneaux and his wife to close their shutters and stay indoors. But at midnight the couple, in their bedroom, heard someone shouting, "Robert! Robert!" Whoever was calling sounded the final "t," which is silent in French but is pronounced in German. With that they heard a crashing in of shutters and windows, as if gun butts were being used on them, and then grenades exploded on the first floor. The house caught fire immediately and

Ravigneaux and his wife barely had time to save themselves. "It must have been the *salauds* from the château," the surly innkeeper says, "because the others wouldn't have known my name. That's what you get for treating the Germans decently. Not that I was ever friendly with them!" he adds hastily when other villagers are listening. He is not a popular man.

The Mayor of Comblanchien, M. Moron, was more fortunate. The Germans came to his house, said they were going to burn it, and ordered him and his wife to get out. Mme. Moron told them that her little girl was ill and had a high fever, and Moron's son, a classmate of the unfortunate Claude Henry at the college in Beaune, talked to them in German. They finally left the house without setting fire to it, but they carried away a small barrel of wine. The survival of the Mayor's residence and his wine warehouse, across the road, did nothing to increase his popularity with his less fortunate fellow-citizens, but it seems to have been sheer chance. Of a hundred-odd buildings in the village, the Germans burned fifty-two, and their decision to spare some was apparently as haphazard as their decision to destroy the others. In addition to killing eight people, the Germans arrested twenty-four men and boys. They put these prisoners aboard the troop train, announcing that they would carry them away as hostages. The selection of the hostages was as inexplicable as everything else about the affair. One of them was a boy of fourteen, and none of them were important citizens—not, for example, the Mayor, the deputy mayor, or the town clerk. Next day, at Dijon, the Germans released twelve of the hostages. All had expected to be shot. The Germans put the twelve others aboard a train for Germany, but when the train was bombed by American planes, two more of the prisoners escaped. They eventually made their way back to Comblanchien. The remaining ten have not been heard from.

The shooting, burning, and looting continued until dawn. In the middle of the night, a truck rolled up from the *Feld-gendarmerie* at Beaune, hauling a field gun. By that time it must have been obvious to all the Germans that they had not been attacked, as they may have thought at first, by the resistance forces, but the gunners fired a dozen rounds at the town hall and church. They hit the belfry of the town hall, knocking off a piece of stone bearing the letters "R.F." (République Française), but did no other damage. Shell cases found on the highway show that the gun was a thirty-seven-millimetre piece. This shelling was probably done for "moral effect." At dawn the truck convoy went on its way, the soldiers in it singing happily. The Germans from the troop train marched back to their cars in cadenced step, singing manly songs about morning in the forest and village maidens with dewy eyes. Oberleutnant Schoning had already gone to the château. In the vineyards, haggard women peered through the leaves at the smoking sockets of their houses.

Toward eight in the morning, it was discovered that the church was burning. The iron grille at the entrance had been locked, and the Germans, after firing a few ineffective shots at the lock in an attempt to break it, had gone off on some other drunken inspiration. But probably an incendiary bullet or grenade, going through a window, had started a smoldering fire that burst into flames hours later. M. Gilles, chief of the commune's volunteer fire company, and M. Chopin, the deputy mayor, went to the Mayor and asked for the key to the engine house, so that they could get out the fire engine. The Mayor said that the Germans had started the fire and might renew the massacre if an attempt were made to save the church. He refused permission to take out the engine, and the church burned to the ground.

Later in the day some of the Germans from the château appeared on the highway. They pointed to the ruins of the town and shouted, "*Boom boom kaput! Terroristen kaput!*" They seemed to find the scene amusing and laughed a great deal, but they made no move to attack any of the people they saw rummaging in the ruins of their houses. Schoning communicated with nobody in the village from then on. During the first week in September he and his Marine detachment evacuated the château and left town. French and American troops arrived in Comblanchien on September 7th.

While the fires were still at their height on the night of the massacre, M. Jordan, the gendarme from Corgoloin, came secretly to Comblanchien to see what was happening there. M. Jordan is a sallow, long-faced man with a hawk nose and a grizzled mustache. He is intelligent and logical and has a professional fondness for phrases like "reconstitution of the crime," since for the past sixteen years he has been a police officer. Until he fled to join the Maquis a couple of weeks before the massacre, M. Jordan had been a *maréchal des logis,* or sergeant, of the national gendarmerie. For the sixteen years of his service he had been stationed at the *gendarmerie* nearest Comblanchien, in the neighboring commune of Corgoloin, so he was intimately acquainted with the district and all its people. During the occupation he had pretended to help the Germans, but he had consistently forewarned everybody he was instructed to arrest. He had salvaged a few weapons so damaged that the Germans had thrown them away, and he had painfully and ingeniously repaired them, so he and the three gendarmes under him were armed with carbines and a submachine gun in addition to the gimcrack revolver and nine rounds per man the Germans allowed French gendarmes to retain. The four gendarmes had gone into the Maquis after they had been warned of an impending raid upon their cache of arms. On the night of the massacre, M. Jordan remained in Comblanchien for an hour watching the Germans. He realized by then that he could do nothing to amend matters, so he crawled off through the vineyards until he got well away, because, even though there was no moon, the flames cast a brilliant light. After the liberation, he returned to the *gendarmerie* at Corgoloin. As soon as he had cleared up a few routine matters, like the arrest of a couple of Germans in civilian clothes who remained in the region, he began a careful investigation of the slaughter of his fellow-citizens at Comblanchien. His findings have not pleased all his neighbors, for people everywhere like to believe in diabolical plots, and M. Jordan has not been able to establish that there was one.

When he began his inquiry, there was already a story in the countryside that the arrival of the train and of the truck convoy at Comblanchien had been coördinated that night for the purpose of making an attack on the village. It had become an article of faith that the few shots before the massacre were a prearranged signal. "The few shots, of course, might have been a signal," Jordan says, "but there had been shots like them in the night on dozens of previous occasions, always proceeding from those nervous Marine patrols. As to the thesis that there really was an attack on the train by men of the resistance and that the Germans fired in defense, I am in a position to say that it cannot be sustained. There were no F.F.I. patrols in Comblanchien that night. Moreover, if the handful of men of Comblanchien had meditated anything so mad as an attack on a two-thousand-man troop train, would Claude Henry, an F.F.I. officer, have been picking string beans in the garden when the train arrived?"

M. Jordan also heard in the countryside a story that people had seen rockets fired from the château before the attack began, but he could never actually find these people. There was also a story that Schoning's Marines had appeared, completely equipped for battle, at the Ravigneaux café an hour before the first shots, but M. and Mme. Ravigneaux and Paul Zenses, the Alsatian interpreter, who subsequently deserted from the German Army and joined up with the French, agreed that Schoning had appeared in the café *after* the firing started. There was also a very persistent report that the German commander of the troop train had insisted, at Corgoloin, the station below Comblanchien, that "the train must go through because we have to get to Comblanchien this evening." The Corgoloin station-master told Jordan that the officer had wanted to get as far as Dijon, not Comblanchien, and that the train had stopped there only because another one was ahead of it. "The strongest argument against the thesis of a deliberate punitive attack on Comblanchien," Jordan says, "is the fact that if they had wanted to kill all the people, the Germans could have remained on the scene the next day and killed them at their leisure. But they didn't. Well, then, there was no premeditation. Well, then, what happened?

"This is what happened. Two detachments of Germans, arriving here simultaneously from two directions, with their customary brutality exacerbated by fear and chagrin, frightened each other into an exchange of shots. The precipitating influence was probably one of the patrols from the château, which were always frightened. The patrol fired two or three shots and soldiers on the train replied with a massive fusillade. Those of the truck convoy replied to this fusillade with a nourished fire. The château joined in. Train and convoy fired on the château. This I know because I have found imbedded in the château two machine-gun bullets that came into it through open windows. No glass is broken, but remember that it was a hot night. One bullet had entered at such an acute upward angle that it was lodged in a ceiling. It must therefore have been fired from the road directly below the château. The other had lodged in a wall almost on a level with the window sill and therefore must have been fired on an only slightly rising trajectory—from the train on the other side of the village. The evidence of a poplar tree, standing between train and convoy, and blasted by fire from the two directions, proves that the Germans fired on each other.

"Now, however, please remark that I do not exonerate these brutes for what they did. Mistakes sometimes occur, even in armies which, like the German, propagate a legend of their own perfect discipline and skill at warfare. If some innocent inhabitants of the village had been caught in the crossfire and wounded, that would have been regrettable but not a crime of war. But notice—the Germans descended from the train and killed eight persons in their houses, firing point blank. These persons were not only unarmed; of the eight, three were men more than sixty years old and two were women, persons unlikely to be dangerous. They did not kill only in the first access of fury, because it was an hour and a half after the first attack that they killed old man Blanc. Long after they discovered their mistake, they continued to burn houses. What was their crime? In my opinion, any court would convict them of murder."

Afterword

I have been advised to write an epilogue to this book to "give it unity" and "put it in perspective," but I find this difficult, because war, unlike drama, has no unities, classical or otherwise. It is discursive, centrifugal, both repetitive and disparate. Also, I have never got it into perspective myself— It is sometimes as much part of now as then, particularly the moment when I saw the blood mixed with milk. ("The symbolism was too obvious," a literary friend said to me afterward, mistaking me for a creative writer.) Also, although I am a rationalist without belief in the hereafter, some of the pieces are irrationally filled with spooks, like the dead airplane crew in "Run," that wanted me to fly with them, and this makes it hard for me to write about these stories—they must speak for themselves.

A.J.L.

NORMANDY REVISITED

To Moran, Frere, and Simone

Contents

FOREWORD

In 1943 I wrote a book called *The Road Back to Paris*, but the title was merely predictive. It was, in fact, about the road I followed from Paris, via the French retreat of 1940, the neutral United States of 1941 in which Lend-Lease had just squeaked through, and England as the English began to get their second wind. The road led to the United States again in an uneventful 42-day convoy, during which the Norwegian tanker crew and I learned through the radio operator that the United States was in the war. Then it led back to Britain, and to North Africa, which was the visible turning. I did not get back to France until June 1944. We moved so fast on the true Road Back then that I had no time to write another book, although correspondents turned them out quickly in those days, throwing the manuscripts over their shoulders in the general direction of the United States while continuing to advance intrepidly for the glory of their employers.

I wrote despatches for *The New Yorker* on fighting, politics, and peasantry (none of the stories I wrote then are in this book) and arrived home three days before Christmas 1944, with a great many memories that it would have done me good to write, if I had been ready.

After my return to peaceable preoccupations, my best therapist was a man named Joe Braun, who, with a partner named Harry Kaplan, runs a place called the Palace Bar & Grill on West Forty-fifth Street, between Longacre Square and Sixth Avenue. On the night of June 6, 1946, the second anniversary of D Day, I was in his place but without good friends and maudlin. Joe, who works nights, is a sallow man, calm, a cigar-chewer, and a speaker of the side-street New York language, which is flattened, unemotional, and unpolluted by Iobraskan or Virgissippian, the *Volksprache* of the Executive Belt to the east of his saloon, or by Hollywood-Jambonian, which is the Swahili of Sardi's, to the west. He talks like my father.

"Have you ever seen a deck awash with blood and condensed milk?" I asked him, as he broke ice cubes apart with the handle of the pick. He put ice in highball glasses, poured the accompanying whisky, and went away to serve the drinks. When he returned he said, "No." Then he moved away to serve more drinks, leaving me embittered by his insensitivity.

But when he came back next time he proved he had been considering what I said. He took his cigar out of his mouth, put it on the bar, and said, "If you seen that, Joe, it will stay with you."

After that, I knew it would, and I might as well leave it alone.

"Leave them alone, and they'll come home, wagging their tails behind them" is particularly true of memories. In time they recur in forms so implausible that you must go back and make sure the events they represent were real.

When this desire grew strong, I returned to a part of France that has a peculiarly personal relation to me, as I hope I make clear in the following narrative.

A.J.L.

"IF ONE American division could beat one German division, I thought then, a hundred American divisions could beat a hundred German divisions. Only the time was already past when Germany had a hundred divisions to spare from the Russian front, plus God knows how many more to fight the British, plus garrison troops for all the occupied countries. I knew . . . that the road back to Paris was clear."

—Last of The Road Back to Paris, *written in August 1943 and published in January 1944. The American division that beat the German division was the 1st Division, at El Guettar in Tunisia, in 1943.*

1 / Weymouth Pier

THE LONDON WEATHER, ominously good in late April, then bad through May, came bright again in the first week of June, reminding me of the stretch of weather before the embarkation for the Allied invasion of France in 1944, when I was in what a girl I knew then called a nugly mood. For at least a month before D Day, I was continuously angry at the press-relations officers of FUSAG (for First United States Army Group), a pre-invasion echelon destined never to function on the Continent under that name. I was equally angry with the correspondents of the major American news agencies and dailies in pre-invasion London, a number of whom I had until then considered my friends. (I now reconsider some of them such, but others I have never forgiven.) This was because the Army Group P.R.O.s, few of whom had ever heard a shot fired in anger—the old taunts come back to mind with the old combinations of initials—refused to let me accompany the 1st Division across the Channel, even though Major General Clarence Huebner, its commanding officer, had invited me. It is painful to let friends go into danger without you; abandoning them later comes easier. It is like knowing that a friend is critically ill in hospital: having visited once or twice, you stay away with relative equanimity. I considered myself bound to the 1st by ties of friendship and honor that dated from the North African campaign. Historical curiosity also entered into my feelings, since, wherever the 1st was, the best story was sure to be. Because it was the most thoroughly tested American division, it had to go into the trickiest place. This saved a reporter the trouble of trying to divine official intentions; while my colleagues stared helplessly at maps depicting German-held Europe from Spitsbergen down to Hendaye, I had only to stick to the 1st and the Great Riddle would come clear in due course.

Some giant mind higher than Army Group, however, had imagined that the way to please the press was to let an association of permanent American correspondents in London decide who might cover the invasion, and how. The members of the association were not military correspondents but sitters at the ends of cable lines. Since, in the nature of things, they worked for the press services and dailies that maintained permanent bureaus in London, they reserved all the good spots for their fellow-employees. (None asked to make the landing personally.) This ridiculous association would do nothing to help me, and I suspected its overcordial dignitaries of promoting a monopoly.

In those pre-invasion days, I used to go for a run every morning in Hyde Park—from Hyde Park Corner to Kensington Palace and back—and as I jogged along I would reflect on the ignominy of being left out of an event to which I had looked forward for four years, ever since the fall of France, a country I had left in June 1940. I was not consoled by the P.R.O.s' assurance that I would get over some time, days or weeks after D Day, or even, perhaps—if I was good—be permitted to witness the event itself from a ship so big that there were butter plates and celery on the officers' dinner table. The running was sensible, because I knew from experience that infantry war takes a lot out of even a spectator's legs. If my permission came through, I wanted to be in shape to take advantage of it. I was four months short of forty, and had been waiting all winter in London, training in pubs and bottle clubs. The greatest benefit of the running, however, was that it helped me work off the surplus adrenal juices that accumulated whenever I thought of the P.R.O.s, for whom I invented appropriate civilian pasts as I ran along. I decided they had been moving-picture press agents, office boys in advertising agencies, or newspaper legmen with metatarsal defects. I also devoted sweaty miles of thought to the press-service bureau chiefs—Sweet Alices trembling at the frown of fatheaded Ben Bolts five thousand miles away. Whenever I invented an insult that especially amused me, I would break my jog and walk a furlong to savor it. One puffball had particularly infuriated me by offering a confidential tip that the Army expected casualties of ninety-five per cent in the first hours. This was not only monstrously untrue but insulting, because it suggested that I could be frightened. I could, of course. As for him, he had not the faintest idea what he was talking about, having never, in the phrase of the immortal Dan De Quille, "seen the elephant nor hearn the owl." This same *bête noire* (or, rather, *bête rose*; he had a pink, snouty face like a Walt Disney porker's) had made up a slogan: "Every typewriter in a landing craft takes up space needed for a machine gun." He was patriotically willing to waive his own claim to passage. "*Ça, ç'est un blasphème*," a Basque major of Zouaves in Tunisia had once said to me of the Vichy generals who didn't want to fight, and I repeated it as I pounded along, regarded without astonishment by old gentlemen feeding the ducks on the Serpentine. London is used to eccentrics.

I lived at a hotel on Half Moon Street, which is one block long and runs from Piccadilly to Curzon Street. My fever came to a head one noon as I walked home through Curzon Street after my run. I was drenched in sweat but still full of rage when I saw a very small English automobile draw up at the curb ahead of me, in front of a house bearing a doctor's doorplate. A woman got out of the driver's seat, opened the door on the sidewalk side, and extracted from the hind portion of the car first a pair of crutches, which she leaned against the hood, and then part of an old man, who was so wedged in that he could get out of his shell only about as far as a periwinkle. I was twenty yards past before it occurred to me that I ought to help—the gaffer didn't look like an AP man. I doubled back, grabbed the bony wrist extruding from the metal carapace, and jerked so violently that he came out flying. (He was an emaciated old gentleman and couldn't have weighed much more than a collie.) When I saw the mingled gratitude and alarm on the woman's face, I realized how mad I must have seemed. A few paces farther on, I began to laugh, and it was then I realized that, for a time, at any rate, I had beaten off paranoia.

I was rescued from my invasion frustration by a pair of Kentuckians in naval uniform—Barry Bingham, of the Louisville *Courier-Journal,* and John Mason Brown, both of them prewar friends of mine—who were running Navy public relations for the great day. When they first proposed that I go as a naval war correspondent I was scornful. But my 1st Division prospects got no better as I pulled successive strings. Instead, as they say in Dublin, they disimproved, because some of the strings got crossed. Brown then artfully suggested that the Navy had little ships as well as big ones. The little ships included LCIs (Landing Craft, Infantry) that would run smack aground in a yard of water to land the troops they carried, beginning within half an hour of the first small-boat landings. Some of the LCIs, Bingham said insinuatingly, would be loaded with 1st Division infantry. I could travel to the other shore on one, and then make up my mind about getting off. If I went ashore, though, he said with regret in his voice, I would not be able to get any dispatches out; the Army P.R.O.s and censors would stop that, he was afraid. If I came back with the LCI—he realized that this was asking a lot, because he knew how anxious I would be to stay on the beach—I *would* be able to write a hell of a story, and the Navy would get it out for me. And, of course, he said, holding up a hand to forestall my protestations of insatiable pugnacity, the LCI, after discharging its first package of soldiers, would go back to the transports lying farther offshore and fetch another load.

"Coming in several times during the day that way, you'll get a splendid idea of how things are going," Bingham said. "You'll be able to judge the intensity of fire at the waterline."

"I could get you on a good early one," Brown said. "I wouldn't want you to miss anything."

So when SHAEF (Supreme Headquarters Allied Expeditionary Forces) summoned us from our hotels for the last time and then shipped us south by bus, my destination was Landing Craft, Infantry, Large (157 feet), No. 88, berthed at Weymouth, in Dorset.

At Weymouth it was instantly plain that there would have been room on LCIL 88 alone for a hundred more passengers. An army does not load its invasion craft like excursion boats but rather to deliver units capable of action to an appointed spot at a useful time in the planned development of battle. It would be murderous, as well as useless, to send in odd lots of troops simply because there was room on the boats. Onshore, they would simply have to stand around and be shot at. I was as welcome as the flowers in May, once the crew knew that I was going across with them. A man who thinks he may have to be a hero is consoled by the thought that his friends may read about it.

The Weymouth pier had landing craft lying alongside lashed together three abreast. The gangplank to the LCI closest inshore would slope down steeply except at extreme high tide; the grumbling soldiers, carrying their gear, plus part of a machine gun or mortar, would fight against slipping, or else, if they weren't too closely packed, come down at a reckless run. The passengers for the two outer boats passed over the inshore one. On the 88, which was next to the pier, it was like living on Route 1. I lived aboard her for four days before we sailed and got to know all her complement of thirty. Three were killed off Omaha Beach at seven thirty-five on the morning of D Day, June 6. Our first trip in was our last for the day; an armor-piercing shell that hit our bow reduced our effectiveness as a landing craft by removing our ramps. When we limped back to Weymouth on Sunday evening, June 11, after five days of shuttling about in the transport area off the beach, I was glad to see the place; but I didn't stay long. Early Monday morning, I took a train for London. I journeyed part of the way with an American soldier who said he had been fished out of the Channel off Omaha Beach and brought back to England by a returning LST. He lacked the guts to rejoin his outfit, he said frankly, and was headed over the hill to an English town where he had a girl. Going back to my own comfortable hotel in London to write my story, I was in no moral position to be censorious. I lent him a pound. He ducked off down the corridor to another compartment when a dazzling Red Cross girl got in at the first station up the line; he was afraid she might ask questions, I suppose. I rode the rest of the way to London with her, practicing the art of heroic understatement as I had studied it in British war films in the Noel Coward manner.

Thinking of all these things in the miraculous London warmth that recalled them, I walked around St. James's Square four times, sniffing the pollen of the mulberry trees, which made me sneeze, without benefit of snuffbox, in the true eighteenth-century style of the quarter. On the façade of Norfolk House, an office building on the east side of the Square, a plaque in polychrome stone relates that within the building, between January 16 and June 6, 1944, General Dwight D. Eisenhower, in conjunction with the heads of the Allied governments, planned and launched the excursion in which I participated. With my sneeze, but without causal connection between them that I can trace, came an impulse to go down to Weymouth again and see what it looked like. It was Saturday, June 4, 1955, and we had sailed from there on the evening of Monday, June 5, 1944. I am fond of anniversaries, although I do not believe in letting them get the better of me. I had never before observed June 5, for example, but that was no reason I shouldn't. A rail strike was on, so I asked Arthur, my hotel porter, to find a man to drive me down to Weymouth next day.

I had often been in the southwest of England in that other spring, when every sizable market town was the headquarters of an American division. As the date set for the invasion neared, the roads choked up with American trucks and tank transporters; Red Cross clubs huddled in the shadows of cathedrals; soldiers from prohibition states drank the pubs out of beer. The gentle West Country girls yielded with increasing facility to the pleas of men unlikely to trouble them again, and a haze of last-minute love hung over the land with the heat. I remembered the bus ride to the embarkation area, with military traffic ever heavier as we neared Weymouth and the adjacent coastal town of Portland. From Dorchester down, the M.P.s worked like cops at a bridge approach fifteen miles long.

On the Sunday of the anniversary, the weather held fair. In the morning, Mr. George Biggs, a staunch friend of Arthur's, came to fetch me in a Vauxhall, a nippy little car manufactured by a British subsidiary of General Motors, and at nine o'clock we set out. The ways in and out of a great city, being so uninteresting in themselves, allow opportunity to get acquainted with a hired driver. Mr. Biggs was a man of conservative aspect, with a gray mustache, glasses, an alpaca jacket, and a cap with a visor. His features underlay a glaze of respectable impassivity, and his opening remarks were not of a startling nature. "Fat pillows of cloud against a blue sky," he said. "I always think they are quite nice, don't you, sir?" And a moment or two later, as he whirled with phlegmatic dash around a mooning family vehicle: "Putterers and picnickers—that's what we shall have to contend with from here to the other side of the New Forest, sir."

After we stopped at Winchester for a nice cup of tea, he loosened up a bit. I remembered when the headquarters of Major General Manton S. Eddy, commanding the 9th Division, had been there. I had known the 9th in Africa, where it depended on half-trained mules and untrained muleteers to bring up ammunition, and had found it again in green Hampshire during the pre-invasion entr'acte. It was a crack division by then, and probably the chief architect of its excellence, next to Eddy, had been a private named Warner and nicknamed Molotov, which was later shortened to Mollie. I had seen him dead by a wadi north of Sedjenane a year earlier. Once Mollie had walked up a *djebel* under fire and captured six hundred Italians by asking them if they weren't tired of acting so miserable. His death resulted from a subsequent similar hunch, which turned out less well. That earlier time in Winchester, I had talked about Mollie with fellows who had been in his company. Now the only strangers in town were weekend putterers like us, who had stopped for elevenses and a look at the cathedral. It was unlikely that they had ever heard of Sedjenane.

All the way from London we had been threading our way among barelegged, bicycling girls. They occur in clubs, as fish do in schools, and once you have sighted the rearmost rump, high off the seat as the owner pushes to keep up, you sometimes run among them for five minutes before you leave the leader's pink, determined face behind. There were also, as one might expect, automobiles of all descriptions, and motorbikes with a girl riding sidecar or pillion, or with two girls riding sidecar *and* pillion, or with mother and baby in the sidecar and dad and the boys on the bike. The motorbike, in all its forms, is to the British highways what the small donkey is to those of North Africa. Buried under a superstructure of humanity and tea things, it snarls along on two, three, or even four wheels. Many an apparent automobile reveals itself, as you come closer, to be a bubble built out from and over a basic motor bicycle, with the rider, his face inside a plastic windscreen, as grave as the front half of a comedy horse. The attractions of the road beckon: "Thirteenth Century Cottage—First Left—Car Park—Teas, Snacks, Fully Licensed"; "Four Hundred Yds. to Fresh-Picked Strawberries"; "Purebred Herefords and Cocker Spaniels." In the New Forest, which was set aside as a royal hunting ground by William the Conqueror when there may have been trees there (the forest visible from the road now looks like Long Island scrub), our progress was further complicated by the New Forest ponies, wild horses of an ancient breed that line the road on Sundays to mooch tea buns from picnickers. English nature lovers have told me that the New Forest pony, with that uncanny instinct for survival that savage creatures develop, has learned to count to seven and never misses a Sunday, frequently turning up at the roadside with a bunch of wild primroses between its teeth to swap for boiled sweets or Yarmouth bloaters. The pony mothers bring their foals along to pose for photographs, knowing that more tea buns are forthcoming from camera amateurs who want the ponies to stand steady than from putterers who have no cameras. They are reported to have followed cars with cameras in them for miles, but this is on the dubious authority of letter writers to the *Times*. In appearance, the ponies are uncommonly hard to tell from small, undistinguished horses that have been left out in the rain. They cross the highway in both directions as they see carloads of tea-bun prospects approaching. The motor vehicles stop when the drivers see the ponies, and, as the drivers of sequential vehicles do not always see them at the same time, this leads to rearend collisions, while squads of children, leaping down and skinning their knees, add further perils to William the Conqueror's old line of country. Mr. Biggs egg-danced among them without hitting a pony, or even a child.

At Wimborne, a few miles beyond the New Forest, Mr. Biggs and I turned with relief onto the byroad that leads to Blandford, a town that once sheltered the headquarters of the 1st Division. This is one of the prettiest bits of road I have seen in England, running in part through an avenue of ancient beeches, which Mr. Biggs, checking by his speedometer, said was two miles long. (A bar waiter in Blandford told me later there were three hundred and seventy-five beeches, and that a society of ladies in Blandford cut the ivy off them every two years; he had a Sam Weller look about him, however, and may well have been in the habit of writing letters to the *Times* himself.) In Blandford there were soldiers in the long street, because the British Army has a permanent camp there, but they wore British battle dress instead of our field jackets.

Blandford is built around the bend of a pleasant small river called the Stour, and the main street, after a few constricted turns, runs over a bridge. "The town contains numerous fine 18th-cent. buildings including . . . the Crown Hotel, most of which were designed by the Bastard brothers."—The Little Guide series; Dorset, page 49. It is an old town, but nothing like as big or historic as Winchester. I bade Mr. Biggs stop for lunch at the Crown, because I remembered it as the principal inn of the place. In its bar, elegant but no longer animated, three or four customers in good jackets were solemnly drinking sherry. I had something stronger and told the gentlewoman behind the bar that I had been there before, with the Americans, and she said that *did* seem a long time ago. I pursued the subject no further, but she must have quoted me to other members of the staff; as Mr. Biggs and I made our way to the dining room a few minutes later, I heard a much younger gentlewoman at the reception desk say over her shoulder, "It was a bit livelier then, I daresay."

The cold meat was quite good, and only the flavor of the brown soup recalled the war. As I tasted it, a tune came into my head (this association of two sensory memories is, I believe, called synesthesia), but I had to down the spoonful of soup and hum two experimental bars before I could identify the air. It was "There'll Always Be an England." Mr. Biggs looked astonished and remarked, "I've always said there's nothing like a dash of high spirits, sir." The gentlefolk at the other tables looked peculiarly depressed, as if they had all come down into the country to hear the wills of relatives who had left them nothing. Mr. Biggs, having finished the last mouthful of the two kinds of potatoes and one kind of cabbage that had accompanied his mutton, looked around him slowly and then back at me. With a flash of perception that surprised me, he said, "We *are* a sad people to look at, aren't we, sir?"

On the sunlit road again, barreling down to Dorchester and Weymouth, I found it hard to keep my mind on the anniversary. There was no weekend traffic here, a hundred miles from London. In those other days, the road had been full of men going to a war, and now it wasn't. King Arthur probably used the same road going up to Badbury Rings, by the avenue of beeches, to whip the West Saxons. "Badbury is identified by Dr. Guest with Mount Badon, or Mons Badonicus. . . . Dr. Guest's case is a strong but by no means overwhelming one." *Op. cit.*, pp. 43-4. That was in circa 520, and there had been operations in between. In the fields by the road, red Devon cattle had replaced the Jerseys and Guernseys nearer London. The country looked less carefully tended, less self-consciously old, than the Home Counties. It has been there so long that there is no need to call attention to a post-Arthurian horror like a thirteenth-century cottage. I could smell the Channel, and Europe across it. This was an illusion based on reality, because for me the smell of the lower Norman coast—sea and broom plant—is the smell of Europe, and Dorset has sea and broom plant, too. For years, I did not know the second ingredient of this smell; it was a botanically informed friend who identified it for me. Last April, at Lanark, in western Scotland, where there is a lot of broom, I smelled Europe all about me. Glasgow does not smell like Europe, but that is because the broom gets no chance. (Broom has a light, pleasant, spicy smell, like fresh-baked ginger cake but enough different so you know it can't be.)

The gaunt boarding villas that lined the highway as it entered the town limits of Weymouth were as lugubrious as the Blandford lunchers, and their looks contrasted pitiably with the names the original proprietors had chosen for them—Bon Repos, Miramar Chalet, and the like. Weymouth in peacetime is more celebrated as a beach resort than as a port. The sea air had already nibbled at the villas' high, late-Victorian façades of brick and stucco, which advertised the dankness within. Nothing ages faster than a jerry-built house by the sea. There are desolations within New York City, by Jamaica Bay, where trees grow out through the glassless windows of facsimile châteaux, and house fronts gape like crazed Faulknerian ladies from behind hedges of privet grown twenty feet high —desolations that I can remember raucous with silk shirts, white flannel pants, buckskin shoes, straw skimmers, gypsy orchestras, and women in pretty good diamonds, forty years ago. Skip painting a house by the shore for one season and it starts to go; ten and it's gone. The pollution of Jamaica Bay and the coming of the automobile did to those shore resorts close to town what Faulkner thinks the Civil War did to Chuggetybug-gety County, which would have gone bust in the natural course of events anyway.

These Weymouth villas had missed a lot of paintings, but somebody had always come along in the nick of time to save them from falling to pieces altogether. I knew that in a shore resort the boardinghouses farthest from the sea are always the shabbiest. Making full allowance for that, I found the approach to the Weymouth harbor sad in the Biggsian sense. I had stopped at Weymouth for tea once on the way down to some landing exercises in Devonshire in early spring, before the genuine embarkation, and I had retained from this visit a memory of a prodigiously long row of gaunt lodginghouses and hotels with nobody in them, staring out to sea across a beach encumbered with barbed wire. Then there had been the second, anxious time, in the LCI, with the beach still deserted but the town rumbling with troops and vehicles headed for the pier, while I, with crew and fellow-passengers, was confined to the 88 from the moment I came aboard. Bon Repos and the rest confirmed those first gloomy impressions. What Mr. Biggs and I saw when we reached the sea front abashed me, and perhaps him, because it was so different.

Weymouth Beach is a semicircle rimmed by an esplanade a mile long. The pier stands out to sea at the south end of the arc, which is the end away from the normal landward approach. The conflicting music of competing roundabouts down on the sand supplied a background to the shouts of children, who yell more and louder when they are by the sea than anywhere else, keeping in touch with one another in the face of bravely imagined dangers. On the breeze blowing from the direction of the pier I could identify occasional strains of band music and the screams of a number of mad sea gulls, inspired to vocalism by the general clamor as they dived for the discarded butts of ice-cream cones. From flagpoles set at intervals of not more than fifty feet along the esplanade fluttered the banners of Uruguay, Norway, Mexico, Italy, and about every other nation with gay colors. The great red brick hotel, the Gloucester, once the summer residence of George III (*Op. cit.*, p. 174), was cheerfully rubicund; the *pensions* with the Pullman-car names—Nyanza Chalet, Windermere Cottage, Tickety-Boo-sur-Mer—flirted discreetly with the day trippers, employing tablecloths instead of handkerchiefs. There were flowers and cones of napery on the tables by their windows, inviting the trippers to the seven-and-six *prix fixe*. I imagined subterranean cisterns of brown soup, h. and c., but for the most part nearly c., supplying taps in all their kitchens; the thought depressed me only momentarily. The tide was low, and not one of the bathers I could descry walking out into the water—some of them mere dots at a distance of a nautical mile—had yet got up to his armpits; but a pedestrian with perseverance and an early start might reach swimmable depths and get back in time for a late tea. Some jolly good sunburns were already on view among the returning footsloggers.

Mr. Biggs parked the Vauxhall at the end of the esplanade farthest from the pier, just by an Italian flag, and we set out on foot. By the time we had gone a sixteenth of a mile, I realized that about every third flag was Italian; the chap in charge of decorations was either an Italian himself or enamored of red, white, and green. Abandoning all thought of finding the car again—I was glad I didn't own it—I strode on happily with Mr. Biggs, who was smiling, too, in a reserved way, past queues for teas and queues for ices at stands on the beach below our path, past queues at bathing tents, which here take the place of bathhouses.

We paused to look down on a Punch-and-Judy show. There was no Judy in it, though; perhaps the Lord Chamberlain had turned thumbs down on the battle of the sexes as entertainment for children. Instead, there was a smarmy male character, who outwitted Punch with the active connivance of the children in the audience. "Not Angles but Angels," St. Gregory said when he saw the captive English children in the slave market; and the small, beautiful faces turned up to the puppet show on Weymouth Beach made it easy to understand him. The smarmy puppet said to Punch, " 'Old out your 'and. I won't 'urt you." He held a sledge hammer behind his back. Punch shrieked apprehensively and waved his hands about his head. Smarmy appealed to the angels. "I won't 'urt 'im, will I, children?" he asked them. "*No!*" they all shouted in chorus, following with an explosion of knowing squeals. Poor Punch wavered. He appealed to his little friends in turn. "Will 'e 'urt me if I put my 'and out, children?" "*No!*" followed by more squeals. "All right, pal. 'Ere's my 'and." He extended his right hand, palm up. Smarmy hit it with the sledge hammer. Punch screamed realistically, and the angels howled so hard with laughter that mummies and nannies had to drag half of them away to public lavatories. Even Mr. Biggs had to laugh. "Children *are* cruel, don't you agree, sir?" he said, when he could control his voice. After that, the puppet man, a topical cove, put on two boxing puppets in the roles of Rocky Marciano (boos) and Don Cockell (excited cheers). Cockell had all the best of it, and the "three-round exhibition" ended with Marciano out on the ropes while Cockell alternately butted him in the stomach and pulled his nose, a historical inaccuracy that the children accepted with enthusiasm.

Farther along, a cathedral builder had finished one half of the façade of Westminster Abbey in wet sand; the model was seven feet high. A placard on an easel said, "Sand and water only used in this construction," and the man was working with a trowel. There was a bit of old carpet on the sand between the Abbey and the esplanade, and passing lovers of the fine arts showered down coins. Like the others, I felt that it was important for the master mason to finish his dedicated labor before high tide reduced it to ruins; a finished work of art, once it has existed, exists forever. I threw the man a sixpence, which landed fair in the middle of the carpet, but when I passed that way again, the Abbey was in the same unfinished state; he knew from experience, I suppose, that if he completed the job, no further appropriations could be expected. His game was to play upon the public anxiety.

At the end of our demitour, we reached the pier. It was a double pier, perhaps a thousand yards long, with a sunken railroad track in the middle. I had not remembered it exactly that way. There was relatively deep water only on the side away from the beach, facing a dredged inlet I did remember, which led into Weymouth's little port, beyond the pier end of the esplanade. The pier was of concrete; I recalled one covered with planks. Tied alongside, where I thought I remembered the LCIs end to end and cheek by jowl, were two steamers. The first, spruce and fairly ambitious, was a passenger liner serving the Channel Islands. The one out beyond her, a low, almost square-bowed coaster, was a potato boat from Jersey, where vegetables are earlier than in England. The potato boat was unloading; Sunday is a working day when there is a question of getting the new stuff to Covent Garden in time for the opening of the Monday market. Farther inshore, at the quayside of the port, a tomato boat from Guernsey was unloading. Mr. Biggs and I picked our way along the pier, among the cranes and lorries and potato sacks, while I tried to reconcile my memories with what I saw. Across from the very end of the pier, and forming the mouth of the inlet with it, was a round fortification dating from Napoleonic times. I remembered that LCIL 88, commanded by Lieutenant Henry Rigg, U.S. Coast Guard Reserve, had passed this fort on the evening of Sunday, June 11, 1944, coming into port with a hole forward and enough of a list to get her sent back from Normandy for repairs. Off the fort, an old fellow had rowed out to us in a boat, shouting greetings and asking after friends of his in the crew. He brought us eleven bottles of beer because the pubs were closed.

Mr. Biggs and I talked to some of the longshoremen. The younger men had themselves been away in service, but a ganger, or foreman, said he remembered the LCIs well; he had worked as a fitter in the engine-repair shops set up for them in Weymouth. As to the exact berth of the 88, which he didn't remember, he said that if I recalled planks she must have lain up the inlet, where the Guernsey boat was now unloading tomatoes. "That quay is concrete now, same as this pier," he said, "but in 1944 there was still planks across the top of it. It's been rebuilt since. This here pier was concrete already then, same as like it is now."

So Biggs and I walked back, I by this time beginning to feel silly about the whole business. If the quay had been rebuilt, as the ganger said, it wouldn't look the same anyway. And what was I going to do if I did find the berth? I asked myself. Put a plaque there like the one on Norfolk House? "At this point in space and history 177 (approx. fig.) men (among many thousands of others) sweated out the invasion of *Festung Europa*, telling what jokes they could think of and playing poker badly for small sums"; or "Sacred to the memories of Moran, Frere, and Simone, whose first names I have forgotten. Moran was going to write a book, and Frere had a girl named Hazel." They hoisted Frere and Simone, dead, aboard a hospital ship, and when I reached up to steady one of the wire baskets, blood poured down in my face. I was soaked in blood, and when I washed it off my glasses I looked down and saw the stuff on the deck. The soldiers, who messed on deck, had left a case of canned milk, and a piece of our shell had opened the cans. We walked down to the tomato boat just the same, and I said it looked like the place all right, but of course it didn't.

We were hot and a bit footsore by that time, so I said to Mr. Biggs that it might be nice to go out to the end of the shallow-water side of the double pier, where there was a band concert, and sit down in deck chairs and have an ice. This side of the pier is divided from the working side by the railroad track and an iron grille. It is an amusement pier, and admission costs eighteen pence. Posters at the entrance said that the concert was being rendered by the Yeovil Workmen's Silver Prize Band. Yeovil is a small city in Somerset, not very far away. The posters did not say who gave the band the prize, or why it was only silver. Mr. Biggs and I walked out to the end again and hired deck chairs for sixpence apiece and sat down. There was a breeze out there. I bought a large-size, sixpenny ice-cream cone filled with brilliantly white ice cream that tasted as American ice cream bought at the beach used to when I was a boy (before the trees grew through the windows). The ice cream tasted of honest mucilage and vanilla, not imitation-rum-chocolate-chip-pistachio-cherry dextrose, like the contemporary variety. The band, which should have had all the prizes going, played a bewitching medley, including "The Maple Leaf Forever," "Widdicombe Fair," "The Minstrel Boy to the War Has Gone," "Rule, Britannia" (which made me feel retrospectively heroic), and, by a special dispensation of chance, "The Ace in the Hole":

> Others have friends in the old Tenderloin,
> That is their Ace in the Hole.

How the Ace got into the Yeovil medley I will never know. I hummed as I licked the delicious white ice cream. Mr. Biggs, that perceptive man, was watching me, although I was not at that moment aware of it. He had declined an ice, preferring to save himself for a nice cup of tea on the road. "The grimmest things, afterward, in the course of time," he said, "are softened, aren't they, sir?"

2 / The Men in the Water

EARLY GEOGRAPHERS had a habit of studding their maps with representations of monsters supposed to exist in the regions they delineated, and my geographical memory works the same way. For eleven years after D Day, the five-mile stretch of beach under the cliffs between Port-en-Bessin and Pointe de la Percée, on the Channel coast of Normandy, was marked in my mind by a line of American soldiers waist-deep in water and immobilized by fear. Descending arcs of tracers were entering the water around them, an LCT (Landing Craft, Tank) was burning nearby, and they could not bring themselves to move. They seemed as permanently fixed in time and space as those Marines in the statue of the flag-raising on Iwo Jima, but the circumstances were different. While the men stood there, the LCIL 88, on which I was a deeply impressed observer, went in on their right and landed its passengers, and then pulled out. That image of the beach, for me, superseded pleasant earlier memories of the same strip of coast. Prior to 1944 I had visualized the water there as blue under a summer sun, as it had looked to me in 1926, when I strolled along the tops of the cliffs behind it. After 1944, I remembered it as gray, except for the lines of the tracers, and disquietingly narrow between the LCIL 88 and the beach.

In 1955, a few days after my run to Weymouth, I went down from Paris to Port-en-Bessin, which is a cinematogenic fishing port, to have another look. D Day had been stormy, but this time the weather was perfect, as it had been in June 1940, when the Germans were on the outskirts of Paris (the weather was seldom on the side of the side I was with). For the expedition, I had hired a Versailles, which is a small car developed in France by Ford but now built by Simca. A Versailles is a sparrow compared to an American Ford, which in France is now a *voiture de grand luxe*, but in relation to other French-built cars it is a giant of the road; when you park one in a provincial town, boys dash out of alleys crying, *"Regardez la Versailles!"* The very small French cars are undoubtedly well adapted to French purchase taxes, French gasoline prices, French village streets, and French distances, but they often remind me of a famous French clown named Toto, who years ago did a standard turn in Keith vaudeville and at the Hippodrome. Toto made his entrance folded up inside what seemed to be a toy sedan, which operated under its own power. After he had extracted himself from it—a thin man, he was fairly tall, or at least he knew how to make himself look so—he would haul out a valise, a string of sausages, a dog, and a feather duster. He was an unrecognized pioneer of the contemporary French automotive industry. The Versailles towers above the Totomobiles one encounters on French highways.

With my elephant of the roads came a mahout—a White Russian named Michel, who took care of it as carefully as if it had been an atom-fueled jet airplane. He changed the oil every seven hundred miles, had the car greased nearly every time we stopped for a beer, and probably slept with it under his pillow. Michel was a polite man, fifty-four years old, with strands of black hair carefully plastered over the bald top of his head and soft brown eyes continually wide with wonder at his escape from the Ukraine in 1920, from Bulgaria in 1928, from the Germans during the occupation of Paris, and from various hotel concierges, who ordinarily clipped him twenty per cent of his fee every time they got him a driving job. (I had hired him through the carhire man, who, Michel said, did not clip him.) For thirty-five years he had lived with all the perils, real and imagined, that beset the life of a permanent foreigner. He still had a Nansen passport; since 1939, his wife, a Pole, had also been without a country. Her brother had been talked into going back to Poland, and the current Polish government wouldn't let him out. All this Michel conveyed to me in pidgin French during the first twenty minutes I knew him. There had been 22,000 White Russians in Paris when he arrived there, he told me—all chauffeurs, taxi drivers, or maîtres d'hôtel— and with 21,999 of his fellow-countrymen to talk to he had never felt the need to learn sequential French. In the summer, he drove American clients who knew no French at all. The concierge in whatever hotel they were staying at would tell him where they wanted to go, and he would take them there. If they had further instructions for him, they could relay them through the concierge at the next hotel. Every time we stopped, Michel would get out, run around the back, open my door for me, and bow. Whenever I got out before he could reach me, I saw he felt snubbed. (It would have been impossible to explain to him that the mannerisms he had learned while driving a Hispano-Suiza were not appropriate to a Versailles, since he thought of the latter as a vast vehicle, pulsating with power.) He won me over our first afternoon out, and from then on I sat and waited for him to come around and open the door.

Michel was a good driver as long as he knew what road he would be on for the next fifty miles. But he expected Americans to travel in their regular orbits—Paris-Deauville, Paris-Biarritz, Paris-châteaux-of-the-Loire —and it disconcerted him to be instructed to leave these known trajectories. He was not much on maps and drove too fast to read the signs at *carrefours,* so he often took us several miles in a wrong direction. When this occurred, he would look at me reproachfully for not having wanted to go to Deauville, and then get out to search for a deaf and dumb old lady or, in her default, the next most unlikely source from whom to request directions. I was unaware of these idiosyncrasies until we reached Caen, a hundred and fifty miles from Paris. Up to that point, it had been main road all the way.

"Where now? Where?" Michel asked, and I said, "Bayeux," which is the nearest town of prominence to Port-en-Bessin. He leaped from the car, ran across a traffic circle to an Algerian rug peddler, and engaged in animated consultation. Then, waving his arms, he abandoned the Algerian and stepped in front of an old gentleman on a bicycle. There was wild pantomime, after which Michel returned, his eyes wider than ever with amazement, which was now mingled with pity. "*N'esista pas, Moosioo,*" he said. "*N'esista pas, Boolioo.*"

It was my turn to be astonished. "No *Boolioo,*" I said, already falling into his gibberish. "*Bayeux!*"

"*Oui, Moosioo, Boolioo, mais n'esista pas,*" he said.

I got out a Michelin road map and pointed to Bayeux on it. Michel carried the map to a nearby café and came back looking disappointed. "Ba-*yeux!*" he said, with an inflection that asked why I couldn't pronounce it properly. "Ba-*yeux!* Ba-*yeux esista.*"

Michel resigned himself to not going to Biarritz, and we drove along the route his consultant in the café had indicated until we saw the towers of the cathedral, indisputably tangible and ferocious. Michel and I had not conversed much after he recited the autobiography that he had succeeded, probably through practice, in organizing into an almost intelligible form. Other attempts at prolonged communication had fallen down, and I was rather glad they had, since I wanted to think about what lay ahead.

I pass as a Francophile, but there are only two parts of France with which I have had more than a fleeting connection. One is Paris. The other is a ragged triangle in Lower Normandy, two of whose sides are formed by the English Channel and the third by an imaginary line drawn from Caen south and west to Mont-Saint-Michel, with a slight deviation to take in Vire and Mortain. All this lies within the departments of Manche and Calvados. The reasons that persuaded me to go there first were sensible but slight. I had two months to spare before the opening of the Sorbonne in the fall of 1926, and I wanted to travel in some part of France that wasn't Paris. Lower Normandy was easy to get to, it had a historic cachet, and I had heard that it was agreeable but not spectacular. Because it was not spectacular, it was not tourist country, and I was terribly afraid of being mistaken for a tourist. At that remote period of my life, I liked to walk fifteen or twenty miles a day, but I wanted a good bed to sleep in at night, and I was a great glutton. I had read Guy de Maupassant in English when I was still in short pants—I was in them again in 1926, but I called them plus fours—and this gave me a feeling of confidence about plunging into Normandy. I knew what to expect of its peasants; they would be like New Englanders. The precipitating pretext for my choice was a mild curiosity about a medieval poet who was supposed to have lived in Vire. When I got there, I found that he was a hoax long since exploded, but the story of the hoax was amiable.

This country, which I had chosen so lightly, gripped me—partly, I suppose, because it was the first foreign land I had traveled in alone. Paris is foreign to no literate person, and the sensation of being abroad is the only pleasure I have never known there. Within my Norman triangle, I noticed differences from, as well as analogies with, home, the beauties of small landscapes, the taste of food prepared in ways new to me. Even the old wheezes of such a land are irresistibly funny, because you have never heard them before. Old jokes survive because they are good jokes; if our own old jokes seem flat to us, it is because we have heard them so often. Coming to a new old city, I would walk all through it, smell it, look at streets house by house, as if I were going to live there all my life. People I saw around me became important. I devoted more reflection, for example, to the possibilities of one waitress in the Hotel du Cheval Blanc in Vire— snub nose, pasty color, in spite of the incredible amount of hard physical work she got through, small eyes, but splendid forearms and legs—than to all the women, some of them dazzling, who passed me on the Champs-Elysées that same summer. I cannot remember now what any one of *them* looked like, though I thought they were all hot stuff at the time. In the mornings, the waitress would wash down the floors of the hotel, and for that she would wear wooden clogs. At lunchtime she would take off the clogs and put on stockings and high-heeled slippers, a gesture of coquetry I can still see her performing. After she had pulled on the slippers, she would wash her hands at the spigot over a painted metal basin that was placed at the entrance of the dining room for the use of fastidious clients. She left an enduring impress on my life, although our relations were always impersonal. At my first meal at the hotel, I asked for a salad plate. She brought it to me, saying, with a superior smile, "*Chacun son pays, chacun sa façon.*" I have taken my salad on my meat plate ever since, dabbling the lettuce in the leftover gravy.

The sojourn had a no less pronounced effect upon my tastes in food. I am still of the opinion that Lower Normandy has the best sea food, the best mutton (from the salt meadows of the Avranches region), the best beef, the best butter, the best cream, and the best cheese in Europe, and that the ideal light lunch is a dozen *huitres de Courseulles,* an *araignée de mer* (spider crab) with a half pint of mayonnaise on the side, a dish of *tripes à la mode de Caen,* a partridge Olivier Basselin, poached in cream and cider and singed in old Calvados, a *gigot de pré-salé,* a couple of *biftecks,* and a good Pont l'Evêque. I can no longer stand up to it in one sitting, as the Irishmen say in the storybooks, but that is not the fault of the menu. It is my metabolism that has collapsed.

The Norman takes his vegetables in the form of animals. "Herbivores eat grass," one hotel landlord told me. "Man, a carnivore, eats herbivores." The Norman takes his fruit in the form of cider and its distillate Calvados. "Those big, beautiful apples are good, perhaps, to look at," the same sage said, "but our little ones make better drinking." I have never wavered since in my belief that old Calvados has a more agreeable bouquet, a warmer touch on the heart, and a more outgoing personality than cognac. It is less precocious, but that is only a confirmation of its more profound character. The barrel of Calvados laid down at an infant's birth matures with him; he is unlikely to need it until he is at least eleven, and by that time it will be passable. If the boy is to drink Calvados at its best, however, it is better to lay down several barrels, so he will still have some when he is fifty.

Because of my feeling about the region, I sneaked back there for a week in the winter of 1939, the first year of the war, and I found that I thought no less of it. Consequently, when, on Friday, June 2, 1944, I learned that the destination of the cross-Channel expedition was my ragged triangle, I felt as if, on the eve of an expedition to free the North from a Confederate army of occupation, I had been told that we would land on the southern shore of Long Island and drive inland toward Belmont Park. It was a British naval officer who briefed my lot of correspondents at Whitehall that Friday morning before they shoved us off to the invasion ports. "If it's a good show, as we rather hope, all will be tickety-boo by D-plus-1," the naval bloke said cheerily. I forget whether he added "Good hunting!" or whether I merely heard that one in a motion picture. From the Whitehall briefing, which gave us the large, inter-Allied naval picture (a British admiral, Sir Bertram Ramsay, was in over-all command of the naval operation), we progressed, after a long bus ride, to another briefing, this one by an American admiral aboard the command ship *Ancon*, off Portland Bill, in Dorset. The Admiral told us about the American half of the project—everything from Port-en-Bessin west to Utah Beach, on the Cotentin peninsula. But it was not until I got to LCIL 88, at Weymouth, that I learned her precise destination—a zone of Omaha Beach known by the code name of Easy Red. The "tickety-boo" stuck; I quoted it numerous times in the following week, and it was taken up by our little social group on LCIL 88. "Tickety-boo on Easy Red" became our catch line, and after the shell hit it acquired piquancy.

Once aboard the 88 and restricted to her small hull, I received all the detailed information I could possibly want—in fact, a bit more about the enemy capabilities than I possibly wanted. The 88 was to land a mixed lot of special units that would be needed early—engineers to blow out obstructions, naval beach-battalion men to guide small-boat traffic, and the like—at a point about three miles west of Port-en-Bessin, where, I remembered at that moment, I had once eaten a magnificent sole *normande*, bedewed with shelled mussels, on the terrace of a restaurant looking out on a summer sea. I asked Lieutenant Henry K. Rigg, the 88's commander, whether I would be able to see Port-en-Bessin from where we were going in, and he said that if the day was clear, I might see the lighthouse and the long west jetty, but he thought I would have a lot of distractions.

The houses of Port-en-Bessin are folded into a draw between two rows of cliffs where a stream, the Dromme, comes down to the Channel. Two stone jetties, or moles, form an artificial outer port, which leads to two inner basins, one behind the other, where the fishing boats tie up. The weather on D Day—a Tuesday—wasn't clear, and Rigg's surmise proved correct; there were so many nearer objects calling for attention that I never looked in the direction of my gastronomic idyl. Before we went back to Weymouth on the following Sunday, I learned that Port-en-Bessin had been captured promptly and without serious damage.

Bayeux has been for many years one of my favorite cities, but as Michel and I neared the sea, my need to look at Easy Red became imperative, so we paused in the town only long enough to drink a glass of beer at the Hôtel du Lion d'Or. When I had last seen the hotel, in 1944, it was Field Marshal Montgomery's headquarters; now there was no trace of the great man, not even a high-pitched echo. When we had finished our beer, I told Michel we would push on. By road, it is 9 k., or five miles and five furlongs, from Bayeux to Port-en-Bessin. The road, bordered sometimes by hedges and sometimes by rows of tall, scraggly poplars, led past a couple of gray stone country churches, nine hundred years old, fields full of white-and-liver-colored Norman cattle, a dappled Percheron mare with her bay foal, and a disconsolate man standing beside a stalled Totomobile (Citroën, two horsepower). We stopped and went back to the man; he was out of gas. "And just to think," he said as he got into our car, "I'm a salesman for a gasoline company."

"It is the son of the cobbler who wears shoes with holes in them," I said, coming up with a Lower Normandy chestnut I had not been able to utilize in the previous quarter of a century. At Port-en-Bessin, he told us, he would buy a flimsy of gas, and have the garageman drive him back to his car. A creature like a weasel ran across the road well ahead of us with something in its mouth—a field mouse or a bird's egg. A similar creature had run across my course on the same road twenty-nine years before, and I had always meant to ask a peasant what it might have been. I made the same resolve about this one and then forgot to ask. I was momentarily saddened by a sign I saw posted in a field. "MYXOMAROSE," it read, indicating the presence of the rabbit disease that had decimated the warrens of western Europe. I suppose the sign was to warn sportsmen of the unhealthy nature of the rabbits to be found there (although if the disease had caught on in the neighborhood, there wouldn't be many), but it reminded me of my baptism of fire, which I underwent in 1926 on the fields atop the cliffs between Arromanches and Port-en-Bessin.

For a week in that magic end of summer, I lived in a hotel at Bayeux and walked almost every day, blackthorn stick in hand, to one of the small shore resorts—Arromanches, Asnelles, or Port-en-Bessin. Turning at the sea, I would proceed along the tops of the cliffs to an adjacent village and then return to Bayeux by a different road. On a Sunday morning, I walked to Arromanches, took a copious *apéritif* there, and then headed along the footpath that led to the sole *normande* I was to demolish and remember. That Sunday was the opening day of the shooting season. Nobody had told me. As I pushed along, I heard what French military communiqués call a "nourished" small-arms fire from the direction in which I was advancing. Of a sudden, but too late, I perceived its source— a rank of sportsmen moving forward in a skirmish line, pressed in from the ends, for want of space, until they were almost elbow to elbow. They were preceded by a stampede of terrified dogs—*briquets*, griffons, and Brittany spaniels—over whose heads they discharged their automatic shotguns as they advanced. They were the sportsmen of Port-en-Bessin.

Had I been on the summit of some distant acclivity, like Napoleon at Regensburg, I would have admired the spectacle. It was magnificent, but it was not hunting; it was rather in the tradition of Fontenoy—the cadenced step and the fire by companies. My position being what it was, however, I beat a retreat, effecting a *repli* sufficiently abrupt upon Arromanches. (The idiom of the communiqué continues to impose itself.) Then I heard, to what had been my rear, a fire equally well nourished and the baying of another pack of dogs. The sportsmen of Arromanches were out, keen on getting their share of rabbits. I ran to the edge of the cliff, but there was no escape in that direction, for the tide was all the way in. I therefore tried to make myself as conspicuous and as unmistakably human as possible. Waving my arms high over my head, with my blackthorn stick clutched in my right hand, I walked deliberately toward the nearer danger—the ambulatory fusillade from the direction of Port-en-Bessin. I did not tie a white handkerchief to the end of the stick; that is merely a detail I invented the fourth time I told the story and have since decided to discard. My approach was observed just before I got within shotgun range. The fire died away; one or two final charges of buckshot whistled high over my head as I reached the line of dogs— merely shots fired at a sea gull somebody had mistaken for an edible lark. I passed through the disgruntled ranks of the *chasseurs*, who leaned upon their *fusils* and did not even say "*Bonjour*." Scarcely had I resumed my promenade when I heard behind me the crash of a new volley. It terrified me to imagine what would happen when the two detachments met, and I hurried on in order to avoid being called as a witness.

I was thinking happily of my miraculous escape from the pothunters when Michel reached Port-en-Bessin. We dropped our passenger at a garage on the outskirts and then continued down the road, which soon changed to Port-en-Bessin's main street, running along the west bank of the two boat basins. Masts rose on one side of the street and on the other were stores and a couple of cafés. "Fishing port," Michel said knowingly, and then, waving his hand at some men on the quay, added, "Fishermen." He pointed to the boats. "For the fishing," he said. Little had changed that I could notice since the day of the rabbit shoot and the sole *normande*.

The quay and the street made a right-angle turn where the outer harbor began, and there, in front of the Hôtel de la Marine, I had a view of the sea—blue again, and smiling. "Little place," said Michel. "Peasants." He inhabits a walkup on a street just off the Champs-Elysées. This has given him a sense of belonging to *le monde chic*. When I was in Port-en-Bessin before, it had 1,334 inhabitants, according to the *Guide Bleu* of 1926; the latest *Guide Bleu* says it now has 1,314. This seems odd, considering the apparently high proportion of children in the population, but it is probable that many of the males drown or enter holy orders, while a good number of the females leave to take jobs inland.

The ground floor of the Hôtel de la Marine is bar, café, and kitchen. At mealtimes, paper tablecloths turn the café into a restaurant. A movable screen partitions off one corner of this room for the group social life of the proprietor and his wife and their swarm of children. He reads a newspaper, she shells peas, and the children make noises. The room above is a long *salle* for wedding and Communion banquets. The kitchen of the Hôtel de la Marine is the cause of innumerable detours from the Route Nationale that joins Paris and Cherbourg. In the *Guide Michelin*, which is the automobilist's vade mecum, Port-en-Bessin is identified on a map of France as a place where one may enjoy "a particularly well-prepared meal, preferably regional in character" at a moderate price. The *Guide* defines a moderate price as seven hundred francs (the equivalent of two dollars, or fourteen shillings), including wine. There are less than a hundred restaurants on this map as compared with nearly seven hundred cited elsewhere in the *Guide* as having outstanding cuisine. Cherbourg, fifty-six miles up the road, is the nearest dot on the moderate-price map. The woman at the desk consented to harbor us for one night, on condition that we not try to stay longer, because all the rooms would be needed for the guests at a Communion banquet on the following day. "After what they will send themselves, it is better that they do not drive," she said.

The upper floors of the Hôtel de la Marine have the excessively bare look common to hotels whose management expects guests to track sand through the halls; they also have showers. It was six o'clock by then, and I was eager to get out on the west jetty, which is a third of a mile long; but it had been hot on the road, and I decided to have a cold shower first. The beach I wanted to see would be just like any other beach, I told myself, and at that distance I would not even be sure where Fox Green ended and Easy Red began. And the men could not have been standing in the water all this time. Somebody would have noticed them and invited them to come ashore and rest up.

I was drying myself with a towel six inches square—the largest available at the Hôtel de la Marine—when a hideous noise broke out, like the quacking of a monster mad duck against the background of the shriek of an air-raid siren. As I was on my way back to my room, a man I passed in the hall told me it was the foghorn of a small lighthouse that stands on the top of the cliffs west of town. I looked out the window, but not far, because a white fog was pressing against the glass. It had come up in a matter of minutes. There was no use going to the jetty now; visibility was about ten feet. The fog, the quacking, and the shrieking went on unabated, and the harmless quality of the place seemed to have vanished with the blue sky. I imagined boats in the fog steering toward the sound and slipping past the fingertips of the men in the water off the beach, who still waited for a lift.

I went down to the café and took a *pastis*. There were four young fishermen there, off a dragger named the *Notre-Dame de la Délivrance*, and they were glad they had made port before the fog set in. The siren, which was driving me mad, did not annoy them; they admired it as a beneficent mechanism. "*Quel potin!*" (What a row!), one of them said. "It makes itself heard eleven miles out at sea." They had brought in a fair catch of *raie* (skate), a fine cash fish in France, this sailor said, and a lot of oddments that also came up in the nets—*tourteaux* (like English or Cuban crabs), *araignées de mer, congres* (conger eels), *encornet* (squid), *carangue* (a small blue fish that the sailor described as "the female of the mackerel"), *limande* (plaice), and a number of species for which I could not recall any familiar counterparts. The price of fish was low, the sailor said, compared to that of the fuel oil needed to propel the boats. The fish "rarefied" themselves more every year, and the boats had to go farther all the time to get them. In winter, they often stayed out ten days. When bad weather caught them off the Cornish coast, the crews sometimes had to put into English ports, where they were *mal vus*—they got hard looks. Fishermen were suspected of smuggling not only in England but in their own *petit pays*. As the sailor was talking, a shadow passed in the fog, close to the window. "Look," he said. "It's the customs guard. Always nosing around for trouble. This is a quiet little place— never a row, no funny business. You never see the nose of a gendarme here from one year's end to the next. But the customs men, they show off. They claim storms drive us too often into Falmouth."

One of the other fishermen, a reserved and, until then, expressionless male-beauty-contest type, said with violence, "They know about storms, the customs men? They're sailors, them? *C'est des Parisiens!*"

"And is there no smuggling off this coast?" I asked, remembering to smile.

"Oh, Monsieur, one isn't living in the eighteenth century," the first sailor said. "There isn't much any more."

One of the sailors was a dark, heavy-set fellow who looked as if he might be from the Midi, but when I asked him, he told me that he had been born in Port-en-Bessin, like all the others. "There are almost no foreigners—that is to say, sailors from other ports—working on our boats," he said. "We are all a little more or less related. Fellows go away from the port, of course, but they come back after they finish their service in the Navy."

There were thirty-odd boats working out of the port, the sailors said, and about three hundred and fifty seamen. "Including engineers and fellows who work in boatyards," the handsome boy, a stickler for exactitude, added.

"But the engineers are marine engineers," the dark sailor said. "They go to sea, what?"

"They aren't sailors," the purist replied. "If you want to call them quasi-sailors, I agree."

I asked the men if they remembered D Day, when, as well as I could judge by looking at them, they must all have been between ten and thirteen years old. They remembered it as a super Fourteenth of July celebration. Not many shells had fallen on Port-en-Bessin, they said, because the Allies wanted to take the port intact. A number of summer villas on the slopes overlooking the town had been destroyed by artillery fire laid down to stop the Germans from moving up supporting units. But no one had been hurt, because it was early in the season and the summer people had not yet moved in. At dawn, the boys had heard the guns on the long beach to the west and had seen a cloud of artificial fog spread over the landing operations. I had forgotten the fog, but it must have added to the gloom of the rainy, windy day.

The scout plane of the *Georges Leygues*—a Free French cruiser in the fleet covering the landings with fire—had flown low over the town, dropping leaflets warning the people to take cover. The *Georges Leygues*, the sailors told me, had fired more shells than any other ship in the fleet. Two of the young men had subsequently done their military service aboard her, and she was a great favorite in Port-en-Bessin. I remember the *Georges Leygues* well—a self-assertive vessel.

Soon after the airplane with the leaflets, British Commandos had appeared on the east jetty and American infantry on the west, the sailors continued. Canadians had moved in on Port-en-Bessin from the land side, and the Germans had not insisted; some took off and others were "done like rats." There had never been many of them in the town—a couple of companies, perhaps.

The sailors went home to their suppers—we had sent ourselves a few by then—and Michel and I now settled down to the selection of a particularly well-prepared meal, preferably regional in character, from the menu presented by Georgette, the waitress, whose name I had learned from my nautical acquaintances. She had red hair and a short upper lip, but the traveler in the Norman triangle must be several days out of Paris before he begins to pay waitresses the concentrated attention I gave the one at Vire. The fog cleared at sunset, as abruptly as it had come, and the foghorn ceased its infernal *potin*.

To insure the regional character of my meal, I ordered an *araignée*, to be followed by *raie au beurre noir*. The *araignée*, a beast of loathly aspect in a state of nature, is a warty, long-legged creature with a carapace resembling a slightly flattened baseball. It looks more like a land crab than a water crab. It is of a despicable khaki color, which gives it protective coloration on mud bottoms, and it has acquired a trick of tangling seaweed around its legs, possibly to make itself appear innocuous or inedible. Whatever its object, it has created the latter impression so successfully on the New England and Long Island coasts that I have never known anybody there to eat one. It is a great bait grabber, and when Americans fishing for blackfish or flounder haul one of these crabs aboard, they consider it a calamity instead of a stroke of luck and dash the crab to death, or stamp on it, before they throw it back into the sea—the men in the party swearing and the women, if there are any aboard, shuddering. What doesn't occur to those fishermen is that the *araignée*, placed in hot water, will turn red like any other crustacean, and so lose its repulsive color. It turns a peculiarly beautiful red, in fact—the color of those old-fashioned rambler roses that smell like raspberries. On the other hand, the *tourteau*, so popular in Britain, where "crab" means only *tourteau*, will blush no deeper than a yellowy pink, attractively set off by black claw tips, while our own blue crab assumes in hot water the angry color of a newborn baby.

Set down on the plate right side up, the cooked *araignée* has the appearance of an ambulant rosy-red apple. The Norman cook has already made a discreet incision around the periphery of the carapace, permitting the spider-eater, after he has sufficiently admired his specimen, to lift the top like a lid and attack the white interior from above. There is a good deal to eat in an *araignée*; while there are none of the large chunks of meat you find in a lobster or *langouste*, every part of it except the lid may be profitably scrunched between molars. The long legs, passed between the incisors, yield their sweet juice to a gentle pressure. Just as the nectarine combines peach and plum, the taste of the *araignée* suggests both lobster and crab, with the tantalizing added suggestion of *oursin*, or sea urchin.

Skate is a less peculiarly regional dish, but in support of my choice of this relative of the shark I appropriate a statement by a woman I once knew about Long Island fluke. "Once plucked from the water, they lose their flavor as quickly as corn on the cob," she said, and the observation is equally pertinent to the skate. The *raie au beurre noir* of West Forty-eighth Street or Soho is to the *raie au beurre noir* of Port-en-Bessin what the Joe Louis of 1951 was to the Joe Louis of 1938. The inland chef's sole recourse in preparing skate is to stoke the *beurre noir* with capers until the *raie* tastes no worse than deep-frozen Pacific Coast swordfish bought in cellophaned slats from a supermarket.

By the time I had finished the skate and a mound of strawberries, Port-en-Bessin seemed to have resumed its harmless quality, even though the foghorn was again raising its benevolent *potin*. I now found the noise agreeable. Michel retired for the night. *"Pas Deauville, Moosioo,"* he said sadly before going. *"Pas Place Etoile."* He could hardly have complained that it was too quiet. I got to sampling the hotel's various Calvados. It was the first night I had spent in the triangle since July 1944, by which time, after six weeks of residence, the Allied forces had drunk up all the Calvados in the region. The new, ten-year-old stuff I was served in the Hôtel de la Marine was rough but showed promise. Presently my fishermen came back and told me what an absurdly puritanical country England was. The cafés close at eleven, they said, and they put you to the door. Georgette threw them out at ten-thirty and then stacked chairs on my table. I went to bed.

The night cleared, and the foghorn fell silent. I was sleeping when it opened up again. It was hard to disregard the quacking of the mad, asthmatic duck when there was neither conversation nor Calvados to cushion the impact on the eardrums. I lay wondering whether I would be able to have my look at the beach next day or whether the fog was going to keep me around long enough to develop an interest in Georgette. Toward dawn, the *potin* stopped, and I fell asleep, as I used to do after the all-clear in wartime London.

Despite my untranquil night, I was up early, and I took a turn by the boat basins, where I joined a knot of men and women around an auctioneer who was just beginning his *marché à la criée* of the fishermen's haul. The boats lay ranged along the main-street quay, their catches spilled out in open crates or baskets that were aligned on the quay in front of them. The auctioneer started with the boat lying nearest the entrance of the harbor and worked his way inland, calling for bids on every lot, even if each consisted of but three lobsters or a couple of kilos of undersized scallops. He was a Norman out of the storybooks—blond, blue-eyed, all his facial capillaries exploded by wet weather and good living and his neck bursting out of the top of his blue shirt like a tree trunk out of a hole in a sidewalk. His clothes appeared to conceal the torso of a Percheron. He was a ringer for a ship's carpenter named Andersen I once knew on a Norwegian tanker called the *C. T. Boe*. If you put the two men together, you would need no further documentation of the story of the Viking migration to Normandy under Rollo.

The auctioneer talked very fast, like his colleagues the world over. As he stopped at each lot, he would begin, *"Mesdames, Messieurs, regardez les belles limandes,"* or *"les beaux turbots"* (there were, unfortunately, not many of these), or *"les belles lamproies,"* or *"les beaux congres,"* or *"les belles roussettes"* (these last three are hideous lampreys, conger eels, and spotted dogfish, with faces like Picasso women of the artist's most misogynistic period). All fish were beautiful to the auctioneer. He would then start at what he considered a reasonable minimum price per kilo. "Eighty francs the handsome Saint-Pierre," he might say, referring to a fish with the retreating forehead of a Chicago alderman. "Eighty-one, eighty-two, ninety," he would patter on mysteriously, as if he were doing the bidding, and then stop just as mysteriously by naming the purchaser, who hadn't said a word. An assistant would write the buyer's name on a chit and throw it in the crate, and the auctioneer would lead the way to the next lot. Most of the prospective buyers ate raw scallops as they walked along, nipping them out of the baskets on the quay. I noticed that one of the bidders, a fishwife, had brightly polished toenails. As the lots were sold, huskies loaded the crates into motor trucks parked on the quay, and after the last lot was knocked down, the trucks roared off for Caen and Paris, the latter less than four hours by road. Large skates, I observed, brought a hundred and eighty francs a kilo, which works out to about twenty-five cents a pound, on the dock. Skate is a poor man's fish the world over. The cost of living is high in France these days.

When the *marché* broke up, I introduced myself to the auctioneer, and he asked me if I had been able to follow him; he was obviously proud of how fast he could talk. So I said that I had not understood a word, and he looked happy. I asked him how he spotted the bids so fast. He said he knew his customers, since they were the same ones every day, and their ways of bidding—by wiggling their thumbs, rubbing their noses, or just winking. There was a *marché* every morning, and Thursday's was the biggest, because it came just before Friday. We were Thursday.

I told the auctioneer that I had been nearby on D Day, in 1944. On a point at the east side of the entrance to the boat basins there was a gaunt and decrepit structure that looked like an abandoned barracks, and I asked him whether it had been a partial casualty of the attack. He said no, that it was an old hotel that had belonged to a rich widow, who had willed it to the state to be used as a school for orphans, on condition that they be taught by Sisters of Charity. It had been assigned, somehow, to the police of Paris for the use of orphans of policemen, but the Prefect of Police had insisted on lay teachers. The lawyers for the widow's estate had sued the government to recapture the building for the residuary heirs, on the ground that the terms of the bequest had been violated. Neither party to the litigation had cared to risk any money on repairs pending the result of the *procès*, which dated back to the time of Tardieu. Consequently, the hotel was falling to pieces.

"The port was little damaged on D Day," the auctioneer said. "It was really in much better shape than it had been six months earlier. The Germans had been working in an endeviled manner to dredge the entrances from the outer port into the inner basins, clear the mudbank from the west quay, and perfect the harbor in every way. They used it for flak barges [the Siebel ferries that were designed for the invasion of England and later converted into floating antiaircraft gun platforms]. It shows how little they expected an attack on this part of the coast. If they had known it was coming here, they would have done all they could to make the port unfit for use in case of capture. There was an English officer, disguised as a German, who needled them to push the work. He had the shoulder tabs of a German staff officer, and he would come here in a big car, as if direct from high headquarters. 'The Führer wants it ready by the end of May,' he would say. '*Allez, hop!* Big things in the wind! Don't mention it even to the Army commander.' "

"You knew he was English?" I asked.

"No, not personally," the auctioneer replied. "But I have a friend who talked to him one day, in English. My friend speaks English well, having been a deck steward on the *Paris* before he retired. The English chap was dressed as a colonel, a Fritz, and he spoke German perfectly, you understand. 'Ah, well,' he said to my friend, 'I am not a German at all. I am a spy, but don't say anything about it.' My friend, naturally, didn't say anything about it, even to me, until after the landings. On the day following D Day, my friend saw the chap again. He was still a colonel, all right, not a doubt. But an English one."

"They're shrewd, the English," I said.

"More than one would think, to look at them," the auctioneer said.

I have made no attempt to verify the story about the British colonel.

We walked across the cobbled street to a small place called the Café du Port, where the auctioneer ordered some kind of poison-green alcoholized "pippermint," because, he said, his doctor had told him coffee was bad for his kidneys. I risked the coffee, but added a jolt of Calvados as a kidney guard.

"Seeing the Germans work so hard to improve the port, we didn't expect the attack here, either," the auctioneer went on. "Still, when we heard the guns at dawn, we said, '*Ça y est.*' But that's all in the past. It's the fish that annoy us now. They rarefy themselves. The total catch of the port is greater than during the between-wars, but that's because there are more boats. The catch per boat is less. And each boat represents such a placement of money! There is a new one in the basin—a seventy-three-footer—with every latest gadget for spotting fish. She must have cost thirty million francs [eighty-five thousand dollars] to build. The owner won't get his money back for twenty years. I used to own two boats, but I sold them."

"Doesn't the Bishop of Bayeux still bless the fleet every year?" I asked.

"Yes, Monsieur," the auctioneer replied. "But the fish have lost the Faith."

Leaving the Café du Port, I walked along the edge of the outer harbor to the beginning of the long west jetty that I might have seen from the LCIL 88 on D Day, had the weather and circumstances been otherwise. The outer harbor was described concisely in a monograph issued in 1944 by Admiral A. G. Kirk, commander of United States Naval Task Force 122. It is a "semicircular basin approximately 1,640 feet E-W and 1,260 feet N-S, encircled by two granite moles. The western mole is 1,490 feet long; the eastern 1,390 feet long. . . . A spur, called the Epi de la Poisson-nerie, extending 312 feet from the shore, divides the basin into two parts, of which only the eastern part is usable. . . . The western portion . . . though larger, cannot be used to secure ships as it is encumbered by a mudbank drying out at 10 to 13 feet. . . . The entrance channel lies be-tween the heads of two curving moles. . . . The width of the channel is 328 feet."

The western part of the basin—the one that dries out, or almost—is the *plage* of Port-en-Bessin, where at low tide children hunt shrimps or pad-dle in the inshore tidal pools and the braver adults venture out into the shallow swimming waters inside the elbow of the jetty, where it swings over toward its fellow. The jetty was built in 1860, out of great, carefully cut blocks of stone. A rampart, also of stone, runs around the outer, seaward edge. The inner side is a steep stone slope, with a few flights of steps cut into it at intervals. Sometimes the children use the steps, but for the most part they simply scramble up and down the seaweed-covered slope like flies on a wall. The tide was low when I began my walk, and the jetty acted as a sounding board to echo the voices of the swarms of juveniles within the amphitheater. Each tidal pool was the center of a band with its own pecking order—very small boys trying to drown very small girls, small girls trying to drown very small boys, and medium-small boys trying to frighten medium-small girls by pretending to drown them. Older, manlier types, from eight to eleven, had stationed themselves on the rampart with long fishing poles, dangling bait in the deeper water outside. They apparently banned girls from this serious activity. Girls of the same age group lay on the sand farther inshore, their skirts drawn up to their underpants, their eyes closed, and their faces toward the summer sun, trying as hard as they could to incubate themselves into women.

I walked out on the jetty to a point just before it turned and looked west toward the sweep of Omaha Beach, with the calm water in front of it and the green cliffs in back. The cliffs were not imposing at that dis-tance. They were no more than a hundred to a hundred and thirty feet high where they flanked Easy Red. I had remembered them swollen with danger. There were a couple of small sails—draggers with auxiliary en-gines, probably—down toward Pointe de la Percée, but although I looked carefully, with racing glasses, I could see no soldiers standing in the water anywhere.

3 / Tickety-Boo on Easy Red

WHEN I FIRST came to the ancient, illustrious, minuscule city of Bayeux, as an American newly entitled to vote, the book I carried in my pocket was the 1926 edition of the Hachette *Guide Bleu* for Normandy. In it, the capsule description of the city began:

> BAYEUX: 7,026 inhabitants (*les Bayeusains*), former capital of the Bessin [the low-lying area between Caen and Isigny], seat of a bishopric, is situated in the verdant plain watered by the little River Aure. Its cathedral is one of the most beautiful of France, and the "tapestry of Queen Matilda" constitutes a curiosity unique of its kind. Bayeux, which is as the bird flies but 7 k. 5 from the sea, is the point of access of the small shore resorts of the Bessin.

After a résumé of the city's two thousand years (it was the Roman city of Augustodurum), the *Guide* threw in a bit of interpretive reporting:

> On the eve of the Revolution the old city was above all a city of the Church. . . . It was also a city of bourgeois and retired government officials. . . . The immense changes of the nineteenth century have hardly touched it; it remains a city of priests and *rentiers*, where the rich stockmen of the region meet on market days. It may be seen what interest Bayeux has for those enamored of the past.

Nearly all the next nine pages were devoted to the cathedral and to the "tapestry," which is, to be more precise, a narrative cartoon strip embroidered on linen, telling Matilda's husband's side of his conquest of England, along with the events leading up to it. At the time the cartoon appeared, her husband, William the Bastard, was just beginning to be known as William the Conqueror. (Lebatard is still a common surname in Bayeux, but those who bear it claim no royal descent.) The tapestry was a publicity release. Because it was in pictures, the vast illiterate majority got the general idea, and the running legend made its points in extremely easy Latin for the benefit of the small literate minority. The cartoon is simple and stylized, with plenty of violent action, like "Smilin' Jack." Matilda and her ladies added a border of uninhibited medieval female fantasies for the beef-cake, or reverse-cheesecake, trade. She had the tabloid formula cold. As a consequence, her version of that prototypical colonial war has prevailed in popular history. Harold, according to

William's wife, was not only a crude fellow but a cad. He maintained a love nest in England while getting himself engaged to a fine, pure girl in Normandy. It was both as a jilted future father-in-law and as a bilked legatee that William launched his expedition, and any attendant territorial acquisitions were purely incidental to his civilizing mission. (In a lost sequel to the tapestry, of which we have only a description by a Norman monk, Matilda is thought to have shown how the Normans improved sanitary conditions in England and taught the natives to wear blazers.)

When I decided to go back to the part of Normandy that includes Bayeux, I bought the latest edition (1952) of the *Guide Bleu*, in order to be prepared for any striking changes. This time I read, under "Bayeux":

> City of 10,246 inhabitants (*les Bayeusains*), former capital of the Bessin, seat of a bishopric, is situated in the verdant plain watered by the little River Aure. Its cathedral is one of the most beautiful of France, and the "tapestry of Queen Matilda" constitutes a curiosity unique of its kind. Bayeux, which is but 7 k. 5 from the sea, is the point of access of the small shore resorts of the Bessin. . . . On the eve of the Revolution, the old city was especially an ecclesiastical city, where the people of the Church supported numerous beggars; it was also a city of retired bourgeois and government officials. . . . The immense changes of the nineteenth century hardly touched it; it remains a city of priests and *rentiers*, where the rich stockmen of the region meet on market days. It may be seen what interest Bayeux has for those enamored of the past.

This reassured me. I had visited the former Augustodurum once between the 1926 and 1952 editions of the *Guide Bleu*, when it was the headquarters of the Allied Twenty-first Army Group, Field Marshal Sir Bernard Montgomery commanding. That was soon after the Allied landing in Normandy in June 1944—the Army group included the British Second and American First Armies—and for a while it looked as if the Field Marshal might install himself there *en permanence*, like William in his English capital city of Winchester long ago. The British occupied Bayeux on June 8, which was D-plus-2. The Germans pulled out of the verdant plain without defending the city, so it was freed without damage. They fell back on the stronger position in front of Caen, fifteen miles to the southeast, where they held for the next seven weeks, penning the British into the Bessin. (It has been contended since by one school of military historians that the Marshal was holding the Germans out of the Bessin, but if he was, it was in the manner of the Rhode Islander who stuck his hand into a hole after a weasel. "Have you got him?" the fellow's brother yelled. The weaseler yelled back, "The sonofabitch has got me!") During all this period—longer than the Austro-Prussian War of 1866—the enemy made no serious bombing attack on Bayeux. Pursuing some higher strategic aim, they forwent attack upon the military vehicles swarming up from the beachhead. As these vehicles arrived, the British military police channeled them into a series of traffic circles around the center of town, and from the air the place must have looked like a shooting-gallery target, with the cathedral in the middle to mark the bull's-eye and the Hôtel du Lion d'Or, which was the Army Group command post, in the next ring outside it. The circles were designed to let the lorries get around the town on their way to forward areas, and the military police maintained the circular pattern so staunchly that visiting jeeps bound for the Lion d'Or were sometimes forced to revolve around the city until their gas ran out or their occupants gave up and went away. A dream of the Bayeux shopkeepers had come true: There were tens of thousands of potential customers. But there was nothing to sell except Camembert cheese, which is produced in the region, and which was prevented by the battle line from taking its normal course toward Paris. A flood of Camembert had backed up on Bayeux. Shopwindows normally devoted to other kinds of merchandise were full of cheese. There is no mass market for Camembert in either the British or the American Army. Caught in an outer eddy of the traffic whirlpool one evening, a jeep driver and I made three two-and-a-half-mile circuits between walls of window-displayed Camembert. I at last got out and bought some, telling the driver to pick me up on his next time around. When we arrived back at the First Army press camp, at Vouilly, near Isigny, I offered to share the cheese with colleagues, jeep drivers, and, finally, in desperation, Army press-relations officers, but none would have any. A supply of Camembert is not the sort of thing you keep under your cot indefinitely, even in a well-aired tent. I wouldn't throw mine away, though, and I didn't have to, because while I slept, the late Ernie Pyle stole it from under me and threw it away himself.

Another of my memories of the city in its phase of atypical animation is an occasion when I allowed myself to believe that even in wartime a French-speaking American willing to pay adequately might find a French meal in Bayeux. I failed miserably, involving in my failure a jeep driver, whom I had kept away from Vouilly and the mess tent. Determined to restore the situation, I thought of M. François Coulet, the former *chef de cabinet* of General de Gaulle, who had been placed at the head of the civil government of liberated France—it consisted entirely of the Sous-Préfecture of Bayeux at the time—by the French Provisional Government, in London. It had been important to the Free French to take over smoothly in Bayeux, in order to set a precedent. The Western Allies, it is painful to recall, had not recognized the Provisional Government as the government of France, even provisionally, and the Free French feared the same kind of *fait accompli* that had faced them after the landings in North Africa. So before anybody in Washington had time to dredge up a Darlan, the Gaullists had popped M. Coulet, a strong personality, into

Bayeux. The *fonctionnaires* there had accepted him without any fuss, and the precedent would be hard to upset as the Armies liberated new territory. Where M. Coulet was, I knew, there would be a square meal, and he did not disappoint me.

Aided by the gathering darkness and a French cop, the driver and I sneaked through the whirling circles and arrived at M. Coulet's residence, a private house that sat behind a walled garden near the cathedral. Coulet is very tall, like his *patron*, and, like him, chilly-mannered for a Frenchman, but he relaxes more easily than the General. Beneath the manner, which is perhaps mimicry, he is a friendly man, lucid and amusing. He had had his dinner, but an old woman servant, the first civilian to cook for me in freed France, produced another—an omelet, veal cutlets, and a salad. She then offered us some Camembert, but we declined it.

After dinner, we talked of politics. The conversation turned on de Gaulle, and I remember two details that may serve some future Plutarch. Coulet said that the General never sweats, even after the most violent exertion, and that he knows all the works of Racine by heart. In circumstances of stress, he said admiringly, the General was likely to break into *alexandrines* he considered apposite. Coulet, recognizing their source, would reply with the next couplet. Master and disciple would go along that way for nine or ten scenes and feel spiritually refreshed. Coulet himself was later French Ambassador in Belgrade, but it is unlikely that he talked to Marshal Tito in couplets.

After I had looked long at the whole sweep of sand that stretched away from the end of the Port-en-Bessin jetty without seeing a single ghost, I told Michel we would go back to Bayeux. I wanted to look at the cathedral, but I didn't tell him so. He already considered me mad for having hired a car and him to bring me down from Paris to look at an empty beach.

"*Après, Moosioo, Deauville?*" he asked insinuatingly. Michel liked destinations where he would be likely to meet hired-car chauffeurs of his acquaintance. Once they delivered their American charges to the concierges of Palace Hotels at the end of each day's driving, the chauffeurs were free for an evening of refreshment and trade talk, the latter in Russian. In this system of transportation, of which I got occasional glimpses during my difficult conversations with Michel, the concierges furnish the sole means of communication between the chauffeurs and their paying prisoners, and levy a heavy commission on both. Once committed to the chauffeurs selected for them by the concierges of their Paris hotels, the Americans, like runaway slaves on the Underground Railroad, are entirely dependent on their silent guides. It is a tribute to the devotion of the concierges of France that few such consignments are lost in transit, although, Michel allowed me to understand when we knew each other

better, the human shipments sometimes arrive at a wrong destination—
Saint-Jean-de-Luz, for example, instead of La Baule, or Ostend instead of
Geneva. *"Pas importa beaucoup,"* he said, with a merry Ukrainian laugh.
"Noo soo rend compta oo sont." (In *langue chauffeuroise,* which has
affinities with both Provençal and Old Slavonic, this means, "It doesn't
matter much. They never catch wise to where they are.") The concierge
of the hotel where they arrive simply readdresses them and forwards
them to where they were supposed to go. In the hotels of *grand tourisme,*
chauffeurs get rooms and meals at a special rate. For Michel this was an
important point, because he had asked me for a flat salary, out of which
he paid his own expenses. In villages like Port-en-Bessin, where no one
was used to chauffeurs, there was no price differential. This increased his
antipathy for his surroundings. *"Paysans,"* he said disparagingly of the
Port-en-Bessin citizenry, as if the Ukraine of his youth had been a land of
private eyes and taxi dancers. *"Chassa poisson."*

"After Bayeux," I told him as we walked toward the car, not wishing to
instill any false hopes, "we are going to a place called Vouilly, but on the
way we are going to stop off at the beach of debarkation—*Plage* Easy
Red." He opened the door at the right of the driver's seat, waited until I
got in, closed it behind me, bowed, and then walked around behind the
Versailles to take his seat at the wheel.

"Après Boolioo," he said with resignation, *"Voolioo."*

There are only two cathedrals I have ever liked in my life. One is Notre-
Dame de Paris, but only at a distance. The other is the cathedral at
Bayeux, which is also called Notre-Dame but is about as ladylike as a
Norman knight whacking off a thane's head. The knights who followed
William the Bastard wore simple shirts of chain mail, like iron mackin-
toshes and about as ornamental; they rode short, strong horses they could
jump down from easily when they saw a dead man with a ring finger
worth chopping off and could jump onto again as nimbly when they saw
his friends coming. They were all muscle and business, like Moon Mullins.
You can see them in Matilda's comic strip. To understand the decline of
Western chivalry as a military force, you need only compare Matilda's
pirates on horseback with the gloriously illuminated fifteenth-century
Livre des Tournois of King René, in which manicured Clydesdales
swathed in *robes de chambre* transport knightly Fancy Dans encased in
patent burglarproof vaults—and at that the passengers used blunted
lances, to be doubly sure of not hurting one another. Off their horses, they
were as helpless as sea turtles turned on their backs, and out of their armor
as vulnerable as hermit crabs drawn from their shells.

The cathedral offers corroborative reading matter for those enamored
of the past. The front consists largely of two great, blocky stone towers,
combinations of skyscraper and donjon, whose façades are broken only

by slits of windows with outlines like armor-piercing shells. These towers remain from the Romanesque cathedral that William the Bastard ordered built after his great amphibious operation. Most of the other elements of the original cathedral were destroyed by fire in 1105—a great pity, because they were replaced with comparatively namby-pamby Gothic. In the two original towers, William built the kind of fortress for God that God would have liked had He been William. They constituted a defensive position a small detachment of angels could hold against all the Powers of Hell, pending the arrival of reinforcements. The Powers must have been easy for William to visualize, because his direct ancestors in the preceding century had been Norse pagans.

The later architecture is a clear record of the progressive enfeeblement of the Middles Ages, like the transition from mail shirts to couturier armor. Early in the thirteenth century, a bishop of Bayeux named Robert des Ableiges surmounted William's savage towers with spires, which was like putting New Year's Eve clown hats on busts of Sulla. In 1099, when William's towers still looked like fortresses, William's son Robert and other rough men stormed Jerusalem; by the late fifteenth century, when Louis XI was adding the last *style-flamboyant* jingle bells to the cathedral, the Turks had taken Constantinople, and Bayeux was a city of priests and *rentiers*.

I reflected on these things as we drove to Bayeux, and Michel, presumably disgruntled, said nothing. At the Hôtel du Lion d'Or, I abandoned Michel and the Versailles and set out on my own, wandering through the town, inspecting the cathedral, and having a glass of Calvados, which was the only new thing since 1926 that I could notice. Then I routed out Michel, and we set off for Easy Red Beach and Vouilly. Just outside Port-en-Bessin, we turned off to the left on a third- or fourth-class road, and presently passed through the village of Sainte-Honorine-des-Pertes, named for the many shipwrecks at the foot of its cliff. We breathed the sea, although we couldn't see it over the tops of the cliffs. On the seaward side of the road, there were wild roses in the pastures, the grass was coarse, and the cattle had a more enterprising, world-conscious look than the inland animals on the other side. At Colleville, five miles along the road, we turned right, onto a miserable downhill dirt track that had once been the subject of exhaustive Intelligence reports. One of the few exits from the beach, it marked the eastern limit of Easy Red, and it was given the name of Exit E-1. The planners depended on these widely spaced primitive exits to get all our vehicles over the cliffs and onto the existing road network. The spire of the Colleville church, seen over the cliffs from the sea, was the marker for E-1, and the Intelligence sheets expressed hope that the spire wouldn't disappear during the preliminary bombardment. When I first saw E-1, a couple of days after the landing, it was lined with signs that read, *"Achtung Minen!"*

Michel went down the hill as cautiously as though it were still mined, for the Versailles, as he reminded me every time we hit a root, was brand-new, and the hired-car man would give him no further jobs if he brought it back with a neurosis. This was its maiden cruise, and despite the fact that I had rented it as a medium of transportation, Michel tried to make me feel that I was merely the chosen instrument of its introduction to life, a Lord Melbourne to this thirteen-horsepower Victoria.

A government or a public-spirited magnate interested in the maintenance of French self-esteem would subsidize the production of a large, fast, beautiful automobile to replace in the world scale of elegance the vanished Hispano-Suizas, Delahayes, and Panhard-Levassors. Never before have the French been at the same time so susceptible and so automobile-conscious, and the fact that the Americans, the British, the Germans, and, latterly, even the Russians, have been building big, luxurious cars contributes to an unavowed feeling of lost status. France is a nation where, more than in any other, inner well-being depends upon outward appearance. The point was well understood by Louis XIV, both Bonapartes, and General de Gaulle. That the popular symbol of success the world over is now a big car may mark a regression from the more sensitive age of Stendhal, for whom it was a good carriage; in any case, it is out of the question for most Frenchmen to make the symbol of success a Cadillac, which in France costs as much as a Rolls-Royce does in America. The Cadillac symbol also adds subtly to the sum of anti-Americanism. The proletarian, unable to afford that good omelet that is not made nowadays without breaking six-cent eggs, sees a rich compatriot in a big American car and thinks of him as a *parasite américanisant*. If he saw him in a big French car, he would still think of him as a parasite but not as an *American*-type parasite. If, for reasons of economy, a French government must choose between subsidizing this car and holding Madagascar, it would do well to drop Madagascar.

By the time we reached the beach and turned onto the rudimentary road, hardly more than a pair of parallel ruts, that follows the high-water mark, Michel was showing symptoms of nervous collapse. Since I was depending on him to get me to Vouilly, I allowed him to stop the Versailles on the safe side of a tidal puddle in the road three-eighths of an inch deep. He sat murmuring *"Waterloo, Waterloo, n'avansa pas,"* which I took to mean *"Voiture lourde"* (heavy car) "can't go farther." To show my displeasure, I got out before he could run around the Versailles to open the door for me.

I walked off along Easy Red, trying to remember how it had been on that rough morning eleven years ago, but it was no use. The tide was far out (at H Hour it had been high), and the sand, smooth and yellow, shimmered in the sun. I walked along a grassy bank, a foot or so high, just above the high-water mark. It had figured prominently in our advance Intelligence, and hundreds of Americans, emerging from the water, had claimed its uncertain shelter. Now it was just a little ledge covered with bunch grass, daffodils, and a kind of yellow ranunculus. There was a single hull still on the beach—an LCT. It looked like an island between sea and grass, equidistant from me and from the blue water. I walked out toward it across the damp, firm sand, crosshatched with tidal rills. The tide was still going out. Offshore, a few concrete chunks of Mulberry, as the artificial port floated over from England was named, still showed above the water. Out on the horizon, where I had seen a big transport, the *Susan B. Anthony*, lift her nose out of the water and settle on her bustle, nothing moved. Swinging on her cable at the turn of the tide, she hit a mine dropped in the water by a German plane the night before, and sank, stern first, in less than fifteen minutes—a gracefully impressive casualty. The water around her boiled with landing craft; never was a crew better-situated to be rescued. That was a couple of days after D Day, when Mulberry was about the busiest port in the world. LCTs, barges, DUKWS, and assault craft ferried men and ammunition, and, farther out, the commandeered merchant ships and the LSTs lay at anchor. Now it was as if I had come back to the Upper Bay and found it empty.

As I started toward the abandoned LCT, I could see a family group— two couples and three or four children—scouting gingerly about her, as if they still feared an explosion. She lay deep in the sand, and in settling had made a shallow moat about her, which retained a few inches of water. A woman started to climb aboard, and one of the men grabbed her arm; I suppose he was telling her some nonsense about booby traps or live shells. The children squatted in the water under her bow. I thought I might join the group and get off a few instructive lines about the way things had gone on the great day—how they could not imagine the difference be- tween that day and this. I was still preparing my little *discours*, which would present me and the heroic American nation in the best light— without pretension, of course, and even with a suspicion of humor—when I saw one of the men, who had been observing my approach, signal to the others in the group. The adult members of his band gathered around him like wild horses around an old stallion with his nose in the wind. All then started to move inshore, herding the children in front of them. They were upwind from me, and as they came abreast of me, I heard this chap say to his probable wife, "It was a near thing. If I hadn't spotted him, we would have been for it. He would have said hello and then told us for the next half hour how he and his pals came ashore on this very spot." They were not French but English. I wished William the Bastard were there to deal with them.

I was amused that the boor should have thought me capable of forcing my company upon strangers. Ignoring him as ostentatiously as possible, I went on to the LCT and regarded it for a long time, as if I had never seen one before, until the trippers were so far away that it was perfectly plain I wanted nothing to do with them. Just as a small boy who knows himself to be safely awake tries to re-establish the mood of a nightmare, I looked back at the cliffs. A couple of nights after the landing, I recalled, Commander Gene Carusi, a Navy beach-battalion C.O. who had crossed with us on the LCIL 88, had been sleeping in a cave on the side of a hill, believing all his troubles were over, when an American antiaircraft shell, fired on a low trajectory from a ship, nearly killed him. Carusi had prematurely white hair, and an Army medic bending over him said to another medic, "It's no use moving that old bastard; he'll die anyway." This interservice irreverence made Carusi so mad that he survived. Looking at Easy Red in the sunlight, I found it impossible to believe that anything violent had occurred there. The great conical bird cage of tracer bullets over Mulberry at night, with the German planes flying between its bars, was hard to hang over the *petite plage du Bessin* in memory. There are places where you can believe in history and others where it is more difficult. We had no Queen Matilda to record our episodes—only millions of photographs, and nobody wants to look at them.

After a while, I headed back for Michel and the Versailles. He greeted me warmly. He had begun to think of me as his only link with the world of private eyes and taxi dancers. I was glad to see him, too. As a sign of reconciliation, I allowed him to get out and open the door for me, and we started back to the road at Colleville, away from Easy Red and bound for the place Michel called *Voolioo*.

4 / Madame Hamel's Cows

ON JULY 18, 1944—a Tuesday, as I remember it—part of the 29th, or Blue-and-Gray, Division, which was formed originally from Maryland, Virginia, and Pennsylvania National Guard units, fought its way into the city of St. Lô, the seat of the prefecture of the Département de la Manche, in Lower Normandy. St. Lô, which had a prewar population of about twelve thousand, was deserted, except for unevacuated German dead. Correspondents—among them me—who entered shortly after the troops saw little, because they either hugged what they hoped would prove to be the lee of a wall or lay flat on their faces during their sojourn. The Germans, having been thrown out of the city, were reacting like a drunk who has been chucked out of a saloon and then throws a beer bottle through the window. Rising briefly to cross a street at an intersection, I saw the assistant division commander, Brigadier General Norman D. Cota, receive a wound in his cane-carrying arm. He shifted his stick to his other hand and stepped inside a gaping shop front while a medic put a dressing on the damaged member. Cota came out in time to see the correspondents departing as rapidly as possible, and my last memory of that victory is of the laughing general waving his stick and yelling, "Don't leave me now, boys! Don't leave me now!" The wound hurt worse later. When I next saw the General, he said, "I was standing out there to give the boys confidence, but it didn't work out right." A couple of days before the wounding, I had encountered him in the wooded country near St. André de l'Epine, a hamlet on the right flank of the German position. He was stopping soldiers who were drifting back from the firing line. "Where are you going, boys?" I heard him ask a pair of stragglers, and they pulled up sharp when they noticed the star on the helmet of the spindle-shanked, Roman-nosed old man alone in the road with his walking stick.

"The Lieutenant bugged out, sir, and we thought we might as well, too," one of them said.

"Harses! Harses!" the General said in a non-Harvard New England accent. "I haven't seen any lieutenant coming this way. Get up there before he notices you've been away." Cota was a Regular, born in Massachusetts. He waved the stick and they went back.

After leaving General Cota in St. Lô, some of the correspondents went to see Major General Charles Gerhardt, the division commander, a couple of kilometres farther back, to congratulate him on his capture of the city, for which the 29th had been fighting hard for a month. General Gerhardt was a sporting type, an old West Point third baseman who had acquired the habit of peppery talk. "Sir," one correspondent said, in a highly technical tone, "could you explain to us the strategic significance of St. Lô? Why has First Army made such a point of capturing it?"

"Well, Peanut," the General said, "it's a catchy name. It fitted well in headlines, and the newspapers took to using it every day. After that, it became a morale factor, so we had to capture it."

The General knew better, but his answer stirred up the sediment of *War and Peace-cum*-Siegfried Sassoon that lies at the bottom of every civilian's thinking about the Military Mind. St. Lô was the confluence of arterial roads from the south and east, through which the enemy might have been able to pour reserves to smother a breakthrough farther west. Its capture was like a tourniquet on an elbow, permitting an operation on the forearm. The General couldn't have said that without giving the next move away, but he might at least have said something Delphic and stuffy that the fellows could have put in their dispatches.

Gerhardt's reactions were snappy, as an infielder's have to be, but he didn't always stop to think of their effect. For example, there was the occasion, after the storming of Brest, when the Division buried a couple of thousand of its dead. The Division's Catholic chaplain told me afterward in Paris, in the bar of the Hôtel Scribe, that, marching the men away from the cemetery, the General had the band play "Roll Out the Barrel." He wanted to change their mood. The chaplain considered it an inappropriate choice. Furthermore, he objected to the prayer the General had offered at the funeral formation; the chaplain thought the General should have left that to the professionals. "He said, 'May the good God in Heaven, if there be one . . .'" the chaplain reported. "Who is he to voice a doubt of the existence of God?" I said it was just a reflex—the General wanted to be sure all bases were covered before he threw the ball. As a matter of fact, Gerhardt used to say grace before every meal in his mess.

When St. Lô fell, there was for the moment nothing for the correspondents to write about, and this was bad for their dispositions. Deprived of the progress-toward-St. Lô report that had been the essential element of their daily stories, my colleagues, especially the press-association men, began to bicker. All of them had used the St. Lô dateline on their stories of the capture (I had seen nobody carry a typewriter into town, much less stay long enough to write a story), but one man was charged by his colleagues with having used the dateline when he had not actually been in the town at all. The others considered this unethical. The press-association boys constantly competed among themselves on a strict time basis, like milers. The day after the capture, a United Press man wandered through my tent and his, carrying a copy of a cable he had received from his home office. "'Beat nearest competitor one minute forty-five,'" he read aloud proudly. "'Kudos, kudos, kudos.'" Then he looked up and asked "What does 'kudos' mean?"

"It means they've decided not to give you a raise," another correspondent said.

The tents were in the First Army press camp, where there were censors and excellent mobile facilities for the transmission of our stuff by Press Wireless. The camp was at a place called Vouilly, which was near Isigny, an early capture, and about fifteen miles north of St. Lô. Vouilly was a crossroads, an old church, a harness-maker's shop, and a grocery-café. Down a wooded private road beyond the crossroads lay a big farm with an immense, moated farmhouse that was known as the Château. In that country of rich peasants and hard-drinking gentry, the line between large farmhouses and small châteaux is seldom clear; houses, like families, cross and recross social lines. Mme Hamel, the proprietress of the Château, made no claim to nobility, but she looked a proper chatelaine—tall and straight, with a high forehead, a long, straight nose, bright-blue eyes, and white hair. She was sixty-two. The living room of the Château, equipped with Army chairs and tables, was our pressroom. It was bigger than the city room of the Providence *Journal & Evening Bulletin* when I worked there a long time ago. The dining room, as long and almost as wide, was never used; Mme Hamel, her son and daughter-in-law, the farm servants, and the neighbors made their headquarters in the kitchen, which was a fine room in itself, with a wall spigot that ran hard cider. Our tents were in front of the house, along the edge of one of the great pastures, which we shared with fifty cows. Every morning during the fighting for St. Lô, we would have a large, hot breakfast in the mess tent and then climb into jeeps, two or three correspondents to a driver, and take off for the battle-field. The mess tent was our ace good-will builder with the farmers; it was run cafeteria style, and all of us generally left a lot on our plates. The swill was of a magnificence unparalleled in that thrifty countryside, and the farmers carted it away for their young pigs and the mothers of their still younger pigs.

By five o'clock in the afternoon, we would be back. It was a sensible way to work, but it created what the quarterly-review fellows call a dichotomy—we were in the war from nine to five and out of it from five to nine. The weakness of the Luftwaffe at that stage increased the dis-crepancy between the front and Vouilly. There was no danger on the roads, and although we maintained a blackout at night, we felt silly about it. The best route to the front was a sunken road that led up through St. André de l'Epine. For days, the progress of the 29th along it was slow, bloody, and sometimes nearly imperceptible. If you stuck to the road in the Division's wake and went slowly, in order not to raise dust, you could not be seen, except at gaps in the high hedges that lined both sides, and there was not much chance of your being hit. There was always fire going over the road, clipping leaves from trees and making you feel important, but you would have needed a stepladder to climb up to it. The Germans believed in firing their weapons often—as advocated by the distinguished American military critic, General S. L. A. Marshall, and numerous Chi-nese tacticians of the fifteenth century—in order to keep their spirits up. When we got to the point where vehicular traffic ended—there was al-ways an M.P. on the spot to say where it was—we would dismount and walk as far up front as the mood moved us. It was on one of these forward excursions that I heard Cota talking to the stragglers. The feature writers would try to cull thrilling incidents from company commanders and walking wounded, and the correspondents from places like Min-neapolis would go around trying to find soldiers from Minnesota to ask them what R. F. D. route they lived on. During the last days of the battle, I had been heartened by the number of abandoned German bodies in the road; it showed that the survivors were moving backward a lot faster than they wanted, or they would have carried their dead with them. They were unlikable people and they had no business in that part of France anyway.

The infantrymen and artillery spotters, who had to fan out in the fields on both sides of the road, naturally were more likely to be hit than we were. The wounded who could walk had their hurts dressed at first-aid stations by the roadside and then hiked, or hitched jeep rides, to the rear. When we turned back at the end of each day's outing, we picked up as many of them as we could. They would sit on the hood of the jeep, embarrassed because they had been hit. "Looks like we might have some rain," they would say, or "Wonder how the Yankees are doing." This embarrassment is the mark of a good competitor. He neither complains nor tries heroically to pretend it was jolly good fun; he feels that he personally is responsible for whatever happened to him. His prototype is General Joe Stilwell, who said, after his eviction from Burma, "I claim we got a hell of a beating"—not "I claim the cards were stacked against us" or "I claim we won a hell of a moral victory."

Driving homeward, we would look into the faces of the infantrymen coming up to the line, in single file, well-spaced, heavily burdened. They were preoccupied faces, neither aggressive nor self-pitying, from a region that was neither Big City nor Wild West. They had been twenty months in Devon before coming to France, and they had fitted in well with the gentle Devon people. "The finest physical men I ever saw," General Cota had told me in England when he first went to the Division. "But there's no meanness in them. I try everything I can think of to make them mean, but it's no use." The General had come from the 1st Division, which was loaded with Brooklyn boys, and they had convinced him that the best premilitary preparation was two brisk battles daily for a seat in the subway. "Those fellows in the First were little, but they didn't care who they stepped on," he said, explaining his theory.

When I got back from my exciting incursion into St. Lô, I rushed to the kitchen of the Château to inform Mme Hamel of our glorious feat of arms. The family still possessed a private stock of old Calvados, and these tidings were, I thought, of a sort to stimulate hospitality. I was in a great hurry to get there before André Rabache, the Agence Française correspondent, who also knew about the Calvados. I arrived to find the Hamels and a large collection of neighbors seated around the long kitchen table. I could sense that they had been engaged in a serious discussion.

"Madame," I said proudly, for I wanted her to think well of the American Army, "I come from St. Lô. The city is ours! Now we can advance!"

"I felicitate you, Monsieur," she said. "I am happy to hear it."

"I also, *mon Commandant*," said a neighboring farmer, whose name was Lesavoureux. "*Correspondant*," which is not a military rank, seldom registered with the Normans, who usually promoted us to *commandant*, or major. "But I ask myself what will happen to the pigs."

"The pigs?" I asked. My mind was still on Cota, directing traffic among the shells.

"Yes, *mon Commandant*—the young pigs who depend for their nourishment on the leftovers of the mess," he said.

The only ray of hope I could offer was that the enemy might make a tenacious defense of the environs.

Mme Hamel, who had the manners of a marquise, came to the rescue. "The pigs are already well launched," she said, turning a disdainful eye in M. Lesavoureux's direction. "They have had a good start in life and will make out for themselves perfectly. Perhaps Monsieur would like a glass of Calvados? The day must have made you some emotion."

The Normans are not a sheeplike people. Give them a lead and they start in the opposite direction. While M. Lesavoureux wanted the Army not to advance, a farmer down the road, whom I visited one night with Hamel *fils*, was irritated by our procrastination. He had part of an armored division in his pasture. "I was extremely pleased to see them arrive," he said, "but they are ruining my hay crop." I had been reliably informed that this farmer owned several barrels of old Calvados, and it was my object to obtain one of them for our mess. To do this, I was prepared to buy one of his pigs, also for the mess. (The correspondents made up a pool for these supplementary purchases and declared the Army personnel in.) The farmer's counterplan was to use a small amount of the Calvados to get me drunk, and then sell me the pig, but no barrel. After a long evening, I came away with neither the barrel, which he wouldn't sell, nor the pig, which I wouldn't buy without the barrel. But I had the makings of a frightful hangover free, and M. Hamel said that nobody else had ever got anything for nothing from the host of the armored division.

I was thinking of all these things as I rode west from Colleville to Isigny with Michel. We were on the road that runs along the top of the cliffs overlooking Omaha Beach, and at Isigny, where our road would end, we would look for a road that led south to Vouilly, where I hoped to find Mme Hamel as magnificent as before. I wondered, too, about the descendants of the pigs. When we got to Isigny, which is famous for producing the thick cream that comes to the table with strawberries in French restaurants ("Isigny: 2,787 inhabitants; specialties: butter, tripe, cream, mussels; sixty per cent destroyed by bombardment on June 8, 1944."—*Guide Bleu, Normandie*), Michel was favorably impressed by the white stone buildings, in the style of Robert Moses comfort stations, that have replaced the sixty per cent destroyed. "*Moderne!*" he said. "*Pas comme Boolioo.*" He had been unfavorably impressed by the fishnet of medieval alleys that entangles the cathedral. Isigny is dominated by the large, modern, double-winged plant of the Reunited Butteries & Creameries, a modern-Norman testimonial to God's bounty. At a quartermaster's dump in Isigny in 1944, I drew the best pair of shoes I have ever owned, free. I was sure that it was no use looking for the quartermaster's dump now, however.

Michel stopped in front of the Reunited Butteries & Creameries and went inside to ask the way to Vouilly. He came out visibly depressed, as always when he had to ask directions. "*N'esista pas, Moosioo,*" he said, in what I had learned to recognize as his notion of French. "*Voolioo, personne a entendoo.*" He stood with folded arms, his great brown eyes liquid with astonishment at his plight, like those of an abandoned straggler from Denikin's army who has heard the first howls of the advancing Bolsheviki. His eyes told me that I had been a fool to leave the caravan routes between Paris and Deauville or Paris and Cannes in order to lead him after a mirage. Nothing to do now but throw our burnooses over our heads and wait for the St. Bernard dogs.

"*Voolioo*, evidently, does not exist," I said to him, in an excessively reasonable tone. "But *Vouilly, Vouilly, Vouilly* exists!" I made a move as if to go myself to ask directions.

"*Ah, Vooyee!*" Michel said, starting back at a run, and adding, over his shoulder, "*Pooquoi Moosioo dit Voolioo?*" Michel had lived in France for twenty-seven years, and it was a point of professional honor that he, the resident, should translate for me, the foreigner. It was a little like traveling through the British Isles with a Gurkha dragoman who insists on carrying on all intercourse with the natives. Michel returned from the Reunited this time with the expression of a Scotland Yard inspector who has cracked a big case. *Ça y est*," he announced. "*Vooyee—ah!*," and he looked at me indulgently before he headed the Versailles in the right direction.

Vouilly is less than a dozen miles inland, but when you get there the sea is forgotten. Bayeux, with its ten thousand inhabitants, seems an incredibly large city in retrospect, and its cathedral, embodying renovations right up through the fifteenth century, is Saarinen compared to the small, unornamented Romanesque church of Vouilly, with its front and rear elevations like equilateral triangles on squares and its tower no higher in proportion than a peaked helmet on a Norman swordsman. The Vouilly church hasn't been changed since the eleventh century. The tower is off to one side of the peaked roof, like a fighter's head tucked in behind his shoulder. It surveys a countryside where the fields are surrounded by ditches and banks of earth, with trees, all ensnarled with vines and bushes, growing out of the tops of the banks—the most ancient of cattle fences. The rain falls most days, the grass grows all through the year, and the cattle turn it into milk. During the fighting in Normandy, the Army Civil Affairs branch tried to evacuate peasants from farms that became battlefields, but they wouldn't go. They said the cows had to be milked. The cattle, in the open all year round, but never out of call of the milkmaid, develop a character that is neither wild, like that of range cattle, nor passive, like the milk factories that spend most of their lives in front of a manger. They are, like the Normans, independent, gluttonous, and indomitable. The Germans defended the hedged fields as fortresses, and the cattle remained in them as audience, chewing the rich grass as the shells burst among them and falling on their sides like vast milk cans. In the immediate vicinity of Vouilly, however, there had been no fighting.

Michel asked a woman at the café the way to the Château, and she said to turn left on the first "avenue" past the crossroads. She meant the first avenue of trees, but Michel was amused. "*Elle appelle 'avenoo' oona toota petita roo*," he said. "*Paysanne*." For Michel, "avenue" was a term reserved for the Avenue des Champs-Elysées, the Avenue Foch, and thoroughfares of equivalent luminosity. He consented to turn down the bucolic version of an avenue, though, and after about a mile I saw the Château in front of me, sleeping among the trees. Its tower was higher than that of the church, but not high enough to rise above the oldest trees around it.

We drove between the hedged fields, over the bridge and into the farmyard. Mme Hamel and her son were sitting under an apple tree, shelling peas. They were surrounded by fat, sleepy hens, among whom walked peacefully a fat, sleepy tomcat. When Michel stopped the Versailles, Madame looked at us, shading her eyes with one strong hand, and called out to her son, "It's he!" She rose—a trifle heavier but even more impressive than I had remembered her—like a great, noble Percheron mare, white with age, getting up in a field, and walked over to the car as I got out. Her son came with her, and as they reached the car, she said to him, "I knew he would come back someday." To me she said, "Why didn't you come last year with the others?" In 1949 and 1954, I knew, airlines had organized two junkets to Omaha Beach for former war correspondents who had been there—and some who hadn't—thus reaping a modest harvest of mentions in news stories. I had not been with either party, and Mme Hamel, in consequence, had felt slighted. She liked all her old guests to come back to her. For five weeks in 1944, the Château had been one of the news centers of the world. Scores of millions of people in America had hung on the stories of the ugly fighting among the dead cattle, and every word had gone out through the mysterious wireless trucks on Madame's farm. She had not been insensible to the honor, or to the excitement of feeling herself in the know, and she had not begrudged us the use of her pastures. All the old guests who made the junkets came back to visit, she said. She remembered me particularly, because I had hung around the kitchen so much, cadging refreshments.

Her son is a quiet man, short, wide-shouldered, and long-armed. He walks with a limp that dates from the time when, as a prisoner of war of the Wehrmacht, he was made to work at clearing French minefields in Alsace. (It was in 1940. Pétain had capitulated, and the Germans were paying only nominal heed to the Geneva Convention rules on the treatment of war prisoners.) Hamel had stepped on some kind of antipersonnel device, crippling himself so badly that the Germans had sent him home during a much-publicized "restoration to their families" of a number of French prisoners incapable of useful labor. The Vichy regime had touted this as a great concession. By 1944, when I first met him, he had got around to thinking of his accident as a stroke of luck. He could walk again—although with a limp—he could work as well as ever, and he was home, on the right side of the Allied line, while the fate of his former fellow-prisoners was dubious. They had already had to undergo four years of heavy Allied air bombardments, and it was still possible that the S.S. would massacre the survivors when Germany was invaded. (As it turned out, they didn't, but the omission was probably due to a loss of nerve.) Hamel *fils,* therefore, didn't hold the minefield incident too strongly against the Germans. Certain aspects of his captivity had even amused him—particularly the fright of the civilian population during the first great air raids.

Every evening, while the correspondents pounded at their typewriters, he would circulate among them with a cup and a jug of milk still warm from the cow, like a hospitable precursor of M. Mendès-France. He was married, but the dowager Mme Hamel remained the chatelaine, and I had only to see the Hamels together to know that nothing had changed since 1944. The pastures stretched green and profitable before us, with not a tent in sight. The cows roamed free over the site of the vanished latrine, a part of the pasture that for some bovine reason they always resented being dispossessed from. They upset the simple installation almost every night, I recalled.

I asked Mme Hamel about the health of some of the cows I remembered: L'Anglaise, so called because she came from the Channel Islands; La Nageuse, who leaped into the moat to cool off; La Nitouche, who pretended a maidenly aversion to the bull. None survived, Madame said, but they had left daughters and granddaughters to make assault upon their records of lactation. She kept a book listing the names, biographies, and milk records of her cows—usually about fifty. I remembered Madame and her lady in waiting, the milkmaid, leading La Nitouche to the bull, who was the terror of the soldiers, even though he was fastened to a stake by a chain and nose ring. "Do you remember the day the bull broke loose and charged the jeep?" she asked me, as if she had been following my unspoken recollections. I remembered, of course. He had knocked out one of his eyes, which occasioned rejoicing among the men.

In the pasture on the other side of the road, where the mess tent had stood, the grass had the look of never having been disturbed by man. I could not help asking the question that had been on my mind all the way from Omaha Beach.

"And the pigs, Madame?" I asked. "The pigs that were fed on the leavings of the *popote* and that we abandoned when the Army was compelled to advance?"

"Most of them died," Madame said. "But of indigestion. They had been *too* well fed. Figure to yourself, Monsieur. A pig fed on pancakes and sirup—God never intended it. It was Providence that the Army advanced when it did, because in three more days they would all have perished." I was happy to learn that, in effect, the interests of First Army and of the pigs of M. Lesavoureux had coincided, although M. Lesavoureux was too shortsighted to recognize it.

The day was hot, and Mme Hamel proposed that we go inside the Château. In the long, cool hall that parallels the front of the house, I felt I had come back to one of my homes. (A mobile man has many. There is, for example, a cabin on a Norwegian tanker that I wake in often, although I haven't slept there for fourteen years.) On one of the great oak doors leading off the hall, a sign reading "Press Room" preserved the memory of the *grande époque*. Mme Hamel led me into the room next to it, the dining room—a symbol that the Château was on a peacetime footing. M. Hamel and Michel trailed along, Michel with his beret in his hand, and looking about him with a new appreciation of the Hamels' status. These were more than *paysans*; they were kulaks.

The dining room was full of furniture I could not remember from the war days; there was a long Norman table of old, scarred oak, surrounded by carved chairs, and a buffet and an armoire, equally old. All were in what I judged to be the style of the late sixteenth or early seventeenth century; the *ferronerie* of the buffet and the chest was of a chaste hammered crudity that proclaimed the age of all the work. "I made them myself, all but the armoire," said M. Hamel soberly. "The armoire is real, of the sixteenth century, and I copied it."

"And the hardware? The handles, locks, hinges?"

"All," he said. "Everything."

"How did you age the wood?"

He smiled. "It's my secret."

On one wall hung a portrait of a rough-coated chestnut foal with upstanding crest and ears. "The colt that was born while you were here," Mme Hamel said. "The foal of the mare the Cossacks abandoned." There had been Cossacks in the region before we came, part of the Vlasov Army of Russian prisoners of war, who had consented—under threat of death, they inevitably said when captured by us—to fight for Hitler. They were an anomaly in the German Army, since the Germans never trusted them sufficiently to issue them any armament that dated from later than the First World War. They had therefore been used principally to garrison and overawe regions where nothing much was expected to happen, and they had a nasty reputation for pillaging. The German soldiers had as low an opinion of them as they had of their Italian allies in the Mediterranean, and when the Allies landed in Normandy, the Russians fought only until it was apparent that the debarkation was no mere raid. Then they quit. Prisoner-of-war pens were full of them well before we began to get genuine Germans in quantity. The Cossack horses wandered through the pastures and mixed in with the herds of cattle. I remembered the mare and her foal, a pair of tolerated free boarders among Mme Hamel's cows. She didn't have the foal any longer, she said, but the old mare was still around. Young Mme Hamel, the daughter-in-law, had painted the picture.

Mme Hamel brought out a bottle of muscat de Frontignan, a cloyingly sweet white wine from the south of France. Wine is a ceremonial drink in Normandy, where none is grown or made. It is not expected to taste good. M. Hamel came to my rescue by bringing out a carved wooden bottle of Calvados. "I remember you always preferred this," he said. "It's some of our own make, ten years old." I reflected bitterly on the greed of all the Americans, including me, and all the British who had passed through in the war years and accepted the one-or-two-drinks-at-a-time hospitality of the Hamels, drying up the prewar stock. This 1945 Calvados was merely promising, but I got a couple of glasses down in order not to offend my hosts. While I was tasting the Calvados and Michel was sipping the horrid wine with the air of a connoisseur, Madame went to the armoire and returned with a great black scrapbook of clippings, like a grand old lady of the theater; she resembles one. These were her clippings of things that had been written about her, unfortunately all in English.

"This is by M. Beyle," she said, and I looked at the byline and saw that it was not by the M. Beyle who took the nom de plume of Stendhal but by M. Hal Boyle, the Associated Press columnist and an old tenter in the pasture, who wrote how glad he was that Madame was alive and well and nicer than ever. There were other clippings of the same tenor; the authors, or other Americans who saw them in print, had evidently sent them to her. On pages where no clippings had been pasted, former guests had written appropriate sentiments and their names and addresses. One of these entries was by Colonel Monk Dickson, the G-2, or head Intelligence officer, of First Army, dated a couple of days after the fall of St. Lô. It said, as nearly as I can remember now, "To the good family of the Château de Vouilly, which was the repository for a week of the secret of Cobra." Cobra was the code name of the breakthrough, on the road that stretched west from St. Lô to Périers, that stove in the left wing of the German Seventh Army. It led to the great hooking movement that rolled the Germans up like a window shade. Dickson's name reminded me of an incident at the Château that I had forgotten. A bit after the capture of St. Lô, General Omar Bradley came there to see the correspondents and tell us about the next move, so that we could prepare to cover it. The tall, long-jawed, gravely humorous Missouri general who was so great a soldier that he never felt compelled to bark to prove it, arrived by jeep with his aide, Major Chet Hansen, and Dickson. Hansen carried a map under his arm. The lecture room in which he chose to announce the impending doom of the German Seventh Army—"I may be sticking my neck out in predicting it," he said, to soften any hint of cockiness—was a shed that had been extended forward with canvas tent sides and roofing to serve as a movie theater for the troops. General Bradley said that he hadn't wanted to trouble us to come over to his headquarters—there were so many of us. It had also been a far better idea, from the point of view of security, for him to disappear from headquarters for an hour than to convoke fifty correspondents and their jeep drivers, which would have given an always possible enemy agent a decided notion that something was up. But Bradley did not mention this second consideration; it was as if he shrank from encouraging the idea that anything he did could be important. General Collins' VII Corps, so reinforced that it virtually constituted an army—four infantry and two armored divisions, I think—was to make the strike, amputating the arm that Gerhardt had bound off. Then Patton's Third Army was to come into official being—it already existed incognito, behind the First Army line—and race through the hole south and west into Brittany. (The plan worked even better than that, of course, but a fighter starting a combination of blows can't know in advance the other fellow's capacity to absorb them.) I suppose that if I had heard Scipio, before the Battle of Zama, describe how he was going to cancel out Hannibal's elephants, I would have thought it a historic occasion, but it took Monk Dickson's handwriting in Mme Hamel's book to remind me that I had heard Bradley call his shot.

"Do you remember when General Bradley came here and spoke in the shed?" I asked Madame.

"Yes," she said. "There were no movies that night."

The breakthrough, I remembered, was originally scheduled for July 21. It was aborted by soaking rain, which spoiled the ground for armor and made it impossible for the bombers in the preparatory air strike to see their targets. So Collins didn't jump off until July 25, when, aided by perfect visibility, the Air Corps inflicted heavy casualties on our 30th Division. I remembered that because I had watched the planes, not knowing where their bombs were falling. We had wondered why the 30th didn't get along and let us move.

I felt that it was time to go, because there was not much left to say. I answered all the usual biographical questions: How was my family? Did I continue to occupy myself with journalism? It was superfluous to ask Madame how she occupied herself: the fifty cows, the hay crop, the chickens answered that. Her son, I was sure, was an excellent farmer, but she would never dissociate herself from any of his farming. Seeking a question slightly less idiotic, I asked her how she amused herself.

"Ah, well, there is always fishing," she said brightly.

This was a side of Madame's personality I had never divined. She scarcely seemed the type to put on waders and dangle feathers at the end of a line.

"Where?" I asked.

"But here, in the dining room," she said. "Look."

She led me to a window, and we looked down at the moat, covered with lily pads, beneath which the water barely moved. It was originally formed by diverting a stream and leading it around the house, but the stream was no Mississippi to begin with.

"It is full of carp," Mme Hamel said. "Every day, I throw bread and bits of potato out the window. The carp accustom themselves to the snack. Then I put a hook in a potato and drop my line from the window. Instantaneously, I have a magnificent carp. You cannot make yourself an idea how good really fresh fish is."

I gazed at her with an admiration whose extent I could not express. No sunburn, no squint from looking at the shimmer on water, no bony shins sticking out of Bermuda shorts—she displayed none of the usual stigmata of the sports fisherwoman, yet her technique was of an intellectual refinement that my friend Colonel John R. Stingo would have appreciated. The Norman carp is a conservative investor, not to be taken in, like a trout, by the flash of an obviously spurious insect flourished under his nose like a prospectus for Montenegran carbuncle mines. The kind of chump who is really worth taking has to be encouraged by a series of unwarranted dividends. "When the habituation is achieved," Colonel Stingo once said to me, describing a parallel process, "the chump, ascribing his success to his own talents, demands a further opportunity to invest. He is then ready for the *coup de grâce.*"

I did not wish to take time to explain to Madame who Colonel Stingo is, so I did not call her attention to their affinity. Instead, I asked another question: "Are there pike?"

"Not here, but in the pond," Madame said. The pond is behind the house, at a distance of perhaps a hundred yards. It is a large pond, shadowed by great willows, and in 1944 we used to swim in it. "My son goes out there," Mme Hamel said. "I don't often have the time. He has also arranged a pair of shooting holes, with sliding shutters, in the back of the carriage house, which is turned toward the pond. When the wild fowl settle on the pond, he goes into the carriage house, slides back a shutter, and shoots them."

It sounded to me like the only shooting and fishing preserve I ever wanted to lease.

The Hamels, *mère et fils*, entreated us to stay for dinner, but I had it in my mind that I wanted to get back to Bayeux before dark.

"Come back soon," Madame enjoined me as we departed. "I am getting old, and who knows?" She looked imposingly durable.

As Michel and the Versailles and I headed back up the avenue of trees, I composed in my mind the text of an advertisement I meant to insert in the *Times* when I was next in London: "Syndicate of keen guns being organized to fish Merovingian carp moat, hunt Gallo-Roman duck bath in attractive country surroundings."

A cow, perhaps a daughter of L'Anglaise or La Nitouche, stopped eating to watch us as we passed, then again put her head down in the grass.

5 / The Communion Card

FOR ELEVEN YEARS, now, I have carried in my wallet, along with a slowly changing repertory of telephone numbers, Irish Sweepstakes tickets, and family snapshots, a fraying card, printed in France, that bears an engraving of a small boy dressed in a black suit of adult cut, with a white sash tied around his left arm, kneeling on a faded pink carpet before a lamentably insipid representation of Jesus, who, standing before an altar, is holding a chalice in His left hand and offering a wafer to the boy with His right. An elderly saint, clutching an Easter lily, stands to the right and rear of the boy, and all three figures are grouped against a background so lacking in the illusion of perspective that it resembles a photographer's prop. At the bottom of this St.-Sulpice buckeye—such cards are sent out by the hundreds of gross from Paris to churches in the provinces to be used as First Communion announcements—is printed this invocation, in French:

Be, O Jesus, present in the Eucharist, the joy, the happiness of all my life. (Abbé Perreyve)

On the other side is written, in the small, Sunday-best hand of a French schoolboy:

Souvenir of my solemn Communion, taken in the church of Barneville the 30 July, 1944. Raymond Legaillard.

Whenever, through the years, I chanced to come across this card, usually while shuffling through the contents of my wallet to find my social security number, a postage stamp, or a theater ticket, it reminded me of a blond boy—pug-nosed and slightly freckled, and dressed like the figure in the Communion scene but not minding it a bit—staring up woozily at me from his seat at a table between two Norman uncles, who had made him ecstatically drunk on Calvados in the dining room of the Hôtel de Paris, in the village of Barneville. The boy was the magnet of all attention for perhaps the first time in his life. He was eleven. His relatives had gathered to do him honor. His uncles, red-faced men with downsweeping mustaches, looked like ancient Gauls, and their wide backs strained the black broadcloth coats they had long ago worn at their weddings and that they would be buried in, by which time their torsos might be sufficiently reduced to be again comfortably encompassed by the garments. They forced great wedges of creamcake and slugs of Calvados alternately upon their nephew. A great-aunt—a wiry, animated old woman who made her living catching lobsters trapped in rock pools when the tide went out—did not disapprove of the way the uncles plied the boy. She took drink for drink with him. The sun beat down on the kernel of Barneville, which consists of a huge old church, two elementary schools—one for boys, one for girls—a market place, and a single business street, a hundred yards long. The town, which by then had been out of the fighting for some weeks, is a shore resort, but the beach and its hotels are a mile away. The boy's sister, a tall girl of seventeen, handsome but already inclined to flesh, sweated candidly through the long-sleeved dress she had worn to church. She was not actively gay; rather, she was solemn, as if drink had made her reflective. Her downy upper lip quivered occasionally as her mood continued to droop. The *patronne* of the Hôtel de Paris, which was the center of the social life of the year-round inhabitants, flitted in and out of the dining room, keeping tabs on the waitress, Andrée, who was very pretty and whom the male guests pinched in the behind at every opportunity.

There were women of all ages in the party, and I asked M. Ribaud, the Barneville electrician, which of them was the boy's mother. It was M. Ribaud who had drawn me, and a jeep driver lent me by the Army, into the Communion party. His wife, who was the teacher at the girls' school, was one of the boy's numerous aunts. I had met M. Ribaud only that morning, in a less chic café, down the street. *Pastis*, patriotism, and then Calvados ripened our friendship quickly. He dragged me and the driver to his home, behind his shop, for the midday meal, explaining that he needed us as tangible excuses for being an hour late; Mme Ribaud had a *gigot* that might by now be overcooked. The *gigot* proved not at all too cooked, because Madame, who understood her husband, had popped it into the oven an hour later than she had told him she would. Afterward the Ribauds had brought the driver and me along to the Communion party—a true Norman *carrousse*, which had begun after the church ceremony with a dinner for all the relatives who didn't live in Barneville proper, and was apparently going to continue forever.

Answering my question, M. Ribaud told me that the boy's mother had died in a hospital in Cherbourg the week before, and that his father, driving a civilian ambulance on a road fairly near the front lines, had been killed only a few days earlier by a strafing airman, either a German or an overenthusiastic Ally. The boy knew of neither death; the sister knew of both.

The boy gave me the card, and I have carried it with me ever since.

While I was in Normandy, I thought I would like to go to Barneville and look up the Ribauds and see what had happened to the boy, Raymond Legaillard, who by that time should have been twenty-two and just what his surname signifies—a brisk strong fellow. Michel and I were at the Hôtel du Lion d'Or, in Bayeux, when I told him of our new destination. He had almost resigned himself to the crisscross cat's-cradle pattern our path made over this part of Normandy. I am not a very imaginative person, and so I am constantly seeking out sequels, instead of taking it for granted that they have taken place and letting it go at that. If I leave a town in flames, for example—as I left La Haye-du-Puits, some twelve miles from Barneville, in 1944—it is likely still to be burning whenever I think of it. So I find it comforting to go back and make sure that somebody has put the fire out. I suppose that what drove Sinbad back to sea all those times was the same inability to let ill enough alone. He was not a creative artist, although posterity has chosen to think of him as a liar. He had the opposite, reportorial deformation—a compulsion to have another look.

Distances are not great in that corner of Normandy, in which the Germans contained the Allied armies between June 6 and the beginning of August 1944. A straight line from just west of Bayeux, in the northeast section of the Cotentin peninsula, to Lessay, in the southwest, is hardly forty miles long. It corresponds roughly to the American front in mid-July of that year. The most direct route from Bayeux to Barneville is by Isigny, but on the morning of this excursion I had Michel make a slight southward loop by way of St. Lô, so that I could again see the new city that has been built on the site of the one I saw destroyed. There are some Norman towns, like Bayeux and Port-en-Bessin and Vouilly, that the war passed over without changing anything essential about them; returning to them, I had been reassured. In St. Lô, however, when the war moved on, it took the scene with it. I recall the disappointment of the Army Civil Affairs team, which spent weeks, while the infantry was fighting for St. Lô, formulating plans for reviving the municipal administration. By the time shells ceased to burst in the streets, there was nothing left to administer. Now I saw that in the years since the war something had been built in the old city's place that was about as Norman and time-hallowed as the Cross County shopping center in Yonkers. Driving through the streets of the new St. Lô with Michel, I felt like the man in Fitz-James O'Brien's story "The Lost Room." This chap is ejected by a group of reveling evil sprites from his furnished room in the New York of 1850 and returns a moment later to discover that the room itself has vanished. I could not find the convent wall against which I had pressed for shelter or the street intersection where I had seen General Cota wounded, because they no longer existed.

"*Beau, beau,*" Michel said as we entered St. Lô. "*Moderne.*" His urban ideal is the Avenue des Champs-Elysées between the Rond-Point and the Etoile. St. Lô was modern enough, but I didn't feel that I had ever been there before. "Don't stop, Michel," I said. "To Lessay and then La Haye-du-Puits." My 1944 jeep driver, an Iowan named Whitey White, used to pronounce the latter town "Hooey da Pooey." Michel pronounced it in precisely the same way. What ancient links between the Ukrainian and Iowan dialects this indicates I am not prepared to discuss. Once I had Michel fairly launched along the road leading from St. Lô to Lessay—the road, incidentally, across which our VII Corps made the first great attack of the breakthrough—I again began to think of Barneville, where I ate every Sunday dinner of that remote July.

The lot of a spot-news war correspondent is trying when his side neither advances nor retreats. There are often intervals of more than a day between events—a truth that the daily paper, by its very nature, must deny, or it would have no excuse for coming out daily. The correspondent can exaggerate whatever is going on, but the official communiqué and the censor are there to cramp his style, and when several days pass without confirmation of his melodramatics, readers yawn and editors give the play to other fronts. The newsman can, alternatively, take the portentous tack, pretending he knows that a sensational development is imminent, but when nothing continues to happen, that peters out, too. The press-association men watch each other morosely, afraid to stray from Army Headquarters lest they miss a small lead. In a better position are the fellows from the dailies and the writers of syndicated features. The hand-out catchers of the press associations will cover the former on any actual new developments, while all the latter have to do is collect anecdotes— humorous or heroic, as the mood or editorial demand moves them. Most fortunate are the writers for magazines, who, when nothing happens, do not have to write about it.

The essential Allied activity in Normandy in early July of 1944 was building up a reserve of supplies and of troops to support an offensive. Nobody, naturally, was allowed to report how that was progressing. There was the ugly, constant, grinding struggle in the apple orchards as our 29th Division of XIX Corps, aided by the 2nd, on its flank, inched its way southward toward St. Lô, but the day-by-day results of the fighting were not spectacular. People reading of them must have thought it was a return to the positional warfare of the First World War, in which gains were measured in hundreds of meters. We correspondents accredited to the First Army, which at that stage was the only active American army in France, went curiously and dutifully into the St. Lô fight several times a week. We also made jeep trips to other parts of the line. It was in the course of one of these diversionary explorations—to VIII Corps, on the extreme right of the American line—that some of us discovered the Hôtel de Paris, in Barneville. As I remember, VIII Corps consisted of two or three inexperienced infantry divisions and one airborne division, and was pushing, but not rushing, southward—"maintaining pressure" is the cliché that comes back to me out of a disused vocabulary. Its right reached to the sea, and there were marshes in front of its left, so all the pressure was maintained in the direction of La Haye-du-Puits, which straddles the one highway south from Barneville.

A colonel who was the chief of VIII's Intelligence section showed us maps and told us that, as far as he could find out, the enemy had less power than VIII, but, having a rather favorable defensive position, was holding—stubbornly and irrationally, in line with Hitler's prescription. Thinking back, I can see that these odd lots of under-strength Wehrmacht divisions and exotic auxiliaries recruited from prisoner-of-war camps, with a stiffening of a few good parachute units, had no future in the region. They were like the blue crab, which stupidly hangs on to an unhooked bit of meat while the crabber slips a scoop net under him. I did not know that Bradley was preparing the net, the handle of which he poked through the German lines below St. Lô approximately four weeks later; the Germans, Balts, Russians, and Mongols comprising this makeshift Nazi left flank were the first crabs to land in the basket. In default of this knowledge my colleagues and I found nothing stimulating in the situation, and after politely excusing ourselves from the midday meal in the VIII Corps mess, which would probably have been no better than ours at Vouilly, we made for Barneville and the Hôtel de Paris, which I had noted from the road. (I once had a flair for making such finds, but it has been destroyed by the *Guide Michelin*. While I have no confidence in the *Michelin*'s stars for superior restaurants, I am touted off the places it doesn't star.)

The meals at the Hôtel de Paris were good indeed. In this corner of the Cotentin there were shellfish and inshore fish to complement the butter and beef that abound in the whole region. The proprietress, the owner of a café in Cherbourg who had taken refuge in Barneville, ran the kitchen with a touch of big-town sophistication. She was a scrawny, enameled ex-soprano, whose extravagant circumspection inspired doubts about her past. In order to get good wines from her (these, unlike the cream and butter, were irreplaceable), we had to pay her a bit of court. The *soi-disant* leading candidate for her favors was Bob Casey, of the Chicago *Daily News* syndicate, who spoke no French but looked like a major general. Casey would roll his eyes and emit terrifying groans, representing passion, and I would order up the last bottles of Nuits-St. Georges '37.

The country around Vouilly had nothing like the Hôtel de Paris, so Sunday trips to check up on VIII Corps became part of the press-camp routine. They continued until the breakthrough, on July 25. The Communion day must have been my last Sunday visit to Barneville, for a week later the war of position was over. The front lines and the press camp alike shifted far forward, and we were Paris-bound. Yet I remember dashing back on a weekday to get some lobsters that the old rock-pool woman had caught and left for me at the Ribauds' electrical shop in a shoe box with holes punched in the lid. They were packed in seaweed. At the shop, M. Ribaud asked me to call on his brother, who was also an electrician, in Villedieu-les-Poêles, on the other side of what had been the front lines, to tell him the Barneville Ribauds were safe and sound. So by then we must have already broken through, and how I managed the trip back for the lobsters, I do not recall. A couple of days later, I got to Villedieu-les-Poêles and delivered the message.

I have written before of the dual character of the Normandy front during the period of buildup and containment—nasty going up front, and lovely, fat, tranquil farming country a couple of miles back, undisturbed by enemy aviation or artillery. I have noted, too, the oddly guilty feeling it gave us, who did not have to remain in the front lines but had the option of going there whenever we pleased. We seldom visited Barneville without also puttering around some spot that we could permit ourselves to consider hazardous. On the afternoon after our first dinner, I remember being in a division's command post—I think it was the 79th's—which was in an apple orchard infested with snipers, who, a colonel informed me, were harmless if you kept moving. Division commanders vied in getting their headquarters as far front as possible. This one, whose name I forget, used to sleep on the ground and make his staff do likewise.

The colonel who reassured me about the snipers was an Ozark type; he said they couldn't have done much shooting before they got into the Army, since they didn't know how to lead a moving target. "If you just keep walking, they almost always shoot behind you," he told me. I looked around, and it was the most perambulatory headquarters personnel I had ever seen. The G-3 and the assistant G-3 were walking arm in arm, discussing something, and the G-4 and the assistant G-4 were walking arm in arm in the opposite direction, discussing something else. Even the warrant officers had for once got up from behind their tables and were walking. "We got some old Missouri squirrel-hunters in this outfit, and we are hunting the snipers down pretty good," the colonel said. "But we could do better if we had dogs."

While these martial memories filled my mind, Michel guided the Versailles west to Lessay, where we turned north, toward La Haye-du-Puits, on the road that parallels the coast. Michel is a comforting companion when you don't want to talk. It is when you try to bring up some mutually comprehensible concept that your troubles begin. "Hooey da Pooey!" he said triumphantly upon spotting the road sign in Lessay, and beamed with the relief of a Captain Frémont whose Indian guide has led him aright. Michel never quite believed in any of the places we set out for until we got to them, but he accepted road signs as favorable omens. The country we now started to drive through is not so rich or so thickly wooded as the land from Bayeux down to St. Lô, but the road is straight and good, running all the way from Mont-St.-Michel to Barneville and beyond with hardly a fork at which a driver has to make a decision—a course that suited Michel's talents. We consequently arrived in La Haye-du-Puits before I'd had time to get myself into a properly somber mood for it.

On July 9—the second Sunday of the month—I had gone down to Barneville with Casey and Hal Boyle, both of whom wrote feature stories, mostly good ones. Stopping in at VIII Corps before dinner, we learned that its forward elements were engaged in cleaning out La Haye, which in the interval since our previous visit had developed into a minor St. Lô. It was smaller than St. Lô and at the extreme western end of our line, so it was hard to ascribe any pivotal importance to it. If its defenders were pushed out, they would simply be shoved straight south on Lessay, where they had another good position. Because of the sea, there was no way of getting around them. But taking La Haye meant as much to VIII Corps as taking St. Lô did to XIX. Casey and Boyle and I all felt it would be callous to tell the G-2 we were cutting his battle in order to eat *sole bonne femme* and *tournedos Choron*. We decided, therefore, to attend the battle, but not until after lunch, when we would be in a better frame of mind for it. The Spartans on the sea-wet rock sat down and combed their hair before Thermopylae, and Casey, Boyle, and I ate *sole bonne femme*.

It was odd, though, finishing the big meal and the wines that went with it (we had white and red Burgundies), and then climbing into our jeep and heading south, past the summer villas in the summer sun, on our way to the fighting. From Barneville down to La Haye is, as I've said, a distance of only twelve miles, and for the first seven of them the road was unencumbered except for a few ambulances we met coming back and a few trucks we passed going forward. We felt none of the apprehension of the North African campaign—that enemy tanks might appear in a place where they were not expected or that planes might come out of the sky and hover on our radiator cap while we scrambled for a ditch. This feeling of security was newly acquired. (I had seen no enemy planes since the night raiders over the ships at Omaha Beach, and saw none until, during the breakthrough, I witnessed one attack by rocket-carrying Messerschmitts. Behind the German lines, things were different, as we discovered by the number of shot-up German vehicles we found along the roads when we advanced.)

As we drove down the road to La Haye that Sunday it was like going to Jamaica in time to have a bet on the third race, when most of the crowd has already gone through. Near La Haye, however, traffic was slower; it is amazing how frequently, when approaching danger, drivers who can read a road map perfectly feel that they must stop and ask directions. We ourselves stopped at a Medical Corps clearing station in a large villa that had a walled garden, where jeeps and ambulances were parked. We wanted to know how far to take our vehicle, but mostly we just wanted to stop.

A couple of big, country-looking soldiers out of one of the new divisions were standing at the south end of the garden, grinding their heads against the wall like little boys having a tantrum. They had the palms of their hands against it, too, and were digging into mortar with their nails, as if clinging for shelter against a hail of bullets, but there was no shooting going on around them. Some medics were trying to talk the pair into getting into an ambulance, so they could take them to the nice, quiet rear, but the men couldn't or wouldn't budge, or even talk. Instead they continued to grind themselves into the wall, sniffling, now, like little boys who have cried themselves out.

We left our jeep and driver in the garden, having been informed by the medics that "it" began just around the next bend in the road. Before long we were angry because they had not told us it was such a long walk.

I remember being in two places in La Haye-du-Puits that day, but I am not sure of the sequence. One was a very big modern house, with landscaped grounds around it (I took it to be a sanatorium or summer hotel), which the Germans had used as a barracks and then as a redoubt. It was foul with the smell that poured out of their abandoned blankets and mess utensils. (The German Army had two smells—one of sour cabbage, which permeated even its sweat-soaked blankets, and one resembling a blend of a camel house and raw ether, which attached even to fragments of shot-down aircraft. I don't know yet what that one was, but it was known from Norway to Cyrenaica as the Boche smell.) There were numerous bodies around the big house, but they hadn't begun to smell dead. I remember particularly a tall German, who had dragged a wicker chaise longue from the house and placed it on a hillock in the garden. There he had sprawled himself, binoculars in hand, to look about for likely places on which to call down fire. It was flat country, and even this slight elevation was serviceable. A fragment from an air burst had saved him the trouble of getting up. There was no fire on this house while we were there, although shellbursts were visible not far away, but I cannot remember whether I was there before or after we went into the town.

There was plenty of shellfire in the streets of the town, whenever it was we went into it, but street fighting, in my limited experience, is not particularly dangerous unless you want to fight personally. Observation for marksmen is limited, and there is defilade everywhere. You sprint from shelter to shelter. Even while I was running, I felt that it was a game that did not in any way affect survival. It is plausible that the basis of many gestures of self-preservation is simply superstition. The man involved feels that if he does not show solicitude for his own skin he will invite the retaliation of a dark power. This mechanism works heavily in favor of the companies that offer one-flight insurance to air travelers. Having taken out sixty-two thousand dollars' worth of insurance for two dollars and a half, the traveler feels sure he won't crash. Sprinting, nevertheless, through the burning town, we reached a company command post in a wrecked café. A Chinese pfc. from Elizabeth, New Jersey, had found an unbroken bottle of Calvados there, but he hadn't saved us any. The company commander was pleased to have visitors. We stayed around awhile, rather at a loss for conversation, and then left, feeling that we had atoned for our good lunch.

The 1955 town had been rebuilt more thoroughly, and also, I thought, more attractively, than St. Lô. We stopped at a café on the Grande Place that may well have been on the site of the one where the Chinese soldier found the Calvados; the new building stone had not had time to lose its first pallor, and the interior was late Third Avenue American, with a jukebox and a pinball game. Leaving Michel there, I walked on to where the road left the north side of town, trying to figure where the big house with the dead Germans around it had been; it was not a long walk. La Haye-du-Puits, like many other war objectives, is of such inconsiderable size that you wonder that it meant so much. There was no big house in sight when I reached the town limits, so I came back to the center of town. There I talked with a dashing man in a tweed jacket, *très anglais*, who was peering through a surveyor's transit, apparently to see if they had got the main street in straight, and he said that he was not familiar with the house I described, but that he was not of the region. He suggested that I inquire at the *mairie*, still housed in a temporary one-story plank building, which stood near the railroad station and was almost the last such structure in town. The municipal authorities must have feared criticism if they got their offices rebuilt before the taxpayers got theirs. At the *mairie*, I talked to the secretary to the *maire*, who corresponds to town clerk. *M. le Secrétaire*, who had a chewed gray mustache and wore spectacles on the end of his nose and a linen duster to protect his clothes, told me that the big house had burned to the ground on the night of the last capture of the town; La Haye had changed hands four times, he said. He himself had managed to avoid being evacuated by the Germans before the fighting began and had lived through it all in his house, a mile or two away. "They were times full of emotion, Monsieur, full of emotion," he added. "We are lucky to have survived them."

We shook hands on that, and I went back to the café, where Michel, neat and citified in his blue suit and white shirt, was keeping watch over the parked Versailles with the manner of a horse holder left alone in Indian country. He smiled gaily to show me how brave he had been, and after a bad beer we headed for Barneville. (You have to go far from the big centers in France now to get the bad old kind of sour French beer— all belch and no body, and served in a *canette* with a porcelain stopper attached to its neck by a wire.)

I was sure Barneville would not have changed outwardly, and I was right. There, on first view, was the surprisingly big eleventh-century

church at the turnoff from the highway. The other buildings of the town
are low and unimpressive, and I cannot think why Barneville should have
rated such a commodious place of worship nine hundred years ago. Then
the Hôtel de Paris, narrower and meaner than I remembered it, caught
my eye, and the triangular market place, with the business street running
out of its pointed end toward the sea. I told Michel to leave the car near
the hotel and come with me, but it was a market day and he said he was
afraid that boys or drunkards would break into the magnificent Versailles
while he was away. Michel treated his mount as if he were Father Divine's chauffeur and the Versailles were Father's Rolls-Royce. So I left him
standing guard over it, a neat and alien figure among the peasants who
were hefting screaming pigs by an ear and the tail. It gave me a holiday
feeling to be in one town that I had never visited except in quest of
innocent pleasure—the only kind any of us ever succeeded in finding
there, because *la patronne* kept such close tabs on Andrée.

The sun beat down as it had on all those successive Sundays in 1944,
and the breeze off the sea came straight from the Channel Islands. I had
no trouble locating the electrical shop of M. Ribaud, but the chap in
charge informed me that M. Ribaud was on a three-week holiday. "You
can find Mme Ribaud at the *école des filles*," he said. "Opposite the
church." I turned back, sorry to miss the electrician but sure his wife
could bring me up to date on the chronicles of Barneville. The town's two
elementary schools stood side by side, each two stories high and narrow
as a small private house. The doors were closed, and I supposed the
summer holidays were on. Nevertheless, I rang the bell at the door of
the girls' school, and a pretty girl opened it—a girl certainly far too young
to be Mme Ribaud, but not young enough to be a pupil in elementary
school. She, it turned out, was the Ribauds' daughter, who had been six
when I last visited the family, and who now, at seventeen, had just passed
her baccalaureate examination in Cherbourg and come home for the summer. I told her who I was, and she called her mother, who came to the
door wiping her hands on her apron, as if she had miraculously prepared
another *gigot* against my arrival. This time, she said, it would be only
beefsteak and fried potatoes, which she had begun to cook for lunch for
her son and daughter; during the summer the Ribauds lived at the school.
The son, who was eighteen, had also passed his baccalaureate a few days
before, and would go to the university in Caen in the fall. The girl was
hesitating between the university and a teachers' college.

Mme Ribaud asked me to stay to lunch, but I said I couldn't. I would
have liked to, but I didn't see how I could ring Michel in on the invitation, and I didn't want to abandon him. We went out to the kitchen,
which was the school's domestic-science room, so Madame could watch
the beefsteaks. She remembered the Sunday of the delayed dinner and
the Communion party. Her daughter said she thought she could remember it, too. Madame also remembered the message to Monsieur's brother.

She said the two brothers were taking their holiday together, driving. Presently her son came in from swimming, having bicycled up from the beach. He was a cheerful lad, wide between the shoulders, like the Norman uncles, but, quite unlike them, wearing shell-rimmed glasses and a crew cut. The mother and daughter—thin, quick, with clever, mobile faces—reminded me by their agility of the lobster lady I remembered so well. Mme Ribaud brought out a sweet white wine of the same genre that Mme Hamel had produced when I visited her in Vouilly. We talked of how I had met M. Ribaud that Sunday morning and of the *gigot*, which Madame insisted, in retrospect, *had* been overdone, and which I assured her hadn't. The children, amused but proud, said it was just like their father, making friends with strangers and inviting them home with him. I told them how much Whitey, whom Madame remembered as *le petit soldat*, had liked the family, although he hadn't been able to converse with them.

Then I asked Madame about her nephew, Raymond Legaillard, the principal figure of the Communion party. "He ought to be a grown man by now," I said.

"He was," Madame said. "He's dead."

"What a pity," I said. "How?"

"There was really nobody for him to live with as he grew up," Madame replied. "So he went up young to naval training school. He did well. He was a specialist and liked submarines. In 1952, he was on the *Sibylle* when she submerged in the Mediterranean and didn't come up. He was a very jolly boy, and very handsome. Wait!" She went upstairs and returned with a full-length portrait photograph of a smiling sailor in a striped *maillot*, white summer ducks, and the beret with the pompon—a wide-shouldered, narrow-waisted, long-legged, and impudent-looking young man. And, as Madame had said, very handsome. I thought of what had happened to his parents and then to him, and remarked, without originality, "He had no luck."

"Evidently," Mme Ribaud said. But when I asked her about Raymond's great-aunt, the old lobster lady, she told me she was doing fine—as spry as a plover.

I took my leave of the three Ribauds, all of whom I thought admirable, and walked back to the Hôtel de Paris. There I found Michel shaking his fist at a small, vague dog, which had been overcuriously inspecting the Versailles. I invited Michel to lunch with me, and he followed me over the threshold, looking back distrustfully at the dog. The enameled *patronne* no longer ran the hotel. Possibly she had gone back to her café in Cherbourg. The present proprietors, a pastry cook and his wife, had partitioned off half the front of the *grande salle* to make a pâtisserie, with a separate entrance from the street, which accounted for the narrowing I had noticed. The new *patronne*, who explained all this to me, was a blonde with a figure like a *vol-au-vent* of generous diameter and a skin like smooth custard. Several dealers from the market were already busy with the regular lunch, and as they appeared to be doing themselves well, I told the *patronne* that we would have the same. It began with a *croûte de volaille*, which, as the Hôtel de Paris presented it, was a bit of crisp, hot pastry with chunks of chicken embedded in it. *"Pirozhki!"* Michel exclaimed. There followed skate, not with the familiar black butter, but with a *sauce matelote*, made with red wine, and, after that, a *contrefilet* of beef, rare and beautiful, and about the best thing of its kind I have had since Barney Gallant closed his restaurant on University Place in 1948— two glorious square slices of beef, each a quarter of an inch thick, with *frites* as crisp as larks' legs. Then came string beans engulfed in butter, a lettuce salad, a Pont l'Evêque, and one's choice of the proprietor's *éclaires* or his *mille-feuilles*, still warm with the breath of the oven. The complete lunch went for five hundred francs a head, and I treated Michel and myself to a bottle of not-bad *muscadet* to accompany it. These, I did not trouble to inform Michel, were the funeral baked meats.

I still have the Communion card in my wallet, although I am afraid it will rub the luck off the Sweepstakes tickets.

6 / The Hounds with Sad Voices

I REMEMBERED another Norman house called a château, where the press lived for a week after the breakthrough, but the memory was like Le Grand Meaulnes' of the house he dreamed. I no longer knew precisely where it was, nor could I recall the surname of the proprietor, though I had one in my mind—de Fives. From Vouilly the press camp moved to a place called Canisy, of which I remember nothing except that the tents were in an apple orchard; and then in a few days to a house on the skirts of the Forest of St.-Sever. It was near a hamlet called Fontenermont, which is near the small ancient town of St.-Sever, which is not far from the small city of Vire.

This was a baroque house, although in rural Normandy, where the baroque lingered, it may have been of the late eighteenth century. It was tall in relation to its length, with a square tower that had a top like an *accent circonflexe* (∧). It was of gray granite, like most of the other buildings of the region of Vire, which is hilly and in many places wooded —the Bocage, or Bosky Land. Compared to the flat and rich Bessin, where Vouilly lay, the Bocage is romantic and energetic. The land is still good, but shading off toward the austerity of Brittany to the south. In the Bocage you begin to smell Brittany. It has a high incidence of small noblemen, of families that officered the Army, the Navy and the Church before the Revolution.

This house might have been built by a retired frigate's captain or a colonel, a younger son of such a family, returned from the wars against the English in the East or West Indies, and content in middle age to follow the staghounds in the Forest of St.-Sever. They hunted the stag with dignity and clamor, the slow, deep-voiced hounds driving him in wide, then narrowing circles, he running from the sound and not the sight of them, working into the center of the deep but not sufficiently entangled woods. At last he would stand exhausted in a clearing, or in a pond, up to his neck in water. Then the hired huntsman would advance and cut his throat, and the bandsmen would play their taradiddles for wind instruments. The horses, never out of a canter all day, would be turned toward home and the waiting holocausts of venison and game birds and the old Calvados, the dice boxes, and the canopied curtained beds closed like confessionals and full of secrets.

This family had enjoyed another period of prosperity in a more recent era, to judge from the vestiges of the chic of the early Third Republic that cluttered the house, like props for the production of a dramatic version of *Bel-Ami*. There were trophies of African spears and Arab scimitars on the walls, which were papered with an imitation of brocade, and faded green plush portieres drooped crazily from valances askew. Notably there was a stuffed leopard, its lips pulled back in a savage snarl from teeth that were no longer present. Age affects the grip even of plaster gums. The background of the leopard's rosettes had faded to the color of bad California white wine. Most of the furniture was crank and perilous to sit upon.

It all reminded me, sadly, of the illustrations in the thirty-volume-or-so set of Maupassant, bound in three-quarter green imitation morocco with gold ornaments on the spine, that had been the chief advertisement of sophistication behind the glass of my parents' Globe-Wernicke sectional bookcases. In those volumes I sought my first clues to sex, and to this day I retain a prejudice that gentlemen with curved jet-black mustaches and long-tailed coats are wickeder than others, and that ladies with big behinds and small feet are the most irresistible. I had arrived, at last, in my chosen décor, but sixty years too late. Maupassant was a Norman, and my long liaison with Normandy began in the Globe-Wernicke mahogany sectional bookcases, and probably in a bad translation.

I thought the proprietor, when young, might have shared the glories of the Normans-transplanted-to-Paris I remembered in the illustrations, slipping from behind portieres exactly like the ones that now hung in shreds, to put their arms about the hourglass waists of chambermaids in white lace caps. I was sure he had slain the leopard and had his photograph published, wearing *le casque tropical*, his feet and the stock of his rifle behind the prostrate victim's head: "M. *le Vicomte de Fives avec une belle pièce de gibier. Ce léopard faisait la terreur des noirs du Limpopo français avant que le sportsman normand l'arretait en pleine fureur avec une balle bien placée dans chaque narine."* But by the time we arrived he had regressed into peasantism. A great, heavy figure of a man, he went about in shirt sleeves, with checked denim trousers held around his pendulous paunch by an old harness strap.

The only vestige of the old chic that I confidently attributed to him was a hard straw hat, a *canotier*, or boater, that he wore indoors and out. (He was probably bald.) The old man's face and wattles were suffused with blood, and his mustache, of the color and aspect of hempen rope, no longer curled upward, as I was sure it must have once, but hung limp under his forceful nose.

The house stood on a low ridge with a higher ridge behind it. Our tents were pitched out behind the house, and to get to it we had to walk across what had once been a garden with flower beds marked out with rocks, and gravel paths between them. These boundaries were wiped out now; the rose bushes had gone to briar, but there were still late-season blooms, falling to pieces on their stalks. Petunias ran as wild as morning glory on a beach, and there were dusty zinnias.

We spent our days upon the roads, now that the war was all of movement, but in the evening we returned, and after supper wrote our dispatches in the blacked-out house, using as typewriter tables Levantine taborets inlaid with mother-of-pearl stars like those that cluttered living rooms from Lodz to Laramie in 1900. They still manufacture them in Damascus, but they must export them to places like the Dominican Republic. The censors and the Press Wireless men were set up amid the shards of elegance as we were.

Between the edge of our camp and the beginning of the garden we had to walk along the outside of a run fenced in with chicken wire, which contained eight or ten gaunt, sad hounds, with long heads and short legs, whose sad voices had the quality, at first emission, of echoes that have bounced around a valley. They were bassets of some kind, I knew at once, but higher on the leg and of a less studiously abnormal appearance than the English sort. Their flanks, as corrugated with ribs as a hunger striker's, were white flecked with black, their long, wide, trailing ears solid black and their faces black flecked with white. They were *bassets de Gascogne*, the old man told some one of us, the only pack of that strain in the northwest of France. I never talked to him myself; he did not invite conversation.

They were so thin, the old man was reported to have said, because under the conditions of the Occupation and rationing, it was hard to get meat to feed them on—even the meat of old horses brought high prices as *filet Longchamp*. (And because of the same phenomenon, I thought uncharitably, he would be sure not to feed them any of his own livestock when he killed.) Because the Germans had allowed the Normans to possess no ammunition for hunting, much less use any, the dogs were unexercised and unhappy. The old man said his hounds were of such an ancient and glorious breed that he could have sold them in couples, or one by one, at whopping prices, particularly to the Germans, but he had not wanted to disperse his breeding stock. I think he fed them on snared rabbits and other oddments as available.

The jeep drivers and cooks, some of whom came from hound-dog country, used to spend a lot of time in front of the chicken wire talking to the dogs, but the bassets were distant and surly. They scorned K rations. They might be down, but they were not so flat as all that.

If the soldiers had been horse cavalry, they might have found an unpopular officer's mount for the hounds to eat, but they had only jeeps. One night somebody stole one of the bassets, but I was away on an overnight trip to the Falaise pocket and so escaped suspicion. The abduction made a great stir. The old man protested to the lieutenant colonel in command of the press camp that it was not a question of the theft of a vulgar dog. His pack was a national historical monument, and Haro XVIII's disappearance reflected the blackness of the error committed by Louis XVI when he temporized with the mob. It was a delayed effect of the Revolution.

The lieutenant colonel made a serious try to find the historic animal, but he failed, as I expected he would. I have seen soldiers carry large dogs aboard a transport slung across their shoulders in barracks bags, and setters abducted from England leap from the cockpits of fighter planes landed on Tunisian airfields. The First Army moved ahead toward the Seine, and the press camp followed to Bagnoles-de-l'Orne, but the fate of Haro XVIII remained a mystery.

My fear of Michel's scorn kept me from trying to rediscover this house unaided. I could foresee his reactions if I asked him to begin inquiring after a house whose owner, of whose name I was uncertain, had once kept dogs with sad voices, or if I even let him know that such was the object of my search. When we arrived at l'Hôtel du Cheval Blanc in the city of Vire, however, I dismissed Michel and the Versailles, lunched, and then went on foot in search of M. Marcel Le Cornec, the publisher and editor of *La Voix du Bocage*—The Voice of the Bosky Country—a newspaper that I have received in New York every week since the conclusion of the war by M. Le Cornec's courtesy.

M. Le Cornec is a man of sensibility as well as intelligence. He respects the capricious forms nostalgia often takes, and when I related to him my desire to see for inconsequential reasons this Château of the Mournful Hounds, he volunteered to help me find it. St.-Sever and Fontenermont are fifteen miles or so from Vire, but well within the zone of circulation and influence of *La Voix du Bocage*, which is the most powerful organ of public opinion between St. Lô and Avranches. But, to begin with, he said, my recollection of the family name as de Fives and of the old man as a Vicomte must be erroneous.

M. Le Cornec is a tall and very handsome man who looks like George Washington *en littérateur*, Roman nose, blue eyes, high complexion, and mane of white hair long in back, over a string tie and corduroy jacket. He is, as his name shows, of Breton family origin, but began life in Paris. There he was a commercial artist during the twenties. He came to Vire to design packages and draw advertisements for a wholesale grocery firm.

Vire, like a number of other Norman towns at rail and road junctions, was destroyed by the Allied air bombardment of June 6 designed to stop the Germans from reinforcing their coastal troops. The city's printing plants disappeared in the ruins. When Vire was freed in August, M. Le Cornec founded its first postwar newspaper, printing at first in a less damaged city, until he could re-establish printing in Vire. I do not remember now, although M. Le Cornec told me, whether the publisher of the prewar paper was killed in the bombardment or disqualified for collaboration. At any rate, M. Le Cornec and his wife, a witty and spirited woman, made a paper with a decided personality.

Since M. Le Cornec is not a native, he takes an objective view of the remarkable world in which he lives. He keeps the paper's face straight, but his amusement sometimes filters through his long and circumstantial accounts of such affairs as the suit for defamation, for endless billions of francs, that a rich farmer brought against *La Voix du Bocage* ten years ago, for printing a speech of the mayor of the farmer's community. In the speech the mayor accused his *administré* of "moistening his milk" before selling it. To moisten milk is, in Norman, to add water to it.

When the farmer sued, *La Voix* recorded the news, along with a restatement of the grounds on which he was suing. He then sued them for a reiteration of libel. But the mayor's speech was an official statement, since he had made it at a meeting of the municipal council. *La Voix* contended that a newspaper must publish official statements. What had loosed the mayor's wrath against the rich farmer was that the rich farmer opposed the use of municipal funds to provide free milk for school children. Reading *La Voix* in New York, I was sure that was why the paper reprinted the story so many times, but they never said so.

Vire was the place where I stayed longest on my first exciting *prise de connaissance* with lower Normandy in 1926. I saw it for only a few minutes in 1944, so dreadfully demolished that I could not bear it for longer. Now a Vire had risen on the old site, solid, ugly, new without being modern. There was, in 1955, still a noise of drills and bulldozers. Construction was going on, but it was already irremediable. Each property owner had wrung as much money as he could from the State for reconstruction of what he said he had had, and then built a house containing the maximum number of cubic feet that could be roofed over, leaving the upper floors to be finished at his leisure in the years to come. One surviving monument was the Tour de l'Horloge, the old Clock Tower, that had once been a gate in the medieval city wall. The rest of the wall had been leveled by Henri IV, after the Wars of Religion.

The tower, with the gateway under it, stood astride the main street of the Vire I knew. Traffic passed between its legs. The bombs had cleared a space around it but left it crazily erect at the hub of the city. The traffic now passed around instead of through, and, indeed, the vibration set up by trucks might have brought La Tour down on the drivers' heads if they had persisted in the old way.

The sixteenth-century clock that banged out the time every quarter of an hour, night and day, was silent, knocked out of time when the bombs fell. The old Hôtel du Cheval Blanc stood next to the clock tower, and a guest unable to fall deeply asleep in fourteen minutes flat had a fat chance of getting to sleep at all. The new Cheval Blanc has been erected fifty yards from the old site, and when I slept there I was willing to forgive the Municipal Council for not having restored the historic chimes. There is a limit to my archaeological purism. But I found it harder to forgive that the surrounding proprietors had been allowed to mass high, bloated new buildings all around the new traffic circle, and that the bit of space remaining in the center was used for parking automobiles, instead of for a plaza or small park. So the Tower stands like a stag at bay in a pond, the ugliness ringing it and closing in, awaiting the inevitable hour when some municipal engineer will declare it a menace and workmen will come to cut its throat. Vire will then be indistinguishable from St. Lô or Isigny or any of the other rebuilt towns of the same size. I spent an unhappy afternoon walking about.

I had M. and Mme Le Cornec to dinner that evening at the new Cheval Blanc. Michel had found himself a cheaper lodging in town. The pre-June 6 Cheval Blanc was a posting inn several hundred years old, but as gradually accumulated as the rest of pre-bombardment Vire. It had an archway leading from the street to the courtyard behind the house, and at the back of the courtyard was the old stable, remodeled into a garage, with a café and a billiard table on the floor above.

You reached the café by a narrow stairway, and once there you drank horrid-tasting French drinks like St. Raphael, Gentiane Suze and Raspail, and talked to commercial travelers from Cherbourg and Le Havre, who voyaged by train and made a point of passing the night at Vire instead of Granville at the end of the line from Paris, because Granville was infested with large, expensive summer hotels. One ate better for less at Le Cheval Blanc or at its rival in Vire, the St. Pierre, they said, and then, one was more at home. On a drummer's earnings, one couldn't rivalize with the swells, "a?" they said, closing the sentence with a sound like the "a" in "at," which is customarily transcribed *hein*. (When I first read the green Maupassants, I thought this ever recurrent *hein* was pronounced like the first syllable in "Heinie." I was disillusioned because I never heard any-body say it.)

The commercial travelers sometimes talked about the miserable Norman character, which impelled their customers to demand goods in niggardly quantities at prices based on shipments in carloads, and even to demand rebates on single shoes because they had sold the other of the pair to a one-legged man who refused to pay for two. But mostly they spoke of hotels where the best and the most food was to be obtained at a fixed price: the Hôtel du Centre et de la Victoire at Caen is one I still remember. Others, widely traveled, would oppose to the best of these Norman bargains the meals, four times as marvelous and only half as dear, to be obtained in other provinces.

At l'Hôtel du Commerce in Vendôme, for example, a fellow told me, one had for lunch a magnificent *hors d'oeuvre—rillettes, paté*, country ham, good things, what? and then *tripes à la mode de Caen* copiously served, a magnificent beefsteak with potatoes, and half a pheasant, followed by *fromage cendré*, the cheese of the country that is lightly coated with ashes, *pommes bonne femme*, and all you could drink of wine.

"It isn't great wine, but it's still better than the cider you get with the *prix fixe* in this region of misers."

"Don't you pay extra for the pheasant at Vendôme?" I asked.

"A small supplementary payment," he admitted.

In the following winter I lunched at the Hôtel du Commerce in Vendôme with a friend who was an instructor in a school for Armenian orphans in a château that a New York rug merchant had bought from the Duc de Dodon Rochefoucauld. The rug man had not thought fit to hire the Duc's chef for the orphans, and my *convive* brought a hearty appetite to the meal, which was served at the head of a long table, with a half dozen *commis-voyageurs* ranged around the other end of the board.

Paniguian, my friend, was twenty-four and I was twenty-three. We were both confirmed gluttons. We ate the precise menu that the *commis-voyageur* at Vire had described, with some amendment in the wine department. We had a bottle of the landlord's best local wine to begin with and then a Corton Clos du Roi with the pheasant. The gentlemen of commerce were patronizing when we sat down and placed our napkins in our laps. They tied theirs around their necks, so that they could forget caution in grappling with their grub. But when we cleaned the serving platters of *rillettes*, of *paté de lièvre*, of *jambon cru du pays*, of *andouilles* (inferior to those of Vire, but acceptable), and even of salt herring and scraps of *gigot* left over from yesterday's Sunday dinner and freshened with onion, they were admirative. They still felt superior, though. One was sportsman enough to warn us, "Attention, there's more to come!"

It was presumption on his part to think we didn't know.

After we devastated the *tripes à la mode de Caen* a look of speculation broke water in their faces, as in a pool shark's when his intended victim runs 15 from the break.

Our performance on the beefsteaks and soufflé potatoes was so apocalyptic that I saw one of them pause, his fork halfway to his mouth, to watch us—a pause so unusual, for a Frenchman eating, that I thought for a moment he had a stroke. When we had eaten five or six beefsteaks apiece while each of them was despatching a humdrum three, the waitress cleared the table, and all of us regarded one another with satisfaction, like men who have rowed a creditable race in the same boat. The drummers' fear that we would eat all the beefsteaks was assuaged. They were full and could afford to be complimentary.

"Here you truly ring the bell!" one drummer said, and another corroborated, "What one sends oneself, it's something!"

The waitress placed a cheese tray and a couple of baskets of Saint-Jeans, which we call seckel pears, before the drummers, and went away.

One called down to us, "Why aren't you having any cheese? Are you full already?"

Then his paternal bonhomie changed to an expression of compound hate, a mixture of xenophobia (the franc was falling) and the Spirit of the Barricades. He saw the waitress bringing in the pheasant, just for us.

It was a remarkable pheasant, served on a skinned and lightly toasted loaf of bread, in which a trough had been made and filled with a salmi of the bird's insides. I have never since believed the legend that all game must be hung, because I had seen the gunner bring in the pheasant early that morning. It remains the best bird in my memory.

Long before we had eaten all and crushed each bone in our teeth, the drummers had disappeared. They could not bear watching us and had elected to take their coffee and *eau de vie* in a café down the street. After we had done full justice to the goat cheese in ashes, the seckel pears and the puckered baked apples with cores of jelly, we called for the *patron* and congratulated him on an unforgettable meal. We offered him a glass of his own best Armagnac, taking a gamble that, since we were not in Normandy, he might respond by buying us the next round.

The *patron* said modestly that it was the regular Monday lunch, all except that little bird that he had been fortunate enough to come by that morning, and it was too bad we hadn't come later in the week, when he made an effort.

"You know how it is on Monday," he said. "After the substantial repasts of Sunday, nobody has any appetite."

This has developed from a merely culinary into a geographical digression, but I can never approach the memory of that meal without wanting to go into it. It has the same attraction for me as Costello's saloon. I seldom encounter a pheasant nearly so good nowadays, and when I do, an *hors d'oeuvre* and possibly the tripe is all I can manage at one meal besides the bird. (I am writing this on a lunch exclusively of turtle soup, as I am trying to take off weight.)

Monsieur Secher, the *patron* of the old Cheval Blanc, was not so lavish with his meals *en pension* as his colleague at Vendôme, although he set what I thought was a remarkable table. Even the travelers admitted it wasn't bad. He stood, in relation to the meals at fixed price, in the position of a great couturier who has consented to sponsor a line of ready-to-wear. He was not truly *engagé* in this mass aspect of his art.

Monsieur Secher lived in his chef's *toque* as the old man at Fontenermont lived in his straw hat. It is conceivable he wore this *toque* to bed, to stimulate dreams about food. He was a tall, slender man, who had performed his military service at the school of cavalry at Saumur in the epoch made familiar to movie-goers by *Les Grandes Manoeuvres*, with Gérard Philipe and Danielle Darrieux, and he wore a waxed mustache and imperial. His primary interest in the hotel was the creation of *spécialités sur commande* for clients with plenty of money, who were rare in those days of relatively limited *automobilisme*. Vire is 150 miles from Paris. What happened upstairs—if the water closets ceased to function or the one electric-light bulb in a bedroom was extinct—was of little moment to him. Sleep was to him a fashion of passing time between meals and love an activity for people without imagination.

From my arrival he cultivated me as a prospective client for one of the *plats* he had presented at a gastronomic exposition in Paris, where he had put on a Day Consecrated to the Classic Cuisine of Vire. He had won a magnificent specimen of calligraphy on parchment attesting his glory. An American, even a young one, must be in at least easy circumstances, he believed. I was not flush, though, and wanted to be sure, before I gave him his head, that I would be able to finish the month out and return by rail to Paris.

When, near the end of the month, I was sure that I had a safe margin of twenty-five dollars, about seven hundred and fifty francs at the rate then, I commissioned a repast *de gala*.

On that evening, when I came to the dining room I was placed at a table by myself, sequestered from the vulgarians of the long table. They had to make do with Cistercian fare such as *potage mongole, merlan en colère*, and *canard aux navets*, followed by a salad. What the meal began with, I am ashamed to say I do not remember, nor how it ended. But the main dish was a partridge Olivier Basselin, cooked in cream and old Calvados, a dish named in honor of a fifteenth-century poet and drunkard reputed to have lived in Vire. The poems formerly ascribed to Basselin are now known to be the work of a hoaxing Virois named Le Houx who lived two centuries later, but Le Houx made use of a name and a tradition already extant. The peculiar glory of the partridge Basselin was that the cream smoothed the Calvados and both impregnated the bird without turning it into a mess like Stroganoff. It tasted like a partridge that had been fed all its life from a bottle of Calvados fifty years old.

Thirteen years later, in the first winter of the Second World War, I returned to Vire and stopped at the Cheval Blanc again, but I learned that M. Secher had sold the hotel and gone to Angers. There he had bought another of the same name, l'Auberge du Cheval Blanc. Two much younger people, a Monsieur and Madame Delaunay, had taken over the Vire Cheval Blanc, but had not changed it. Vire, too, was the same.

Early in 1940 I went from Paris to Angers to prepare a story on the Polish Government-in-Exile, which had set up its capital there, and naturally I went to the Angevin Auberge du Cheval Blanc. Monsieur Secher was himself an Angevin.

Angers is a great city compared to Vire. It had then perhaps 100,000 inhabitants—Vire had 5,000. It had a great cathedral, that of St. Maurice, a Château-Fort that is one of the marvels of France, a municipal theater, a night life centering around the Place du Ralliement, a diplomatic corps accredited to the Polish Government, two or three restaurants renowned throughout France, and a history that once encompassed that of England. (It was the Angevin Henry II who became King of England, not an Englishman who became Count of Anjou.) All this, I thought, must have produced some effect on M. Secher, who was on his native soil again.

The Auberge du Cheval Blanc at Angers was even older and more intricately accumulatively constructed than the one at Vire. Part of it dated from the thirteenth century. It had a courtyard, and in a small glassed-in office adjoining it sat Monsieur Secher, still wearing a *toque*.

I went in and reintroduced myself. He professed to remember me, and we chatted awhile about Vire and the war. I asked him if he preferred Angers to Vire; I expected he would. He thought a moment and then said, "It is difficult to say. The chickens here are better, beyond discussion. They are more delicate and symmetrical. The vegetables are also better, and the fruit, there's no comparison. But the *charcuterie* of Vire is hard to beat. And the cream, the butter, the cheese! What a delight! Not a bad country for game, either, you know. Monsieur, your question is very hard to answer."

7 / *The Farmer's Boy*

THE NEW Hôtel du Cheval Blanc has a round lobby with high walls, like a well, and in the center there is a smaller well with the reception desk in it. The walls are stuccoed glaring white, and off the lobby is the café, with a bar *américain* all succedaneum chromium and *veritable* plastic. Over the back bar there is a striped tent, as in similar decorating jobs from Tel-Aviv to Wichita. The architect has tried to create the new Cheval Blanc in the mood of *Match*, the French picture-weekly equivalent of *Life*. To what degree he has succeeded I am incompetent to say, but I wish he hadn't tried.

Monsieur Delaunay, who was still the proprietor as of June 6, 1944, was killed in the bombardment, which knocked the old hotel to bits. It was beyond the power of his widow to reconstitute the old warren even if she had wished. I am sure she was advised that the day of the *commis-voyageur* was over, and that to prosper a *hotelier* must appeal to the taste of the motorized bar trade, which is the same everywhere. And still . . .

When I came downstairs to await the Le Cornecs in the café that evening, the chromium-fluorescent bait had brought in two couples who sat up at the bar. The women's tight, round little bottoms perched up on the bar stools like the tops of swizzle sticks. The V-backs of their motoring dresses started just above the caudal cleft, their hair was rose platinum, and their voices suggested they wore microphones in their garter belts. They and the men, who looked like *compères* in a Marseillais road show, were drinking Scotch, as everybody does in France now who does not wish to be taken for a tourist. Their dialogue, aimed to impress the barmaid and me, was full of allusions sealed to any except the two million readers of the gossip columnists in *France-Soir*. They claimed all the columnists' subjects as close friends. Their main subject, though, was the rusticity of the surroundings. They gave the impression that they were in a goatherd's hut in the Cevennes.

Madame Le Cornec arrived alone, bringing her husband's excuses because he was still writing the editorial for the paper that was going to press. She herself, she said, had just finished writing the court column headed *"Tribunal, or En Correctionelle,"* which is my favorite reading in *La Voix du Bocage*. She is a slender, resilient woman, with a thin, pretty face, and she said she enjoyed court reporting more than anything else she did.

"This afternoon, for example, we had two farmers' wives in court who charged each other and were charged by the court with reciprocal assault and damages to the person. I thought they would fight again in court. The husbands were there, great hulks of men, in their town clothes, each trying to avoid his woman's eyes. They were intimidated by the law, the men, they wanted to keep the fines as low as possible. They testified that they had taken no part in the fight, and when they said that you should have seen the wives look at them!

"They had just stood there while the women fought, one man said—it must have interested them!—and then, when the hair began coming out in handfuls, and 'it looked like there might be breakage,' he had taken his wife up by the waist and his neighbor had taken his, and they had carried them away—'like two hens that are quarreling.' The intervention was understandable; a woman is a useful animal on a farm too. But you could see that the women thought their men should have stood up for them. Murders have grown from such disputes!"

"And what was the fight about?" I asked.

"It appears there is a rill of water that runs down through the farmyard of the neighbor higher up the slope and across the farmyard of the lower neighbor—very advantageous for the ducklings and the chickens. But there is bad blood between the two women—an old story of one having accused the other's brother of slander. So the higher-up woman dammed the rill with stones and turned it out of its course so the water would stay longer on her land. The other woman crossed the property line and took the stones away—trespass! Now they will have a long civil suit. That will please them."

"And what was the verdict today?"

"The judge fined them ten thousand francs apiece with suspended sentence and adjunction not to recommence. I think the husbands will make them keep the peace. Ten thousand francs, after all, it's ten thousand francs."

During Madame Le Cornec's *compte-rendu*, the sophisticates at the bar continued to bray. When she finished, she regarded them for the first time.

"We have a saying here," she said. "Africa begins at Paris."

I told her that in her collected court columns of ten years she must have the makings of a hundred short stories as dry and as high in flavor as an *andouille de Vire*, the smoked sausage made of tripe cased in tripe that is the specialty of the city. Maupassant used just such anecdotes as the bases of some of his best stories.

"Some of the best ones I can't write in their entirety in the columns of *La Voix du Bocage*, which is, after all, a family journal," Madame Le Cornec said. "Although in this country, where everybody knows the principals, each reader fills in the details for himself. There was, for example, one that I wanted to send to you for publication in the journal *The New Yorker* of which you are the director."

(This is an illusion the Le Cornecs have had for years; my copy of their paper always arrives addressed to me as Director of *The New Yorker*, and I do not want to tell them that I am not because they might then send it to the real editor instead.)

I urged her to tell me the story now that she had the chance, and she said, "It concerned a rich farmer with a jealous wife. He wanted a divorce, but naturally on the best terms for himself. So he put the eighteen-year-old farm boy in her way as much as possible, gave them all opportunity, and naturally he caught them one day *en flagrant délit*.

"He frightened the boy into signing a long confession, and as further punishment made him agree to work two months without wages. But the woman denied everything, and the farmer was afraid that when the case came to trial the boy would repudiate his confession. So he took the boy on a tour of the neighboring farms one Sunday, ordering him to repeat the story of his adulteries at each farm, so that he could call the neighbors to testify that they had heard the boy tell all without duress.

"Well, the reaction was what you would expect. At the first farmhouse, when he announced the purpose of his call, the peasant howled with laughter. He invited his wife and all his sons and sons-in-law and their wives to hear this wonderful *divertissement*. They plied the farmer and the boy with Calvados, with old hard cider for a chaser. The reception was the same at each house. It was an ovation, a triumphal progress!

"The boy, timid at first, saw that he was the leading man. He felt a hero. Pretty soon he began going into details, a bit boastful. He was drunk. He extolled the virtuosity of the farmer's wife; everybody clapped him on the back and asked for more information. The farmer, in rage, knocked the boy down and began to beat him. 'I brought you here as a witness,' he roared, 'not to make commentaries!'

"Then it was the boy who became the plaintiff. He brought the farmer into court for aggravated assault with outrage and withholding two months' wages. The wife was summoned as a witness for both sides. She sat there in the court, with a long curved feather in her hat, like a plumed serpent, fixing both with her hard, glittering eyes. She hated her husband for himself, and the boy as much for blabbing. The boy lost the case. The court acquitted the farmer and allowed him to keep the unpaid wages as balm for conjugal wrongs.

"The farmer obtained the divorce, but when he drives up to a farm-house now, he risks to have the neighbor call out: 'Say, *Aimable*, have you brought the boy along to tell us some good ones?'"

The platinized Paris women and their *mecs* continued to gabble at the bar, but they were no longer the loudest element of sound in the café of the Hôtel du Cheval Blanc.

Between twenty and thirty male and female Germans of matched un-attractiveness, alike monochromatic—hair, hides, and trenchcoats of the same tint, and all equally hard-jawed, bespectacled, thick in the middle, and hung about with cameras—had entered the café. They moved three or four tables end to end to form a long single *Stammtisch*, and seated themselves around it. They were a party, traveling by chartered motor-bus, of veterans of the war of 1939–45 and their wives. The husbands were revisiting the scenes in which they had passed so many happy Occupation hours, and bringing the wives to share their sentimental journey—"There is some portion of a foreign land das immer und immer Deutschland ist," I suppose they were snorting at each other across the beer. (I had heard of one such group that swarmed all over the monument to the hostages executed by the Gestapo at Chateaubriand in Brittany, taking photo-graphs.) The lot at Vire did nothing particularly awful, beyond being there. They didn't sing marching songs or yodel, but drank their beer and communicated in their sniffling, bitter howls. When they returned to Germany, I imagined, they would say they had been well received, that the inhabitants looked fondly back on the days of the beneficial Occupation, and that the time appeared ripe for the resumption of their civilizing mission.

Happily Monsieur Le Cornec arrived, to rescue me from further consideration of these *revenants*, carbon copies of remembered corpses. ("Why isn't it as natural for a German as for an American to wish to revisit his old battlefields?" any one of them would have said, if aware of my irritation. It would have seemed to him a parallel.)

Monsieur Le Cornec said he had just written an editorial about an agitation to drive from popular usage the term Basse-Normandie—Low Normandy—for the departments of La Manche and Calvados. Vire is the seat of one of the *arrondissements*, or administrative subdivisions, of Calvados.

"It has been Basse-Normandie forever," M. Le Cornec said, "and its people have been Bas-Normands, and proud of it, but now the Syndicates of Initiative and Tourism have decided that 'low' has a connotation of inferiority. It is a movement that began in other parts of France—for example, the Department of Seine-Inférieure, in the other part of Normandy, has changed its name officially to Seine-Maritime, to escape the imputation that it is 'inferior' to the Department of Seine, which includes Paris. Basse-Normandie, however, is not an official but a historic, a popular, appellation. What shall we call ourselves, if not Low Normans? Surely we do not wish to be confused with the inhabitants, mediocre in all respects, of the three eastern departments, Orne, Eure and Seine *soi-disant* Maritime? Bocains? Bretons Supérieurs?

"Our Mayor, Monsieur Halbout, the pharmacist, says the solution is simple. 'Let us call ourselves simply Normans,' he says. 'The other three departments aren't Norman at all. They are by this time suburbs of Paris. Normandy begins at Caen.' But unfortunately, I told him, they will continue to call themselves Normans anyway. 'Get a court order,' he says, 'or a law of regional appellation.'"

"The boundaries of Africa are expanding," I said, "if Africa begins at Paris and Paris begins at Caen!"

"The boundaries of barbarism are indeed expanding," said M. Le Cornec, serious now. "It is an age of the Ram, violence, and upheavals are inescapable." He is the exponent of a Zodiacal system of historical inevitability, which does not interfere with his practical sense as a newspaper proprietor. "My wife is shrewd but not intelligent," he sometimes says. "She does not share my wider views."

We went in to dinner, which, if not up to the glories of Monsieur Secher's time, was at least honorable. The *charcuterie de Vire*, featuring the renowned *andouilles*, was as remarkable as always. We agreed that

Michel and I, with the Versailles, should pick up M. Le Cornec at his printery the following mid-morning, and that we should set out together in quest of the château with the stuffed leopard and the sad baritone hounds.

"It would be well, I think, to consult the Colonel de Petiville," M. Le Cornec said. "He lives between Vire and St.-Sever, and his mind contains an Almanach of the nobility of the region. If there is a Vicomte de Fives at Fontenermont, he will know him. The Colonel de Petiville is a brother of the Marquis de Petiville, and is my most popular collaborator on *La Voix du Bocage*. He contributes long essays on the antiquities of Vire— 'Trade Guilds in Vire in the Eleventh Century,' for example—but he takes a strong political slant. The decadence of France was determined, according to *M. le Colonel*, when the barons declined to follow Louis IX en masse to the Seventh Crusade in 1270. He says the Sieur de Joinville was an archetypical liberal. The Baron's refusal announced a national surrender to egoism, and everything that has happened since has but confirmed the deplorable symptomatology. It is a comfortable point of view, because it blames neither the Communists nor the parties of the Right Center, the Center-Right, and the Right-of-Center Left, which are, in that order, the strongest in the region, except when they group, in face of the Communists, to form a Center-Center lightly to the left of Right."

When we arrived at the entrance to the Colonel de Petiville's estate next morning, however, a chain lay on the ground across the roadway, an indication, M. Le Cornec thought, that the Colonel was from home. We drove on up to his house, hoping to leave a message for him with the caretaker—Monsieur Le Cornec said the Colonel had a peasant farmer who worked the estate—but we found the place garrisoned exclusively by peacocks. It was a high, narrow stone house, smaller but more graceful than the one at Fontenermont, and I noticed that the stoop and balcony were ornamented with graceful wrought iron painted white, as on houses in New Orleans. Save for the cries of the peacocks, silence reigned under the great trees that shaded the house.

"The Colonel has perhaps gone to Vire, to carry me his weekly essay," M. Le Cornec said. "I think he was contemplating something on the disastrous amiability of Louis XVI when he omitted to have the Swiss Guard shoot all the delegates of the Third Estate as a prophylactic measure. But since he is not here, we will have to continue our quest alone." And he directed Michel toward Fontenermont. Michel, incredulous as always, pointed the Versailles along the obviously dead-end road M. Le Cornec indicated. Before we started off, however, he turned upon me a monumental, Champs-Elysian wink, to show he wasn't being fooled. It was a typical beginning of a day with me, he seemed to say—a visit to an empty house—and now we would go somewhere equally ridiculous.

I rode in front with Michel, and as we proceeded on this new wild-goose chase he told me about his evening in Vire. He had found lodging over a stationery and newspaper store and had attended a moving picture, about an American gangster trafficking in *stupéfiant* drugs, who disguised himself as an agent of the police of *stupéfiants* in order to drag down another gangster who had stolen from him his mistress and 500 kilos of *schnouf*. In so doing he enlisted the sympathies of a young female American, *très chic*, the daughter of a millionaire, but when he admitted that he had abused her confidence—he was in fact not an agent but a gangster—she said not to be put out, because she was in fact not a *jeune fille* but a feminine ace of the police. I said it sounded sufficiently complicated, and he agreed.

"She couldn't arrest him, of course," Michel said. "They were in bed together. Figure to yourself."

I don't know the answer yet, because M. Le Cornec advised that we stop at a roadside store where he thought the people might know of a man at Fontenermont who kept hounds. "The man here is a great hunter," he said, "President of the Circle of Hunters and Fishermen with the Pole of Saint-Sever." The shopkeeper, who also exercised the trade of blacksmith, told us there was no Vicomte, or Comte, or even simple Monsieur de Fives at Fontenermont, but in the matter of hounds practicing hunting by pursuit there was in effect a Monsieur de Carville! In effect, a great gray house! He had never been asked in, so he couldn't say whether there was a straw-filled leopard. He gave directions to M. Le Cornec—in effect, on the very edge of the Forest of Saint-Sever, the last house on the road before the forest began. We drove three miles or so along a road I now began to think I recognized and took a private road through a copse not yet continuous with the Forest. And there, beyond the trees, I saw the house I remembered. It stood, against the un-Norman background of hill and forest, as when I had left it for Bagnoles de l'Orne.

The house was silent, and I suggested we drive down to the barns, where we could see a couple of men fiddling about as farmers do.

"We will be able to ask them if the proprietor is about," I said. I could see the chicken wire not far from the barns, and as the Versailles approached, a baritone psalmody rose on the air, as if the dogs were rehearsing the "Pilgrims' Chorus" from *Tannhäuser* in the original language. We stopped the Versailles near the barn, and the men interrupted their agricultural routine—taking hay out of the barn or putting hay into the barn—which they may have pursued throughout the intervening eleven years, for all the sense my urban eye could make of it.

I asked for Monsieur de Carville, and they said he was off in the field on the other side of the house, harrowing. That indicated to me that it couldn't be the old man, and when I asked, they said, sure enough, that the old man was dead. The present proprietor was his son, who had also been here when the Americans were here. The working men themselves had not been on the farm then, they said—they had been prisoners in Germany. One of them came along back to the house with us. He left the car on the driveway and went off across the field to get M. de Carville, whom we could see in the distance, atop the two-wheeled, one-horse harrow. When the man got within shouting distance of the harrow, he stopped, and shortly thereafter we saw the driver head the horse toward us. It was a bay at least eighteen hands high, and a good ton on the hoof. When he got within fifty yards of the car M. Le Cornec and I walked out to meet him.

As we came even with the horse, the driver stopped, and M. Le Cornec introduced himself and me. It was the editor who made the impression. M. de Carville, who was wearing a straw boater—possibly inherited from his father—removed it with *empressement*. "I have never before had the pleasure of meeting you," he said, "but of course I have heard a great deal about you. I am a constant reader." I was well sponsored.

M. de Carville was a man in his early forties, lean, tanned, fair-haired and blue-eyed, with a hard New England look about him. He was in his shirt, with his sleeves rolled up and held by elastic bands, and his forearms and wrists showed that he had driven a lot of big horses in his time. But his profile was, as M. Le Cornec observed, *racé*, and his language was courteously old-fashioned.

M. Le Cornec explained who I was, and M. de Carville said that he remembered the Americans and added courteously that he thought he recalled me. (I had forgotten him entirely, remembering only the gross old man.) I said that I would like to see the stuffed leopard again, and he invited us inside, jumping down from the harrow and turning the horse over to the farm hand. We went around to the rear of the house, where the garden still agonized, and entered through the kitchen, a vast raftered room hung with hams and shotguns. There was a cot in one corner. "I live here now," M. de Carville said. "I'm alone, and it isn't worth the trouble to keep up the rest of the house." The old disorder was gone, though. The combination gun room, larder, kitchen, dining room and bedroom was of an ascetic neatness.

The sun was blazing in the field, as I remembered it eleven years before, but in the dark kitchen there was a welcome coolness, and M. de Carville said, "I'll show you into the rooms you remember, and then I'll go down cellar and get a bottle of old *cidre bouché*. It's an occasion." He opened a door and led us through the great living room to the dining room. The shutters were closed, and the rooms were semi-dark, but I could see the leopard. It was really a small specimen, a half-grown male or a young female, looking a bit like the ones you used to see in side-street furriers' windows.

Seeing me pause before it, Monsieur de Carville said, "Father Dupuy, a missionary, sent it to my father from Conakry in West Africa a long time ago." He thus shattered my fantasy that the old Vicomte, who, it now appeared, hadn't been a Vicomte either, had personally killed the leopard. Nor had I thought of the old rip as an associate of missionaries.

The room, like the kitchen, was clean now. There had been no attempt to restore the old fripperies, but they had been shoved decently aside and were evidently dusted sometimes. It was a rectangular room, and in each of the four corners was neatly wedged a great high-backed sofa, like a triangular segment of a pie, with a curved outer edge. The backs, of conforming shape, rose to the ceiling, where they had apparently been sawed off. I did not recall them specifically, and I now looked at them with such interest that M. de Carville said, "They are the four quarters of a round sofa, with a high upholstered pillar in the middle, that the Imperial Russian Ambassador in Paris had had made for the Embassy in the last century. When it was finished he found he couldn't get it into the Embassy, so he sold it at auction at the Salle Drouot. Naturally there were few bidders, but my grandfather, who was there, couldn't bear to pass up a bargain. He bought it and had it sawed into quarters, from top to bottom. Then all he had to do was trim off a metre or so at the tops, and the pieces fitted in very nicely. What my grandmother said I don't know."

He showed us into the dining room, and M. Le Cornec, Michel, and I took seats at the table, in the dark streaked with sun that came through cracks in the shutters.

"I saw you drive in," M. de Carville said, "but I didn't come to meet you because I suspected you were city people looking for antiquities. They bother me a lot in the summer, driving up and demanding to know what I have to sell. When I tell them, nothing, they insist on coming into the house anyway. 'You may have something of great value that you don't know about!' they say, as if I were a noodle. They can be quite rude."

He went in search of the cider, and M. Le Cornec said, "It is as you remember it?"

I said, "Essentially. But less remarkable."

Michel said, "He needs a wife. He must have to pay a servant quite a lot."

Monsieur de Carville returned with the litre of cider and four glasses. The cider was cool from the cellar, and the bubbles in it carried an overpoweringly intoxicating smell of decaying apples into the drinker's nostrils. *Cidre bouché* can be a mighty drink, as strong as a generous wine. We drank it gratefully, but when we finished, M. de Carville offered no second bottle. He had the rest of his harrowing to do.

"I remember the day the Americans came," he said. "We had a family of friends from Caen staying with us, and when the Germans fell back from their first line they took the house as a battalion headquarters. It was full of them. I got away and walked into Vire, where I heard the Americans had already arrived, to tell them how things were. I didn't want them blundering into the Germans and having a battle in my house; it would have been a ruin. Luckily I encountered a French liaison officer with the Americans who was an old friend. He assured them that I was not a spy, but they didn't look too convinced. M.P.s are all alike, be they of France or of Navarre. I didn't get back here for twenty-four hours, and then in a jeep with some hard-looking boys. But the Germans, fortunately, had decamped. It was after that the Americans decided to put the press camp here."

"Your pack of hounds has survived," I said. "Always the same strain, I see."

"Yes," M. de Carville said. "It is easier to find food for them now, but expensive. They are marvelous dogs."

"Do they track?" I asked.

"Infallibly," M. de Carville replied. "They drive out all sorts of game, foxes, pheasants, rabbits, boars—it remains only to shoot it. I have five couples."

'There was some *histoire* about a soldier who stole one of the dogs while I was here," I said.

"It was not a soldier," said M. de Carville with conviction. "It was a correspondent. An Englishman. He begged my father to sell him a dog. My father, naturally, refused. The morning this Englishman went away, the dog disappeared."

From the tone in which M. de Carville said "Englishman" I could tell there was no use arguing with him. The English had taken Canada from Normandy. Why not a *basset de Gascogne*?

I longed to ask M. de Carville the history of his family, down to, and especially, his father's generation. But he was too well bred, and too occupied with his farm. We said polite goodbyes, and half an hour later we were back in hot, white Vire, with its smells and noises of construction.

8 / Michel's Mountain

THE GERMANS had gone, perhaps to Omaha Beach and Easy Red, to tell their feminine counterparts how they had repulsed the invasion, only to be betrayed by the Jewish General Rommel, who ordered them to advance in the wrong direction. After that they would have a picnic with cervelat and *bierkase*. The Parisians had also gone, perhaps to a seaport where the men would book the women as "entertainers" for a tour of South America. I felt small desire to stay in the new Vire, and so we said goodbye to M. Le Cornec and pushed on for Mont-Saint-Michel, where I had decided to pass the weekend and then return to Paris.

Michel was pleased when I told him where we were going. Mont-Saint-Michel is a standard attraction for American tourists, and he was sure to meet other White Russian tourist-wranglers there, freshly arrived from Paris with convoys of sightseers they had turned over to the concierge of La Mère Poularde Hôtel. He in turn would hand them over to licensed guides who would make them climb all the stairs and stumble down them again. In the meanwhile the chauffeurs, peaceably remaining at the base of the mount, would drink *pastis* together, eat at the chauffeurs' half-rate table d'hôte in the hotel, and exchange stories of the accidents of the route, like the crews of slavers after having discharged their cargoes at São Paulo or Belem in the reign of the good Dom Pedro. The inhabitants of the Rock are accommodating, particularly the chambermaids who come over from the mainland to work the summer season in the hotels.

Headed for such a haven, the Versailles sped along like a livery hack pointed in the direction of the stable. We reached the coast road at Granville and turned due south, with the Channel at our right hands, where it is more than 100 miles across to the invisible Devon shore. We came down through a row of small summer resorts, Carolles and St.-Jean de Thomas, favored by the English in pre-B.E.A. days, when it was less easy than now to reach more distant and exotic places. The sea was sometimes far below us and sometimes close. I remembered swimming at Carolles in that magic summer after the breakthrough. (The swims of wartime were memorable because so widely spaced: Tabarka in Tunisia in April 1943, Carteret and Carolles in 1944. I do not count the pond in back of Madame Hamel's, or a brook nine feet wide in Berkshire, because they were not salt water; nor the wadi at Gafsa where the jeeps washed away and we scrambled among the floating cadavers of camels.) The road led through Avranches, *chef-lieu* of an *arrondissement*, like Vire. Through Avranches Bradley had funneled Patton's new army into Brittany, a subcutaneous injection from which the Germans never recovered, and in Avranches I had slept in September 1926, in the hotel on top of the hill that has a view over Mont-Saint-Michel and a garden with fig trees. When the Germans put in their big counterattack against the road through Avranches in 1944, against the advice of all the surviving German generals who have written their memoirs, including General Speidel, the commander in chief of ground forces of NATO in Europe, Bradley stood it off with one division, the 30th, at Mortain, a town I walked to from Vire in 1926. The distance, which I have checked, is 27 kilometres—16⅞ miles. I had an excellent meal in the Hôtel de la Poste at Mortain; I remember the brook trout still. Then I hired the local taxi man to drive me home to the Cheval Blanc.

(I was getting into the lift at the Fifth Avenue Hotel in New York in the spring of 1945 when I saw a young fellow-guest who had obviously been badly shot up not long before. I asked him where he had been, and he said Mortain. This proves (a) that the world is a diminutive place, and (b) that a town does not have the same associations for everybody.)

From Avranches in 1926 I went to the village of Genêts (the Broom-

plants) and hired a carriage to take me across the sands at low tide to
Mont-Saint-Michel. There were men in the village who made their living
that way. There was, of course, already an automobile causeway to the
Mont, but it seemed more authentic to cross the sands in the *calèche*,
with its wide-rimmed sand wheels. There was no danger of being engulfed by the incoming tide or *enlisé* in the quicksands, but my world was
so without peril in 1926 that I found it pleasant to conjure up small
shudders.

In 1944 a couple of battered old correspondents I knew crossed the
same sands in a jeep, and arrived at the Mont in time to liberate it—the
only Germans there, a weather-observation unit, had left, and the official
Army had not arrived. I believe they had a good welcome. Hemingway
made the Hôtel de la Mère Poularde his headquarters after that. He had
a good time and wrote and recruited his strength for his dash on Paris. I
went there myself once or twice that August and had a pleasant time.
Nothing was important to us then—to Hemingway and the rest who had
lived in Paris—but getting back there. The war was winning itself; the
Germans were on the run. When we encountered officers we knew from
divisions we had been with in the hard days, the stories they had to tell
were of scooping up prisoners at will, and their only complaints were of
failures in supply that impeded their advance—some other sonofabitching
Army, or Army Corps, was getting all the gas. The infantry thought the
armor was hogging it all, but the armor thought it must be going to the
British, who were sitting on their asses as usual, waiting for a lead.

It would have been difficult for me to communicate these varied memories to Michel, so I maintained what must have been a welcome silence,
never breaking it to suggest he go down some side road in quest of a
farmhouse I thought I remembered. We went to the Mont by the causeway this time, because the Versailles was no sand-wagon. Michel parked
outside the walls of the great fortress and the porters came to lug my bag,
as they had thirty years before. The Hôtel Poularde is just inside the
gates, and built *en espalier* against the side of the rock, like everything
else in the place. It is a good hotel, well modernized. It is now operated
by a hotel chain, perhaps Swiss, which exploits skiing in one succursal,
cave drawings in another—at the Mont, omelets and ecclesiastical architecture. The *patron* and *patronne* of 1944, great friends of Hemingway's,
were gone, but the omelets were as good as ever.

The Abbey, built up artfully over a nub of rock like a resplendent
porcelain dental cap over a spike of tooth, was again on the basis of 1926,
pure honky-tonk, which I find soothing. I went up on the ramparts, as I
always do, skirting the ammoniac places under the arches, and at first
resisting the solicitations of the proprietors of the small hotels that have
cafés opening onto the ramparts. There they sell little Cancale oysters all
summer through, with *palourdes* and *praires*, the French cousins of the
Rhode Island quahog, which is the cherrystone or little neck of New York

and points south. You can walk from the ramparts into the upper floors of these hotels and so on down two or three flights of stairs to the narrow, slithery, slanting, cobbled street. At the third or fourth café I sit down and begin eating the sea-water-salt shellfish and drinking muscadet. I look over the mud flats to Normandy, if it is low tide, and think I smell Jamaica Bay, in New York City, where as a small boy I used laboriously to dig my own clams, a score or so at a time, and then with other boys roast them in a fire to kill the germs, since our elders assured us that the waters were polluted. There was an old drunk who lived along the shore by crabbing and fishing, who used to chase us because we called him Chewterbacker. "Chewterbacker, Chewterbacker, here he comes! Run!" The age of the cigarette had arrived, and it seemed to us grotesque that he spat tobacco juice. We were snobs.

It was a Saturday evening. Mont-Saint-Michel, like Brighton, Rockaway Beach, Block Island and South Bend, is afflicted with rainy Sundays. The weather for a week or more had been superb, but now it began to mist up, and soon to rain. The merchants of *crustaces* and crucifixes and souvenirs made of synthetic cockleshells, crouching in their recesses like hermit crabs to dart their pincers at the Sunday visitors, began their almost weekly moan. The season is so short, rents, taxes, high, and all the *fric* must be extracted on the weekends. As for the tourists who come to the hotels, the hotel-keepers englobe their last *sou*. When the weather is good, the Sunday trippers, bound for the Abbaye on top of the island, linger along the steep path, stopping frequently to get their wind, and then they look in the fronts of the shops selling religious goods and, for the English-language trade, the novels of Henry Miller. They pause at the cafés and can be pulled in to have *apéritifs* at double the mainland price, or even meals. But when it rains, they pull their coats about their faces and push along grimly, to get under cover at the top of the path, where the uniformed attendant with his diploma from the Service of Historic Monuments will take them over and hustle them through the cloisters, the refectory, the Merveille, stumbling up and down dark staircases, until he turns them out again after they have bought all the post cards and guide books they are ever likely to want. Once they have been through his mill, they are no market for the shopkeepers' similar wares.

They hurry down the hill, slipping and sliding and turning their ankles, for the main and only street of the Mont is, like the Lewes racecourse in Sussex, not only sloping but tilted to one side. They are by now wet through and eager to reach the charabancs parked on the causeway. The chartered charabancs will take them home. No good trying to get them into cafés to wait for the rain to abate; they've had it now. Perhaps, at the very bottom, they stop for a shot of calva, and that's all the hermit crabs' take for the day. A miserable life, Monsieur.

It isn't the aspect of Mont-Saint-Michel that excited Henry Adams;

but he was, on the subject of the Middle Ages, what Monsieur de Carville calls a noodle. You may be sure that in the centuries when there were pilgrims there were hermit crabs, and that the monks shook visitors down for alms, for the noble purpose of adding another story to the skyscraper. And as for the skirmishes between French subjects of the French-speaking kings of England and French subjects of the French-speaking kings of France that enlivened the history of the rock, they decided nothing and were, you may depend on it, miserably contested, with a maximum of irresolution and confusion, like medieval warfare in general. It was a time when panic decided five battles out of six, the nadir of the military art in Christian countries until the Hussites and the Swiss revived it.

The Middle Ages were neither brave nor spiritual, but full of cunning, lechery, speculation unlimited by knowledge, and the passionate enjoyment of good things as available, because they so irregularly were. A gorge of salt fish or a whack at a girl under a bush were opportunities that might not come again in a lifetime. The stones of medieval cities, and of Mont-Saint-Michel, exude the sweat and smell of that time, which is why I love them.

In the evening, in the restaurant of the Hôtel Poularde, a shrill American couple arrived with three specimen demons from a breeding farm run by Hieronymus Bosch. They had apparently crept in and out of the woman's womb and convinced her they were human children. All, the woman recited in a monotonous imitation of a train whistle, had been on the road all day, coming from Paris. They probably had tried to do the Château district on the way. It was nine o'clock, and she demanded that her children be fed instantly. The children saw a large *langouste*, whose fiery hue possibly reminded them of their last pre-earthly habitat. They screamed that they wanted for their supper "lobster," and the mother shouted that they never liked lobster, reminding them how they had spewed it out at Dinard, and how deathly sick it had made them at Plymouth. The father said what the hell was the use, let them have lobster, but not cold. They wanted it broiled. The *maître d'hôtel* had learned his English in England—he might have understood "grilled," but broiled stopped him—and the woman screamed that none of these stinkers could understand English, that "they" had sworn in Paris that this was a good hotel, and here were her little children starving to death. The director of the hotel came and understood that they wanted hot lobster— it would demand thirty minutes, he said. Nothing else would do.

The children, waiting, screamed continually, and one of them lay under the table, kicking his father's shins. The director of the hotel suggested the permissive pair remove the children from the dining room; he would serve the hot lobster, which he of course realized they would reject in some disgusting manner, in their living quarters. At that, the woman went off her chump completely. I left, and when I returned at midnight, after a discreet patrol of the hermit crabs' bars, I heard the woman howling still, in her bedroom, that she would not stay the night in a hotel where they insulted her li'l children. Her husband, I judged from the cadence of her howls, was slugging her by now, and I went to sleep hoping he would kill her, strangle the incubi and commit suicide.

On Monday morning Michel and I left for Paris in the Versailles. He said he had encountered a chauffeur friend since boyhood days in the Ukraine, who told Michel that he had arrived from Paris transporting a mad American couple and three children. But when Michel awoke Sunday morning, his friend and the friend's clients had disappeared. I suppose they decided they had seen enough of Mont-Saint-Michel.

Michel and I parted on excellent terms, and he said he hoped he would have the pleasure some day of driving me to St. Jean-de-Luz or Deauville.

9 / Days with the Daydaybay

READING A French newspaper in a restaurant in Paris one winter, I came upon a heading of a kind that would not ordinarily interest me: "*Ventes de Charité.*" I had time to spare, however, having asked for my check while the waiter was skinning a *truite au bleu* for another customer, so I read the first item in the column. (After all, the waiter was quite right: the *truite*, if abandoned, would get cold, and the check wouldn't.) The item stated:

> The sale for the benefit of the Veterans of the 2nd Armored Division will open today in the salons of the Sorbonne (entrance: Rue des Ecoles). Presiding will be Mme la Maréchale Leclerc de Hauteclocque, who will direct a booth devoted exclusively to souvenirs of the General. Numerous booths will be devoted to exotic products and artifacts. At the book booth authors such as André Maurois and Louise de Vilmorin will autograph their works.

I divined without trouble that Mme la Maréchale was the widow of General Leclerc, who had been made a Marshal of France after his death in an airplane accident in Algeria, in 1947. Leclerc's name in obscurity, before he escaped to England to join General de Gaulle in 1940, had been de Hauteclocque—Philippe-François-Marie de Hauteclocque, to give him his full due. De Hauteclocque was a name that had marked him from school days as an unreformed aristocrat. In England, taking a pseudonym to protect his family from reprisals, he had chosen a common French name, the exact equivalent of Clark. Changing from de Hauteclocque to Leclerc was like shucking tails for a sweatshirt. Once, in 1944, as a correspondent with the American First Army, I asked him what his real name was. It was an awkwardly worded question, because everybody knew by that time. All I really wanted was to verify the spelling; those two "c"s are tricky.

"What does my name matter as long as I fight?" he asked. He had been affable up to that point, or as affable as he knew how to be, but the question about the name nettled him. I thought that he was like the countless little boys who have wished, and have gone on wishing all their lives, that they hadn't been named Elwyn or Abbott.

We were in a field near Fleuré, in the Département de L'Orne in Normandy, and all around us were vehicles that the Americans had supplied to the Deuxième Division Blindée, or D.D.B.—pronounced by the French as a single word, "Daydaybay." The Daydaybay was known to the American forces as the French 2nd Armored Division; there was an American 2nd Armored Division in western France, too. Fleuré, which is so small that if you are driving fast you are likely to miss it entirely, is near Argentan, which was then the southern jaw of the pincers that Bradley and Montgomery were trying to close on the escaping Visigoths of the Seventh Army and the Fifth Panzer Army. The Daydaybay, pushing out into the middle of the receding Germans, joyfully managed to get itself surrounded, and killed a great many of the enemy before being called back to the American side of the gap. Leclerc, a red-haired little man with a long nose and a bristling red mustache, reminded me of an interrupted terrier that sniffs more rats under a barn door.

Like so many quests for simplicity, Leclerc's, I noted with regret while still awaiting the check for my meal, had ended only in further complication. As a surname, Leclerc de Hauteclocque is even more of a mouthful than de Hauteclocque. Moreover, I reflected, there is by now hardly a town in what became the Daydaybay's path across France—from the Cotentin to the Rhine—that is without its Avenue du Général Leclerc, a name that is perpetuated because "Avenue du Maréchal Posthume Leclerc de Hauteclocque" just won't fit on a street sign.

Then, remembering a journey I had once made in attendance upon the Daydaybay, it occurred to me that I might as well go over to the Sorbonne and spend a few francs with my old fellow-travelers. I had nothing else in the world to do except go back to my hotel room and work, and I hate that. When I was at last allowed to pay for my simple repast—a dozen oysters followed by a pair of thrushes roasted with juniper berries —I decided to walk to the Sorbonne in order to prolong my respite. I find it hard to deter myself from walking in Paris, with or without a pretext. There was a time when I thought I might never walk in Paris again, for it had fallen under a spell that was supposed to last a thousand years, and now, I suppose, I walk its streets for reassurance.

From the restaurant, which is at the Fontaine Gaillon, I walked up the Rue Saint-Augustin and turned down the Rue de Richelieu, a narrow gulch of one-way, hornless traffic these days, where, if you step off the meager sidewalk to let an old woman with a market basket pass, you risk silent obliteration by a motorized baby buggy magniloquently called an automobile. One of the unadvertised benefits of the law forbidding Parisians on wheels to sound their horns is the increased pleasure of the driver, who is now under mandate to sneak up without warning on his prey. This swells his *tableau de chasse*, or total bag. (The highest award of the Friendly League for the Ecrabouillement Piéton, or Squashing of Pedestrians, goes to the member who succeeds in killing a man with a motor scooter, which is considered comparable to getting an elephant with a bow and arrow.) I followed the street down past the discouraging baroque bulk of the Bibliothèque Nationale and the charming front of the Hôtel de Malte, which received its first guests in 1777. As I approached the Rue de Rivoli, I passed under the colonnade of the Comédie Française, with its wall medallions of Molière, Racine, and the rest, in a Hydrox Biscuit style of sculpture, and its yellow *affiches* announcing the casts of next week's *Cinnas* and *Athalies*. Coming out from under the colonnade, I paused in front of a bust of Alfred de Musset to read again on its socle one of my favorite cheer-up bits of literature:

> *Les plus désespérés sont les chants les plus beaux*
> *Et j'en sais d'immortels, qui sont des purs sanglots—*

which might be freely translated as

> The most utterly lachrymose lyrics are frequently good jobs,
> And I could cite some deathless instances that are unadulterated sobs.

I repeat the couplet to myself when I am feeling low, and it works as well as three fingers of bourbon.

On reaching the Seine, I walked past the fishing-tackle shops and the bird stores to the Pont au Change, at the Châtelet, and then across the Ile de la Cité, past the Préfecture of Police, where the Paris police barricaded themselves against the German garrison and raised the tricolor on August 19, 1944, setting off the week of insurrection. When I got over on the Left Bank, I ascended the Boulevard Saint-Michel as far as the big, brassy Restaurant Dupont, at the corner of the Rue des Ecoles. The Dupont never fails to enrage me, because it occupies the disfigured former premises of the Taverne Soufflet, an establishment of majesty and tranquility, which in 1926, when I first stayed in the Latin Quarter as a casual student at the Sorbonne, was still the exact image of the French cafés Maupassant had taught me to expect.

In the Soufflet, the long banquettes were upholstered in garnet plush, with backs topped by a manger of brass rails, into which the customers tossed their overcoats after crumpling them up into the smallest possible bundles. The tables in front of the banquettes had white marble tops and were placed end to end, with no space between. There were vast mirrors, which permitted refracted flirtation. The waiters were individualists who improved on acquaintance; they had little use for a newcomer until he had been in the Quarter long enough to achieve their own cultural standing. The girls who frequented the Soufflet did not frequent the Café d'Harcourt or the Source, farther up the Boulevard, nor did the demoiselles of the d'Harcourt or the Source invade the Soufflet. Each habitual customer at the Soufflet had his table, and each girl had hers. There she would arrive in mid-afternoon and begin to write on stationery furnished by the house. The girls were as prolific as a pack of Mme de Sévignés, but none of them was ever seen to affix a postage stamp to an envelope. Perhaps they were diarists. Any one of them could nurse an infusion of peppermint through a long afternoon; it was the *consommation* that she felt the least temptation to finish, and so the one that enabled her to hold the franchise longest. Male acquaintances would pause by the girls' tables to shake hands, to chat, and, rarely, to stand treat. The girls knew the limitations of the academic budget. They snubbed nobody because he bought seldom. They were young, averaging only a year or two older than the students, and not particularly pretty.

The students in the cafés were exclusively male. A number of coeds attended lectures, but they used no makeup, wore cotton stockings, took masses of notes, and disappeared as soon as class was over. They went straight home, I imagine, or else to a room in some dark and hideous *pension de famille,* with a window giving on a court into which boys threw lynched cats. I used to suspect that in order to win their parents' consent to such unwomanly careers the coeds had to make a show of being completely uninterested in sex, like nuns, and that in default of a habit they utilized steel barrettes and straight hair to advertise this indifference. Nowadays there are almost as many *étudiantes* as *étudiants* in the cafés of the Quarter—a lot of them married and living with their husbands, and others still single but living *en ménage.* The *petites femmes* of the kind I remember, a species peculiar to the environs of the university, have been eliminated, like the Soufflet. Many of the women students today are prettier than the Soufflet girls, but they are more intimidating.

"*Ce n'était pas vraiment du vice,*" a very old friend of mine who still inhabits the Quarter said recently, reminiscing. "*C'était une espèce d'artisanat."* From the point of view of the bashful foreigner, one advantage of the *petite* who could always be found in the same place was that he could observe her at leisure—for several evenings, if he chose. He might learn to like the way she looked up to greet fellows she knew, or the way her head sat on her neck or her neck on her shoulders. That would achieve what Stendhal baptized the "crystallization." By the time the young man approached, he felt that he knew her as well as the girls in his high-school class, whom he had first observed in the same manner. He would find her receptive but not precipitate, practical but not rapacious. The greatest treat he could offer, within what the boys on the quarterlies would now call the Soufflet's frame of reference, was the *prix-fixe* dinner on the wide balcony that overhung the *grande salle*. (It was not reasonable to assume that a customer who could afford better would be at the Soufflet at all.) The *prix fixe* more than nourished the girl; it raised her standing with the management and with her other male acquaintances. Best of all, it infuriated her colleagues who had not been invited anywhere and who bitterly watched her as they masticated the sandwiches that hunger had at length impelled them to order grudgingly for themselves. The *prix fixe*, at sixteen francs, comprised a choice of soup or a spectacular *hors d'oeuvre varié* and then fish, entrée, vegetable, salad, and cheese and fruit or dessert. Wine was included, but coffee wasn't. The franc was twenty-five to the dollar.

I cannot truthfully say that I think of all these details specifically whenever I see the Restaurant Dupont on the site of the Taverne Soufflet, but I have thought about one or another of them so often on reaching that corner that the memory of the whole scene hits me ready-blended, like a smell. As for the Dupont, it is one of a chain of restaurants, all flaunting the disputable slogan *"Chez Dupont, Tout Est Bon."* It has fluorescent lighting overhead and electric lamps, with candy-striped shades, on wall brackets. The walls are further decorated with posters displaying offensive colored photographs of fried eggs and blobs of pink ice cream and conveying such inspirational messages from the management as "Eat Oysters—Good for Your Health" and "The Management insists upon impeccable courtesy and compliance on the part of its employees—Messieurs les Clients are urgently recommended to report with exactitude any infraction of servility." The Dupont waiters, naturally, pay no attention to the latter poster, but they tolerate it. Those of the old Soufflet would have ripped it from the wall and made Messieurs les Clients eat it.

In front of the Dupont I paused to look across the Boulevard Saint-Michel at the *pâtisserie* in the building that, shaped like a flatiron, stands where the Rue Racine and the Rue de l'Ecole de Médecine converge. The *pâtisserie*, which used to be open all night, closes early now, but it is still there, and that is something. Above the bargain bookstore in the acute angle of the Rue Racine and the Boulevard is the Hôtel de la Faculté, where, in the fall of 1927, I last saw Angèle, one of the pleasantest girls at the Soufflet. Angèle was twenty years old and chunky, and she had a snub nose. On this occasion she complained of having a fever and said she was going to die. Three or four of us from the Soufflet, sitting on her bed, assured her that she would be up and around in a few days. Shortly thereafter she died, and since then I have wondered sometimes what a girl with a snub nose has to do to be taken seriously. In the Rue de l'Ecole de Médecine, from which the Medical School has departed, is a plaque marking the birthplace of Sarah Bernhardt, who made hundreds of thousands of people cry by merely pretending to die. She had the profile for it.

When I had had my look, I turned, entered the Rue des Ecoles, and walked on, past the entrance to the narrow Rue Champollion and past the Brasserie Balzar, another surviving landmark. Outside the Sorbonne I saw posters bearing the emblem of the Daydaybay—a white silhouette map of France with the Cross of Lorraine on a blue field superimposed. A blue banner hung above the door, and on the wide steps in front of it there was a double stream of well-dressed people, some making for the entrance and the others leaving it. Those going in were empty-handed; those coming out carried amateurishly wrapped packages. Inside the door, I found myself in the high marble vestibule at the foot of the Grand Escalier of the Sorbonne, a place I hadn't been in for nearly thirty years. It looked just about the same.

In 1926, all an American needed in order to matriculate at the Sorbonne was a diploma from an American university. The old fellow who took your minuscule matriculation fee wouldn't even make you unroll the diploma. "Ahbay?" he would ask, signifying Bachelor of Arts, and if you said "Ahbay," he would nod knowingly and extend to you the privilege of listening to the big-league medievalists. (At least, that was the privilege I was interested in.) Ahbay was the only American degree the old boy had heard of, and it served no useful purpose to open your diploma and explain that it was Bay anything else.

M. Ferdinand Lot, the professor who in those days taught the Dawn of the Middle Ages, gave out a bibliography as long as my two arms. When I went to the library to get started on it, I saw a considerable number of my fellow-students—who, unlike me, were working for degrees—standing in line and waiting for books that other students were reading, several of them sitting on the floor, for lack of seats. This made me feel guilty, so I bought some of the books from dealers and took them to my room to read, and soon I stopped going to Professor Lot's lectures. I was afraid of being found out as a dilettante. Another of my lecturers was Professor Antoine Thomas, who taught Old Provençal. I remember that he had a spade-shaped white beard and that he accused Professor Anglade, of the University of Toulouse, his rival in their common field, of approaching the origin of a verb I have forgotten *"avec sa légèreté coutumière"* ("with his habitual frivolity"). What an epithet can be derived from that—"Frivolous philologist!" For thirty years I have been waiting for a chance to use it, but every time I get into an argument with a savant, he turns out to be of some other persuasion—a psychologist, perhaps, or a podiatrist. The neck my knife would fit has never presented itself.

When I had whiffed all these matters, in the same manner that I had my memories of the Soufflet, I climbed a flight of white marble stairs that leads off to the left of the Grand Escalier and takes one to the salons where the charity sale for the benefit of the Daydaybay was being held. The salons of the Sorbonne are a set of high-ceilinged rooms, each about forty feet by sixty, arranged *en suite* for exhibitions and academic receptions. Outside the entrance to the sale, I perused a panel listing the maids and matrons who were serving at various booths and counters. A high proportion of the names were *en courants d'air*—spread out in bits, with drafts through them—like Leclerc de Hauteclocque. I could see that Mme la Maréchale had built up a social cachet for the Daydaybay in the years following the General's death. I observed none of the Corsican, Mussulman, and Jewish names that had been so common in the ranks. Nearly every counter—toys, comestibles, books, perfumes, yard goods, flowers—was garrisoned by women with horse-cavalry surnames, usually a promise of a high standard of good looks.

Inside, I made a clockwise tour of the counters and bought a book, entitled *Leclerc et Ses Hommes* and illustrated in color, from its tall and distinguished-looking author, identified by a card on the table in front of him as Pierre Nord. I told M. Nord that I had accompanied the Daydaybay into Paris on August 25, 1944, the day of the Liberation. M. Nord informed me that he was a colonel in the Regular Army, and that Nord was a nom de plume. He is not the sort of author who dismisses customers with a mere signature, and after a moment of thought he wrote in my book, "In homage to a sincere fraternity of arms, to the American friend and war correspondent of our difficult years. Faithfully, Pierre Nord (Colonel Brouillard)." It made me inflate my chest, and I went and bought a flask of white pepper, a carton of matches, and a can of pineapple, each from a different pretty girl. The salons were crowded, and the warm air, heavy with the evaporation of samples at the perfume counter, made me sweat; I took off my hat, which happened to be what elegant Londoners call a titfer (tit fer tat, bowler hat) and the French a *melon*. Try, sometime, taking off a hard hat, holding it, and wiping your brow with a handkerchief while grasping a book and a flask of white pepper in one hand and a can of pineapple and a carton of matches in the other. Of course, the dicer fell to the floor, where it rolled between a woman's feet. In attempting to get to it, I bumped into her. *"Polisson!"* she said firmly.

The situation was saved by a one-legged chap on crutches, who swung down like a bird from a perch and retrieved my hat for me. He was selling copies of a publication entitled *L'Amicale Sportive des Mutilés de*

France. I bought one and asked if he had been with the division at the Liberation. "No, Monsieur," he said apologetically. "I joined up after the division got here. I was wounded in front of Strasbourg." He was embarrassed by not having lost his leg soon enough.

I had somehow had an idea that the benefit would be like the reunion of an American division, with a lot of old noncoms lined up at a bar to exchange lies, and, as a possible French variant, a continuous raffle for ducks and geese. But the *vente* for the Daydaybay was exactly like a *vente* for any other charity with excellent social sponsorship. Except for a number of amputees selling *L'Amicale Sportive,* there was nobody present who looked to me like a former noncom or enlisted man. That is probably the way a charity sale should be in order to turn a profit for good works, but it did not correspond with my recollections of hot roads, dead Germans, and cheering crowds. I therefore descended the white marble stairs, carefully re-enthroning my titfer when I got beyond jostling range, and walked over to a place called L'Alsace à Paris, a few blocks away, which has nothing in particular to recommend it except that the proprietor, Robert, used to be the *patron* of the Taverne Soufflet. The waiters, who are not Alsatians, wear red waistcoats, as in all Paris Alsaces; the prices are fairly stiff, and there are no little women. "This is a more serious affair than the old place," M. Robert says. He still has the same students among his clientele—students of the twenties, grown into bald dentists and sedate *avocats.* I ordered a *formidable,* which is a litre of beer in a stone mug, and, while rehydrating, reviewed the recollections that my late experience did not correspond with.

On Monday evening, August 21, 1944, I attended a press conference that was addressed by the then Lieutenant General Omar Nelson Bradley at Laval, a town in the Département de la Mayenne, in western France. Bradley, whose infrequent lectures I had been following with rapt attention ever since he took over II Corps in North Africa, in April 1943, had in sixteen months progressed from the command of a corps through that of an army (the First) to that of an army group (the Twelfth), but his manner—benevolent, pedagogical, and slightly apologetic—had not changed. A month before the Laval press conference, I had listened to him in a shed behind Mme Hamel's at Vouilly, as he outlined to correspondents the plan for the First Army's new offensive. Before that, I had heard him at Béja, in Tunisia, explaining how he was going to try to take Bizerte, and then in Bryanston Square, London, offering his opinion, take it for what it was worth, that we would get ashore in France. At Laval, everybody knew that the most recent effort, like the ones previously adumbrated by the General, had come off nicely. It had been set back a couple of days by rain and had then wheezed a bit when the most impressive assemblage of air power ever up to then on view outside a

Howard Hughes production flew over from England and, getting mixed up, dropped a lot of its bombs on the American 30th Division instead of on the Germans, just beyond. But, once under way, the offensive had discombobulated all the German defensive arrangements in the West and had changed the war of position into one of pursuit, with the First, now confided to Hodges, sweeping north behind the German Seventh Army and Fifth Panzer Army and joining the British, Canadians, and Poles in a grand *battue* of fugitives at the Argentan-Falaise escape gap while Patton's newly activated Third dashed southwest and then east.

As Group Commander, Bradley controlled both the First and the Third, and he had selected Laval as the headquarters of the moment because it was approximately behind the point where the zones of the two armies overlapped. Laval was a good long jeep ride from First Army Headquarters and press camp, at Bagnoles-de-l'Orne, in central Normandy. It was equally far, I suppose, from Third Army Headquarters, although I have no idea where the Third was. (To judge by the telling of it by Third Army correspondents, its advance elements were already on the outskirts of Vienna, but you couldn't believe everything those fellows said.) As the conference wouldn't be over until after dark and none of us First Army correspondents wanted to ride any farther than we had to on a road full of blacked-out trucks and tanks, my colleagues had entrusted me with the mission of reserving promising billets for them in hotels and inns along the way back to Bagnoles-de-l'Orne. I had done that, saving for an officer friend—Lieutenant Roy Chitterling—and myself accommodations in a small town called Ernée, whose hotel looked too comfortable to tell the others about.

It was the most cheerful briefing I had yet attended. Tall, bespectacled, and Missouri-speaking, Bradley had the pleased look of a Sunday-school superintendent announcing that the cake sale had brought in eleven dollars and fifty cents more than anticipated. The German Seventh Army was in a satisfactory state of disintegration, he said, although "annihilation" might be too rosy a term to use in describing it yet, since a number of its men, abandoning their equipment, had made their way out through the gap. A part of our First had crossed the Seine between Mantes and Vernon, northwest of Paris, and the Third was hooking around Melun, south of Paris. We all knew there had been an American landing in the south of France on August 15, and we assumed that up north Montgomery's Britons and Canadians were barreling along at last. They constituted the Twenty-first Army Group, and Bradley's briefing did not cover them.

The General said, with a smile, that he knew what we all wanted to find out was when did we get to Paris. Well, the important thing was to destroy the German armies, and the next after that was to secure Paris as nearly intact as possible. So we would just hook around Paris, north and south, he said, and the German garrison would probably pull out to avoid capture, since, with Americans across the Seine both above and below the city, it would have no military usefulness, as the Germans were sure to see. A Third Army correspondent said that General Patton had bet him five dollars the Third would be in Paris before the First, and General Bradley remarked that he might just take it into his head to tell General Patton to go someplace else. First Army people present regarded this as a good omen. One thing we could be sure of, Bradley said—we weren't going to make a rush for Paris.

Bradley has what psychiatrists call a therapeutic personality. We all shook hands with him after the briefing, like members of a congregation shaking hands with their minister, and one of the First Army correspondents said, "General, I'm always glad to see you, because you always make me feel good." Then Chitterling and I got on the road at the head of our motorcade, and started dropping jeeps off a couple at a time—each jeep containing three or four correspondents and a driver—as we came to the various *auberges* in which we had booked rooms. After we had dropped the last one, we pushed on to Ernée. Since General Bradley had assured us that there was no hurry about Paris, Chitterling and I played hooky the next day, pursuing some projects that failed to pan out, and did not get back to Bagnoles until Wednesday. There seemed to be no reason for haste; from a journalistic point of view, the war was marking time. You could drive in a jeep all day without finding any rational German resistance, although you might run into a band of vindictive fugitives and so get yourself shot. Or you might find isolated groups shooting away their stocks of ammunition because their commanding officers had listened to too much Wagner, like the drunken *Kommandant* of the fort at Saint-Malo who had made a senseless four-day stand against an all-out barrage and had then capitulated, contrary to the orders of the Führer. But such episodes were anodyne after the events of the breakthrough; the next big story coming up was the redemption of Paris, which the General had told us wouldn't occur immediately. It would be the biggest story of all for me, because I had left the city on June 10, 1940, when crowds of would-be refugees were overflowing into the streets around the railway stations. In my mind, the war would pretty well end with the road back to Paris. The rest would be epilogue.

I was bowled over, therefore, when, on returning to the press camp Wednesday afternoon, Chitterling and I found that it had been deserted by the other correspondents. Bagnoles-de-l'Orne is a summer resort of the most grisly vintage and variety, encumbered with great clapboard-and-stucco hotels of the early days of the Third Republic. The hotels are built around shallow lakes, which, while the press camp was there, at least, were so choked with the stems and leaves of water lilies that they were no good for swimming. I believe that when the place is operating normally, the guests at the hotels partake of purgative waters and talk about their insides, but by the time the First Army reached the town, in the summer of 1944, the hotels had been abandoned, and we roosted in them, doubly depressed by the lack of running water because the bathtubs reminded us of comforts we had almost forgotten.

Now only a few of the officers and enlisted men in the press-relations detachment were still around, and they were packing. In a few minutes, they informed Chitterling and me, they would be off for Paris, where they were to set up a new press headquarters in the Hôtel Scribe, near the Opéra. All my fellow-correspondents, they further related, were probably there already. What had happened, we gathered, was that the forces of the Resistance had unexpectedly risen in Paris and thrown the Germans out. They had then sent a messenger to Bradley asking him to come in fast and save them from the kind of revenge the Germans were currently visiting on Warsaw. The road to Paris was clear. The messenger had arrived in Laval after we left, and the General had revised all his thinking about Paris. I was consequently in a fair way to being scooped on the story I had been looking forward to for four years, two months, and thirteen days. As for Chitterling, my fellow-sybarite, he not only had missed the takeoff but was in Dutch with his superior officers.

I ran upstairs to the room I had shared with another correspondent, grabbed my sleeping bag off the floor, tied up all my junk in it, and came down demanding instant transportation to Paris. Chitterling would have been glad to take me, but, being in the doghouse, he had already been condemned to some menial task like checking the inventory of bales of carbon paper. There was, however, a young first lieutenant named Jack Roach, formerly a press-association reporter in Philadelphia, who controlled, on a provisional basis, a magnificent conveyance—a Chevrolet touring car built in Belgium before the war. It had been liberated from the Germans, and somehow or other Roach had got it. I can't for the life of me remember who was in command of the rear echelon of First Army Public Relations, which was rapidly dwindling as its officers, in order of seniority, provided themselves with missions to Paris. The command may have got down as far as Roach himself by that time.

At any rate, Roach and I took the Chevrolet and set out for La Ville Lumière, figuring we ought to hit it that evening if the roads ahead were as clear as had been rumored. That, I thought, would not be too late for the best of the celebration. We were intensely excited. How many times in his life does a man start out for what he is certain is going to be a phenomenally happy occasion? I don't think that Roach, who was in his middle twenties, had ever been in Paris, but that gave his anticipation a special quality. And for me, at forty, and with nearly half that many years of scattered memories of Paris behind me, it was like finding my Annabel Lee again. All the previous spring, in London, I had been reading clandestine newspapers smuggled out of France. I had cried over them. I do not regret my sentimentality; I wish I had something now that I could be as sentimental about.

When Roach and I had gone a fair piece of the way, we realized that we had brought no food along, either for ourselves or for hungry people we might meet. Living off the country was all very well in Normandy, Brittany, and Anjou—rich farming provinces unable to reach their customary markets and surcharged, like unmilked cows, with their own products. But Paris, we expected, would be short of food. We found the solution of our supply problem on the road ahead of us: a two-and-a-half-ton truck stacked high with cases of K rations, which were flat waxed-cardboard packages—thirty-six to a case—each containing the ready-to-eat components of a nourishing, harmless, and gastronomically despicable meal, calculated, I always supposed, to discourage overindulgence. (Among troops actively engaged, a K ration beat nothing to eat, but it was a photo finish.) These components were a round tin of alleged pork and egg, ground up together and worked to a consistency like the inside of a sick lobster's claw, and tasting like boardwalk cotton candy without any sugar in it; a few sourballs or other boiled sweets (I remember one particularly horrid variety that was flavored with root beer); four cigarettes; and a pinch of soluble coffee, dehydrated vegetarian bouillon, or lemonade powder. You sometimes had to open six packages to find one with coffee in it, and smokers had to open five to get the equivalent of a pack of cigarettes. The rest of a K ration so opened was then chucked away, except in Arab countries, where it could be traded for shell eggs, fowl, or little girls.

Atop the stacks of cases on the truck, at least ten feet above the road, stood a Negro soldier of the Quartermaster Corps. The crown of his helmet was a good sixteen feet above where he would land if he fell. His driver, I saw when we had overtaken the truck and were passing it, was another Q.M.C. soldier. But we did not overtake it until we had witnessed an extraordinary spectacle. There were a lot of jeeps on the road whose occupants had taken off, like us, à l'improviste, and as these vehicles passed the truck, the soldier up top would throw cases of K rations down into their rear seats. It was the way he did this that was remarkable. The truck was going about forty miles an hour, and a jeep would pull up on it, going about forty-five. As it did so, the soldier, standing up there, facing the rear—his feet spread wide apart to brace him on his gradually diminishing platform—would yell "How many?" and the jeep driver would hold up one, two, or three fingers, usually three. The soldier would have the first case already in the air, leading the driver, who would instinctively hunch forward over the wheel. But the case would fall harmlessly behind him every time. The second would land right on top of it. The third might land a couple of inches farther back, or even hit the stern end of the jeep and carom in, since by now the Q.M.C. bombardier would have to twist and throw it after the passing vehicle. These near misses must have pained him, for he was clearly a precisionist. He raised each successive case high above his head before he sent it crashing down, like an Old

Black Jove hurling well-meant thunderbolts. I watched him until we had got our share, and then I turned my head and looked over my shoulder until we lost him from sight, some time afterward, and I never saw him conk anybody or throw any groceries out into the road. The driver was good, too; he held the same even course and pace, like a well-trained circus horse. It was, of course, a wholly unauthorized distribution of Army supplies, and maybe when that talented team reached the end of their run, some niggling quartermaster lieutenant chewed them out because they were a few hundred cases short, but I would have given them the Legion of Merit. Their gesture was so lordly that when I heard our cases crash behind me on the floor of the Chevrolet, I momentarily believed that they might contain fresh caviar, *écrevisses à la nage,* and a covey of smoked partridges.

I remember no other incident between Bagnoles-de-l'Orne and Chartres, a journey that, as the *Carte Michelin* reminds me now, is about a hundred and sixty kilometres, or a hundred miles. All the way to Chartres, we accepted our hot tip at its face value and assumed that we were going straight through into Paris that night. I recall the excitement of seeing the first stone road markers that gave the distance not only to Alençon and Chartres but to Paris. The excitement increased as the number of kilometres decreased. When we reached Chartres, we were nearly two thirds of the way from Bagnoles to Paris and we had a couple of hours of daylight left, but there we were held up. Army was moving divisions from north to south and south to north, passing them through each other like a dealer giving cards a fast shuffle—the kind of *passe-passe* that is a good G-3's delight and that it sometimes seemed to me the boys did just for the hell of it. To Roach and me, it was like being caught on the wrong side of a St. Patrick's Day parade. Then, in the mixed crowd of soldiers and civilians that was packed around the principal *carrefour* of the city, half a dozen blocks from the Cathedral, I noticed a small private, first class, gesticulating and running toward us. As he approached, I saw he was Allan Morrison, a soldier-reporter for the *Stars & Stripes,* who has since become New York editor of the picture magazine *Ebony,* an ameliorated Amerafrican version of *Life.* He was the diagnostician who first divined the reason for the protracted resistance of the fort at Saint-Malo. "The C.O. is loaded," he said. "When he finishes his last bottle of sauce, they'll run up a white flag."

Morrison was hitchhiking, so I beckoned him aboard, and he climbed over the side and perched on our stack of K rations. A moment later, I recognized the lieutenant colonel who was out in the middle of the *carrefour* directing traffic, and I was able to surmise, correctly, that the shuffling of troops was not being run off in strict accordance with standard practice. The lieutenant colonel was a 1st Division fellow named Chuck Horner, and he was letting an endless column of his own people through; the only trucks that were moving were full of 1st Division soldiers. This was an old 1st Division trick. Army M.P.s were supposed to handle such matters, but those assigned to the task were usually enlisted men. If one of them showed up and tried to stop a 1st Division column to let the vehicles of some other outfit through for a while, a 1st Division lieutenant colonel, or even a higher officer in the outfit, would pull rank on him. I knew a 1st Division colonel who became a major general and got a division all his own. Once, when I was stuck for half an hour in a column halted at a road intersection, I got out of my jeep and walked up ahead to see what was happening. It was the major general personally passing his whole division through. I was glad he had not acquired a corps.

I had last seen Horner in North Africa hunting for enemy parachutists, who turned out to be soldiers of the Twelfth Air Force shooting tracers to celebrate Christmas Eve. ("It's the Air Force mentality," Horner said when he had finished his reconnaissance. He was very vexed.) I now reminded him of the occasion, and he agreed to let us through the 1st Division column. The 1st was not going into Paris, Horner told me; it would cross the Seine farther south, where there was still serious opposition. "Wouldn't you know it?" he said. "The bad divisions always get the soft jobs." The 1st pitied itself for being indispensable.

After we got on the Paris side of Chartres, traffic thinned out, and before long we were alone. "If everybody is going into Paris, I don't see why we're the only ones on the road," Roach said, with what made excellent sense. Morrison gave us the benefit of his inquiring reportorial mind by asking, "Who told you the way was clear all the way into Paris?" When we replied that everybody at Bagnoles-de-l'Orne had said so, Morrison asked, "Who told *them?* That's a long way back from here." Roach, who was not going to succumb to a climate of anxiety set up by an enlisted man, said, "Well, if the other correspondents didn't go into Paris, where are they? We haven't passed any on the road." This prompted Morrison to remark, "Maybe some prison-camp paper in Germany is going to have a hell of a staff." Twilight was coming on, and it suddenly seemed to me that my conversation with Lieutenant Colonel Horner had been a long while ago. There have been times in my life when I have missed the 1st Division more than anything else on earth.

When I was a boy member of the St. Agnes Branch of the New York Public Library, I enjoyed reading about Jeb Stuart and imagining myself in his position, but by 1944 I no longer thought of myself as a man to lead a raid behind enemy lines, and our 1937-or-so Chevrolet was no armored division. As an assimilated captain (the grade bestowed on all war correspondents), I was the senior member of the expedition. Lieutenant Roach, the ranking active soldier, had received most of his battle training in the Philadelphia Bureau of the United Press, and his combat effectiveness was not enhanced by an oversized helmet that was likely to fall over his eyes if he moved suddenly. Pfc. Morrison's attitude was that of an objective observer, exactly as it is taught in schools of journalism. He was our whole enlisted strength.

"If we keep on going, we're bound to meet someone," I said decisively.

"That is exactly what I am afraid of," Morrison said.

To turn back was unthinkable, but we continued in a mood of modified rapture. I remember getting to a spot where a road branches north toward Rambouillet. That, we later learned, was the way most of the correspondents ahead of us had gone. But we held straight on. After a while, we came upon a couple of American soldiers in a jeep, which encouraged us. They said they were members of a troop of motorized cavalry belonging to the 7th Armored Division and that their outfit was a couple of miles down a side road, preparing to spend the night there. Roach said their commanding officer ought to be able to give us some dope about what lay ahead. If the cavalry, which was made up of reconnaissance troops, was bedding down forty or fifty miles short of Paris, it hardly seemed likely that anybody had gone into the city by that route. We thought we might as well ask, though, so we turned down the side road and found the outfit, with its vehicles dispersed in a field.

"How much of our stuff is there out ahead of us, Lieutenant?" I asked the boy who was in command.

"Nothing," he replied. "Why should there be?"

I felt as mad as a man who is about to take a dip in a swimming pool and discovers that somebody has let all the water out of it. "Then why isn't there a sign on the road, or an M.P., or something?" I demanded. "After all, somebody might get captured this way."

"Ain't no Germans, either," the lieutenant replied reasonably. "We've had patrols up that road twenty miles. Can't find any."

"Well, it's a hell of a way to take Paris," I said. "Back at Bagnoles, they told us we were going right into Paris today."

"Bagnoles?" the lieutenant said. "Where's that? I'd like to go to Paris myself someday. Always heard it well spoken of."

"It's all right to go on, then?" Roach asked.

"You'll be safe enough along the main road," the lieutenant replied. "But don't go down any of the side roads, because there might be stray krauts along them, trying to escape. And don't try to drive after dark, because the country is full of F.F.I. [Forces Françaises de l'Intérieur], and they shoot at everything."

It was nearly dark by then. We could have slept out in the field, but there didn't seem much point to that when we could probably find beds at some hotel a little farther along the highway. Besides, I wanted to be as close up as possible in order to rush into the capital the next morning. So after we got back on the highway, we pushed on as far as the first crossroads agglomeration—I think the town was called Bonnelles—where there was a building that we thought might be a hotel. It was blacked out, of course, but light leaked defiantly from around every door and window. As soon as we got inside, we could see that we were in the provinces no longer but within the Sunday-outing belt of a big city. The name of the hotel was something like Au Retour de la Chasse et Rendez-Vous des Pêcheurs à la Ligne. There was a big, bare, partly dismantled dining room that was really just a boarded-in porch—obviously designed for use only in summer, the season of *boulistes* and lovers. There was also a bar, the full length of which would be required only on Sundays during the hunting (rabbit) and fishing (carp) seasons, when the sportsmen returned to discuss their evil luck over a *pastis* before reintegrating with their socially mediocre *arrondissements*. (The huntsmen and fishermen of the better neighborhoods miss bigger game with more expensive weapons at a greater distance from the city.) Since neither ammunition nor gasoline had been available for recreational purposes during the four years of the Occupation, business had been subnormal, and the place looked it. The barnlike ground floor was overrun with young men and women wearing the tricolor armbands of the Resistance. Each of the fellows had one or two weapons; German pistols (stolen) and tommy guns (parachuted) predominated. We got a big welcome.

Part of the difficulty of trying to reconstruct the days preceding the Liberation is that one now knows too much; I have since heard and read so often about what happened in Paris between August 15, when the police went on strike, and August 25, when the German garrison surrendered, that it is hard to recall the state of ignorance in which Roach and Morrison and I approached the city. It must have been there at the crossroads hotel, on the night of Wednesday, August 23, that we first heard any of the details. There were still some organized groups of Germans in the suburbs between where we were and Paris, the F.F.I. people told us, but there was no continuous line, and some of the kids we talked with had been in and out of the city several times during the past week, to help in the fighting and share in the excitement. News of the battle was on tap in the hotel twenty-four hours a day, the very shapely sweater-girl daughter of the proprietor informed me, since the telephone lines into Paris were still open; all you had to do was call and ask the *téléphonistes* what was happening. The German officers in control of the French telephone system either had skipped or, in the confusion, had lost track of which telephone centrals were now outside the rapidly shrinking Wehrmacht orbit. It must have been at the hotel, too, that we first heard how open fighting had begun in Paris on the previous Saturday, when the Germans gave the order to disarm the French police. The latter, refusing to be disarmed, had begun the defense of their headquarters, on the Ile de la Cité. Resistance groups had seized several other strong points, and the garrison had besieged them. On Monday, it seemed, there had been an abortive armistice. A distorted account of this development, trickling through to Bagnoles, had given rise to the report that the road was clear.

But the fighting had continued, and now, as the Germans were pulling out, leaving only a rear guard, the Resistance, in turn, was besieging these hind-end Charlies.

"All these years, I have dreamed of seeing my first Allied soldier," the proprietor's daughter said. "This morning I saw him. He was alone in a jeep—a scout. He stopped in front of the door to ask directions. I rushed out, I precipitated myself on him, I threw my arms around him, I kissed him. I broke his glasses. He was furious."

That night, Roach, Morrison, and I slept in beds. The young F.F.I.s stayed up, because they were too excited to sleep, like children on the night before Christmas. They didn't even have a collaborator to shoot as a means of passing the time, an F.F.I. lieutenant told me shortly before I retired. "This is such a dreary little place," he said apologetically. "We had only a few *collabos* to start with, and now they've all skipped."

I shared the young F.F.I.s' excitement, although I realized how irrational it was, for, no matter how delighted, I was still capable of realizing that the liberation of Paris would not solve all the problems of the world, or even terminate the war. Nevertheless, before I fell asleep I saw American planes burning on the ghostly hills above the phosphate mine at Metlaoui, in Tunisia, and remembered the names of the pilots in them. Our side had come a long way around.

When I went downstairs next morning, a couple of jeeps bearing the emblem of the Daydaybay were parked in the garage with our Chevrolet. A French captain, a medic, was shaving painstakingly, a basin of hot water on the hood of a jeep in front of him, his field mirror hanging from a nail on a post. The captain said the Daydaybay was going to liberate Paris. When the Allied command advanced the date of the Liberation, the Daydaybay, officially attached to V Corps of the First Army, was resting after some hard fighting at the Argentan-Falaise gap, which it had helped to seal. The Daydaybay had been on the road all night long, the captain said, and by now its tanks were up ahead of us. The captain's report banished any misgivings I may still have had about those groups of Germans between us and Paris and also explained the paucity of American troops on the Paris side of Chartres. It was through the captain that I got my first hint of the Allied command's decision to have the only French division in the north rescue the capital, instead of ordering an American division straight in. It was one of the wisest decisions of the war, helping to compensate for a thousand wounding stupidities in Anglo-American relations with the French. For all practical purposes, it constituted recognition of General de Gaulle's Provisional Government as the government of France, because Leclerc was more Gaullist than his chief. The presence of the Daydaybay in Paris would preclude any last-minute State Department–Foreign Office deal with collaborationists anxious to hedge their bets, like Darlan in Africa. We had nourished angry suspicions of such a deal by declining to recognize the Provisional Government officially.

The captain was making a careful toilette for his *rentrée* into Paris, which he expected to celebrate that evening. He was a specialist in colonial medicine, he told me, and at the time Paris fell, he was in Equatorial Africa, whence he had returned by stages—Lake Chad to Fezzan, Fezzan to Tunisia, Tunisia to Morocco (where the Daydaybay was put together and given its equipment), Morocco to England, and England to Bonnelles. All these steps had been made in the train of Leclerc, who had accumulated rank and firepower as he moved along, beginning as a thirty-eight-year-old major and winding up as a forty-one-year-old general of a division. Leclerc and the captain had left Chad in 1942 with the equivalent of one weak regiment—thirty-five hundred men in all, including three thousand Central African Negroes. Now they were on the outskirts of Paris surrounded by a magnificent division. It was a unique example of attrition in reverse. The captain's and my routes back to Paris had coincided once before. That was at Enfidaville, when the Allies were beginning their final drive to Tunis and Leclerc's troops were attached to the 4th Indian Division of the British Eighth Army. At Enfidaville, I nearly had my first encounter with Leclerc, who was sleeping in a Ford sedan out beyond his front line—"*pour être tranquille,*" his aide informed me—while mortar shells burst on all sides of his improvised dormitory. The aide said that if I wished to wait around until the General awoke, the General would be glad to talk to me. I replied that I had nothing important to discuss, and went back to have tea at Division.

Leclerc had brought his officers and noncoms along with him to stiffen the cadres of his new division, but he had left his black soldiers in North Africa. Although there were thus only a few hundred Chadians in the Daydaybay, it remained, in the popular imagination, "Leclerc's Army from Chad." I had seen the division on the road above Avranches on August 8, on its way to the front. The men were exuberant, sprawling over their tanks—all span-new Shermans—like kids on a hay ride. They had painted the sides of their vehicles with the names of French towns, regions, and rivers (Tarbes, Cévennes, Moselle, La Villette, and so on), and had topped their tankers' uniforms with the forage caps of their former branches of the service—red for the artillerists, blue for the chasseurs and marines. They were all volunteers, and, on the entire western front, they were the only soldiers in either the Allied or the Axis armies who were fighting on their home territory. They were also the only ground soldiers I remember during the war who were eager to fight. Ten days after I came across the division near Avranches, I had my talk with Leclerc in the field at Fleuré. In the meanwhile, the Daydaybay had flung itself in the path of the retreating German armies, got itself surrounded, cut its way out again, sunk its teeth in their hams, and kicked them in the ankle. It was the occasion when I asked the General about his name. I

also asked him how his fellows compared with the blacks he had left in
Africa. He replied that they fought as well but had less discipline.

When Roach and Morrison and I got out on the road that morning, we
found ourselves in the midst of the armored infantry regiment of the
Daydaybay, which was traveling in open half-tracks. Now that the tanks
of the Daydaybay had gone through, the citizens of the populous countryside had no fear that the Germans would return, and so they turned
out en masse to line the road as their men rode by. We were in the truck-
gardening belt that surrounds Paris, and about all the inhabitants had to
offer their liberators was tomatoes. While I know of few simple gastronomic pleasures comparable to a raw ripe tomato, I will concede that
eight or ten such vegetables, coming at a soldier simultaneously from
different directions, soon detract from his military appearance, and this
the troops in the half-tracks, though appreciative of the generous spirit
behind the gesture, were discovering.

Above Arpajon, where the long snake of vehicles from the west de-
bouched into the north-south highway that connects Paris with Orléans,
we passed a middling-pretentious villa, set back from the highway. A long-
legged young woman in a bathing suit was lounging in a deck chair by
the front door, her bare toes pointing at the oncoming column as she
waved a promise—purely symbolic, of course—of what the young men in
the half-tracks had been dreaming for four years of getting back to. Three
small children clustered about her knees, discouraging a too personal
reaction. The Daydaybay crawled by—fifteen thousand men on a moving
belt of appetite.

I have read since that it rained during the night and early morning,
while the Daydaybay was moving toward Paris. But mood and weather
were in accord now, and the three of us in the Chevrolet tried to get
along to the homecoming celebration quickly. Since we were attached to
none of the division units, we were not obliged to stay in place in the line,
so Roach began to weave his way forward, at first past half-tracks and
then past tanks, scooting along the shoulders of the road when there were
any and then ducking back to travel in the wake of the armor, until
another opportunity presented itself. Our appearance helped. We were
Americans, and Roach's First Army shoulder patch and my correspondent's green flash gave the impression that we were on an urgent mission.
I encouraged this by asking French M.P.s along the way where General
Leclerc found himself. Every time I asked, they waved us forward, which
didn't surprise me, remembering my near encounter with him at Enfidaville.

The solidity and nonchalance of the column, now within twenty miles
of Paris, convinced me that the Germans had simply skedaddled. I surmised that as we entered the Porte d'Orléans, they would be going out the

Porte de la Villette, on the other side of town. I have always preferred to enter a beleaguered city in this fashion. Violence interferes with the enjoyment of the sentiments appropriate to such an occasion; shooting, if bilateral, spoils everything. As we skittered happily along in the Chevrolet, the only question in my mind was whether Leclerc would retain enough sense of *noblesse oblige* to share with those American allies who found themselves by chance in his immediate vicinity the *vin d'honneur* that was sure to be offered him as he entered the city.

We passed the tank that was leading the procession, and Morrison, from the rear seat, asked me if I didn't think I might have received another wrong steer. For some time, as we pushed along, the welcoming throng had been thinning out, and now it had dwindled to nothing. This, of course, is always an ominous sign. No one had thrown a tomato to us for a couple of miles when, suddenly, we spotted two jeeps ahead of us, one of them flying a general's fanion. "Don't get ahead of him," I told Roach. "He might be offended." Just as we began to pull up on the jeeps, they stopped. There was the sound of an *arrivée*—an incoming shell—and then a spout of dirt and smoke two hundred yards to the right of the highway; it had clearly crossed over the road between us and the jeeps. Leclerc got out of his jeep—we knew it was he because he carried a cane—and began to look about him with interest. He did not look long; within a few seconds we saw him wave his cane, like a pointer, in the direction he evidently thought the shell had come from. Then he hopped back into his jeep, and both vehicles turned around and started toward us, the General undoubtedly pleased as Polichinelle at having spotted an antitank gun before it could hurt one of his cherished armored vehicles. He was the only divisional commander I ever saw use himself as a decoy to draw fire. Roach asked if I thought Leclerc would be angry if we preceded him back down the road. I replied that in retreat the place of honor is in the rear, and we might as well leave it to the General.

We soon reached the main body of vehicles again, and saw that the parade had temporarily disbanded; deploying from the Paris-Orléans highway, the tanks were taking off along feeder roads and the half-tracks across fields, as if preparing to pinch in on the point of resistance. Leclerc, after a brief pause at the first tank he came to, headed down a tarred crossroad. "Maybe he's going to try another way through," Roach said. "Let's follow him." Not being able to read Morrison's mind, I couldn't tell whether Roach's proposal represented the inclination of the majority, and I was ashamed to suggest putting the matter to a vote. So we hustled along after the General.

I have no coherent recollection of the next few hours, which we spent running up and down crossroads, hoping they would lead us to a nice, clear, Franco-American-held path into Paris, or else following half-tracks loaded with infantrymen along minor lanes that ran parallel to the main highway. The men in the half-tracks were passing wine bottles from hand to hand, for the inhabitants of the region, having run out of tomatoes, had levied on their cellars to produce new offerings, and there was a festival atmosphere. Each time we attached ourselves to a company of vehicles, one of us would say, "Maybe this outfit will go all the way through," but each time, after a mile or two, there would be a barrage of antitank *arrivées* and the vehicles would stop and fan out from the road.

An armored division is a superior instrument for long sweeps across open country but ill-adapted to fighting in the suburbs of a great city. Between Arpajon and Paris the terrain is finely veined with roads and closely dotted with villages. Roads converge upon each village, and every village crossroads offers an ideal emplacement for a concealed antitank gun, which an approaching tank, hemmed in by buildings on either side, must face head on. In such circumstances, the safe, cautious procedure is to stop the tanks, call up the half-tracks, and deploy infantrymen around each strong point, but there were two persuasive arguments against such strategy on that August 24. One was that there were so many antitank emplacements and so few infantrymen—since the Daydaybay, as an armored division, carried with it only one infantry regiment—that the thrust would have slowed to a crawl, and the other was Leclerc's and the whole Daydaybay's overpowering haste to get into Paris. The Germans, rightly calculating that the Allies would never again bomb them in Paris, had dismantled all their antiaircraft defenses in the zone, and the weapons taken from those installations gave them an abundance of the deadliest kind of antitank artillery. Rommel, it is now known, had wanted to bring this stuff forward months earlier and use it on the battlefield, but he had been overruled. Antiaircraft belonged to the Luftwaffe, the Luftwaffe belonged to Goering, and Goering hated Rommel.

The Daydaybay's irregularly progressing advance elements were followed by a great wheeled throng, including us, that was always just far enough back not to be shot at, which meant not quite far enough forward to see what was going on, with the result that nobody could understand why the headway being made was so intermittent; it was like a huge crowd following a pack of coon hounds by their sound, unaware that the dogs have met up with a wildcat. In the throng, in addition to the supply and ammunition trains and all the other rear elements of the division, were many vehicles whose occupants, whether military or civilian, had no connection with the Daydaybay. There were, for example, increasing numbers of American trucks carrying provisions for Paris, because Group had envisaged the possibility that the city would be found on the verge of famine, and of civilian charcoal-fueled trucks, mounting odd revolving chimneys that belched stinking smoke, and jammed with delegations of F.F.I. from behind the Allied lines. The F.F.I., who were willing enough, could have been used as infantry if the division staff had had liaison with them, but it is hard to improvise such an arrangement on a battlefield. So they mostly just followed along with the rest of us, though occasionally some of them dismounted to hunt down a German in a haystack after the tanks had cleaned out a gun position. There were Army jeeps from all over the front, carrying officers who, like those at Bagnoles-de-l'Orne, had invented missions for themselves that would take them to Paris. And there were the correspondents, military and civilian, too. Morrison and I spotted jeeploads of our colleagues at every turning, giving me happy reassurance that I had made up the head start that so appalled me the day before.

The many tangential roads were a constant challenge, and Roach, Morrison, and I kept trying new ones, always figuring that we might still come on one that was clear all the way into Paris. But whatever road we tried led us to fighting. We could tell that the advance units were moving nearer Paris all the time, though, because at each try we got farther from our line of departure, which was where the parade had come to a halt. After we explored all the accessible roads, we went back over those on which we had first run into fighting, and here the evidence of progress was all about us, in the form of burned-out vehicles (most of them, unfortunately, bearing the Daydaybay emblem), knocked-out antitank guns, and German dead and wounded, lying by the roadside with their feet toward the pavement, waiting to be picked up, sometime, by French ambulances. They had been laid out there in orderly fashion, as if they had dressed their lines, by German prisoners, working in pairs under the orders of F.F.I. boys with tommy guns. It must have been disquieting to a member of the Führer's master race to feel, as he walked along holding a leg of a wounded man in each hand, that there was within kicking distance of his rear a seventeen-year-old with a tommy gun pointed at his kidneys and a wild desire to use it. We came across unwounded and unutilized prisoners, too, holding their hands high over their heads and doing a shoeless goose step in response to the orders of their F.F.I. guards. (Boots of real leather had become extremely scarce in France, and the F.F.I.s figured that since the collective Occupant was responsible for this state of affairs, it was fair enough to glom the individual Occupant's boots when he was taken prisoner.) The prisoners' faces had the same color as those of the dead Germans—greenish-white under the dust from the road—as if, physiologically, the processes of death had already begun, a reaction to an anticipated situation. Yet I saw only one Frenchman justify such a reaction. A wounded German was lying, quite still, by the roadside, when two armed civilians approached him. One pulled at his boots and the other pointed an automatic—German—at his head and fired. There was no excuse for it.

The Daydaybay's infantrymen, in their half-tracks, followed the tanks at a distance of a little less than a mile. The commander of each combat group—four or five tanks and as many half-tracks—committed his infantry only when he had to, since to detruck and deploy them, move them up on foot, envelop a position, and then take it by small-arms fire might require anywhere from fifteen minutes to an hour. That accounted for the heavy losses of the tankers and for the boredom of the infantry, who, in their open vehicles under a baking August sun, began to sweat wine. I remember two troglodytic types—an Arab and a Frenchman from some part of the Mediterranean littoral—locked in unfraternal combat while their *compagnons de voiture* tried unsuccessfully to pry them apart. *"Tapette!"* each of the contestants shouted in one of the other's ears as they struggled. The insult, which is French slang for "homosexual," was never used with less apparent foundation. They looked like pithecanthropi with gold teeth. (I did not see either of them at Mme la Maréchale's recent party.)

On each road we tried, we met jeeploads of correspondents and of officers attempting to maintain liaison with Division, but the jeep we met most frequently was General Leclerc's. Leaning forward as he sat, tapping on the floor with his cane, he looked as if he were riding the jeep toward an obstacle on a steeplechase course. Leclerc was forty-one, a year younger than the Ulysses S. Grant of the Wilderness Campaign, and, like Grant, he was by training and predilection a horseman. Watching him in his jeep made me realize for the first time how valuable a horse must have been in the old days as an outlet for the emotional energy of a fretting commander. The constant conflict of wills, on a level slightly below that of thought, and the horse's reflexes, impossible to ignore even during great crises, must have offered a distraction from the pressures of the moment. Leclerc, I knew, had been a cavalryman, and I have since learned that when he first saw action, as a lieutenant in Morocco in 1926, he had two horses killed under him. And now he had only a jeep to sit, and a jeep is insensitive to the eager tremolo of the legs. Still, he was riding it as best he could. To be so near Paris and not yet have it made him strain the long nose and the bristling red mustache in close pursuit of the point of the visor of his three-star-general's kepi.

I had, it is true, been talking with Leclerc only a week or so earlier, but now, as we passed and repassed each other on the road, I never found what I deemed a suitable opportunity to remind him of our acquaintance, and the same diffidence restrained me even when, just beyond a railroad culvert, his vehicle and ours stopped close together in deference to a shelling by an unanticipated battery. During a pause in the shelling, he continued on his way, but we decided to turn back and try some other route, and presently we met a jeep carrying an American brigadier general from V Corps, the unit of which the Daydaybay was theoretically a part. The general waved to us to stop, and when we did, he got out in the road and asked us if we had seen Leclerc. He was a very precise-looking brigadier general, with rimless glasses and a neatly trimmed black mustache, and he carried a well-filled map case under his right arm. We pointed in the direction in which we assumed Leclerc was still riding, if his luck had held out, and the brigadier sighed. "I've been looking for him at what is supposed to be Division Headquarters, and they told me they hadn't heard from him for hours," he said. "The division isn't where it's supposed to be, and I can't find Leclerc to tell him so. God damn it," he added, with unexpected warmth, "this isn't an advance at all! It's the march of a gypsy band." The brigadier turned, the set of his shoulders a form of professional reproof, climbed back into his vehicle, and took off after the unhorsed cavalier, who, as a matter of principle, tried to stay out of touch with Corps as much as possible. He loathed receiving orders. "He was a commander who knew how to make himself adored without making a single concession to popularity," a man who served under him said to me once. "Whenever he did a kindness, he always covered it with a hard word."

Late in the afternoon, having worked all the subsidiary roads in vain, we went back to the Paris-Orléans highway and found it clear for at least ten miles beyond where we had left it that morning. There was almost the fine free feeling of our ride to Chartres the day before as we raced up past Montlhéry and into Longjumeau, an ancient town that chiefly consists of a single endless street, walled on both sides with houses. In the coaching days, Longjumeau was the last change of horses before Paris. On its interminable street, we came upon the tail end of a long string of motionless vehicles. The Germans were making another stand up ahead, at Fresnes, where they were using a prison as an antitank fort. I acquired from a source that I believed authentic—and it turned out to be so—the information that the division would not go into Paris until the next morning. It is strange that I cannot remember now who told me, because it must have been somebody I trusted like my mother, or Roach, Morrison, and I would have waited in the street all night. The fighting at Fresnes, which we did not try to see, was savage.

Longjumeau, with its locked and tightly shuttered house fronts, offered small promise of an entertaining billet, so we turned back toward more open country and took the turnoff to the Tower of Montlhéry. A difference between the Paris suburbs and those of New York is that in the former, crabbed old medieval towns are interspersed with the latest jerry-built speculative developments. The town of Montlhéry, huddled on the slope of a hill a mile or so east of the highway, might as well be, from its appearance, in a remote corner of Burgundy as where it is, thirteen miles from the Porte d'Orléans. On the other side of the highway is the Montlhéry automobile race track, an incongruous annex to the ancient commune. We took the road that leads up through the steep, narrow streets of the town to the ancient Tower, on the top of the hill. (*Monument historique*, completed 1015 A.D., 137 metres above sea level at its base, 168 at its summit, it says in the guidebooks.)

Only the Tower remains of a castle that dominated the southern approach to Paris for six centuries, served as a fortress for insurrectionary French lords in a drawn battle against Louis XI in 1465, and was finally dismantled by Henry IV in 1591, so that it could never again be used as a center of rebellion. The four encircling walls have long since disappeared, the stones having been carted away by thrifty housebuilders. Trees have grown up over most of the site. After passing through the town, the road skirts the outline of the vanished outermost wall. In peacetime, Sunday motorists park their cars along it and walk up to where the Tower stands solitary on the wooded hilltop. To cater to these visitors, a rustic restaurant and bar, called the Auberge de la Tour, has been built near the road, with a wide concrete terrace that affords a view in the direction of Melun and Fontainebleau, and it was here that we stopped.

The interior of the Auberge de la Tour (*"Terrasse—Jeux—Panorama Splendide"*), like that of our stopping place the night before, was in a state of ecstatic ebullition. M. Bertrand, the *patron*, by whom we were made welcome, is one of those Frenchmen who wear a cap and sweater in all seasons and invariably speak in a deep baritone. His eyes bulge in a friendly but disillusioned manner, advising the world that he is not a man to be taken in. His handclasp is strong and his conversation informed and libidinous, as an innkeeper's should be. His chalet is crowded with paintings in which he descries the hands of Old Masters. M. Bertrand is the *crieur aux ventes*, or auctioneer, of the district, which is in itself an assurance that he is a glib fellow. In selling the effects of the deceased, he told me over our first glass of wine, he was occasionally able to come by some good things; he was, after all, the only connoisseur between Melun and Saint-Michel. He bought not for resale, he said, but as an investment, with a view to creating an estate for his descendants.

"That Géricault there, for example," M. Bertrand said, pointing to a dark oil painting of a lean young thoroughbred in a stall. "There aren't many *guinguettes* where you'd find a Géricault. It's unfortunate he didn't sign it, but it's the real thing. I know his style." Mme Bertrand, a stout, red-faced woman with high cheekbones and narrow eyes, produced a bottle of a dreadful sweet *apéritif* wine called Cap Corse—the only prewar *apéritif* in the house, she said—which she had saved for this great day. We all felt obliged to smack our lips over it.

An F.F.I. boy asked me if Morrison was "an American colonial." I told him no, he was an American, just like Roach and me—we came all colors. So the boy said that if Morrison was that sort of American, he must be conversant with the latest *tendances du jazz hot*. As it happened, Morrison was, and the boy went to a cupboard and fetched a clarinet. Then Roach, Morrison, and I and the boy, and about five other F.F.I. youngsters in shirt sleeves went out on to the *terrasse* with the *panorama splendide* in the late twilight and pulled up chairs around a couple of tables. The clarinetist put his feet up on his table, tilted his chair back, and announced that he was going to play *"Dans l'Ambiance"*—or, as he translated it, "Een de Mud." Then he lifted the clarinet to his lips and played "In the Mood" while Morrison encouraged him with the whole sectarian gamut of facial appreciation and a few quiet, satisfied groans. "Een de Mud" sounded better than any other music I've ever heard. The clarinet gloated over the routed Ostrogoths. The thin sound, wriggling up toward the old Tower, woke birds that had turned in for the night. M. Bertrand's son, a slight youth of eighteen, said the Germans had disapproved of jazz, regarding an interest in it as evidence of Allied sympathies, and had forbidden it to be played in public places. The *zazous*, or hepcats, however, were not discouraged by this from playing at dances but, instead, amused themselves by working out musical arrangements that began as Viennese waltzes, then switched to jazz and back again before any Germans present could call the turn. The *zazous* also affected *le genre jazz* in their clothes, the Bertrand boy said; they wore what Americans call zoot suits. There was nothing much *l'Occupant* could do about that.

In time, the clarinetist finished his recital. It was full dark by then. I could tell by his voice when he spoke that it had done him good to get that dissident music out of him, blasting it forth into the night after the hour of the Occupation curfew. He told us he was not a professional musician—as we had all suggested he must be—but a typewriter repairman. There had been no new typewriters in Paris since the Occupation, he said, and the maintenance of the old ones had become a fine art. I asked him what my banged-about portable Underwood would bring on the black market, and he said, readily, fifty-six thousand francs, which, at the going rate of fifty to the dollar, would have been eleven hundred and twenty dollars.

The jazz connoisseurs of Montlhéry had not been completely cut off from the *potins* and *nouvelles tendances* of the American jazz world, the lads said. They had had not only the *émissions* of the London radio but reports on the situation from four American and two Canadian aviators and jazz fanciers who had lived in the village for several weeks after being shot down over France and who had departed only that afternoon, when an American detachment showed up there. The airmen had reached Montlhéry by a branch line of the underground railroad that was washed out a short while after their arrival in the village. "They were all *fanatiques du jazz*," young Bertrand said. "Unhappily, they spoke hardly any French, but by whistling, tapping with the foot, and now and then a word, we could make ourselves understood to one another."

Until D Day, Allied airmen shot down over France and retrieved by the Resistance were frequently taken to Paris and thence rerouted toward the Spanish frontier. Paris was the turntable. The Allied landings, however, had made communications between Paris and the rest of France uncertain, and from then on most of the Allied fliers who were shot down had to sit it out where they were until they were rescued. The *fanatiques du jazz* stranded in Montlhéry were in this position. All our airmen who flew over France carried photographs of themselves taken in civilian clothes and suitable for attaching to *cartes d'identité*. The Resistance supplied the *cartes*—forged, of course, and usually describing the bearer as a deaf-mute. The high incidence of deafness and mutism in Occupied territory might have astonished an Occupant with more intellectual curiosity. The airmen in Montlhéry had been dressed in French clothes and billeted with "relatives." It became easy to explain newcomers after the landings by saying they were fugitives from the war area.

"The Sunday afternoon before last, we gave a concert on the terrace here," young Bertrand said. "No jazz on the program, of course, but we had a very good crowd and had a lot of fun—all except for the best-known *collabos*. The *collabos* were feeling sick. We were very gay, because we knew by word of mouth and through the B.B.C. how fast the Americans were advancing. *Les Fritz* were furious, but they couldn't forbid innocent amusements without acknowledging that their position was becoming critical. Officially they were still saying the offensive was a local attack that would be contained. The airmen came to the concert and mingled with us young people—all pals of theirs. If a Gestapo man had asked them for their cards, he would have made the discovery that deaf men are crazy about music. Those aviators were nice boys. The town won't be the same without them. It is the only regrettable result of the Liberation."

The night was black and quiet. If there was sporadic shooting up ahead, as there must have been, the wind was wrong, for we heard none. We might have been sitting out under the trees on a New England lawn. There wasn't a uniform in the Auberge, except for Roach's, Morrison's, and mine, in which (I feel safe in speaking for my two companions) none of us had ever felt natural. We were as tired as if we had spent all day swimming, and tired in the same contented way.

I was up early next morning, and while waiting for the others to turn out, I climbed up the fifty yards or so to the Tower, traversing the remains of a causeway that crosses the remains of a moat. The top of the hill is the highest point between Montlhéry and Paris. A very informative booklet, which I did not have then but which I recently bought, for fifty francs, says that the Tower is 24.111 kilometres from the Panthéon and dominates it by 31 metres. Because of its height, the booklet adds, it was a station on the semaphore-telegraph line that linked Paris with the Spanish border in the days before the electric telegraph made the service obsolete, and in 1874 scientists used the Tower to measure the speed of light. One could hardly imagine the Germans' passing up a bet like that, and, sure enough, they had built a brick observation-and-listening post on a flat stretch beside the Tower. I was staring up at the Tower, the first ruin I had seen in months that didn't look as if it could be blamed on the Allied Air Forces, when I heard an American voice say, "Good morning!" Turning, I saw that the voice emanated from a Signal Corps lieutenant, who, I suppose, had emanated from the brick building. Neither voice

(Philadelphia, perhaps) nor lieutenant (five ten, pale under a black stubble, serious mouth) was distinctive, but he was a man I won't forget.

"I've been up here since yesterday morning, sir," he said. "Recon troop brought me up here with a couple of other men, so we could look around. I haven't been of any use, but I've been having a wonderful time looking at Paris through a good glass. I've never been to Paris, but I've been reading about it all my life. I know it by heart, from the maps. Just where everything is. And there it is! God, I just can't take my eyes off it! Come over here and I'll show it to you." He handed me his binoculars, a magnificent Signal Corps pair, and led me over to the northern edge of a broken parapet. Paris was there, all right—there in the same place I had left it four years, two months, and fifteen days before.

"I got the map right here," the lieutenant said, and he unrolled it and laid it out on a flat stone. Then he straightened up and said, "But I don't need the map, because I've got all the landmarks cold. Now, over there," he went on, pointing to the dome of the Invalides, "is the Opera House. Once you get that clear, you have your orientation. And over there," he continued, pointing now to the Opéra, "is the City Hall—you know, the Chamber of Deputies. Isn't it beautiful?"

"It's beautiful," I said, and meant it.

The lieutenant got the Eiffel Tower right. "I suppose you know what that beautiful white church is up on the hill?" he next said, swiveling my elbow into line with Sacré-Coeur. I was going to name it, but something warned me not to, so I shook my head. "Why, it's Notre Dame, of course!" he said, and I was glad that I had kept my mouth shut.

"I can't wait to get down there," the lieutenant said. "It's the most beautiful city in the world."

I thanked him from the bottom of my heart. I hope he made it.

10 / The Navel of the Loire

AUGUST 25, the day that began on the hill of Montlhéry, was to be one of the happiest of my life. The day is celebrated in history also as that of the Liberation of Paris. As a redundant stroke of luck, beyond mathematical probability, I was to see General von Choltitz, the German Military Governor of Paris, sign the surrender of the city and its recent jailers to Leclerc.

In Paris now there is more agreement about what went on under the Merovingians than what happened in the years between 1940 and 1944. The former Vichy people have worked so hard to deny the Resistance, and the Communists to prove there never was a liberation in which the

United States had a part, that often I have found myself searching for tangible evidence of what I think I remember. I was happy, therefore, when, beside an exit from a train platform in the waiting room of the Gare Montparnasse, I came upon a plaque reading:

"Here, the 25th of August, 1944, at 17 o'clock, General Leclerc received from the German Military Governor von Choltitz the act of surrender consecrating the Liberation of the City by the People of Paris and the Allied Armies."

The Gare Montparnasse, I hear, is to be torn down soon, and then not even the plaque will remain. It was not conspicuous, and to find it I had to ask my way at the information counter. The first clerk I spoke to there, a young one, had never heard of either the surrender or the plaque, but a senior colleague said "Gate Thirty-three," and led me to it. The authorities might have given it more splash, I thought; it isn't every day a French general receives the surrender of Paris. But at least I knew now I had not suffered a hallucination.

I remembered the German staff officers—a dozen of them—in their flat, visored caps and shiny boots and the neat uniforms their batmen must have pressed for them in the beleaguered *Kommandantur* at the Hôtel Meurice so that they would have something fresh to surrender in. After von Choltitz, a worried, fat little soldier, had signed, he and his officers were ordered into command cars, in which, accompanied by officers of the Daydaybay, they were driven off to carry the news to German strong points that were still holding out.

It was by sheer chance that I got to see the ceremony. Roach, Morrison, and I entered Paris early in the afternoon, and by the time we reached the Gare, which was the temporary headquarters of the Daydaybay, the streets around it were *en fête*, and the sidewalk tables of the cafés facing it were jammed with jubilants. (There was the sound of desultory shooting fairly close—presumably spite sniping by collaborationists—but nobody paid it any heed.) After gawking about for a short while in a couple of cafés, where white wine, a rarity in Paris then, was being sold to celebrate the victory, we started down the Rue de Rennes toward the Seine. Clinging to the old Chevrolet were three or four frantic young boys of the F.F.I., who acted as guides, and they soon got us into a zone where there was nobody on the streets—a bad sign. Then we ran into shooting, so we drove back to the Gare to ask at Division if there was a safe route across the Seine. Leaving our car at the entrance to the station, we climbed the long flight of stairs to the waiting room, and there were Leclerc and the Germans.

We had seen Leclerc so often on the roads that we felt we knew him, although he never said hello. The last time, before the surrender, had been that morning in a suburb called Antony, less than five miles outside the city. The General's jeep started toward the city, and Roach, who was doing our driving, had begun to follow him, but a large, officious French captain, who looked like United States District Court Judge Thomas F. Murphy, stopped us and said we could not go on in, because we were not correspondents assigned to the division. (No American correspondents were assigned to it.) So we had had to go back six or seven miles to the headquarters of the First Army's V Corps, to which the Daydaybay was attached, and get a *laissez-passer* from the G-2 there. When we returned to Antony with this document, the officious captain was gone, and nobody wanted to see our credentials. But by then the highway leading to the Porte d'Orléans was choked with vehicles, lined up bumper to bumper, and we could advance only a few yards at a time. The German rear-guard action that had slowed the Daydaybay's advance the day before had collapsed, and there was nothing ahead to worry us but traffic. From the hill, the city looked exactly as it had when I last left it, on June 10, 1940. For four years now, however, I had been wondering what was happening to people I knew in Paris, and I wouldn't find that out until we got there. Apparently the Germans had not—as yet, at least—demolished anything, and I could see from the hill no clouds of the sort of smoke that might indicate explosions. But there was no telling what the Nazis might do at the last minute, when they saw Paris escaping them. General Hans Speidel, who was Chief of Staff of Rommel's Army Group B, has since written that von Choltitz had orders from Hitler to blow all the bridges across the Seine, and that after he surrendered the city, he was condemned, *in absentia*, by a Nazi court-martial for failing to do so. Since Leclerc sent von Choltitz a warning that he would hold him personally responsible for any damage to the city, it is possible that the German preferred the *in absentia* kind of trouble.

My anxiety increased after we left the Auberge de la Tour to continue toward our goal, and it wasn't until I saw the glum krauts in custody at the Gare Montparnasse that I was sure we and Notre Dame and the festive crowds wouldn't all go up in a cloud of black smoke. Every delay on the road, especially our reluctant rearward trip to Corps, sharpened our impatience. The endless queue of vehicles moved, but, it seemed, ever more slowly. In Longjumeau a woman rushed out of a house and presented Roach with a magnificent tricolor, big enough to drape a hearse. The flag made us look extremely impressive.

During the long crawl, I had time to think back on the events that preceded my 1940 departure from Paris, at the same jammed-road tempo. I remembered the morning when, from my window in the Hôtel Louvois, I saw the Luftwaffe make its first reconnaissance in force over the city. The Hôtel Louvois faces the Bibliothèque Nationale across the Square Louvois, a park that covers a block in front of the library and has in its center a heroic fountain ornamented with four nearly nude female figures, representing four great rivers of France. They have chests like old-fashioned contraltos. La Loire, who has faced me, off and on, for protracted periods during the last seventeen years, has a lower torso like one of the oil jars in which Ali Baba's handmaiden discovered the thieves. All four ladies hold their heads and shoulders back, in order to support the upper basin of the fountain, which is topped by a Grecian urn—a position that requires them to throw their abdomens forward, as if they were doing bumps. In summer, the water in the fountain cascades past the dryads' noses and splashes in their navels, which are as large as halves of coconut shells.

On the morning the planes came—May 10, 1940—all the inhabitants of the three more or less residential sides of the Square Louvois stood at their wide-flung windows and looked up, sensing that the *drôle de guerre* (the non-fighting one) was over even before they heard the news on their radios that the Germans had invaded the Low Countries. The planes were flying quite high, glinting like metal spinners in the sky, amid puffs of white antiaircraft smoke. One of the spectators on the Square Louvois was a woman who appeared on the narrow balcony in front of her window still wearing her nightgown. She had a figure like La Loire in flood, and she waved toward the unattainable Messerschmitts an arm like one of the statue's legs. *"Courage!"* she cried. *"On les aura!"* And now, as Roach and Morrison and I inched along toward the Square Louvois, four years and three and a half months later, her prediction had come true. I hoped the balcony lady had been patient.

When I prepared to leave Paris, just a month after the balcony scene, I was one of the last half-dozen guests at the Hôtel Louvois, which had a hundred and eighty rooms. The management had been closing floors successively, working from the top down. By the time of my departure, only the entresol and the ground floor were in use, and there remained but five or six employees; the manager, a *valet de chambre*, a *femme de chambre*, the young woman who kept the books, and the night porter, Fernand, are those I remember. Fernand was the oldest and spunkiest. The bookkeeper, Mlle Yvonne, was a good-humored girl, ash blond and plump. *"Au revoir,"* I said to her as I went out the door, but I didn't think it would be soon. I headed south with a broadcaster named Waverley Root and a *Herald Tribune* man named John Elliott, who had a broken leg. I saw a great many things happen in the following four years. While I can't say that I recalled all of them there on the slow, hot road, they all jointly affected my mood.

The Square Louvois, which is again under my window as I write, is a park of modest dimensions—probably no more than a hundred and fifty feet wide or deep—with fourteen full-grown trees, as well as some bushes, and a circular path surrounding a lawn and the fountain. The park occupies one of the former sites of the Théâtre National de l'Opéra, which stood there from 1794 to 1820 and gave the neighborhood a gay Italianate flavor that Henri Beyle found congenial. The operatic flavor persists in the names of the surrounding streets—Lulli, Rameau, Cherubini. The Square has the same character as the central *place* of a provincial town. There is a school at one side, which also serves as a meeting hall and polling place, and we have a bookshop, a cobbler, and several bars. A butcher and a baker have shops in the block-long Rue Rameau, running off the Square, so, all in all, the people who live around it have little need for the rest of Paris. *Pour la vie intellectuelle,* there is the Bibliothèque.

Pigeons roost in the trees of the Square Louvois; even when the temperature is near zero, they seem none the worse for it, and no less amorous. The pigeons are collateral descendants of those I used to see there in 1940, the latter having been eaten during the Occupation. (The same people who treacherously devoured those birds now try to make it up to their successors by feeding them crumbs of *croissants* left over from breakfast.) "My God, those pigeons were tough!" says Fernand, the old night porter. "Real athletes! And with the rationing, we were hardly strong enough to chew them." Fernand has a long, downturned mustache *à la Vercingétorix* and a limp that I have always assumed is a souvenir of Verdun. (I have never asked him, for fear he might avow a less romantic etiology.) He parts his hair in the middle, wears glasses, and has one of those angular faces that anonymous sculptors used to carve over cathedral doors. He speaks with a harsh *Berrichon* accent. Back in the winter of 1939–40, whenever there was an air-raid alert and nothing happened, Fernand would take it as a personal insult. *"Ah, les salauds!"* he would fume, sounding like a band saw in need of oil. "They disturb us, but they don't come!" He believed that it was the Germans who set off the sirens, in the manner of a drunk leaning against a doorbell.

Fernand's spirit of high indignation has not diminished. Every night, when he brings a bottle of Vichy to my room, it is as if the all-clear had just sounded after a bombless alert. *"C'est la pagaille!"* he exclaims on entering, which means it's an intensified, botched-up rat race. Fernand then identifies the particular *pagaille* he is talking about, which may be local, national, or international, on a moral, governmental, or meteorological level. One evening he explained that the concierge had left word the night before for him to waken the man in No. 210 at five-thirty and take him coffee, and that when he had knocked at 210's door, 210 had "screeched like a cow." It turned out that it was 310 who had left word to be wakened, and 210 had complained to the management. *"Ah, quelle pagaille!"* Fernand wailed, stumping out, perhaps to administer a *cataplasme sinapisé,* or mustard plaster, to another guest he has known a long time; he is the unofficial house doctor. The results of the January 1956 election brought Fernand to my room crying, *"C'est la pagaille!* These elections, it's impossible! A country without a government! We'll be back at the voting urns within six months. *Ah, quelle pagaille!"* He tugged at his collar to indicate that he was choking with rage. And on the evening after Scotland beat the French Rugby team, 12–0, Fernand's reaction was "A defeat without parallel in history! They marked not one point! *C'est la pagaille!"* I couldn't sleep without my nightly dose of *pagaille*. But Fernand is right: *la pagaille* is in the air. The quintessential expression of it, of course, is Poujadisme, a political movement with as much intellectual content as a scream.

I had thought of the whole war as a road back to Paris, and now that I was on the real one, I momentarily felt let down. The car barely crept; I might as well have been riding home to Manhattan on a Sunday night from a weekend in Norwalk. After we got through Longjumeau, though, we made better time, and then, as we approached the Porte d'Orléans, we began to meet cyclists coming out from the city to greet us. These cyclists (the only ones I recall, anyway) were all women, the most beautiful I have ever seen. It is an established fact that women look better at some times than at others. I once knew a chap, for instance, who claimed that a woman is never so attractive as just after a severe bout of flu, because it makes her more ethereal, and when I was a young reporter, I used to think that women looked their best in a house where a man had just died. All such previous theories of environmental cosmetology blew up, however, when I saw the Parisiennes on their bicycles. To make a woman really beautiful, liberate her. It brings her up pounds on any kind of track. She visibly exudes a generalized good will that makes you want to kiss her.

These women wore long, simple summer dresses that left their bodies very free. (Elastic for girdles had disappeared from Occupied France years earlier.) Their bare legs were more smoothly muscled than Frenchwomen's before the war, because they had been riding those bicycles or walking ever since taxis vanished from the streets of Paris, and their figures were better, because the *pâtissiers* were out of business. It was a tribute to the French frame that none of them looked scrawny or knobby. Their hair was done up high on their heads, without silly little ponytails, and they wore wooden platform shoes, because there was no leather. As they bore down upon the oncoming jeeps, I understood how those old Sag Harbor whalers must have felt when the women of the islands came swimming out to them like a school of beautiful tinker mackerel. None of ours came aboard though. They couldn't abandon their bicycles. One evening after the war, Roach and I were reminiscing about our arrival in Paris, and he told me that I cried. I have no doubt that I did, but I do not remember when.

In the Place d'Orléans, just within the city limits, we came upon a sight unique in my experience—thousands of people, tens of thousands, all demonstratively happy. In any direction we looked, there was an unending vista of cheering people. It was like an entry into Paradise, and all the sweeter because we didn't deserve it. A man goes through life feeling that he is never getting sufficient credit for what he has done, and few are ever cheered for something they haven't done. Neither Roach nor Morrison nor I had fired a single shot, but there was adulation enough for everybody. General Omar Nelson Bradley, who was not there to receive any of it, could have moved an American division into Paris twenty-four hours sooner, but instead he had sent to Normandy for the Daydaybay, because he wanted a French unit to disengage the capital. It was the most potent lift that French morale received during the war. The people crowded about the troops in the trucks and half-tracks and jeeps, sometimes making it impossible for them to move. At one point our Chevrolet was so weighted down that it came to a dead stop.

There were police lines, but the police were celebrating, too. They couldn't find it in their hearts to step on anybody's feet. Resistance organizations of Left, Center, and Right had united in the final insurrection of Paris, and the display of exuberance was therefore that rare phenomenon in France—a demonstration without a counter-demonstration. An open truck crossed the Place loaded with police, all of them carrying Sten guns. The crowd cheered madly: *"La police à l'honneur!"* The police had been the collective heroes of the uprising; they had raised the tricolor over the Préfecture of Police on August 19 and had held it against all attacks. Nobody called them *flics* or *poulets* or *la flicaille*. In a city where cop-hating is a tradition, such cordiality was without precedent. *"La police à l'honneur!"* It was like a dream.

There were considerable numbers of Moslems in the Daydaybay, but nobody was calling them *bicots*, which is the contemptuous French slang word for North Africans. It was not until a week later that I met a man, in a black-market restaurant near the Bourse, who said he thought it had been a mistake to let *indigènes*—"natives"—take part in the Liberation of Paris. It might make them uppity, he felt. I did not ask him what barricades he had stormed, for I was being friends with everybody, and so, still, was almost everybody else. But the sour note he injected into the general rejoicing was bleakly symptomatic of many things to come. Those things—some of them, at any rate—were probably inevitable. The mood of the first few days after the Liberation could not, in the nature of man, have been expected to last. It was too beatific, and the victory that we were all looking forward to did not arrive soon enough to act as a booster shot; cold weather and physical discomfort arrived first, and dampened the August enthusiasm. Nevertheless, when I left Paris, three months after the Liberation, the romance was still on. Simply being an American predisposed Parisians in your favor.

Between late 1944 and my present visit, I returned to Paris only once—for ten days in 1948, during which I had little chance to do more than say hello to old friends. But after I came back and settled down for a while, I found it hard to believe that the girls on bicycles had ever ridden out to greet us. Although the old friends were as warm as ever, the city itself made me feel a bit like a man returning after a dozen years to a former love and finding that she is married, has four children, is worried about money, and devotes all her afternoons to the Parent-Teacher Association, the Ladies' Village Improvement Society, the Friends of Krishnamurti, and the American Red Cross. She is not hostile; she just has no time to waste on past performances. This always astonishes the man, although it shouldn't.

Such a man is likely to try to reconstruct a picture of things as they were. In a similar frame of mind during the last few months, I have occasionally felt impelled to make small expeditions in quest of the past, like Réstif de la Bretonne circumambulating the Ile Saint-Louis to read the inscriptions he had scratched on walls there on evenings when Sara was kind. (That was how I came to look up the plaque in the Gare Montparnasse.) On one of these excursions, my destination was the Boulevard Saint-Michel, in the student quarter, where I spent a good deal of time during my first visit to Paris, as a student myself, in 1926. Setting out from my hotel, I walked through the Square Louvois to the Bibliothèque and turned down the Rue de Richelieu toward the Seine, stopping, as usual, in front of the building at No. 69, where in 1830 Stendhal wrote *Le Rouge et le Noir*. It was No. 71 in his day and a hotel, like almost every other place he ever lived in. He was correcting the proofs of *Le Rouge et le Noir* when he heard the first shots of the July revolution, which substituted Louis-Philippe for Charles X on the throne. It was Stendhal's lucky year. He put on one of his light-cinnamon frock coats, for which it is highly improbable he had reimbursed his tailor, and went out to root for the mob. Two months later he had a consulate, which supported him for the rest of his life. (*Le Rouge et le Noir* was not a serious money-maker; it brought him a total of something under a thousand dollars.) A few rods farther on, I passed No. 61, where, in the eighteen-twenties, when it was No. 63, he lived in what he insisted was not sin with Mme Giuditta Pasta, the prima donna of the Théâtre-Italien.

I crossed through the Tuileries, where the 1830 shots were fired, and, when I got to the Left Bank, walked on to the Odéon, a brisk half hour's going. Leaving the Place de l'Odéon, I had a choice of several tangential streets by which to reach the Boulevard Saint-Michel. I chose the Rue Racine, and presently stopped in front of the window of a bookshop where a copy of a new collection of French cartoons was on display. The cover drawing showed a lanky, goofy-looking American soldier sitting in a swivel chair with his feet up on a desk and holding a telephone to his ear. The caption was *"Toujours occupé"*—a pun in French but not in American, since we say a country is "occupied" but a telephone line is "busy." (The English, who are foreign to both of us, say "engaged.") Pinned to the G.I.'s shoulder was a tag reading, "Go home," but he was fatuously unconscious of it. The artist had clearly been influenced by Sad Sack. It is one of the dilemmas of the young Western European anti-American that in any popular art he must express himself in an American idiom or lose his audience. Jazz, the movies, and the ten thousand pseudo-Hemingways, half of whom are European, have formed the mold. The other side has nothing to offer as an alternative. It is impossible, for instance, to imagine a young Western European cartoonist adopting the manner of the Soviet's *Krokodil,* which is that of *Punch* or *Puck* in 1905, or a Russian folk-dance ensemble taking the play away from Lionel Hampton's band at a Parisian music hall. It is our misfortune both that we have not more to offer and that the others have so much less. Everything we do is overconsidered by Europeans, like the performances of a fair three-year-old in a nothing year. An American B picture is reviewed at solemn length, as if it were a novel by an Academician, and the critic comes up at the end of two columns with the verdict that *Flaming Guns,* or whatever, is not the kind of first-rate art that one might expect from a country "with the pretension of instructing a Europe that has, after all, let us not forget, produced Corneille, Euripides, Sartre, and Shakespeare." (Jazz alone has a consistently good press, because of the rationalization that it is the exclusive product of mutilated Negroes, who compose it on their way to the stake.)

I continued up the street to the Boulevard Saint-Michel, where thirst and curiosity prompted me to stop in at a café I had once known. Since I had last seen it, in 1944, the place had been sold and the new boss had called in a decorator to slick it up, turning the pleasant, easygoing, old-style French café into a restaurant de luxe—a cocktail lounge on Route 4 in New Jersey. The bar, too, had gone *discret,* with recorded piano music and tropical fish. The music was schmalz, and consisted of selections whose lyrics are familiar to anybody of an age that I don't like to be reminded of: "I'll see *yew* again"—things like that. The barman served cognac in a *ballon,* a burlesque gesture unless the cognac is highly distinguished, and even then it would be better off in a brandy glass of a size a man can warm in one hand. I remembered a fat French engraver named Gillet, who used to cadge drinks there back in my student days, and I couldn't imagine him at home in a bar such as this. Gillet was a fat man with a scraggly chin beard like Verlaine's, and his fingers were always blue from acid. He wore a *vie de bohème* hat—high crown and wide brim—and there were always buttons off his overcoat, because of the trouble he had in drawing it together across his belly. Gillet would have hated the music—"I'll see *yew* again." Go home, indeed! What need to, if on the Boulevard Saint-Michel they were going to change good cafés into muted mood joints?

When Roach at last succeeded in inching the Chevrolet through the crowds in the Place d'Orléans, we headed for the center of town along the

Avenue d'Orléans, through more scenes of frenzied excitement, and came out on the Place Denfert-Rochereau—the first spot we reached in Paris that I distinctly remembered having been in before. It is a big *carrefour*, where six or seven boulevards and avenues converge. There are *brasseries* all around its perimeter, and in the middle of it is the bronze statue of the couchant Lion de Belfort—a memorial to the garrison of the one French fortress that held out through the war of 1870–71. The sculptor was Bartholdi, who did the Statue of Liberty, but the Lion is a better job. Bartholdi was stronger on animals than on goddesses. (If Klagmann, who did the four rolling rivers in the Square Louvois, had got the contract for Liberty, she would attract more attention.) Beneath the Place there is an old quarry full of bones removed from cemeteries that were abandoned in the eighteenth century. Although I didn't know it as we drove past, this catacomb was still serving as the headquarters of Colonel Rol, the Communist who commanded the combined forces of the Resistance during the insurrection of Paris. *Dans le civil,* he was a metalworker in the Renault automobile plant. I met Rol a couple of weeks later, when the Era of Good Feeling was still on and the Jesuit Père Philippe was speaking from the same platforms as the Communist Louis Aragon. It was the period of the Front National, which seems as distant now as Mistinguett's First Communion.

We drove down the Avenue Denfert-Rochereau, an austere thoroughfare lined with religious institutions. Most of them, housed in seventeenth- and eighteenth-century buildings behind high walls, are Catholic—an orphanage, a convent, a home for old priests, and the like. Among them, however, there used to be an American Baptist Center, with a small gymnasium and shower room at the far end of a baroque courtyard. Every Wednesday afternoon during my student days, I would walk to the gymnasium from the less bracing surroundings of the Taverne Soufflet and the d'Harcourt, in the Latin Quarter, where I spent most of my leisure. There I would have a workout and a cold shower. I did not admit these infantile regressions to anyone—not even to Angèle, my favorite companion at the Taverne Soufflet. I would as soon have had her catch me eating puffed rice with sliced bananas. But one Wednesday afternoon when I walked into my hotel, on the Rue de l'Ecole de Médecine, my right eyelid was studded with metal clamps, installed by a doctor after a Mormon missionary and I bumped heads while boxing, and I stood exposed.

The fellows I met at the Center were Americans, most of whom were living in Montparnasse and were writing or trying to learn how to paint. None of them was trying to learn how to write, because in the twenties that was supposed to come naturally, like falling off a bar stool. There were also fellows, among them the missionary, who were studying at the Sorbonne. Most of these were taking the packaged course in French culture and living with nice French families. Basketball and handball were the popular games, but I usually found somebody to box with. After a workout, several of us would walk down the Avenue Denfert-Rochereau, which at its tip merges with the Avenue de l'Observatoire, as far as the Closerie des Lilas, where we would stop in for a vermouth cassis together. Then my friends would head for the Dôme or the Sélect, on the Boulevard du Montparnasse, while I would start back for the Soufflet or the d'Harcourt, on the Boulevard Saint-Michel. I was priggishly determined not to waste my year abroad on fellow-Americans; Wednesday afternoons were simply exceptions.

The Closerie stood by itself, with gravel and trees all around it; quiet and cool, it had a touch of class. The noisy geniuses you heard at the Vikings and the Sélect and the Dôme considered it *vieux jeu* and did not frequent it. The place had a brisk, knowing barman named Dominique, a Catalan from Barcelona, who would have been a natural for a good speakeasy in the States. Sometimes, after my friends had left, I switched to hard liquor and stayed on talking to him. These interludes were part of my small weekly concession to a nostalgia I wouldn't have avowed. The most memorable customer was a Canadian painter named John Russell, who always wore a bowler hat and a Chesterfield with velvet lapels. He wasn't imitating the Edwardians; he was one. Russell was in his late forties and not yet decrepit, and this reassured me. I was twenty-two, and worried, because I associated thirty with dotage. Looking at Russell, I could see that I might still have a couple of years left to work in. Russell had white hair, which he wore rather long in back, black eyebrows, a red face, and a profile like that of an old tragedian. He was critical and imperious, and also often abusive, because he was a solvent portrait painter, producing pictures that brought high prices but that his avant-garde colleagues contemptuously referred to as "good likenesses." (They were mostly portraits of wealthy Anglo-Canadians, dressed as Masters of Foxhounds, and their wives, to whom Russell gave a telling hint of family resemblance to Queen Mary.)

"They all sneer at Bouguereau, but I'd like to see one of them paint a hand with five fingernails and polish on them," Russell used to say. "They" meant the avant-garde. Once, in 1927, I went to the Salon de Printemps to see a picture he was showing. It was of a smart nude lying on a sofa in front of a full-length mirror, which was so convincing that I caught myself looking into it to straighten my tie. In front of the sofa stood a coffee table inlaid with mother-of-pearl, and on the table was a cloisonné vase containing four flowers, all different. It must have taken a lot of doing. *Ce vieux Russell* was often accompanied by a tail of French painters, more advanced but less pecunious, for whom he bought drinks. They didn't needle him, as the young Americans did—partly, no doubt, because they spoke no English and Russell's French was limited, but also, I suspect, because they respected his bag of tricks, even if they didn't like them. And maybe they did like them. Then, too, he was paying for the drinks.

In a way, I was aware of all these matters as Roach turned the Chevrolet down the Avenue Denfert-Rochereau, although, naturally, I said nothing about them. It would have been hard to explain why I should recall such trivia on the day of the Liberation of Paris, which was History with a capital "H." But they increased my excitement. We stopped for a couple of minutes at the corner of the Avenue de l'Observatoire and the Boulevard du Montparnasse, to consider our further course. Before leaving Bagnoles-de-l'Orne, Roach and I had been told that the press would set up shop in the Hôtel Scribe, on the Boulevard des Capucines, near the Opéra. Roach wanted to report there as soon as he could, but we had no means of knowing whether the way was clear. I thought our best bet would be to turn west on the Boulevard du Montparnasse, which we could see was peaceful, and then head down toward the Seine when we were approximately opposite where we wanted to go. During our halt, while Roach consulted a street map, I noted with satisfaction that the Closerie was intact, although black-out blinds had been drawn behind its plate-glass windows. Then we started up the Boulevard, past the Nègre de Toulouse, the Jockey, the Sélect, the Dôme, and the other landmarks of the prohibition emigration, all of them closed. It was a quarter I had never fancied, but I felt a certain emotion about it just the same. Any liberated place acquires a special charm, like a kitten recovered from the town dump. In the immediate neighborhood of the Gare Montparnasse, with Daydaybay vehicles parked in the adjacent streets, things were just as festive as they had been in the Place d'Orléans. And so, after turning back from our attempt to get through the Rue de Rennes with the help of the F.F.I. boys, we returned to the train shed in time for the surrender.

We were, it developed, in plenty of time, for Leclerc, ordinarily so impatient, was holding up the ceremony until General de Gaulle could get there. With the approach of the Daydaybay, one of the division's intelligence officers told me, the German garrison had given up trying to reduce Resistance strong points within the city and had been besieged in its turn, in perhaps a dozen redoubts of its own. (Von Choltitz had a rather better chance of being shot if he retreated than if he didn't, for Hitler, it was later disclosed, had directed him to fight to the last man. I think if I had known then what lay behind that troubled soup plate of a German face, I would have felt a little sorry for Von.) Leclerc had ordered an attack on the Meurice, on the Rue de Rivoli, in order to bring in von Choltitz, the only man in Paris who was qualified to sign the surrender. When the German Military Governor felt himself safely surrounded by French regulars, he had come out. All the Germans had a deadly fear of being lynched by the F.F.I.

Lieutenant General Leonard T. Gerow, of V Corps, was at the Gare. He was a tall, dry man, who might have thought that since the Dayday-bay was part of his corps, *he* was the liberator of Paris, but Leclerc kept him in his place. (Paris, like practically every other town in France, has since named a street for Leclerc; it is the former Avenue d'Orléans, along which Roach drove us on the great day. The Avenue du Général Leclerc is wide but not chic, being bordered by cheap department stores and cut-rate retail markets.) Finally, de Gaulle arrived—stiff-backed, as usual, but very nearly smiling—and the surrender was signed. De Gaulle wore the expression of a poker player hauling in his first pot of the evening and trying not to show how good he feels. It was politically important, from the point of view of the Free French, that de Gaulle be on hand, because up to the last minute they were afraid that our State Department would produce somebody like Camille Chautemps or Georges Bonnet to usurp his place. They couldn't forget Darlan.

While we and von Choltitz were still waiting for de Gaulle, two more American correspondents arrived—Paul Gallico, who was writing for a monthly magazine, and Harold Denny, of *The New York Times*. They had been traveling together in a jeep, with a soldier driver, and had run into the same sort of perplexity as we had in trying to get across town. When Denny spotted the Germans, he reacted like a redbone hound to a tree full of raccoons. He saw that he had a scoop of historic dimensions, since he was the only correspondent for a daily publication present. Denny, who was one of the best reporters I have known, broke out his typewriter and went to work. The rattle of the keys, echoing under the train shed, cheered him on. He lit a cigarette, ran a hand through his hair, filled a sheet of paper, and instinctively yelled "Boy!" Only there was no boy to pick up his copy. It was then that he realized he was faced with the problem of how to get his copy from the Gare Montparnasse to a censor and a wire.

We all knew that if an American communications center had been set up in Paris, it would be at the Hôtel Scribe. The obvious person to take Denny's copy there was Roach, who, as a public-relations officer, could expedite its transmission, and who, moreover, felt obligated to get there at the earliest possible moment. I therefore agreed to give up my de luxe transportation—it was but justice—and to pig in with Gallico and Denny in their jeep. After the German surrender party had been marched away, I went downstairs and got my typewriter, sleeping bag, and musette bag out of the Chevrolet. Despite the extreme revulsion I experience at the mere thought of K rations, I took a couple of those waxed-cardboard cartons charged with soapy cheese, vegetarian bouillon powder, and simi-lar delicacies from the supply that the lordly Negro had thrown into our car a couple of days before. Since arriving in Paris, we hadn't seen any-body who looked hungry enough to want them, and now that I figured my days in the field were about over, I was resolved never again to allow myself to get that hungry, either. Still, I thought it prudent to be prepared for the worst.

That was the end of our small Bagnoles-Chartres-Paris task force. Morrison shouldered his musette bag and went out into the streets to collect paragraphs for *Stars & Stripes*, and after Denny finished his story, Roach, with a Daydaybay soldier for a guide, left us to take it to the Scribe. There, we learned later, he found a press center installed and functioning normally—so normally that it managed to lose poor Denny's exclusive eyewitness story of the surrender. At any rate, the *Times* never received it. When the first copies of the August 26 issue of the *Times* reached Paris, flown in by the Air Transport Command, we were dismayed to see that the big story about the surrender was an Associated Press dispatch that read as if it had been assembled in London. It was the worst luck I have heard of a reporter's having. Denny died a little less than a year later. He was fifty-six—older than almost any other American correspondent in France, although he looked younger than the majority of us—and his heart failed him. I've sometimes wondered how much the lost scoop had to do with it.

Since we had no idea that the story was going to be lost, Denny and Gallico and I were in high good humor as we left the Gare. But it was getting on toward six, and they said they were tired, as I certainly was, so we decided to seek a lodging for the night. From the moment of our appearance in the station, we had been attended by a bevy of F.F.I. lads wearing tricolor brassards and strung with bandoleers and lethal weapons, mostly captured Wehrmacht machine pistols. They told us they belonged to the Service de Presse des Forces Françaises du Quartorzième Arrondissement. I asked a fellow who seemed to be their commanding officer if he could find us a billet. He replied that a hotel had been set aside for the accommodation of *La presse étrangère*—the Hôtel Néron, near the statue of the Lion de Belfort. It was an appetizingly wicked name; a good orgy would be appropriate on such a night.

Our progress to the Néron was a dashing cortege—a cross between an Arab fantasia and the reception accorded Adah Isaacs Menken by the silver miners of the Big Bonanza. Six or eight F.F.I.s, each carrying at least three firearms, hung on to the sides of our jeep, which was preceded by one captured Volkswagen and followed by another, both loaded to the Plimsoll with effervescent firepower. The Néron, despite its name, turned out to have nothing *louche* about it. Standing on a side street off the Avenue d'Orléans and a couple of hundred yards beyond the Lion, it was neither dilapidated nor elaborate. The Fourteenth Arrondissement is a neighborhood of low-salaried white-collar people, mostly civil servants, and the chief peacetime clientele of the Néron, I thought, must have consisted of old bachelor or widower postal clerks and railway conductors. Now the hotel was a combination of barracks and arsenal, with young men in berets, shirt sleeves, and pistol belts bounding up the stairs three at a time, for no apparent reason, and then dashing down again. The soldiers of the night were strutting openly at last, and enjoying it.

Two ecstatically beaming elderly women were standing in the office downstairs when we arrived at the Néron—the *patronne* and her maid, delighted to be in the midst of such excitement. The hotel, I noticed on the way to my quarters, had a bathroom, and I was soon gratified to discover that the taps worked, although they both ran cold. In all the other French cities I had been through, the Germans had succeeded in blowing the water systems before leaving. The best I had been able to manage at Bagnoles was a swim in a spinachy pond.

I had an invigorating soak, got dressed, putting on a fresh pair of socks—the only change in attire my musette-bag wardrobe permitted—and sallied out into the dusky streets, home again. It was not quite dark, and the *bistros* on either side of the Avenue d'Orléans and on the Place Denfert-Rochereau were full of men—some with F.F.I. brassards and some without—*discutant le coup*, as after a football match. I went into a bar and had one of those sticky red *apéritifs* that partly refute the notion that the French have sensitive palates. It cost a hundred francs, which was two dollars then. I was getting hungry, and looked for a place to eat, but I saw none that was open; the reports of a food shortage in Paris were evidently well founded, and I began to think grimly about my K rations. Walking along the Avenue Denfert-Rochereau, I searched for the plaque that had marked the gatepost of the American Baptist Center, and, unable to find it, presumed that the Germans had closed my old health resort during the Occupation.

By now, it was beginning to be really dark. From the direction of the Luxembourg came the sound of steady firing—small-cannon as well as machine-gun; apparently, the Germans inside hadn't listened to the officers sent out from Leclerc's headquarters. I mention this firing because it seemed part of the summer night, like thunder. There was no menace in the sound, and if it were not for plaques on the walls of houses in various parts of Paris that now commemorate the deaths of Frenchmen on that very night, I would find it difficult to believe there was real combat on the evening of my stroll. I walked on down as far as the Closerie des Lilas and crossed the Boulevard du Montparnasse to have a better look at the place. The French were never as thorough as the English were about blackouts, and I could soon see, through chinks in the curtain of a window near the side door of the café, that there was a blue light—a *veilleuse*, or night lamp—burning within. I banged on the door and shouted, in French, "It's an old customer! An old customer! An American! An American!" I thought that would interest whoever was inside, and it did, but not immediately. After I had shouted it a dozen times, the door opened a crack and a barman I had never seen looked out. I said to him, "Dominique? Where is Dominique?" I couldn't remember the boss's name. For all I knew, Dominique might have been gone seventeen years, for I hadn't visited the Closerie since 1927. In that case, the current barman might never even have heard of him. But I was in luck. Dominique had not left until 1940, when the Germans came in, and this barman had known him. "Dominique went back to Barcelona in 1940," he said. At least, I had established myself as a former customer.

I could hear another man behind the fellow at the door, talking to him, and now a new face, which I recognized as that of the *patron*, appeared at the crack. "I used to come here with Russell," I said. "*Le vieux Russell.* With the *chapeau melon.* Is he still in Paris?"

The *patron*'s face split in a grin."*Ah, sacré Russell!*" he said. "He went to England. Come in." He opened the door.

There were no customers in the Closerie—only the *patron*, his wife, the barman, and a waitress. Once inside, I talked to them of Russell, of the celebration at this very bar of Lindbergh's safe arrival in Paris in 1927, of the perils of D Day and the hardships of the road, and of the outstanding character of General Leclerc. It took. The four of them were preparing to dine at one of the deserted tables, and as the waitress brought in a great terrine of potato soup, the boss asked me if I had eaten. I magnanimously consented to join them, even though his wife warned that there would be nothing to follow but an omelet and a salad; the *patronne*, it was plain, had never sampled a K ration.

The firing around the Luxembourg continued. "Apparently they're still holding out," I said.

"A lot of good it will do them," the *patron* observed, with relish. "A shot of red?" He filled my glass with Bordeaux, and, as he did so, his name came back to me—M. Colin. "Do you remember how Russell used to talk about Bouguereau?" he asked. "How he was all for Bouguereau?"

"*Sacré vieux Russell!*" I said. Never had an acquaintance served me better. The omelet was as big as an eiderdown.

"The Americans will be back soon," I said. "It will be like old times here at the Closerie."

"But you are the first," M. Colin said, in a voice that had taken on a tone of significance. Up to that point, our talk had been friendly but casual, with nothing about it to suggest that we were reunited on a historic occasion. Now, however, M. Colin said, "Monsieur, at the moment of the débacle, when the future looked blackest, I set aside two bottles against the arrival of the first American customer to return here. One is a bottle of *véritable* pernod and the other contains Black and White. Later, such bottles became impossible to find in Paris. They were beyond price. But I have never opened either. Which bottle will you drink?"

I chose the whisky, because I knew I could drink more of that, and after we had finished the wine and the omelet and the salad, M. Colin put the bottle on the table. It was the only trophy or award I won during the war, and I wouldn't have traded it for the D.S.O. We drank to Russell and Bouguereau and Lafayette and General de Gaulle, and to Angèle, upon whom I had once prevailed to accompany me as far out of the student quarter as the bar of the Closerie, where she immediately became homesick for the Taverne Soufflet, half a mile away. "She said whisky smelled of bedbugs," I recalled sentimentally. "But she admired the stimulating effect it had on me. She has been dead for seventeen years." By that time, my new honors were beginning to overwhelm me.

"A chagrin of love never forgets itself," the waitress said. "You must not make bile about it."

When we had imbibed the last of my glory, I look an effusive leave and went out into the dark street. The bars that I had passed earlier were still busy, but I had no inclination to enter. Any further drinking that night would have been a letdown. I made but one brief pause—to roar at the Lion. He wouldn't roar back, and I continued to the Hôtel Néron, which I found as easily as if I had lived there all my life.

Next morning, Denny, Gallico, and I rose early and drove across town to the Scribe. There was not even token firing now; the city was calm but exhausted, like Manhattan on a New Year's morning. I left my gear in a room at the Scribe, but I didn't bother to unpack. I knew where I was going to stay, unless something had happened to it. I went down to the street and walked by the Café de la Paix, where a few of my colleagues were already seated waiting for everybody they knew to pass. I turned down the Avenue de l'Opéra and left on the Rue Saint-Augustin, then right for one block on the Rue Sainte-Anne, and left again, and found myself staring at the navel of La Loire, who hadn't straightened her back since I last saw her. I counted the trees in the Square. There were still fourteen. The pigeons, of course, were gone, but I can't say that at that moment I really missed them.

I exchanged lubricious smiles with La Loire and then walked into the lobby of the Hôtel Louvois, for the first time in four years, two months, and sixteen days. Mlle Yvonne was sitting behind the desk, going over her accounts. "*Bonjour*, Monsieur Liebling," she said, barely looking up. It was as if I had just stepped out for a walk around the fountain.

BETWEEN MEALS:
AN APPETITE
FOR PARIS

to Yves Mirande

Contents

1 / A Good Appetite

THE PROUST *madeleine* phenomenon is now as firmly established in folk-lore as Newton's apple or Watt's steam kettle. The man ate a tea biscuit, the taste evoked memories, he wrote a book. This is capable of expression by the formula TMB, for Taste > Memory > Book. Some time ago, when I began to read a book called *The Food of France*, by Waverley Root, I had an inverse experience: BMT, for Book > Memory > Taste. Happily, the tastes that *The Food of France* re-created for me—small birds, stewed rabbit, stuffed tripe, Côte Rôtie, and Tavel—were more robust than that of the *madeleine*, which Larousse defines as "a light cake made with sugar, flour, lemon juice, brandy, and eggs." (The quantity of brandy in a *madeleine* would not furnish a gnat with an alcohol rub.) In the light of what Proust wrote with so mild a stimulus, it is the world's loss that he did not have a heartier appetite. On a dozen Gardiners Island oysters, a bowl of clam chowder, a peck of steamers, some bay scallops, three sautéed soft-shelled crabs, a few ears of fresh-picked corn, a thin sword-fish steak of generous area, a pair of lobsters, and a Long Island duck, he might have written a masterpiece.

The primary requisite for writing well about food is a good appetite. Without this, it is impossible to accumulate, within the allotted span, enough experience of eating to have anything worth setting down. Each day brings only two opportunities for field work, and they are not to be wasted minimizing the intake of cholesterol. They are indispensable, like a prizefighter's hours on the road. (I have read that the late French professional gourmand Maurice Curnonsky ate but one meal a day—dinner. But that was late in his life, and I have always suspected his attainments anyway; so many mediocre witticisms are attributed to him that he could not have had much time for eating.) A good appetite gives an eater room to turn around in. For example, a nonprofessional eater I know went to the Restaurant Pierre, in the Place Gaillon, a couple of years ago, his mind set on a sensibly light meal: a dozen, or possibly eighteen, oysters, and a thick chunk of steak topped with beef marrow, which M. Pierre calls a *Délice de la Villette*—the equivalent of a "Stockyards' Delight." But as he arrived, he heard M. Pierre say to his head-waiter, "Here comes Monsieur L. Those two portions of *cassoulet* that are left—put them aside for him." A *cassoulet* is a substantial dish, of a complexity precluding its discussion here. (Mr. Root devotes three pages to the great controversy over what it should contain.) M. Pierre is the most amiable of restaurateurs, who prides himself on knowing in advance what his friends will like. A client of limited appetite would be obliged either to forgo his steak or to hurt M. Pierre's feelings. Monsieur L., however, was in no difficulty. He ate the two *cassoulets*, as was his normal practice; if he had consumed only one, his host would have feared that it wasn't up to standard. He then enjoyed his steak. The oysters offered no problem, since they present no bulk.

In the heroic age before the First World War, there were men and women who ate, in addition to a whacking lunch and a glorious dinner, a voluminous *souper* after the theater or the other amusements of the evening. I have known some of the survivors, octogenarians of unblemished appetite and unfailing good humor—spry, wry, and free of the ulcers that come from worrying about a balanced diet—but they have had no emulators in France since the doctors there discovered the existence of the human liver. From that time on, French life has been built to an increasing extent around that organ, and a niggling caution has replaced the old recklessness; the liver was the seat of the Maginot mentality. One of the last of the great around-the-clock gastronomes of France was Yves Mirande, a small, merry author of farces and musical-comedy books. In 1955, Mirande celebrated his eightieth birthday with a speech before the curtain of the Théâtre Antoine, in the management of which he was associated with Mme. B., a protégée of his, forty years younger than himself. But the theater was only half of his life. In addition, M. Mirande was an unofficial director of a restaurant on the Rue Saint-Augustin, which he had founded for another protégée, also forty years younger than himself; this was Mme. G., a Gasconne and a magnificent cook. In the restaurant on the Rue Saint-Augustin, M. Mirande would dazzle his juniors, French and American, by dispatching a lunch of raw Bayonne ham and fresh figs, a hot sausage in crust, spindles of filleted pike in a rich rose *sauce Nantua*, a leg of lamb larded with anchovies, artichokes on a pedestal of foie gras, and four or five kinds of cheese, with a good bottle of Bordeaux and one of champagne, after which he would call for the Armagnac and remind Madame to have ready for dinner the larks and ortolans she had promised him, with a few *langoustes* and a turbot—and, of course, a fine *civet* made from the *marcassin*, or young wild boar, that the lover of the leading lady in his current production had sent up from his estate in the Sologne. "And while I think of it," I once heard him say, "we haven't had any woodcock for days, or truffles baked in the ashes, and the cellar is becoming a disgrace—no more '34s and hardly any '37s. Last week, I had to offer my publisher a bottle that was far too good for him, simply because there was nothing between the insulting and the superlative."

M. Mirande had to his credit a hundred produced plays, including a number of great Paris hits, but he had just written his first book for print, so he said "my publisher" in a special mock-impressive tone. "An informal sketch for my definitive autobiography," he would say of this production. The informal sketch, which I cherish, begins with the most important decision in Mirande's life. He was almost seventeen and living in the small Breton port of Lannion—his offstage family name was Le Querrec— when his father, a retired naval officer, said to him, "It is time to decide your future career. Which will it be, the Navy or the Church?" No other choice was conceivable in Lannion. At dawn, Yves ran away to Paris.

There, he had read a thousand times, all the famous wits and cocottes frequented the tables in front of the Café Napolitain, on the Boulevard des Capucines. He presented himself at the café at nine the next morning —late in the day for Lannion—and found that the place had not yet opened. Soon he became a newspaperman. It was a newspaper era as cynically animated as the corresponding period of the Bennett-Pulitzer-Hearst competition in New York, and in his second or third job he worked for a press lord who was as notional and niggardly as most press lords are; the publisher insisted that his reporters be well turned out, but did not pay them salaries that permitted cab fares when it rained. Mirande lived near the fashionable Montmartre cemetery and solved his rainy-day pants-crease problem by crashing funeral parties as they broke up and riding, gratis, in the carriages returning to the center of town. Early in his career, he became personal secretary to Clemenceau and then to Briand, but the gay theater attracted him more than politics, and he made the second great decision of his life after one of his political patrons had caused him to be appointed *sous-préfet* in a provincial city. A *sous-préfet* is the administrator of one of the districts into which each of the ninety *départements* of France is divided, and a young *sous-préfet* is often headed for a precocious rise to high positions of state. Mirande, attired in the magnificent uniform that was then de rigueur, went to his "capital," spent one night there, and then ran off to Paris again to direct a one-act farce. Nevertheless, his connections with the serious world remained cordial. In the restaurant on the Rue Saint-Augustin, he introduced me to Colette, by that time a national glory of letters.

The regimen fabricated by Mirande's culinary protégée, Mme. G., maintained him *en pleine forme*. When I first met him, in the restaurant, during the summer of the Liberation, he was a sprightly sixty-nine. In the spring of 1955, when we renewed a friendship that had begun in admiration of each other's appetite, he was as good as ever. On the occasion of our reunion, we began with a *truite au bleu*—a live trout simply done to death in hot water, like a Roman emperor in his bath. It was served up doused with enough melted butter to thrombose a regiment of Paul Dudley Whites, and accompanied, as was right, by an Alsatian wine—a Lacrimae Sanctae Odiliae, which once contributed slightly to my education. Long ago, when I was very young, I took out a woman in Strasbourg and, wishing to impress her with my knowledge of local customs, ordered a bottle of Ste. Odile. I was making the same mistake as if I had taken out a girl in Boston and offered her baked beans. "How quaint!" the woman in Strasbourg said. "I haven't drunk that for years." She excused herself to go to the telephone, and never came back.

After the trout, Mirande and I had two meat courses, since we could not decide in advance which we preferred. We had a magnificent *daube provençale*, because we were faithful to *la cuisine bourgeoise*, and then *pintadous*—young guinea hens, simply and tenderly roasted—with the first asparagus of the year, to show our fidelity to *la cuisine classique*. We had clarets with both courses—a Pétrus with the *daube*, a Cheval Blanc with the guineas. Mirande said that his doctor had discounseled Burgundies. It was the first time in our acquaintance that I had heard him admit he had a doctor, but I was reassured when he drank a bottle and a half of Krug after luncheon. We had three bottles between us—one to our loves, one to our countries, and one for symmetry, the last being on the house.

Mirande was a small, alert man with the face of a Celtic terrier—salient eyebrows and an upturned nose. He looked like an intelligent Lloyd George. That summer, in association with Mme. B., his theatrical protégée, he planned to produce a new play of Sartre's. His mind kept young by the theater of Mme. B., his metabolism protected by the restaurant of Mme. G., Mirande seemed fortified against all eventualities for at least another twenty years. Then, perhaps, he would have to recruit new protégées. The Sunday following our reunion, I encountered him at Longchamp, a racecourse where the restaurant does not face the horses, and diners can keep first things first. There he sat, radiant, surrounded by celebrities and champagne buckets, sending out a relay team of commissionaires to bet for him on the successive tips that the proprietors of stables were ravished to furnish him between races. He was the embodiment of a happy man. (I myself had a nice thing at 27-1.)

The first alteration in Mirande's fortunes affected me so directly that I did not at once sense its gravity for him. Six weeks later, I was again in Paris. (That year, I was shuttling frequently between there and London.) I was alone on the evening I arrived, and looked forward to a pleasant dinner at Mme. G.'s, which was within two hundred metres of the hotel, in the Square Louvois, where I always stop. Madame's was more than a place to eat, although one ate superbly there. Arriving, I would have a bit of talk with the proprietress, then with the waitresses—Germaine and Lucienne—who had composed the original staff. Waiters had been added as the house prospered, but they were of less marked personality.

Madame was a bosomy woman—voluble, tawny, with a big nose and lank black hair—who made one think of a Saracen. (The Saracens reached Gascony in the eighth century.) Her conversation was a chronicle of letters and the theater—as good as a subscription to *Figaro Littéraire*, but more advanced. It was somewhere between the avant-garde and the main body, but within hailing distance of both and enriched with the names of the great people who had been in recently—M. Cocteau, Gene Kelly, la Comtesse de Vogüé. It was always well to give an appearance of listening, lest she someday fail to save for you the last order of larks *en brochette* and bestow them on a more attentive customer. With Germaine and Lucienne, whom I had known when we were all younger, in 1939, the year of the *drôle de guerre*, flirtation was now perfunctory, but the *carte du jour* was still the serious topic—for example, how the fat Belgian industrialist from Tournai had reacted to the *caille vendangeuse*, or quail potted with fresh grapes. "You know the man," Germaine would say. "If it isn't dazzling, he takes only two portions. But when he has three, then you can say to yourself . . ." She and Lucienne looked alike—compact little women, with high foreheads and cheekbones and solid, muscular legs, who walked like *chasseurs à pied*, a hundred and thirty steps to the minute. In 1939, and again in 1944, Germaine had been a brunette and Lucienne a blonde, but in 1955 Germaine had become a blonde, too, and I found it hard to tell them apart.

Among my fellow customers at Mme. G.'s I was always likely to see some friend out of the past. It is a risk to make an engagement for an entire evening with somebody you haven't seen for years. This is particularly true in France now. The almost embarrassingly pro-American acquaintance of the Liberation may be by now a Communist Party-line hack; the idealistic young Resistance journalist may have become an editorial writer for the reactionary newspaper of a textile magnate. The Vichy apologist you met in Washington in 1941, who called de Gaulle a traitor and the creation of the British Intelligence Service, may now tell you that the General is the best thing ever, while the fellow you knew as a de Gaulle aide in London may now compare him to Sulla destroying the Roman Republic. As for the women, who is to say which of them has resisted the years? But in a good restaurant that all have frequented, you are likely to meet any of them again, for good restaurants are not so many nowadays that a Frenchman will permanently desert one—unless, of course, he is broke, and in that case it would depress you to learn of his misfortunes. If you happen to encounter your old friends when they are already established at their tables, you have the opportunity to greet them cordially and to size them up. If you still like them, you can make a further engagement.

On the ghastly evening I speak of—a beautiful one in June—I perceived no change in the undistinguished exterior of Mme. G.'s restaurant. The name—something like Prospéria—was the same, and since the plate-glass windows were backed with scrim, it was impossible to see inside. Nor, indeed, did I notice any difference when I first entered. The bar, the tables, the banquettes covered with leatherette, the simple décor of mirrors and pink marble slabs were the same. The premises had been a business employees' bar-and-café before Mme. G., succeeding a long string of obscure proprietors, made it illustrious. She had changed the fare and the clientele but not the cadre. There are hundreds of identical fronts and interiors in Paris, turned out by some mass producer in the late twenties. I might have been warned by the fact that the room was empty, but it was only eight o'clock and still light outdoors. I had come unusually early because I was so hungry. A man whom I did not recognize came to meet me, rubbing his hands and hailing me as an old acquaintance. I thought he might be a waiter who had served me. (The waiters, as I have said, were not the marked personalities of the place.) He had me at a table before I sensed the trap.

"Madame goes well?" I asked politely.

"No, Madame is lightly ill," he said, with what I now realize was a guilty air.

He presented me with a *carte du jour* written in the familiar purple ink on the familiar wide sheet of paper with the name and telephone number of the restaurant at the top. The content of the menu, however, had become Italianized, the spelling had deteriorated, and the prices had diminished to a point where it would be a miracle if the food continued distinguished.

"Madame still conducts the restaurant?" I asked sharply.

I could now see that he was a Piedmontese of the most evasive description. From rubbing his hands he had switched to twisting them.

"Not exactly," he said, "but we make the same cuisine."

I could not descry anything in the smudged ink but misspelled noodles and unorthographical "*escaloppinis*"; Italians writing French by ear produce a regression to an unknown ancestor of both languages.

"Try us," my man pleaded, and, like a fool, I did. I was hungry. Forty minutes later, I stamped out into the street as purple as an *aubergine* with rage. The minestrone had been cabbage scraps in greasy water. I had chosen *côtes d'agneau* as the safest item in the mediocre catalogue that the Prospéria's prospectus of bliss had turned into overnight. They had been cut from a tired Alpine billy goat and seared in machine oil, and the *haricots verts* with which they were served resembled decomposed whiskers from a theatrical-costume beard.

"The same cuisine?" I thundered as I flung my money on the falsified *addition* that I was too angry to verify. "You take me for a jackass!"

I am sure that as soon as I turned my back the scoundrel nodded. The restaurant has changed hands at least once since then.

In the morning, I telephoned Mirande. He confirmed the disaster.

Mme. G., ill, had closed the restaurant. Worse, she had sold the lease and the good will, and had definitely retired.

"What is the matter with her?" I asked in a tone appropriate to fatal disease.

"I think it was trying to read Simone de Beauvoir," he said. "A syncope."

Mme. G. still lives, but Mirande is dead. When I met him in Paris the following November, his appearance gave no hint of decline. It was the season for his sable-lined overcoat à l'impresario, and a hat that was a furry cross between a porkpie and a homburg. Since the restaurant on the Rue Saint-Augustin no longer existed, I had invited him to lunch with me at a very small place called the Gratin Dauphinois, on the Rue Chabanais, directly across from the building that once housed the most celebrated sporting house in Paris. The Rue Chabanais is a short street that runs from the Square Louvois to the Rue des Petits Champs—perhaps a hundred yards—but before the reform wave stimulated by a Municipal Councilor named Marthe Richard at the end of the Second World War, the name Chabanais had a cachet all its own. Mme. Richard will go down in history as the Carry Nation of sex. Now the house is closed, and the premises are devoted to some low commercial purpose. The walls of the midget Gratin Dauphinois are hung with cartoons that have a nostalgic reference to the past glories of the street.

Mirande, when he arrived, crackled with jokes about the locale. He taunted me with being a criminal who haunts the scene of his misdeeds. The fare at the Gratin is robust, as it is in Dauphiné, but it did not daunt Mirande. The wine card, similarly, is limited to the strong, rough wines of Arbois and the like, with a couple of Burgundies for clients who want to show off. There are no clarets; the proprietor hasn't heard of them. There are, of course, a few champagnes, for wedding parties or anniversaries, so Mirande, with Burgundies discounseled by his doctor, decided on champagne throughout the meal. This was a drôle combination with the mountain food, but I had forgotten about the lack of claret when I invited him.

We ordered a couple of dozen escargots en pots de chambre to begin with. These are snails baked and served, for the client's convenience, in individual earthenware crocks, instead of being forced back into shells. The snail, of course, has to be taken out of his shell to be prepared for cooking. The shell he is forced back into may not be his own. There is thus not even a sentimental justification for his reincarceration. The frankness of the service en pot does not improve the preparation of the snail, nor does it detract from it, but it does facilitate and accelerate his consumption. (The notion that the shell proves the snail's authenticity, like the head left on a woodcock, is invalid, as even a suburban housewife knows nowadays; you can buy a tin of snail shells in a supermarket and fill them with a mixture of nutted cream cheese and chopped olives.)

Mirande finished his dozen first, meticulously swabbing out the garlicky butter in each *pot* with a bit of bread that was fitted to the bore of the crock as precisely as a bullet to a rifle barrel. Tearing bread like that takes practice. We had emptied the first bottle of champagne when he placed his right hand delicately on the point of his waistcoat farthest removed from his spinal column.

"Liebling," he said, "I am not well."

It was like the moment when I first saw Joe Louis draped on the ropes. A great pity filled my heart. "*Maître*," I said, "I will take you home."

The dismayed *patronne* waved to her husband in the kitchen (he could see her through the opening he pushed the dishes through) to suspend the preparation of the *gendarme de Morteau*—the great smoked sausage in its tough skin—that we had proposed to follow the snails with. ("Short and broad in shape, it is made of pure pork and . . . is likely to be accompanied . . . by hot potato salad."—Root, page 217.) We had decided to substitute for the *pommes à l'huile* the *gratin dauphinois* itself. ("Thinly sliced potatoes are moistened with boiled milk and beaten egg, seasoned with salt, pepper, and nutmeg, and mixed with grated cheese, of the Gruyère type. The potatoes are then put into an earthenware dish which has been rubbed with garlic and then buttered, spotted with little dabs of butter, and sprinkled with more grated cheese. It is then cooked slowly in not too hot an oven."—Root, page 228.) After that, we were going to have a fowl in cream with *morilles*—wild black mushrooms of the mountains. We abandoned all.

I led Mirande into the street and hailed a taxi.

"I am not well, Liebling," he said. "I grow old."

He lived far from the restaurant, beyond the Place de l'Etoile, in the Paris of the successful. From time to time on our way, he would say, "It is nothing. You must excuse me. I am not well."

The apartment house in which he and Mme. B. lived resembled one of the chic modern museums of the quarter, with entrance gained through a maze of garden patches sheathed in glass. Successive metal grilles swung open before us as I pushed buttons that Mirande indicated—in these modern palaces there are no visible flunkies—until we reached an elevator that smoothly shot us upward to his apartment, which was rather larger in area than the Square Louvois. The décor, with basalt columns and floors covered with the skin of jumbo Siberian tigers—a special strain force-fed to supply old-style movie stars—reminded me of the sets for *Belphégor*, a French serial of silent days that I enjoyed when I was a student at the Sorbonne in 1926. (It was, I think, about an ancient Egyptian high priest who came to life and set up bachelor quarters in Paris in the style of the Temple of Karnak.) Three or four maids rushed to relieve

Mirande of his sable-lined coat, his hat, and his cane topped with the horn of an albino chamois. I helped him to a divan on which two Theda Baras could have defended their honor simultaneously against two villains of the silents without either couple's getting in the other's way. Most of the horizontal surfaces in the room were covered with sculpture and most of the vertical ones with large paintings. In pain though he was, Mirande called my attention to these works of art.

"All the sculptures are by Renoir," he said. "It was his hobby. And all the paintings are by Maillol. It was *his* hobby. If it were the other way around, I would be one of the richest chaps in France. Both men were my friends. But then, one doesn't give one's friends one's bread and butter. And, after all, it's less banal as it is."

After a minute, he asked me to help him to his bedroom, which was in a wing of the apartment all his own. When we got there, one of the maids came in and took his shoes off.

"I am in good hands now, Liebling," he said. "Farewell until next time. It is nothing."

I telephoned the next noon, and he said that his doctor, who was a fool, insisted that he was ill.

Again I left Paris, and when I returned, late the following January, I neglected Mirande. A Father William is a comforting companion for the middle-aged—he reminds you that the best is yet to be and that there's a dance in the old dame yet—but a sick old man is discouraging. My conscience stirred when I read in a gossip column in *France-Dimanche* that Toto Mirande was convalescing nicely and was devouring caviar at a great rate—with champagne, of course. (I had never thought of Mirande as Toto, which is baby slang for "little kid," but from then on I never referred to him in any other way; I didn't want anybody to think I wasn't in the know.) So the next day I sent him a pound of fresh caviar from Kaspia, in the Place de la Madeleine. It was the kind of medication I approved of.

I received a note from Mirande by tube next morning, reproaching me for spoiling him. He was going better, he wrote, and would telephone in a day or two to make an appointment for a return bout. When he called, he said that the idiotic doctor would not yet permit him to go out to a restaurant, and he invited me, instead, to a family dinner at Mme. B.'s. "Only a few old friends, and not the cuisine I hope to give you at Maxim's next time," he said. "But one makes out."

On the appointed evening, I arrived early—or on time, which amounts to the same thing—*chez* Mme. B.; you take taxis when you can get them in Paris at the rush hours. The handsome quarter overlooking the Seine above the Trocadéro is so dull that when my taxi deposited me before my host's door, I had no inclination to stroll to kill time. It is like Park Avenue or the near North Side of Chicago. So I was the first or second guest to arrive, and Mme. B.'s fourteen-year-old daughter, by a past marriage, received me in the Belphégor room, apologizing because her mother was still with Toto—she called him that. She need not have told me, for at that moment I heard Madame, who is famous for her determined voice, storming at an unmistakable someone: "You go too far, Toto. It's disgusting. People all over Paris are kind enough to send you caviar, and because you call it monotonous, you throw it at the maid! If you think servants are easy to come by . . ."

When they entered the room a few minutes later, my old friend was all smiles. "How did you know I adore caviar to such a point?" he asked me. But I was worried because of what I had heard; the Mirande I remembered would never have been irritated by the obligation to eat a few extra kilos of fresh caviar. The little girl, who hoped I had not heard, embraced Toto. "Don't be angry with *Maman!*" she implored him.

My fellow guests included the youngish new wife of an old former Premier, who was unavoidably detained in Lille at a congress of the party he now headed; it mustered four deputies, of whom two formed a Left Wing and two a Right Wing. ("If they had elected a fifth at the last election, or if, by good luck, one had been defeated, they could afford the luxury of a Center," Mirande told me in identifying the lady. "*C'est malheureux*, a party without a Center. It limits the possibilities of maneuver.") There was also an amiable couple in their advanced sixties or beginning seventies, of whom the husband was the grand manitou of Veuve Clicquot champagne. Mirande introduced them by their right name, which I forget, and during the rest of the evening addressed them as M. and Mme. Clicquot. There was a forceful, black-haired man from the Midi, in the youth of middle age—square-shouldered, stocky, decisive, blatantly virile—who, I was told, managed Mme. B.'s vinicultural enterprises in Provence. There were two guests of less decided individuality, whom I barely remember, and filling out the party were the young girl—shy, carefully unsophisticated and unadorned—Mme. B., Mirande, and me. Mme. B. had a strong triangular face on a strong triangular base—a strong chin, high cheekbones, and a wide, strong jaw, but full of stormy good nature. She was a woman who, if she had been a man, would have wanted to be called Honest John. She had a high color and an iron handgrip, and repeatedly affirmed that there was no affectation about her, that she was *sans façon*, that she called her shots as she saw them. "I won't apologize," she said to me. "I know you're a great feeder, like Toto here, but I won't offer you the sort of menu he used to get in that restaurant you know of, where he ruined his plumbing. Oh, that woman! I used to be so jealous. I can offer only a simple home dinner." And she waved us toward a marble table about twenty-two feet long. Unfortunately for me, she meant it. The dinner began with a kidney-and-mushroom mince served in a giant popover—the kind of thing you might get at a literary hotel in New York. The inner side of the pastry had the feeling of a baby's palm, in the true tearoom tradition.

"It is savory but healthy," Madame said firmly, setting an example by taking a large second helping before starting the dish on its second round. Mirande regarded the untouched doughy fabric on his plate with diaphanously veiled horror, but he had an excuse in the state of his health. "It's still a little rich for me, darling," he murmured. The others, including me, delivered salvos of compliments. I do not squander my moral courage on minor crises. M. Clicquot said, "Impossible to obtain anything like this *chez* Lapérouse!" Mme. Clicquot said, "Not even at the Tour d'Argent!"

"And what do you think of my little wine?" Mme. B. asked M. Clicquot. "I'm so anxious for your professional opinion—as a rival producer, you know."

The wine was a thin *rosé* in an Art Nouveau bottle with a label that was a triumph of lithography; it had spires and monks and troubadours and blondes in wimples on it, and the name of the *cru* was spelled out in letters with Gothic curlicues and pennons. The name was something like Château Guillaume d'Aquitaine, *grand vin*.

"What a madly gay little wine, my dear!" M. Clicquot said, repressing, but not soon enough, a grimace of pain.

"One would say a Tavel of a good year," I cried, "if one were a complete bloody fool." I did not say the second clause aloud.

My old friend looked at me with new respect. He was discovering in me a capacity for hypocrisy that he had never credited me with before.

The main course was a shoulder of mutton with white beans—the poor relation of a *gigot*, and an excellent dish in its way, when not too dry. This was.

For the second wine, the man from the Midi proudly produced a red, in a bottle without a label, which he offered to M. Clicquot with the air of a tomcat bringing a field mouse to its master's feet. "Tell me what you think of this," he said as he filled the champagne man's glass.

M. Clicquot—a veteran of such challenges, I could well imagine—held the glass against the light, dramatically inhaled the bouquet, and then drank, after a slight stiffening of the features that indicated to me that he knew what he was in for. Having emptied half the glass, he deliberated.

"It has a lovely color," he said.

"But what is it? What is it?" the man from the Midi insisted.

"There are things about it that remind me of a Beaujolais," M. Clicquot said (he must have meant that it was wet), "but on the whole I should compare it to a Bordeaux" (without doubt unfavorably).

Mme. B.'s agent was beside himself with triumph. "Not one or the other!" he crowed. "It's from the *domaine*—the Château Guillaume d'Aquitaine!"

The admirable M. Clicquot professed astonishment, and I, when I had emptied a glass, said that there would be a vast market for the wine in

America if it could be properly presented. "Unfortunately," I said, "the cost of advertising . . ." and I rolled my eyes skyward.

"Ah, yes," Mme. B. cried sadly. "The cost of advertising!"

I caught Mirande looking at me again, and thought of the Pétrus and the Cheval Blanc of our last meal together *chez* Mme. G. He drank a glass of the red. After all, he wasn't going to die of thirst.

For dessert, we had a simple fruit tart with milk—just the thing for an invalid's stomach, although Mirande didn't eat it.

M. Clicquot retrieved the evening, oenologically, by producing two bottles of a wine "impossible to find in the cellars of any restaurant in France"—Veuve Clicquot '19. There is at present a great to-do among wine merchants in France and the United States about young wines, and an accompanying tendency to cry down the "legend" of the old. For that matter, hardware clerks, when you ask for a can opener with a wooden handle that is thick enough to give a grip and long enough for leverage, try to sell you complicated mechanical folderols. The motivation in both cases is the same—simple greed. To deal in wines of varied ages requires judgment, the sum of experience and flair. It involves the risk of money, because every lot of wine, like every human being, has a life span, and it is this that the good vintner must estimate. His object should be to sell his wine at its moment of maximum value—to the drinker as well as the merchant. The vintner who handles only young wines is like an insurance company that will write policies only on children; the unqualified dealer wants to risk nothing and at the same time to avoid tying up his money. The client misled by brochures warning him off clarets and champagnes that are over ten years old and assuring him that Beaujolais should be drunk green will miss the major pleasures of wine drinking. To deal wisely in wines and merely to sell them are things as different as being an expert in ancient coins and selling Indian-head pennies over a souvenir counter.

Despite these convictions of mine about wine, I should never have tried a thirty-seven-year-old champagne on the recommendation of a lesser authority than the blessed M. Clicquot. It is the oldest by far that I have ever drunk. (H. Warner Allen, in *The Wines of France*, published circa 1924, which is my personal wine bible, says, "In the matter of age, champagne is a capricious wine. As a general rule, it has passed its best between fifteen and twenty, yet a bottle thirty years old may prove excellent, though all its fellows may be quite undrinkable." He cites Saintsbury's note that "a Perrier Jouet of 1857 was still majestical in 1884," adding, "And all wine-drinkers know of such amazing discoveries." Mr. Root, whose book is not a foolish panegyric of everything French, is hard on champagne, in my opinion. He falls into a critical error more common among writers less intelligent: he attacks it for not being something else. Because its excellences are not those of Burgundy or Bordeaux, he under-rates the peculiar qualities it does not share with them, as one who

would chide Dickens for not being Stendhal, or Marciano for not being
Benny Leonard.)

The Veuve Clicquot '19 was tart without brashness—a refined but
effective understatement of younger champagnes, which run too much to
rhetoric, at best. Even so, the force was all there, to judge from the two
glasses that were a shade more than my share. The wine still had a
discreet *cordon*—the ring of bubbles that forms inside the glass—and it
had developed the color known as "partridge eye." I have never seen a
partridge's eye, because the bird, unlike woodcock, is served without the
head, but the color the term indicates is that of serous blood or a maple
leaf on the turn.

"How nice it was, life in 1919, eh, M. Clicquot?" Mirande said as he
sipped his second glass.

After we had finished M. Clicquot's offering, we played a game called
lying poker for table stakes, each player being allowed a capital of five
hundred francs, not to be replenished under any circumstances. When
Mme. B. had won everybody's five hundred francs, the party broke up.
Mirande promised me that he would be up and about soon, and would
show me how men reveled in the heroic days of *la belle époque*, but I had
a feeling that the bell was cracked.

I left Paris and came back to it seven times during the next year, but
never saw him. Once, being in his quarter in the company of a remarkably pretty woman, I called him up, simply because I knew he would like
to look at her, but he was too tired. I forget when I last talked to him on
the telephone. During the next winter, while I was away in Egypt or
Jordan or someplace where French papers don't circulate, he died, and I
did not learn of it until I returned to Europe.

When Mirande first faltered, in the Rue Chabanais, I had failed to
correlate cause and effect. I had even felt a certain selfish alarm. If eating
well was beginning to affect Mirande at eighty, I thought, I had better
begin taking in sail. After all, I was only thirty years his junior. But after
the dinner at Mme. B.'s, and in the light of subsequent reflection, I saw
that what had undermined his constitution was Mme. G.'s defection from
the restaurant business. For years, he had been able to escape Mme. B.'s
solicitude for his health by lunching and dining in the restaurant of Mme.
G., the sight of whom Mme. B. could not support. Entranced by Mme.
G.'s magnificent food, he had continued to live "like a cock in a pie"—
eating as well, and very nearly as much, as when he was thirty. The
organs of the interior—never very intelligent, in spite of what the psycho-
somatic quacks say—received each day the amount of pleasure to which
they were accustomed, and never marked the passage of time; it was the
indispensable roadwork of the prizefighter. When Mme. G., good soul,
retired, moderation began its fatal inroads on his resistance. My old
friend's appetite, insufficiently stimulated, started to loaf—the insidious
result, no doubt, of the advice of the doctor whose existence he had

revealed to me by that slip of the tongue about why he no longer drank Burgundy. Mirande commenced, perhaps, by omitting the fish course after the oysters, or the oysters before the fish, then began neglecting his cheeses and skipping the second bottle of wine on odd Wednesdays. What he called his pipes (*"ma tuyauterie"*), being insufficiently exercised, lost their tone, like the leg muscles of a retired champion. When, in his kindly effort to please me, he challenged the *escargots en pots de chambre*, he was like an old fighter who tries a comeback without training for it. That, however, was only the revelation of the rot that had already taken place. What always happens happened. The damage was done, but it could so easily have been averted had he been warned against the fatal trap of abstinence.

2 / *Its Corollary*

M. MIRANDE had an equally rich life between meals. He had pleasure of women. Currently pleasure and women are held matters incompatible, antithetical, and mutually exclusive, like quinine water and Scotch. Mirande also gave women pleasure; many women had pleasure of him. This is no longer considered a fair or honorable exchange. Women resent being thought of as enjoyables; they consider such an attitude an evidence of male chauvinism. They want to be taken seriously, like fallout.

The function of the sexes, if I read the authors of the age aright, is mutual boredom.

It has become customary to write freely of the sexual connection; but always with solemnity. One may respectably write of his sexual initiation, provided it was a disaster. Holden Caulfield never got to the post. Henry Miller may write about revelers self-woven into a human hooked rug, because his ecstasy is solemn. (Arriving in Paris at thirty-nine, he wrote about *la noce* like a child making a belated discovery of the banana split.) *Lady Chatterley's Lover* is acceptable because it is "a *serious* work of art." It is impossible, for the best of reasons, to prove it is a work of art, but it is easy to show that it is serious, the legalizing word. The jocund work of art is still beyond the pale. This is no damn joke.

The wretched how-to-do-it books about copulation are serious in intention, solemn in tone; the do-it-yourselfs will soon be with us.

The one thing about the glorious diversion that is no longer written, or if still written never published, is that it remains the most amusing as well as the most instructive of human activities, and one of the most nearly harmless. The same thing has happened in France, and it used to enrage Mirande.

"If I were a *tapette* writing plays about incest instead of simple fornication, I would have been a member of the Académie for the last twenty years," he once said to me.

The Académie has made posthumous amends by electing to membership Marcel Achard, Mirande's friend and disciple, who is a comic writer. M. Achard inherited M. Mirande's library, which will never be on exhibition at the Bibliothèque Nationale.

Nevertheless, Mirande was devout; he was as regular in attendance at mass Sunday morning as at the races in the afternoon. I imagine the Sieur de Brantôme was a good Catholic too.

There is in Mirande's *Souvenirs* a bewitching account of his visit to the leading lady of one of his great hits shortly before the First World War. He had a habit then of renting magnificent furnished flats and getting locked out of them. With three or four shows running on the Boulevards each season, he made a great deal of money, but it came in irregular spurts, and he had costly tastes and gambled high. He always left landlords to the last in paying up. He loathed them.

In this particular hour before the dawn, returning from Maxim's, he found that an especially spiteful landlord had chosen that night to invoke the law against him. Mirande was in evening clothes and had no place to take them off. From a telephone in an all-night bar he called the actress. Could he come up and sleep? Fortunately she was alone; she said she would be delighted. He stayed the heeltap of the night and half the next day with her. There was no spare room.

Early in the afternoon they were awakened by the actress' maid, who was in a state of extreme agitation. She excused herself for disturbing them but said there was a grave emergency: a man in the drawing room who said he would remove all the furniture if her mistress did not pay his bill, long overdue. She presented an official-looking *facture*, impressively decorated with legal stamps.

This was a piece of business the cast of two regularly acted out for rich admirers who stayed overnight for the first time. The actress' role called for her to burst into tears after receiving her cue, denounce herself as a silly, extravagant woman, and appeal to the admirer to save her from disgrace in the eyes of the quarter. (The scenario provided Mirande with an idea for a first act.)

This time, however, the actress turned on her maid with contempt.

"Imbecile!" she cried. "Can't you see that this is my *author*?"

The notion of getting money out of an author being obviously imbecilic, the maid had no riposte.

"And besides, that envelope is getting pretty gray. Provide yourself with some new stationery before the next time. And go!"

It was the kind of situation that Mirande loved. He especially loved the actress for keeping in form by acting even on days without a matinee.

He would not have understood the battle of the sexes. He saw life as their kindly collaboration. When Mirande was a boy of seventeen, fresh from Lannion, older women—demidowagers in their twenties—made love to him and taught him. When he was a ripe man he returned the favor by making love to the young.

Mirande boasted that he was good to the last. An expeditionary to Hollywood in his green youth, at sixty, he returned with a full *tableau de chasse*, and at eighty, just before the closure of the restaurant of Mme. G., he was meditating another invasion.

"We Frenchmen make love with our brains," he once said to me.

"We others utilize the traditional material," I said. It was the only time I ever had him.

After I published my first study of Mirande in *The New Yorker* I received an avalanche of letters—at least a dozen—from English-reading admirers of the great man, adding reminiscences that would have increased his stature if it were possible to do so.

"After all, he was the lover of the great star X," a woman wrote to me, "and that is nothing to sneeze at."

"I once asked him how X was to make love to," she continued, and he said, 'She is as randy as a pregnant cat.'"

Achard told me that Mirande, like many abnormally productive authors, was lazy. He would accumulate as many advances as possible before honoring any of his commitments and would then wait until the day before first rehearsal before beginning to write. He was confident, from experience, that an idea would occur to him when he needed it.

"Once he waited a day too long and appeared at rehearsal with a number of sheets of paper that he would allow nobody to read because he said they were so scribbled that only he could make them out. He made up the play as he went along, starting from the title, and it was a great success—*My Friend's Wife*. You can imagine the plot. He was a genius."

M. Achard, seeing that I thought that a bit strong, defined his terms.

"You know what is a genius?" he inquired. "Jacques Deval has said it: 'A genius is an author who writes not always flops.'"

"Mirande once said to me that he did not enjoy love with society women," he said, reverting to another aspect of our old friend's genius. "He said they kissed as if they were sipping *crême de menthe* through a straw."

3 / Paris the First

MY PERSONAL Paris is like Byblos in Lebanon, a pile of cities stacked in order of seniority, the oldest at the bottom. Byblos has its culinary associations, too, because the low strata are peppered with large casseroles containing skeletons of a people who boiled their dead and folded them. I know, because I have been told, that I was in Paris in 1907, when I was three, at a hotel on Cours-la-Reine, but I remember nothing about that earliest visit. The first Paris I remember was a colonnaded city, like a stage set of a street with one side perpetually cool shade and the other bright, hot sun. In the middle of the street there was a cuirassier, the nearest thing to a knight in armor I had seen outside a picture book, immense in his plastron and boots. He sat a horse with two tails, one in the usual place and one hanging from the back of the man's helmet. This was the Rue de Rivoli in the dog days of 1911, when my family paused there on the way home to New York from a holiday in Europe proper, or *odiosa*, a place where the inhabitants spoke German, as did my oppressors, the Frauleins. Fraulein, to me, had the strong specific meaning of nursegirl. It was to be years before I realized that it could be applied to an unmarried woman not in service. Many Frauleins *in* service must have been married, but I never thought of one as *Frau*. Frauleins were my immemorial enemies, interposed between my parents and me, like wicked bailiffs between kind barons and their serfs. They were the bad doorkeepers of a benign sultan. Without their officious intervention, I was sure, I could have been with my parents twenty-four hours a day, and they would have been charmed to have me. There were two incidents of the 1907 trip that I did remember in 1911, and remember still, but they happened in Germany.

In Wiesbaden in 1907 a Fraulein named Martha had dragged me at unforgettable speed, my feet touching the ground only occasionally, through what I remembered as a mile of streets, to see a tall man in a white uniform with a cape, sitting in a white automobile on some hideous *Platz*, surrounded by a cheering crowd. He was, she told me in hysteric shrieks, the Kaiser. Her tone would have been appropriate to announce the Second Coming. Martha ranked in the Frauleinian dynasty like Caligula among Roman emperors. She was one of the worst. In Nuremberg that same summer she had packed me off to the torture tower in the old keep to see the Iron Maiden, a hinged hollow figure lined with spikes. The guide-lecturer said that prisoners were put inside and then squashed and blinded simultaneously. I understand now that the Maiden was a fake, but it was a *German* fake. Then they showed me the mouth of the well down which the torturers used to drop the broken bodies. The guide held a lighted candle and Martha held me in her arms and let me look down. Then he chucked a stone in and we waited an impressively long time before we heard it hit the water.

"It happens to naughty children, too," Martha said.

She bought me a miniature Iron Maiden as a souvenir.

My wars against the Frauleins left me with a blurred recollection of injustice and struggle, like the collective memory of the Irish, for whom I have an anomalous sympathy at their most difficult. We are like the children of long, hard deliveries, incredulous of our freedom even when we reach the clear. The Fraulein, I have thought often since, was a remarkably effective device for siphoning off from the parents the hostility that analysts assure us is the parents' due. Careful bootleggers in Harlem during Prohibition used to pass suspect alcohol through an old felt hat, on the theory that the poison would remain there. The Fraulein had the function of the felt hat. As full of the discharged hostility as the hat was of fusel oil, she shifted to another job when the child outgrew her. She left it as harmless to its parents as a baby rattlesnake milked of venom. To the child who began conscious life under the rule of a Fraulein, even the least bearable mother appeared an angel.

The device seems to me, looking back, more sensible than that of the kind nanny described in English novels. The nannies siphon off not the hostility, but the affection, leaving the protagonists incapable of liking anybody else for the rest of their lives. (Anticipating that these notes will be utilized at some future date by biographers, some analytically oriented, I shall make their path clearer by expositions like the above from time to time.)

It never occurred to me to wonder why my parents paid the Frauleins who deprived them of the pleasure of my constant company. I was sure the witches, like those in the fairy tales with which they tried to terrify me, had imposed themselves on the kind king and queen by some cunning swindle. We had a Fraulein with us even in Paris, although, to defend my pride, I insisted she was there only to take care of my sister, who was two and change. I was nearly seven. In fact, though, Fraulein had authority over me, too, especially in my parents' absences. I was only fourth in the chain of command, and my sister, the only member of the party I outranked, was too dumb to take orders from me.

France was better than Europe proper, because it was on the way home from it. The language sounded better, although I couldn't understand what people said in it. We lived at the Hotel Regina, where the Place des Pyramides debouches into the Rue de Rivoli, and when we went out on foot we stayed under the colonnade because of the heat. We seldom got beyond the Place de la Concorde, because my sister, who in later years became as nimble as a roebuck, could not then walk worth a damn.

For years afterward I thought of Paris as a city mostly roofed over, like a *souk*. I don't know why I think of the cuirassier as a permanent feature of the set. There may have been a fixed guard in front of one of the hotels because a visiting royal personage or head of state was in residence. But it is possible that I saw the soldier only once, and was so impressed that I never forgot him.

My parents abandoned the three of us often and went out into un-roofed regions in a fiacre or a taxi. Hippomobile and automobile ages overlapped; it was no longer dashing to motor, nor yet quaint to prefer a carriage. My own prejudice in favor of horses was so strong that when I chanced to be with my parents they deferred to it.

All of us had stayed four weeks at Marienbad, a spa in Bohemia that is now known by some Slavic name, while Mother reduced her weight. Having reduced, she had an excuse to gather a wardrobe for her new figure before we went home. (She was sure to put the weight back on before the *Kaiserin Augusta Victoria* docked in Hoboken, nine days after leaving Cherbourg, but the dresses could always be let out.) Father had to accompany her to see how pretty she looked and to authorize expenditures that he would have rejected in horror if he had not been there to see her. He was not only proud of her looks—"A regular Lillian Russell," he would say—but sensitive to the good opinion of the mannequins and *vendeuses*. The sight of a pretty woman had an airborne chemical effect, like nerve gas. It relaxed the rubber band around his wallet. He was, moreover, helpless in Paris without Mother because he did not have French and thought she was fluent in it. It was an illusion she maintained as long as they traveled together.

"If you talk English to them they double the price," he used to say.

He did not suffer from this disadvantage in Europa Odiosa, since he spoke German, but it gave him little pleasure. What I principally remember him talking about in Marienbad was how a waiter captain had tried to swindle us by putting twenty-three rolls on our breakfast bill when we had taken only twenty-one. Mother, when on a diet, limited herself to three rolls.

Once that summer they took me, unforgettably, to Napoleon's tomb, where the gold light, the marble, and the massed battle flags made an image of Napoleonic glory that has always helped me understand the side of Stendhal that is least rational. If brief exposure to the glories of the Empire, a hundred years later, could so dazzle me, I find it easy to pardon the effect upon a lieutenant of dragoons eighteen years old, riding in the midst of the Sixth Light Dragoons, uniform bottle-green, red waistcoat, white breeches, helmet with crest, horsetail, and red cockàde.

Napoleon's name and general repute were already known to me. He was a deity of the small personal Olympus I was putting together for myself, like a collection of the pictures of baseball players that then came in packages of cigarettes. The captain of the team was George Washington, and there were also Miss Russell (Aphrodite) and Enrico Caruso (Pan). Washington was Zeus, or boss god. His stern virtue—"I cannot tell a lie"—put him above me and everybody else I knew, because we all lied frequently. His hatchet inspired a terror I could not then explain to myself. I can see now that his craggy *old* face under the white hair—I had no notion then that he wore a powdered wig—equated him with the Old Man of the Tribe, or father-persona, vested with power symbolized by the ax. He looked mean enough to use it. The cherry tree, of course, is a son-substitute—Isaac is to Abraham as cherry tree to Washington—and even the merest fool can see what the candied cherries are, symbolically speaking. (The show windows of the Platt-Deutsch and Greek confectionery stores in New York were full of candied cherries, cardboard or chocolate hatchets, and cardboard cherry trees, bearing edible cherries, for a week before Washington's birthday. Here we have the personae and materia of a cult, with a built-in miracle play.) I knew Miss Russell, like Washington, only by hearsay. In my cosmogony she was already a figure of the past, associated with my prehistory and my parents' salad days, because they talked about her that way. I was astonished, on checking her dates when I wrote this, to read that she retired from the stage only in 1912, at the age of fifty-one. In 1911, although no longer in perihelion, she was an undefeated champion still, about to retire into wealthy marriage with a Pittsburgh publisher. Miss Russell had been the reigning American Beauty, on and off stage, since about 1885. She was a butterscotch sundae of a woman, as beautiful as a tulip of beer with a high white collar. If a Western millionaire, one of the Hearst or Mackay kind, could have given an architect carte blanche to design him a woman, she would have looked like Lillian. She was San Simeon in corsets.

Mother, who was seventeen years younger, had bloomed in an age when all blond little girls with blue eyes wanted to grow up to be Lillian Russells. At puberty, if the girls were still pretty, their relatives began to compare them to their model.

Miss Russell embodied a style. Her hats were famously enormous and beplumed, even in an era of big, feathered hats. In photographs she seems to be wearing a forest of ostrich plumes above a mesa with an underbrush of satin bows. Her contours did not encourage fasting among her imitators. In building up to a similar opulence, I suppose, a younger woman developed eating habits that were hard to curb after she reached the target figure. That may have been Mother's difficulty.

A popular dessert named for the star, the Lillian Russell, was a half cantaloupe holding about a pint and three quarters of ice cream. If an actress had a dish named after her now, the recipe would be four pheno-barbital tablets and a jigger of Metrecal. The consecrated silhouette was an hourglass. Hence, I imagine, rose a dietary dilemma. A woman had to eat to stay plump above and below the pinch and slender in between.

Corsets afforded only partial and painful aid. I remember, as a small child, that in the bathing pavilion at Far Rockaway, the women, before going out on the beach, would summon the locker man, a leathery old drunk, to pull the strings of their corsets tight. In cinching them up, he would sometimes place his bare foot in the small of a whaleboned back. They tipped him for doing them this violence. People then were willing to go to more pains than now in order to look nice. The women were not alone in this. Marshal Mannerheim in his *Memoirs* recalls that officers of the Russian Imperial Guard used to put on their doeskin trousers, sit in a bath, and then let them dry tight to the skin.

Miss Russell and her imitators held their beautiful chins high, to arch the neck and prevent wrinkles. It was no time for an undecided profile. Throats, arms and backs counted more points than they do today because women wore low-necked gowns more often. People dressed for the dress circle in the Metropolitan Opera House then, for example, where now they wear street clothes in the boxes. Merely well-off couples, like my parents, with no social pretensions, often dressed just to go to friends' houses for dinner. I can remember Mother pausing in my bedroom to show herself off on some of these occasions in a white gown with gold sequins or a lilac with silver. I agreed with Father that she was a regular Lillian Russell.

Miss Russell, as reflected in my mother, furnished my basic pattern of feminine beauty. But the type already trembled on the brink of the archaic in 1911, like silent films the year before sound came in. Irene Castle lurked just around the corner of history, light of foot, long-legged and sparse, and by the early twenties, when I began to look purposefully at females, I would not find a Russellinear woman anywhere. (To this sharp bend in the river of womanly morphology I sometimes attribute my insatiable nostalgia for the past: I have a fixation on a form of animal life that no longer exists.)

Caruso, the fourth in my pantheon, was a Disembodied Voice, which is an essential feature of the history of any religion. His, with which I was familiar, came out of the horn, shaped like a morning-glory, of our Victrola. I could not understand what he said, which made it more awesome. Mostly, it seems to me now, he sang "E Lucevan le Stelle." I can identify it, at fifty years' distance, by the place where Cavaradossi sobs. Caruso sobbed louder than any other tenor, and when he did, my father always said, "That's art. You can tell a real artist by touches like that."

Tosca, Father used to say, was the touchstone for sopranos, too. "When she lays Scarpia out and puts the candles by the corpse, you can tell whether she can act," he would say. "She's just stabbed him, you know, and then she gets superstitious."

The only reason I would have liked to go to the Metropolitan in person was to see the stabbing; I wondered how they managed the blood. The music, I judged from the phonograph records, was something one could easily have too much of. The description "a regular Caruso" was as valid praise as "a regular Lillian Russell," but neither meant that the person so qualified was literally a deity—just that the amateur could sing well, or that the girl was a peach. There had been a third god on the same level, but his foot had slipped.

"A regular Jim Jeffries" no longer meant, in 1911, what it had before 1910, when that Caucasian Colossus had lost to Jack Johnson. You couldn't very well say that a white boy was a regular Jack Johnson.

Caruso was also a Pan-god, or satyr. Everybody knew that he had once followed a woman into the monkey house at the Central Park Zoo and pinched her in the rear. The woman had had him arrested. The incident had filled headlines; it had become legend. Thirty years later I was to learn that it was a press agent's trick, put up to attract attention to the tenor's appearance in a new role, Rodolfo in *La Bohème*. But then it was a myth that I accepted as fully as the story of George Washington and the cherry tree. Caruso, again like Miss Russell, was a deity often made manifest to my parents, more worthy than myself. Home from the Opera, they talked about his tonsils as if they were my Uncle Mike's.

In those days the people of New York saw its gods in the flesh, on the stage of the Met or the Colonial Theatre, or strutting in front of Kid McCoy's saloon, according to the departments over which they presided. They were not a reconstituted mess of dots on a screen.

Culture impinged on daily life. My father, when shaving, sang the Toreador's air from *Carmen* every morning while stropping his razor. I associated this habit of his with the Caruso cult, too, but erroneously. Father, like Escamillo, was a baritone. There was only one word in his version of the song, and that deformed by a feminine ending that he dragged in for euphony:

"To-reea-Dora" . . .

He sang the rest of the music to a devocabularized lyric—"Ta, ra, ta, ra, *tah.*"

He could shave with a straight blade on a transatlantic liner in a storm. The electric razor fosters no comparable talents.

I do not denigrate my pantheon of fifty years ago. An aesthetic taste founded on the gold light in the tomb and Lillian Russell's figure and Caruso singing Cavaradossi—and Sousa's Band and the Buffalo Bill show —is bound to be big and rich. It can be pruned down afterward.

In the Paris evenings, Father and Mother dined *en ville*, leaving the three of us to take supper in our room. Fraulein and I would share some uninspiring dish like cold cuts or an omelet, and my sister would have consommé and a soft-boiled egg, which made her unhappy. This particular Fraulein was rather nice, the only one I remember without distaste. I had, in any case, attained an age that forbade the worst personal indignities. (The most annoying was when they got the wash rag into your ear, meanwhile pulling the lobe with their other hand, but the most publicly humbling was when they spit on a handkerchief and wiped a smudge off your nose.) This Fraulein was Volks-Deutsch, from northern Hungary, and looked more Hungarian than German, with a good figure, ruddy complexion, and heavy black eyebrows. The room waiter was an Alsatian and won her confidence by speaking German. On the first night we were there, though, when he came back for the dishes after my sister and I were in our beds, he showed he was just like all the other Frenchmen, Fraulein told my mother the next day. He got fresh. Thereafter, she told him to leave the dishes for the maid to collect next morning, and she barricaded the door with chairs.

"But what could he do to you, Fraulein?" I asked her.

We nagged the poor girl so, during those hot days, that Mother advised her to take us to Rumpelmayer's *confiserie* under the colonnade, near the Hotel Continental, for what we had seen advertised on a window card as an American ice-cream soda. Fraulein could build a whole day of peace around the excursion, keeping us in line during the morning by threatening not to take us if we weren't good, then making us have a nap after lunch as preparation for the treat. Afterward we might, if she was lucky, be sick, and she could put us to bed again.

The day came, and we went. Fraulein and I had the sodas, but they were not, in my opinion, up to the standard of the West Side of New York. Trying, at this long distance in time, to appraise the trouble, I do not think Rumpelmayer's had a genuine soda-fountain pump to gas them up with. I suspect that famous *salon de thé* of slopping a bottle of Perrier over a parfait. Boys liked their sodas very gassy then, with a sharp, metallic bite that reminded me of the smell of a bicycle-repair shop. My sister was allowed, I suppose, to have some of the ice cream out of my soda. Then the waitress brought the bill. Fraulein, who had expected they would cost ten cents, like the ones at home, did not have enough French money with her to pay it.

There was a conference, made more memorable because Fraulein spoke no French, and they trusted nobody who spoke German. The allegorical statue of Strasbourg among the cities of France in the Place de la Corcorde was draped permanently in black; it was knee-high in funeral wreaths. We had once walked that far. *La revanche* was in the air, like humidity. Finally, Fraulein and the management reached a *Konkordat*: she was to go back to the hotel and change some Austrian *Kronen*— Rumpelmayer's wouldn't. She was to take Norma, who was already howling, with her. I was to be left as collateral.

She explained the deal to me before she left. I did not like it; I proposed we leave Norma. She said patiently that the reason Rumpelmayer's was releasing her even temporarily was to get Norma out of there. I demanded a supplement of pastry on the principle of extra danger pay, but Fraulein said that the management would advance no further credit.

So there I sat, for what seemed the second seven years of my life, my apprehension steadily growing, while she walked the couple of hundred yards back to the Regina and took Norma to the bathroom and came back. Before she made it I decided a dozen times that she wouldn't. When at last she reappeared, she asked me not to tell my parents what had happened, and I blackmailed her out of an éclair.

It was a prophetic trauma. I have spent a large aggregate portion of my life since in situations that repeated the quarter hour at Rumpelmayer's, waiting for a loan to bail me out. No matter how sure I am that the money will arrive, I have the same anxiety. My first stay in hock should have infected me with a horror of Paris forever, but it didn't, although I did not know how deeply I was in love. There would come a time when, if I had compared my life to a cake, the sojourns in Paris would have represented the chocolate filling. The intervening layers were plain sponge. But my infatuations do not begin at first taste. I nibble, reflect, come back for more, and find myself forever addicted.

I remember, from that first Paris, the gold light in the tomb, the cuirassier, and the *vespasiennes* where no Fraulein could pursue me. Finally, there were two toys that I bore off with me to the *Kaiserin Augusta Victoria*. One was a chef *legumier* who hacked away at a carrot with a big knife—another version, had I but recognized it, of the George Washington myth. The other was a scale fire engine with hose no thicker than vermicelli through which I could pump real water.

The chef symbolized in my unconscious Paris, *ville gastronomique*, and the engine with its squirt Paris, *ville d'art*. The graphic arts had their origin in the free patterns made in the snow by Ice Age man with warm water. This accounts for the fact that there have been few good women painters. Lot's wife, who looked behind her, may have been a pioneer, but we had a head start of several million years.

The years from 1911 to 1924 were plain sponge, yet that dull stratum clinched my allegiance. Nineteen-fourteen was the year of transition to Francophile from mere Germanophobe. On August 1, Fraulein Germania's armies crossed the frontier, and the "Marseillaise" became my favorite tune. I was by that time already a compulsive newspaper reader instead of a tentative one, as I had been in 1911. I counted on Papa Joffre and the cuirassier to avenge my early indignities. Joffre's face reminded me of Santa Claus, a pleasant association, although I had long ceased to believe. (When I saw Santa Clauses on street corners, I knew I would soon get a lot of presents, and it set up a pleasant mood. When I see them now, I know I will have to give a lot, and I am filled with bile.) All through August, though, the French retreated. The Germans—I forget when they became Huns—advanced toward Rumpelmayer's and the Hotel Regina. It was a personal humiliation, because in America I was surrounded by German rooters.

We were quartered at a hotel called Schaefer's in Lake Hopatcong, a hot summer resort in New Jersey. Schaefer's was a German-American kind of place, as much roadhouse as hotel, built on the side of a hill, with a dark, cool bar on the lowest level. There was a fruit machine in this crypt, and I would play it every day, until I had lost the last nickel I could wheedle or extort from my mother. Then I would drink sarsaparilla and eat Swiss cheese sandwiches on rye while I read the Waverly Novels. The sarsaparilla and sandwiches went on the bill. The novels came from a mission-oak bookcase in the hall outside the dining room. When Fraulein —the Paris one was still with us—would drive me into the distasteful fresh air, I would walk down to a pier, sit down again, and fish for perch. I never caught one big enough to eat.

A bar, aromatic of stale beer, presented an aspect of Teutonic culture I could appreciate, and my antipathy might have shaded into indifference if the war hadn't started. When it did, though, Otto, the bartender, and Fred and Karl, the waiters, began to crow offensively about their national superiority to everybody else. The French, they said, betrayed themselves from fear, and the English were fairies. As I was a great reader of G. A. Henty, this involved me on a second front.

Victory followed victory, and as the help's chests swelled, Fraulein's bosom heaved with them. She was an Austro-Hungarian subject, and an ally. Karl was cockeyed and he pinched lady guests' bottoms when he thought he could get away with it. He had long hinted he was a remittance man, and he now professed to have been an officer on a U-boat. Fraulein looked at him otherwise than she had upon the Alsatian waiter in Paris. My attitude toward her was now ambivalent, for I had begun to take a sneaking interest in women and half regretted that I no longer shared a room with her and Norma; I would have welcomed the opportunities for observation. I therefore resented Fraulein Fasching's interest in Karl. Patriotism, I sensed, could be employed for ulterior purposes. I told her that if he was so brave he should go home and join the navy. She explained that since the cowardly English held the sea he couldn't—he was breaking his heart over it. But it was hardly worth regretting, because even if there were boats going, the Germans and Austrians would win the war before Karl could get there. He was having his *Schnecke* and eating it. I longed for Joffre to turn the tables, but he looked to be two out and ten runs behind in the last half of the ninth inning. The Marne determined my second nationality forever. I became a Frenchman at one remove.

By that time, I think, we were back in our house at Far Rockaway, a boundary province of Greater New York on Long Island. Like all frontier dwellers I was chauvinistic, and I thought of people who lived across the street in Nassau County as hicks. It was a tall, gaunt house, painted dark green and darkened by oaks that stood too close. (Thirty years later I saw it again and it had been divided into flats.) There Fraulein, reeling under the shock of Joffre's and my combined attack, received fresh support from Louis, our houseman, a Tyrolese from Meran. He had been working as a waiter in another summer hotel while we were away.

Louis was as Pan-German as Fraulein. He predicted that the Marne was only a temporary setback. The French were merely a kind of Wops—I would see. He had his own kind of frontier chauvinism—anti-Italian. He had an impressive trick of jumping out of a third-floor window, grabbing a limb of an oak tree, and swinging his way down by changing hand-holds, like a pre-Weissmuller Tarzan.

I was then in 5B. The war enlisted me and filled my proxy life for four years. When it ended I was a sophomore in high school. I grew up in it, transferring in fantasy from the cuirassiers, when I saw cavalry wouldn't do, to the heroic poilus, defenders of Verdun. I served a brief period as an officer of heroic Senegalese, and a short bit with the heroic Escadrille Lafayette. I also did a turn as liaison with our gallant allies, the heroic Brusiloff's heroic Cossacks. It is more vivid to me, even now, than the following World War; that is because I saw it through the eyes of correspondents who knew how to use their imaginations. Each fall, when the offensives that had begun so optimistically bogged down, I would say to Fraulein and Louis, like a Dodger fan, "Wait till next year." It was no longer fun for Fraulein—her brother was a surgeon with the Austrian army in Galicia, and after the sinking of the *Lusitania* it was clear which side was out of favor here.

Then in the Verdun spring—1916—while I walked along the parapet of my trench to show my fellows the Huns couldn't shoot, I began to feel queer and got sent home from school. Mother put me to bed, and it shortly transpired that I had typhoid fever. I had caught it by eating oysters from polluted waters—they had not been sold as such, of course—and I soon drifted into delirium, where I stayed for weeks of combat service on several fronts I had not yet visited. I had a particularly arduous indefinite period as a Serbian army horse, being ferried across a river as one in a bunch of bananas. On arriving at the other side of the river I was presented at a formal review of cuirassiers, where General Nivelle, the heroic commander of Verdun's heroic defenders, decorated me with the Médaille Militaire, which he attached to my right horse-ear by a safety pin. I put the medal under my pillow.

I had two trained nurses who lived in the house and worked around the clock—my parents didn't think well of the local hospital. As I achieved a patchy lucidity, I became aware of Miss Galt and Miss McCarthy as nurses in a military hospital. (I had stopped being a horse, but still had the medal, safe under the pillow.) They were kind, but I was peevish, and they sometimes said the conventional things.

Once, then, when the fever had departed and they thought I was quite all right in the head again, I gagged or whimpered at some measure of therapy, and Miss McCarthy said, "Don't be a crybaby."

It roused the *grand decoré*, in me, and I yelped, "Crybaby? How do you think I got that medal under my pillow?"

"Medal under what pillow?" she asked.

I lifted myself on an elbow and turned the pillow over, but my decoration wasn't there.

I was never so disappointed in my heroic life.[*]

4/Just Enough Money

IF, AS I was saying before I digressed, the first requisite for writing well about food is a good appetite, the second is to put in your apprenticeship as a feeder when you have enough money to pay the check but not enough to produce indifference to the size of the total. (I also meant to say, previously, that Waverley Root has a good appetite, but I never got around to it.) The optimum financial position for a serious apprentice feeder is to have funds in hand for three more days, with a reasonable, but not certain, prospect of reinforcements thereafter. The student at the Sorbonne waiting for his remittance, the newspaperman waiting for his salary, the free-lance writer waiting for a check that he has cause to believe is in the mail—all are favorably situated to learn. (It goes without saying that it is essential to be in France.) The man of appetite who will stint himself when he can see three days ahead has no vocation, and I dismiss from consideration, as manic, the fellow who will spend the lot on one great feast and then live on fried potatoes until his next increment; Tuaregs eat that way, but only because they never know when they are going to come by their next sheep. The clear-headed voracious man learns because he tries to compose his meals to obtain an appreciable quantity of pleasure from each. It is from this weighing of delights against their cost that the student eater (particularly if he is a student at the University of Paris) erects the scale of values that will serve him until he dies or has to reside in the Middle West for a long period. The scale is different for each eater, as it is for each writer.

Eating is highly subjective, and the man who accepts say-so in youth will wind up in bad and overtouted restaurants in middle age, ordering what the maître d'hôtel suggests. He will have been guided to them by food-snob publications, and he will fall into the habit of drinking too much before dinner to kill the taste of what he has been told he should like but doesn't. An illustration: For about six years, I kept hearing of a restaurant in the richest shire of Connecticut whose proprietor, a Frenchman, had been an assistant of a disciple of the great Escoffier. Report had

---

[*] Thirty-six years later, in 1952, I got a French decoration for the most disappointing of reasons: being a writer—I sometimes take it surreptitiously from its case and stare at it, pretending that I won it by jumping a horse over the bayonets of a British square at Waterloo and, once in, decapitating a Colonel the Honorable Something-or-Other, a Tory back-bencher in the House of Commons.

it that in these wilds—inhabited only by executives of the highest grade, walking the woods like the King of Nemi until somebody came on from Winnetka to cut their throats—the restaurateur gave full vent to the creative flame. His clients took what he chose to give them. It they declined, they had to go down the pike to some joint where a steak cost only twelve dollars, and word would get around that they felt their crowns in danger—they had been detected economizing. I finally arranged to be smuggled out to the place disguised as a *Time-Life* Executive Vice-Publisher in Charge of Hosannas with the mission of entertaining the advertising manager of the Hebrew National Delicatessen Corporation. When we arrived, we found the Yale-blue vicuña rope up and the bar full of couples in the hundred-thousand-dollar bracket, dead drunk as they waited for tables; knowing that this would be no back-yard cookout, they had taken prophylactic anesthesia. But when I tasted the food, I perceived that they had been needlessly alarmed. The Frenchman, discouraged because for four years no customers had tasted what they were eating, had taken to bourbon-on-the-rocks. In a morose way, he had resigned himself to becoming dishonestly rich. The food was no better than Howard Johnson's and the customers, had they not been paralyzed by the time they got to it, would have liked it as well. The *spécialité de la maison*, the unhappy *patron* said when I interrogated him, was jellied oysters dyed red, white, and blue. "At least they are aware of that," he said. "The colors attract their attention." There was an on-the-hour service of Brink's armored cars between his door and the night-deposit vault of a bank in New York, conveying the money that rolled into the *caisse*. The wheels, like a juggernaut's, rolled over his secret heart. His intention in the beginning had been noble, but he was a victim of the system.

The reference room where I pursued my own first earnest researches as a feeder without the crippling handicap of affluence was the Restaurant des Beaux-Arts, on the Rue Bonaparte, in 1926–27. I was a student, in a highly generalized way, at the Sorbonne, taking targets of opportunity for study. Eating soon developed into one of my major subjects. The franc was at twenty-six to the dollar, and the researcher, if he had only a certain sum—say, six francs—to spend, soon established for himself whether, for example, a half bottle of Tavel *supérieur*, at three and a half francs, and braised beef heart and yellow turnips, at two and a half, gave him more or less pleasure than a *contre-filet* of beef, at five francs, and a half bottle of *ordinaire*, at one franc. He might find that he liked the heart, with its strong, rich flavor and odd texture, nearly as well as well as the beef, and that since the Tavel was overwhelmingly better than the cheap wine, he had done well to order the first pair. Or he might find that he so much preferred the generous, sanguine *contre-filet* that he could accept the undistinguished *picrate* instead of the Tavel. As in a bridge tournament, the learner played duplicate hands, making the opposite choice of fare the next time the problem presented itself. (It was seldom as simple as my

example, of course, because a meal usually included at least an hors
d'oeuvre and a cheese, and there was a complexity of each to choose
from. The arrival, in season, of fresh asparagus or venison further complicated matters. In the first case, the investigator had to decide what course
to omit in order to fit the asparagus in, and, in the second, whether to
forgo all else in order to afford venison.)

A rich man, faced with this simple sumptuary dilemma, would have
ordered both the Tavel *and* the *contre-filet*. He would then never know
whether he liked beef heart, or whether an *ordinaire* wouldn't do him as
well as something better. (There are people to whom wine is merely an
alcoholized sauce, although they may have sensitive palates for meat or
pastries.) When one considers the millions of permutations of foods and
wines to test, it is easy to see that life is too short for the formulation of
dogma. Each eater can but establish a few general principles that are true
only for him. Our hypothetical rich *client* might even have ordered a
Pommard, because it was listed at a higher price than the Tavel, and
because he was more likely to be acquainted with it. He would then never
have learned that a good Tavel is better than a fair-to-middling Pommard
—better than a fair-to-middling almost anything, in my opinion. In student restaurants, renowned wines like Pommard were apt to be mediocre
specimens of their kind, since the customers could never have afforded
the going prices of the best growths and years. A man who is rich in his
adolescence is almost doomed to be a dilettante at table. This is not
because all millionaires are stupid but because they are not impelled to
experiment. In learning to eat, as in psychoanalysis, the customer, in order
to profit, must be sensible of the cost.

There is small likelihood that a rich man will frequent modest restaurants even at the beginning of his gustatory career; he will patronize
restaurants, sometimes good, where the prices are high and the repertory
is limited to dishes for which it is conventionally permissible to charge
high prices. From this list, he will order the dishes that in his limited
experience he has already found agreeable. Later, when his habits are
formed, he will distrust the originality that he has never been constrained
to develop. A diet based chiefly on game birds and oysters becomes a
habit as easily as a diet of jelly doughnuts and hamburgers. It is a better
habit, of course, but restrictive just the same. Even in Paris, one can dine in
the costly restaurants for years without learning that there are fish other
than sole, turbot, salmon (in season), trout, and the Mediterranean
rouget and *loup de mer*. The fresh herring or sardine *sauce moutarde*; the
colin froid mayonnaise; the conger eel *en matelote*; the small fresh-water
fish of the Seine and the Marne, fried crisp and served *en buisson*; the
whiting *en colère* (his tail in his mouth, as if contorted with anger); and
even the skate and the *dorade*—all these, except by special and infrequent invitation, are out of the swim. (It is a standing tourist joke to say
that the fishermen on the quays of the Seine never catch anything, but in

fact they often take home the makings of a nice fish fry, especially in winter. In my hotel on the Square Louvois, I had a room waiter—a Czech naturalized in France—who used to catch hundreds of *goujons* and *ablettes* on his days off. He once brought a shoe box of them to my room to prove that Seine fishing was not pure whimsey.) All the fish I have mentioned have their habitats in humbler restaurants, the only places where the aspirant eater can become familiar with their honest fishy tastes and the decisive modes of accommodation that suit them. Personally, I like tastes that know their own minds. The reason that people who detest fish often tolerate sole is that sole doesn't taste very much like fish, and even this degree of resemblance disappears when it is submerged in the kind of sauce that patrons of Piedmontese restaurants in London and New York think characteristically French. People with the same apathy toward decided flavor relish "South African lobster" tails—frozen as long as the Siberian mammoth—because they don't taste lobstery. ("South African lobsters" are a kind of sea crayfish, or *langouste*, but that would be nothing against them if they were fresh.) They prefer processed cheese because it isn't cheesy, and synthetic vanilla extract because it isn't vanillary. They have made a triumph of the Delicious apple because it doesn't taste like an apple, and of the Golden Delicious because it doesn't taste like anything. In a related field, "dry" (non-beery) beer and "light" (non-Scotchlike) Scotch are more of the same. The standard of perfection for vodka (no color, no taste, no smell) was expounded to me long ago by the then Estonian consul-general in New York, and it accounts perfectly for the drink's rising popularity with those who like their alcohol in conjunction with the reassuring tastes of infancy—tomato juice, orange juice, chicken broth. It is the ideal intoxicant for the drinker who wants no reminder of how hurt Mother would be if she knew what he was doing.

The consistently rich man is also unlikely to make the acquaintance of meat dishes of robust taste—the hot *andouille* and *andouillette*, which are close-packed sausages of smoked tripe, and the *boudin*, or blood pudding, and all its relatives that figure in the pages of Rabelais and on the menus of the market restaurants. He will not meet the *civets*, or dark, winy stews of domestic rabbit and old turkey. A tough old turkey with plenty of character makes the best *civet*, and only in a *civet* is turkey good to eat. Young turkey, like young sheep, calf, spring chicken, and baby lobster, is a pale preliminary phase of its species. The pig, the pigeon, and the goat—as suckling, squab, and kid—are the only animals that are at their best to eat when immature. The first in later life becomes gross through indolence; the second and third grow muscular through overactivity. And the world of tripery is barred to the well-heeled, except for occasional exposure to an expurgated version of *tripes à la mode de Caen*. They have never seen *gras-double* (tripe cooked with vegetables, principally onions) or *pieds et paquets* (sheep's tripe and calves' feet with salt pork). In his book, Waverley Root dismisses tripe, but he is no plutocrat;

his rejection is deliberate, after fair trial. Still, his insensibility to its charms seems to me odd in a New Englander, as he is by origin. Fried pickled honeycomb tripe used to be the most agreeable feature of a winter breakfast in New Hampshire, and Fall River, Root's home town, is in the same cultural circumscription.

Finally, to have done with our rich man, seldom does he see even the simple, well-pounded *bifteck* or the *pot-au-feu* itself—the foundation glory of French cooking. Alexandre Dumas the elder wrote in his *Dictionary Cuisine*: "French cooking, the first of all cuisines, owes its superiority to the excellence of French bouillon. This excellence derives from a sort of intuition with which I shall not say our cooks but our women of the people are endowed." This bouillon is one of the two end products of the *pot*. The other is the material that has produced it—beef, carrots, parsnips, white turnips, leeks, celery, onions, cloves, garlic, and cracked marrowbones, and, for the dress version, fowl. Served *in* some of the bouillon, this constitutes the dish known as *pot-au-feu*. Dumas is against poultry "unless it is old," but advises that "an old pigeon, a partridge, or a rabbit roasted in advance, a crow in November or December" works wonders. He postulates "seven hours of sustained simmering," with constant attention to the "scum" that forms on the surface and to the water level. ("Think twice before adding water, though if your meat actually rises above the level of the bouillon it is necessary to add boiling water to cover it.") This supervision demands the full-time presence of the cook in the kitchen throughout the day, and the maintenance of the temperature calls for a considerable outlay in fuel. It is one reason that the *pot-au-feu* has declined as a chief element of the working-class diet in France. Women go out to work, and gas costs too much. For a genuinely good *pot-au-feu*, Dumas says, one should take a fresh piece of beef—"a twelve-to-fifteen-pound rump"—and simmer it seven hours in the bouillon of the beef that you simmered seven hours the day before. He does not say what good housekeepers did with the first piece of beef—perhaps cut it into sandwiches for the children's lunch. He regrets that even when he wrote, in 1869, excessive haste was beginning to mar cookery; the demanding ritual of the *pot* itself had been abandoned. This was "a receptacle that never left the fire, day or night," Dumas writes. "A chicken was put into it as a chicken was withdrawn, a piece of beef as a piece was taken out, and a glass of water whenever a cup of broth was removed. Every kind of meat that cooked in this bouillon gained, rather than lost, in flavor." *Pot-au-feu* is so hard to find in chic restaurants nowadays that every Saturday evening there is a mass pilgrimage from the fashionable quarters to Chez Benoit, near the Châtelet—a small but not cheap restaurant that serves it once a week. I have never found a crow in Benoit's *pot*, but all the rest is good.

A drastically poor man, naturally, has even less chance than a drastically rich one to educate himself gastronomically. For him eating becomes merely a matter of subsistence; he can exercise no choice. The chief attraction of the cheapest student restaurants in my time was advertised on their largest placards: *"Pain à Discrétion"* ("All the Bread You Want"). They did not graduate discriminating eaters. During that invaluable year, I met a keen observer who gave me a tip: "If you run across a restaurant where you often see priests eating with priests, or sporting girls with sporting girls, you may be confident that it is good. Those are two classes of people who like to eat well and get their money's worth. If you see a priest eating with a layman, though, don't be too sure about the money's worth. The fellow *en civil* may be a rich parishioner, and the good Father won't worry about the price. And if the girl is with a man, you can't count on anything. It may be her kept man, in which case she won't care what she spends on him, or the man who is keeping her, in which case she won't care what he spends on her."

Failing the sure indications cited above, a good augury is the presence of French newspapermen.

The Restaurant des Beaux-Arts, where I did my early research, was across the street from the Ecole des Beaux-Arts, and not, in fact, precisely in my quarter, which was that of the university proper, a good half mile away, on the other side of the Boulevard Saint-Germain. It was a half mile that made as much difference as the border between France and Switzerland. The language was the same, but not the inhabitants. Along the Rue Bonaparte there were antiquarians, and in the streets leading off it there were practitioners of the ancillary arts—picture framers and bookbinders. The bookshops of the Rue Bonaparte, of which there were many, dealt in fine editions and rare books, instead of the used textbooks and works of erudition that predominated around the university. The students of the Beaux-Arts were only a small element of the population of the neighborhood, and they were a different breed from the students of the Boulevard Saint-Michel and its tributaries, such as the Rue de l'Ecole de Médecine, where I lived. They were older and seemingly in easier circumstances. I suspected them of commercial art and of helping Italians to forge antiques. Because there was more money about, and because the quarter had a larger proportion of adult, experienced eaters, it was better territory for restaurants than the immediate neighborhood of the Sorbonne. I had matriculated at the Faculté des Lettres and at the Ecole des Chartes, which forms medievalists, but since I had ceased attending classes after the first two weeks, I had no need to stick close to home. One of the chief joys of that academic year was that it was one long cut without fear of retribution.

I chanced upon the Restaurant des Beaux-Arts while strolling one noon and tried it because it looked neither chic nor sordid, and the prices on the menu were about right for me: *pâté maison*, 75 centimes; sardines, 1 franc; artichoke, 1.25; and so on. A legend over the door referred to the proprietor as a M. Teyssedre, but the heading of the bill of fare called him Balazuc. Which name represented a former proprietor and which the current one I never learned. I had a distaste for asking direct questions, a practice I considered ill-bred. This had handicapped me during my brief career as a reporter in Providence, Rhode Island, but not as much as you might think. Direct questions tighten a man up, and even if he answers, he will not tell you anything you have not asked him. What you want is to get him to tell you his story. After he has, you can ask clarifying questions, such as "How did you come to have the ax in your hand?" I had interrupted this journalistic grind after one year, at the suggestion of my father, a wise man. "You used to talk about wanting to go to Europe for a year of study," he said to me one spring day in 1926, when I was home in New York for a weekend. "You are getting so interested in what you are doing that if you don't go now you never will. You might even get married."

I sensed my father's generous intention, and, fearing that he might change his mind, I told him that I didn't feel I should go, since I was indeed thinking of getting married. "The girl is ten years older than I am," I said, "and Mother might think she is kind of fast, because she is being kept by a cotton broker from Memphis, Tennessee, who only comes North once in a while. But you are a man of the world, and you understand that a woman can't always help herself. Basically . . ." Within the week, I had a letter of credit on the Irving Trust for two thousand dollars, and a reservation on the old *Caronia* for late in the summer, when the off-season rates would be in effect. It was characteristic of my father that even while doing a remarkably generous thing he did not want to waste the difference between a full-season and an off-season passage on a one-class boat. (He never called a liner anything but a boat, and I always found it hard to do otherwise myself, until I stopped trying. "Boat" is an expression of affection, not disrespect; it is like calling a woman a girl. What may be ships in proportion to Oxford, where the dictionary is written, are boats in proportion to New York, where they nuzzle up to the bank to feed, like the waterfowl in Central Park.)

While I continued to work on the Providence paper until the rates changed, Father, with my mother and sister, embarked for Europe on a Holland-American boat—full-season rate and first class—so that my sister might take advantage of her summer holiday from school. I was to join them for a few days at the end of the summer, after which they would return to the United States and I would apply myself to my studies. Fortunately, I discovered that the titulary of a letter of credit can draw on it at the issuing bank as easily as abroad. By the time I sailed, I was eight hundred dollars into the letter, and after a week in Paris at a hotel off the Champs-Elysées I found, without astonishment, that I had spent more than half of the paternal fellowship that was intended to last me all year. The academic year would not begin until November, and I realized that I would be lucky to have anything at all by then. At this juncture, the cotton broker's girl came to my rescue in a vision, as an angel came to Constantine's. I telegraphed to my parents, who were at Lake Como, that I was on my way to join them. From my attitude when I got there— reserved, dignified, preoccupied—my father sensed that I was in trouble. The morning after my arrival, I proposed that we take a walk, just the two of us, by the lake. Soon we felt thirst, and we entered the trellised arbor of a hotel more modest than ours and ordered a bottle of rustic wine that recalled the stuff that Big Tony, my barber in Providence, used to manufacture in his yard on Federal Hill. Warmed by this homelike glow, I told my father that I had dilapidated his generous gift; I had dissipated in riotous living seventy-two per cent of the good man's unsolicited benefaction. Now there was only one honorable thing for me to do—go back to work, get married, and settle down. "She is so noble that she wouldn't tell me," I said, "but I'm afraid I left her in the lurch."

"God damn it," he said, "I knew I should never have given you that money in one piece. But I want you to continue your education. How much will you need every month?"

"Two hundred," I said, moderately. Later, I wished I had asked for fifty more; he might have gone for it. "You stay in Paris," he said—he knew I had chosen the Sorbonne—"and I'll have the Irving send you two hundred dollars every month. No more lump sums. When a young man gets tangled up with that kind of women, they can ruin his whole life."

That was how I came to be living in Paris that academic year in a financial situation that facilitated my researches. Looking back, I am sure my father knew that I wanted to stay on, and that there was no girl to worry about. But he also understood that I couldn't simply beg; for pride's sake, I had to offer a fake *quid pro quo* and pretend to myself that he believed me. He had a very good idea of the value of leisure, not having had any until it was too late to become accustomed to it, and a very good idea of the pleasure afforded by knowledge that has no commercial use, having never had time to acquire more than a few odd bits. His parents had brought him to America when he was eight years old; he went to work at ten, opened his own firm at twenty-one, started being rich at thirty, and died broke at sixty-five—a perfect Horatio Alger story, except that Alger never followed his heroes through. At the moment, though, he had the money, and he knew the best things it would buy.

The great day of each month, then, was the one when my draft arrived at the main office of the Crédit Lyonnais—the Irving's correspondent bank—on the Boulevard des Italiens. It was never even approximately certain what day the draft would get there; there was no air mail, and I could not be sure what ship it was on. The Crédit, on receiving the draft, would notify me, again by ordinary mail, and that would use up another day. After the second of the month, I would begin to be haunted by the notion that the funds might have arrived and that I could save a day by walking over and inquiring. Consequently, I walked a good many times across the river and the city from the Rue de l'Ecole de Médecine to the Boulevard des Italiens, via the Rue Bonaparte, where I would lunch at the Maison Teyssedre or Balazuc. There were long vertical black enamel plaques on either side of the restaurant door, bearing, in gold letters, such information as "Room for Parties," "Telephone," "Snails," "Specialty of Broils," and, most notably, "Renowned Cellar, Great Specialty of Wines of the Rhone." The Great Specialty dated back to the regime of a proprietor anteceding M. Teyssedre-Balazuc. This prehistoric *patron*, undoubtedly an immigrant from Languedoc or Provence, had set up a bridgehead in Paris for the wines of his region of origin.

The wines of the Rhone each have a decided individuality, viable even when taken in conjunction with *brandade de morue*—a delightful purée of salt codfish, olive oil, and crushed garlic—which is their compatriot. *Brandade*, according to Root, is "definitely not the sort of dish that is likely to be served at the Tour d'Argent." "Subtlety," that hackneyed wine word, is a cliché seldom employed in writing about Rhone wines; their appeal is totally unambiguous. The Maison Teyssedre-Balazuc had the whole gamut, beginning with a rough, faintly sour Côtes du Rhône— which means, I suppose, anything grown along that river as it runs its three-hundred-and-eighty-mile course through France. It continued with a Tavel and then a Tavel *supérieur*. The proprietor got his wines in barrel and bottled them in the Renowned Cellar; the plain Tavel came to the table in a bottle with a blue wax seal over the cork, the *supérieur* in a bottle with a purple seal. It cost two cents more a pint. I do not pretend to remember every price on the card of the Restaurant des Beaux-Arts, but one figure has remained graven in my heart like "Constantinople" in the dying Czar's. A half bottle of Tavel *supérieur* was 3.50; I can still see the figure when I close my eyes, written in purple ink on the cheap, grayish paper of the *carte*. This is a mnemonic testimonial to how good the wine was, and to how many times I struggled with my profligate tendencies at that particular point in the menu, arguing that the unqualified Tavel, which was very good, was quite good enough; two cents a day multiplied by thirty, I frequently told myself, mounted up to fifteen francs a month. I don't think I ever won the argument; my spendthrift palate carried the day. Tavel has a rose-cerise *robe*, like a number of well-known racing silks, but its taste is not thin or acidulous, as that of most of its mimics is. The taste is warm but dry, like an enthusiasm held under restraint, and there is a tantalizing suspicion of bitterness when the wine hits the top of the palate. With the second glass, the enthusiasm gains; with the third, it is overpowering. The effect is generous and calorific, stimulative of cerebration and the social instincts. "An apparently light but treacherous *rosé*," Root calls it, with a nuance of resentment that hints at some old misadventure.

Tavel is from a place of that name in Languedoc, just west of the Rhone. In 1926, there were in all France only two well-known wines that were neither red nor white. One was Tavel, and the other Arbois, from the Jura—and Arbois is not a rose-colored but an "onion-peel" wine, with russet and purple glints. In the late thirties, the *rosés* began to proliferate in wine regions where they had never been known before, as growers discovered how marketable they were, and to this day they continue to pop up like measles on the wine map. Most often *rosés* are made from red wine grapes, but the process is abbreviated by removing the liquid prematurely from contact with the grape skins. This saves time and trouble. The product is a semi-aborted red wine. Any normally white wine can be converted into a *rosé* simply by adding a dosage of red wine* or cochineal.

In 1926 and 1927, for example, I never heard of Anjou *rosé* wine, although I read wine cards every day and spent a week of purposeful drinking in Angers, a glorious white-wine city. Alsace is another famous white-wine country that now lends its name to countless cases of a pinkish cross between No-Cal and vinegar; if, in 1926, I had crossed the sacred threshold of Valentin Sorg's restaurant in Strasbourg and asked the sommelier for a *rosé d'Alsace*, he would have, quite properly, kicked me into Germany. The list is endless now; flipping the coated-paper pages of any dealer's brochure, you see *rosés* from Bordeaux, Burgundy, all the South of France, California, Chile, Algeria, and heaven knows where else. Pink champagne, colored by the same procedure, has existed for a century and was invented for the African and Anglo-Saxon trade. The "discovery" of the demand for pink wine approximately coincided with the repeal of prohibition in the United States. (The American housewife is susceptible to eye and color appeal.) In England, too, in the same period, a new class of wine buyer was rising with the social revolution. Pink worked its miracle there, and also in France itself, where many families previously limited to the cheapest kind of bulk wine were beginning to graduate to "nice things."

Logically, there is no reason any good white- or red-wine region should not produce equally good *rosé*, but in practice the proprietors of the good vineyards have no cause to change the nature of their wines; they can sell every drop they make. It is impossible to imagine a proprietor at Montrachet, or Chablis, or Pouilly, for example, tinting his wine to make a Bourgogne *rosé*. It is almost as hard to imagine it of a producer of first-rate Alsatian or Angevin wines. The wines converted to *rosé* in the great-wine provinces are therefore, I suspect, the worst ones—a suspicion confirmed by almost every experience I have had of them. As for the *rosés* from the cheap-wine provinces they are as bad as their coarse progenitors, but are presented in fancy bottles of untraditional form—a trick learned from the perfume industry. The bottles are generally decorated with art

---

* "Some [peasants] will give you a quick recipe for *rosé* which shall not pollute these pages."—The late Morton Shand's classic, *A Book of French Wines*, Jonathan Cape, Ltd., London, 1960 edition.

labels in the style of Robida's illustrations for Rabelais, and the wines are peddled at a price out of all proportion to their inconsiderable merits. There is also behind their gruesome spread the push of a report, put out by some French adman, that while white wine is to be served only with certain aliments, and red wine only with certain others, rosé "goes with everything," and so can be served without embarrassment by the inexperienced hostess. The truth is, of course, that if a wine isn't good it doesn't "go" with anything, and if it is it can go in any company.* Tavel though, is the good, the old, and, as far as I am concerned, still the only worthy rosé.**

At the Restaurant des Beaux-Arts, the Tavel *supérieur* was as high on the list as I would let my eyes ascend until I felt that the new money was on its way. When I had my first supersensory intimation of its approach, I began to think of the prizes higher on the card—Côte Rôtie, Châteauneuf-du-Pape, and white as well as red Hermitage, which cost from three to five francs more, by the half bottle, than my customary Purple Seal. Racing men like to say that a great horse usually has a great name—impressive and euphonious—and these three wines bear similar cachets. The Pope's new castle and the Hermitage evoke medieval pomp and piety, but the name Côte Rôtie—the hillside roasted in the sun—is the friendliest of the three, as is the wine, which has a cleaner taste than Châteauneuf and a warmer one than Hermitage. Châteauneuf often seems to be a wine that there is too much of to be true, and it varies damnably in all respects save alcoholic content, which is high. Red Hermitage is certainly distinguished; as its boosters like to say, of all Rhone wines it most resembles a great Burgundy, but perhaps for that reason it was hardest for a young man to understand. It was least like a *vin du Rhône*. As for the scarce white Hermitage, of which I haven't encountered a bottle in many years, it left a glorious but vague memory. Côte Rôtie was my darling. Drinking it, I fancied I could see that literally roasting but miraculously green hillside, popping with goodness, like the skin of a roasting duck, while little wine-colored devils chased little nymphs along its simmering rivulets of wine. (Thirty years later, I had a prolonged return match with Côte Rôtie, when I discovered it on the wine card of Prunier's, in London. I approached it with foreboding, as you return to a favorite author whom you haven't read for a long time, hoping that he will be as good as you

---

* Mr. Frank Schoonmaker, a writer on wine and a dealer in it who has done much to diffuse rosé in this country, wrote to me after the first appearance of this statement that I "surely wouldn't want to serve a good claret with sardines or a Montrachet with roast beef." To this I must answer that I wouldn't serve a Montrachet or any other good wine of *any* color with sardines, since they would make it taste like more sardines. Beer might be a better idea, or in its default, rosé, and I offer, without charge, the advertising slogan "Rosé, the perfect companion for fish oil."

** The eminent Shand, in 1960 (*A Book of French Wines*), wrote with more authority but no less bitterness of the Pink Plague: "Odd little rosés were belatedly exhumed from a more than provincial obscurity to set before clamorous foreign holiday parties; or if none such had ever existed steps were speedily taken to produce a native rosé."

remember. But I need have had no fear. Like Dickens, Côte Rôtie meets the test. It is no Rudyard Kipling in a bottle, making one suspect a defective memory or a defective cork.)

On days when I merely suspected money to be at the bank, I would continue from the Restaurant des Beaux-Arts to the Boulevard des Italiens by any variation of route that occurred to me, looking in the windows of the rare-book dealers for the sort of buy I could afford only once a month. Since on most of my trips I drew a blank at the Crédit Lyonnais, I had plenty of time for window-shopping and for inspection of the book-stalls on the quays. To this I attribute my possession of some of the best books I own—the *Moyen de Parvenir*, for example, printed at Chinon in the early seventeenth century, with the note on its title page: "New edition, corrected of divers faults that weren't there, and augmented by many others entirely new."

On the *good* day, when I had actually received the notification, I had to walk over again to collect, but this time I had a different stride. Simply from the way I carried myself when I left my hotel on the Rue de l'Ecole de Médecine, my landlord, M. Perès, knew that I would pay my bill that night, together with the six or seven hundred francs I invariably owed him for personal bites. He would tap cheerfully on the glass of the window that divided his well-heated office and living quarters from the less well-heated entrance hall, and wave an arm with the gesture that he had probably used to pull his company out of the trenches for a charge at Verdun. He was a *grand blessé* and a Chevalier of the Legion of Honor, *à titre militaire*, with a silver plate in his head that lessened his resistance to liquor, as he frequently reminded Madame when she bawled him out for drinking too much. "One little glass, and you see how I am!" he would say mournfully. In fact, he and I had usually had six each at the Taverne Soufflet, and he convived with other lodgers as well—notably with an Irishman named O'Hea, who worked in a bank, and a spend-thrift Korean, who kept a girl.

At the restaurant, I would drink Côte Rôtie, as I had premeditated, and would have one or two Armagnacs after lunch. After that, I was all business in my trajectory across Paris, pausing only nine or ten times to look at the water in the river, and two or three more to look at girls. At the Crédit, I would be received with scornful solemnity, like a suitor for the hand of a miser's daughter. I was made to sit on a bare wooden bench with other wretches come to claim money from the bank, all feeling more like culprits by the minute. A French bank, by the somber intensity of its addiction to money, establishes an emotional claim on funds in transit. The client feels in the moral position of a wayward mother who has left her babe on a doorstep and later comes back to claim it from the foster parents, who now consider it their own. I would be given a metal check with a number on it, and just as I had begun to doze off from the effects of a good lunch, the Côte Rôtie, the brisk walk, and the poor ventilation, a *huissier* who had played Harpagon in repertoire at Angers would shake me by the shoulder. I would advance toward a grille behind which another Harpagon, in an alpaca coat, held the draft, confident that he could riddle my pretensions to the identity I professed. Sometimes, by the ferocity of his distrust, he made me doubt who I was. I would stand fumbling in the wrong pocket for my *carte d'identité*, which had a knack of passing from one part of my apparel to another, like a prestidigitator's coin, and then for my passport, which on such occasions was equally elusive. The sneer on Harpagon's cuttlefish bone of a face would grow triumphant, and I expected him to push a button behind his grille that would summon a squad of detectives. At last, I would find my fugitive credentials and present them, and he would hand over the draft. Then he would send me back to the bench, a *huissier* would present me with another number, and it all had to be done over again—this time with my Kafka impersonation enacted before another Harpagon, at another grille, who would hand out the substantive money. Finally, with two hundred times twenty-six francs, minus a few deductions for official stamps, I would step out onto the Boulevard des Italiens—a once-a-month Monte Cristo. "Taxi!" I would cry. There was no need to walk back.

5 / La Nautique

Mens sana in corpore sano is a contradiction in terms, the fantasy of a Mr. Have-your-cake-and-eat-it. No sane man can afford to dispense with debilitating pleasures; no ascetic can be considered reliably sane. Hitler was the archetype of the abstemious man. When the other krauts saw him drink water in the Beer Hall they should have known he was not to be trusted.

I, once, at fifty-two, committed myself voluntarily to a slimming prison in Switzerland, but I was suffering from only temporary insanity. I soon repented, but I stayed in because I had paid two weeks' nonboard in advance, and I didn't want to forfeit the fee, which was rather more than four meals a day would have cost me at Pierre's on the Place Gaillon, each with a half-bottle of Corton Charlemagne, another of La Mission Haut-Brion, and three healthful drinks of Calvados to follow.

It was like a mental hospital where, as a result of a mutiny, the inmates had taken over from the staff, and now addressed one another as "Doctor." All the kind, fat, sensible people like me, who longed for something decent to eat, were under restraining orders, while the *soi-disant* doctors, who were free to eat normally, chose to drink rosehip tea and eat muck made of apple cores and wheat germ. They permitted us to eat only minuscular quantities of that. The nurses and therapists ate in the same ironically denominated *Speise-sal*, and except that they had larger portions than we, appeared to slop in identical slop. (Once, as a special reward for fortitude, I got three peeled hazelnuts.)

The only sane man on the place, aside from us, was the masseur, a big Swiss named Sprüdli.

"And thou, eat thou this crap?" I asked him in my imperfect but idiomatic German.

"No," said Sprüdli, as he plucked my biceps like harp strings and let them snap. "I need my strength. I eat to home."

"And what has thou to home yesterday evening eaten?"

"*Blutwurst*," he said, "and *Leberwurst*."

I wished I hadn't asked, but masochism feeds on itself, especially when there is nothing else to eat. I had an appetite for self-inflicted pain that since then has helped me understand the submissiveness of prisoners in concentration camps.

"And what has thou to home yesterday evening drunk?"

"*Wein*," he said, "*und Bier*."

He wrenched one of my knees out of joint, then put it back in the socket with the gesture of a man making a massé shot at billiards.

Tears of hunger and pain filled my eyes.

Sprüdli was, after all, like the majority of Swiss, a German. Once he knew my hurt, he made a point of telling me at each visit his menu for the previous day.

"Good morning," he would say. "Calves' hocks have I yesterday at lunch to home eaten, with potato dumplings, and to dinner spring chicken with another time dumplings." Then he would laugh, even before I winced, because he was so sure I would. Good old *Schadenfreude*.

When I had served my time in this ruinously expensive para-Buchenwald, I set out for Pontarlier, on the French side of the border, where I had friends I had not seen since the war. To get there I had to change trains at Bern. By the time I reached that city I had the flu, and when I got through the customs barrier on the station platform at Pontarlier I tottered into France and fell into my friends' four arms. I still weighed quite a lot. They bore me home in the Peugeot and put me to bed, where I shivered under eight or nine bankets. I knew I would recover when I heard, as through a deep fog, the voice of that good Doubsien doctor, who reeked congenially of kirsch and pipe tobacco.

"But the man has been starved!" he said. "His constitution has been mined! You must give him to eat—but do not commence brutally; he could not support it. A guinea hen or two the first day, and some brook trout."

"And wine?" asked my angelic hostess. "He can have wine? He adores it."

"He mustn't exaggerate," Hippocrates said. "No more than two litres a day, and nothing heavy—perhaps a Mercurey. If his pulse is low, a little *marc d'Arbois*. No *fondues* until tomorrow. Then we can begin feeding him up!"

I left Pontarlier, like Mother after her reducing tours long ago, pounds heavier than when I flew to Zurich to get weight off. This episode has remained unique in my life: it is the only time I yielded to the temptation to give myself pain. I found others harder to resist.

In 1926, though, I had another route to keeping my weight within bounds. I liked to box, and I had an illusion that if I boxed a lot, I could eat and drink a great deal and even stay up late with the girls. The exercise would burn all that out. I was too young to know that if you do those three things often you will feel with increasing infrequency like boxing, and boxing is no fun unless you feel like it. This is because boxing makes you want to eat, but eating does not make you want to box. I had not yet heard the great Sam Langford say: "You can sweat out beer and you can sweat out whiskey, but you can't sweat out women." Sam had never had to contend with my toughest opponent of all, sheer gluttony.

At thirteen, when my Uncle Mike from San Francisco inducted me into the rudiments of the dulcet art, I was not a drinking man or a rake. Later, at college and even in Providence, temptation had been sparse. On the *Journal* I worked a night shift for forty dollars a week. That meant I got a full sleep after work and ate plainly. Most days I hit the YMCA gym about noon and sparred a few rounds or jogged a couple of miles before going into the newspaper office. I weighed between 160 and 170 pounds. In Paris my only exercise was walking. For a while that was enough, and then I began to feel guilty. Ralph Henry Barbour and G. A. Henty were among the moralists in my background; they had succeeded George Washington. The heroes of their screeds were constantly in hard physical condition so they could play left end or undertake dangerous missions behind enemy lines. No overlay of Rabelais or Stendhal could eradicate their depraved influence.

Uncle Mike, my mother's slightly younger brother, was not one of the relatives who had "done well." He had a pinched, Cruikshank kind of face that had remained small while the jowl grew and solidified around it, until it looked like a small print in a large mat. The character he had chosen for himself—the hot sport of 1900—likewise became set in the fat of respectability as he settled down. He should have been a vaudeville actor or a confidence man, but both his sisters had married good providers, and he had formed the bad habit of working for relations.

Mike was therefore a disappointment to his kin, but he was an inspiring pedagogue. The academic life might have suited him, now that I think of it, but he had not pursued Minerva beyond the portals of Lowell High School, preferring to scuttle down an alley in pursuit of burlesque girls. The object of boxing, Mike made clear from the first, was not self-defense. It was pleasure, like ocean swimming.

You do not go into the ocean to defend yourself from drowning. Indeed, the chances are slightly greater that you will drown if you go in than if you don't. Neither do you box to save yourself from getting a black eye.

The satisfactions outweigh the risks. Boxing is more social than swimming or poetry, because it is a dialogue. An infelicitous line invokes a disastrous rhyme.

I was an awkward child, fat from sitting still and reading, and had to learn all from the beginning, even to keeping my eyes open when popped on the nose. I talked learnedly about the names on the sports page, indeed, and when Mike asked me if I could box, I answered with assurance that I could, But I then stood up with my right hand forward and my feet close together. It was a moment of humiliation, but a good place to start from. I knew nothing at all. Mike taught me to stand, to move, to hit, always in the short line, but most important, the theme of boxing, which is, as in chess, annihilation.

Defense is either a preliminary to attack or an interlude between attacks. You move to beat the other fellow, not to avoid being beaten. Safety, relative though it be, lies in attack, too. You are safer inside a punch—which means inside its arc—than stepping away from it, and possibly into its sweep.

More, if you are inside a punch you are in position to strike, but if you are outside it, you have merely escaped. This is the simple essence. Whatever other inferences may be drawn from it are optional and incidental.

Mike taught me, I am sure, less than he knew, but everything he gave me was right, or within good arguing distance thereof. To hunch the left shoulder over the jaw, for example, does not suit all styles, but he said it was Jim Jeffries' way. To half-rotate the arm while jabbing is considered by some purists an affectation, but Mike said it was Kid McCoy's corkscrew, and that made its appeal to me irresistible. He had the marks of California's Golden Age clear on his style. The Californians were like their contemporaries the Impressionists, graceful, direct, and full of light.

What charmed me more than anything was the craftily circumventional trick Mike taught me of catching the other fellow's best hand under your armpit and swinging him off balance, meanwhile punching away.

"Holding with one hand and hitting with the other is a foul," Mike explained, "but if the guy gets his glove caught under your armpit, how can you help it? And if you accidentally hit a guy in the mouth with the top of your head, bring your head up again to say you're sorry. If you are lucky you might catch him in the same place." This made me feel wise as well as brave.

My wisdom redounded to my disadvantage once during that soft Paris year, when I was boxing with a young Mormon missionary at the American Baptist Center gym on the Rue Denfert-Rochereau. We both had our heads down and brought them up simultaneously. He must have had another Uncle Mike. The right side of his head hit the right side of mine. We split each other's right eyelids, from brow to lash, neatly and identically. The blood ran as from two faucets; there was no pain, but the mess was ridiculous. Amateur first aid was hopeless. It would have posed a problem to a professional cut man like Whitey Bimstein. So we set out just as we were, in sweat shirts and gym pants, and ran to a hospital on the Avenue de l'Observatoire, not far away. We left a bloody trail as we jogged.

The Mormon was at the Sorbonne taking a course in French culture so he could convert a better class of people. He looked a real Joe College, with slicked blond hair, but was a nice enough kid. By now he must be a bishop.

We had a great reception at the hospital, where nurses and interns found us *rigolo*—victims of our passion for healthful exercise. There a resident closed the long vertical cut in my lid with small metal clamps, which he put in with an instrument like a stapler. It was too near the eye for sutures, he said, and the stapler was quicker and less painful. An old doctor at Cherbourg took the last dressing off several weeks later and left the clamps in. His theory was perhaps that they would dissolve. The skin in time grew over them, and the hair-thin white line, gravelly to the touch, is the nearest thing that I have to a dueling scar by which to remember my university days. It is also the nearest thing I have to a mining claim; grains of metal have continued through the years to work their way up to the surface, and I sometimes suspect that they breed or multiply by parturition.

My appearance when I returned to the Hotel Saint-Pierre kept M. Perès in laughs for a month.

That was the most animated episode of my athletic life in Paris. I had found the Center through a two-line ad in the Paris *Herald*. It had a small gymnasium with a basketball court and showers, but they were in use by French Baptist children most of the week. There may have been a school there as well as a church. I was not nosy.

For a minute fee, we non-Baptists were allowed to work out on Wednesday afternoons, and it was a bargain, because if you lived at a hotel you had to pay each time you took a bath. The weekly shower alone amortized your dues at the Center. Some of the odd lot who turned up made do with that one a week. Some played basketball or volleyball, but I was the only Centrist keen on boxing. I owned the only gloves, and my efforts to proselyte were viewed with suspicion.

A few of the young painters and students were athletic, but putting on gloves intimidated them and they froze. There is no fun in boxing with a nonboxer: you feel silly hitting him, and then, when you let down, he catches you an awkward blow that hurts, and you have to say "Good man!" when you want to murder him. I have read in numerous reminiscences since of the American Artists' Club, on the Boulevard Raspail, where literary figures like Hemingway and Morley Callaghan and Bob Coates beat each other's brains out constantly, but I never found that one. Raspail was far off my beat, and I don't suppose they would have boxed with anybody who hadn't published. The only American writer who used the Center was Joe Gollomb, a hairy, heavy-set, kindly man who ground out whodunits. He was thirty-eight, and I could not conceal my incredulity when he told me that he still had a sex life. There was also a thin, prim young man from Kansas named Harold Callender, who was a correspondent for *The New York Sunday Times Magazine*. He would not, I remember, take a drink, and would cause me embarrassment by sitting with us in a café and asking for a glass of water. When I last saw him, a few years ago, he was chief of the *Times* bureau in Paris and a reformed character. He bought me a splendid lunch and drank almost as much as I did.

When we had finished our moderate Wednesday exertions—mine grew more moderate by the week—three or four of us would walk together as far as the nearest café. Rue Denfert-Rochereau runs from the Lion de Belfort to a confluence with Avenue de l'Observatoire, which arrives almost instantly thereafter at the juncture of the Boulevards Montparnasse and Saint-Michel. (Avenue de l'Observatoire is, except for its name, a continuation of Saint-Michel—or Saint-Michel of Observatoire, if you start at the other end.) Denfert-Rochereau was an austere street with several convents, but no bars. So we had to walk to the junction of the boulevards for our drink, at the Closerie des Lilas. All of us had to walk that far together anyway, before our paths diverged.

By then it would be time for the *apéritif*, and we would all feel virtuous because we had performed the clean-life equivalent of attendance at mass. We had made our peace, for the week, with Ralph Henry Barbour.

We would knock off a couple of vermouths cassis, and then my acquaintances would turn off west along Montparnasse to join the other Americans, while I would turn down Saint-Michel alone, firm in my resolve to live the life of the French. I did not, of course, but I lived with them and among them, and among other assorted foreigners of the Quarter.

I liked the sensation of immersion in a foreign element, as if floating in a summer sea, only my face out of water, and a pleasant buzzing in my ears. I was often alone, but seldom lonely; I enjoyed the newspapers and books that were my usual companions at table, the exchanges with waiters, barmen, booksellers, street vendors, the old voices of the old professors in the lectures I irregularly attended, the sounds of the conversations of others around me, and finally, the talk of the girls I ended some evenings by picking up. This isolation dispensed me from defending my whims.

I was free to attend the operetta theaters, like the Mogador and Gaîté-Lyrique, without fear of being called corny, or the Grand-Guignol without being reminded that it was *démodé*. One of the delights of Paris then was that several theatrical pasts coexisted with the present; one was not limited to a choice of contemporary or classic theater. Besides Romains and Giraudoux at the Théâtre des Champs-Elysées, and Molière and Racine at the State Theaters, there were constantly on tap the operettists of the early Third Republic, the bedroom farces and the Guignol of before the 1914 War, the classic clowns of the Cirque Medrano. Each had its public, and only segments of the public overlapped. That of the operettists consisted of nostalgics and provincials, proper old couples and their grandchildren come to celebrate their name-days. But seeing and hearing each of these theatrical modes for the first time and without preconception, I got the same lift out of *Les Cloches de Corneville*, let us say, as had Planquette's first audience in 1877, when it was as new as *No, No, Nanette* in 1927. The French circus burst on my vision as freshly as on that of Toulouse-Lautrec twenty-five years earlier. I was to recognize it later in the drawings that when I discovered the *cirque* I had not seen. The bedroom situations of the Théâtre du Palais-Royal struck me as of the utmost originality, and the surviving *chansonniers* in the manner of Aristide Bruant delighted me—I did not have the advantage of possessing friends *à la page* who could have told me they had gone out.

I remember the tender reverence with which I heard Xavier Privas, the *Roi des Chansonniers*, a beautiful old man with a white spade beard, intone, at the tiny Théâtre des Noctambules in the Quarter:

"Pour qui sait aimer, les heures sont roses. . . ."

Pour qui savait some other infinitive, the hours were some other color. I forget what colors went with what particular hours, except for the *aimer-rose* link, but he ran through the spectrum: *penser, mourir, attendre; grises, blanches*, and perhaps *chartreuses*. I thought Privas had written the air as well as the lyrics, and it was not until long afterward that I learned it was the most hackneyed Brahms "Lullaby."

The Noctambules was a hall with a platform at one end and a bar at the other. It was in the Rue Champollion, an alley two blocks long bearing the name of the man who deciphered the Rosetta Stone. Champollion covertly paralleled the Boulevard Saint-Michel, sneaking like an assassin behind the Boul's back from the Rue des Facultés as far as the Rue Cujas, named for an illustrious jurist of the sixteenth century. The names of the streets of the Latin Quarter are designed to facilitate the acquisition of culture, like the noodles in alphabet soup. Gypsy's Bar, of which more hereafter, stood at the Cuja end of Champollion, and midway in the alley there was the Hotel Champollion, where the *séjours*, like an analyst's sessions, lasted fifty minutes, which permitted the couples to leave before they had to pay for another hour.

Besides Privas, the apostle of the noble and pathetic, I heard at the Noctambules an old rascal named Georges Polin, who did a number in an ill-fitting French uniform of the red-pants era before 1914—the sort that

must have looked so odd on the fastidious conscript Proust. Polin's material was drawn from Courteline, bespattered with latrine humor. His
stage character was the clodhopping conscript, slyly stupid, lecherous, and
confident, even after he had been had, that he had had the other fellow. It
was clear that it was old, older than the red pantaloons of the costume. It
had become so familiar to the great public that he could find no bookings
in larger theaters, but like a *cassoulet* long on the stove, it was better than
ever. Here, before the students who had never seen him in his glory, he
was irresistible, like those potpourris of cuttings from silent film comedies
that convulse present audiences. So I enjoyed not only what amused my
Paris, but what had amused several earlier ones.

This living retrospective of the theater is something New York has
never provided, except for films. The New York theater has always
rejected the past, although with the slimmest imaginable justification,
to judge from its output season by season. Paris was then a city of
constant artistic innovation—of which I was unconscious, and if I hadn't
been, would have been distrustful. But there was a past *concurrent* with
the present. This is more nourishing than revivals, which tend to be arch
and patronizing. Polin's bulbous red *trogne* with the pendulous upper lip
and Privas' pretentious profile belong to the nineties, but I remember them
as well as Maurice Chevalier and his wife of my era, Yvonne Vallée,
framed in the spotlight of prime success at the Casino de Paris, singing
"Leendy, Leendy, sweet as the shoogar can," and "Valentine." "Valentine,"
incidentally, is the ten thousandth version of *La Belle Heaulmière*. "*Elle
avait*, etc.," *Mais où sont les et cetera de 1926?*

In the affairs of the ring there was the same place reserved for age.
Georges Carpentier was all through—you couldn't have got him a match
in the United States in 1926–7 if you were Al Capone—but I saw him box
an exhibition at the Salle Wagram with a mulatto named Jack Walker,
and the exhibition topped a card of in-earnest bouts. From having seen
him work the four rounds, without pressure, I can remember, and testify,
that he had a fluent, beautiful style, with extremely fast reflexes—he
seemed to be pouring into his man, like a curving stream, the blows
winding around elbows and under arms and slipping like eels into the
great breadbasket sea, then leaping like salmon across the dropped shoulder to the chin. I could see what he must have been when he still could
take a punch. I have never thought since that the great American fighters
he met before World War I carried him—he must have been a bit of a
phenomenon, as a middleweight. Dempsey was a stream, too, but like a
jet out of a fire hose, a straight-at-you flattener. I think Carpentier at his
best would have been harder to elude although less instantly fatal. Of
course he never was very big.

Walker, his foil at the Wagram, was a magnificently made light-
heavyweight, who moved well in a style rather like Carpentier's—after

all, the latter had set a fashion for the boxing generation that followed him. But Walker, I have heard since, lacked heart; he was a sparrer rather than a fighter.

The Carpentier style produced patterns that Dunoyer de Ségonzac caught in line drawings of a grace unequaled by any other draftsman of the ring. A hundred years after Thomas Rowlandson's "Cribb and Molyneux," Ségonzac made his fighters move like fighters. There was nobody in between. The lugs in "A Stag at Sharkey's" are just pushing. Bellows painted fights the way Jack London wrote about them. Thomas Eakins, though he did fine ring scenes, never showed his fighters in motion—one would be down, as in "Taking the Count," or both in their corners, or about to enter the ring.

The French style then coming in was the antithesis of Carpentier's—it was constricted, sly, and almost surly. The boxer, leaning slightly forward, walked in with elbows high and forward, the line from elbow to fist almost vertical. He conducted his operations from this cage, usually offering the top of his head as part of his defense. It was a style set, I believe, by an old-timer named Professor Fernand Cuny, who coached the French Olympic team. The new French fighters were beginning to come out of the amateurs instead of directly from the back alleys.

One of the toughest was Edouard Mascart, a knotty featherweight who on the night of January 25, 1927—a date I have verified from the *Ring Record Book*—took on Panama Al Brown at the Cirque d'Hiver, a building designed, as its name indicates, to house an indoor circus. It was high, because it featured aerial acts, and narrow, because real estate was valuable, and I remember that I climbed hundreds of meters of stairs to attain a height from which I looked down at the fighters' heads and shoulders. Brown was an oddity in more ways than one—he was five feet eleven inches tall and could make 112 pounds ringside. Withal he was a remarkably good boxer, one of those self-taught artists, like Kid Chocolate from Havana, who came out of the Caribbees letter perfect, as if they had, in one adolescence, invented for themselves all the developments of the last fifty years. He had first shown in New York in 1923 and gone almost three years without losing. He had then begun to take on heavier men, and good ones, and he lost several decisions. (There were rumors that in some of these bouts he was handcuffed by agreements he had to make in order to get work.) When he turned up in Paris he allowed his weight to rise to 118, and the extra six pounds endowed him with a punch like a welterweight. He was black, skinny, and had a long, pointed head. Two thirds of his length was legs, and he had long arms swinging from shoulders like a crossbeam. His torso was so narrow that his heart had standing room only. Mascart was ten pounds heavier and eight inches shorter.

It was not an epic battle. Mascart advanced behind the top of his head surrounded by the cage, but when he pulled a bar out of the cage to strike, Brown would insert a long left into the vacancy left by the displacement. Mascart would stagger back across the ring, amid the mad clamors of the crowd, astonished that he held his feet.

"*Il tient! Il tient!*" they chorused. "He stays, he resists!"

And "*Vas-y,* Mascart!"—"Hop to it."

He would put his head down and rush again, and this time Brown would pull him in with the left and uppercut with the right, lifting him off his feet. It was murder; Mascart might as well have been fighting a power mower with his face. The weight advantage, his lower center of gravity, and the constitution of an ox prolonged his suffering. It was one of the fanciest beatings I ever saw a man take, and the crowd cheered throughout, not because he was winning, but because Brown didn't knock him out.

"*Il tient, il tient, il tient encore!*"

It was one of those situations that stay graven on the mind. Always now, when things are going wrong one after another, I rally myself with the cry "*Il tient!*"

In the fifth round *pouvait pas plus*—Brown hit him an uppercut that sedated him completely. When disaster starts throwing combinations, fortitude will not suffice. Yet, had Mascart held a moment longer, fate might have intervened. Hardly had the Frenchman subsided flat on his back when the admiring shouts changed to screams of vituperation against Brown. Everybody in the balconies threw something, and one *deus ex galleria* hit Brown with an apple, right on the point of his head. Panama Al's seconds led him to his corner, as deep in dreams as his victim. The moral, I suppose, is: Never despair; perhaps God will throw an apple.

Had I had a companion in my wanderings, his reactions would have differed from mine and perhaps spoiled them. The matter of how much discomfort a man is prepared to undergo for an experience depends on how much it is worth to him. The best of friends can seldom agree on the price. (This is true even of a price in money.) Excursions are likely to become compromises, gratifying the full taste of neither. The man who pokes around alone may take a wrong turning at the junction of two streets and return from his ramble disappointed, but never recriminative. He has nobody to blame for his mistake. This is also a superiority of boxing over, say, bridge or football. There is no colleague to throw off on.

Granted that in later life a man will have to learn to get along with other people—I learn with horror that the knack is now taught in high school as a "social study"—that is all the more reason there should be a period in his life when he has to get along with nobody but himself. It will be a sweetness to remember.

I was not entirely a free particle in Paris, however, without touch with a French heart or *droite d'entrée* to a hearth. There was a family where I had the quality of an almost-relative. Monsieur and Madame, with their children, Suzette, seventeen, and Jean-Paul, fifteen, inhabited a vast apartment on the Avenue de la Motte-Picquet, near the Champ de Mars.

I had known them since my childhood, because they had lived near us on Long Island in what was then a fairly far-out but is now a very near-in suburb of New York. Monsieur had been sent to America before the 1914 War as sales manager for a great French silk mill. He had returned to fight, leaving Madame in what she considered straitened circumstances, and she had then given French lessons to the local ladies. My mother had been her star pupil. Suzette had gone to school with my sister. After the war Monsieur had returned, half-ill from the effects of gas. We had become friends, despite the difference in age. He was full of a suppressed Bohemianism, of the vintage of 1900. He looked like Don Quixote, as tall as de Gaulle, with a long drooping mustache *en grenadier*.

In 1925 he had been called back to France to a very good place in the old firm. For him America had been a place of Bithynian exile, but for Madame, to hear her talk after she got back, it had been a giddy whirl, an exotic paradise. Happiness, for her, was always some place where she used to be. One disaster, from Madame's point of view, was that they were again within the orbit of Monsieur's mother, who according to Madame had always favored his two brothers since Monsieur had married her. On the surface, though, all was smooth—the family was reunited, and, since Monsieur was prosperous, his mother could not bully him. Monsieur liked me because we had felt ourselves castaways in suburbia, and Madame loved me as a visible symbol of that glorious world in which she convinced herself she had recently existed. As a matter of fact, she had been most unhappy there. It was through Monsieur that I joined La Société Nautique de la Marne, one of the two chief rowing clubs of the region. It was my last gesture of appeasement toward Ralph Henry Barbour and *Mens sana*.

The coach, a M. Parisot, was my direct sponsor, in spite of the fact I never saw him before I became a *sociétaire*. For years he had been chief clerk of an importing house in the Cité Bergère, one of the partners in which was one of the brothers of Monsieur. The brother, who first talked to Parisot about my *adhésion* to La Nautique, informed Monsieur, who informed me, that Parisot had been knocked in the eye at the prospect of having an American oarsman for the objective race of the season—against La Nautique's rival, the Rowing Club de la Seine.

Two years before, M. Parisot had witnessed the triumph of Yahlé, the American crew at the Olympics of 1924, and he expected to see a Yahlé type of oarsman when I reported at the clubhouse of La Nautique on the following Sunday. He was not completely disappointed in me. I wasn't as big as a varsity oarsman, but I was a lot bigger than most of the other *sociétaires*. His first deception, as he expressed it, came when I told him I had never rowed in my life, even in a skiff. He was of the opinion, however, that with application I would be able to figure in the debutant eight of the Nautique on the day of the great race and that in another summer I might be ripe for the senior boat. M. Parisot was a ruddy little man with a bristly black-and-gray mustache, a deep voice, and an air of command, which he had acquired in early life when he had been a coxswain. He was a Southerner, I believe, and on Sundays always wore a steamer cap pulled down over his eyes and a gray turtleneck sweater, to indicate the completeness of his release from sedate importing-office ways. M. Parisot, as *barreur*, which is French for cox, had once directed the unsuccessful activities of a French crew at Henley.

"It wasn't because of more savant manipulation of the oar that they beat us," he informed me on that first morning of our acquaintance, "but because of a superiority of brute force. They were horses, my lad."

The Société Nautique de la Marne had its seat at Joinville-le-Pont, which is a little suburban town that you reached from the Gare de Vincennes. The Société occupied an island in the Marne, accessible by a stairway from the stone bridge that gives Joinville-le-Pont its name. One of the first things I noticed about the Marne was that there did not seem to be much water in it. What water there was appeared to be full of long green weeds, and I wondered how I would ever be able to pull an oar through them. This problem turned out to have no importance.

Before inducting me into the mysteries of the sweep, M. Parisot said (I had sought him out as soon as I arrived on the island) it would be his pleasure to present me to my fellow *sociétaires* and, he hoped, my team-mates of the future. When the presentations were finished it was time for dinner. I learned from a young man named Morin, to whom I had been presented, that the crews of the Société practiced only on Sundays when the weather was pleasant; there was consequently no time to waste on elaborate dinners. The *sociétaires* did not insist upon formalities, what the devil, one wasn't *chez* Foyot, what? So we had, as hors d'oeuvre, only a crock of duck *pâté*, a crock of *pâté* of hare, a few tins of sardines, muzzle of beef, radishes, and butter. Morin, who sat next to me, was almost abjectly apologetic. Two little girls in pigtails served the dinner. They were the daughters of the caretaker. He was not the best of caretakers, Morin said, but his wife, the little girls' mother, was an excellent cook. Morin was a handsome fellow and wore a royal-blue sweater with the arms knotted negligently around his neck even while he ate. The colors of the Société were blue and white. After the hors d'oeuvre we had a potato soup, then a *buisson de goujons*, a mound of tiny fried fish, for each of the *sociétaires*. After that, a leg of mutton with roast potatoes, a salad, cheese, and fruit. Red and white wine were there to take *à discretion*, and most of the *sociétaires* had a brandy with their coffee as a digestive.

Naturally, one did not attempt violent exercise after such a meal. It would not be healthy, M. Parisot explained. A group of us took a stroll about the island. A *sociétaire* named Leclerc, the *chef de nage*, or stroke, of the senior eight, said that he didn't think he'd row that afternoon.

"What the devil!" he said. "One works hard all week. Why sweat when you don't have to?"

We interrupted our walk to watch the shell of the Femina Sports, a women's athletic club which also went in for rowing. The shell was being towed upstream by a motorboat. The girls sat with their feet on the gunwales in order not to wet their slippers; their thighs were ravishing. I still remember the girl who sat at bow. She wore her hair, which was ash-blond, in a high mound on top of her head, and she had long earrings. When the girls got about a quarter of a mile above the island they decided not to row anyway, so the motorboat towed them back to their own float, a bit farther downstream. We of the Nautique were disappointed.

Toward half past four M. Parisot suggested that I essay the club's rowing machine. I planked myself down on the sliding seat. It was on a float on the side of the island away from Joinville. The motion of the float, it was explained to me, would partially accustom the beginner to the swell of the river. I seized the dummy sweep, and M. Parisot, pausing frequently lest I break into perspiration—the weather was as yet a trifle raw—began to impart to me that *savant* stroke of the oar which had discomfited the Rowing Club de la Seine on innumerable occasions. "Lengthen out," he adjured me. "Lengthen out. All the way back until you regard the types who pass on the bridge!" Since the float was fairly close to the bridge, I had to lie back until my head almost touched the float in order to regard the pedestrians. This was at the bottom of my stroke. It is known technically, I learned afterward, as a long layback. I performed the *savant* stroke of the oar several times to M. Parisot's satisfaction. Then he began to notice an unusually long pause at the end of the layback. A girl was crossing the bridge who I thought looked as if she might be the bow oar of the Femina Sports. She was walking with a soldier from the school for army physical instructors at Joinville, and I could not help watching them.

M. Parisot decided I was tired. "Rest," he said. "It is sufficient for the first day."

On the next Sunday it rained. I telephoned to the clubhouse. One of the caretaker's little girls informed me that there would be no practice. "*Crotte!*" she said. "It isn't worth the trouble to come. It's a pity, because *Maman* had bought three fine suckling pigs."

The races, debutant and senior, against the Rowing Club de la Seine were to take place on July 14. It was only mid-April then, but I began to count the intervening Sundays: not more than twelve! Allowing for a certain amount of rain, we would have time for not more than ten practices, probably. According to American standards, I thought, this would be hardly enough. On the third Sunday I reported to the clubhouse early, in time for an *apéritif* before dinner.

"Today," M. Parisot said, "if you indicate sufficient progress, we launch you on the river. In a yawl for two—there's no place in the debutant eight, unfortunately. You will have Poirier as your comrade."

He presented Poirier. I can see him still—a pale, long-legged boy of about eighteen, with lank blond hair combed straight back. We shook hands like men about to embark on a desperate adventure. I wondered if Poirier could swim.

In turn we performed our exercises on the rowing machine for M. Parisot. He expressed himself as satisfied. The sky clouded over and a few drops of water fell.

"*Attendez!*" said M. Parisot. "You can take an *apéritif en attendant.*"

He held up a finger to the wind and looked dubiously at the Marne, which stretched at least ten yards from the island to the right bank. Fifteen minutes later, as Poirier and I sat in the clubhouse over two vermouths cassis, M. Parisot entered.

"The river is too turbulent, my boys," he said. "Another time, what the devil! Drownings, you know—that does a rowing club no good. Better luck the next time."

I rode back to Paris with Poirier in third class. Poirier was a nice fellow, an apprentice ironworker. At the Gare we had another vermouth cassis and parted with a promise to brave the Marne together next Sunday, come what might. The next Sunday it rained. The one after that was Easter and I wanted to spend it with friends in Neuilly. On the Sunday after Easter I suffered from *la gueule de bois*, which is French for hangover. A week later I decided that it was no use going out to Joinville because I had probably lost my form. That was the end of the athletic phase of my *vie parisienne*.

6 / The Modest Threshold

IN 1927, when I was on the Left Bank of the Seine learning to eat, Root, whom I did not then know, was champing his way through his own delightful and necessary apprenticeship on the opposite side of the river. (I use the verb "to eat" here to denote a selective activity, as opposed to the passive acceptance and regular renewal of nourishment, learned in infancy. An automobile receiving fuel at a filling station or an infant at the breast cannot be said to eat, nor can a number of people at any time in their lives.)

Root (we have since compared notes) was twenty-four—a year or so my senior—and was a copyreader on the Paris edition of the Chicago *Tribune*, a daily later merged with the New York *Herald Tribune*'s Paris *Herald*. It astonished many that the Chicago *Tribune*, with its phobia about foreign entanglements, should maintain a Paris affiliate. The immortal Colonel Robert R. McCormick, the parent *Tribune*'s publisher, had divided feelings about this himself, and he satisfied his conscience by keeping the Paris by-blow on the stingiest footing possible. Most of the American employees were stranded expatriates, who came cheap, because they were always in oversupply while prohibition lasted.

The future author of *The Food of France* was earning fifteen dollars a week, which then worked out to about four hundred francs—considerably less than the grant-in-aid I was receiving from my father for doing nothing, or next to it. Being obliged to work six nights a week, Root had less opportunity to spend money; because he was paid fortnightly, he had a maximum of one night every two weeks when he wasn't broke. The gastronomic secondary school that he attended was a small café kept by a couple named Gillotte in back of the printing plant that Colonel McCormick's least favorite child shared with a French newspaper.

The Gillottes offered the indispensable advantage of credit, which made up for a lack of variety in their menu. What there was was good, though, Root says now—"They would give you a good honest *gigot* with *haricots blancs* for almost nothing, which was what we could afford to pay." On his one flush night off, he would stop by the Gillottes' to pay his tab and have one on the house, but he would not stay to dine. He could afford more advanced instruction then. On the other nights, in the intervals between writing heads on cable stories, he would think of his menu for the magic evening, revising it five or six times, so that he had considerable pleasure even out of the dishes he decided not to order. So the bibliophile steals pleasure from a catalogue, the lover from his fantasies.

The cable news served up to Americans in Paris in 1927, as I remember it, consisted—apart from the inevitable sports results—of cheap shootings in Chicago, Jimmy Walker's didos in New York, and the grim, persistent efforts of the press to read humorous profundity into Calvin Coolidge's dim silence. Confinement with these items made Root understandably reckless; sometimes he and whatever colleagues were free on the one great night would venture higher than I ever dared—to Lapérouse, where, according to my bedside book, the *Guide du Gourmand à Paris* (1925 edition), the average price of a meal was thirty-five francs, or a dollar thirty-five.

The franc fluctuated, and the *Guide* was always a bit optimistic about the price you could get away for, even "without doing anything lavish." Actually, a meal at Lapérouse was likely to cost at least two dollars. For that I could get a slap-up dinner for myself *and* a girl at the Taverne Soufflet, on the Boulevard Saint-Michel. But since I had all my evenings free, I had to spread the money around.

Root's judgment is independent and frequently sound, but when he holds, in *The Food of France*, that Lapérouse is still out of the ordinary, I think it is a case of his memory's clouding his comprehension of the present. When I was there last, not even the *oeufs en gelée* were a success; the yolks were hard, inside a casing of aspic without flavor, although a proper *oeuf en gelée*, runny *à l'intérieur* and savory, is within the competence of any respectable charcutier. And the matelote of eels was not as good as you'd get in any Sunday fishermen's tavern along a riverside; in depressing fact, it was bad. There are certain simple and unavoidably cheap dishes that are the I-beams of French cookery and are not to be tampered with; wine and eels and bacon and onions and herbs and judgment go into a matelote, and the eels should be fresh. The wine can be as old as you please. Within these classic limits, as within the rules of a game, there are gradations of success, dependent on the quality and proportion of the ingredients and on the thermotactic gift, since no two stews reach their nearest approach to perfection in the same number of minutes—or, to be meticulous, of seconds. The good cook, like the good jockey, must have "a clock in his head."

Failure in rudimentary things is typical of large restaurants now, in France as well as here. The reason is the happy improvement in the human economic condition; it is harder every year to recruit boys of superior, or even of subnormal, intelligence for the long, hard, dirty apprenticeship, at nominal pay—or none, in the early years—that makes a cook. Nowadays, a boy is likely to spend those years in school and go directly into a factory or office job that pays better than the kitchen. The apprentices became journeyman cooks, rising through the echelons. Without these, it is impossible to staff a large kitchen properly. A *saucier* now, if under forty, is likely to be a fellow who has learned, *en vitesse*, to make a few sauces. (If he is over forty and still a *saucier*, he is probably a drunk.) The fish cook who has learned as hastily and then practiced may be able to fillet a sole, but neither can do the other's work, or anyone else's, because neither is a rounded artisan, which is a necessary preliminary to bucking for artist. (There is a saying that, by exception, one is born a *rôtisseur*, but I should hate to entrust a guinea hen to a baby.) Nobody learns to boil an egg or watch a pot nowadays, because that isn't anybody's job in particular. Needless to say, none of these assembly-line cooks would ever be able to run a kitchen, but that is not yet the critical problem; the fellow at the top of the heap in a large French restaurant may even today be a great man, since the chances are that he started his apprenticeship forty years ago. But he cannot do all the cooking, and the effectiveness of supervision is limited by the capacity of those exposed to it. He is like a choreographer without executants, an Omar Bradley without officers of field or company grade.

In 1948, Gaston Magrin, then commodore-chef of the French Line and on the point of retirement, told me that if he were to open a restaurant it would have fifty seats at most, because that was the maximum number of clients one man could "responsibly" care for. Since then, the situation has deteriorated; there are even fewer experienced and dependable *sous-chefs* to be had. The small restaurants where a talented owner and his wife have direct control of the kitchen produce the best food in France now, though in most cases it is far from cheap. (The "good little holes where you eat well for nothing" have vanished, like the stately restaurants where you ate superbly for a fortune.) In such families, the proprietor is sometimes aided by his progeny; the children have an inducement to learn the profession the hard way, because they hope to inherit a profitable business. The impetus seldom lasts more than one generation, though; the children never resist the temptation to expand and spoil the joint.

Not all Root's nights of glory were spent in spheres as exalted as Lapérouse; sometimes, he tells me, he would dine in small restaurants that are now defunct or that he can no longer find. The small restaurant is evanescent. Sometimes it has the life span of a man, sometimes of a fruit fly. In these lost Atlantises, Root and his friends would eat dinners ordered in advance and built around some special discovery of the proprietor's, like a haunch of illegally killed venison. (Poachers' cars had powerful headlights, and the deer would stand dazzled by the road.) "These feasts were rare occasions, and we always had to keep the price in mind when we arranged them," Root wrote me not long ago. "They bear out perfectly your theory that the rich can be only dilettante eaters." (The eater's apprenticeship, though less arduous, must be as earnest as the cook's.) "But also, of course, the nonfeast level was very high. Even at the present expensive rates, though, it's pretty rare nowadays to have a memorable meal. I did have one pretty good one at the Relais Fleuri, in Rouen, not so long ago—all Norman. First that cream-of-mussel soup, then *canard au sang*, then what was about the best Pont-l'Evêque I ever encountered, finally a Norman soufflé, and after it a subtle Calvados. I had run into plenty of good strong Calvados before, but this was the first time I had come across one that could hold its own against a really topnotch brandy."

The letter indicates that Root, at sixty or so, has not yet fallen completely for the hepatic fallacy, or obsession with the liver, which has taken so much of the fun out of French life. His note on the Calvados is the most encouraging bit of news I have heard from that country in years. Evidently the casks that the British Army overlooked are beginning to mature. (The Americans, in their zone of Normandy, left none.) Root's notion that Calvados, at its best, is not better than brandy, however, is an indication only of the truth that no one man can be expected to know everything. Like the Norman, Calvados matures slowly and pays no taxes, but it is full of craft; brandies are precocious and superficial by comparison. As for the soufflé, I should have omitted it and preceded the rest of the meal with a dozen Norman oysters. I should also perhaps have introduced a bit of turbot (not more than a pound) between the mussel soup and the duck, to bring myself more gradually up the evolutionary scale— mollusks, fish, bird. In a menu so unpretentious, the cheese must represent the world of mammals from which it is a derivative. Root's weakness for soufflés, I suspect, traces back to the soda fountains of Fall River, but despite this sentimental lapse—like the *lapsus lapérouse*—Root is no indiscriminately indulgent lip-smacker. For example, he attacks the touted cuisine of Lyons as sharply as G. G. Coulton having a crack at a Catholic medievalist:

> My personal experience has been never to have eaten a really good meal in Lyons [he writes in his book, insuring an auto-da-fé if he ever goes there under his own name]. Lyons is a heavily bourgeois city . . . which has always vaguely reminded me of Philadelphia . . . [and] the cooking of Lyons fits the character of the city—it is hearty rather than graceful, and is apt to leave you with an overstuffed feeling. [It may be seen by his Rouen menu, however, that Root does not stuff too easily.] The cooking of Burgundy is hearty, too, but there is a livelier imagination connected with it. This is not to say that Lyonnaise cooking is not good of its kind, but its kind is not spirited. . . . One of the commonest dishes associated with the city's name—*pommes lyonnaises*—means simply German-fried potatoes cooked with onion. . . . When Lyonnaise cooks set out to be elaborate, they produce rich, liver-assaulting dishes [this is the first known instance of Root's acknowledging that he has a liver], even with such a simple start as chicken—for instance, *poularde demi-deuil*, fowl in half mourning, in which the bird is accompanied by sweetbreads of lamb and slices of truffles cooked in Madeira. . . . Considering the heaviness of the cooking of Lyons, it seems somewhat astonishing that the Pyramide, at Vienne, so nearby . . . manages to get so much subtlety into its cooking. Even so, the local tradition of richness remains. When the Pyramide attacks trout, possibly the most delicately flavored of all fish, it stuffs it and then braises it in port wine—a triumph, but of the Lucullan rather than the purist school, which takes its trout *au bleu*—very fresh and boiled, with no adornment to detract from the basic flavor of the fish itself. Finally, the conclusion of a Pyramide attacks trout, possibly the most delicately flavored of all of tempting little cakes and pastries of every imaginable variety, is calculated to send the diner away some pounds heavier than when he came.

Root admires La Pyramide, on the whole, but he holds that no restaurant on a byway can be called truly great, since its clients come a long way to eat its specialties and it need scarcely ever change its menu. The truly great restaurateur is the one who can please essentially the same clientele week after week without boring or disappointing it. *La cuisine française* is not one cuisine but a score, regional in origin, shading off into one another at their borders and all pulled together at Paris. Since certain of these cuisines are almost antithetical to certain others, the self-styled lover of *la cuisine française* without qualification is simply admitting that he has no taste at all. He is like the French majors at American colleges; in order to get all A's, in one year they profess a profound admiration for Racine and in another for Stendhal, who found Racine an inexpressible bore. (The worst offenders in this branch of conformity, though, are *lycéens* in France, who, to obtain the grades on which their future careers largely depend, swallow whole the glories of every writer celebrated in a rigid curriculum. The savagery with which French scholars turn upon their predecessors in their own specialty is a direct result of the exaggerated subservience demanded on the way up.)

It is possible, of course, to like something in the cuisine of any province —or, rather, nearly impossible not to. Any sensitive eater, though, must prefer the essential line of some regional cuisines to that of others. I agree with Root that Dijon, for example, seems to have no bad restaurants and that the good Burgundian cook "achieves . . . a trumpeting perfection." This good man, or woman, Root says, "does not take a delicate trifle and, by the subtle application of refined seasonings, transfigure it with an ethereal sauce into a whispering perfection." (He here defines a kind of cooking for which he and I have a limited regard.) Burgundian food, he says, "is the *cuisine bourgeoise* at its best, or peasant cooking elevated to its greatest possible heights. It is often said that you need a solid stomach to live on Burgundian cooking, but Burgundian cooking develops solid stomachs."

And yet Dijon and Lyons are little more than a hundred miles apart—a safe distance between sound and unsound cultures in the Middle Ages but an insufficient barrier against contamination since the coming of the motorcar.

Thirty-five years ago, at Mâcon—a third of the way north from Lyons to Nuits-Saint-Georges, which is where I place Burgundy's heart—I had an alarming experience of the encroachment of the Lyonnais. The proprietor of the small city's leading hotel was a magnificent figure of a man who wore a chef's toque two feet high. (It was in those times a favorable sign when a hotel owner wore cook's garb; the beds might prove hard, but the food would be good. Lately, it seems to me, all hotel owners dress that way—it is a come-on.) Monsieur B. was sincerely a cook, but the axis of his culinary eye had shifted until he saw the main body of dinner as a perfunctory hors d'oeuvre to the sweets. His preliminary menu—consommé with shredded carrots, sole slicked with sauce (and this in a town by a river full of humbler, tastier fish), and, finally, veal *glacé*—reminded me depressingly of the Hamburg-American Line. Then squads of assistants, also in toques, would begin to roll in trolleys of pastry and confectionery—*vacherins, suissesses, mille-feuilles, meringues, îles-flottantes de Tante Marie*, and hundreds of sugary kickshaws I was unable to identify. Monsieur B. personally plied me with these, in the manner of a soprano volunteering unsolicited encores. I, at twenty-three, had not the nerve to turn him down; it was the first time I felt sick on *la cuisine française*. After this honeyed surfeit, at which I displayed hypocritical delight, the *patron* imposed himself upon me while I had a drink on the house. (He was astonished that I preferred cognac to Bénédictine or Cointreau.) "It is not in this little region that one could learn to cook so," he said with complacency. (I sadly thought that there was probably not a woman in town who couldn't cook more to my taste.) "I retired here and bought this hotel at the beginning of the war. Until then, for twenty years, from the time I left Lyons as a young *chef pâtissier*, I was chief cook for *le Kaiser Guillaume II*." In the years since, this somber episode has helped me define what I don't like about *la cuisine lyonnaise*.

The dinner at Mâcon peculiarly distressed me because it was one of my constantly fewer chances to further my education before leaving France, and it was wasted. The academic year at the Sorbonne was over, and I was in full retreat from Paris to Providence, via Marseille, where I was to embark on the *Patria*, of the Fabre Line. I had chosen Marseille as a port of departure because it would give me an excuse to eat and drink my way through Burgundy en route—or at least to nibble and gulp at a small part of its glory. My father, a grim chancellor now, had cut the fiscal supply line, and I had arranged by letter to resume my old employment at the Providence *Journal*, at the increased salary of sixty dollars a week. This would not have been a bad prospect to look forward to, if I had not been quitting one so much more splendid.

I descended from the Paris-Marseille express at Dijon to eat the first rear-guard action of my anabasis. There was one advantage in my position: I had more than sufficient money for the limited time left to me. I could afford some good bottles. At the Restaurant Racouchot, in the Place d'Armes, at Dijon, I made the acquaintance of *caille vendangeuse* and drank a bottle of Corton Clos du Roi. Having demonstrated my taste for the beautiful, I asked the waiter to recommend a small inn among the vineyards, where I might eat and drink well between long walks, or take long walks between heavy meals. Pedestrianism was always my balance for voracity; they were countervailing joys. Walking, I consumed what I had eaten, built up appetite for more, had noble thoughts, and spotted likely-looking restaurants.

The waiter recommended the Auberge de l'Etoile, at Gevrey-Chambertin, a village of blessed associations. At the Auberge, I fell in with the greatest host in my life—a retired second lieutenant *de carrière* named Robaine, who had risen from the ranks in the course of thirty years in the colonial Army. Robaine took me to all the cellars of the commune and the communes adjoining, representing me as a rich American bootlegger come to the Côte d'Or, the Golden Slope of Burgundy, to buy wine for the cargo of a fabulous *bateau-cave*—a wine-cellar ship that would be sailed into New York Harbor and hoisted by night ("like a lifeboat but on a huge scale, understand?") into a skyscraper with a specially prepared false front. In that way, I got to drink more good wine than most men are able to pay for in their lives, and Robaine drank along with me—"pushing" the merchandise as he drank, and winking grossly at the proprietors of the vineyards, to indicate that he was conspiring with *them* to get a good price from *me*. At night, I would stagger home to eat the *jambon persillé*—parsley-flavored ham with mustard and pickles—that every meal began with, followed by hare or beef or fowl in a sauce of better wine than you could buy in other regions in labeled bottles. All the good wine I could drink came with the meals, but Robaine had invented the bootlegger story to get at the superlative wine of the vineyardists. He was a Lorrainer, from Nancy or Metz, and so an outsider, possessing no vineyards of his own.

One day, I varied the hospitality of the *cavistes* of Gevrey-Chambertin, Fixin, and Vougeot, the nearest communes, with a pedestrian expedition to Nuits-Saint-Georges, six miles away. There, in the restaurant of one of the two local hotels, I sat at the common table, where I was soon joined by a young man of my own age—a scholarly chap interested in foreigners— who said that he was bookkeeper-manager for a local wine merchant. Presently, he asked me how I liked the wine I had before me. The wine was a superb bottle of Grands-Echézeaux, but with a presence of mind learned from Robaine, I said that while it was good, it had limitations. Prodded, I even confessed to a trifle of disappointment. I said I had drunk as good bottles of Burgundy in Paris, even in Ireland; one expected that when one came to the birthplace of wine and asked the proprietress to furnish her best bottle . . . It was one of the most mendacious moments of my life.

The young Frenchman, appalled, said that he would speak to Madame. I begged him not to. He bit his lip. Finally, he said, "I cannot tolerate that you should carry away such a mediocre impression of our cellars. I invite you to sample what we call good wines at *our* place." Looking at the label on my now empty bottle—which was fortunately not that of his firm—he whispered, "Between you and me, the fellow who bottled that, although he is my boss's cousin, is a sharp chap. Doubtful integrity." After that, of course, he had to start me off on something that he considered better than the wine I had downed.

The afternoon I spent in the cellars of his firm was one of the happiest of my life. I regret that I have forgotten the firm's name. I was lucky to remember my own. After sipping the first glass he poured for me, I said, "It certainly beats the other for velvet, but the Echézeaux had a certain vigor, all the same, that is not to be despised." The next, I conceded, had an eternally youthful masculinity—but the Echézeaux, much as I had depreciated it, had had a certain originality. When I had drunk myself as tight as a New Year's Eve balloon, I admitted that the last wine he offered was indeed clearly superior to the bottle at the hotel. This was polite, but a lie. *"That,"* I said, "is what I call Burgundy." It was a Romanée-Conti of some sort, and first-rate. "Well worth a voyage from North America to taste. Thunderously superior to that stuff I had with lunch." My benefactor was pale with gratitude. But the bottle at the hotel had been the best of the day.

That short week, thirty-five years ago, was my true initiation into the drinking of Burgundy. My introduction to the wine at its best and in profusion can only be compared to the experience of a young woman I know who, having attended progressive schools all the way to college, had her first massive introduction to Shakespeare *and* the Old Testament in the same year. My introduction was a bit overwhelming, but I had had a stout preparation for it during the academic year at the Sorbonne, when I passed my oenological novitiate experimenting among the Tavels and Côte Rôties of the Restaurant des Beaux-Arts. Drinking Richebourg without this training would have been like a debutant prizefighter's meeting Archie Moore in a feature bout; he would not be up to it and would never know what hit him. Burgundy has the advantage—to which a young palate is particularly sensitive—of a clear, direct appeal, immediately pleasing and easy to comprehend on a primary level. This is a quality compatible with greatness. Shakespeare and Tolstoy, because more accessible, are not necessarily inferior to, say, Donne and Dostoevski. The merits of the Parthenon sculptors are not inferior to those of the primitives for being easier to recognize. Burgundy thus has two publics: one (which it shares with Bordeaux) that likes it for its profound as well as its superficial qualities, and one that likes it only because it is easy to like. This second public is its monopoly, and has increased vastly since the Second World War, with the wide dissemination of money among Frenchmen unused to affluence, and the new tourism, spurred by the airlines in both Britain and America, that is made up of people whose holidays were never before long enough to allow them to penetrate the Continent. The double public has, in my view, made Burgundies double the price of equally good clarets—a condition clearly reflected in the prices of wines exported to America. (That is, if you like both clarets and Burgundies, you can do as well with two dollars invested in a bottle of claret as with four dollars invested in Burgundy.*)

In Paris itself, Burgundies are so far out of sight that even expensive restaurants feature peripheral and approximative growths—some good, some merely not bad, and nearly all claiming a relationship to "the Beaujolais." (If the Beaujolais region were to produce all the wines, bottled and *en carafe*, that are sold in its name, it would have to be larger than Alaska. One reason the French held on to Algeria so stubbornly was

---

* The disparity is less now (late 1962) than when this was first written, but, I think, still exists—A.J.L.

that with its loss three-quarters of "the Beaujolais" would disappear.) The essentials of these wines are a "fruity" taste and a liberal degree of alcohol.

And yet Burgundy is a lovely thing when you can get anybody to buy it for you. Root, I think, is still a Burgundy man. "Bordeaux," he writes, "from the ancient city of Romans—inheritor of the sophisticated Latin tradition—is grown in the region of a great port which has known an urban and cosmopolitan civilization for centuries; it is suave, polished, civilized. Burgundy, from the region of the swashbuckling Grand Dukes of the West, the lusty sons of inland soil, grown where men lived close to the land, remained rustic in richness, and exerted their own influence outward more readily than they welcomed other influences directed inward, is full-bodied, strong, earthy."

It is much easier to prove a relation between the chemical composition of the soil and the kind of wine it produces, though, than between the nature of the wine and the local civilization. Hymettis, for example, which grows on a mountain overlooking Athens, has no hint of philosophy or ancient civilization in it. The best wine grown near Rome is no great shakes, either; the marble in the soil that was grand for sculpture is not much good for the vine. As for the vintages of Lebanon, which was Phoenicia, and of Egypt, the cradle of the oldest civilization, they are less suave and polished than wine grown on the islands of Lake Erie.

In Marseille, waiting for my ship to sail, I paddled about in bouillabaisse. The *Patria* was of Marseille, the owners were Marseillais, and the officers were Corsicans, with the exception of the doctor, who did fine needlework. The crew on deck were Italianate Frenchmen from the Old Port, and the stokers were Senegalese. She was a delightful Conrad kind of ship that took the dull certainty out of peacetime sea travel. (Eventually, she exploded and capsized in Haifa, killing scores of homeless Jews who had been refused admission to Palestine.) Providence was to be her first port of call in the United States, and she went by way of Genoa, Naples, Palermo, Madeira, and the Azores—nineteen days. This was the direct express route; other Fabre liners had more circuitous itineraries. When I got back to Providence, I was met by a fellow worker on the *Journal*, who helped me smuggle five bottles of champagne and several of cognac past the customs men and prohibition agents. I knew I was home again.

Root, meanwhile, remained in Paris, where I had not known he was. He ate assiduously and judiciously, improving his circumstances after the Paris edition of the Chicago *Tribune* folded and left him free to earn a living. When I returned, early in October of 1939, both our situations were different, and so was that of Paris. A war, such as it was, had begun, and both of us were correspondents—he for a tabloid known as the Chicago *Times*, a Copenhagen newspaper, and the Mutual Broadcasting System, concurrently. At that stage it was such an equivocal war, and had so limited an interest for neutrals, that none of Root's employers thought it justified sending a full-time representative. Root was what newspapers call a stringer.

The war's touch on Paris was so light that the government continually organized tours of the front for French *littérateurs en vue,* in the course of which a conducting officer would show them the Germans and remind them that although few shots were being fired—and those through nervousness or inadvertence—both antagonists were armed. Returning to the Berkeley Restaurant or the Pavillon de l'Elysée, the men of letters would assure their colleagues that there was a war, and then, in long articles in the dozen or so popular newspapers, tell the readers of the emotions they had experienced in the contemplation of what might happen. The government was less eager to send neutral correspondents on such tours; they might not have been so easily impressed. It kept most foreign correspondents hanging about Paris, allowing only a few at a time to go up and see the sights—a selected portion of the impregnable Maginot Line, the Rhine bridge at Kehl, and the like. It was the most gradual introduction to warfare imaginable, and when, in the following May, the war became *de facto,* we were as unprepared for it as the poor old generals and their bored troops. The correspondents who had succeeded in staying on edge through the intervening months—the prophets of doom—were justified, but it had required effort or a built-in neurosis.

When I arrived in Paris, I was excited and apprehensive, and determined, if I got the chance, to sell my life dearly at my French friends' side. I had the scene by heart in fantasy: I would snatch up the rifle dropped by a falling *tirailleur* and die lying on my belly on a ridge, in the manner of Robert Jordan in *For Whom the Bell Tolls,* meanwhile snuffing out Huns like candle flames in a shooting gallery (where I had practiced several times before embarking). It is an image of his own demise that often occurs to the writer militant; Mathieu, in Sartre's long novel *La Mort dans l'Ame,* does it that way, firing from a belfry. But after several months of *attente* in a near-normal Paris, unbombed and unexcited, I began to hope that the whole thing would blow over, leaving me with the glory of having covered a war and none of the inconveniences possibly to be anticipated.

During this doldrum period, I met Root for the first time; it was at a weekly luncheon meeting of the Anglo-American Press Association of Paris, at the Restaurant Drouant, which has good oysters. Soon he became a familiar; we had a passion in common. His face in those days was the precise color of the inside of a *châteaubriand* that is between rare and medium rare. His firm and broad-based jaw appeared to be an ideal instrument of mastication, but his rounded chin and friendly eyes announced a man readier to crunch a lark's carcass than tear a tiger's throat. A kindly and humorous man of wide and disparate interests, he could talk well of many things, but our conversations, from the day I met him, were preponderantly about what we had eaten, or were about to eat, or wished to eat—a topic varied by discussions of what we had drunk or would like to drink with it.

I could now afford to eat wherever I cared to. During my American interim, my appetite had been sharpened; now, returned to Paris, I was ready to fly with the wings of larks, pheasants, and woodcock. I took up quarters at the Hôtel Louvois, on the little square that faces the Rue de Richelieu, thus abandoning the quarter haunted by Villon in favor of one that is sacred to the memory of Stendhal. Villon, although there are no contemporary portraits of him, is conventionally represented by illustrators as he described himself: "Lean, sunken cheeks, starved belly." His passion for good food was a fixation on the unattainable, like Rudel's for La Princesse Lointaine, or Chartier's for La Belle Dame Sans Merci. Stendhal, however, enjoyed having his picture painted and left many likenesses. They all agree in the convexity of his front elevation—a magnificent background for a watch chain, an advantageous stuffing for a brocaded waistcoat. The difference in the profiles of the resident ghosts symbolized the gastronomic disparity between their respective neighborhoods. The Square Louvois was surrounded by fine restaurants.

In the twenties, the Rue Sainte-Anne, a narrow street running from near the Théâtre Français end of the Avenue de l'Opéra to the Rue Saint-Augustin and skirting the Square Louvois *en passant*, had been rendered illustrious by a man named Maillabuau, a gifted restaurateur but a losing horseplayer who had no money to squander on décor. He turned his worn tablecloths into an asset by telling his customers that he wasted none of their contributions on frills—all went into the supreme quality of his materials and wines. A place with doormen in uniforms, he would say—a place with deep carpets and perhaps (here a note of horror would enter his voice) an orchestra—was *ipso facto* and *prima facie* a snare. He would then charge twice as much as any other restaurant in Paris. My memories of visits to Maillabuau's—visits that I had enjoyed only by stratagem—were so pleasant that I had chosen the Hôtel Louvois in order to be near it.

All during my year at the Sorbonne, the *Guide du Gourmand à Paris* had served as the Baedeker for my exploratory splurges when I had money enough to try restaurants off my usual beat. The author addressed his book to the gourmand, rather than to the gourmet, he said, because it was impossible to like food if you did not like a lot of it; "gourmet" was therefore a snob word, and a silly one. This predisposed me in his favor. But it was his subject matter that held me captive. The restaurants were categorized as "of great luxury," "middling-priced," "reasonable," and "simple," but all were warranted "good," and there were about a hundred and twenty-five of them. At the head of the "luxury" group was a "first platoon" of six restaurants (of which today only one survives, and that scarcely worthy of mention). Maillabuau, despite the worn tablecloths, figured among the ten others in the "luxury" group. In my own forays, "reasonable" was my ceiling, but I liked to read about the others—those financially unattainable Princesses Lointaines. I knew the description of Maillabuau's by heart:

> Sombre, almost lugubrious front. If the passerby is not warned, never will he suspect that behind that façade, having crossed that modest threshold, he can know the pure joys of gastronomy! How to know, if one is not a gourmand, that here the sole is divine, that the *entrecôte Bercy* has singular merits, that the pâté of venison is beyond equal, that the burgundies (especially the Chambertin) are of the year that they should be, and that the *marc* resembles embalmed gold? How to know that only here, in all Paris, are made ready the fat squab guinea-hens anointed with all the scents of the Midi? Staggering bill, which one never regrets paying.

I had no thought of crossing that modest threshold myself until one warm morning in the late spring of 1927, when it occurred to me that my father, mother, and sister would be arriving in Paris in a few weeks—they were waiting only for the beginning of the summer holiday at the Connecticut College for Women, where my sister was now a sophomore—and that in the natural course of events they would ask me, the local expert, where to dine. My mother and sister favored the kind of restaurant where they saw pretty dresses and where the *plat du jour* was likely to be called "Le Chicken Pie à l'Américaine," but my father had always been a booster for low overhead and quality merchandise; they were the principles that had guided his career as a furrier. Russian sable and ermine—with baum or stone marten if a woman couldn't afford anything better—had always been his idea of decent wear. His views on fur were a little like J. P. Morgan's on yachts—people who had to worry about the cost shouldn't have them. Foxes began and ended, for him, with natural blacks and natural silvers; the notion of a fox bred to specifications would have filled him with horror. Seal had to be Alaskan seal, not what was called Hudson seal, which meant muskrat. Persian lamb had to be *unborn* Persian lamb, not mutton.

As I had anticipated, when my family arrived in Paris they did indeed consult me about the scene of our first dinner together. So Maillabuau's it was. When we arrived before the somber, almost lugubrious front, my mother wanted to turn back. It looked like a store front, except for a bit of scrim behind the plate glass, through which the light from within filtered without éclat.

"Are you sure this is the right place?" she asked.

"It's one of the best restaurants in the world," I said, as if I ate there every day.

My father was already captivated. "Don't give you a lot of hoopla and ooh-la-la," he said, with approval. "I'll bet there are no Americans here."

We crossed the modest threshold. The interior was only half a jump from sordid, and there were perhaps fifteen tables. Old Maillabuau, rubicund and seedy, approached us, and I could sense that my mother was about to object to any table he proposed; she wanted some place like Fouquet's (not in the *Guide du Gourmand*). But between her and Maillabuau I interposed a barrage of French that neither she nor my sister could possibly penetrate, though each chirped a few tentative notes. "I have brought my family here because I have been informed it is the most illustrious house of Paris," I told him, and, throwing in a colloquialism I had learned in Rennes, a city a hundred years behind the times, I added, "We desire to knock the bell."

On hearing me, old Maillabuau, who may have thought for a moment that we were there by mistake and were about to order waffles, flashed a smile of avaricious relief. Father, meanwhile, regarding the convives of both sexes seated at the tables, was already convinced. The men, for the most part, showed tremendous *devantures*, which they balanced on their knees with difficulty as they ate, their wattles waving bravely with each bite. The women were shaped like demijohns and decanters, and they drank wine from glasses that must have reminded Father happily of beer schooners on the Bowery in 1890. "I don't see a single American," he said. He was a patriotic man at home, but he was convinced that in Paris the presence of Americans was a sign of a bunco joint.

"Monsieur my father is the richest man in Baltimore," I told Maillabuau, by way of encouragement. Father had nothing to do with Baltimore, but I figured that if I said New York, Maillabuau might not believe me. Maillabuau beamed and Father beamed back. His enthusiasms were rare but sudden, and this man—without suavity, without a tuxedo, who spoke no English, and whose customers were so patently overfed— appeared to him an honest merchant. Maillabuau showed us to a table; the cloth was diaphanous from wear except in the spots where it had been darned.

A split-second *refroidissement* occurred when I asked for the *carte du jour*.

"There is none," Maillabuau said. "You will eat what I tell you. To-night, I propose a soup, trout *grenobloise*, and *poulet* Henri IV—simple but exquisite. The classic *cuisine française*—nothing complicated but all of the best."

When I translated this to Father, he was in complete agreement. "Plain food," he said. "No *schmier*." I think that at bottom he agreed that the customer is sure to be wrong if left to his own devices. How often had the wives of personal friends come to him for a fur coat at the wholesale price, and declined his advice of an Alaskan seal—something that would last them for twenty years—in favor of some faddish fur that would show wear in six!

The simplicity of the menu disappointed me; I asked Mallabuau about the *pintadou*, fat and anointed with fragrance. "Tomorrow," he said, posing it as a condition that we eat his selection first. Mother's upper lip quivered, for she was *très gourmande* of cream sauces, but she had no valid argument against the great man's proposal, since one of the purposes of her annual trips to Europe was to lose weight at a spa. On the subject of wines, M. Maillabuau and I agreed better: the best in the cellar would do—a Montrachet to begin with, a Chambertin with the fowl.

It was indeed the best soup—a simple *garbure* of vegetables—imaginable, the best trout possible, and the best boiled fowl of which one could conceive. The simple line of the meal brought out the glories of the wine, and the wine brought out the grandeur in my father's soul. Presented with one of the most stupendous checks in history, he paid with gratitude, and said that he was going to take at least one meal a day *chez* Maillabuau during the rest of his stay. The dessert, served as a concession to my sister, was an *omelette au kirsch*, and Maillabuau stood us treat to the *marc*, like embalmed gold. Or at least he said he did; since only the total appeared on the check, we had to take his word for it. The *omelette au kirsch* was the sole dessert he ever permitted to be served, he said. He was against sweets on principle, since they were "not French," but the *omelette* was light and healthy. It contained about two dozen eggs.

The next day we had the *pintadou*, the day after that a *pièce de bœuf du Charolais* so remarkable that I never eat a steak without thinking how far short it falls. And never were the checks less than "staggering," and never did my father complain. Those meals constituted a high spot in my gastronomic life, but before long my mother and sister mutinied. They wanted a restaurant where they could see some dresses and eat *meringues glacées* and *homard au porto*.

So in 1939, on my first evening in wartime Paris, I went straight from the Louvois to the Rue Sainte-Anne. The Restaurant Maillabuau had vanished. I did not remember the street number, so I walked the whole length of the Rue Sainte-Anne twice to make sure. But there was no Maillabuau; the horses at Longchamp had eaten him.

7 / The Afterglow

WHEN I RETURNED to Paris in the fall of 1939, after an absence of twelve years, I noticed a decline in the serious quality of restaurants that could not be blamed on a war then one month old. The decline, I later learned, had been going on even in the twenties, when I made my first studies in eating, but I had had no standard of comparison then; what I had taken for a Golden Age was in fact Late Silver. Like me, Root, when he made his first soundings in the subject in 1927, was unaware that the watershed was behind us and that we were on a long, historic downslope. Enough of the glory remained to furnish us with memories by which to judge the punier times ahead, though; the food of France in 1926–27 still constituted the greatest corpus of culinary thought and practice anywhere. The only touted challenger for the lead then was China, and the only touts were people who wanted to let you know they had been there. When you got these Orientalized *fines gueules* to a table where they had to use a knife and fork instead of chopsticks, they could not tell the difference between a Western sandwich and a *darne de saumon froid sauce verte*. In most cases, their sole preparation for gourmandizing had been a diet of institutional macaroni in a Midwestern seminary for medical missionaries, and any pasture the Lord led them to was bound to be better.

Chinese *haute cuisine* is unlikely to improve under the austere regime of Mao. The food of France, although it has gone off disastrously, is still the best there is. But we are headed for a gastronomic Dark Time, such as followed the breakup of classical civilization, and nobody younger than Root and I are can remember the twilight.

My lamented mentor, Mirande, could remember the full glow of the sun, before the First World War. "After the First War, everything had already changed," Mirande wrote in 1952, when he was seventy-seven. "The mentality of today began to show the tip of its ear." One thing that changed early was the position of the women he called *les courtisanes de marque*—the famous women of the town—and this had a prodigious, if indirect, effect upon the sumptuary arts. "Yes, Paris was radiant, elegant, and refined," Mirande wrote of his heaven before 1914. "In the world and in the half-world, feasts followed upon feasts, wild nights upon vertiginous suppers. It was the courtesans' *grande époque*. Innocent of preoccupation with the future, they had no trace of a desire to build up an income for old age. They were gamblers, beautiful gamblers, with a certain natural distinction in their ways and a *je ne sais quoi* of good breeding—the bonnet thrown over the windmill, but without falling into vulgarity or coarseness. They had a tone—a tone as distinct from the society woman's as from the fancy girl's. All the successful demimondaines ordered their clothes from the great couturiers. Their carriages were splendid, better turned out for a drive in the Bois than those of duchesses and ambassadors." Moreover, these town toasts ate magnificently, and boasted of the quality of the meals their admirers provided for them. It was the age not only of the dazzling public supper but of the *cabinet particulier*, where even a bourgeois seduction was preceded by an eleven-course meal. With these altruistic sensualists, a menu of superior imagination could prove more effective than a gift of Suez shares; besides, the ladies' hosts had the pleasure of sharing the meals they had to pay for.

The *courtisanes de marque* were substantial in a Venus de Milo-y, just short of billowy way. Waists and ankles tapered, but their owners provided a lot for them to taper from. Eating was a *soin de beauté* that the girls enjoyed.

The successful Frenchman of the early nineteen-hundreds was fat; it was the evidence of his success, an economic caste mark. To be thin at thirty was a handicap in the world of affairs, the equivalent in our culture of driving a year-before-last automobile. It indicated that one had never been in a position to eat one's fill. Caricature accents but does not reverse reality, and I cherish a special twenty-four-page number of *L'Assiette au Beurre,* a journal of savage caricature, printed in 1902 and devoted to "*Le Singe,*" which was, and is, argot for "the employer." Every successful *singe* in the issue—rapacious, lecherous, murderous—is fat. The only unfat *singe* is the one on the last page—an obviously unsuccessful pimp who is beating up a thin girl, clearly not a *courtisane de marque.*

By 1927, however, the celebrated belles, amateur and professional, had become even more skeletal than they are today. Lady Diana Manners and Rosamond Pinchot, the international beauties paired in Max Reinhardt's *The Miracle,* for example, were as leggy and flat as a pair of handsome young giraffes. It was no longer any use taking a woman to a great restaurant except to show her off. She would not eat, and, out of ill temper disguised as solicitude for her escort's health, she would put him off his feed as well. The chic restaurants of Paris—which were none of my or Root's concern at the moment—were already beginning their transition from shrines of *dégustation* to showcases for the flapper figure. The men, too, had turned to the mortification of the flesh, though less drastically. Without exception, the chaps who emerged from the trenches at the end of the war had lost weight, and at such a time everyone wants to resemble a hero.

Of the victorious commanders, only Joffre and Sarrail had figures like Napoleon's, and they had not been conspicuously successful. Foch and Pétain were ramrods, like Pershing. Also, *le sport,* which before the war had been considered a form of eccentricity, was now taken seriously. When Lacoste, Cochet, and Borotra beat the United States for the Davis Cup that very spring, the sensation was greater than when Lindbergh completed his transatlantic flight. There was also a wave of that endemic European malady *americo-mimesis;* the attack in the twenties is often forgotten by contemporary Europeans in their rage against the bigger one now in progress. The infection then was carried by jazz and by American silent moving pictures, which had nearly wiped out European films. (The injection of the human voice into movies and the resultant language barrier gave the foreign cinema a reprieve that became permanent.) And, finally, there was the legend of the Perpetual Boom. America, it appeared, was the country that had discovered an infallible system for beating the races. This made Americans, in the abstract, as unpopular as we eventually became in the forties, but it also spurred imitative identification. The silent-film comedian Harold Lloyd, who played go-getting young businessman types, energetic to the point of acrobacy, was the pattern-symbol of the Frenchman disgusted with old methods. Even a dilettante can still spot Frenchmen of that vintage by their tortoise-shell glasses and their briskness. (Jacques Soustelle is a classic specimen.) Their costume has become fixed, like the Sikh's turban. The crash of 1929 discredited the original motivation of the mimesis, but the Frenchman trapped by habit behind his tortoise-shells had forgotten why he put them on.

In 1927, these changes were beginning to be reflected in the composition of the restaurant world. The 1925 edition of the *Guide du Gourmand à Paris* listed six restaurants as its *"peloton de tête,"* or leading platoon: Montagné, Larue, Foyot, Voisin, Paillard, and La Tour d'Argent, all "temples of gastronomy" for serious feeders. (Of the first five, all venerable, four ceased to exist even before the declaration of the Second World War. Larue maintained its majestic style through the winter of the *drôle de guerre,* 1939–40, but has disappeared since, to be replaced by an establishment called Queenie's, whose name, as the French say, is a program. La Tour d'Argent, in order to continue, has gone in heavily for public relations, and floodlights itself at night, like a national monument. Such expedients may be justified as being necessary to survival, but they cast a shadow on the age that renders them necessary.)

The specialties that the *Guide* listed as the glories of these great houses in their declining years were not of a sort to accord with low-calorie diets or with the new cult of the human liver. Before the First World War, the doctors of France had been a submissive and well-mannered breed, who recognized that their role was to facilitate gluttony, not discourage it. They returned to civilian life full of a new sense of authority, gained from the habit of amputation. Instead of continuing, as in the past, to alleviate indigestion, assuage dyspepsia, and solace attacks of gout, they proposed the amputation of three or four courses from their patients' habitual repasts. Since the innovators were, as always, the doctors most in fashion, the first patients to be affected were the most fashionable—precisely those who patronized the most expensive restaurants. The *Guide* listed Montagné's greatest attractions as "meats and fish under a crust of pastry; salmon, turbot, prepared *à l'ancienne,* in a sheath of dough; venerable Louis-Philippe brandy. And the coffee!!!" (The Montagné was the same who edited the great "Larousse Gastronomique.") This is a catalogue of horrors for a man worried about his weight and works, but it was a program of delight for an eater of Mirande's *grande époque.*

The constant diminution of the public that was interested in flamboyant food ended the economic justification of the restaurants staffed to supply it; the new doctrines had the same effect on temples of gastronomy that the Reformation had on the demand for *style-flamboyant* cathedrals. At first, the disappearance of the expensive restaurants was not felt at the lower levels where Root and I reveled, but it slowly became evident, as the disappearance of the great opera houses would become evident in the standards of professional singing; with no Metropolitan to aspire to, the child soprano of Boulder, Colorado, would have no incentive to work on her scales. As a career for the artistically ambitious, cooking became less attractive just at the moment when alternative means of earning a living grew more numerous for the offspring of the proletariat. Child-labor laws and compulsory education were additional obstacles in the way of the early apprenticeship that forms great cooks.

One of the last of the Fratellini family of clowns, an old man, made a television address in Paris a few years ago in which he blamed the same conjunction of circumstances for the dearth of good young circus clowns. "When I was a child, my father, bless him, broke my legs, so that I would walk comically, as a clown should," the old man said. (I approximate his remarks from memory.) "Now there are people who would take a poor view of that sort of thing."

In another area of the arts, Rocky Marciano's preceptor, Charlie Gold-man, a septuagenarian, says that there will never again be great boxers, because such must begin their professional careers before the age of puberty, while they can keep their minds on their business. (Marciano, who began late, was a fighter, not a boxer, and fighting is more a knack than an art.) When Persian carpets were at their best, weavers began at the age of four and were master workmen at eleven.

During the twenties and thirties, the proportion of French restaurants that called themselves *auberges* and *relais* increased, keeping pace with the motorization of the French gullet. They depended for their subsistence on Sunday and holiday drivers, who might never come over the road again, and the *Guide Michelin,* the organ of a manufacturer of automobile tires, ominously began to be the arbiter of where to dine—a depressing example of the subordination of art to business. By 1939, the shiny new "medieval" joints along the equally new highways had begun to supplant the old hotels, across the road from the railroad stations, that in the first quarter of the century had been the centers of good, solid provincial eating.

The hotel proprietors' living depended on the patronage of traveling salesmen, whose robust appetites and experienced palates had combined with their economical natures to maintain the standards of honest catering. But the drummers no longer moved by train, doing one large town or small city a day and staying overnight at the Hôtel du Commerce or the Lion d'Or. They were now motorized, and scooted about the highways in minute Citroëns and Arondes, managing to get home to their bases in the larger provincial cities at the day's end. They lunched in a hurry—"like Americans"—and the rural hotels began to die. When the peasants, too, started to become motorized, the small towns themselves began to die. The small-town and small-city merchants had pushed a bill through the

Chamber of Deputies prohibiting the great retail chains, like Monoprix, from opening stores in cities of less than ten thousand population, and one result was to accelerate the desertion of the small towns by shoppers; to get the variety and lower prices of the chain stores, they passed up the old centers altogether.

By 1939, the country coyness of the *auberges* and *relais*, with their pastiche medieval décors and their menus edited with fake-archaic whimsey—the equivalent of "ye" and "shoppe"—had even invaded the capital. *"Humectez vos gousiers avec les bons vins du noble pays du patron en actendant les chatouille-gencives du Maistre Queux,"* a Paris restaurant menu was likely to read, in place of the 1926–27 *"Vins en carafe—rouge ou blanc, 50 centimes. Saucissons d'ail, 50 centimes. Sardines . . ."* The new baby-talk Rabelais was about as appetizing as, and on a level with, some of our own bill-of-fare prose: "Irrigate the li'l ol' red lane with some of our prime drinkin' whiskey and branch water while the Chef Supreme rustles up an Infra-Red popover Salad Bowl."

The Rue Sainte-Anne is a medium-long street, narrow and totally without distinction, that begins near the Rue de Rivoli end of the Avenue de l'Opéra and runs north toward the Grands Boulevards; it roughly parallels the Rue de Richelieu, at a remove of a couple of squalid blocks, but it has no Comédie Française to illustrate its beginning and no Bibliothèque Nationale to lend dignity to its middle. A block or two before it reaches the Boulevards, it takes the name of the Rue de Gramont. It is lined with uninviting hotels, cobbler's shops, neighborhood hairdressers, and establishments that sell the drab sundries of wholesale businesses—wooden buttons and hat blocks, patterns for dresses, office supplies—and with restaurants that feed office workers at noon. Among all the restaurants, there is frequently a good one, but it never lasts long. The Rue Sainte-Anne is the kind of street that seems to attract independent spirits. A talented cook who opens there is an Expressionist; he feels no need of a public. There Maillabuau had practiced his art. An American I know once walked in on him between meals to order a dinner for a special celebration. He found the wizard cooking a *choucroute*, or sauerkraut, well *garnie* with *pâté de foie gras*, for three French senators. As my acquaintance watched, he poured in a whole bottle of ancient cognac to improve the flavor. His prices approximated Picasso's.

Yielding to hunger at last, on that evening in 1939 when I walked the Rue Sainte-Anne looking in vain for Maillabuau's, I entered another restaurant, of the same unpromising aspect—a store front muffled in curtains because of the blackout but extruding a finger of light to show that it was open for business. (Everybody in France, at that stage, waged a war of small compromises.) A shabby exterior is no guarantee of good food—perhaps more often it is the contrary—but I was too hungry by then to leave the neighborhood. Nor were the streets hospitable in the dimout. There were no cruising taxis.

Thus it was that I stumbled into the family circle of M. Louis Bouillon, a native of Bourg-en-Bresse, which is the eating-poultry capital of France and in the home province of the great Brillat-Savarin, who was born in Belley. M. Bouillon was a small man with bright, liquid eyes, a long nose, like a woodcock's, and a limp, drooping mustache that looked as if it had been steamed over cook pots until it was permanently of the consistency of spinach. When I entered, he was sitting with his elbows on a table and his head in his hands, contemplating a tumbler of *marc de Bourgogne* as if trying to read the fate of France in an ink pool. Around the table, with newspapers and coffee, were seated Mme. Bouillon; Marie-Louise, the waitress; the Bouillons' daughter, Dominique, a handsome girl of eighteen; and their son, not yet called up for service. (I did not know their individual identities yet, but I soon learned them.) Mme. Bouillon brightened, and Marie-Louise rose and came to meet me. "Sit where you wish, Monsieur," she said. "You have your choice."

There had been a scare at the very beginning of the war, and a great many people had left Paris, expecting it to be bombarded. They had not yet quite decided to come back—it was in the first week of October 1939—and business was, in consequence, dead. I have seldom been so welcome anywhere, or got so quickly acquainted. And I had fallen luckily. M. Bouillon was a great cook. He was not, however, like Maillabuau, a great character actor. His son was in apprenticeship at the Café de Paris, one of the few remaining big classic restaurants. His daughter, that paragon, could make a soufflé Grand Marnier that *stood up on a flat plate*. M. Bouillon told me that he had only recently taken over the restaurant. The rickety cane chairs and oak sideboard looked bad enough to have come from Maillabuau's dispersal sale. But there was food. "The markets are full," M. Bouillon said. "Game, shellfish—everything you can think of. It's customers that lack." I forget what I had at that first meal—a steak *marchand de vin,* or a *civet* of hare, perhaps, before the soufflé, which I ordered to see Dominique do her trick. Then I settled down to drinking with M. Bouillon. He was somber at first. What kind of a war was this, he wanted to know. When would we go out and give them a crack on the snout? In *his* war, the horizon-blue war, the Boche had come as far as the Marne and been stopped within six weeks of the beginning. That put people in the proper cadence. This war set one's nerves on edge. It was the British, he felt sure, who were responsible for the delay; they were perhaps negotiating with Fritz. A war that could not make up its mind had a funereal effect on commerce. The Americans were different from the English, but they weren't in the war. M. Bouillon and I grew sentimental, optimistic, bellicose, and, finally, maudlin. I had a hard time finding my way home, although my hotel, the Louvois, was only a hundred and fifty yards away—a straight line with one turn to the right.

After that, M. Bouillon's restaurant became my advanced field head-quarters while I vainly tried to get an *ordre de mission* to go to the front, where nothing was happening anyway. Conditions rapidly simulated normal. The Parisians came back. An ill-founded feeling of satisfaction succeeded the alarm and puzzlement of the first days; the Allies might not be hurting the Nazis, but at least the Nazis weren't hurting the Allies. There was a growing public hunch that the "real" war would never begin. Often, M. Bouillon took me with him on his buying trips to Les Halles, so I could see that the Germans weren't starving Paris. On these trips, we would carry a number of baskets, and, as we filled one after another with oysters, artichokes, or pheasants, we would leave them at a series of bars, in each of which we had one or two *Calvas*. The new Calvados sold at the market bars was like a stab with a penknife, and at some bars we would drink Pouilly-Fumé by the glass for a change of pace. The markets were overflowing; I recall that there was fruit from Mussolini's Italy and fine poultry from Prince Paul's Yugoslavia. M. Bouillon drew my attention to the chickens, which he said were as handsome as those of Bresse but inferior in flavor. There was transport, apparently, for everything but war materials. (I drew the wrong conclusion, naturally; if there was transport for the superfluous, I inferred, the essential must already have been taken care of.)

The Bouillon theory was that when we had completed our round of Les Halles, we would circle back on our course to pick up the baskets, with a courtesy round at each port of call, and thus avoid a lot of useless toting. It worked all right when we could remember the bars where we had left the various things, but sometimes we couldn't, and on such occasions M. Bouillon would cry that *restauration* was a cursed *métier*, and that if the government would permit, he would take up his old Lebel rifle and leave for the front. But they would have to let him wear horizon blue; he could not stand the sight of khaki, because it reminded him of the English.

Of all the dishes that M. Bouillon made for me, I remember with most affection a *salmis* of woodcock in Armagnac with which I astounded a French friend—a champagne man—whom I entertained in the little restaurant. I'm sure that it was the best I've had in my life, and M. Bouillon could do almost as well with a partridge, a beef stew, or a blood pudding with mashed potatoes. My Frenchman, as a partner in a good firm of champagne-makers, had to get around to an enormous number of restaurants in a normal year, so when he acknowledged M. Bouillon's greatness, I felt the same gratification that I felt much later when Spink's, of London, authenticated a coin of Hadrian, minted at Gaza, that I had bought from an Arab in Gaza itself. M. Bouillon was my discovery, and the enjoyment of a woodcock signed "Bouillon" was an irreplaceable privilege.

Like most fine cooks, M. Bouillon flew into rages and wept easily; the heat of kitchens perhaps affects cooks' tear ducts as well as their tempers.

Whenever we returned to the restaurant from Les Halles minus some item that M. Bouillon had paid for and that Madame had already inscribed on the menu, there would be a scene, but on the whole the Bouillons were a happy family—Madame and the children respected Monsieur as a great artist, though the son and daughter may have thought that he carried temperament a bit far. It was an ideal family unit to assure the future of a small restaurant; unfortunately, the war wiped it out. When the fighting began in earnest, in May 1940, the customers again left Paris. The son was mobilized, and the rest of the family went away to work in the canteen of a munitions factory. When I re-entered Paris at the Liberation, in 1944, I looked them up and found that they had returned to the quarter but that they no longer had the restaurant. To conduct a restaurant successfully under the Occupation had called for a gift of connivance that poor M. Bouillon didn't have. Since August 1944 I have lost sight of them.

It was in 1939, too, that I was first introduced to M. Pierre and his establishment on the Place Gaillon. (The fact that the restaurant is not on the Rue Sainte-Anne but some two hundred meters from that street of transition perhaps accounts for the fact that M. Pierre is still in business.) It is my favorite middle-sized restaurant; the cuisine has a robust, classic clarity, like a boxing style based on the straight left. Everything is done the way it says in the book, without neologisms or deviations. The matériel is of the best, the service is deft, and the prices are rather stiff. M. Pierre has the appearance of a distinguished sinner in a René Clair movie; in 1939 he had prematurely white hair (to which his age now entitles him), a high complexion, and an upright backbone. His elegance was acquired not at the Quai d'Orsay but in the métier in which he made his début, at fourteen. Our first bond was my discovery that he is a Norman, and from the proper part of Normandy—he is from Avranches, across from Mont-Saint-Michel—and, consequently, an amateur of Calvados, which, to my taste, is the best alcohol in the world. He sometimes spends weekends calling on peasants in his automobile and trying to wheedle from them a few bottles or—wild dream—a small keg of the veritable elixir of Eden. (Every Norman knows that the apple of the Bible is symbolic; it stands for the distilled cider that will turn the head of any woman.) Good Calvados is never sold legally. The tax leaves a taste that the Norman finds intolerable, like the stuff that wives put in whiskey to cure alcoholics. And only a few of Pierre's clients know what they are drinking from his precious bottles; not everybody has had the advantage of a good early soaking in the blessed liquid. Millions of Frenchmen are obtuse enough to prefer cognac, and of late a lot have switched to Scotch.

Even in 1939, Pierre, master of the whole classic repertoire of cooking, admitted that the elaborate numbers in it were no longer in demand. At noon, his restaurant sometimes had the aspect of what Americans were just beginning to call a steak house. "Only twenty-five per cent of my customers order a *plat du jour*," he said to me one day. "The rest take grilled things. It's the doctors, you know. People think only of the liver and the figure. The stomach is forgotten." He tried his best to modify the rigors of this cowboy diet—like a modiste adding a button or a ribbon to soften what the fashion writers call a stark line—by offering superb steak *au poivre*, steak *Diane*, steak *maison* (with a sauce made on a white-wine base), and steak *marchand de vin* (red-wine ditto), but a growing number of customers kept demanding their steak *nature*. "Oysters and a steak, a bit of *langouste* and a mixed grill, a *salade niçoise* and a lamb chop—it's to die of monotony," Pierre said. "If it were not for you and a few like you, I'd drop the *cassoulet* on Tuesday—it's a loser."

The trend has continued since. One evening in 1956, I entered M. Pierre's honest, soothing precincts. The headwaiter—old, gentle, dignified, with the face of a scholarly marquis—led me into the largest room, and in passing I observed a group of six (doubtless three couples) around a table at which a waiter was serving a magnificent *plate côte de bœuf*, while a colleague, following in his wake with the casserole from which the meat had been recovered, ladled onto each plate the leeks, the carrots, the onions, and the broth to which the beef had given its essential tone. The men, I could see, had acquired their jowls, their plump hands, and their globular outlines, uninterrupted by necks—as well as their happy faces— in an age before the doctors had spread the infection of fear; the wives had won their husbands' love, and learned to feel secure in it, before the emergence of the woman with a flat basic figure, on which she simulates a pectoral bulge when Balenciaga's designs call for it, and a caudal swelling when fashion goes into reverse.

When I arrived at my table, I did not even look at the *carte du jour;* my nose was full of the delectable steam of the boiled beef. I said, "For me, a dozen *pleines mers*"—oysters that are a specialty of Pierre's *écailleurs*, the men who stand out in the cold and open them—"and the *plate côte*."

An expression of sorrow elongated the old-ivory face of the maître d'hôtel. "I am desolated, M. Liebling," he said, "but the boiled beef is not on the menu. It was prepared *sur commande*—the party over there ordered it two days in advance."

That the humble glory of the classic French kitchen should have to be ordered two days in advance in one of the best restaurants in Paris is evidence of how far *la cuisine française* has slipped in the direction of short-order cooking. Beef boiled in its bouillon was the one thing that in the seventeenth and eighteenth centuries, before the development of true restaurants, the traveler was sure of finding at the lowliest inn, where the "eternal pot," drawn upon and replenished but never emptied, bubbled on the low fire that was never allowed to die. "Soup [the *pot-au-feu*] is at the base of the French national diet, and the experience of centuries has inevitably brought it to its perfection," the divine Brillat-Savarin once wrote.

"If there is any left over," the maître d'hôtel told me, looking toward the table of the happy six, "I will be glad to bring it to you. But I strongly doubt there will be."

And now one final instance of lost love on the Rue Sainte-Anne. In June of 1955, I discovered a small establishment there, completely without charm and crowded at noon with employees of neighboring business houses, which posted prices so low that I knew the fare could not be out of the ordinary, though it must have been good value to attract so many people. In the evening, however, when the quarter was quiet and customers few, the proprietor, I learned, could perform marvels. He was a Greek, born in Cairo, who had served his apprenticeship in the kitchens of Shepheard's Hotel and then worked in good restaurants in France before the First World War. Enlisting in the French Army, he had won naturalization, he said, and after the war he had worked in most of the good kitchens that he had not been in earlier. On sampling his work, I gave his story full credence, although it was not apparent to me why he had not risen higher in his profession. His explanation was that he had always been an independent soul—*une forte tête*—and had preferred to launch out for himself. He had mounted small restaurants in Paris, in Le Havre, in Granville—a little bit of everywhere. He liked to be his own boss. An imposing man, he must have measured six feet eight inches from the soles of his shoes to the top of the chef's toque that he always wore—one of the starched kind, shaped like an Orthodox priest's hat. He had a face that a primitive Greek sculptor might have intended for either a satyr or a god—terra-cotta red under an iron-gray thatch. His hands were as big and as strong as a stonecutter's, and his manner in the kitchen was irascible and commanding. He could be observed in the opening in the top half of the kitchen door, through which he thrust the steaming *plats* when they were ready to serve— and also often thrust his head, toque first, to bellow at the waitress when she did not come quickly to retrieve the evening masterpieces he extended. He would have to duck, naturally, to get the toque through. The round white top would appear in the aperture first, like a circular white cloud, and then, as he moved his neck to the vertical, his face would shine out like the sun—round, radiant, terrible—to transfix the waitress. The girl, bearing the deliciously heavy trays to table, would murmur, to excuse him, "By day, you know, he isn't at all like that. What he cooks for the day customers doesn't excite him— and then it must be said that he hasn't the same quantity of cognac in him, either. The level mounts." The Greek must have been in his middle sixties; his wife, an attractive Frenchwoman some twenty years younger, minded the bar and the cash and the social relations of the establishment; she, too, was fond of brandy. He could produce an astonishing *langouste à l'américaine* and a faultless pilaf to accompany it; I have never known a man who could work with such equal mastery in the two idioms, classic and Levantine.

The pre-eminent feature of any kind of lobster prepared *à l'américaine* is the sauce, which, according to *The Food of France*, contains white wine, cognac, fish bouillon, garlic, tomatoes, a number of herbs, the juices of the lobster itself, and the oil in which the lobster has been cooked before immersion in the liquid. (I have never personally inquired into the mysteries of its fabrication; I am content to love a masterpiece of painting without asking how the artist mixed his colors.) Early in his great work, Root disposes magisterially of the chauvinistic legend, invented by followers of Charles Maurras, that lobster *à l'américaine* should be called *à l'armoricaine* (from "Armorica," the ancient name for Brittany), simply because there are lobsters (*langoustes* as well as *homards*) on the coast of Brittany. "The purists," he says, employing a typically mild designation for these idiots, "do not seem to have been gastronomes, however, or they might have looked at the dish itself, which is obviously not Breton but Provençal, the lobster being cooked in oil and accompanied lavishly with tomatoes—and, indeed, until the middle of the nineteenth century, virtually the same dish was known as *homard à la provençale*. The most reasonable explanation for this name seems to be the one which ascribes it to a now vanished Parisian restaurant called the Américain, which is supposed to have made a specialty of it."

In general, the Bretons practice only one method of preparing their lobsters, true or spiny—boiling them in sea water, which is fine if what you want to taste is lobster. In lobster *à l'américaine*, on the other hand, the sauce, which cannot be produced without the lobster, is the justification of the indignity inflicted on him. If the strength of this dish, then, lies in the sauce (as I deem indisputable), its weakness, from a non-French point of view, lies in the necessity of mopping up the sauce with at least three linear meters of bread. Bread is a good medium for carrying gravy as far as the face, but it is a diluent, not an added magnificence; it stands to the sauce of lobster *à l'américaine* in the same relationship as soda to Scotch. But a good pilaf—each grain of rice developed separately in broth to the size of a pistachio kernel—is a fine thing in its own right. Heaped on the plate and receiving the sauce *à l'américaine* as the waitress serves the lobster, the grains drink it up as avidly as nymphs quenching their thirst. The grains do not lose form or identity, although they take on a bit of *rondeur*. Mere rice cooked any old way won't do the trick; it turns to wallpaperer's paste. The French in general are almost as bad with rice as the Chinese, who are the very worst. The Armenians, Greeks, and Turks are the best with it. The conjunction of my Greek cook's *langouste* and his pilaf was a cultural milestone, like the wedding of the oyster and the lemon.

At the end of July, six weeks and several dozen *langoustes* after making the Greek's acquaintance, I left Paris. I came back in November, arriving at the Hôtel Louvois on a chill evening. I left my bags unopened and hurried through the chill to the little shrine I had discovered. *Langouste* was too much to hope for at that season, but the Greek also made an excellent couscous—a warming dish on a cold night, because of the fiery sauce you tip into the broth—and he was sure to have that on the bill. The aspect of the restaurant had not changed. There were still paper tablecloths, a zinc bar, a lettered sign on the window proclaiming "*Grande Spécialité de Couscous.*" But the faces—one behind the bar and the other framed in the kitchen window—were not the same. They were amiable faces, man and wife, but amiability is no substitute for genius. I ordered couscous, but it was a mere cream of wheat with hot sauce and a garniture of overcooked fowl—a *couscous de Paris*, not of North Africa, where the Greek had learned to make his. I had a drink with the new *patron* and his wife when I had finished. They were younger than their predecessors, and said that they knew and admired them. They would "maintain the same formula," they promised. But restaurants don't run by formula. The Greek had sold out to them, they told me, because he and his wife had quarreled.

"Why did they quarrel?" I asked.

"Because of their art," the new woman said, and smiled fondly at her husband, as if to assure him that nothing so trivial would come between them.*

In 1927, the crepuscular quality of French cooking was not discernible to Root and me, because the decline was not evident at the levels at which we ate. The cheap and medium-priced restaurants that we patronized held good; slimming and other eccentricities affected only the upper strata, and only the rich had automobiles. Motoring and eating were still separate departments. Root, remaining in France during the dozen years that followed, was perhaps less aware than I of what my lamented Dublin friend Arthur McWeeney would have called the "dis-improvement" of French cooking. The experiences of an individual do not follow precisely the descending curve of a culture. A man as wily as Root—gastronomically speaking—might eat so well every day that he would be insensible to the decreasing number of good restaurants. The

---

* One added, final example of the ill luck that haunts *la restauration contemporaine.* After the tragedy of the Greek joint, I found another marvel, the name of which I did not disclose in my *New Yorker* pieces because I wanted to keep it to myself. It was a restaurant of undistinguished, though not sordid, aspect on the Rue des Petits-Champs, near the Bourse.

At noon it was *plein à craquer* with *cambistes* and their employees, which insured its prosperity, but in the evenings serene and almost deserted, which insured admirable service. The *patron*, a real talent, was in his early thirties, the *patronne*, a doll, in her late twenties. They were ambitious and acquisitive; the life expectancy of the restaurant looked, therefore, long. When I returned in 1960, I had the same experience as in the Rue Sainte-Anne. The new owners said that my couple had prospered so that they went in for winter sports. Both had suffered severe skiing injuries and had had to give up the business! "*Ils sont très handicappés,*" the new *patronne* said.

number was still high then—and is, even now, although, naturally, there are fewer today, and the best aren't as good as the best used to be, or the next-to-best as good as the next-to-best used to be, and so on down the line. Good bottles, however, persist, especially among the classified growths of the Bordelais. The proprietor of a legally delimited vineyard, constrained to produce his wine on the same few acres every year, cannot change his ingredients to fit deteriorating public taste. Good year, bad year, the character of his wine, if not its quality, remains constant, and the ratio of good and bad years is about the same every century. (The quantity of bad wine sold annually in France has certainly increased, but that is another matter; it is sold under labels of vague or purely humorous significance, or *en carafe* as something it isn't.) When the maligned Second Empire delimited and classified the vineyards of Médoc in 1855, it furnished French culture with a factor of stability, such as it furnished Paris when it made a park of the Bois de Boulogne. Both were ramparts against encroachment.* Wine drinking is more subjective than horse racing and nearly as subjective as love, but the gamble is less; you get something for your money no matter what you pick.

So Root the individual was eating voraciously and perceptively, and with total recall, all during that twelve-year interval, and laying the basis for his masterpiece. (I don't think he will ever write a book on the food of Britain. In his monumental treatise, he says, "I used to think . . . that the English cook the way they do because, through sheer technical deficiency, they had not been able to master the art of cooking. I have discovered to my stupefaction that the English cook that way because that is the way they like it.") Root and I, during the *drôle de guerre*, shared some good meals; then for a month, between May 10, when the Germans invaded the Low Countries, and June 11, when the French government quit Paris, we had more pressing preoccupations. (I still remember with gratitude, though, a meal of fresh brook trout and still champagne taken at Saint-Dizier, behind the crumbling front; a good meal in troubled times is always that much salvaged from disaster.) When the government pulled out, Root invited me to accompany him in pursuit of it in a small French automobile. "Maybe we can find some good regional food on the way," he said. I left France for the United States eleven days later; Root, with his French wife of the epoch and their infant daughter, followed in a month. He returned to France when the war was over, and has spent most of his time there since. *The Food of France* is a monument to his affection for a country as well as for its art. He has another French wife now.

The originality of Root's approach to his subject is based on two propositions. The first is that regions compel the nature of the foods produced in them, which is only partly and sketchily true, and, by extension, that the characters of the foods, the wines, and the inhabitants of any one

* There is a move on to reclassify the growths. I distrust it.

region interact and correspond, which makes for good anecdote but is pure whimsey. (De Gaulle has not a poor mind, although his province, Flanders, has a relatively poor and restricted cuisine; Camus' mind was balanced, not overseasoned like the food of his native Algeria; Mauriac's is thin and astringent, not voluptuous like his native *cuisine bordelaise*, which he adores.) Root's erudition is superior everywhere but at its best south of the Loire. Alsace and Normandy haven't his heart, although he tries to be fair, and he doesn't perform a sufficient obeisance to Anjou; on Provence, Nice, and the Central Plateau he is superb, and in his attack on the cooking of the Lyonnais heroic. Still, to call the cuisine of Alsace an offshoot of German cooking, as he does, is as unfair as it would be to dismiss French culture as an offshoot of Roman civilization. A lot has happened since the shooting in both cases.

In Provence, though, where he has sunned his well-covered bones during much of the past decade, Root is without peer:

The grease in which the food of a country is cooked is the ultimate shaper of its whole cuisine. The olive is thus the creator of the cooking of Provence. A local saying points this up. "A fish," it runs, "is an animal that is found alive in water and dead in oil. . . ." Garlic may not belong to Provence alone, but at least it gets special recognition there. It has even been called "the truffle of Provence." A third element must be noted as particularly typical of Provençal cooking —the tomato, which manages to get into almost everything. . . . The rabbits of this area hardly need herbs; having fed all their lives on thyme, they have inbred seasoning. . . . Artichokes . . . are ubiquitous in the region. . . . In the Vaucluse area you may be surprised if you order something listed on the bill of fare as *asperge vauclusienne*, for it is a joking name in the tradition of Scotch woodcock or prairie oysters, and what you will get is not asparagus at all but artichoke. It will be a very festive artichoke, however, stuffed with chopped ham and highly seasoned with a mixture of those herbs that seem to develop particular pungency in the dry, hilly terrain of upper Provence.

This is the lyric portion of the book; it is in Provence that Root's New England heart now lies.

The sounder of Root's two propositions, in my opinion, is his division of all French cooking into three great "domains," in accordance with his dictum that the grease in which food is cooked is the "ultimate shaper" of the cuisine. Root's "domains" are that of butter (northeastern and northern France, the Atlantic coast to below Bordeaux, and the center as far south as Lyons), that of fat (Lorraine, Alsace, and the Central Plateau); and that of oil (Provence and the County of Nice). The Basque coast has a mixed cuisine based on all three media and so refutes the universality of the system. It is true that the old division of France by orthodox *fines gueules* into gastronomic "regions" (in many cases smaller than *départements*, of which there are ninety in Continental France) has been in the process of breaking down since the remote date when the abolition of serfdom made it legitimate for the population to move around. The Revolution, the diligence, the railroad, and, finally, the automobile ended the pinpoint localization of dishes and recipes—and in any case, as Root shows, these traditional ascriptions of dishes to places are often apocryphal.

Repeatedly, as he leads the reader about France, he points out instances where adjoining provinces dispute the invention of a dish, and where a province that didn't invent a dish does it rather better than the one that did. There are, however, broad similarities in the cooking of certain subdivisions of France that are larger than the old provinces or the modern *départements*. These similarities (and differences) do not follow any purely geographic lines, and Root's "domains" are an ingenious beginning of a new taxonomy; he is like the zoologist who first began to group species into genera, observing that while a cat, a monkey, a man, and a tiger are different things, a man is rather more like a monkey than a cat, and a cat rather more like a tiger than a man. Somebody had to start, and Root is a true innovator. Whether the cooking of Périgord really is more like the cooking of Alsace (because both use the fat of the goose and the pig) than like that of the southwest (which, like Périgord, uses garlic) is another question; some future scientist of taste may attempt a new grouping on the basis of seasoning. If the inventor of the new system has as much love for his subject and as much learning as Root, the result can only be another good book, as rich in the marrow of argument as *The Food of France*.

Now that Root's monument has been erected for the ages—a picture of a cultural achievement, fixed to history's page before the snack bars and cafeterias and drive-ins could efface it from men's minds—he seems a trifle melancholy. "It's hard to find such good eating in the provinces nowadays, even at the present high rates—or maybe I'm just getting old and cranky," he wrote me not long ago. "The fact is that it's a long while since I have come upon one of those bottles of wine that make you sit up and take notice, and it's even pretty rare nowadays to have a memorable meal." Here, however, he was unduly somber. There will still be enough good bottles and good meals to last us all a few more decades; it is only that they are becoming harder to find. The rise and fall of an art takes time. The full arc is seldom manifest to a single generation.

8 / Passable

FOLLOWING THE publication of some of the foregoing papers I had an avalanche of letters—perhaps a half dozen—asking scornfully whether, in my student days in Paris, I did nothing but eat. I tried conscientiously to think of what I did between meals in the years 1926–7, when I was twenty-two–three, and it seems to have been quite a lot. For one thing, in those days young men liked women. We did not fear emasculation. We had never heard of it. This would today be considered a subliterary approach, but there it was. Havelock Ellis was the sage who made authority in the dormitories. Freud had not yet seeped down to the undergraduate level. Molly Bloom was the pin-up girl of the *nouvelle vague*, and we all burned to beat out Blazes Boylan.

Women offered so much fun from the beginning that further possibilities appeared worth investigating. For this we considered acquaintance, or even marriage, with an undergraduate of the opposite sex insufficient. We assumed, perhaps overoptimistically, that the possibilities of the subject were limitless. They may not be, but no finite man will ever be able to brag that he has exhausted them.

For the beginning student of all essential subjects, the Latin Quarter was an ideal school. The Restaurant des Beaux-Art, as I have indicated, was a great place to learn to eat because the items on the menu were good but simple. The cafés on the Boulevard Saint-Michel offered self-instruction of another kind, but similarly within the grasp of the beginner. You could find any feature of a beauty queen in our cafés, but they were all on different girls. A girl who was beautiful all over would pick a better neighborhood. So, just as at the restaurant, you had to choose a modest but satisfying agenda. In doing that you learned your own tastes.

It was trickier than that because a woman, unlike a *navarin de mouton*, has a mind. A man may say, when he begins to recognize his tastes, "Legs, on a woman, are more important to me than eyes." But he has to think again when he must choose between a witty woman with good eyes and a dull one with trim legs. Give the witty woman a bad temper and the dull one constant good humor and you add to the difficulty of the choice. To multiply the complexity the woman, unlike the *navarin*, reacts to you. She may be what you want, but you may not be what she wants. In such a case she will turn out to be not what you wanted at all.

The unimaginative monogamist has none of these perplexities, but I doubt that he has fun either. I attribute the gloom of many young novelists to an adolescent mistake made at a church. Afterward belated curiosity clashes with entrenched ignorance and produces that *timor mundi* which is the *mal de siècle*. "Ain't It Awful, Mabel?" is their strange device, instead of "Up in Mabel's Room."

The girls would arrive at their customary tables soon after lunch, in late afternoon, and establish themselves with a permanent *consommation*, something inexpensive and not tempting, for they would make it last until somebody treated them to something better. This might be a long time, and they had a skill in husbanding the drink that would have stood them in good stead if they had been airmen downed in the Sahara. When treated, they exhibited another desert talent, the opportunism of the camel. They drank enough to last them to the next oasis.

They spent the afternoon writing on the house stationery. If the waiter caught them doodling or doing ticktacktoes he would cut off their supply. With the hour of the *apéritif* came animation and hope. After the dinner hour, if they had not been invited to eat, there remained animation. It could always happen that, if they kept up their spirits, some late customer would offer them a sandwich. The girls were like country artisans; they took money for their services, but only when they felt like working. On occasion they would accept payment in kind—a dinner or a pair of stockings—but then, as often as not, they would ask you to lend them their current week's room rent.

I suppose some of them had sweet men, but these must have been *dilettanti* too. No protector worthy of the name would have tolerated such irregularity. He would have said the girls of the Boulevard Saint-Michel were not serious. And he would have starved on a percentage of their earnings, like a literary agent who depended on poets. All the girls were young. It was easy to comprehend that this was a phase without a future; there was no chance to accumulate. Where they went after they disappeared from the Quarter I do not know. They were brisk rather than chic, and they made up without exaggeration. My memory is not tenacious in matters of dress, but I am sure the girls wore short skirts—I remember the legs. One girl helped me select a hat for a woman in America, and this would not have been possible except in a period when all hats were essentially alike. It was the age of the face *sous cloche*.

The *cloche* was an enlarged skull cap, jammed down on the head like an ice-cream scoop on a ball of vanilla. For the rest, their clothes were not elaborate, with the short skirt, a short blouse and short jacket, and underneath a *soutien-gorge* and *pantalon*. Having the *points de repère* once well in mind, one saw at a glance what was what.

Sometimes a girl would enter *en ménage* with a student, usually a Romanian or an Asiatic. If it was one of the latter, with an allowance from home, the girl would disappear from her customary café for a while or appear there only with him. If it was a Romanian, she would be on the job more regularly than before. Often a girl would make such an arrangement to gain the status of a kept woman, which would protect her from the jurisdiction of the *police des moeurs.*

Once the cops of this unsavory group picked up a girl without visible means of support they would force her to register. Then they would give her a card that subjected her to a set of rules.

"Once a girl has the card she is bound to infract the rules," the girls said. "We are all so lazy. She misses a couple of visits; she is subject to heavy penalties. Then comes blackmail. The police put her to work for chaps who give them a cut. *Hop*, then, no more chattering with student friends who have no money.

"It's the pavement for her, and turn over the receipts to the mackerel at five o'clock in the morning. The police have opened another account."

I was glad to know how things were. It made me feel like an insider, and it helped me understand cops, who run to form everywhere.

Our girls were not intellectuals. None was a geisha primed with poems, nor were there hetaerae who could have disputed on equal terms with Plato, or even with Max Lerner. But all served as advisers on courses of study. They knew the snaps and the tough ones in all faculties, which professors were susceptible to apple polishing and which the most resolutely *vache.* Above all, they had anticipated a theory that was to be imparted to me later as a great original discovery by T. S. Matthews, an editor of *Time*, who told me that the content of communication was unimportant. What did count, Matthews said, was somebody on one end of a wire shouting, "My God, I'm alive!" and somebody on the other end shouting, "My God, I'm alive too!"

It was a poor prescription for journalism, but a good program for conversation between the sexes. (The girls did not keep us at the end of a wire.)

To one I owe a debt the size of a small Latin American republic's in analysts' fees saved and sorrows unsuffered during the next thirty-odd years. Her name was Angèle. She said: *"Tu n'es pas beau, mais t'es passable."* ("You're not handsome, but you're passable.")

I do not remember the specific occasion on which Angèle gave me the good word, but it came during a critical year. I am lucky that she never said, *"T'es merveilleux."* The last is a line a man should be old enough to evaluate.

My brain reeled under the munificence of her compliment. If she had said I was handsome I wouldn't have believed her. If she had called me loathsome I wouldn't have liked it. *Passable* was what I hoped for. *Passable* is the best thing for a man to be.

A handsome man is so generally said by other men to be a fool that in many cases he must himself begin to believe it. The superstition that handsome men are dull is like the prejudice that gray horses quit. Both arose because their subjects were easy to follow with the eye. The career of the late Elmer Davis, a handsome but intelligent man, was made more difficult by his good looks. Favored with a less prepossessing appearance, he would have won earlier acceptance. There are homely fools too, and quitters of all colors.

Women who are both randy and cautious, and therefore of the most profitable acquaintance, avoid handsome lovers because they are conspicuous. He who is *passable* escapes attention. To be *passable* is like a decent suit. It gets you anywhere. *Passable* and *possible* are allied by free association. A young man wants desperately to be considered at least a possibility. But it is the only game in which there is no public form, and he can't present a testimonial from his last employer. He is like a new player in a baseball league where there are no published batting averages. To be *passable* gets him in the ball park without arousing inflated expectations. The ugly man is the object of a special cult among women, but it is relatively small. He runs well only in limited areas, like a Mormon candidate in Utah.

A heartening fact, if you are *passable*, is that there are more *passable* women than any other kind, and that a *passable* man establishes a better rapport with them. Very pretty girls are preferable, of course, but there are never enough to go around. Angèle was *passable* plus—a woman who looks pretty at her best and *passable* at her worst. Her legs, though well-tapered, were a trifle short and her round head a trifle large for good proportion with her torso, in which there was no room for improvement. It was solid Renoir. Her neck was also a bit short and thick—a good point in a prizefighter but not in a swan. She had a clear skin and a sweet breath, and she was well-joined—the kind of girl you could rough up without fear of damage. Angèle had a snub nose, broad at the base, like a seckel pear tilted on its axis.

It was a period when the snub nose enjoyed high popular esteem. The fashions of the day called for a gamine, and a gamine cannot have a classic profile. A retroussé nose, for example, looked better under a cloche. The cloche made a girl with an aquiline nose look like the familiar portrait of Savonarola in his hood. It gave her the profile of that bigot or a spigot.

I had an early belief that I could get along with any woman whose nose turned up. This proved in later life to have been a mistake based on a brief series of coincidences, but when I knew Angèle it still influenced me. Among snub-nosed idols in the United States we had Mary Pickford, Marion Davies, Mae Murray, and Ann Pennington, to name a few I remember. The last two were dancers, and when they kicked, the tips of their noses and their toes were in a straight line. In France they had Madge Lhoty and a girl named Lulu Hegoboru.

Here memory, furtive and irrelevant, interpolates a vision of La Hegoboru taking a refrain of "Tea for Two" in English, in the Paris production of *No, No, Nanette*: "I will back a sugar cack—" as she jumped right, kicked left.

We have no such artists today. The profession of ingenue exists no longer. There was a girl in *Little Mary Sunshine* who had the gist of it, but she will have no chance to develop. In her next job she may have to play an agoraphobic Lesbian in love with her claustrophobic brother. The tragic siblings will be compelled to tryst in a revolving door. It is the kind of play people like to write now, because it can be done in one set, in this case the door.

Angèle had large eyes with sable pupils on a pale-blue field, and a wide mouth, and a face wide at the cheekbones. Her hair was a black soup-bowl bob, as if she had put a cloche on and let a girl friend cut around it. (Girls in the United States went to barber shops for their haircuts.) The corners of her mouth were almost always turned up because Angèle was of a steady, rough good humor. Angèle was a Belgian; half the girls in Paris were Belgians then, and all of them said their parents had been shot by the Germans in World War I.

I met Angèle at Gypsy's Bar on the Rue Cujas, a late place outside the circle of tranquil cafés in which I usually killed my evenings. Most of the time I tried to live like a Frenchman, or, rather, like my idealized notion, formed at home, of how a Frenchman lived. The notion included moderation: I would drink only wine and its distillates, cognac, Armagnac and marc. I did not class French beer among alcoholic drinks. In the United States I had been accustomed to drink needle beer, reinforced with alcohol; a six-ounce glass for twenty-five cents hit as hard as a shot of whiskey for half a dollar.

I did not get drunk as long as I followed what I imagined was the French custom. I thought a sedentary binge effeminate. Now and then, though, I would suffer from a recurrent American urge to stand up and tie one on. It was like the *trouvère's* longing to hear the birds of his own province:

> *The little birds of my country,*
> *They sing to me in Brittany;*
> *The shrill-voiced seagulls' cries among*
> *Mine ears have heard their evensong,*
> *And sweet, it was of thee.*

When this yearning struck during the solvent week of my month—the first after receiving my allowance—I would go to Gypsy's and drink Scotch. The bar was in the Quarter but not used by students. It was too dear. There were even gigolos there—what student would tip a gigolo? I shall not try at this distance in time to guess the nature of Gypsy's sustaining clientele. There may have been a *spécialité de maison*, but I never learned what. I would stand at the bar and think my own thoughts, clear and increasingly grandiose as the level dropped in the bottle. People whose youth did not coincide with the twenties never had our reverence for strong drink. Older men knew liquor before it became the symbol of a sacred cause. Kids who began drinking after 1933 take it as a matter of course.

For us it was a self-righteous pleasure, like killing rabbits with clubs to provide an American Legion party for poor white children. Drinking, we proved to ourselves our freedom as individuals and flouted Congress. We conformed to a popular type of dissent—dissent from a minority. It was the only period during which a fellow could be smug and slopped concurrently.

Angèle impinged on my consciousness toward the end of one of these reveries. She said that I needed somebody to see me home. In Tours the previous summer, a girl making a similar offer had steered me into the hands of two incompetent muggers. Angèle was of a more honorable character. She came home with me. In the morning, when we had more opportunity to talk, we found that we were almost neighbors. She had a room in the Hôtel des Facultés, where the Rue Racine and the Rue de l'Ecole de Médecine form a point they insert in the Boulevard Saint-Michel. My room, one of the pleasantest of my life, was on the fifth (by French count) floor, front, of the Hôtel Saint-Pierre, 4 Rue de l'Ecole de Médecine, next door to a Chinese restaurant that had dancing. At night, while I read, the music from the dancing would rise to my window and a part of my brain would supply the words to the tune as I tried to maintain interest in the *Manual of Provençal Documents* of Monsieur Maurice Prou. One that recurred often was *"Oh, les fraises et les framboises, le bon vin qu'nous avons bu,"* from *Trois Jeunes Filles Nues*, one of Mirande's great hits.

It was an atmosphere not conducive to the serious study of medieval history, which was my avowed purpose in the Quarter.

Angèle not only lived by day on the same street, but frequented by night the same cafés I did—the Taverne Soufflet, La Source, the Café d'Harcourt, all strung along the Boulevard Saint-Michel. She made her headquarters in the d'Harcourt, where it was the merest chance that she had not remarked me, she said. She had so many friends, she explained, there was always somebody engaging her attention.

I said that in any case I spent most of my time in the Soufflet, where the boss was a pal of my landlord. But after that I would go to the d'Harcourt whenever I wanted to see her. It had a favorable effect on her standing if I bought her a drink there, and none on mine if I took her to the Soufflet. If she was not at her post, her waiter would take her messages. He would also tell her to dress warmly in winter and not get her feet wet, to take sufficient nourishment to keep up her strength, and not to be beguiled by clients who had to his experienced eye the aspect of musclemen recruiting for a brothel. It was a relationship already familiar to me from New York, where a waiter was the nearest thing to a mother lots of girls had.

When we had established the similarity of our *frequentations*, Angèle and I marveled that we had to go all the way to Gypsy's, a good fifty meters from the Boulevard, to find each other. We sounded like the traditional New Yorkers who inhabit the same apartment house but meet for the first time in Majorca.

After that I was with her often. I do not know if she had a heart of gold, but she had what I learned long years later to call a therapeutic personality. She made you feel good.

When I took her out in the evening we sometimes strayed from the Quarter. This was like taking a Manhattan child to the Bronx Zoo. Girls did not shift about in Paris. Clienteles were localized, and so were usages. Montparnasse, although not a long walk away from the Quarter, had all the attributes of a foreign country, including, to a degree, the language.

In Montparnasse the types in the cafés spoke English, American, and German. The girls there had to be at least bilingual. In the Quarter, the languages, besides French, were Vietnamese, Spanish, Czech, Polish and Romanian. But the specimens of all these nationalities spoke French at least passably. The girls consequently could remain resolutely monolingual. The clients were students, or simulated students, at the University. Those were the days of the Little Entente, and France set the cultural and military pattern for the East Europe that is behind the Curtain now. Romanian students came to French universities as freely as if they had done their secondary work in France.

The pre-eminence of the University of Paris was acknowledged as it had been in the Middle Ages. All the tribes rescued from the Austro-Hungarian and Turkish Empires flocked there—Serbs and Croats, Egyptians, Greeks, Armenians, along with Haitians and Koreans, Venezuelans and Argentines. There were also, of course, the North Africans. It would have been a great place to form friendships that would serve in the convulsive years to come. But I thought, if I thought about it at all, that regional convulsions were as out-of-date as *écriture onciale* or horse armor.

Our foreignness made each more confident of his speech than he would have been among the French. From my first appearance in the Quarter, my French was no worse than that of a White Russian or a Czech, and I rose rapidly and successively through the grades of being mistaken for a Hungarian, German Swiss, Alsatian, and Belgian from the Flemish-speaking provinces. Beyond that point I have not since progressed, except in Algeria, where I am mistaken for an old lag of the Foreign Legion who has all kinds of accents so inextricably mixed that it is hopeless to attempt to disassociate them.

Angèle did not like Montparnasse. Neither did I. I had come to France for the same reason that at home I would go out to a beach and swim out just beyond the breakers. There I could loaf. Lying on my back, I would paddle just enough to keep out of the pull, and draw my knees up to my chin and feel good. The Americans in Montparnasse, sitting at their tables in front of Le Sélect and talking at each other, reminded me of monkeys on a raft. They were not in the water at all. One reason I didn't think I liked them was that they had all decided they were writers, or painters, or sculptors, and I didn't know what I was. During my residence in the Hôtel Saint-Pierre I never heard of Gertrude Stein, and although I read *Ulysses*, I would as soon have thought of looking the author up as of calling on the President of the Republic.

Angèle disliked Montparnasse because the people looked at the same time too prosperous and too bizarre. The American women, she said, did not look like Frenchwomen and the Frenchwomen did not look like other Frenchwomen. There were no serious bookstores stacked with doctoral dissertations and tributes to deceased savants. (She herself was not a reader, but she liked academic surroundings.) The types appeared smug and possibly addicted to narcotics. The waiters in the cafés were insolent and Italian, and the *consommations* were overpriced. There were too many fairies and they gave her *drôles* of looks. Let them not fear, she was not in competition. We wound up our tour at the Closerie des Lilas, the border post, at the corner of the Boulevard Montparnasse and our own Boulevard Saint-Michel. The Montparnassiens occupied the post—its tariff was too high for the Quarter. I offered her a whiskey there, but she said it smelled of bedbugs. Now all the French drink Scotch.

Angèle could not get back to the d'Harcourt with sufficient celerity, but once there, it pleased her to have voyaged. She talked as if she were home from a world cruise. But when we went to Montmartre, she was in her glory. She had talked all her life about the *nuits blanches* of Montmartre but had never been there. I took her to Zelli's and we drank several bottles of champagne. She was a solid drinker. All her appetites were robust. In bed she was a kind of utility infielder. She made me buy half a dozen flashlight photographs of us and the bottles, like sportsmen and sailfish, to serve as documentation when she recounted our adventure. Her room, in the prow of a ship-shaped building, was barely wide enough for a single bed. I was there only once, in September of 1927, when she was ill. Half of the mirror was covered with photographs of us at Zelli's.

Aside from her concession that I was passable, which is wrapped around my ego like a bulletproof vest riveted with diamonds, I retain little Angèle said. The one other exception is a report so vivid that I sometimes confuse it with a visual memory.

Angèle told me one morning that she and a number of her colleagues had been playing cards in her room. There were a couple of girls sitting on her bed, a couple more on the bureau, one on the only chair and another on her trunk, when one took off her shoes.

A second girl said, after a moment, "It smells of feet in here!" The shoeless girl said, "Say that once more and you will say *Bon jour* to the concierge."

"You get it?" said Angèle. "The concierge is on the ground floor, we are on the sixth. She will throw her down the stairs. The other comrade who commenced says again, 'It smells of feet.'

"So the other hooks on and drags her out on the landing, and they roll down the stairs together, interscratching with all claws. On the fifth, two law students, interrupted in their studies, pull them apart from each other. The girls couldn't work for three nights afterward.

"One student took up for the girl he had pulled upon, and the other took up for the adversary. Now the students have quarreled, and the girl whose feet smelled has moved in with one of them at the Facultés, while the other student has moved in with the girl whose nose was delicate. It is romance in flower."

Life in the Quarter was a romance that smelled of feet.

I am afraid that I do not succeed in making Angèle's quality come clear. To attempt a full description of a woman on the basis of a few fragmentary memories is like trying to reconstruct a small, endearing animal from a few bits of bone. Even some of the bits are not much help. My arms try to remember her weight—I should say 118, give or take two pounds.

It makes me wince, now, to recall that she used to butt me in the pit of the belly, quite hard, and that we both thought it chummy. My point of view has changed with the tone of my muscles.

Yet she existed. The proof is that my old landlord, Perès, remembers her well. I sometimes meet Perès at a brasserie called l'Alsace à Paris. The proprietor there is M. Perès' old friend, the former owner of the Taverne Soufflet, which failed in 1931 because he had a wife who did not keep her mind on the business. (It is too much to expect the *patron* of a café to keep his mind on the business himself.) Now M. Robert, whose last name I have not learned in thirty-six years of greeting him, has an excellent wife who does not have to keep her mind on the business. It goes as if on rollers.

M. Perès, who retired from the management of the Hôtel Saint-Pierre shortly after World War II, continues to live in the Quarter because, he says, it keeps him young. He has recently been made an Officer of the Legion of Honor. He was a Chevalier, *à titre militaire*, as I have said before, when I first came to live under his roof in 1926, having distinguished himself by courage in World War I. I always suspected him of trying to give the impression, however, that he had won the ribbon for some discovery in Aramaic intransitive verbs or the functioning of the gall bladder. This would have been more chic in his neighborhood. During World War II he served as a captain of infantry, at fifty-one, and distinguished himself again.

"I was a bit put out," he said to me when I congratulated him on his new rosette, "because my promotion was slow in arriving. A man of seventy in the vicinity of the University who has only the ribbon has the air of a demifailure. But the delay was occasioned by the nature of my business. The Chancellery of the Legion is cautious in awarding the higher grades to hotelkeepers, because the hotel may be a *maison de passe*. Once I announced my retirement, the rosette was not long on the way."

M. Perès, in thirty years at the Saint-Pierre, lodged an infinity of students. It makes him think of himself as a housemaster. "One of our fellows is raising the question of confidence in the Chamber today," he may say when you meet him, meaning a Deputy who used to live at the Saint-Pierre as a student. "He has gone farther than I would have predicted." Or, "One of our fellows is now the leading internist in Port-au-Prince—I had a card last week." Or, "One of our chaps who is the professor of medieval history at the University of Jerusalem has, it appears, achieved a remarkable monograph on secular law in the Latin kingdom of Acre. He had your room about ten years after you left. He, at least, worked from one time to another." It is M. Perès' contention that I was a *farceur*, a donothing, because we sneaked out so often for a drink at the Soufflet when his wife was in bad humor.

The Anciens de l'Hôtel Saint-Pierre is the sole alumni association of which I would willingly attend a reunion; unhappily it does not exist. If it did, it would include the ladies' auxiliary, *bien entendu*; the girl who lived with the Korean on the floor below me, the mistress of the Dane upstairs, Angèle and subsequent and preceding Angèles of all promotions, and the two little maids from Dax, Lucienne and Antoine, who led the way to the bathroom, which was on the third floor, when the client had ordered a bath. They then allowed themselves to be trapped long enough for an invigorating tussle.

M. Perès remembers Angèle almost as well as if she had made a name for herself as a comparative zoologist in Peru.

She died in the winter of 1927–28, not of a broken heart, but flu. I was no longer in Paris, but in Providence, Rhode Island, where I had returned to a job on the Providence *Journal* and *Evening Bulletin*, and Perès included word of her death, along with other neighborhood news, in a letter that he sent me.

"She had a felicity of expression," he said of her one day thirty years later. "Once she said to me, 'Head of a ruin, how much do you extort for your cubicles?' There wasn't a sou's worth of harm in her. What a pity that she had to die. How well she was built!" he said in final benison.

"She was *passable*," I said.

I could see that M. Perès thought me a trifle callous, but he did not know all that *passable* meant to me.